TRUST
IN
ORGANIZATIONS

To Gene Webb

TRUST
IN
ORGANIZATIONS
FRONTIERS OF THEORY AND RESEARCH

RODERICK M. KRAMER
TOM R. TYLER

SAGE Publications
International Educational and Professional Publisher
Thousand Oaks London New Delhi

HM
131
.T715
1996

For information address:

 SAGE Publications, Inc.
2455 Teller Road
Thousand Oaks, California 91320
E-mail: order@sagepub.com

SAGE Publications Ltd.
6 Bonhill Street
London EC2A 4PU
United Kingdom

SAGE Publications India Pvt. Ltd.
M-32 Market
Greater Kailash I
New Delhi 110 048 India

Printed in the United States of America

Library of Congress Cataloging-in-Publication Data

Trust in organizations: Frontiers of theory and research / edited by
Roderick M. Kramer, Tom R. Tyler.
p. cm.
Includes bibliographical references and index.
ISBN 0-8039-5739-4 (cloth: alk. paper). — ISBN 0-8039-5740-8 (pbk.: alk. paper)
1. Social groups. 2. Trust (Psychology). 3. Community. 4. Organization. 5. Organizational behavior. I. Kramer, Roderick Moreland, 1950- . II. Tyler, Tom R.
HM131.T715 1995
302.3'5—dc20 95-20967

This book is printed on acid-free paper.

96 97 98 99 10 9 8 7 6 5 4 3 2 1
Sage Production Editor: Gillian Dickens

Contents

Preface

In May 1994, a 2-day conference on trust in organizations was held at the Stanford University Graduate School of Business. A primary goal of that conference was to bring together social scientists interested in studying trust in organizations from a variety of disciplinary perspectives. The theoretical and empirical contributions in the present book are a result of this effort. Any book is a collective enterprise, but this is especially true of an edited volume. Accordingly, there are many players, both front stage and back stage, whose contributions we would like to acknowledge.

First, we are grateful to Joanne Martin, Gene Webb, and Mike Spence for their help in obtaining funding for the conference. We also acknowledge the generous support of the Miller Fund, the Dean's Office of the Stanford University Graduate School of Business, and the Institute for Personality and Social Research at the University of California, Berkeley. The conference was inspired, at least in part, by a very exciting and successful interdisciplinary seminar on trust and norms that was organized by Jim Baron several years ago, and we acknowledge our intellectual debt to him. We also thank Ben Hanna, Peter Degoey, and Lupe Winans for their help in making the conference happen.

Finally, the professional staff at Sage Publications was extraordinary and we are grateful for their efforts. We especially acknowledge our editor, Harry Briggs, for his enthusiastic advocacy and stoic patience. And thanks to Maureen, Matthew, and Catherine for making such labors worthwhile. And to Ben and Jan for being good friends with whom such accomplishments can be shared.

Roderick M. Kramer
Tom R. Tyler

Whither Trust?

TOM R. TYLER
RODERICK M. KRAMER

Within the United States both intellectual discourse and the development of social policy have been dominated in recent years by the "rational choice" model of the individual. This model argues that people are motivated to maximize their personal gains and minimize their personal losses in social interactions (i.e., by self-interest) and react to other individuals, organizations, authorities, and rules from a self-interested, instrumental perspective. The rational choice perspective focuses on (a) individual gains (Stigler, 1950) and (b) the exchange of material resources (Laver, 1981). This intellectual vision has had an enormous impact on conceptualizing issues within law (in the "law and economics" movement) and shaping agency theory, transaction cost perspectives, and theories of collective action in organizational analyses (Eisenhardt, 1989; Hirsch, 1990; Olson, 1965). It has also dominated the formulation of public policy in areas as diverse as criminal justice, welfare policy, and philosophies of taxation.

Typical of the literatures dominated by rational choice models is the study of negotiation. This rapidly burgeoning field has been based generally on rational choice models of the person. In conflicts of interest between rational people, the problem for all parties is to gain for themselves what might be realistically achieved. People are faced with the cognitive problem

1

of effectively managing a solution to such "mixed motive" interactions. People have, in fact, been found to have difficulty effectively building cooperation in negotiations with others. The negotiation literature links these problems to failures to understand effectively the contingencies involved in particular negotiation problems and to people's inability to accurately understand their self-interests (Neale & Bazerman, 1985). Consequently, it proposes that improvement in the conduct of negotiations will flow from more sophisticated cognitive awareness and better framing of negotiation problems (Bazerman & Neale, 1992; Fisher & Ury, 1991; Neale & Bazerman, 1991).

The rational framework underlying negotiation research is typical of a broader effort to understand the problems of social interactions based on the assumption that the root of the problem lies in the limits of human cognition— an inability to understand the contingencies of the problem or "do the math" correctly when handling complex information (Dawes, 1988; Hogarth, 1980; Kahneman, Slovic, & Tversky, 1982; Thaler, 1992). For example, extensive literatures document both people's distortion of objective utilities (e.g., prospect theory) and their use of suboptimal decision heuristics (e.g., availability, representativeness, anchoring and adjustment).

The rational framework has led to a number of important findings. It has also led to a restricted focus on the efforts of self-interested individuals to achieve optimum outcomes in interactions with particular others. The larger social framework within which social interactions occur has been generally ignored (although not completely; e.g., see Pruitt & Carnevale, 1993). Consequently, efforts to explain the crime rate have focused on rational choice-based deterrence mechanisms (Gibbs, 1982; Melton, 1985), as have efforts to explain cooperation (Axelrod, 1984), understand social policy support (Laver, 1981; Mueller, 1979), and explore the dynamics of hierarchies (Miller, 1992).

In the wake of the social excesses and business abuses of the 1980s (Bach, 1985; Burrough & Helyar, 1990; Lewis, 1989), the decline in the legitimacy of social institutions (Lipset & Schneider, 1983), and the emergence of political problems of social inequality, economic discontent, and public fears over health and public safety, there has been a convergence toward questioning the adequacy of the rational choice model—with its individualistic, materialistic focus—as an intellectual model for understanding social interaction in natural settings and as a basis for social policy (Cook & Levi, 1990; Mansbridge, 1990; Tyler, 1990). A chorus of recent writers has argued for greater attention by scholars to the social context within which individuals behave (Bellah, Madsen, Sullivan, Swindler, & Tipton, 1985; Etzioni, 1988; Kramer & Messick, 1995; Selznick, 1992; Wilson, 1993) and by political leaders for a renewal of moral socialization (Bennett, 1993). Kramer (1994) labels such an approach "social contextualism" because it views "individuals as fundamentally and essentially social decision makers" (p. 349).

Understanding about how a consideration of social context would change the focus of attention is provided within the negotiation literature. In contrast to seeing the problem of suboptimal cooperative agreements as one of cognitive limits, the problem would be conceptualized as one of changing social con- ditions (Granovetter, 1985). Such analysis moves beyond viewing the indi-vidual as "atomistic" and "undersocialized" (Granovetter, 1985, p. 483). Consider how negotiation might be shaped by social context. American society is moving away from supporting long-term social connections between individuals and between individuals and organizations. In the family arena, the emergence of no-fault divorce discourages long-term interpersonal commitments. In work, the development of the "contingent workforce" discourages loyalty to work organizations. In this evolving world, people increasingly cannot count on loyalty to others as a basis for reciprocity. They cannot trust others. A wife, for example, cannot point out to her husband that she abandoned her career to raise their family and expect to invoke an obligation that will be honored, just as workers cannot loyally support their organization over the years and expect that organization to place a high priority on their pension needs. In a world without such reciprocal obligations, it is hardly surprising that people are interested in learning how to negotiate effectively to protect their self-interests (Rubin, 1985). However, the underlying problem is organizational—why has faith in the binding power of obligations declined?

A similar change in the structure of society is identified by Sheppard and Tuchinsky (Chapter 8, this volume). They argue that hierarchies are increasingly being replaced by lateral alliances and social relations. In such relationships, individuals are again thrown into situations in which "formal controls and sanctions do not exist" (p. 153). As a consequence, they have yet another reason to hone their negotiating skills. As with the previously outlined changes, these changes reflect an evolution in the social structure and in the form of social relations within which people function. It seems likely that lateral alliances themselves will increasingly suffer from problems of exploitation and "free-riding" and, as a consequence, develop over time the formal and informal social mechanisms that enable trusting behavior to flourish.

The chapters in this volume demonstrate the growth of trust as a central topic in recent social science research. The importance of trust in social, economic, political, legal, and organizational relations has been increasingly recognized (e.g., see Bianco, 1994; Blumberg, 1989; Brown, 1994; Garment, 1991; Miller, 1992; Putnam, 1993; Sitkin & Roth, 1993). Why is trust becoming more important? One perspective on the evolving social landscape and the consequent emergence of trust as a social issue is linked to rational choice. Axelrod (1984) argues that cooperation is sustained by the "shadow of the future." It is the expectation of an ongoing relationship that sustains trust in the actions of others. This rational perspective recognizes that declining trust in the existence of long-term exchange relationships increases transaction costs, because people must engage in self-protective actions and be "continually making provisions for the possibility of opportunistic behavior" by others (Limerick & Cunnington, 1993, pp. 95-96; see Lewicki & Bunker, Chapter 7, this volume). From a rational perspective, trust is a calculation of the likelihood of future cooperation (Williamson, 1993). As trust declines, people are increasingly unwilling to take risks, demand greater protections against the possibility of betrayal, and increasingly insist on costly sanctioning mechanisms to defend their interests.

Central to changing conceptions about the risks involved in trusting others are changes in the social institutions that sanction those who violate trust. Most exchanges occur among people who have long-term social relationships and operate within a stable social group. Hence, social institutions can exert both formal and informal control over the behavior of individuals, making untrustworthy behavior costly. For example, regulatory agencies and civil laws allow those wronged in commercial transactions to complain or sue and possibly collect not only actual but also punitive damages designed to discourage violations of trust. Informally, social groups sanction rule-breakers by refusing to deal with them. For example, lawyers refuse to negotiate with other lawyers who violate agreements, forcing untrustworthy lawyers into the costly behavior of taking all their cases into formal courts (Ross, 1980). As a consequence, people value their reputations and act to protect them.

The occurrence of reputational effects depends on the existence of ongoing interactions and stable social networks through which reputational information can be spread. Hence, trusting is linked to social context, and trusting behavior changes as social context changes. In the practice of law, for example, "claims that the conduct of litigation has become uncivil and unprofessional, and that lawyers' conduct has deteriorated in ways that increase the contentiousness of civil litigation, are now standard fare for lawyer convocations" (Gilson & Mnookin, 1994, p. 511). This change in behavior reflects declines in the stability of social networks and an increase in the number of one-shot interactions among lawyers as well as changes in the nature of business and the practice of law (e.g., increased competitiveness in both fields).

For example, in commercial litigation, where many abuses are reported,

the enormous growth in size of large law firms that provide legal representation in most substantial commercial litigation has undermined the effectiveness of the reputational market . . . [because] the number of times that one lawyer has the experience of litigating against another lawyer in a community is a function of the size of the community—the smaller the community, the easier it is for lawyers to learn about the predilections of their adversaries toward cooperation. (Gilson & Mnookin, 1994, pp. 537-538)

In contrast, in family law, where abuses are much rarer, "the institutional structure of family law practice appears to allow lawyers . . . to create and sustain reputations for cooperation (and noncooperation) . . . [because] local specialists repeatedly deal with one another" (Gilson & Mnookin, p. 543). Furthermore, a formal organization—the American Academy of Matrimonial Lawyers—provides a structure for allowing an "efficient reputational network among family lawyers" (p. 543).

These structural approaches are useful in that they extend the horizon that decision makers use when thinking about whether to trust. However, they still reflect an essentially calculative conception of trust. In other words, they reflect the assumption that the decision to trust is predicated primarily on the computation of risks, albeit a computation that favors trust in the near term if the "shadow of the future" looms sufficiently large.

Social Conceptions of Trust

In addition, trust can be conceptualized as an orientation toward society and toward others that has social meaning beyond rational calculations. The idea of internalized orientations toward others is rooted in the psychological literature on moral development (Rushton, 1980; Staub, 1978, 1979). Studies of moral development demonstrate that, irrespective of the original motives for acquiring attitudes about one's obligation to others, those attitudes develop a functional autonomy over time. They become distinct from short-term calculations of self-interest. Hence, people help others and/or their group because they feel it is the morally appropriate action.

The literature on social dilemmas provides evidence that social trust mechanisms play an important role in cooperative behavior. In a social dilemma situation, for example, when the fish within a lake are being rapidly depleted, a person's rational actions will be governed by his or her expectations about how others will behave. Ideally, everyone would eat less fish, allowing the pool to restock. However, if others continue to overuse the resource, an individual should also make a grab for the few remaining fish. Interestingly, research suggests that people do not behave in this instrumental manner.

Evidence of the noninstrumental nature of people's cooperation in social dilemmas is provided by the important role that identification with the group plays in facilitating cooperation (Brewer & Kramer, 1986; Kramer & Brewer, 1984, 1986). As Dawes and Thaler (1988) summarize in their review of cooperation, "Group identity appears to be a crucial factor" in lessening competition (p. 195). Although one aspect of this effect is instrumental, with group identity increasing expectations that others will reciprocate (Brewer, 1981), expectations of reciprocity do not fully account for this effect. Those who trust others are found to continue to cooperate, irrespective of the behavior of others in the group (Brann & Foddy, 1988; Messick et al., 1983). This trusting behavior reflects a "moral duty or commitment" (Kramer & Goldman, 1995). Similarly, cooperators do not leave groups when it is in their interest to do so (Orbell, van de Kragt, & Dawes, 1988). Dawes, van de Kragt, and Orbell (1990) suggest that identification increases cooperation "in the absence of any expectation of future reciprocity, current rewards or punishments, or even reputational consequences" (p. 199). In other words, instrumental models are inadequate to explain people's trust in others.

The Dynamics of Trust

Overall, two key issues have emerged as central to the analysis of trust. One is an understanding of the dynamics of trust in organizations. On the macrolevel, this issue involves a concern for the influence of social organization on patterns of trust. On the mesolevel, it involves an exploration of social networks. Finally, on the microlevel, it involves consideration of the psychological basis of trust and distrust. The second issue is understanding why people trust. Consideration of this issue involves microlevel comparisons of rational and social motivations for trust. First, consider the dynamics of trust.

Macrolevel Analysis

Two issues are important: (a) Has trust declined? and (b) how can trust be rebuilt? These questions can be addressed on an institutional or organizational level by examining how trust is related to organizational dynamics or management philosophy. In Chapter 2 of this volume, Creed and Miles show how the nature of the trust issues that arise in organizations is shaped by evolution in organizational forms and management philosophies. For example, traditional models of authority assume that workers lack the ability for self-direction, find their work distasteful, and are instrumentally motivated. Hence, managers must closely supervise their employees and cannot trust them. In contrast, more recent human resource models assume that workers can be creative and self-directed, enjoy their work, and motivated by interest in work tasks. In this view, managers need to create an environment in which workers can be trusted.

Kipnis (Chapter 3) also links the nature of trust issues to the organization of work. However, he focuses on stages of technology. He argues that there are three stages in the evolution of technology: from craft production, to mechanized production, to automated production. Each stage presents managers with unique problems of trust. In the craft production stage, managers must ultimately trust employees to produce quality products, whereas mechanized production requires little trust, and automated production requires high trust in the reliability of employees. Interestingly, Kipnis argues that trustworthiness is central to craft production, but Creed and Miles argue that managers during this era regarded workers as having limited ability for self-direction and self-control.

Mesolevel Analysis

Powell (Chapter 4) also focuses on the context within which trust emerges, but his concern is with the mesolevel issue of networks of collaboration. He argues that four types of collaborative network exist, each with unique sources of trust. The first network is linked to ties to place and kinship, the second to common membership in a professional community, the third to shared historical experiences and the utilitarian advantages of group membership, and the fourth to mutual dependencies. These four categories represent four different pathways to cooperative social relationships, each with a distinct basis for trust.

Like Powell, Burt and Knez (Chapter 5) focus on the production of trust in interpersonal networks. They examine the effect of gossip in communicating reputational information through organizations. Their study is based on a study of managers in a large high-technology firm. They find that social relationships, indexed by frequency or duration of contact or emotional closeness, lead to greater trust of others. This effect is reinforced by indirect connections. On the other hand, distrust of another leads to diminished contact. Although trust and distrust are found to have opposite effects, their influence is not symmetrical. Instead, trust builds incrementally, but distrust has a more dramatic "catastrophic" quality.

Finally, Zucker, Darby, Brewer, and Peng (Chapter 6) explore the influence of the structure of scientific fields on patterns of collaboration within those fields. Their study of the field of biotechnology suggests that when a field highly values intellectual capital, people are likely to have a larger number of collaborators. However, those collaborators are more likely to be contained within the same organization. The findings suggest that organizational boundaries are important, because being a member of the same organization generates trust. This trust is more important when a field is competitive.

Microlevel Analysis

Trust can also be addressed on the individual level by considering the psychology of the individual. Such a psychological model considers why people trust and why their trust declines or increases. Common to these analyses is the recognition that organizations have generally experienced declines in their perceived trustworthiness in the eyes of both employees and the members of other organizations. This declining trust reflects both a general social phenomenon (Lipset & Schneider, 1983) and is the result of widely publicized organizational practices, such as the high compensation of CEOs (Sheppard, Lewicki, & Minton, 1992).

Lewicki and Bunker (Chapter 7) point out the centrality of trust to emerging organizational forms and seek to understand how trust can be developed. They argue for a three-stage model underlying the development of trust. The first stage, deterrence-based trust, links the willingness to trust to the belief that there is a credible threat of punishment for failure to cooperate. This dynamic is consistent with already outlined rational models. The second stage, knowledge-based trust, links the willingness to trust to the belief that other people's dispositions are well-known enough that their behavior can be reliably predicted. Again, this model is consistent with rational choice motivations. The third stage, identification-based trust, occurs when people have taken on the needs and desires of others as personal goals and act in ways that consider joint gains. This model, which suggests that people have noninstrumental motivations, leads to a series of predictions about how damaged relationships can be made more trusting.

Sheppard and Tuchinsky (Chapter 8) also focus on the evolution of new forms of economic exchange. They explore the implications of the movement away from hierarchy and market to more lateral forms of organization. Much of current organizational behavior focuses on managerial control over subordinates, a topic of lesser importance in lateral organizations that emphasize interaction among "relative equals." In such situations, they see the three bases of trust outlined by Lewicki and Bunker (drawn from Shapiro, Sheppard, & Cheraskin, 1992): deterrence, knowledge, and identification. Research suggests that through these forms of trust there can be trust in long-term non-hierarchical relationships.

Like the authors in Chapters 7 and 8, Meyerson, Weick, and Kramer (Chapter 9) believe that organizations are moving away from formal hierarchical structures to more flexible and temporary groupings around particular projects. Such rapidly converging groups require methods for developing "swift trust." Paradoxically, temporary groups often exhibit behavior that presupposes trust, without having any of the traditional sources of trust. This seeming paradox is resolved by the recognition of a new form of trust characteristic of such groups—swift trust. Such trust involves a series of hedges in which people behave in a trusting manner but also hedge to reduce the risks of betrayal. It also centers around the competent and faithful enactment of clear roles and their associated duties.

Unlike Lewicki and Bunker, who examine how to rebuild trust, several chapters explore how trust is undermined or destroyed. Sitkin and Stickel (Chapter 10) explore the dynamics of distrust in an organization that attempts to impose a "Total Quality Management" program on a group of creative scientists. Their case study nicely illustrates how misperceptions between managers and researchers develop and documents the insidious effects of such misperceptions on trust between groups within an organization.

Along similar lines, Kramer (1993) investigates how trust and distrust are construed in hierarchical relationships. He characterizes individuals in a trust relationship as "intuitive auditors" who maintain mental accounts regarding the perceived history of trust-related behaviors involving self and others. He argues that an individual's location in a power-status relationship influences how such information is processed, leading to divergent perceptions and systematic asymmetries in the construal of trust and distrust. These divergent perceptions, in turn, lead to reciprocal disappointments and decline in trust.

Bies and Tripp (Chapter 12) explore individuals' responses to the betrayal of trust. In particular, their study of revenge examines how people react when they are betrayed by others with whom they believe they have a trusting relationship. Their chapter maps the geography of revenge, exploring the actions that provoke revenge, the attributions that govern interpretations leading to revenge, and the types of revenge that people engage in. Two harms result from trust violations—a damaged sense of civic order through the failure of others to follow social rules and a damaged identity or social reputation. Interpretations of and responses to those harms take a variety of forms.

Mishra (Chapter 13) uses interviews with managers to identify four dimensions of trust: competence, openness, concern, and reliability. Competence rests on the belief that managers will make correct decisions. For example, companies may not check the reliability of shipments from companies they trust. Openness and honesty reflect the belief that managers will give straightforward accounts of events. Concern indicates the belief that a manager acts in ways designed to benefit employees. This means not taking advantage of others and involves acting in employees' interests as well as one's own. Finally, reliability reflects the degree to which people's statements and their actions are consistent (e.g., preaching concern for the company but acting to serve one's own interests).

Mishra also examines the influence of trust on key behaviors of organizational actors during times of crisis. Those behaviors include the decentralization of decision making, undistorted communication, and collaboration. Mishra argues that trust between managers, workers and managers, and workers, managers, customers, and suppliers all have a positive influence on these three aspects of responses to crisis. Trust facilitates decentralization, it increases truthful communication, and it leads to collaboration over the allocation of scarce resources. Consequently, organizations with high levels of trust are more likely to successfully survive crises. Webb (Chapter 14) presents another perspective on the role of trust in organizational crises, noting how crisis elevates the importance of trust but at the same time makes it more problematic.

Cummings and Bromiley (Chapter 15) also identify several aspects of trust. The first involves the belief that others make a good-faith effort to behave in accordance with their commitments. The second concerns honesty in negotiations. The third involves not taking excessive advantage of others when opportunities are available. It is demonstrated by using confirmatory factor analysis that these concerns represent three distinct aspects of trust. Furthermore, each aspect of trust has affective, cognitive, and behavioral intention components that are similarly distinct. Finally, it is shown that these trust measures are distinct from, but related to, actual behavior.

Why Do People Trust?

Many of the chapters in this volume are based on the underlying assumption that trust is rationally based. In other words, people's decisions about whether to cooperate—for example, their willingness to trust others—are based on their estimates of the probability that others will reciprocate that cooperation. Hardin (1993) refers to this rational perspective as an "encapsulated interest" perspective on trust. Coleman (1990) defines trust as "an incorporation of risk into the decision of whether or not to engage in the action" by acting based on estimates of the likely future behavior of others (Coleman, 1990, p. 91). Although widespread, these assumptions that the motives for trusting are instrumental typically are not empirically tested.

Two chapters make an effort to compare the rational and social models of trust. Tyler and Degoey (Chapter 16) first show the importance of trust in managerial, political, and family authorities by demonstrating that evaluations of the trustworthiness of authorities are a key antecedent of the willingness to accept decisions voluntarily and of feelings about the obligation to obey the law. They then address the instrumentality of trust. Several types of evidence are put forward to suggest that trust in others is not explainable in instrumental terms.

The first evidence Tyler and Degoey put forward for the inadequacy of an instrumental model of trust is that trust is important only when people have social relationships. This argument reinforces the findings of Kahneman, Knetsch, and Thaler (1986a, 1986b) that people apply moral standards in market settings to protect existing social relationships. For example, a landlord has an obligation to an existing tenant and cannot raise rents to reflect market values. However, if the tenant leaves, the landlord then raises the rent to reflect market values for the new tenant. Unfortunately, the motivation for this variation is unclear and could reflect either feelings of moral obligation to social relationships or changes in judgments about other people. In the social dilemma literature, for example, an increased willingness to cooperate is found when people have a social bond with others in their community (e.g., they identify with others; see Tyler & Dawes, 1993). Although seeming to suggest noninstrumental motivations, as previously noted, this change in the willingness to cooperate could either reflect feelings of moral obligation to others or the belief that others with whom one shares a social bond are more likely to reciprocate cooperation.

The argument that patterns of trust support a noninstrumental perspective on the motivations underlying trust is supported by a second Tyler and Degoey finding: Trustworthiness is more central to the willingness to defer to authorities than is competence. Here, people do not seem to be focusing on instrumental concerns in reacting to authorities. This finding seems difficult to explain in instrumental terms.

Another type of evidence put forward by Tyler and Degoey more directly tests the argument that trust is noninstrumentally based. Their analysis demonstrates that people rely on trust in situations in which they draw identity-relevant information from their interactions with group authorities. In other words, noninstrumental concerns frame the importance of trust. Conversely, instrumental concerns are shown not to influence the importance of trust. These findings directly link trust to issues of identity formation and change (Tajfel & Turner, 1979) and not to the material concerns that have been the focus of social exchange theories (see Cook & Levi, 1990).

Trust concerns are further linked to noninstrumental motivations in another type of evidence provided by Tyler and Degoey. The criteria by which people evaluate trustworthiness are not instrumental in character. In other words, people do not focus on their control over outcomes and/or on the favorability of those outcomes. Instead, they focus on the "relational" issues of neutrality and status recognition (see Tyler & Lind, 1992).

Kramer, Brewer, and Hanna (Chapter 17) echo the theme of moving away from a purely calculative or expectation-based view of trust. Their chapter draws attention to motivational and affective dimensions of trust that might prompt people to engage in trust behavior, especially in collective action contexts. In particular, they suggest that identification with a group or collective enhances concern for collective processes and outcomes. From this perspective, collective trust becomes, itself, a public good that individuals are motivated to develop and maintain.

Brockner and Siegel (Chapter 18) also argue for the importance of trust. They suggest that issues of trust underlie the important role of procedural and distributive justice in shaping people's reactions to their social experiences. Studies of justice suggest that distributive and procedural justice interact, with procedural-justice judgments shaping the favorability of participants' reactions primarily when outcomes are unfavorable or unfair. Brockner and Siegel argue that, in fact, trust, a key antecedent of procedural justice, causes this relationship to occur. They suggest that trust has both instrumental and noninstrumental components.

Of course, it is important to avoid thinking of the exploration of the psychological antecedents of trust as a struggle between two mutually incompatible models—the instrumental and the noninstrumental. The studies in this volume suggest that each model explains behavior in some settings. Hence, future research might most profitably explore the *situational* dimensions that shape the importance of instrumental and noninstrumental concerns.

It is also important to identify different types of noninstrumental motivations underlying trust. One motivation involves identification with others. Another involves internalized moral values about what is right and wrong. A third involves identity concerns in dealings with group authorities, for example, the use of the information contained in social interactions to define identity and self-worth. Although each of these motivations is important in at least some settings, the range within which each of these noninstrumental concerns shapes trust is unexplored.

Similarly, the domain of various types of instrumental motivations underlying trust needs to be examined. In its most direct instrumental form, trust is viewed as the expectation that specific others will reciprocate trusting behavior. In other words, people think they know what others will do so they can adjust their level of cooperative behavior and precaution taking. However, people might also regard at least some level of initial cooperative behavior as a generally effective instrumental strategy, irrespective of the expected behavior of particular others (Axelrod, 1984). Furthermore, people may take a long-term perspective on their gains and losses in social interaction, codifying rules of exchange in moral norms enforced by informal and formal sanctions (Tyler & Smith, in press).

Viewed in the aggregate, the contributions to this volume draw attention to a rich and still emerging body of theory and evidence regarding the role of trust in organizational life. Much of this work reflects the theme—sometimes explicitly stated and sometimes only implied—that many extant models of trust from the social sciences provide inadequate or incomplete foundations for an organizational theory of trust.

References

Axelrod, R. (1984). *The evolution of cooperation.* New York: Basic Books.

Bach, S. (1985). *Final cut: Dreams and disaster in the making of* Heaven's Gate. Beverly Hills, CA: Sage.

Bazerman, M. H., & Neale, M. A. (1992). *Negotiating rationally.* New York: Free Press.

Bellah, R. N., Madsen, R., Sullivan, W. M., Swindler, A., & Tipton, S. M. (1985). *Habits of the heart: Individualism and commitment in American life.* Berkeley: University of California Press.

Bennett, W. J. (1993). *The book of virtues: A treasury of great moral stories.* New York: Simon & Schuster.

Bianco, W. T. (1994). *Trust: Representatives and constituents.* Ann Arbor: University of Michigan Press.

Blumberg, P. (1989). *The predatory society: Deception in the American marketplace.* New York: Oxford University Press.

Brann, P., & Foddy, M. (1988). Trust and the consumption of a deteriorating resource. *Journal of Conflict Resolution, 31,* 615-630.

Brewer, M. B. (1981). Ethnocentrism and its role in interpersonal trust. In M. B. Brewer & B. E. Collins (Eds.), *Scientific inquiry and the social sciences* (pp. 214-231). San Francisco: Jossey-Bass.

Brewer, M. B., & Kramer, R. M. (1986). Choice behavior in social dilemmas: Effects of social identity, group size, and decision framing. *Journal of Personality and Social Psychology, 50,* 543-549.

Brown, P. G. (1994). *Restoring the public trust.* Boston: Beacon.

Burrough, B., & Helyar, J. (1990). *Barbarians at the gate: The fall of RJR Nabisco.* New York: Harper & Row.

Coleman, J. S. (1990). *Foundations of social theory.* Cambridge, MA: Harvard University Press.

Cook, K. S., & Levi, M. (Eds.). (1990). *The limits of rationality.* Chicago: University of Chicago Press.

Dawes, R. M. (1988). *Rational choice in an uncertain world.* Orlando, FL: Harcourt Brace.

Dawes, R. M., & Thaler, R. (1988). Anomalies: Cooperation. *Journal of Economic Perspectives, 2,* 187-197.

Dawes, R. M., van de Kragt, A. J. C., & Orbell, J. M. (1990). Cooperation for the benefit of us—not me, or my conscience. In J. Mansbridge (Ed.), *Beyond self-interest* (pp. 16-55). Chicago: University of Chicago Press.

Eisenhardt, K. M. (1989). Agency theory: An assessment and review. *Academy of Management Review, 14,* 57-74.

Etzioni, A. (1988). *The moral dimension: Towards a new economics.* New York: Free Press.

Fisher, R., & Ury, W. (1991). *Getting to yes* (2nd ed.). New York: Penguin.

Garment, S. (1991). *Scandal: The culture of mistrust in American politics.* New York: Random House.

Gibbs, J. P. (Ed.). (1982). *Social control: Views from the social sciences.* Beverly Hills, CA: Sage.

Gilson, R. J., & Mnookin, R. H. (1994). Disputing through agents: Cooperation and conflict between lawyers in litigation. *Columbia Law Review, 94,* 509-566.

Granovetter, M. (1985). Economic action and social structure: The problem of embeddedness. *American Journal of Sociology, 91,* 481-510.

Hardin, R. (1993). The street-level epistemology of trust. *Politics and Society, 21,* 505-529.

Hirsch, P. (1990). Rational choice models for sociology: Pro and con. *Rationality and Society, 2,* 137-141.

Hogarth, R. (1980). *Judgment and choice.* New York: John Wiley.

Kahneman, D., Knetsch, J. L., & Thaler, R. H. (1986a). Fairness and the assumptions of economics. *Journal of Economics, 59,* 285-300.

Kahneman, D., Knetsch, J. L., & Thaler, R. H. (1986b). Fairness as a constraint on profit seeking: Entitlements in the market. *American Economic Review, 76,* 728-741.

Kahneman, D., Slovic, P., & Tversky, A. (1982). *Judgment under uncertainty: Heuristics and biases.* Cambridge, UK: Cambridge University Press.

Kramer, R. M. (1993). Cooperation and organizational identification. In J. K. Murnighan (Ed.), *Social psychology in organizations: Advances in theory and research* (pp. 244-268). Englewood Cliffs, NJ: Prentice Hall.

Kramer, R. M. (1994, October). Integrative complexity and conflict theory: Evidence of an emerging paradigm. *Negotiation Journal,* pp. 347-357.

Kramer, R. M., & Brewer, M. B. (1984). Effects of group identity on resource use in a simulated commons dilemma. *Journal of Personality and Social Psychology, 46,* 1044-1057.

Kramer, R. M., & Brewer, M. B. (1986). Social group identity and the emergence of cooperation in resource conversation dilemmas. In H. A. M. Wilke, D. M. Messick, & C. G. Rutte (Eds.), *Experimental social dilemma* (pp. 129-137). Frankfurt: Verlag Peter Lang.

Kramer, R. M., & Goldman, L. (1995). Helping the group or helping yourself? Social motives and group identity in resource dilemmas. In D. A. Schroeder (Ed.), *Social dilemmas.* New York: Praeger.

Kramer, R. M., & Messick, D. M. (Eds.). (1995). *Negotiation as a social process.* Thousand Oaks, CA: Sage.

Laver, M. (1981). *The politics of private desires: The guide to the politics of rational choice.* New York: Penguin.

Lewis, M. (1989). *Liar's poker: Rising through the wreckage of Wall Street.* New York: Norton.

Limerick, D., & Cunnington, B. (1993). *Managing the new organization.* San Francisco: Jossey-Bass.

Lipset, S. M., & Schneider, W. (1983). *The confidence gap: Business, labor, and government in the public mind.* New York: Free Press.

Mansbridge, J. (Ed.). (1990). *Beyond self-interest.* Chicago: University of Chicago Press.

Melton, G. (Ed.). (1985). *The law as a behavioral instrument.* Lincoln: University of Nebraska Press.

Messick, D. M., Wilke, H., Brewer, M. B., Kramer, R. M., Zemke, P. E., & Lui, L. (1983). Individual adaptations and structural change as solutions to social dilemmas. *Journal of Personality and Social Psychology, 44,* 294-309.

Miller, G. J. (1992). *Managerial dilemmas: The political economy of hierarchy.* Cambridge, UK: Cambridge University Press.

Mueller, D. C. (1979). *Public choice.* Cambridge, UK: Cambridge University Press.

Neale, M. A., & Bazerman, M. H. (1985). Perspectives for understanding negotiation: Viewing negotiation as a judgmental process. *Journal of Conflict Resolution, 29,* 33-55.

Neale, M. A., & Bazerman, M. H. (1991). *Cognition and rationality in negotiation.* New York: Free Press.

Olson, M. (1965). *The logic of collective action.* New Haven, CT: Yale University Press.

Orbell, J. M., van de Kragt, A., & Dawes, R. M. (1988). Explaining discussion-induced cooperation. *Journal of Personality and Social Psychology, 54,* 811-819.

Pruitt, D. G., & Carnevale, P. J. (1993). *Negotiation in social conflict.* Pacific Grove, CA: Brooks/Cole.

Putnam, R. (1993). *Making democracy work.* Princeton, NJ: Princeton University Press.

Ross, H. L. (1980). *Settled out of court.* Hawthorne, NY: Aldine.

Rubin, J. Z. (1985). Editor's introduction. *Negotiation Journal, 1*(1).

Rushton, J. P. (1980). *Altruism, socialization, and society.* Englewood Cliffs, NJ: Prentice Hall.

Selznick, P. (1992). *The moral commonwealth: Social theory and the promise of community.* Berkeley: University of California Press.

Shapiro, D. L., Sheppard, B. H., & Cheraskin, L. (1992). Business on a handshake. *Negotiation Journal, 8,* 365-378.

Sheppard, B. H., Lewicki, R. J., & Minton, J. W. (1992). *Organizational justice: The search for fairness in the workplace.* Lexington, MA: Lexington Books.

Sitkin, S. B., & Roth, N. L. (1993). Explaining the limited effectiveness of legalistic "remedies" for trust/distrust. *Organizational Science, 4,* 367-392.

Staub, E. (1978). *Positive social behavior and morality. Vol. 1: Social and personal influences.* San Diego: Academic Press.

Staub, E. (1979). *Positive social behavior and morality. Vol. 2: Socialization and development.* San Diego: Academic Press.

Stigler, G. J. (1950). The development of utility theory. *Journal of Political Economy, 58,* 307-321, 373-396.

Tajfel, H., & Turner, J. (1979). An integrative theory of intergroup conflict. In W. G. Austin & S. Worchel (Eds.), *The social psychology of intergroup relations.* Pacific Grove, CA: Brooks/ Cole.

Thaler, R. H. (1992). *The winner's curse: Paradoxes and anomalies of economic life.* New York: Free Press.

Tyler, T. R. (1990). *Why people obey the law.* New Haven, CT: Yale University Press.

Tyler, T. R., & Dawes, R. (1993). Fairness in groups: Comparing the self-interest and social identity perspectives. In B. Mellers & J. Baron (Eds.), *Psychological perspectives on justice: Theory and applications.* Cambridge, UK: Cambridge University Press.

Tyler, T. R., & Lind, E. A. (1992). A relational model of authority in groups. *Advances in Experimental Social Psychology, 25,* 115-191.

Tyler, T. R., & Smith, H. J. (in press). Social justice and social movements. In D. Gilbert, S. T. Fiske, & G. Lindzey (Eds.), *Handbook of social psychology* (4th ed.). New York: McGraw-Hill.

Williamson, O. E. (1993). Calculativeness, trust, and economic organization. *Journal of Law and Economics, 34,* 453-502.

Wilson, J. Q. (1993). *The moral sense.* New York: Free Press.

Trust in Organizations

A Conceptual Framework
Linking Organizational Forms,
Managerial Philosophies, and
the Opportunity Costs of Controls

W. E. DOUGLAS CREED
RAYMOND E. MILES

Interest in the concept of trust has grown throughout the 1980s and into the 1990s. At the societal level, the interest in trust appeared, at least in part, as a "communitarian" response to the self-serving materialism of the Reagan and Bush era (Etzioni, 1988) and as a return to social concern (Bellah, Madsen, Sullivan, Swidler, & Tipton, 1991).

Among organizational scholars, trust has received attention as a mechanism of organizational control and more specifically as an alternative to price and authority (Bradach & Eccles, 1989), as a response to the emphasis on opportunism that pervades agency theory and transactions cost economics (Bromiley & Cummings, 1992; Etzioni, 1988), as a key factor in managerial beliefs and philosophies (Miles & Creed, 1995; Sitkin & Roth, 1993), and as a necessary element in the operation of network forms of organization (Miles & Creed, 1995; Miles & Snow, 1992; Powell, 1990). In at least some of these cases, the focus has been on the inadequacies of the assumptions that underlie organizational economics, including the failure to recognize an impetus for human "betterment" (Whitehead, 1929) that belies notions of negative opportunism (Griesinger, 1990).

Within the ranks of managers, trust has been recognized as a major issue in building supplier relations ("Learning from Japan," 1992); the starting point for problem-solving sessions across work groups and between firms, their customers, and suppliers (Malnight, 1989; Tichy & Charan, 1989); a key outcome of building relationship understandings prior to the start of large projects (Associated General Contractors of America, 1992); and a means of facilitating high-tech industry growth and success (Yoffie, 1994).

However, despite the outpouring of interest in trust, there does not yet appear to be a consensus on the role of trust in organization theory. Theories of its role range from viewing trust as the most general of three classes of control mechanism—price, authority, and trust (Bradach & Eccles, 1989)—to viewing trust as the essential factor that permits all forms of risk taking in any social system (Luhman, 1988). Trust functions, according to Powell, as "a remarkably efficient lubricant to economic exchange [that] reduces complex realities far more quickly and economically than prediction, authority, or bargaining" (1990, p. 305). In line with these notions of the essential nature of trust, Bromiley and Cummings (1992) argue that the level of trust and trustworthiness in organizations affects their structures and processes. Trustworthy behavior, according to these two scholars, actually reduces transaction costs.[1]

This chapter builds on our earlier work (Miles & Creed, 1995; Miles & Snow, 1994) and suggests a conceptual framework that explores organizational trust through the attitudes and behaviors of managers and highlights the interactive role of trust in managerial philosophies and organizational forms. It offers general propositions concerning the differential trust requirements of alternative organizational forms. In addition, it suggests a conceptual calculus for considering the costs of failing to meet the minimum level of trust for each organizational form. Finally, this chapter describes the forces shaping an emerging new managerial philosophy that focuses explicitly on trust and trust investments.

General Concepts and
Sources of Trust in Social Settings

Trust is both the specific expectation that another's actions will be beneficial rather than detrimental (Gambetta, 1988) and the generalized ability to "take for granted, to take under trust, a vast array of features of the social order" (Garfinkel, 1967, ctd. in Zucker, 1986, p. 57). A level of trust is a fundamental element of the social fabric and a factor in all market transactions (Etzioni, 1988). Individual and market freedoms, such as those presumed to exist in many market economies, are inconceivable without a social order rooted in community norms, including trust (Etzioni, 1988; Granovetter, 1985).

In general, the social sciences view trust as emerging through a variety of mechanisms.[2] For the purposes of this chapter, we draw on a sociological perspective, Zucker's (1986) characterization of three central mechanisms of "trust production" in economic structures as process-based, characteristic-based, and institutional-based trust. It should be noted that although these categories stem from a sociological perspective, there are clear common-alities with the perspectives found in developmental and social psychology and economics.

Our initial focus is on the first two of these three modes of trust production. In the process-based mode, trust arises either through the personal experience of recurring exchanges, such as gift exchanges, or in expectations based on reputation.[3] Reciprocity is at the heart of this process.[4] If a long-term balance emerges, such repeated exchanges create a system of diffuse social norms of mutual obligation and expectations of equitable treatment (Malinowski, 1922; Zucker, 1986). Through this process, transactions become embedded in a social context where the personal overlaps with the economic (Bradach & Eccles, 1989; Granovetter, 1985, 1992). In organizations, such repeated contact through time suggests a long-term commitment (Arrow, 1984; Powell, 1990), with the opportunity for incremental increases in risk and cooperation (Good, 1988; Lorenz, 1988). In short, the security and stability of such recurring reciprocal exchanges enable learning and engender trust (Powell, 1990).

Characteristic-based trust is based on norms of obligation and cooperation rooted in social similarity—the expectation that a person can or cannot be trusted because of family background, age, social or financial position, ethnicity, and so forth. Characteristic-based trust may extend broadly within a society (e.g., Japan) and may be reinforced by ritual and symbolic behaviors (Dore, 1987) that emphasize common membership and familiarity (Good, 1988). Common characteristics may provide an inclination to trust and, because trust begets trust (Bradach & Eccles, 1989; Gambetta, 1988), may initiate a positive, self-reinforcing process of interaction. (The third mode is institutional-based trust. Here, trust is tied to formal societal structures, depending on individual or firm-specific attributes; e.g., certification as an accountant, or intermediary mechanisms, such as use of an escrow account.)[5]

As suggested, both process-based and characteristic-based trust are em-bedded in the broader social fabric of a society and vary across communities and states and, from time to time, within communities and states (e.g., between the pre- and post-Vietnam/Watergate periods in the United States). This embeddedness suggests that one can develop hypotheses concerning the impact across societies of differing economic and governance systems on the development of individuals' predispositions to trust or distrust.

In sum, we believe one can usefully conceive of trust as a simple function, with the amount of trust varying as the result of some combination of characteristic similarity and positive relational experience, with broad societal norms and expectations setting a baseline or intercept—the initial expectations of general trustworthiness.

$$\text{Trust} = f\{\text{embedded predisposition to trust,}$$
$$\text{characteristic similarity,}$$
$$\text{experiences of reciprocity}\}$$

This function presumes that trust can be influenced by increasing perceived similarities and the number of positive exchanges. Clearly, educational programs designed to enhance acceptance of diversity aim at improving trust by reducing the barrier of characteristic dissimilarity. Similarly, efforts to build relational experiences—for example, putting police officers back on walking beats or assigning them to neighborhood substations—are undertaken with the intent of improving trust (through both reducing perceived dissimilarity and increasing the opportunities for experiences of reciprocity and mutuality).

Managerial Philosophies and
the Organizational Trust Function

Within organizations, managers obviously play a central role in determining both the overall level of trust and the specific expectations within given units. Managers initiate most vertical exchanges; thus, whatever level of trust or mistrust is evident in their actions may well be reciprocated. Moreover, managers design reward and control systems that are visible displays of base levels of trust or mistrust within departments or the organization as a whole. Agency theory focuses on this very issue, based on assumptions of untrustworthiness and manifest opportunism. In addition, managers control the flow of certain types of information and the opportunities to share or not share key information in ways that influence the level of trust between or across organizational levels or units (Pfeffer, 1992). Finally, managers are the primary designers of the total organizational form employed—the combination of strategy, structure, and internal mechanisms that provide the overall operating logic and resource allocation and governance mechanisms of the organization.

Based on the nature of their role relative to trust in organizations, managers affect trust levels in several ways that work along the lines of the three factors identified earlier in the general trust function. First, managers' beliefs and actions directly and indirectly influence both process-based and characteristic-based trust in organizations. They can increase or decrease the opportunities for exchanges that could increase trust levels, and they can diminish or increase characteristic differences—for example, increasing or decreasing status symbols between levels or employing means of organizational socialization that emphasize shared values. Perhaps more important, as suggested in the earlier examples, managers' overall attitudes and behaviors determine the initial levels of trust expectations within the organization, in effect enacting the context within which organizational processes will be embedded. Thus, inside organizations one can conceptualize the trust function as having both characteristic and process variables, with managers' core beliefs setting the overall predispositions for trust or distrust.

Trust in Organizations = $f\{$

> **embedded predisposition** (a function of managerial philosophy and its structural manifestations),
>
> **characteristic (dis)similarity** (which is affected by organizational actions and structure),
>
> **experiences of reciprocity** (which are affected by the organization context for reciprocity/mutuality)$\}$

These core beliefs are referred to as managerial philosophies. Managerial philosophies are the mechanisms that serve to focus expectations about people and so shape trust in organizations. Multifaceted managerial philosophies are at once statements about the nature of interactions and the possibility of reciprocity within the organization, the manifestation of norms, and "institutionalized" attributions about people's abilities and values. In addition, they are subject to cognitive biases (Good, 1988) and reflect the ideological climate of the times (Bendix, 1956; Miles & Creed, 1995).

Elsewhere (Miles & Creed, 1995) we have argued that managerial philosophies have evolved over time as a response to *ideological forces* (managers' needs to rationalize their authority and its uses), *operational forces* (the demands placed on managerial behavior by the adoption of new strategies and organizational forms), and *sociocultural forces* (the pressure placed on managers by broader societal movements and reforms). We have described (following Bendix, 1956) the evolution from the traditional social Darwinist philosophy of the 19th century to the human relations philosophy that was commonplace from the early 1900s through the 1940s and early 1950s. We have hypothesized a similar pattern of evolution from the human relations philosophy to the human resources philosophy in the late 1950s and early 1960s and the emergence of a new set of beliefs that we have called the human investment philosophy in the late 1980s and early 1990s.[6]

TABLE 2.1 Evolution of Forms and Philosophies

	Product-Market Strategy	Organizational Form	Management Mechanisms	Managerial Philosophies
1800	Single product or service Local or regional markets	Agency	Direct, personal control	*Traditional*
1890-1920	Limited, standardized product or service line Regional-national markets	Functional	Central plans and budgets. Departments run by staff specialists	*Human Relations*
1920-1960	Diversified, changing product or service line National and international markets	Divisional	Corporate goal setting. Operating decisions at division level	*Human Relations/ Human Resources*
1960-1990	Standard and innovative products or services Stable and changing markets	Matrix	Temporary teams and lateral resource allocation tools, such as internal markets or joint-planning systems	*Human Resources*
1990-2010	Product or services produced by market-linked units	Network	Broker-assembled temporary systems with shared information systems for trust and coordination	*Human Investment*

Source: Miles and Creed (1995).

As we have already described, managers' philosophies flow from basic assumptions about organizational members. Following McGregor (1960) and others, we have specified the key assumptions as those dealing with the trustworthiness of subordinates and rank-and-file organizational members and with their reliability, particularly in terms of their capabilities and their potential for exercising responsible self-direction and self-control. These assumptions are thus virtually identical to the two aspects of trust that Sitkin and Roth (1993) see as operating in organizations: (a) a belief in an employee's task reliability and (b) expectations of value congruence between a manager and his or her subordinates and between peers.

Alternative philosophies emerge in different periods and tend to become the dominant written and spoken philosophy around which an individual manager's beliefs vary. Thus, the prevalent spoken and written view of 19th-century managers emphasized the limited competence of the rank and file (as evidenced by their lack of achievement) and stressed the differences in values and motivation between managers and employees. These assumptions began, as do modern concepts of agency theory and transactions cost

TABLE 2.2 Managerial Philosophies: Assumptions, Policies, and Expectations

Traditional Model	Human Relations Model	Human Resources Model
Assumptions:	*Assumptions:*	*Assumptions:*
1. Work is inherently distasteful to most people.	1. People want to feel useful and important.	1. Work is not inherently distasteful. People want to contribute to meaningful goals that they have helped establish.
2. What workers do is less important than what they earn doing it.	2. People desire to belong and be recognized as individuals.	2. Most people can exercise far more creative, responsible self-direction and self-control than their present jobs demand.
3. Few want or can handle work that requires creativity, self-direction, or self-control.	3. These needs are more important than money in motivating people to work.	
Policies:	*Policies:*	*Policies:*
1. The manager's basic task is to supervise closely and control his or her subordinates.	1. The manager's basic task is to make each worker feel useful and important.	1. The manager's basic task is to make use of his or her "untapped" human resources.
2. He or she must break down tasks into simple, repetitive, easily learned operations.	2. He or she should keep subordinates informed and listen to their objections to his or her plans.	2. He or she must create an environment in which all members may contribute to the limits of their ability.
3. He or she must establish detailed work routines and procedures and enforce these firmly but fairly.	3. The manager should allow his or her subordinates to exercise some self-control on routine matters.	3. He or she must encourage full participation on important matters, continually broadening subordinate self-direction and control.
Expectations:	*Expectations:*	*Expectations:*
1. People can tolerate work if the pay is decent and the boss is fair.	1. Sharing information with subordinates and involving them in routine decisions will satisfy their basic needs to belong and feel important.	1. Expanding subordinate influence, self-direction, and self-control will lead to direct improvements in operating efficiency.
2. If tasks are simple enough and people are closely controlled, they will produce up to standard.	2. Satisfying these needs will improve morale and reduce resistance to formal authority—subordinates will "willingly cooperate."	2. Work satisfaction may improve as a by-product of subordinates making full use of their resources.

Adapted from Miles (1975).

22

economics, from a position of distrust, emphasizing the likelihood and/or potential for opportunistic behaviors.

Human relations writers and spokespersons argued against the prevailing criticisms of workers and portrayed them as similar to managers in their needs for belonging and recognition—as willing and eager to respond to encouragement, respect, and the opportunity to discuss work issues. Workers were viewed as basically trustworthy, though still needing thoughtful and supportive direction and control. Human resources advocates moved beyond the human relationists' assumptions, arguing that most organizational members shared not only managers' needs to belong and be recognized but also their desires for achievement—the opportunity to develop and use their skills and creativity in the service of organizational and personal goals. In this view, beliefs about task capabilities (and employees' potential) were significantly enhanced, and value and goal congruence was seen as either existing or able to be developed through such mechanisms as management by objectives.

In sum, in society at large, broad patterns of values and norms embedded in governance and economic institutions shape a general baseline of trust—a shared set of expectations and predispositions. In organizations, we contend, the predisposition to trust or distrust is embedded in managers' philosophies and has been displayed throughout time in the different organizational structures and mechanisms that their philosophies prescribe and/or accommodate.

Forms, Philosophies, and the Impact of Trust

Over the past decade there has been a growing recognition of the role of trust and distrust in organizational design. For example, Bradach and Eccles (1989) see trust as a pervasive factor in organizational design and as the most general class of organizational control mechanisms. "Prices and authority are specialized control mechanisms created for and attached to each transaction," but trust works across transactions and throughout relationships (Bradach & Eccles, 1989, p. 104).[7] As noted, agency theory focuses on the design of organizational controls and incentives to combat the purported tendency of agents to engage in suboptimal and/or self-serving behaviors (Eisenhardt, 1989); in this case, of course, distrust plays the pervasive role in organizational design. In contrast, Bromiley and Cummings (1992) suggest that because the average levels of both trustworthiness and guilefulness vary across organizations, they affect organizational outcomes differentially. Furthermore, they suggest that increases in trust reduce transactions costs and thus presumably (though they do not state so specifically) reduce the pressure for vertical integration. Trust also affects investment decisions. Lorenz (1988) argues that trust enables effective investment in assets by assuring parties there will be no abuse of bargaining power after making an agreement.

It is our view that the link between trust and organizational design is broader and more encompassing than the conceptualizations offered to date. Specifically, each alternative organizational form carries a specific set of minimal requirements for trust, and failures to meet these minimums have predictable, differential consequences for the several common forms.

Elsewhere (Miles & Creed, 1995) we have traced (following Chandler, 1962, 1992) the evolution of organizational forms from the owner-managed firm of the 19th century, through the emergence of the large-scale, vertically integrated functional form in the early part of this century, and to the decentralized, divisional form that flourished in the 1940s and 1950s. And, following Davis and Lawrence (1977), Galbraith (1974), and Miles and Snow (1992), we traced the evolution of the mixed matrix form in the 1960s and the network form in the 1980s. Furthermore, we have sought to link the evolution of organizational forms to the emergence of managerial philosophies, both chronologically and causally, offering hypotheses concerning the requirements each form places on managers' philosophies of management.

Given that trust is a key factor in managerial philosophies, we believe the linkage between trust and organizational forms is clear and compelling. Borrowing in part from our earlier work, we suggest the following form or trust relationships.

Owner-Managed Entrepreneurial Form

In the entrepreneurial form common during the 19th century, the owner exercised direct supervision and made all decisions. Employees were considered extensions or agents of the owner's will. In this form, although trust or distrust clearly could have an impact on morale, given the scope of the form, it does not have a clear impact on operating mechanisms. In short, the success of this organizational form appears to pose no clear requirement for trust.

Vertically Integrated Functional Form

The functional form benefits from delegating short-term operating responsibility to functional specialists within the constraints of centrally set schedules and budgets. The form functions perhaps most effectively when managers intercede only in an exceptional case—when schedules are not met or budgets are exceeded—which is why management texts widely used the term *management by exception* to refer to this approach. Managers whose trust levels will not permit them to achieve this level of delegation will lose some of the benefits of subordinate expertise and may cause some delays as a result of centralizing routine operating decisions. Moreover, there may be morale costs from over-management. Nevertheless, a lack of trust places only limited operational constraints on the already centrally planned and controlled functional form. A trust level comparable to that implied in the human relations philosophy of management would appear to meet the minimum requirements of this form; managers must believe, in other words, that employees are willing to be responsive and cooperative when treated properly.

Diversified Divisionalized Form

The divisionalized form succeeds by clustering sets of self-sufficient resources around a particular product, service, or geographic area. Divisions are expected to respond nearly autonomously to their specific markets and be evaluated periodically on the basis of their performance. Corporate managers, whose levels of trust in division management do not allow operating decisions to be made at the division level within normal operating periods, sacrifice the key operating advantage of the divisional form—the potential for rapid, customized responsiveness to specific markets. Thus, divisionalized forms with low trust at the corporate level pay the costs of arraying redundant administrative resources around various markets while receiving minimal benefits in return.

Within divisions, low levels of trust may be expected to have effects similar to those described earlier for the functional form. Thus, corporate managers in this form would appear to need a trust level comparable to that implied in the human resources model if the full benefits of decentralization are to accrue. At the very least, corporate managers need to believe that division managers have adequate technical and business capabilities and share the same values and goals. At the division level, a trust level equivalent to that implied in human relations philosophy—a belief in employees' willing responsiveness and cooperativeness—might meet minimum requirements.[8]

Mixed Matrix Form

The matrix form is designed to achieve frequent and rapid lateral resource allocations, often between stable functional departments and temporary project groups or between global product divisions and local or regional organizations. If matrixes are at all complex, centralized control of these allocations is costly and time-consuming. Indeed, matrixes tend to succeed to the extent that corporate management creates mechanisms that allow resource allocation decisions to be made at lower levels through joint planning, negotiation, or even market devices. Attempts to operate matrixes with low levels of trust lead to decision centralization and/or delays and a loss of both operating efficiency and responsiveness. Thus, in the matrix form, as in the divisionalized form, a general trust level comparable to that implied in the human resources philosophy would appear necessary to meet minimum requirements for effective operation.

Network Form

There is little question that within the network form trust requirements are high and the consequences of failing to meet them severe. Network members are expected to "forego the right to pursue self-interest at the expense of others" (Powell, 1990, p. 303) and recognize their codependence with upstream and downstream partners. Within networks, trust allows reduced transactions costs (Bromiley & Cummings, 1992) and assures "those contemplating a long-term relationship that adaptations to future contingencies will be made in a jointly optimal way" (Lorenz, 1988, p. 201). Networks depend on minimal transactions costs for both their responsiveness and efficiency.

Moreover, as Miles and Snow (1994) and others (e.g., Perrone, 1992) have discussed, the internal structure of network firms must be highly adaptive to facilitate rapid external responsiveness. Thus, both external relationships between network partners and internal arrangements in network firms are dependent on high levels of trust. Indeed, if managers attempt to operate in network settings with low levels of trust, failure appears almost certain. In fact, as we will discuss in subsequent sections, it seems likely that even the level of trust implied in the human resources philosophy may not be sufficient to meet the long-term minimal requirements of the network form.

In sum, as the previous paragraphs indicate, we believe it is possible to predict rather precisely the trust requirements of alternative forms, the point of impact of trust failures, and their relative costs. Comparatively, in functional forms, trust failures reduce efficiency; in divisional forms, they reduce effectiveness and raise costs; in matrix forms, they cause the form to fail; and in networks, they cause the firms to fail.

Costs and Investments:
The Calculus of Trust and Controls

Our arguments concerning the differential requirements for trust in alternative organizational forms imply a schedule of costs associated with failing to meet minimum trust requirements. The suggestion that there may be actual, measurable dollar costs associated with the failure to meet minimal trust requirements is a significant departure from the manner in which the costs and benefits of trust and distrust have generally been approached.

For the most part, organizational scholars have viewed the cost and benefits of trust and distrust in terms of control costs (e.g., as a trade-off relative to the costs of risk minimization), with the cost of monitoring trustworthy individuals likely to be less both in terms of direct costs and the costs of losses (Bromiley & Cummings, 1992; Lorenz, 1988). In addition, some organizational scholars have suggested what some of the opportunity costs might be. For example, although promoting trust is costly in that it requires time to establish personal rapport as well as an attitude and policies consistent with the notion of partnership, according to Lorenz (1988), the lack of trust is costlier still. Lack of trust reduces cooperative efforts of all kinds (Bromiley & Cummings, 1992). In contrast, organizations with high levels of trust can embark on more types of cooperative efforts, incurring lower transaction costs in the process, whereas the strategic options for organizations with low levels of trust are diminished (Lorenz, 1988).

Yet despite these consequences, trust is viewed in much of the organizational literature as an exogenous factor, something of benefit if it should be present but not as a "hard" asset of major financial consequence. In contrast, our view is that it is quite possible to suggest a conceptual calculus with regard to the cost trade-offs associated with investments in trust and controls. For each organizational form, we believe it is both possible and useful at least to consider (a) estimating the costs of standard control mechanisms associated with the forms; (b) estimating the costs of failures to meet minimal trust requirements, either in the form of performance failures or in the form of costs associated with additional controls substituted for trust; and (c) estimating the costs of building trust to meet minimal requirements (i.e., investing in trust).[9] In the following paragraphs, we will discuss more specifically the consequences of trust deficits in each of the organizational forms, considering investments in additional controls and investments in trust as alternative solutions. The juxtaposing of these alternative solutions is the starting point for a true calculus of trust investment.

The Functional Form: The Costs
of Trust Deficits and Solutions

A trust deficit in this form is likely to be manifested in a failure to move responsibility for technical decision making from corporate management to functional specialists. When adequate trust in functional specialists is absent, the typical response is to invest in improved vertical information systems that increase corporate managers' ability to monitor the decisions of those functional specialists. Estimating the costs of creating and operating both the core control system and these expanded information systems is a relatively simple task. Indeed, such cost estimates are commonly drawn up to support proposed additional investments in information gathering and performance measurement. These are the direct costs of trust deficits in the functional form. Firms interested in such estimations might well seek control cost comparisons with peer firms. Firms with higher costs or more elaborate control systems might well be motivated to consider investments in trust as a possible substitute for high-cost controls with uncertain returns.

Estimating the indirect and opportunity costs of trust failures in this form is more difficult, because they may well be hidden in the guise of lower levels of commitment and underused expertise. The impact may be most consequential at the upper levels of the functional form, where senior management's increased monitoring of functional specialists and management professionals is likely to constrain the employees' ability to make valuable contributions to the firm's operations and trigger disaffection. To the extent that senior management's implicit view of subordinate trustworthiness is enacted throughout the firm, the consequence of a trust deficit will be felt at the level of the rank and file as well.

In contrast, investment in trust building can occur at both upper and lower levels of the firm. In this and in all the other organizational forms, trust building requires that senior management be the "first mover" in the trust investment strategy, incurring the "set-up costs" of cooperation and commitment (Baloff & Miller, 1992). For the functional form, this entails bona fide delegation of functional responsibilities and accountability to functional managers and investment of time, energy, and resources in a system of joint problem solving involving senior managers and staff specialists. At lower levels of the organization, it is likely to entail investing in quality circles and other forms of team building.

The Divisional Form: Trust Deficits and Solutions

In divisionalized firms, manifest trust deficits involve, at the upper levels of the organization, a failure to delegate to division executives all facets of operating decision making. Within the divisions, the manifestations of trust deficits look very much like those in the functional form and have the same deleterious effects. For these reasons, it may well be possible to estimate both the current costs of operating controls and the possible costs of failures to meet minimum trust requirements, particularly at the corporate level. Staff duplications at the corporate and division level are usually an indication of control efforts unwarranted by the form, or conversely, of trust levels below those implied by the form. So, as with the functional form, the upper levels of the organization are where the trade-offs between the costs of a trust deficit and the questionable benefits of additional controls are most apparent. In fact, staff duplications and the associated additional controls actually undermine the strategic benefits the divisionalized form is designed to offer.

These redundancies make it quite possible to conceptualize a "control audit" that compares existing controls and their costs with those that would be expected in an efficiently functioning, decentralized, divisional form. Through benchmarking with the cost structures of similarly situated firms that have implemented the divisionalized form effectively, managers could calculate both the costs of an excess control-trust deficiency and the expected costs of building trust to meet the form's requirement. Investing in trust building at the upper levels of a divisionalized firm will entail creating a real system of joint goal setting—in effect, practicing management by objectives as it is practiced by a firm such as Johnson & Johnson (Arguilar & Bhambri, 1983). At the lower levels, as with the functional form, it will entail team building and creating such structures as quality circles.[10]

The Matrix Form: Trust Deficits and Solutions

In effective matrix organizations, the presence of real trust is seen both in the degree to which senior management creates the mechanism for decision making at the level of the project team and the degree to which they allow the mechanisms to function autonomously. A trust deficit is perhaps less easy to pinpoint than in the divisional form (with staff redundancies as the clear evidence), but it is possible to gauge the degree to which upper levels of management are involved in resource allocation decision making that should be taking place at the project team level. Effective matrixes attempt to operate with minimum delays for the upper-level review of lateral resource transfers. The higher the level at which transfer decisions are made or reviewed, the more costly the system and the lower its effectiveness. Although ultimately the cost of a trust deficit will be the failure of the matrix form, the more immediate costs will result from schedule slippage, possibly ill-advised reversals of team-level decisions, project cost overruns, and even failed projects.

In light of these possible consequences, estimating the opportunity costs of a trust deficit along with the direct costs of unwarranted reviews and the operation of inappropriate control systems is possible. For example, matrixes require larger lateral information systems to promote shared understandings, and the costs of these can be compared with alternative vertical information system designs. In addition, it is standard business practice to track project costs relative to the budget. Although it is clearly a more complex task to determine where cost overruns stem from inappropriate interventions by senior management in the workings of the matrix, at the very least, the time spent by senior management in reviewing project decisions can be translated into dollar figures based on both the cost of capital and executive compensation.

In contrast, estimating the direct costs of building levels of trust required for the effective operation of a matrix organization entails assessing the cost of investing in integrative mechanisms that enable project teams to function (Galbraith, 1974) and the cost of the time spent in allowing teams to adapt to the demands of a particular project.

The Network Form:
Trust Deficits and Solutions

In the network form, efforts to apply traditional control mechanisms are generally ineffective. As noted earlier, there is broad agreement that trust requirements are high for networks to perform effectively, and the impacts of trust failures, as we have discussed in detail elsewhere (Miles & Snow, 1992), are clear and calculable. Indeed, it is our view that both across the firms within a network and within the various network firms, there is little choice but to consider trust building and maintenance to be as essential as control system building and maintenance are viewed in the functional form. That is, the functional form is designed to operate with centrally set schedules and budgets. If control is not exercised, the form may fail. The network form is designed to operate with jointly set schedules, individually monitored. If the parties do not trust one another to perform and instead act according to this lack of trust, the form will fail.

Because the costs of trust failures are so visible in the network form, both scholars and managers appear willing to treat trust building and trust maintenance as normal and expected managerial behaviors (Lorenz, 1988; Miles & Snow, 1994; Powell, 1990). In fact, as we suggested earlier, if one examines the statements of many modern managers and management scholars, one can infer the emergence of a new managerial philosophy that we have termed, appropriately to this discussion, the *human investment philosophy*. We will discuss the process of investing in trust in the network form subsequently.

The Human Investment Philosophy

Elsewhere we have described in detail the shape of the emerging human investment model (Miles & Creed, 1995; Miles & Snow, 1994) and approaches managers and firms are taking to apply it, primarily in network settings. For our purposes here, it is enough to consider the trust implications apparent in the philosophy and how these relate to current and future research and management actions.

The key characteristic of the human investment philosophy is a willingness to invest in education designed to enhance the technical competencies, business understanding, decision-making abilities, and the self-governance capa-

TABLE 2.3 The Human Investment Model

Assumptions:

1. Most people not only want to contribute and have untapped capabilities, but they also have the potential to continually develop their technical skills, their self-governance competency, and their understanding of business issues.
2. Most people are both trustworthy and anxious to be trusting in their relationships. They can and will develop broad interpersonal and interorganizational interaction skills with education and encouragement.

Policies:

1. The manager's basic task is to prepare the organization's human and technical resources to respond effectively and efficiently to current and future demands within the organization's scope of operation.
2. The manager must make both current and long-term investments in technical-skill upgrading and general business and self-management knowledge for every organizational member.
3. The manager must give subordinates every opportunity to practice new skills and exercise new knowledge; the manager must view human capabilities entrepreneurially—as assets to be invested.
4. Managers must be prepared to make investments in both technical and governance skills across organizational units within other network member firms.

Expectations:

1. Investments in human capabilities, including self-governance and competence, build adaptive capacity and create a learning organization.
2. The more competent the manager's own organization, the more facile and effective the network linkages that can be made.

Source: Miles and Creed (1995).

bilities of all members of one's firm and the willingness to make explicit investments in similar competencies across firm lines within the network. Such investments make sense only if managers have high confidence in both the educational potential of organizational members (within and across firms) and their trustworthiness.

The human resources model stresses confidence in the willingness and capability of organizational members to exercise more creative and productive self-direction than managers typically believed and organizational structures typically allowed. The human investment model goes beyond confidence in current capabilities such as these and even beyond the willingness to train members to meet foreseeable organizational needs. That is, neither using current capabilities nor providing training for current needs represents an investment. The concept of investment implies risk taking—a hope for returns to capital above its costs and proportionate to the risks involved. Expenditures for job redesign and team building to allow the use of existing capabilities may carry little if any risk (although most such investments are broadly advocated and appear to bring positive returns). Similarly, training for existing needs is usually argued for as necessary and fail-safe. However, a different perspective is required if an organization invests in educating organizational members for technical demands that exceed all current needs, a business understanding that seems to go beyond the scope of an employee's job, and self-governance skills that extend beyond work team issues to customer, supplier, and interfirm relationships. Clearly, expenditures across firm lines—for example, to assist a potential upstream partner to upgrade its technical competency or to help construct a network-wide information system—demand an investment mentality and a high level of trust.

Given that the network organization form, in its several variations, is still evolving, the final shape of a supporting managerial philosophy is not yet visible. Nevertheless, it seems clear that the form demands a high level of initial trust, which is itself an investment (Baloff & Miller, 1992), and its evolution and effectiveness depend on a continuing willingness to expand trust and trust-building investments.

Investing in Trust in the Network Form

In the network form, investing in trust occurs at all levels of the organization. This differs from the other forms, where in some cases the consequences of and the corrections for a trust deficit are more manifest at the interface of senior management and functional specialists (the functional form), of senior management and division executives (the divisionalized form), and between senior management and project teams (the matrix form). Nonetheless, investment in trust has common attributes at each level. First, regardless of the organizational level, building trust depends in part on the emerging knowledge of mutual interests (Gambetta, 1988) and a genuine concern for the well-being of organizational participants (Rousseau & Parks, 1993). Cooperative actions, which give rise to a sense of obligation and so create the fabric of an embedding atmosphere of trust, must precede trust rather than be a precondition of it (Gambetta, 1988). In addition, being the first mover in trust building (Baloff & Miller, 1992) entails being open to the evidence of trustworthiness—to learning and overcoming cognitive inertia and biases for the familiar (Good, 1988). Gambetta refers to this often difficult task as activating "dormant preferences for cooperation tucked under the seemingly safer blankets of defensive-aggressive revealed preferences" (Gambetta, 1988, p. 235).

Investing in Capabilities and
Trust at the Individual Level

At the individual level,[11] the human investment model implies an approach akin to that common across the professions and the highest levels of skilled artisans. In such groups, a combination of broad educational opportunities serve to develop both individuals' intellectual muscle and the ability to learn. Although training and education focus on specific skills and know-how, apprenticeship relationships provide role models, inculcating the values and expectations embedded in the occupation.

The "apprentice" emerges from a long process of investment to become the skilled journeyman, a professional in his or her own right, responsible for adding value in every work setting in which he or she is involved. In general, as a society, we trust professionals to act out the values of their profession, giving us full return for our investment. However, just as competence is built through education and training, trust is built by trusting. When the "master" professional treats the apprentice as a colleague from the beginning, he or she is taking a risk in the hope that such trust will both elicit greater trustworthiness and will be returned. Clearly, during the professional socialization process, some apprentices falter, but the process itself provides for correction and the continuing building of professionalism on which trust can grow. In firms, at the individual level, as at all levels, managers unwilling to risk trusting will not be likely to gain full returns from their investments in skills and abilities.

Investing in Capabilities
and Trust at the Team Level

In terms of human capital investment, team building probably reaches its zenith in the extended process of creating self-managing work teams in both plants and offices. In these settings, team builders routinely invest heavily in team skill development, particularly the cross-training needed to develop team flexibility and an understanding of the total production and business process. Prior to technical skill training, team builders often put newly formed teams through a variety of exercises to build awareness of common responsibilities and foster the skills needed for self-governance, including the ability to manage interteam relations. In the most advanced applications, investments in self-governance skills, along with job process skills, are viewed as a continuous process with corresponding continuous returns.[12]

Investing in Capabilities
and Trust at the Firm Level

Investments in trust at the individual and team levels, of course, accumulate into an investment in trust for the entire firm. As almost all discussions of trust suggest, trust begets trust. It is at the level of the firm that the need for management to begin the process of activating "dormant preferences for cooperation" (Gambetta, 1988, p. 235) is most visible. Employees exhibit a clear preference for viewing the employment relationship as a social as well as an economic exchange; this ready-made predisposition for trust can be undermined, however, by evidence of management's lack of concern for the well-being of the employee and inequitable treatment (Rousseau & Parks, 1993). Investing in trust at the firm level entails then not only investing in trust at the individual and team levels but also hoping for the effects to diffuse throughout the organization. It also involves management taking seriously its responsibility to be what Rousseau and Parks (1993) refer to as "good generals," the managerial mirror image of the employee as a good soldier.

Investing in Capabilities and Trust at the Network Level

At the network level, the key trust investments are made across firms (or, in the internal network [Miles & Snow, 1992], across commonly owned but independently managed organizational units). Some of these investments are in actual dollars. For example, Novell, the computer software company, has gained recognition for its willingness to assist suppliers in need of financial help by buying their inventory in advance and settling accounts when deliveries are made.

A similar investment practice is common at Motorola, though it does not involve out-of-pocket dollars. To maintain the flow of new equipment it needs to build and test microchips, Motorola has established strategic partnerships with small, highly competent firms specializing in developing such state-of-the-art equipment. These small firms, however, may not have the cash to invest in the design and construction of expensive new manufacturing equipment. Motorola has in several instances extended purchase orders for the future output of these firms. These purchase orders then can be used as collateral by the supplier firms to obtain the funding needed to meet the joint needs of the alliance. Thus, Motorola is investing in trust by taking the risk that suppliers ultimately will be able to deliver on their state-of-the-art designs and never-before-built products (Miles & Snow, 1992).

Concluding Comments

We have argued that trust can be profitably approached in organization theory through the interaction of organizational forms and managerial philosophies. Alternative forms have, we believe, clear trust requirements, and managerial philosophies have clear levels of implied trust. As already noted, elsewhere we have argued that forms and philosophies can be brought together in a configurational theory that has great potential for improving the predictive content of existing contingency approaches. One can easily disaggregate our broader arguments to focus primary attention on trust. We believe that such an exercise is valuable to make explicit some direct effects of trust levels on organizational performance and give trust a level of objectivity comparable to that assigned to controls and incentives. Recognition of the explicit trust requirements of alternative organizational forms should give trust the economic substance it has always deserved but seldom received. As is often the case, variables such as trust only gain major attention when they move from the category of ethical "oughts" to the category of "economic musts."

Notes

1. Bromiley and Cummings (1992) propose a model for the optimal choice of control systems based on the expected losses, given the cost of control and the level of trustworthiness.

2. See Lewicki and Bunker (Chapter 7, this volume) for a discussion of the approach of different disciplines—ranging from developmental psychology to economics—on the mechanisms and forces that give rise to trust.

3. This is akin both to the idea found in personality and social psychology that trust is a generalized response based on the reinforcement history inherent in previous social interactions (Rotter, 1971) and to the idea found in developmental psychology that the early experience of such reinforcement is linked to the presence of an individual's "personal philosophy" regarding people's trustworthiness (Bowlby, 1973; Erikson, 1963; Wrightsman, 1966, 1972).

4. See Powell (1990) for a discussion of different social scientific perspectives on reciprocity.

5. Zucker (1986) suggests that in preindustrial economies, perhaps the most basic and widespread forms of trust were process-based and characteristic-based trust. Process-based trust, according to Zucker, was more likely between smaller numbers of parties because it relied on extensive, long-term interaction and clearly shared expectations of what constitutes a fair exchange. However, in more complex social systems, she argues, uniformity of expectations is more difficult to attain and process-based trust will likely narrow its scope to exchanges between those with prior exchange histories. In homogeneous communities, characteristic-based trust was common because it was easy to take for granted many facets of the social order. However, Zucker argues that in industrial America, the normal production of characteristic-based trust was disrupted by increased social heterogeneity due to increased immigration and other economic factors such as labor force mobility.

Alternative mechanisms of "trust production" arose to replace the levels of trust taken for granted in more homogeneous and less complex communities. "The central fact of the transformation of the U.S. economic system," according to Zucker, "is the proliferation of the production of trust and creation of an active market for institutional-based trust" (1986, p. 100). Although an Industrial-Age substitution for both trust founded on social similarity and trust stemming from the direct experience of successful exchange relationships, institutional-based trust still enabled the individual, in the act of trusting another party, to take for granted certain normative constraints on self-interested behavior.

6. In light of management's impact on trust within an organization, one could argue that management institutionalizes its collective view of trust and trustworthiness by enacting the organizational context for intramural exchanges, communication, and fair dealing. In effect, within organizational settings, core structural features have embedded in them the mechanisms for producing a certain level of trust and so create the foundation for taking for granted that

exchanges of particular sorts will occur. This use of institutionalization differs from its use in the term *institutional-based trust* (Zucker, 1986), where an alternative mechanism of "trust production" arose to replace the levels of trust taken for granted in more homogeneous and less complex communities.

7. Bradach and Eccles (1989) emphasize the importance of plural forms—forms that combine more than one of the three classes of control mechanisms. They argue that transactions that are ostensibly controlled by one mechanism are nonetheless profoundly affected by simultaneous use of an alternative control mechanism. Thus, even when a transaction makes extensive use of price or authority, trust is also likely to be operative.

8. It is an interesting empirical question, however, whether different levels of trust can coexist in a single, effective organization.

9. It may well be possible to go further with this concept and estimate the less tangible costs of distrust on morale and commitment (e.g., Etzioni, 1988) and the possible returns from investing in trust beyond the minimums required by the different forms. However, for this chapter, we will focus on the key estimations specified.

10. The organizational development literature is replete with approaches to building organizational trust. In many instances, trust-building investments are simply the obverse of control system investments. For example, control designers emphasize information systems that collect data from lower-level units and distribute them to higher levels to monitor performance. Trust designers emphasize information systems that pass information from higher levels to lower-level units to clarify organizational goals and needs. Similarly, control designers emphasize decision rules for managers to take corrective action. Trust designers emphasize consultative mechanisms for joint problem solving or team building for self-governance. It is our view that one way of approaching trust investments is to consider those expenditures that might reduce characteristic dissimilarities and those that might increase positive exchange experiences. Information sharing may well operate on both sources of trust. Joint goal setting and review sessions may do the same. A simple willingness on the part of management to take the initiative in trusting may be an important initial investment (Baloff & Miller, 1992).

11. Much of the following discussion of trust investments at different levels in the organization appears in Miles and Snow (1994).

12. For an example of a company committed to investing in trust at the work group level, see the discussion of Chapparel Steel in Forward, Beach, Gray, and Quick (1991).

References

Arguilar, F. J., & Bhambri, A. (1983). *Johnson & Johnson (A & B)*. Boston: HBS Case Services.

Arrow, K. (1984). *The limits of organization*. New York: Norton.

Associated General Contractors of America. (1992). *AGC's partnering: A concept for success* [Videotape].

Baloff, N., & Miller, G. (1992, June). *Getting to commitment: Lessons from economic game Theory*. Working paper.

Bellah, R. N., Madsen, R., Sullivan, W., Swidler, A., & Tipton, S. M. (1991). *The good society*. New York: Knopf.

Bendix, R. (1956). *Work and authority in industry*. New York: Harper & Row.

Bowlby, J. (1973). *Attachment and loss. Vol. 2: Separation: Anxiety and anger*. London: Hogarth Press and the Institute for Psychoanalysis.

Bradach, J. L., & Eccles, R. G. (1989). Price, authority, and trust: From ideal types to plural forms. *Annual Review of Sociology, 15*, 97-118.

Bromiley, P., & Cummings, L. L. (1992). *Transactions cost in organizations with trust* (Discussion Paper #128). Minneapolis: University of Minnesota, Strategic Management Research Center.

Chandler, A. D., Jr. (1962). *Strategy and structure: Chapters in the history of the industrial enterprise.* Cambridge: MIT Press.

Chandler, A. D., Jr. (1992). Corporate strategy, structure and control methods in the United States during the 20th century. *Industrial and Corporate Change, 1*(2), 263-284.

Davis, S. M., & Lawrence, P. R. (1977). *Matrix.* Reading, MA: Addison-Wesley.

Dore, R. (1987). *Taking Japan seriously.* Stanford, CA: Stanford University Press.

Eisenhardt, K. M. (1989). Agency theory: An assessment and review. *Academy of Management Review, 14*(1), 57-74.

Erikson, E. G. (1963). *Childhood and society.* New York: Norton.

Etzioni, A. (1988). *The moral dimension: Toward a new economics.* New York: Free Press.

Forward, G. E., Beach, D. E., Gray, D. A., & Quick, J. C. (1991). Mentofacturing: A vision for American industrial excellence. *Academy of Management Executive, 5*(3), 32-44.

Galbraith, J. R. (1974). Organization design: An information processing view. *Interfaces, 4*(3), 28-36.

Gambetta, D. (1988). Can we trust trust? In D. Gambetta (Ed.), *Trust: Making and breaking cooperative relations* (pp. 213-237). Oxford, UK: Basil Blackwell.

Garfinkel, H. (1967). *Studies in ethnomethodology.* Englewood Cliffs, NJ: Prentice Hall.

Good, D. (1988). Individuals, interpersonal relations, and trust. In D. Gambetta (Ed.), *Trust: Making and breaking cooperative relations* (pp. 31-48). Oxford, UK: Basil Blackwell.

Granovetter, M. (1985). Economic action and social structure: The problem of embeddedness. *American Journal of Sociology, 91*(3), 481-510.

Granovetter, M. (1992). Economic institutions as social constructions: A framework for analysis. *Acta Sociologica, 35,* 3-11.

Griesinger, D. W. (1990). The human side of economic organization. *Academy of Management Review, 15*(3), 478-499.

Learning from Japan. (1992, January 27). *Business Week,* pp. 52-60.

Lorenz, E. H. (1988). Neither friends nor strangers: Informal networks of subcontracting in French industry. In D. Gambetta (Ed.), *Trust: Making and breaking cooperative relations* (pp. 194-210). Oxford, UK: Basil Blackwell.

Luhman, N. (1988). Familiarity, confidence, trust: Problems and alternatives. In D. Gambetta (Ed.), *Trust: Making and breaking cooperative relations* (pp. 94-108). Oxford, UK: Basil Blackwell.

Malinowski, B. (1922). *Argonauts of the Western Pacific.* London: Routledge & Keagan Paul.

Malnight, T. W. (1989). *GE—Preparing for the 1990s.* Boston: HBS Case Services.

McGregor, D. (1960). *The human side of enterprise.* New York: McGraw-Hill.

Miles, R. E., & Creed, W. E. D. (1995). Organizational forms and managerial philosophies: A descriptive and analytical review. In B. M. Staw & L. L. Cummings (Eds.), *Research in organizational behavior* (Vol. 17, pp. 333-372). Greenwich, CT: JAI.

Miles, R. E., & Snow, C. C. (1992). Causes of failure in network organizations. *California Management Review, 34*(4), 53-72.

Miles, R. E., & Snow, C. C. (1994). *Fit, failure, and the hall of fame: How companies succeed or fail.* New York: Free Press.

Perrone, V. (1992, August). *The double net: Exploring intra-organizational conditions for effective n-form organizations.* Paper presented at the annual meeting of the Academy of Management, Las Vegas, NV.

Pfeffer, J. (1992). *Managing with power.* Boston: Harvard Business School Press.

Powell, W. W. (1990). Neither market nor hierarchy: Network forms of organization. In B. M. Staw & L. L. Cummings (Eds.), *Research in organizational behavior* (Vol. 12, pp. 295-336). Greenwich, CT: JAI.

Rotter, J. B. (1971). Generalized expectancies for interpersonal trust. *American Psychologist, 26,* 443-452.

Rousseau, D. M., & Parks, J. M. (1993). The contracts of individuals and organizations. In B. M. Staw & L. L. Cummings (Eds.), *Research in organizational behavior* (Vol. 15, pp. 1-43). Greenwich, CT: JAI.

Sitkin, S. B., & Roth, N. L. (1993). Explaining the limited effectiveness of legalistic "remedies" for trust/distrust. *Organizational Science, 4*(3), 367-392.

Tichy, N., & Charan, R. (1989, September-October). Speed, simplicity, self-confidence: An interview with Jack Welch. *Harvard Business Review,* pp. 112-120.

Whitehead, A. N. (1929). *The function of reason.* Boston: Beacon.

Wrightsman, L. S. (1966). Personality and attitudinal correlates of trusting and trustworthy behaviors in a two-person game. *Journal of Personality and Social Psychology, 4,* 328-332.

Wrightsman, L. S. (1972). *Social psychology in the seventies.* Pacific Grove, CA: Brooks/Cole.

Yoffie, D. B. (1994). *Strategic management in information technology.* Englewood Cliffs, NJ: Prentice Hall.

Zucker, L. G. (1986). Production of trust: Institutional sources of economic structure, 1840-1920. In B. M. Staw & L. L. Cummings (Eds.), *Research in organizational behavior* (Vol. 8, pp. 53-111). Greenwich, CT: JAI.

Trust and Technology

DAVID KIPNIS

Trust has been studied from a variety of perspectives over the past several decades. Some studies ask about the antecedents of trust (Christie & Geis, 1970; Deutsch, 1962; Rotter, 1971; Strickland, 1958). Other studies ask about the consequences of maintaining (or failing to maintain) trusting relations (e.g., Bromiley & Cummings, 1992; Cook & Wall, 1980; Rousseau, 1989). Research in such diverse areas as marriage, interpersonal relations, and in organizations report that trust between people, and/or between people and organizations, is a necessary precondition for the establishment of harmonious social relations and the elimination of destructive conflicts (Deutsch, 1962; Gamson, 1968). Value-laden terms such as *good, virtuous,* and *moral* are used to describe trusting behavior, and equally value-laden terms such as *evil, immoral,* and *Machiavellian* are used to describe violations of trust.

In short, social science research agrees that trusting behavior is good and distrusting behavior is bad. If everybody agrees with this generalization, one wonders why it is necessary for so many people—theologians, politicians, psychotherapists, business executives—to continually urge their constituents

AUTHOR'S NOTE: I wish to thank Ralph Rosnow and Rod Kramer for their helpful reviews of this chapter. I also thank Don Hantula, whose observations about current trends in selection were the basis for this chapter's discussion about selection tests.

to be more trusting. One would think that, by now, everybody would have learned that nothing good can come from something as bad as not trusting.

One possible explanation for people's failure to learn is that problems are associated with trust, which most people intuitively know, but these tend to be ignored by social theorists.

The purpose of this chapter is to explore, in a business setting, the assumption that people are bothered by the need to trust others. Although offering no direct proof of this assumption, this chapter will cite business actions that appear consistent with this assumption. In particular, the chapter will examine how technology influences management's concerns about trust—sometimes increasing and sometimes decreasing these concerns. Technology is defined as the use of systematic procedures to produce intended effects (Kipnis, 1991).

Two Components of Trust

Reciprocal trust relations can be divided into two components. These components partially overlap with Bromiley and Cummings's (1992) description of two kinds of trust.

The first component concerns how we feel about being trusted. I believe that most people like to be trusted. To be trusted means that you are capable of managing resources that other people value. Stated another way, it means that you have power over others—certainly not an unpleasant position to be in. It also means that you are a good person. It is generally agreed that positions of trust are given to dependable people. Of course, these positive responses may sour if being trusted includes excessive responsibilities. However, I shall ignore these negative issues in this chapter.

The second component of trust concerns how we feel about having to trust other people. My assumption is that having to trust other people is bothersome. Sometimes this bother is experienced as anxiety and sometimes as feelings of deference, fear, or anger. But whatever the label, the feelings are negative. The reason for these feelings is that most of us are socialized to value autonomy. We believe it is better to control our world than for our world to control us. The requirement that we trust others introduces unwanted uncertainty into our lives. It means that other people control outcomes that we value. It gives people power over us. And, as I will discuss subsequently, people and organizations often go to extraordinary lengths to be rid of the uncertainty that accompanies the need to trust.

Antipathy toward trust is, of course, not inevitable. I am sure that many of us can offer instances where people take great pleasure in trusting others. However, it seems to me that distrust of trust may be particularly prevalent in Western cultures, because we frequently have to trust strangers to get things done. In day-to-day transactions, people must trust lawyers, salespeople, stockbrokers, doctors, druggists, companies that produce products of unknown reliability, strangers on the street, repairworkers, neighbors, and others too numerous to mention. In other words, we have to trust people who are neither close friends, family, nor members of the same tribe or caste. Stated in evolutionary psychology's terms, we have to trust people who do not share the same gene pool as ourselves.

Trust under these circumstances may be unnatural. I am sure that a simple survey would confirm that friends and kin are trusted most often, people who are similar to us next most often, and all others who are outside of this circle least often. If we applied this hypothesis to business settings, it would suggest that trust levels are lowest in work settings in which diversity (gender, culture, and race) is highest.[1] Perhaps the major exception to this exclusionary assumption is that we trust, with cautious faith, people who have interacted reliably with us in the past (Bromiley & Cummings, 1992).

Why Do We Have to Trust?

Before describing the relation between technology and trust, I want to consider briefly why we must trust each other. Trust, as we all know, arises out of our dependency on other people. Because we have needs that require the services of other people, we must deal with issues of trust. Currall (1990) described this relation more fully when he defined trust as an individual's reliance on another person under conditions of dependence and risk. Currall goes on to define reliance as behavior that allows one's fate to be determined by another. Dependence means that one's outcomes are contingent on the trustworthy or untrustworthy behavior of another, and risk means that one would experience negative outcomes from the other person's untrustworthy behavior.

Eliminating Trust

Currall's linked definitions nicely capture the dilemmas of people when they have to trust. That is, when we trust, we also have to give the trustee power over us. Furthermore, the more important the outcomes mediated by the trustee, the greater will be our dependency on him or her, and, by definition, the more power the trustee will have over us (Emerson, 1962). As a consequence, we must be nice to them or they will betray us. Furthermore, we have to waste time thinking about them. We have to worry about their actions. If they betray us, it can be very costly. Who needs these headaches? Who needs trust?

Based on these considerations, I suggest that people prefer to avoid or get out of trusting relationships. This may be particularly true when one has to trust people who are neither friends nor family. And, if it is not possible to avoid trusting, there are several ways in which people and organizations try to contain the suspected costs of trusting other people.

Give Up Wanting

One way is to stop wanting. After all, the more we want, the more we depend on the services of other people. If we could eliminate our many appetites, we would not have to concern ourselves with issues of trust and distrust. To paraphrase Tennessee Williams, we would not have to depend on the kindness of strangers. Thus, giving up wanting frees us from the need to trust or distrust others. I might mention another benefit of giving up wanting things that require the services of others—we free ourselves from other people's power. Paradoxically, then, concerns about trust and power both originate from people's dependence on each other.

Reducing Dependence

Giving up wanting to solve concerns about trust is an unlikely solution for most people. Before taking such a drastic step, most look for ways to minimize any potential damages that may result from having to trust others. One strategy is to reduce our dependence on those we must trust. This alternative is suggested by Pfeffer (1992) in his discussion of how managers consolidate their organizational power. So, for instance, a manufacturer may develop relations with several supply sources and in this way reduce dependence on a single supplier.

Control the Trustee

In many instances, however, it is not possible to reduce our dependence on the trustee. We must play the game with the cards that we are dealt. Under these circumstances, a very popular strategy is to try to control the trustee's actions. If we can somehow guarantee that the trustee will live up to his or her obligations, then we no longer have to worry about trust. There is considerable evidence that individuals choose this strategy of control in everyday life and in organizational settings. There is, however, a major difference between these two settings.

Control in Everyday Life. In everyday life, people have far less power to directly control the behavior of trustees. That is, they have neither the legitimate right nor the coercive power to directly control the behavior of people they must trust. Therefore, control tends to be exercised by making untrustworthy behavior costly for trustees. Regulatory agencies, professional boards of ethics, and civil laws have been created in response to people's urgent demands that physicians, drug companies, contractors, companies that pollute, manufacturers, and the like be controlled through threats or actual fines, prison terms, or loss of license for untrustworthy behavior. I would describe these regulatory agencies as the outward manifestation of people's inner disquiet at the need to trust others.

Control in Business Settings. In business settings, management has the coercive and legitimate power to control directly the behavior of employees it must trust. And, as we all know, the history of labor-management relations is filled with accounts of management's many attempts to exercise such control. Deploying technology to control has the advantage of being impersonal and precise. Furthermore, it avoids public condemnations that predictably follow attempts to control employees by more coercive means, such as guns, threats, or strikebreakers.

Classification of Technology

Before describing how technology is used to control, I must address the rather obvious objection that technologies are not developed simply because management does not trust employees. Technologies are developed to reduce variability in production, reduce costs of labor and materials, facilitate communication, improve feedback systems, develop new products, use materials more efficiently, help reduce the time needed to plan and manufacture new products, coordinate and integrate the actions of units, and for many other reasons.

Whatever their reasons for development, however, most technologies also provide management with the added control of employees.[2] The significance and the variance of employee inputs are reduced through such means as transforming the nature of work, altering the workplace, setting new selection standards for employees who do the transformed work, reducing the number of employees, and developing means to monitor employee behavior. These transformations reduce management's dependence on the skills, teamwork, judgments, and efforts of employees. And as dependence declines, by definition, so too does the need to trust.

To place these methods in perspective, I first describe William Faunce's (1981) model of how technologies develop. Faunce (1981) described the evolution of industrial technology as originating from craft production, in which dependence on the skills of people is almost complete to mechanized production, in which dependence on the skills of people is reduced to automated production, because in mechanized production, computers, robots, computer-assisted design technology, numerically controlled machining, and office automation assume almost complete responsibility for the work that is done. In this last stage, human work becomes reactive rather than proactive. That is, humans monitor the work of machines, which do the actual work.

In a previous article (Kipnis, 1991), I suggested that Faunce's stages in technology can be coordinated with changes in social behavior. The following sections apply this analysis to changes in management's need to trust employees.

Skill-Demanding Technologies

In Faunce's first stage, companies must depend on the skills and abilities of employees to achieve satisfactory performance. As a result, management must trust employees, perhaps far more than they might wish. Although management can use sanctions and employ supervisors to monitor employee performance, ultimately performance outcomes are in the hands of employees. Under these circumstances, I would predict that if we asked managers what kinds of employee issues worry them the most, high on the list would be concerns about whether employees can be trusted to produce quality goods and services and whether they can be trusted to work without any slackening of effort.

Routinized Technologies

In the second stage of the development of technology, performance depends on the efficiency of machines rather than on employee skills. As a consequence of this shift in technology, management should be less concerned with the need to trust their employees. Furthermore, trust issues that do arise in this stage differ from those expressed in the first stage. That is, in the second stage, I would predict that management should express concerns about employee honesty and/or how to prevent employees from stealing company goods. Borrowing ideas from behavior-setting theory (Wicker, 1979), the prediction is that changes in technology should shift management's concerns from issues of employee abilities to issues of employee character.

As a final comment on this stage, the routinization of work should not be regarded as a "blip" in the history of work that will soon disappear as we shift to a postmodern industrial society (Faunce, 1981). As Ritzer (1993) observes in *The McDonaldization of Society,* the use of technology to standardize procedures and eliminate reliance on employee skills and judgment is still very much with us. It simply has moved from large factories to restaurants, shopping malls, chains that specialize in "quickie lubes," mall-type doctor and dentist offices, and much more. Such McDonald-type jobs are becoming an important source of employment for both high school and college graduates. There is also an increasing trend for solid middle-class jobs to be McDonaldized. Computer programs that replicate the labor-intensive work of professionals, such as teachers, accountants, and perhaps psychotherapists, are now being introduced or are in use. The advantages of work simplification, as ever, are minimal costs, control, efficiency, and the elimination of dependence on employees.

Third-Stage Technology

In this stage, managerial dependence on employees and its corresponding need to trust employees once again increase. This is because employees must be trusted to regulate the computers, robots, and other automated machines that are now doing the work. Employee failures can result in major costs for management.

Third-stage technology, then, reactivates management concerns about trusting employees. Employees in this stage have more responsibility and yet are working either by themselves, without direct supervision, or in self-monitoring groups. This has occurred because advances in technology have encouraged the elimination of many first- and second-line supervisory positions. As a result, we should find increased managerial interest in the question of how to make employees more trusting and more trustworthy. Managerial concerns about trust at this stage should focus on the issue of employee failure to monitor the business's technology.

I should also mention that although third-stage technology increases management's concerns about trust, it also provides several ways in which these concerns can be reduced. For one, blue-collar workers and unions make up an increasingly small fraction of third-stage employees. Rather, employees are selected from a pool of professionally and technically trained applicants. As a consequence, their values and ideologies of work are far more similar to management's than those of employees previously hired. Faunce (1981) describes third-stage employees as professionally trained, intrinsically interested in doing good work, and likely to do their best work in the absence of traditional bureaucratic controls. Such similarities in interest and values, as I suggested earlier in this chapter, should make it easier for management to trust employees.

A second reason why management's concerns about trust are buffered is that third-stage technology requires fewer employees to do the work. Hence, fewer employees have to be trusted. Furthermore, technology at this stage continually allows management to downsize its workforce. This results in even fewer employees to trust. So, for example, rather than employing 50 blue-collar machinists, who in the worst-case scenario (from management's perspective) might have been union members, management now employs four technicians to write computer programs and monitor machine performance. In turn, the computers do the actual work of running the lathes, milling machines, and drill presses. Soon, as further improvements in technology are achieved, even these technicians will be gone. My guess is that such reductions in the workforce allow management to retain only employees who are reliable and productive and who can be trusted. Concerns about job security should also motivate the remaining employees to send signals to management that they can be trusted.

Surveillance

Recent technological developments allow management to unobtrusively monitor the performance of its employees by means of computers, electronic reporting devices, videorecording machines, and even through satellite tracking systems. Clerical and factory workers, long-distance truck drivers, telephone sales solicitors, executives, and employed physicians are only a few of the many employees whose actions are now placed under surveillance. Electronic monitoring has become popular largely due to the rapid computerization of the modern workplace and the development of computer network technology. Aiello (1993) reports that more than 70,000 U.S. companies spent more than $500 million on surveillance software between 1990 and 1992, and that by 1990 more than 10 million workers were under electronic surveillance.

What has surveillance to do with trust? Does it reduce or increase management's concerns about trusting employees? Unfortunately, I am not aware of any systematic studies that might provide answers to these questions. Perhaps the most extensive research on the effects of computer surveillance has been reported by Aiello and his colleagues (e.g., Aiello, 1993; Aiello & Shao, 1993). Aiello's research, however, has focused on how employees, rather than managers, react to the use of electronic surveillance.

Some insights are provided, however, by the early research of both Strickland (1958) and Kruglanski and Cohen (1973) as well as by the case studies of Zuboff (1988). This research suggests that being able to watch people, without their awareness, depersonalizes social relations. To illustrate, a manager in Zuboff's case studies of computer surveillance reported,

If I didn't have the Overview system, I would walk around and talk to people more. I would digress, like asking someone about their family. I would be more interested in what people are thinking about. (p. 331)

Strickland's research also suggested that unobtrusive surveillance causes observers to distrust those they are watching. That is, the very act of secretly observing people promotes the belief that they are not to be trusted. After all, if they could be trusted, why would you be watching them?

These findings suggest two tentative hypotheses. First, the use of surveillance systems should heighten management's distrust of employees. Second, surveillance should serve to reduce management's distrust, because it appears to provide precise information about what employees are doing.[3] For example, a manager in Zuboff's study said, "Its beautiful now. I can track my people's work . . . how he is progressing . . . what is his productivity" (p. 331). Another manager said that he disciplined and fired people based on information from the surveillance system.

A further bonus of surveillance is that employees become more trustworthy. Employees who know their behavior is being watched are found to conform closely to what they perceive as management's standards (Aiello, 1993).

Screening for Trustworthy Employees

Another way in which management can reduce concerns about trust is by hiring trustworthy people. Selection tests that identify untrustworthy job applicants are being used with increased frequency in industry. A recent National Public Radio estimate suggested that 87% of all major companies screen at least some of their job applicants for drug use. Paper-and-pencil tests designed to identify an applicant's reliability and honesty are widely marketed. For example, Science Research Associates is marketing The Personal Outlook Inventory, designed to assess the likelihood that a potential employee will steal. Another means of screening for reliability is by searching an applicant's past credit history to determine whether he or she defaulted in meeting credit obligations. Although I have no direct information, I suspect that most of these tests of character are used to screen applicants for second-stage technology positions.

Some Suggested Research

Status, position, and power are prerogatives that generally prevent close personal relations from forming between employees and management. Consequently, management must trust persons who are not quite strangers but who are less than friends. This chapter has examined how changes in technology may shape management concerns about trusting "less than friends." My views are summarized in the following hypotheses.

Hypothesis 1. Negative affect is associated with the need to trust. This negative affect varies as a function of our relations with the trustee. Least discomfort will be experienced when trusting family and friends; the next level of discomfort will be experienced when trusting persons who are similar to us; and the most discomfort will be experienced when trusting everybody outside of this circle.

Hypothesis 2. As discomfort over the need to trust increases, so too will the inclination to control those we must trust.

Applying these ideas to business suggests the following hypothesis:

Hypothesis 3. As organizational diversity increases, there will be increasing attempts by management to control employees they must trust. Management will experience the most discomfort when trusting employees who are dissimilar to themselves on such measures of diversity as culture, class, race, background, gender, and work ideologies.

The remaining hypotheses examine how the use of technology shapes management's strategies in the area of trust. These hypotheses are based on the assumption that many of our thoughts and feelings are formed by the technologies that we use and that changes in technology change our thoughts and feelings (Kipnis, 1994).

Hypothesis 4. There is a curvilinear relation between trust and stage of technology. Management concerns about trust will be highest in the first stage of technology, lowest in the second stage, and rise again in the third stage.

Hypothesis 5. The nature of the trust issues of concern to management will vary by stage of technology. In the first stage, management will be concerned with issues of employee skills; in the second stage, management will be concerned with issues of employee character and honesty; in the third stage, concerns will center on how to make unsupervised employees trustworthy—more specifically, how to ensure employee reliability when they are monitoring technology.

The next hypothesis is based on research by Driscoll (1978), who studied the relation between employee trust and job satisfaction. Driscoll reported that faculty members who trusted their superiors had high job satisfaction. If we extend this idea to management's trust of subordinates, the following hypothesis is suggested.

Hypothesis 6. Stage of technology mediates the relation between trust and job satisfaction. A strong, positive relation exists between management's trust of employees and management's job satisfaction in the first stage of technology; no relation exists between these two variables in the second stage; and a strong positive relation exists in the third stage.

Hypothesis 7. Managers who use electronic monitoring techniques will express the most distrust of their employees and the least concern about the potential of their employees to carry out untrustful actions.

In a previous article, I suggested that the topics studied by social and organizational psychology are based on problems experienced by the major institutions in society (Kipnis, 1994). Applying this generalization to the study of trust suggests the hypothesis that research on the topic of trust in organizations should be increasing. This is because organizations are increasingly using third-stage technologies, which in turn focus management's concerns on the issue of trust.

As a rough check on this question, the psychology abstracts (*Psyclit*) were searched to determine how often the topic of trust has been studied in organizations over the past 20 years. I began my search with research reported in 1974. From 1974 to 1977, 13 studies examined issues of trust in organizations, 21 studies from 1978 to 1981, 22 studies from 1982 to 1985, 38 studies from 1986 to 1989, and 50 studies from 1990 to 1993. This fourfold increase in studies of trust over the past 20 years can be interpreted in many ways. Needless to say, I favor the view that the causal path goes from changes in technology to managerial concerns about trust to research studies about trust.

Hypothesis 8. As increasing numbers of organizations move from the second to the third stage of technology, there will be increased support for research on ways to encourage employee trust and trustworthiness.

Notes

1. This hypothesis is a simple extension of the well-documented generalization that organizational members respond negatively to dissimilar others or to those who do not share common goals (Kramer, 1991; Stephan & Stephan, 1985).

2. The major exception to this relation between technology and control is when new technologies are introduced. New technologies usually increase management's dependence on their employees' expertise. However, dependence inevitably decreases as technologies are improved (Faunce, 1981).

3. R. Kramer (personal communication, 1994) has suggested to me that surveillance systems may also create a false sense of security among managers. This is because dishonest or untrustworthy employees can usually find ways to "beat the system."

References

Aiello, J. R. (1993). Computer-based monitoring: Electronic surveillance and its effects. *Journal of Applied Social Psychology, 23,* 499-507.

Aiello, J. R., & Shao, M. (1993). Electronic performance monitoring and stress. The role of feedback and goal setting. In G. Salvendy & M. Smith (Eds.), *Human computer interactions: Software and hardware interface*. Amsterdam, the Netherlands: Elsevier Science.

Bromiley, P., & Cummings, L. L. (1992). *Transaction costs in organizations with trust*. Minneapolis: University of Minnesota, Department of Strategic Management and Organization.

Christie, R., & Geis, F. (1970). *Studies in Machiavellianism*. San Diego: Academic Press.

Cook, J., & Wall, T. (1980). New work attitude measures of trust, organizational commitment and personal need nonfulfillment. *Journal of Occupational Psychology, 53*, 39-52.

Currall, S. C. (1990). *The role of interpersonal trust in work relationships*. Unpublished doctoral dissertation, Cornell University.

Deutsch, M. (1962). Cooperation and trust. In M. Jones (Ed.), *Nebraska symposium on motivation* (pp. 275-320). Lincoln: University of Nebraska Press.

Driscoll, J. W. (1978). Trust and participation in organizational decision making as predictors of satisfaction. *Academy of Management Journal, 21*, 44-56.

Emerson, R. M. (1962). Power dependence relations. *American Sociological Review, 27*, 282-298.

Faunce, W. A. (1981). *Problems of an industrial society*. New York: McGraw-Hill.

Gamson, W. A. (1968). *Power and discontent*. Homewood, IL: Dorsey.

Kipnis, D. (1991). The technological perspective. *Psychological Science, 2*, 62-69.

Kipnis, D. (1994). Accounting for the use of behavior technologies in social psychology. *American Psychologist, 49*.

Kramer, R. M. (1991). Intergroup relations and organizational dilemmas. In B. M. Staw & L. L. Cummings (Eds.), *Research in organizational behavior* (Vol. 13, pp. 191-228). Greenwich, CT: JAI.

Kruglanski, A., & Cohen, M. (1973). Attributed freedom and personal causation. *Journal of Personality and Social Psychology, 26*, 245-250.

Pfeffer, J. (1992). *Managing with power*. Boston: Harvard Business School Press.

Ritzer, G. (1993). *The McDonaldization of society*. Newbury Park, CA: Pine Forge.

Rotter, J. B. (1971). Generalized expectancies for interpersonal trust. *American Psychologist, 26*, 443-452.

Rousseau, D. (1989). Psychological and implied contracts in organizations. *Employee Rights and Responsibilities Journal, 2*, 121-139.

Stephan, W. G., & Stephan, C. W. (1985). Intergroup anxiety. *Journal of Social Issues, 41*, 157-175.

Strickland, L. (1958). Surveillance and trust. *Journal of Personality, 26*, 245-250.

Wicker, A. W. (1979). *An introduction to ecological psychology*. Belmont, CA: Wadsworth.

Zuboff, S. (1988). *In the age of the smart machine*. New York: Basic Books.

Trust-Based Forms of Governance

WALTER W. POWELL

Why has there been such considerable scholarly interest in collaboration among business firms? Over the past decade, scholars have documented the burgeoning of a wide array of interfirm relationships, ranging from research partnerships, to joint ventures, to complex manufacturing and marketing agreements (Badaracco, 1991; Hagedoorn, 1993; Mowery, 1988). The motives for this upsurge in cooperative competition are perceived as strategic: risk sharing; access to markets, technologies, and complementary skills; shortened innovation cycles; and enhanced learning. Thus we know that varied forms of cooperation among business enterprises are not that rare. Indeed, several decades ago, Macaulay (1963) detailed a broad range of business practices that fall outside the details of a contract, and he reinvigorated discussions found in classical social theory (Durkheim, 1893/1964) of the noncontractual elements of a contract (Stinchcombe, 1985). It is the larger theoretical questions raised by collaboration between ostensibly proprietary and self-seeking business units that animate much of the current research on networks of production. These questions cut right to the core of some of the most vexing

AUTHOR'S NOTE: This chapter builds on, and uses material from, the discussion of networks of production, which was a short section in a longer review essay titled "Networks and Economic Life," written with Laurel Smith-Doerr, in *The Handbook of Economic Sociology* (pp. 368-402), edited by N. J. Smelser and R. Swedberg, Princeton University Press, 1994. Used with permission.

issues in the social sciences (Axelrod, 1984; Coleman, 1990; Gambetta, 1988; Hirschman, 1984; Putnam, 1993; Scharpf, 1993; Stinchcombe, 1986): Can cooperation come about independent of trust? Can trust be a result rather than a precondition of cooperation? Is cooperation a strategic, self-interested calculation?

Trust and other forms of social capital are particularly interesting because they are moral resources (Hirschman, 1984) that operate in a fundamentally different manner than physical capital. The supply of trust increases, rather than decreases, with use; indeed, trust can become depleted if not used (see Putnam, 1993, especially chap. 6). Thus, once trust is operable, it may prove durable. But how can trust be introduced into antagonistic situations? If social norms are part of the reason for the presence of trust, how can it be manufactured (Elster, 1983)? Game theory provides important leads here. To be sure, a key lesson from game theory is that cooperation is exceedingly hard to establish even when it would benefit most of those involved (Axelrod, 1984). But under certain conditions even enemies—such as soldiers in rival armies facing one another across trenches (Axelrod, 1984, pp. 73-87)—may learn to cooperate. When there is a high probability of future association, people are not only more likely to cooperate with others, but they are also increasingly willing to punish defectors. When parties recognize that they have common interests, cooperative relations more readily ensue.

Trust does not imply blind loyalty, however. Thoughtful commentators stress that trust must be deliberate or even studied (Axelrod, 1984; Sabel, 1993; Scharpf, 1993). Cooperation entails moving to a vulnerable position; such a risky move requires creating governance structures that allow for constant monitoring and consultation. The key point is that monitoring is both easier, more natural, and vastly more effective when done by peers rather than by superiors (Powell, 1990). As Sabel (1993) observes, monitoring reduces not only the possibility of duplicity, but it also serves the more important function of routinizing contact between parties. Such consultation minimizes errors and misreadings and allows for adjustments to be made to the relationship. Taken together, these arguments suggest that research on organizational collaboration is appealing because it offers insight into building trust in which consensus emerges as a by-product of success rather than as a precondition for it (Sabel, 1993).

Seen in this light, various forms of interorganizational collaboration that exemplify trust-based governance have a considerable advantage. Generalized expectations of cooperation radically reduce the uncertainty associated with most business dealings. But not all forms of trust-based governance operate in the same fashion. In this chapter, I argue that the sources of good faith vary significantly with respect to the kinds of cooperation being pursued. I review four types of network-based collaborations. In industrial districts, the bonds of community are forged from ties of place and kinship. Here, trust builds on norms of reciprocity and civic engagement (Putnam, 1993); hence, it is "thick" (Williams, 1988). Research and development partnerships build on common membership in a professional community; this serves as an initial commitment to a relationship. The multiplex ties of extended business groups rely on shared historical experiences and the obligations and advantages of group membership. Moreover, group membership is enforced through benevolent authority (Dore, 1987). And last, strategic alliances and collaborative manufacturing emerge out of mutual dependencies. If these ventures are to last, trust must be created.

Industrial Districts: Networks of Place

The most discussed exemplars of new forms of flexible production are found in the industrial districts of north central Italy and in Baden Württemberg in southwest Germany (Piore & Sabel, 1984). These districts are composed of socially integrated, small-scale, decentralized production units. In key respects, they resemble the late 19th-century industrial districts described by the British economist Alfred Marshall, where the matrix of production was the region, not the individual firm (Becattini, 1978; Marshall, 1919). The modern success of industrial districts reminds us that business practices guided by trust-based governance structures are not novel. Given different historical background characteristics, such alternatives to mass production may well have developed in many regions (Sabel & Zeitlin, 1985). Whether in the late 19th or late 20th centuries, networks of loosely linked but spatially clustered firms create a distinctive "industrial atmosphere" where the "secrets of industry are in the air" (to use the language of Giacomo Becattini [1978], who, borrowing from the writings of Marshall, captures the shared access to innovative business practices found in such regions).

The *modus operandi* of the industrial districts rests on a very different logic from that found in the vertically integrated mass-production firm. In the "Third Italy," the small firms are commonly grouped in zones according to their product: knitwear in Modena; bicycles, motorcycles, and shoes in Bologna; food-processing machinery in Parma; and woodworking machine tools in Capri (see Brusco, 1982). Within the region, firms specializing in a product congregate in a specific area, serving to link industry and region closely. Work is carried out through extensive, collaborative, subcontracting agreements. Only a portion of the firms market final products; the others execute operations commissioned by a group of firms that initiate production. The owners of small firms typically prefer subcontracting to expansion or integration (Lazerson, 1988). The use of satellite firms allows them to remain flexible and preserve their legal and organizational structure as small companies. Though closely related and highly cooperative, the firms remain strictly independent. The time horizons for collaboration are long. Subcontractors and suppliers have diverse interfirm linkages, thus developing a wide range of products within a given line of activity.

A strong feature of the research on industrial districts is its keen attention to the social and political aspects that buttress collaborative production. Herrigel (1990) points to the wide range of support services—excellent technical colleges and vocational training institutes, small banks willing to loan funds to local businesses, specialized industry research programs—that strengthen the social structure in Baden Württemberg and encourage cooperative relations that attenuate cutthroat competition. In the Third Italy, decentralized production also depends on a combination of familial, legislative, political, and historical factors. Extended kinship bonds create economic relations based on cooperation and help the search for new employees through family and friendship networks (Lazerson, 1988). Family labor is widespread—making up about 39% of all employees in the knitwear sector (Lazerson, 1990, p. 123). In addition, several trade associations provide small artisanal firms with such services as accounting, guaranteeing loans, marketing information, and assistance in forming cooperatives (Best, 1990; Pyke, 1992). As a result, many of the risks of business enterprise are attenuated through building a cooperative infrastructure. Reciprocity is thus central to the technological dynamism of industrial districts because it both reduces the risk of new investments and discourages the prospect of competition through lower prices or wages.

Saxenian (1994) contends that Silicon Valley, that narrow strip running from Palo Alto to San Jose, California, evinces many of the same characteristics as the European industrial districts. She suggests that Silicon Valley represents an industrial order that promotes collective learning among specialist producers of a complex of related technologies. In this decentralized system, dense social networks and open labor markets encourage entrepreneurship and the ongoing mobilization of resources. Companies compete intensely, but they simultaneously learn about changing markets and technologies through informal communications, collaborative projects, and common ties to research associations and universities. High rates of job mobility spread technology, promote the recombination of skills and capital, and aid the further development of the region. Silicon Valley companies, just as those in Germany or Italy, trade with the whole world, but the core of knowledge and production remains local.[1]

The logic of the industrial districts is self-reinforcing. The more distinctive each firm is, the more it depends on the success of other firms' products to complement its own. Repetitive contracting, embedded in local social relationships cemented by kinship, religion, and politics, encourages reciprocity.

Monitoring is facilitated by these social ties and constant contact. Indeed, trust-based governance seems easy to sustain when it is spatially clustered. But proximity, as is found in north central Italy or Silicon Valley, seems to be both too strong and too weak an explanation for trust. Too strong in that the apparent advantages of the industrial districts seem insurmountable. How could models of production that are not as spatially concentrated generate comparable levels of reciprocity and trust? But, then, too weak in that other regions that combine similar skills and advantages do not reproduce comparable levels of reciprocity and civic engagement. The simple fact of proximity between companies reveals little about their mode of organizing. The vibrancy of the districts is due not to their geography alone but to their social practices as well. What other kinds of social arrangements, then, are likely to generate trust?

R&D Networks

Common membership in a technological community generates a type of precommitment (Powell, 1993). Bonds of professional membership greatly expedite the formation of collaborative research and development (R&D) networks. The sense of common association with a technological, intellectual, or scientific community is a kind of glue that "thickens" cooperation. Membership in scientific or industrial associations is ongoing and occurs outside of commercial relationships. Consequently, members observe how individuals behave and learn about their reputations. The result of such sustained contact is that one's standing in a technological community shapes one's reputation for business practice.

Angel (1991) highlights a different aspect of Silicon Valley, asserting that employees and their experiential knowledge pass freely through open labor markets there. This interfirm movement is made possible because the intellectual community focuses on the advancement of semiconductor technology in general rather than allegiance to a single firm. This "trading" of information and people is a key to the "innovative milieu" of Silicon Valley, because technological know-how is often tacit and is best transmitted through personal relationships (Angel, 1991; Clark & Staunton, 1989).

Innovation often lies at the interstices of firms' knowledge (Gadde & Håkansson, 1992; Håkansson, 1990). When an R&D network brings firms together, sharing different competencies can generate new ideas (DeBresson & Amesse, 1991; Fujita, 1991; Imai & Baba, 1989; Semlinger, 1991). In rapidly developing fields, organizations are compelled to join networks to access relevant expertise. For example, innovative science-based firms need linkages to research institutes and universities to foster their own R&D (Clark &

Staunton, 1989). Moreover, without such ties, firms find it exceedingly difficult to recruit new scientists. Consequently, the reputations of individuals and organizations are intertwined. Von Hippel (1988) argues that learning by a firm is enhanced by allowing highly skilled employees to collaborate with like-minded people at ostensibly competing firms.

The general movement among companies toward stronger involvement in external relationships also reflects the fact that the institutional sources of innovation have become much more diverse and firms can no longer learn internally all they need to know (Nelson, 1990; Powell & Brantley, 1992). Indeed, in many high-tech fields, companies must become expert in both in-house research and cooperative research with external parties (e.g., universities, research institutes, R&D-driven start-up firms, and even competitors). Mowery and Rosenberg (1989, p. 13) capture this process nicely in their depiction of basic research "as a ticket of admission to an information network." Research done in-house and research done externally can no longer be viewed as substitutes but as complements. Internal R&D is necessary to be able to monitor and evaluate research done elsewhere. Collaborative research is critical to exploit new knowledge that is being developed outside the firm. External linkages are thus a competitive form of learning; they are both a means of gaining access to new knowledge and a test of the quality of internal expertise.

The flow of information through R&D networks produces certainty for members in the face of technological uncertainty. Because no single firm has all the relevant pieces of information or can readily access them, the company is faced with doubt about its ability to keep pace with the competition. Building on the preexisting ties of its scientists, a company can gain through cooperation. Von Hippel (1988) contends that industries with free-flowing information trading, such as he observed among engineers in the mini-mill segment of the steel industry, have lower search costs and find that innovation comes easier. Innovation is more than new ideas; for a new technology to catch on, there must be broader normative support, which R&D networks of production provide as well. Networks help garner backing for introducing new ideas (DeBresson & Amesse, 1991; Håkansson, 1990). But much of R&D collaboration is not calculative; rather, it is emergent. Research and development outcomes can rarely be forecast in advance; much of what emerges from discovery is unanticipated. Thus the ability to learn from surprises depends, in part, on trust that the partner will pursue collaboration with a similar zeal. In a survey of Swedish companies, Håkansson (1990) found that about half of developmental resources went into collaborative efforts, but he characterizes the collaborations as "organic"—informal, initiated out of existing ties, and not premeditated. When R&D networks are based on common membership in a technological community, collaborations occur more readily and seem more "natural."

The dynamics of cooperation are, in important ways, endogenous to high-technology fields in which intellectual advances fuel new capabilities, which in turn require novel forms of collaboration. Freeman (1991) nicely captures this dialogic process in his discussion of information technology, in which new applications are found in a wide range of products and processes. The technology simultaneously reshapes every function within a firm as well; consequently, the technology is diffused through collaboration and its further development necessitates new forms of network relations. Freeman (1991, p. 508) points out that new technology paradigms change "the common sense rules of behavior for engineers, managers, and designers." Networks of cooperative R&D become breeding grounds for both further formal cooperative ventures and the expansion of all manner of informal networks of collaboration. In this manner, the "natural" collaboration among members of a technological community and the "unnatural" cooperation among business enterprises are joined.

Business Groups

Another type of production network that seems "naturally" based on affiliation or common membership (rather than on physical proximity) is the diversified business group. In many respects, the diversified industrial group has been the core institution of successful late-developing nations (Amsden, 1989). Simply put, a business group is a network of firms that regularly collaborates over a long time. The groups combine relatively egalitarian, horizontal interorganizational ties and more hierarchical vertical linkages (Gerlach, 1992a). The boundaries of business groups are much clearer than in other networks of production. Even though the members of a group may remain autonomous, the business grouping is viewed as a community.

The best known example of business groups is the Japanese *keiretsu* (literally meaning societies of business). Seen through a U.S. lens, in which interfirm cooperation has been viewed suspiciously from both legal and business viewpoints (Jorde & Teece, 1992), the diversified business groups seem puzzling and forbidding. And there is little doubt that the cohesiveness of Japanese business groups is, in large part, responsible for the difficulties that foreign firms have had in cracking the Japanese market. The extensive reach of the *keiretsu* in Japan, as well as the *chaebol* in Korea, suggests that business enterprises can be organized along a very different set of principles, what Gerlach (1992a) terms *alliance capitalism.* Indeed, the Japanese economy runs on network principles, in three key respects: (a) The large Japanese companies are much more decentralized than their Western counterparts (Aoki, 1990), (b) a great deal of production is contracted out to complex networks of specialist suppliers (Friedman, 1988; Fruin, 1992; Nishiguchi, 1993), and (c) the identity of a firm is closely tied to the identity of the larger business grouping with which it is affiliated (Dore, 1987; Gerlach, 1992a).

Painted in broad strokes, the Japanese economic landscape is dominated by two main network structures.[2] The large, family-run, pre-World War II *zaibatsu* were ostensibly disassembled after the war by the American occupying forces. But six kinship-centered holding companies, such as Mitsubishi and Sumitomo, reemerged. By some estimates, the big six account for nearly one fifth of Japanese economic activity (Ferguson, 1990). Operating according to the principle of one finger in every pie (or *wan setto shugi*), each *keiretsu* operates one company in nearly every major Japanese industry. Each *keiretsu* also has a lead bank, and the financial institutions play a critical role in linking the corporate network altogether, although they remain relatively silent in the decisions of individual firms (Gerlach, 1992b; Glasmeier & Sugiura, 1991). Alongside the six *keiretsu* are a number of large industrial groupings, often termed supply *keiretsu,* that operate in industries, such as automobile, heavy machinery, and electronics, where the parent (e.g., Toyota, Hitachi, or Sony) is the final assembler of complex parts, and subassemblies are supplied by affiliates and subcontractors. In both cases, the large networks of producers look like complex, extended families, organized either in a cobweb-like fashion or as a vast holding company with financial institutions at the apex. In some respects, the family analogy can be stretched further, because even though the *keiretsu* are a complex mix of vertical and horizontal affiliations, authority is exercised with benevolence by the most powerful.

There is little doubt that principles of obligation (Dore, 1983) and reciprocity (Gouldner, 1960) are infused in Japanese business practices. But what is striking, however, is how those principles have been translated into business strategies that have proven to be immensely productive and innovative. Consider the case of subcontracting relationships. Back in the 1950s and early 1960s, when Japanese firms competed on the basis of lowest cost, relationships with subcontractors were hierarchical and asymmetrical. But as firms increasingly competed on the basis of quality and innovation, the complex, multitiered supply relationships underwent significant change. These relationships remain hierarchical in two key respects: (a) The larger firm has a significant financial stake in the supplier or affiliate, and (b) the large firm initiates the production process. But today the asymmetry has been considerably reduced. The suppliers, in an effort to remain competitive, make significant investments in new equipment, constantly upgrade workers' skills, and take on more and more critical aspects of the assembly process (Sako, 1992). The subassembler's stake in the production process can be considerable: Van Kooij (1990) estimates that 75% of the value of Japanese color television production is contracted out. In turn, the large firms offer long-term contracts, share employees and provide technical assistance, and make financial investments to fund equipment upgrades. This is not, however, a cozy, harmonious world. It is an intensely pressurized world in which the smaller partners, or associates, as they are called, constantly strive to improve performance and remain attractive to the large companies. But by spreading their large corporate arms benevolently, the parents wrap the smaller firms under a blanket of protection that enhances their reputations, improves their ability to attract high-quality labor, and generates more business for them. Indeed, a few suppliers, such as auto parts producer Nippondenso, have become powerful multinational companies, providing subassemblies for multiple, competing parents.

On the production side, the network structure looks like one in which the principal and the agent, or the parent and the sibling, have increasingly reversed roles. But this reversal of control can be illusory; authority remains solidified by hierarchical financial control. In other words, capital flows down from the top of the network, and sophisticated industrial products flow back up (Gerlach, 1992b; Lincoln, Gerlach, & Takahashi, 1992). Moreover, because of extensive cross-shareholdings, the majority of the stock in the giant *keiretsu* is not publicly traded, affording the large companies the long time horizons that permit their investments in small-firm upgrading to show results.

Given the dramatic success of Japanese industry, attempts are being made almost everywhere to imitate some features of Japanese network practice, and hybridized versions are also spread by direct Japanese investment, such as in the Japanese transplant to auto factories in Britain, Canada, and the United States. The Japanese system, obviously, has some built-in liabilities (see Sabel, 1994, for a thoughtful discussion of these potential weaknesses), but the network principles employed by Japanese business groups have proven to be remarkably capable of competing on the basis of quality and speed. In this setting, trust emerges out of a complex mixture of obligation, common membership, opportunity, and vigilance.

Strategic Alliances and Collaborative Manufacturing

Members of a diversified business group possess a shared normative foundation; partners feel that they are following a common set of rules. Trust is "in the air." But can cooperative networks of production be established without either proximity or a sense of common membership? Alliances are yet another form of cooperation, albeit one that is calculatively formed, with details of the relationship typically spelled out in a contract.[3] Because strategic alliances lack the "natural" basis of trust that other networks possess, they rely on contractual agreements to curb potential opportunism. Monitoring tends to be more formally structured as well, with prearranged progress reports and milestone dates. As a rule, strategic alliances are short-term agreements designed for specific purposes—to produce a subassembly, establish a joint venture, or enter a new market. Under such settings trust is not easily established; fear and uncertainty must be overcome before information can be shared. But once a strategic alliance is successfully pursued, further cooperation with the same partner becomes easier; moreover, participants may develop reputations as reliable partners. The process is iterative—the level of cooperation increases with each agreement between the same partners, and individual partners become more skilled at learning through alliances.

Strategic networks have been described as relationships between autonomous firms that allow them to be more competitive in comparison with nonaffiliated "outsiders" (Jarillo, 1988; Sydow, 1991). Although strategic alliances are often formed to share information and produce innovation, they differ from R&D networks in their level of intensity. In strategic alliances such as joint ventures and licensing agreements, the depth of information transferred is seldom as great or as proprietary as with R&D collaborations (Hagedoorn & Schakenraad, 1990). The decision regarding whom to cooperate with is based on calculation of resource needs. When partners have complementary resources—from information and technology to materials and labor—they are, sometimes, willing to forego fears of vulnerability and collaborate.

Sydow (1991) argues that managerial functions change when organizations become involved in alliance networks. As firms pursue external collaborations, they attend more to interorganizational politics and assign greater importance to boundary-spanning personnel. Kanter and Myers (1991) also suggest that partnerships with others transform the internal organization of firms (see also Håkansson & Snehota, 1989) and that when strategic alliances are formed, personnel involved closely with external partners assume more salience within the firm. A key consideration, then, is which interests are being pursued: those of the firm? the alliance? an individual's career? the rather intangible quantity of learning that results from multiple collaborations across firm boundaries? As firms come to grips with involvement in a web of external relations, calculations of strategy and interests become much more complex.

Is it possible to be simultaneously strategic and cooperative? A good place to examine these calculations is in subcontracting relationships, which are presently being redefined throughout Europe and the United States. No doubt part of the impetus for change comes from awareness of the key role that subcontractors play in the Japanese just-in-time system. Yet introducing voice into a system that has long been dominated by exit is exceedingly difficult (Helper, 1993). The broad contours of the changing relationships between suppliers and assemblers are clear. In addition to age-old demands about keeping prices down, expectations that subcontractors will operate under shorter time frames, provide greater variety in product design, and deliver higher-quality products are now standard. In return, the larger firms are now more reliant on single-source suppliers and offer longer-term contracts (Helper, 1993; Semlinger, 1993). To cope with these more intense demands, subcontractors must spend more on R&D, and both parties require constant communication, even involving direct access to one another through data-sharing electronic information networks. Yet both partners remain autonomous. Indeed, the larger firms expect subcontractors to supply several competing firms. This increases their capacity for cross-learning, or so the expectation goes. Both parties depend on the sale of the final product; in this sense, they have a shared interest, but the smaller subcontractor has little protection against future cuts in demand. Clearly, the smaller firm is in a more vulnerable contractual position. The strategy of the large firm, in many cases, has been to improve its efficiency, reduce its costs, and increase its flexibility by shifting more of the risk onto the subcontractors.

But the movement toward substituting outside procurement for in-house production can be a double edge for the large firm as well. Once key suppliers have responsibility for delivering entire subassemblies, it is sensible for the larger firm to allow the smaller partner to modify components further if such changes reduce costs or improve performance. As Sabel, Kern, and Herrigel (1991) point out, such efficiency-enhancing moves may then entail further alterations that can have systemic effects. There is, as they point out in an intriguing paper on "collaborative manufacturing," no natural stopping point in this chain of decisions. Once again, we reach a point where agency and control can be reversed. Collaborative manufacturing begins, suggest Sabel et al. (1991), when the flow of knowledge from key suppliers to the final assembler is "such that the latter could not in reasonable time teach itself what its subcontractors are currently teaching it" (p. 209).

The subcontracting case illustrates a larger point about alliances: Motives are a weak guide to outcomes. Imagine two rationales for collaboration—reduced costs and enhanced capability. The former might lead to a strategy of forcing subcontractors to take on more of the risks and costs of product development, but the latter could conceivably dissolve the boundaries of the enterprise. At first glance, the former strategy seems to be a power move and the latter a cooperative one. Yet *either* approach could create a circumstance in which, despite considerable differences in the size and resources of the parties, the smaller and initially more vulnerable one now has possession of key knowledge that the larger one is vitally dependent on. Consequently, a relationship of power contains within itself both the seeds of transformation and the risk of severe failure. In the case when the relationship began out of an awareness of mutual need, the outcome could be greater trust that further sustains the relationship. Now recognize that every large firm has a dozen or more such complex linkages with companies of varying sizes, with different capabilities and varied motives for collaboration. Then you begin to see how the quantity (i.e., the number of alliances) might shape quality (i.e., the nature of partnerships). Through experimentation with new forms of organizing, firms are discovering that their identities are being altered in a manner they may not have even anticipated.

Summary and Implications

These four types of contemporary business practice illustrate different pathways to cooperation. Each relationship is based on an open-ended association in which organizational boundaries are permeable and joint activities and mutual learning are a sustaining force. But in another respect, these diverse forms of economic organization appear to be characterized by different degrees of openness as well as divergent rationales for reciprocity. The casual reader or observer might be inclined to say fundamentally different types of trust are present. By way of conclusion, I follow this argument to see where it goes, and then I turn back and comment on why it is not only analytically misplaced but is also an inaccurate understanding of trust and present-day realities.

Trust is a concept with considerable appeal. It suggests the virtues and autonomy of self-organizing, minus both the heavy hand of third-party oversight and the harsh competition of the marketplace. But trust is also exceedingly elusive (Gambetta, 1988), so much so that Williamson (1993) has argued that much of the discussion of trust ought to be recast as an analysis of risk. If we return to the opening arguments, trust has been viewed in two ways—as a rational outcome of an iterated chain of contacts in which farsighted parties recognize the potential benefits of their continued interaction and as a by-product of the embeddedness of individuals in a web of social relations such that values and expectations are commonly shared. The difficulty is that the rational or calculative view and the cultural or social norm view lead to similarly unappealing conclusions. In the former, trust is exceedingly hard to generate among antagonists, and, in the latter case, those communities well endowed with trust will reap the benefits of cooperation while those without it are doomed to suffer.

Thus trust seems merely a fortuitous by-product of certain forms of cooperation. Indeed, one could read the above summaries as evidence for such a view. In the industrial districts, trust is somehow "in the air" and widely available. In close-knit professional communities, trust flows from common dedication to professional goals. In the large trading groups, trust is a by-product of a system in which all of the parties have a strong interest in maintaining reputations and meeting obligations. Finally, in the case of the proliferating array of business alliances, parties learn to trust one another out of mutual need and a calculation of the benefits of continued interaction.

Yet I think such arguments are inadequate, both conceptually and historically. Social norm-based conceptions of trust miss the extent to which cooperation is buttressed by sustained contact, regular dialogue, and constant monitoring. Clearly, not all regions that evince strong homophily in cultural values produce high levels of trust. Moreover, as Sabel (1993) argues, the industrial districts so celebrated for the "relational glue" that holds them together were once centers of discord and conflict. The key is that the social norms are reinforced through ongoing debate. Without mechanisms and institutions that sustain such conversations, trust does not ensue.

Similarly, the rational or calculative view of trust, which seems such an apt explanation for business groups or interfirm alliances, overstates the extent to which the continued success of a relationship is based on the ability of parties to take a long-term view and practice mutual forbearance. Recall that I stressed that motives are a poor guide to outcomes. Baier (1986) reminds us that trust is quite different from promise keeping. The key element of these business relationships, and the one that many parties find so disconcerting, is the very indefiniteness of what one party is counting on the other party to do. Motives are a weak starting point because the parties are learning by doing. And in the process, common purposes, shared interests, and reputation become entangled with friendship, past experience, and future incentives such that the identities of the parties may be transformed.

In short, I think it is misleading to regard trust as either an outcome derived from calculation or a value traced to culture. To be sure, both the institutional context and the reputation of individual parties may provide the grounds for anticipating whether commitments are likely to be fulfilled (Hardin, 1993). But we need to recognize the extent to which trust is neither chosen nor embedded but is instead learned and reinforced, hence a product of ongoing interaction and discussion.

Notes

1. Saxenian's (1994) fascinating comparison of the fluidity of Silicon Valley with the rigidity of Route 128 in Massachusetts raises a general question about the boundaries of industrial districts. Harrison (1994) argues that studies of industrial districts focus only on "the good jobs" but ignore the low-wage subcontracting work performed outside the district. A more abstract taxonomic debate has developed over what exactly qualifies as a district. This argument is at least as old as Marshall's original writings, but its contemporary relevance is heightened by the apparent fiscal

health of the more notable districts. But even in the Third Italy, there are debates over where exactly districts are located (see Sforzi, 1990). And is the concept stretched beyond elasticity when such diverse activities as electronics and aeronautics in Southern California (Scott, 1990) or mechanical engineering in Lyons, France (Lorenz, 1988), are regarded as operating according to principles similar to those found in industrial districts?

2. In this discussion, I draw freely on several key sources: Dore (1987), Fruin (1992), Gerlach (1992a), Lincoln et al. (1992), and Sako (1992).

3. Recall that the term *alliance* comes from international politics, where it describes temporary affiliations in times of warfare or cooperative relations among states in an anarchic world.

References

Amsden, A. H. (1989). *Asia's next giant: South Korea and late industrialization.* New York: Oxford University Press.

Angel, D. P. (1991). High technology agglomeration and the labor market: The case of Silicon Valley. *Environment and Planning A, 23,* 1501-1516.

Aoki, M. (1990). Toward an economic model of the Japanese firm. *Journal of Economic Literature, 28,* 1-27.

Axelrod, R. (1984). *The evolution of cooperation.* New York: Basic Books.

Badaracco, J. L. (1991). *The knowledge link: How firms compete through strategic alliances.* Boston: Harvard Business School Press.

Baier, A. (1986). Trust and antitrust. *Ethics, 96,* 231-260.

Becattini, G. (1978). The development of light industry in Tuscany: An interpretation. *Economic Notes, 2*(3), 107-123.

Best, M. (1990). *The new competition: Institutions of industrial restructuring.* Cambridge, MA: Harvard University Press.

Brusco, S. (1982). The Emilian Model: Productive decentralization and social integration. *Cambridge Journal of Economics, 6,* 167-184.

Clark, P., & Staunton, N. (1989). *Innovation in technology and organization.* London: Routledge & Kegan Paul.

Coleman, J. S. (1990). *Foundations of social theory.* Cambridge, MA: Harvard University Press.

DeBresson, C., & Amesse, F. (1991). Networks of innovators: A review and introduction to the issue. *Research Policy, 20,* 363-379.

Dore, R. (1983). Goodwill and the spirit of market capitalism. *British Journal of Sociology, 34,* 459-482.

Dore, R. (1987). *Taking Japan seriously.* Stanford, CA: Stanford University Press.

Durkheim, E. (1964). *The division of labor.* New York: Free Press. (Original publication 1893)

Elster, J. (1983). *Sour grapes.* New York: Cambridge University Press.

Ferguson, C. H. (1990, July-August). Computers and the coming of the U.S. keiretsu. *Harvard Business Review,* pp. 55-70.

Freeman, C. (1991). Networks of innovators: A synthesis of research issues. *Research Policy, 20,* 499-514.

Friedman, D. (1988). *The misunderstood miracle.* Ithaca, NY: Cornell University Press.

Fruin, M. W. (1992). *The Japanese enterprise system.* New York: Oxford University Press.

Fujita, K. (1991). A world city and flexible specialization: Restructuring of the Tokyo metropolis. *International Journal of Urban and Regional Research, 15,* 269-284.

Gadde, L. E., & Håkansson, H. (1992). Analysing change and stability in distribution channels—A network approach. In B. Axelsson & G. Easton (Eds.), *Industrial networks: A new view of reality.* London: Routledge & Kegan Paul.

Gambetta, D. (Ed.). (1988). *Trust: Making and breaking cooperative relations*. Oxford, UK: Basil Blackwell.

Gerlach, M. L. (1992a). *Alliance capitalism: The social organization of Japanese business*. Berkeley: University of California Press.

Gerlach, M. L. (1992b). The Japanese corporate network: A blockmodel approach. *Administrative Science Quarterly, 37*, 105-139.

Glasmeier, A., & Sugiura, N. (1991). Japan's manufacturing system: Small business, subcontracting and regional complex formation. *International Journal of Urban and Regional Research, 15*, 395-414.

Gouldner, A. W. (1960). The norm of reciprocity: A preliminary statement. *American Sociological Review, 25*, 161-178.

Hagedoorn, J. (1993). Understanding the rationale of strategic technology partnering: Interorganizational modes of cooperation and sectoral differences. *Strategic Management Journal, 14*, 371-385.

Hagedoorn, J., & Schakenraad, J. (1990). Inter-firm partnerships and co-operative strategies in core technologies. In C. Freeman & L. Soete (Eds.), *New explorations in the economics of technical change* (pp. 3-37). London: Pinter.

Håkansson, H. (Ed.). (1990). Technological collaboration in industrial networks. *EMJ, 8*, 371-379.

Håkansson, H., & Snehota, I. (1989). No business is an island: The network concept of business strategy. *Scandinavian Journal of Management, 5*, 187-200.

Hardin, R. (1993). The street-level epistemology of trust. *Politics and Society, 21*, 505-529.

Harrison, B. (1994). *Lean and mean: The changing landscape of corporate power in an age of flexibility*. New York: Basic Books.

Helper, S. (1993). An exit-voice analysis of supplier relations: The case of the U.S. automobile industry. In G. Grabher (Ed.), *The embedded firm: On the socioeconomics of industrial networks*. London: Routledge & Kegan Paul.

Herrigel, G. (1990). *Industrial organization and the politics of industry: Centralized and decentralized production in Germany*. Doctoral dissertation, Department of Political Science, MIT.

Hirschman, A. O. (1984). Against parsimony: Three easy ways of complicating some categories of economic discourse. *American Economic Review Proceedings, 74*, 88-96.

Imai, K., & Baba, Y. (1989, June 6). *Systemic innovation and cross-border networks: Transcending markets and hierarchies to create a new techno-economic system*. Paper presented at the International Seminar on Science, Technology and Economic Growth, Paris.

Jarillo, J. C. (1988). On strategic networks. *Strategic Management Journal, 9*, 31-41.

Jorde, T. M., & Teece, D. J. (Eds.). (1992) *Antitrust, innovation, and competitiveness*. New York: Oxford University Press.

Kanter, R. M., & Myers, P. S. (1991). Interorganization bonds and intraorganization behavior: How alliances and partnerships change the organizations forming them. In A. Etzioni & P. R. Lawrence (Eds.), *Socioeconomics: Toward a new synthesis*. Armonk, NY: M. E. Sharpe.

Lazerson, M. H. (1988). Organizational growth of small firms. *American Sociological Review, 53*, 330-342.

Lazerson, M. H. (1990). Subcontracting in the Modena knitwear industry. In F. Pyke, G. Becattini, & W. Sengenberger (Eds.), *Industrial districts and inter-firm co-operation in Italy* (pp. 108-133). Geneva, Switzerland: International Institute for Labor Studies.

Lincoln, J. R., Gerlach, M., & Takahashi, P. (1992). Keiretsu networks in the Japanese economy: A dyad analysis of intercorporate ties. *American Sociological Review, 57*, 561-585.

Lorenz, E. (1988). Neither friends nor strangers: Informal networks of subcontracting in French industry. In D. Gambetta (Ed.), *Trust: Making and breaking cooperative relations* (pp. 194-210). Oxford, UK: Basil Blackwell.

Macaulay, S. (1963). Non-contractual relations in business: A preliminary study. *American Sociological Review, 28,* 55-67.

Marshall, A. (1919). *Industry and trade.* London: Macmillan.

Mowery, D. C. (Ed.). (1988). *International collaborative ventures in U.S. manufacturing.* Cambridge, MA: Ballinger.

Mowery, D. C., & Rosenberg, N. (1989). *Technology and the pursuit of economic growth.* New York: Cambridge University Press.

Nelson, R. R. (1990). U.S. technological leadership: Where did it come from and where did it go? *Research Policy, 19,* 119-132.

Nishiguchi, T. (1993). *Strategic industrial sourcing.* New York: Oxford University Press.

Piore, M., & Sabel, C. (1984). *The second industrial divide.* New York: Basic Books.

Powell, W. W. (1990). Neither market nor hierarchy: Network forms of organization. In B. M. Staw & L. L. Cummings (Eds.), *Research in organizational behavior* (Vol. 12, pp. 295-336). Greenwich, CT: JAI.

Powell, W. W. (1993, May). *The social construction of an organizational field: The case of biotechnology.* Paper presented at conference on Strategic Change at Warwick Business School, Warwick, UK.

Powell, W. W., & Brantley, P. (1992). Competitive cooperation in biotechnology: Learning through networks? In N. Nohria & R. G. Eccles (Eds.), *Networks and organizations: Structure, form and action* (pp. 366-394). Boston: Harvard Business School Press.

Putnam, R. (1993). *Making democracy work: Civic traditions in modern Italy.* Princeton, NJ: Princeton University Press.

Pyke, F. (1992). *Industrial development through small-firm cooperation.* Geneva, Switzerland: International Labor Organization.

Sabel, C. F. (1993). Constitutional ordering in historical context. In F. W. Scharpf (Ed.), *Games in hierarchies and networks* (pp. 65-123). Boulder, CO: Westview.

Sabel, C. F. (1994). Learning by monitoring: The institutions of economic development. In N. Smelser & R. Swedberg (Eds.), *The handbook of economic sociology* (pp. 127-165). Princeton, NJ: Princeton University Press.

Sabel, C. F., Kern, H., & Herrigel, G. (1991). Kooperative produktion: Neue formen der zusammenarbeit zwischen endfertigern und zulieferern in der automobilindustrie und die neuordnung der firma. In H. G. Mendius & U. Wendeling-Schroder (Eds.), *Aulieferer im netz: Neustrukturierung der logistik am beispiel der automobilzulieferung* (pp. 203-227). Cologne: Bund Verlag.

Sabel, C. F., & Zeitlin, J. (1985). Historical alternatives to mass production: Politics, markets and technology in 19th century industrialization. *Past and Present, 108,* 133-176.

Sako, M. (1992). *Prices, quality and trust: Inter-firm relations in Britain and Japan.* Cambridge, UK: Cambridge University Press.

Saxenian, A. (1994). *Regional networks: Industrial adaptation in Silicon Valley and Route 128.* Cambridge, MA: Harvard University Press.

Scharpf, F. (1993). Coordination in hierarchies and networks. In F. W. Scharpf (Ed.), *Games in hierarchies and networks* (pp. 125-165). Boulder, CO: Westview.

Scott, A. J. (1990). The technopoles of Southern California. *Environment and Planning A, 22,* 1575-1605.

Semlinger, K. (1991). New developments in subcontracting—Mixing market and hierarchy. In A. Amin & M. Dietrich (Eds.), *Towards a new Europe: Structural change in the European economy.* Aldershot, UK: Edward Elgar.

Semlinger, K. (1993). Small firms and outsourcing as flexibility reservoirs of large firms. In G. Grabher (Ed.), *The embedded firm: On the socioeconomics of industrial networks* (pp. 161-178). London: Routledge & Kegan Paul.

Sforzi, F. (1990). The quantitative importance of Marshallian industrial districts in the Italian economy. In F. Pyke, G. Becattini, & W. Sengenberger (Eds.), *Industrial districts and inter-firm co-operation in Italy* (pp. 75-107). Geneva, Switzerland: International Institute for Labor Studies.

Stinchcombe, A. L. (1985). Contracts as hierarchical documents. In A. L. Stinchcombe & C. Heimer (Eds.), *Organizational theory and project management* (pp. 121-171). Oslo: Norwegian University Press.

Stinchcombe, A. L. (1986). Norms of exchange. In *Stratification and organization* (pp. 231-261). New York: Cambridge University Press.

Sydow, J. (1991). *On the management of strategic networks.* Working paper 67/91, Institut für Management, Freie Universitat, Berlin.

Van Kooij, E. (1990). Industrial networks in Japan. *Entrepreneurship and Regional Development, 2,* 279-301.

Von Hippel, E. (1988). *Sources of innovation.* New York: Oxford University Press.

Williams, B. (1988). Formal structures and social reality. In D. Gambetta (Ed.), *Trust: Making and breaking cooperative relations* (pp. 3-13). Oxford, UK: Basil Blackwell.

Williamson, O. (1993). Calculativeness, trust, and economic organization. *Journal of Law and Economics, 36,* 453-486.

Trust and Third-Party Gossip

RONALD S. BURT
MARC KNEZ

Trust plays an ambiguous role in contemporary images of organization. Trust is essential to the loose coupling that makes network organizations more adaptive to changing environments. But the dense relations argued to sustain trust also produce the tight-coupling rigidity for which trust and loose coupling are the cure.

Much of the ambiguity about organizing to produce trust is resolved by focusing on the simplest social conditions for trust, then studying how trust changes as the simple conditions aggregate into social structures. The simplest context for trust is an isolated dyad—two people disconnected from others. Their relationship is the cumulative result of their exchanges, or interaction

AUTHORS' NOTE: This chapter is an introduction to a story completed elsewhere. Burt and Knez (1995a) describe how positive and negative gossip are associated with different kinds of third parties. Burt and Knez (1995b) generalize to kinds of network structures and reinforce the analysis with results on simulated networks and game experiments. We owe a note of gratitude to the Kramer and Tyler conference participants for the lively debate over social context that sharpened the argument. In particular, discussion with Bob Gibbons sharpened the argument describing how third parties amplify trust and distrust; discussion with Rod Kramer sharpened our analysis of cliques and group affiliation effects; and Blair Sheppard's and Bob Bies's comments sharpened our discussion of how distrust accumulates within exclusive third parties to define the "ambient heat" of an organization.

games, with one another. Their games are private—their behavior displayed only to one another. Trust is by definition interpersonal but rarely private. The usual context for trust is an embedded dyad—two people surrounded by their variably interconnected friends, foes, strangers, and acquaintances. The two people play their games in public, a public composed of the third parties surrounding them. What produced trust between two people now involves third parties.

Using network data on a probability sample of senior managers from diverse functions, we describe the extent to which trust depends on the direct connection between two people versus their indirect connections through third parties and the conditions in which the dense indirect connections that enhance trust reverse their effect to create distrust. Our argument and evidence are summarized in two trust predictions: Direct connection affects trust level, and indirect connection affects trust intensity.

Trust in Private Games

Exchange theory has trust produced in private games by a simple stimulus-response logic. The theory, rooted in turn-of-the-century British anthropology, is most associated with Homans's (1961) two-party analyses of social behavior and Blau's (1964) two-party analyses of social exchange (see Ekeh, 1974, pp. 81-187, for historical exegesis of the individualistic British American version of exchange theory contrasted with the French collectivist variant represented by Durkheim and Lévi-Strauss). Blau (1964, pp. 112-113) argues that trust develops because social exchange involves unspecified obligations for which no binding contract can be written. When you exchange sensitive information with someone, for example, trust is implicit in the risk you now face that the other person might leak the information. Putting aside Blau's moral obligation aspect of exchange to focus on parameters of cost-benefit calculation (cf. Ekeh, 1974, p. 175), Coleman (1990, chap. 5) captures trust more concretely for his systems of two-party exchange and provides the metaphor for our analysis—trust is committing to an exchange before you know how the other person will reciprocate. Coleman focuses on social factors in the decision to trust (and we will return to his analysis to describe public games), but his crisp definition of trust is also useful for analyzing private games. The essential tension of trust in private games is illustrated by the decision rule in a prisoner's dilemma game.

Relations built from private games can be analyzed as the outcome of repeated prisoner's dilemma games, each game another cycle of social exchange (see Hardin, 1990, p. 364ff, on the social exchange substance of the game). Axelrod's (1984) simulation of cooperation in two-person games is intriguing and widely cited evidence for arguments that trust emerges with cooperation in repeated games. Two players choose in each game to cooperate or not. Both players get a high payoff if they both cooperate. Both get a low pay-off if both choose not to cooperate. The maximum payoff occurs when one person cooperates and the other doesn't. The cooperator gets the "sucker's pay-off" and the defector gets the maximum payoff. Tension exists because players decide whether to cooperate or not before they know what the other will do. The decision to cooperate is a decision to trust. If you do for the other, will he or she do for you or yours in the future? Axelrod's analysis shows how trust can emerge as the dominant form of interaction between a pair of people. Across the spectrum of concepts spanned by Barber's (1983) distinctions between trust as moral order, competence, and obligation, we have reduced trust to a humble level: Trust is anticipated cooperation. We have two reasons. First, we want to keep trust a simple concept to focus more clearly on the complexity of social structural effects. More complex images of trust can emerge from complex structural effects producing trust. Second, anticipated cooperation is much of the trust essential to organization. The issue isn't moral. It is office politics. Can you trust me to cooperate with your initiative?[1]

Viewed as anticipated cooperation, trust is twice created by repeated interaction—from the past and from the future. From the past, repeated experience with a person is improved knowledge of the person. Cooperation in today's game is a signal of future cooperation. Across repeated games with cooperative outcomes, one builds confidence in the other person's tendency to cooperate. From tentative initial exchanges, one moves to familiarity and more significant exchanges. The gradual expansion of exchanges promotes the trust necessary for them. From past cooperation, one expects future cooperation (cf. Stinchcombe, 1990, p. 164ff, on the information advantages of current suppliers for building trust; Zucker, 1986, on process-based trust). Furthermore, the history of cooperation is an investment that would be lost if either party behaved so as to erode the relationship—another factor making it easier for each party to trust the other to cooperate (see Larson, 1992, for discussion and anecdotal evidence on the importance of the long-term trust between firms). Blau (1968, p. 454) summarizes the process as follows:

> Social exchange relations evolve in a slow process, starting with minor transactions in which little trust is required because little risk is involved and in which both partners can prove their trustworthiness, enabling them to expand their relation and engage in major transactions. Thus, the process of social exchange leads to the trust required for it in a self-governing fashion.

Although sociological models explain trust emerging from past exchanges, economic models look to the incentives of future exchanges (e.g., Axelrod,

1984; Gibbons, 1992, p. 88ff; Kreps, 1990). The expectation that violations of trust will be punished in future games leads players to cooperate even if defection would be more profitable in a single play of the game. From a game-theoretic perspective, the information contained in past experience and the potential for future interactions are inextricably linked. A player's willingness to forego short-term gains is based on the expectation that his or her current behavior will be used to predict his or her behavior in the future.

The prediction for private games is that trust and relation strength are correlated. Repeated cooperation strengthens the relationship between two people, increasing the probability that they "trust" each other. Their strengthened relationship in turn makes future cooperation more likely.

Trust in Public Games

Put the two-person game in a social context of one or more third parties to the game between ego and alter. What was a private game is now public.

Passive Third Parties Watch

With third parties now watching ego's game with alter, ego's behavior affects more than the probability of future alter cooperation—it also affects future cooperation with the third parties. Ego's cooperation signals to the third parties that ego is cooperative, adding to ego's "reputation" for being cooperative. If ego anticipates future interaction with the third parties, then ego has a reputation incentive to cooperate with alter. If ego believes that alter is similarly aware of the third parties, then ego can see alter's incentive to cooperate. Therefore, ego-alter cooperation and trust are more likely with third parties watching ego's game with alter.

This is a small step. Trust is produced by the same stimulus-response mechanism that drives private games (e.g., see Blau, 1964, p. 37ff, on impressing others; Kreps, 1990, on reputation effects). Players act cooperatively in the short-term because future partners use their current behavior to predict their future behavior. In a single interaction between ego and a particular alter, the third parties don't say or do anything. They are passive bystanders whose mere presence as future (active) players affects ego's behavior. By this argument, trust could be created simply by convincing ego that there are third-party witnesses with whom ego and alter will play later (e.g., point videocameras at ego and alter during game play). This model ignores the issue of transmission. Past ego and alter behavior is assumed to be transmitted accurately to every other player. How is transmission affected when it occurs through a network of variably accurate third parties?

Active Third Parties Gossip

Let the third parties talk. Even such a minimal assumption of active third parties creates enormous complexity for theoretical analysis because so many conversation topics are possible (e.g., see White's, 1992, magisterial work on stories and structure). We focus on one topic: gossip about alter. The third parties have knowledge of alter that they can communicate to ego in stories about games that alter has played.

Third-party gossip is variably relevant to two-person games. The social structure of third parties means that some ego-alter pairs of people hear numerous stories about one another while others hear few stories. A strong relation means three things: (a) The connected people have interacted cooperatively in the past, (b) there is some level of trust, and (c) they have some interest in one another (or else their tie would be weak). In looking for information on alter, ego turns to trusted contacts with knowledge of alter, and those contacts continue their cooperative relation with ego by sharing what information they have. The people who are likely to have knowledge of alter and communicate it to ego are strongly tied to both ego and alter. So the stronger the indirect connection between ego and alter through mutual friends and acquaintances, the more interaction stories they will hear about one another.

The implication is that indirect connections "lock in" relationships at positive and negative extremes by making ego more certain of his or her trust in alter. The implication follows whether stories are relayed with full or partial disclosure.

Full-Disclosure Gossip

Full disclosure has third parties telling complete and accurate stories. Imagine that the stories about alter's interaction games let ego participate vicariously in those games in the sense that vicarious play is in some ways emotionally the same as actual play. The social structure of third parties relaying the stories is like a broadcast system—reaching an audience of ego "armchair quarterbacks." For a game played, signal diffuses in stories about the game create in ego a feeling of replicated game play. The more third-party indirect connections between ego and alter, the more replicating accounts ego hears about alter—and so the more certain ego is of his or her trust in alter.[2]

Partial-Disclosure Gossip

Partial disclosure has third parties telling incomplete stories about alter's past behavior. The following assumption provides a rationale for partial disclosure and provides some predictions of its impact through alternative third-party structures. Assume that the third party can strengthen his or her relation with ego by highlighting the similarity of their opinions of other people (a concrete indicator that the third party's values are consistent with ego's). Ego's tentative view of alter is apparent from a variety of cues ranging from the subtle nuance of a raised eyebrow or a skeptical tone when describing alter, to the blatant signal of expressing a positive or negative opinion. To strengthen his or her own relation with ego, the third party relays stories about alter that are consistent with ego's tentative view. If ego seems to trust alter, the third party relays stories of games in which alter cooperated. If ego seems to distrust alter, the third party relays stories in which alter defected. The more third-party indirect connections between ego and alter, the more replicating accounts ego hears that support his or her view of alter. The replicating accounts, like replicating signals from a sequence of actual games with alter, make ego certain that alter is to be trusted (repeated stories of alter cooperating) or distrusted (repeated stories of alter violating trust).[3]

Positive and Negative Effects in Related Work

Economic and sociological analyses disproportionately concern the positive effect of dense networks. The trust between two strongly connected people is even more likely when the people are embedded in a network of mutual friends and acquaintances. Examples are numerous (e.g., see Bradach & Eccles, 1989; Nohria & Eccles, 1992; Swedberg, 1993; and several chapters in the Smelser & Swedberg, 1994, handbook, especially Powell & Smith-Doerr). Two widely known arguments for a positive correlation between trust and network density are Coleman's (1990, chaps. 5, 8, 12) analysis of trust and social capital and Granovetter's (1985, 1992) discussion of trust emerging from "structural embeddedness" (trust is more likely between people with mutual friends):

> My mortification at cheating a friend of long standing may be substantial even when undiscovered. It may increase when the friend becomes aware of it. But it may become even more unbearable when our mutual friends uncover the deceit and tell one another. (Granovetter, 1992, p. 44)

This is a sociology analog to Kreps's (1990) reputation effect. Indirect connections through mutual friends and acquaintances make game behavior more public, which increases the salience of reputation, making ego and alter more careful about the cooperative image they display, which increases the probability of ego-alter cooperation and trust. Here again is the future-past difference between economics and sociology. Where sociologists ensure trust with a dense network of past exchanges, economists look to the incentives of future exchanges with third parties. The difference is not in concept so much as in research design. The sociological analysis is keyed to network data, which will let us estimate reputation effects and so reveal social structural primitives to inform economic analysis.

Because scholars focus on when it is safe to trust (dense network) rather than when it is advantageous to trust (sparse network), there is relatively little attention to the dark side of network density.[4] However, the certainty produced by dense indirect connections can be negative or positive. Depending on the frame through which ego sees alter, alter can be trustworthy or treacherous.[5] By the gossip argument, stories from third parties make ego more certain in his or her view of alter. The social process that makes ego more certainly positive can in the same way make for negative certainty.

The central conclusion from the gossip argument is that indirect connections affect trust intensity, not direction. The direction depends on conditions between ego and alter. It is this contingency on existing conditions that makes the gossip argument a rational-choice intruder within institutional theory. Ego chooses whether or not to trust alter, but the choice menu is indirectly contingent on existing conditions through the gossip of interested third parties. Where ego has reason to suspect alter, indirect connections through mutual contacts will convey stories that corroborate the suspicion—making ego certain that he or she should distrust alter. Where ego has a strong relation with alter, indirect connections will convey stories that corroborate the strong tie—making ego certain that he or she can trust alter.

Evidence

Our data come from a study of network structure and manager success (Burt, 1992, chap. 4). The data are useful here because (a) the manager respondents are a probability sample, (b) the data have been gathered from a heterogeneous population of senior managers, and (c) the data describe numerous kinds of relations, including indicators of trust and distrust. Here is a brief introduction to the data: The managers operate at the top of one of America's largest high-technology firms (over 100,000 employees at the time of the study). The study population—3,000 people just below vice-president —is heterogeneous in the sense of being scattered across regions of the country and corporate functions (sales and service, engineering, production, finance, human resources, marketing, and management). The stratified probability sample of 284 managers who completed survey questionnaires is an unbiased sample from the population. Managers described their networks of key contacts in and beyond the firm (7 contacts minimum, 22 maximum, 12.6 average). Contacts were identified with nine name-generator sociometric questions concerning diverse relations, such as informal discussion and socializing, past political support, critical sources of buy-in for projects, authority relations, and so on (Burt, 1992, p. 123, lists the questions).

Strong and Weak Relations

The 3,584 cited contacts are displayed in Figure 5.1 by the strength of their relationship with the manager. The networks are a mix of strong and weak relations that show the managers maintaining relations with distant contacts. The most typical relation inside the firm (813 of 2,939 relations) involves infrequent contact (monthly or less) with people known a long time (6 or more years). Over "Frequency" to the left of Figure 5.1, managers speak with a fourth of the contacts every day (860 relations, or 25%) but speak monthly or less often with almost half (48%). Over "Duration" in the center of Figure 5.1, half of the contacts are people the manager has known for more than 5 years (51%), but many are new acquaintances first met this year or last (21%). Over "Emotion" to the right of Figure 5.1, a third of the relations are "especially close" (32%), but almost another third are at the other extreme of "less close or distant" (28%).

The graph to the far right of Figure 5.1 distinguishes relations by relative strength within each manager's network. Emotional closeness response categories are given quantitative values, then divided by the sum of a manager's relations to indicate the proportion of the manager's network time and energy allocated to each of the manager's contacts. This will be our primary measure of relationship strength. It offers fine-grain distinctions between levels of strength, corresponds to our data on relations between the contacts in a manager's network, provides the strongest association with trust and distrust, and was used successfully in the original study to predict manager success.[6]

Trust

The main result in Figure 5.1 is that the data are consistent with a repeated game's image of trust. The probability of trust increases up the vertical axis. Reading from left to right, solid lines describe how trust is more likely in stronger relations. Dashed lines describe how distrust is less likely in stronger relations. For example, of the 1,685 relations at the extreme left of the graph, with contacts met once a month or less often, 289 are people cited for trust (square on the solid line is at .172 on the vertical axis) and 176 are people cited for distrust (circle on the dashed line is at .105). Trust is more likely with contacts met every day (.172 increases to .322), and distrust is less likely (.105 decreases to .027).

None of the sociometric items are worded in terms of trust—"Who do you trust?" or "Who do you most trust of the people you named?"—but two

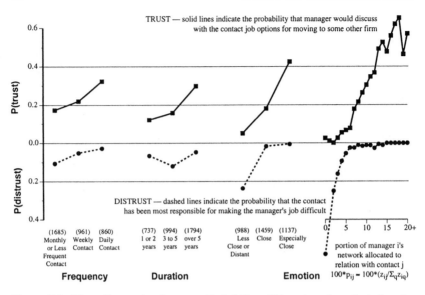

Figure 5.1. Direct Connection Increases Probability of Trust (number of relations in parentheses)

questions have face and construct validity as indicators of trust. Construct validity will become apparent from the correlations with other variables. Face validity is as follows.

Our indicator of trust was discussing job options in other firms: "If you decided to find a job with another firm doing the kind of work you do here, who are the two or three people with whom you would most likely discuss and evaluate your job options? These could be people who work here, or people outside the firm such as friends, family, or people who work at other firms." Managers responded with an average of three names (zero minimum, five maximum). This isn't a comprehensive indicator. Managers probably trust people with whom they wouldn't expect to discuss job options. Job option discussion is nevertheless a trust indicator in this study population. There is a hubris to making it in the firm (as in elite university departments). Employment is more than a contract, it is membership. Moving to another firm repudiates membership—especially for senior managers. Threatening to leave has implications for how you are treated. If word gets around that you want to leave the firm, you are irrelevant to the circulation of opportunities. You become a subject of, rather than a player in, the office gossip that builds solidarity among your colleagues. Your exit creates new opportunities, quickly carved up among your erstwhile colleagues, making it difficult for you not to leave the firm. In short, you don't discuss leaving the firm with just anyone.[7]

The solid lines in Figure 5.1 show that the probability of discussing job options in other firms increases with the strength of a relationship. It increases with the frequency of contact. It increases sharply if the manager has known the contact for more than 5 years. It increases most clearly with emotional closeness; job option discussion is eight times more likely in especially close relations than in less close or distant relations (.42 vs. .05). The graph to the far right of Figure 5.1 shows near-zero trust with the most distant contacts, increasing to over .5 with the closest contacts.

Distrust

Our indicator of distrust was a citation in response to asking managers, "Who has made it the most difficult for you to carry out your job responsibilities?" Citations were few. The usual response was to cite one person. One manager cited 2 people, 22 managers cited no one, and everyone else cited 1 contact who had made their jobs most difficult (for a total of 263 distrust citations from the 284 managers).

The wording doesn't indicate distrust, but managers were asked to explain why they cited the person they did, and their explanations indicate distrust, at least distrust of the repeated game kind. The content analysis of their reasons is reported in detail elsewhere (Burt & Celotto, 1992). The gist of the analysis is that the cited contacts were viewed as uncooperative. All kinds of contacts in the firm were cited. The typical explanation for citing a supervisor was his or her failure to lead: "no support, no coaching, no feedback," "didn't explain the firm's system/culture and advise me," or "egotistical, self-oriented liar—worst manager I've ever met." Undermining teamwork was the typical explanation for citing a colleague in the manager's own function: "not a team player; does only what is good for himself." The problems were colleagues who pursued their "own agenda" rather than the interests of the group, were "proprietary" rather than cooperative, did not "follow through on their commitments," and could not be "trusted." Typical explanations for citing peers in other functions included frustration over being denied political support: "didn't support my proposals," "had great power and withheld help," "high rank but doesn't open door; in fact he gets in the way," or "tree hugger; do it his way or don't do it at all." In short, the cited contacts were people viewed as routinely uncooperative (cf. Sitkin & Roth, 1993).

We expect relations with uncooperative contacts to be weak because managers have little incentive to maintain them. Dashed lines in Figure 5.1 show the expected negative correlation. The probability of being cited for failing to cooperate decreases with the strength of relation between manager and contact. It is most likely with contacts met monthly or less. It is less likely with contacts known for a long time. Distrust is most likely with contacts to

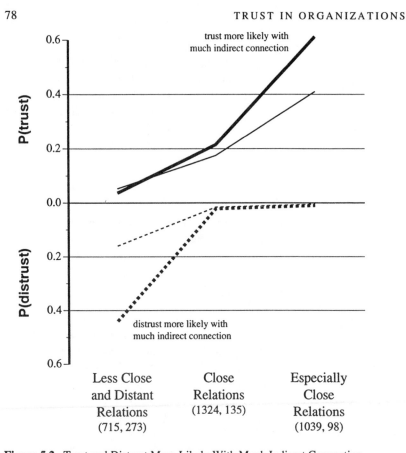

Figure 5.2. Trust and Distrust More Likely With Much Indirect Connection

NOTE: Solid lines show probability of trust; dashed lines show probability of distrust; thin lines describe relations embedded in little indirect connection (private games); bold lines describe relations embedded in much indirect connection (public games); parentheses contain number of relations embedded in (little, much) indirect connection.

whom the manager feels less close or distant, which isn't surprising given the manager explanations quoted above.

Third-Party Effects

In Figure 5.2, the Figure 5.1 association between trust and direct connection is displayed for two social contexts—little versus much indirect connection (the little-much distinction is explained in note 6). Thin (bold) lines describe relations embedded in little (much) indirect connection.

The solid lines at the top of Figure 5.2 show trust amplified within strong relations. The thin and bold lines are similarly close to zero over weak relations.

TABLE 5.1 Loglinear Trust Effects

Effect	τ	All Dyads Effect Z-Score	Within Firm Effect Z-Score	Comments
TRUST	0.49	−18.4	−18.0	Trust occurs in a minority of relations.
TRUST with DIRECT				
Less close or distant	0.47	−12.2	−12.0	Probability of trust increases significantly with relation strength.
Close	1.03	0.6	0.9	
Especially close	2.07	14.7	13.4	
TRUST with INDIRECT	1.06	1.4	2.2	Trust is slightly more likely with indirect connection.
TRUST with INDIRECT by DIRECT				
Less close or distant	0.82	−3.1	−3.0	Trust is less likely with indirect connection around weak relations but more likely with indirect connection around strong relations.
Close	1.04	0.7	0.6	
Especially close	1.17	3.2	3.0	

NOTE: These are effects in a saturated loglinear model of three dyad variables in a tabulation of all 3,584 manager relations (see Figure 5.2) and a tabulation of the 3,015 relations within the firm. TRUST is a contact with whom the manager would discuss job options for moving to some other firm (yes, no), DIRECT is the strength of relation with the contact (especially close, close, less close, or distant), and INDIRECT is the distinction between little and much indirect connection with the contact ($\sum_q p_{iq} p_{qj} < .15$ is little, else much). Three-way interaction is significant by routine statistical inference (likelihood ratio chi-square with 2 d.f. is 10.0 for all relations, 10.7 for relations within the firm; $p < .01$).

Trust is unlikely in weak relations regardless of indirect connection through third parties. Both lines are higher for stronger relations, with the bold line much higher than the thin over especially close relations. Of 1,039 especially close relations surrounded by little indirect connection, managers cited 41% as trustworthy. The odds increase to 61% of especially close relations embedded in extensive indirect connection.

The dashed lines at the bottom of Figure 5.2 show distrust amplified within weak relations. The thin and bold lines are similarly close to zero over close and especially close relations. Distrust is unlikely in strong relations, regardless of indirect connection through third parties. Distrust is more likely in less close and distant relations, especially if the weak relation is embedded in extensive indirect connection. Distrust increases from 16% of the weak

TABLE 5.2 Continuous Trust Effects

	Trust		Distrust		Combined	
	All Dyads	Within Firm	All Dyads	Within Firm	All Dyads	Within Firm
Dyads	3,584	3,015	3,584	3,015	3,584	3,015
Multiple correlation	.39	.39	.47	.47	.51	.51
Intercept	−5.55	−12.25	3.25	4.73	−5.03	−9.50
DIRECT connection	2.55	2.67	−1.21	−1.54	1.99	2.28
	(12.0)	(12.6)	(−8.5)	(−8.8)	(12.5)	(13.1)
					[12.1]	[12.8]
INDIRECT connection	0.19	0.58	0.84	0.96	−.30	−.18
	(0.9)	(2.9)	(6.3)	(6.1)	(−2.3)	(−1.3)
					[−0.6]	[−0.1]
INDIRECT × STRONG	1.51	1.34	—	—	0.60	0.44
	(9.7)	(8.3)		(6.7)	(4.4)	
					[5.7]	[3.7]
INDIRECT × WEAK	—	—	1.10	0.95	−.57	−.47
			(11.0)	(8.2)	(−5.8)	(−4.6)
					[−5.7]	[−4.7]

NOTE: These are ordinary least-squares estimates of regression coefficients with routine *t*-tests in parentheses and *t*-tests adjusted for autocorrelation in brackets (see note 10). TRUST is 100 if the manager trusts the contact, 0 otherwise. DISTRUST is 100 if the manager distrusts the contact, 0 otherwise. COMBINED is 50 if the manager trusts the contact, −50 if the contact is distrusted, 0 otherwise. From manager to a specific contact, DIRECT is 100 times the proportional strength of the direct connection (p_{ij}), INDIRECT is 100 times the portion of relations that lead indirectly to the contact ($\Sigma_q\, p_{iq}\, p_{qj}$), STRONG is a dummy variable equal to 1 if the manager is especially close to the contact (0 otherwise), and WEAK is a dummy variable equal to 1 if the manager is less close or distant from the contact (0 otherwise). The metric coefficients are therefore the points of change in trust expected from a one-point increase in direct or indirect connection.

relations surrounded by little indirect connection to 44% of the weak relations with extensive indirect connection.

Is the amplification statistically significant? Table 5.1 contains trust effects in a loglinear model of the data in Figure 5.1. Table 5.2 contains regression results with continuous predictors. The metric coefficients are points of change in trust or distrust associated with a one-point increase in direct or indirect connection. The "combined" results are for a three-category dependent variable that varies from 50 for trusted contacts, −50 for distrusted contacts, and 0 for relations between the two extremes.[8]

The effects are significant, and their significance remains if relations outside the firm are ignored,[9] if we use a logit model,[10] or if we control for autocorrelation.[11]

Direct connection predicts trust. Trust is likely in especially close relations (13.4 loglinear z-score in Table 5.1, t-tests of 12.0 and 12.6 in Table 5.2; $p <$ .001) and unlikely in less close or distant relations (-12.0 z-score in Table 5.1, t-tests of -8.5 and -8.8 in Table 5.2; $p < .001$).

The third-party effects of indirect connection are also apparent. The trust likely in an especially close relation is significantly more likely when the relation is embedded in extensive indirect connection (3.0 loglinear z-score in Table 5.1, $p = .001$; t-tests of 3.7 to 6.7 in Table 5.2, $p < .001$). The trust unlikely in a weak relationship is significantly less likely if the relation is embedded in extensive indirect connection (-3.0 z-score in Table 5.1, $p = .001$; t-tests of -4.6 to -5.8 in Table 5.2, $p < .001$).

The Probability of Trust

Figure 5.3 provides a better substantive feel for the effects. The graph shows how the probability of trust and distrust change as two people get closer—with and without indirect connections through third parties. The horizontal axis is relationship strength measured as in Figure 5.1 and Table 5.1 by the proportion of a manager's network invested in the relationship. Relations in our data vary from near-zero ($p_{ij} < .01$) to a third ($p_{ij} = .33$). Based on the displayed logit models, the vertical axis in Figure 5.3 is the probability of trust (top) and the probability of distrust (bottom). Thin lines show how probabilities change with a strengthening relationship between two people in isolation. Bold lines show the same probabilities—but for people embedded in extensive indirect connection through third parties.[12]

Two substantive points are illustrated in Figure 5.3. The first is that trust builds incrementally, but distrust is more catastrophic. The solid lines at the top of Figure 5.3 show the probability of trust building slowly and continuously across increasing levels of relation strength. The dashed lines at the bottom of the figure show that the probability of distrust is near-zero across decreasing levels of relation strength, then increases sharply in especially weak relations.

The second point illustrated in Figure 5.3 is the disproportionately negative effect of third parties. Third parties seem to be more alert to negative information, or prefer negative gossip to positive, because indirect connection amplifies the distrust associated with weak relations much more than it amplifies trust within strong relations. This is apparent in Figure 5.3 from the longer gray arrows for distrust. Indirect connection moves the bold line further away from the thin line. Looking back, the larger distrust effect can be seen in Table 5.2. In the first column of Table 5.2, a 1-point increase in direct connection generates a 2.6-point increase in trust. A 1-point increase in

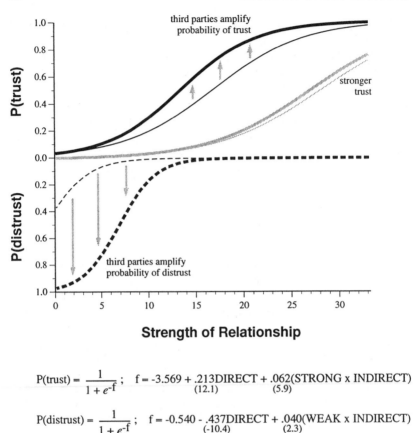

$$P(\text{trust}) = \frac{1}{1 + e^{-f}} \; ; \quad f = -3.569 + .213\text{DIRECT} + .062(\text{STRONG} \times \text{INDIRECT})$$
$$\phantom{P(\text{trust}) = \frac{1}{1 + e^{-f}} \; ; \quad f = } (12.1) (5.9)$$

$$P(\text{distrust}) = \frac{1}{1 + e^{-f}} \; ; \quad f = -0.540 - .437\text{DIRECT} + .040(\text{WEAK} \times \text{INDIRECT})$$
$$\phantom{P(\text{distrust}) = \frac{1}{1 + e^{-f}} \; ; \quad f = } (-10.4) (2.3)$$

Figure 5.3. The Probability of Trust in Private and Public Games

NOTE: Solid lines show probability of trust; dashed lines show probability of distrust; *t*-tests are in parentheses; thin lines describe isolated relations (private games); bold lines describe embedded relations (public games).

indirect connection around an especially close relationship generates a smaller 1.7-point increase in trust (.19 + 1.51). Relative magnitudes are the opposite for distrust. In the third column of Table 5.2, a 1-point increase in direct connection generates a 1.2-point decrease in distrust. A 1-point increase in indirect connection around a weak relationship generates a larger 1.9-point increase in distrust (.84 + 1.10). Not only do we find evidence of the predicted dark side to network density, but it turns out to be more potent than the familiar positive side in which extensive indirect connections increase the probability of trust within strong relationships.[13]

SUMMARY

We have described how trust varies with the strength of a relationship and its location in social structure. The simplest social context for trust is an isolated dyad—two people away from others. Their interaction games are private. The more usual context is two people surrounded by variably close friends, foes, and acquaintances. The two people play their games in public—a public composed of the third parties surrounding them. We argue that third parties telling stories about past interactions with ego and alter are biased toward stories consistent with their view of the existing ego-alter tie. Third-party gossip thus serves to reinforce existing relations, making ego and alter more certain of their trust (or distrust) in one another. This contingency on existing conditions makes the gossip argument a rational-choice intruder within institutional theory. Ego chooses whether to trust alter, but the choice menu is created by the gossip of interested third parties, which is contingent on ego's existing relationship with alter. Where ego has reason to suspect alter, indirect connections through third parties convey stories that corroborate the suspicion, making ego certain that he or she should distrust alter. Where ego has a strong relation with alter, indirect connections convey stories that corroborate the strong tie, making ego certain that he or she can trust alter.

We draw two broad conclusions from an analysis of network data on a probability sample of diverse senior managers: (a) Trust is associated with relation strength, as expected in private games. Figure 5.1 shows the effect of alternative meanings of a strong relationship. (b) As predicted by the gossip argument for public games, trust is significantly amplified by third parties. Third parties have a positive effect on trust within strong relations and a negative effect on trust within weak relations. Figure 5.2 shows the effect, and Figure 5.3 shows how the probability of trust and distrust are affected by indirect connections at different levels of direct connection.

Although both trust and distrust are amplified as expected, they are affected in different ways. First, trust builds incrementally, but distrust has a more catastrophic quality. The solid lines at the top of Figure 5.3 show how the probability of trust between two people builds slowly and continuously across increasing levels of relationship strength. The dashed lines at the bottom of the figure show that the probability of distrust remains near-zero across decreasing levels of relationship strength, then increases sharply in especially weak relations. Second, third parties seem more alert to negative information, or prefer negative gossip to positive, because indirect connection amplifies the distrust associated with weak relations much more than it amplifies trust within strong relations. This is apparent in Figure 5.3 from the longer gray arrows for distrust. Indirect connection moves the bold line further away from the thin line. In short, not only do we find evidence of the predicted dark side to network density, but it turns out to be more potent than the familiar positive side in which extensive indirect connections increase the probability of trust within strong relationships.

Notes

1. Williamson (1993) offers a thorough conceptual review showing how many popular images of trust are images of calculated risk in which the trust factors involved are transaction cost factors limiting risk. He proposes that trust be reserved for the act of taking a risk for personal reasons, evident because no transaction factors minimize the risk (see Williamson, 1994, pp. 97-98, for a summary statement). We admire the intent of Williamson's analysis and would have no issue with taking risk as a dependent variable. Our substantive concern is why a manager gives someone else control over resources, believing that the other person won't act against the manager's interests. This is the exchange with time asymmetry that Coleman (1990) takes as his site for studying trust. Like Williamson, we turn to the social context of the decision to discover collateral conditions that facilitate or inhibit the risky exchange. However, we also believe that the cat is out of the bag on calling the exchange a question of trust. For better or worse, our audience for this analysis is more likely to engage in an argument about trust than in the same argument phrased in terms of risk.

2. The full-disclosure argument can be stated in terms of full information. No individual knows everyone else. Indirect connections between ego and alter provide alternative communication channels and so increase the probability that ego is fully informed about alter's past behavior. Fully informed means that ego is more certain of his or her trust in alter. Whether the stories relayed through indirect connections improve ego's information on alter or give ego a feeling of vicarious play in repeated games with alter, the end result is the same—ego is more certain of his or her trust in alter.

3. The step from full disclosure to partial disclosure introduces the complication of predicting what is disclosed and what is not disclosed. We make two key assumptions for this introductory analysis: (a) Ego, accustomed to using third parties as background informants on other people, is similarly affected by full and partial disclosure of third-party stories about alter. (b) Third parties, to sustain and strengthen their relation with ego, are more likely to disclose to ego experiences with alter that are consistent with ego's opinion of alter. We make these assumptions because we believe they are by and large correct, and our principal analytical concern is to establish third-party effects, postponing for future research the task of elaborating how third-party effects vary across (a) managers variably susceptible to third-party gossip and (b) third parties who selectively communicate stories consistent with ego's opinion of alter and strategically communicate stories to revise ego's opinion to be more consistent with the third party's opinion. We provide detailed discussion of these issues elsewhere (Burt & Knez, 1995a, 1995b).

4. Although not directly concerned with trust, two lines of work describe a dark side to network density relevant to our analysis of trust. One concerns the extent to which a person is subject to the social pressure of interpersonal influence and sanctions. With interpersonal influence stronger within dense networks, it is easier to impose sanctions within a dense network. This is the subject of a rich literature in political science and sociology, but Coleman's (1990, chap. 11) analysis of social norms is a rational choice exemplar. Small (incremental) sanctions within a dense network can aggregate to a large effect (e.g., p. 278ff on negative reputation and p. 284ff on gossip-facilitating sanctions by creating or clarifying norms). If distrust is the emotion that accompanies sanction, then dense networks, by intensifying sanctions, intensify distrust. So viewed, our positive and negative density effects on trust merely combine and give functional

form to what Coleman has already analyzed but as separate phenomena—trust strengthened within dense networks and sanctions strengthened within dense networks.

Network theories of competition are a second caveat to our statement about the neglect of density's dark side. Reversing the concerns of the work just described, this line of work concerns the extent to which a person can negotiate the social pressure of interpersonal influence and sanctions. Building on Simmel's (1922/1955) and Merton's (1957/1968) analyses of conflicting affiliations, network theories of competition describe the information and control advantages of building relations with contacts in disconnected groups (e.g., Burt, 1992, pp. 30-36, on structural holes and entrepreneurs). Sparse networks provide broader information access and more opportunities to control exchange relations. Illustrations are Cook et al.'s (1983) experiments showing how resources accumulate to people at the crossroads in networks, Krackhardt and Stern's (1988) experiments showing higher group performance with cross-group friendships, or Burt's (1992) and Podolny and Baron's (1994) manager surveys showing the promotion advantage of having strong connections to otherwise disconnected groups. Direct application to trust production implies that successful managers build trust in private games (maintaining a sparse network of nonredundant contacts), but less successful managers find themselves in public games (which results in a dense network of mutual friends). Results on the managers studied here are interestingly more complex and available elsewhere (Burt & Knez, 1995b).

5. Lindenberg and Frey (1993) discuss more general parameters in ego's rational choice of frame. Our argument is that ego's frame on alter, whatever it is, is reinforced in conversations with third parties. This alleviates the monitoring problem that Hechter (1987, 1990, pp. 243-244) highlights in his argument about dependence and formal control being necessary conditions for group solidarity. Hechter (1987, pp. 73-77) takes issue with Axelrod's (1984, chap. 4) use of the live-and-let-live system of trench warfare to illustrate the idea that cooperation emerges in even the most difficult circumstances if players anticipate future interaction with one another. Hechter stresses the implicit monitoring necessary to the live-and-let-live system, the difficulty of monitoring even between the two armies that is analogous to a two-player game, and the implausibility of that monitoring (without formal controls) in games of more than two players. In other words, cooperation is more difficult in larger groups. Hechter's argument presumes the perfect information condition that everyone monitors everyone else, where monitoring is more difficult in larger groups. The gossip argument is less demanding. Everyone is relatively ignorant but more informed by third parties with increasing indirect connection. All it takes is one third party to relay stories between a pair of people. Systemic properties of amplified trust and distrust emerge from the microsocial context around individual pairs of people. The monitoring problem reduces to realistic proportions. The whole population doesn't monitor one's behavior, just one's closest friends and coworkers (cf. Janowitz & Shils, 1948/1991, on why the German Wehrmacht continued to function despite repeated defeats during World War II—monitoring was between buddies in the squad, and the army was a system of interlocked squads).

6. Let z_{ij} be the intensity of closeness between persons i and j, scaled from the response categories describing relations with and among manager contacts (Burt, 1992, pp. 125-126). The proportional strength of manager i's relation with contact j (p_{ij}) is z_{ij} divided by the sum of the manager's relations ($\sum_q z_{iq}$). The indirect connection between manager i and contact j is measured as in the original study by the proportion of a manager's network that leads through intermediaries q back to contact j ($\sum_q p_{iq} p_{qj}$, q ≠ i,j). We multiply the proportional strength measures by 100 to discuss points of change. Direct connection varies from 1 to 25 points with a mean of 7.9, and indirect connection varies from 0 to 32 points around a mean of 11.7 points. To create the dichotomy between little and much indirect connection for Figure 5.2, we graphed probabilities of trust and distrust across levels of indirect connection. Cutting the data where the lines of trust and distrust cross, we treat less than 15 points of indirect connection as little and above that as much. This justifies our cut-point between much and little indirect connection by the shift in its effect on trust. We also ran the analysis with slightly higher and lower cut-points and obtained the

same results. We don't want to make too much of the little-much distinction. The point introduced in Figure 5.2 is supported by the results in Table 5.2 with continuous measures of indirect connection.

7. Unless you have no future in the firm. The citations to people for job option discussions could be from managers so unhappy in the firm, or so unsuccessful, that they have nothing to lose by talking about moving to another firm. This doesn't seem to be the case. First, most managers have someone they would turn to. All but three managers cite contacts with whom they would discuss job options. Only 22 limit that discussion to contacts outside the firm. Second, there is no tendency for satisfied or successful managers to cite fewer contacts. Satisfaction is uncorrelated with the number of people cited for job option discussion (.02 correlation). Managers are distinguished in Burt (1992, pp. 126-131) by the extent to which they were promoted early to their current job. This measure of manager success, strongly correlated with network structure, has no correlation with the number of people cited for job option discussion (.05 correlation).

8. Two potential complications turn out to be minor in these data: (a) the assumed equal intervals between trust, neutral, and distrust and (b) managers who cite a person for both trust and distrust. On issue (b), seven contacts are cited for trust and distrust and the circumstances vary. The one thing consistent across the seven trust-distrust relations is extensive indirect connections. The manager didn't trust the contact but would have to let him or her know about plans to move to another firm. Taking the distrust component more seriously, we assign the seven trust-distrust relations to the distrust category. This seems a minor issue because we get the same pattern of t-tests in Table 5.2 if the seven trust-distrust relations are coded as trust relations or neutral relations. Discriminant analysis provides a more sophisticated solution to issues (a) and (b). The discriminant function is the linear combination of the four network variables in Table 5.2 that best predicts two dependent variables—trust and distrust. There is no assumption that the trust-neutral interval equals the interval between neutral and distrust because separate effects are estimated for trust and distrust. The seven trust-distrust relations remain as trust relations in the trust variable and as distrust relations in the distrust variable. Most of the effect variation is captured in the first discriminant function (.53 canonical correlation, 82% of the covariance described by the two canonical correlations). Because there is so little overlap between trust and distrust, however, not much is gained with discriminant analysis. The discriminant function scores are correlated .985, with scores for the three-category trust variable predicted from the regression model in Table 5.2. The Table 5.2 regression model is simpler, easier to use for significance tests, and yields predictions almost identical to the more sophisticated discriminant function model. We use the Table 5.2 regression model, but note that collapsing trust and distrust into a single variable will not be reasonable in all study populations.

9. Tables 5.1 and 5.2 report results for relations within and beyond the firm. Limiting the analysis to relations within the firm could matter because the kinds of people cited outside the firm are likely to be trusted (close friends and spouse), and the questionnaire item eliciting the distrust citations is focused on work. No one outside the firm is cited for making the manager's job difficult (although one manager cited his wife as the primary problem, and two managers cited themselves as the biggest problem—all three of whom are treated in this analysis as citing no one for distrust). Including contacts outside the firm could exaggerate the trust effect from direct connection (spouse and outside friends tend to be especially close contacts and trusted) or depress the trust effect from indirect connection (spouses and outside friends tend to be trusted but have little indirect connection to contacts within the firm). Compare the "all dyads" and "within-firm" effects in Tables 5.1 and 5.2. The effects are very similar. There is no evidence of external relations distorting the results.

10. Trust and distrust are extremely skewed binary dependent variables: 791 of the 3,584 contacts in and beyond the firm are cited for trust (22.1%), and only 263 are cited for distrust, all of whom are within the firm (7.3% of contacts, 8.7% of contacts within the firm). The loglinear results in Table 5.1 correspond to logit results, which eliminates the limited dependent variable

problem, but the binary coding of direct and indirect connection ignores much of the available information on strength of connection. Logit results for the continuous variables in Table 5.2 yield the same relative magnitudes of test statistics for trust (12.3 t-test for direct connection, 7.8 t-test for indirect connection around strong relations) and similar test statistics for distrust (−10.6 t-test for direct connection, 2.6 t-test for indirect connection around weak relations). We focus on OLS results in the text because the metric regression coefficients are more likely to be familiar to readers, and we reach the same conclusions with logit results. The results for the "combined" variable in Table 5.1 are valuable because we can take advantage of the ordering between trust and distrust responses to create a less skewed criterion variable more appropriate for OLS estimators.

11. We have 3,584 relationships elicited from 284 managers. The effect estimates are based on the assumption that each relation is an independent observation. The managers are a probability sample, but their cited relationships are a cluster probability sample (each manager's network a cluster). If relations are autocorrelated within clusters (e.g., a manager has a high threshold for trust or a low threshold for distrust), the number of independent observations is less than 3,584, and test statistics based on dyad counts are exaggerated. We reestimated the equations by predicting the three-category trust variable, adding 283 dummy variables to distinguish managers. There is autocorrelation, but it is concentrated in a minority of managers. There are 70 managers whose dummy variable increases or decreases trust by more than one point, and the weakest of these is statistically quite negligible (1.74 effect; 0.1 t-test). We get the bracketed t-tests in Table 5.2 when dummy variables for all 70 managers are included in the model.

12. The displayed logit equations contain effects estimated from the data in Table 5.2 on relations within the firm. The effects are significant (12.1 and 5.9 t-tests for trust equation, −10.4 and 2.3 t-tests for distrust equation; cf. note 10 for similar tests when effects are estimated from relations within and beyond the firm). To generate the probability of trust and distrust between isolated pairs of people (thin lines in Figure 5.3), we computed probabilities with INDIRECT set to zero, which means the interaction term drops out of each logit equation (leaving a single predictor, DIRECT, which is $100p_{ij}$). To illustrate amplification through indirect connections (bold lines in Figure 5.3), we (a) don't know whether relations are especially close or less close, so we let STRONG and WEAK be a continuous function of relation strength (STRONG = p_{ij}, WEAK = $1-p_{ij}$) and (b) set indirect connection to the maximum possible given the proportion of a manager's network allocated to direct connection (INDIRECT = $100 - 100p_{ij}$).

13. Social structure's different associations with the positive and negative in Figure 5.3 are suspicious. The different functional forms are consistent with the different measurement criteria in these data. Trust is measured with a criterion of discussing job options. Distrust is measured with a more severe criterion of naming the manager's most difficult coworker. The incremental change in trust across levels of relation strength in Figure 5.3 could reflect the less severe criterion for citing contacts as trustworthy. To test this, we reestimated the Figure 5.3 logit model for trust with a more severe criterion. A relationship contains trust only if the contact is cited as trustworthy *and* as the manager's "single most important contact for your continued success within the firm." Of the 3,015 relations with other employees, 98 meet this more severe criterion for trust (vs. 544 trustworthy contacts in the Figure 5.3 logit model). The result is the pair of gray solid lines in Figure 5.3. Third parties contribute less to this higher level of trust (1.9 t-test), but the essential point is that the functional form is again a slow incremental increase with increasing relation strength (6.2 t-test). The higher criterion for trust has merely shifted the function to the right (i.e., trust at the more severe criterion happens in stronger relationships). In short, the different functional forms for trust and distrust in Figure 5.3 are not created by the different criteria for positive and negative relationships.

References

Axelrod, R. (1984). *The evolution of cooperation.* New York: Basic Books.

Barber, B. (1983). *The logic and limits of trust.* New Brunswick, NJ: Rutgers University Press.

Blau, P. M. (1964). *Exchange and power in social life.* New York: John Wiley.

Blau, P. M. (1968). Interaction: Social exchange. In *The international encyclopedia of the social sciences.* New York: Free Press and Macmillan.

Bradach, J. L., & Eccles, R. G. (1989). Price, authority, and trust: From ideal types to plural forms. *Annual Review of Sociology, 15,* 97-118.

Burt, R. S. (1992). *Structural holes.* Cambridge, MA: Harvard University Press.

Burt, R. S., & Celotto, N. (1992). The network structure of management roles in a large matrix firm. *Evaluation and Program Planning, 15,* 303-326.

Burt, R. S., & Knez, M. (1995a). Kinds of third-party effects on trust. *Rationality and Society, 7,* 255-292.

Burt, R. S., & Knez, M. (1995b). *Trust and third parties: The social production of cooperation.* Chicago: University of Chicago, Graduate School of Business.

Coleman, J. S. (1990). *Foundations of social theory.* Cambridge, MA: Harvard University Press.

Cook, K. S., Emerson, R. M., Gilmore, M. R., & Yamagishi, T. (1983). The distribution of power in exchange networks: Theory and experimental results. *American Journal of Sociology, 89,* 275-305.

Ekeh, P. P. (1974). *Social exchange theory.* Cambridge, MA: Harvard University Press.

Gibbons, R. (1992). *Game theory for applied economists.* Princeton, NJ: Princeton University Press.

Granovetter, M. S. (1985). Economic action, social structure, and embeddedness. *American Journal of Sociology, 91,* 481-510.

Granovetter, M. S. (1992). Problems of explanation in economic sociology. In N. Nohria & R. G. Eccles (Eds.), *Networks and organization.* Boston: Harvard Business School Press.

Hardin, R. (1990). The social evolution of cooperation. In K. S. Cook & M. Levi (Eds.), *The limits of rationality.* Chicago: University of Chicago Press.

Hechter, M. (1987). *Principles of group solidarity.* Berkeley: University of California Press.

Hechter, M. (1990). On the inadequacy of game theory for the solution of real-world collective action problems. In K. S. Cook & M. Levi (Eds.), *The limits of rationality.* Chicago: University of Chicago Press.

Homans, G. C. (1961). *Social behavior: Its elementary forms.* New York: Harcourt Brace & World.

Janowitz, M., & Shils, E. A. (1991). Cohesion and disintegration in the Wehrmacht in World War II. In J. Burk (Ed.), *On social organization and social control.* Chicago: University of Chicago Press. (Original publication 1948)

Krackhardt, D., & Stern, R. N. (1988). Informal networks and organizational crisis: An experimental simulation. *Social Psychology Quarterly, 51,* 123-140.

Kreps, D. M. (1990). Corporate culture and economic theory. In J. Alt & K. Shepsle (Eds.), *Perspectives on positive political economy.* New York: Cambridge University Press.

Larson, A. (1992). Network dyads in entrepreneurial settings: A study of the governance of exchange relationships. *Administrative Science Quarterly, 37,* 76-104.

Lindenberg, S., & Frey, B. S. (1993). Alternatives, frames, and relative prices: A broader view of rational choice theory. *Acta Sociologica, 36,* 191-205.

Merton, R. K. (1968). Continuities in the theory of reference group behavior. In R. K. Merton (Ed.), *Social theory and social structure.* New York: Free Press. (Original publication 1957)

Nohria, N., & Eccles, R. G. (Eds.). (1992). *Networks and organizations.* Boston: Harvard Business School Press.

Podolny, J. M., & Baron, J. N. (1994). *Make new friends and keep the old?: Social networks, mobility, and satisfaction in the workplace.* Stanford, CA: Stanford University, Graduate School of Business.

Powell, W. W., & Smith-Doerr, L. (1994). Networks and economic life. In N. J. Smelser & R. Swedberg (Eds.), *The handbook of economic sociology.* Princeton, NJ: Princeton University Press.

Simmel, G. (1955). *Conflict and the web of group affiliations* (K. H. Wolff and R. Bendix, Trans.). New York: Free Press. (Original publication 1922)

Sitkin, S. B., & Roth, N. L. (1993). Explaining the limited effectiveness of legalistic "remedies" for trust/distrust. *Organization Science, 4,* 367-392.

Smelser, N. J., & Swedberg, R. (Eds.). (1994). *Handbook of economic sociology.* Princeton, NJ: Princeton University Press.

Stinchcombe, A. L. (1990). *Information and organizations.* Berkeley: University of California Press.

Swedberg, R. (Ed.). (1993). *Explorations in economic sociology.* New York: Russell Sage.

White, H. C. (1992). *Identity and control.* Princeton, NJ: Princeton University Press.

Williamson, O. E. (1993). Calculativeness, trust, and economic organization. *Journal of Law and Economics, 36,* 453-486.

Williamson, O. E. (1994). Transaction cost economics. In N. J. Smelser & R. Swedburg (Eds.), *The handbook of economic sociology.* Princeton, NJ: Princeton University Press.

Zucker, L. G. (1986). Production of trust: Institutional sources of economic structure, 1840-1920. *Research in Organizational Behavior, 8,* 53-111.

Collaboration Structure and Information Dilemmas in Biotechnology

Organizational Boundaries as Trust Production

LYNNE G. ZUCKER
MICHAEL R. DARBY
MARILYNN B. BREWER
YUSHENG PENG

Science norms urge sharing of information, science rewards require publication in refereed journals, and science training generally includes student access to new information as active components of ongoing research teams. In most sociology of science, it is assumed that the information being created has value but is treated as a public good: Scientists both contribute to and draw

AUTHORS' NOTE: This chapter is a product of the project on "Intellectual Capital, Technology Transfer, and the Organization of Leading-Edge Industries: The Case of Biotechnology," by Lynne G. Zucker, Marilynn B. Brewer, and Michael R. Darby, Principal Investigators. Our project is part of the Organizational Research Program, Institute for Social Science Research, UCLA, and the research program in productivity at the National Bureau of Economic Research. Our research has been supported by grants from the National Science Foundation (SES 9012925), the University of California Systemwide Biotechnology Research and Education Program, the University of California Systemwide Pacific Rim Research Program, the UCLA Center for American Politics and Public Policy, and the UCLA Institute of Industrial Relations.

from a common resource pool that consists of discoveries and refinements of those discoveries. In most economic treatments, it is assumed that scientific discoveries have only fleeting value unless formal intellectual property rights mechanisms are used to prevent use of the information (i.e., absent patents, trade secrets, or actual secrecy); the value of a discovery erodes quickly as the information diffuses.

We have quite a different view. Scientific discoveries vary in the degree to which others can be excluded from making use of them. Inherent in the discovery itself is the degree of *natural excludability:* If the techniques for replication are not widely known prior to the discovery, then any scientist wishing to build on the new knowledge must first acquire hands-on experience.[1] If he or she cannot gain access to a research team or laboratory setting with that know-how, then working in that area may be difficult if not impossible. We argue that it is primarily in collaborations that the fine details and hands-on knowledge to conduct cutting-edge bioscience are transmitted; only in collaborations are all biological materials freely shared, although requirements for making them more widely available once research is published are growing (Eisenberg, 1987, pp. 197-205, 229-231).

Trust is extraordinarily important in communicating discoveries in biotechnology because of their high scientific and commercial value. The resulting intense competition produces an information dilemma, with contradictory incentives to communicate the new knowledge and withhold it (Schneider, 1990; Schneider & Brewer, 1987).[2] In brief, if a scientist communicates usable information about a new discovery, the benefits associated with exclusive access to that information are compromised.[3] But withholding information about the new discovery may slow progress in the field as a whole.

Information dilemmas, usually couched as conflict between individual self-interest and group interest, can be resolved by relying on close-knit collaborations, sharply limiting with whom the new discovery is shared. Although the information is not shared with the field as a whole, it is shared with a group of collaborators that tends to grow over time. The information boundaries that these collaboration structures define determine the extent of diffusion of the new discovery. Because organizations have both established internal exchange relations and enforcement mechanisms, we expect that trust among members of the same organization will be significantly higher than trust among members of different organizations and thus that organizational boundaries are efficient *information envelopes.* In general, the higher the value of the intellectual capital, the more likely organizational boundaries are used to limit its diffusion.

Thus, we can extend our argument one step further to the effects of organizational boundaries on diffusion of information. If trust is produced and information flow is in fact restricted along organizational lines, then diffusion should slow differentially. Specifically, within a geographic area, the higher the proportion of same-organization pairs of coauthors, the less information should diffuse within that area. Indeed, our final model explains nearly all of the variation in diffusion to new coauthors of scientific articles between geographic areas, with significant amounts explained by variables related to the value of intellectual capital and the resultant patterns of collaboration within or between organizations.

Trust Production in
Information Dilemmas

Trust production can occur when an individual is *open to social influence* from another individual or when a third party with whom both individuals are open to social influence intervenes to mediate (Zucker, 1986). This reframes the trust problem substantially, focusing attention on the mechanisms by which an individual becomes more or less open to social influence from another individual (or the interaction becomes mediated). Predictably or certainty is *not* sufficient for trust production, contra the Williamsonian (1979) argument; for example, a narcissistic individual will behave predictably in his or her self-interest, but this consistent behavior will on average produce distrust, because much of the self-interested behavior is not open to influence by the other person in the exchange and ignores the other person's interests.

Trust, by defining the group of others who are likely to be open to social influence reciprocally, determines where the information boundaries will be drawn. The higher the value of the information, the more likely trust production will be a central concern. Trust production is often based on institutional mechanisms, including in-group preference and formal rules and procedures defined by formal organization boundaries (Brewer & Silver, 1978; Zucker, 1983, 1986).[4] We expect that organizational boundaries will heavily determine with whom to share recombinant DNA (rDNA) sequence discoveries.

In the economic literature, Darby and Karni (1973); Klein, Crawford, and Alchian (1978); and Darby and Lott (1989) have studied the use of third-party experts as one means to create trust for parties to act more in maximizing group values rather than simply pursuing myopic self-interest. Trusted agents receive a higher income from their "brand-name capital," which is reduced or lost if they do not behave consistent with that trust. Also, when a third party is not available to monitor the exchange, anthropologists (e.g., Geertz, 1978) find that a combination of repeat exchange and expected future exchange best produces trust (see also Kollock, 1994).

Within organizations, of course, both repeated and future exchange are common, as is third-party intervention, or at least the possibility of it. Senior managers, for example, are trusted experts with organizational and self-interests aligned who potentially can apply substantial sanctions in the face of self-seeking behavior. To the extent that within-organization collaborations involve a third party, whether explicitly or only implicitly, organizational involvement will help to increase the self-enforcing range and thus produce a higher rate of collaboration within organizational boundaries.[5] Although we do not measure these effects directly, our indirect measurement provides substantial support for this line of argument.

Production of trust, then, involves information boundaries that are at least partially constructed by collaborating within the same organization (university, research institute/hospital, or firm). We in fact demonstrate that specific characteristics of other scientists, generally those indicating the potential value of their discoveries, lead them to be included more often in scientific collaborations and be more often in collaborations with scientists working in the same organization. Our finding is consistent with expectations derived from the transaction cost approach, where the boundaries of the firm are determined by the relative costs and benefits of using markets or the firm's own hierarchy to govern each exchange (Coase, 1937, 1988; Williamson, 1979, 1991). If similar exchanges exist both within and between organizations, the higher costs involved in transacting across organizational boundaries should imply that these transactions will have higher value or not occur.

Cost and Demand in Trust Production

Social agency is required to *produce* trust. Human action is required to form repeat collaborations or collaborations within an organization and exclude alternative forms of action. As Zucker has argued elsewhere (Tolbert & Zucker, 1995; Zucker, 1986; Zucker & Kreft, 1994), this social agency involves activity that is costly, requiring human time, attention, and resources, and thus there must be some *demand* for trust before it will be produced. Yet social scientists often unrealistically treat social process and the resulting structure as if they were simply by-products of human activity, as ubiquitous as air, and therefore costless (Granovetter, 1985). In contrast, we argue that deciding to produce trust incurs drawing the opportunity cost of resources away from other activities. It is unlikely that such resource flow will occur in the absence of identified demand.[6] We will first examine costs involved in production of trust in the biosciences and then the effects of the value of the information on generating demand for trust.

Costs may not be simply the human energy and money expended, but also other opportunities lost. In the case of bioscience collaborations, for example, a colleague in the same institution may become a coauthor for the reasons outlined above yet not be the ideal choice as a coauthor in terms of potential intellectual contribution to the project. Other bioscientists who might make a much more significant contribution to the project are not included because their trustworthiness is too costly to establish compared to the alternatives.

Costs also are incurred because defining who is trusted sufficiently to include in a collaboration simultaneously defines a much larger group of scientists who are excluded. Although science norms call for *inclusion* of a large circle of trusted colleagues in an "invisible college" model of both the high-volume and high-velocity exchange of scientific information/discovery (Crane, 1969, 1972; Gaston, 1973; Merton, 1938, 1957), considerable evidence shows that whenever the discoveries have significant value, whether as pure science or as a commercial product, some scientists will exploit nonpublic knowledge for personal gains—monetary or nonmonetary (Taubes, 1986; Watson, 1968). If the excluded scientists recognize the value, they become angry and voice complaints; much time and energy are spent responding to these complaints and either resolving specific difficulties or creating new structures designed to define the amount of exclusion permitted. In a thorough review of the early controversies in bioscience, Rebecca Eisenberg documents the kinds of disagreements that occurred over access to cell cultures that, if access is denied, make actual replication of the published research and later extension of it close to impossible (1987, pp. 197-205, 214-216, 229-231, and examples throughout).

In the face of these costs of trust production, some positive demand must exist for trust to be produced. Our hypothesis is that the major demand for trust in scientific research is derived from the potential value of the specific discoveries.

**Value of Intellectual
Capital and Demand for Trust**

Let us define *intellectual capital* as the value of nonpublic information possessed by an individual in excess of the costs of learning the information (see Zucker, Darby, & Brewer, 1994). We conceive of translating nonmonetary returns to the information, such as prestige and professional advancement to monetary equivalents, and then taking the present value of the sum of the monetary value of all future monetary and nonmonetary returns and subtracting the cost of learning the information.[7] So defined, intellectual capital is the wealth value of the knowledge to an individual who makes a significant discovery or to whom the information discovered is transmitted before it has diffused sufficiently to earn only the normal returns to the cost of learning the information.

As information diffuses after a discovery, the associated intellectual capital of a person who embodies the information declines both because the supranormal returns decline as more scientists use the information competitively and less time remains until the information is part of routine science and thus no longer capable of earning supranormal returns. The value of intellectual capital created by a new discovery increases because the discovery involves techniques that must be learned firsthand through collaboration or apprenticeship, that is, to the extent that they possess the "natural excludability" necessary for relatively long-lasting supranormal returns.[8]

Scientists incorporate the information—transiently both nonpublic and yielding supranormal returns—as part of their human capital. The returns to this information may come from other scientists in the form of citations, promotions, job offers, and so on. These returns may also come from commercialization of the discovery in the form of consulting income, patent royalties, ownership interest in the firm, and so on. In Zucker, Darby, and Brewer (1994), we demonstrate that intellectual capital in conjunction with active publishing is a strong predictor of founding new biotechnology enterprises. This reward structure encourages other scientists to invest in learning the know-how to obtain the supranormal returns, although as more come to know the information its capital value falls.

Students have especially strong incentives to work with scientists on the leading edge, from whom they can gain knowledge that is not available from other scientists. As Harriet Zuckerman (1967, 1977) discovered in her study of Nobel laureates, scientists working at the intellectual frontier can obtain the best students, another form of capital, by diffusing the knowledge to them. Zuckerman's pathbreaking work establishes as a central research question the differences in scientific production between the first-rank scientist in terms of quality and those lower down in the prestige hierarchy of science.

We argue that the higher the value of the intellectual capital, the greater the demand for production of trust and the use of information boundaries to create it. The value of intellectual capital varies along many dimensions, four of which we will examine empirically in this chapter:

1. *Quality of the individual scientist:* We identify "star" scientists in terms of their productivity in biotechnology and study these stars and their collaborators. The quality of intellectual output generally will be higher if two star scientists collaborate than if one star scientist collaborates with graduate students, postdoctoral students, and/or other less distinguished scientists.

2. *Quality of the university:* We identify scientists in terms of their location at 1 of 18 top-quality universities, defined by having exceptionally high-ranking biochemistry, microbiology, and/or molecular biology programs (see below). Working

in one of these top-quality university departments indicates expected high-quality intellectual output and greater use of information boundaries.

3. *Time:* As the discovery diffuses, the value of the intellectual capital declines. Over time, then, we expect that information boundaries will be relaxed.

4. *Appropriation regime:* Firms are generally able to appropriate the value of new discoveries more successfully than universities or research institutes, and thus we expect greater use of information boundaries in firms.

Scientific Discovery and Collaboration Structure in Biotechnology

Discovery. Gene splicing was an extremely significant discovery that set off a cascade of research in biotechnology (see Cohen, Chang, Boyer, & Helling, 1973). Although other very significant discoveries were made in biotechnology at about the same time, only genetic-sequence discoveries were exhaustively cataloged in a data file, GenBank, which was created for bioscientists.[9] Gene splicing has the distinction of being a scientifically valuable innovation that has a virtually complete record of subsequent discoveries of genetic sequences, so that the timing, extent, and other characteristics of its diffusion can be tracked. We extensively reprogrammed the original GenBank files to identify 327 "top-producing" scientists: those scientists who discovered at least 41 genetic sequences from 1968 to 1990. Because some sequences are harder to unravel, we added to these "star" scientists another 22 who published 20 or more articles identifying gene sequences, which made them among the most productive scientists, but reported fewer genetic-sequence discoveries per article. Thus, the star scientists we identify worldwide total 327 and are listed as authors on 4,061 distinct published articles in major journals.[10] The distribution of these publications over time can be seen in Figure 6.1, along with the distribution for the 208 stars who ever work in the United States.

At the beginning of the time period, in 1967, it was exceedingly difficult to make a genetic-sequence discovery. Gradually, it became easier to sequence genes, and now these discoveries are a part of normal science. Between 1967 and 1990, there were both increasing diffusion of the ability to gene sequence and a decreasing value of the related techniques. Indeed, by 1987 or 1988, discovering a gene sequence could no longer earn a PhD at any of the major U.S. research universities. At the same time, machine-based technology was becoming more reliable and relatively inexpensive.[11]

The reorganized GenBank data files contain a great deal of information on the characteristics of the discoveries, including the list of authors who collaborated in making the discoveries. These scientists are coauthors of our 327 star scientists but do not themselves meet the "star" criteria. These *col-*

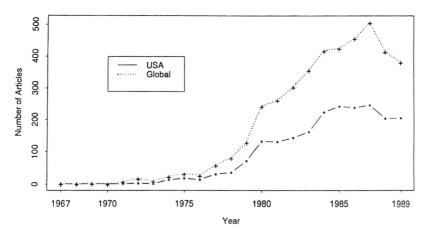

Figure 6.1. Total Number of Articles Reporting Sequence Discoveries Authored by Stars: Total and United States Only, 1967-1989

laborators number 7,825, with 4,012 of them ever working in the United States. Because we are examining the effects of collaborating within the same organization on fine-grain diffusion patterns, we will focus only on scientific collaborations in the United States in our analyses in this chapter.

Without adding to the original GenBank files, we are able to study the general pattern of diffusion. But information on the organizational membership (same vs. different; type of organization, including university, research institute or hospital, and firm) and the geographic location of the scientists is not contained in GenBank, nor is it available except for the first author in any on-line database (see MedLine). If star scientists always appear first, the use of MedLine affiliation would at least permit the study of the top producers. But our informal information proved more accurate: Star scientists most often appear last, so that among articles with U.S. stars, 71.2% of last authors are stars, compared to 16.4% of first authors.

Organizational Location and Characteristics. Because our major hypotheses concerning the role of trust in collaborations rest on organizational location, we pulled each of the 4,315 articles identified as containing "high-quality" intellectual capital and coded institutional affiliation and location of each author, including any dual affiliations and changes in affiliation, from the headings of the articles. From these data, we find that intellectual capital is rather concentrated: In the United States, only 264 distinct organizations— 149 universities, 71 research institutes and hospitals, and 44 firms—were given at any time through 1990 as affiliations of any of the stars or collaborators in our articles' data set.

Our university data consist of all U.S. institutions listed as granting the PhD degree in any field in the Higher Education General Information Survey (HEGIS), Institutional Characteristics, 1983-1984.[12] Each university is assigned an institutional ID number, a university flag, and is located by zip code based on the HEGIS address file. Additional information was collected for those universities granting the PhD degree in biochemistry, cellular/molecular biology, and/or microbiology that we define as *biotech-relevant fields* (see Jones, 1964). In our analyses here, we rely only on the National Academy of Science measure of university department quality, a scholarly reputation rating based on responses from approximately 15% of the faculty in the fields studied. Because we were interested in identifying the very best programs, we considered only the highest-rated biochemistry, cellular/molecular biology, and/or microbiology programs offered by a particular university. Whether any specific star or collaborator in the United States is located in one of the most highly rated programs (rated above 4) is our variable TQU (top-quality university).[13]

Firms and research institutes (including hospitals) listed as affiliations in the article data set received an institutional ID number and an institute/hospital flag and gave an address with a zip code as required for geocoding. For a review of additional data and sources not used in the analyses presented in this chapter, including non-U.S. information, see the Data Sources section at the end of the reference list in this chapter and Appendix A in Zucker, Darby, and Brewer (1994).

Collaboration Structure. We now introduce a further refinement to our measurement of collaborations. Because our sample is selected based on star scientists, and sequence-reporting articles by collaborators appear in our sample only if one of our star scientists is an author, we define the collaboration as all possible pairs of coauthors that have at least one star in it. Our basic unit is thus the number of coauthor pairs in a collaboration that have at least one star. By examining coauthor pairs, we are able to model explicitly the selection criteria used in generating our sample: Each pair must have at least one star. Most of these coauthor pairs consist of one star and one collaborator, for a worldwide total of 20,595, with 9,025 of those having both scientists located in the United States and 10,514 having at least one scientist in the United States. Two-star pairs constitute 2,044 of the worldwide pairs and 904 pairs with at least one star in the United States (820 both in the United States).

The distribution of coauthor pairs and the increasing number over time may be attributed both to a dense interaction network of lab-based collaborations and to the diffusion of the new technology.[14] But this is where our story really begins.

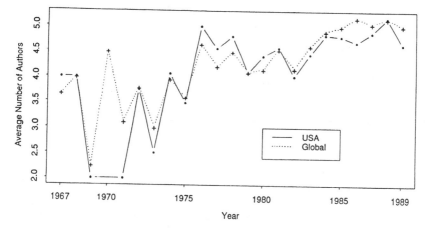

Figure 6.2. Average Number of Authors per Article Published by Stars, 1967-1989

Organizations as Information
Envelopes: Value, Trust, and Diffusion

Changes in patterns and relationships among bioscientists occur over time, reflecting changes in the value of the information and the consequent demand for trust production. Two aspects of the information flow identify gradual changes in the use of information boundaries consistent with the initial high value of intellectual capital and subsequent decline in its value:

- The number of coauthor pairs increases over time in part as a result of increasing average collaboration size, such that wider access is being given to the new scientific discoveries as the area develops. This suggests that the value of the intellectual capital produced is falling. Figure 6.2 shows the increasing average number of authors per article worldwide, smoothed to reduce the effects of very small numbers of articles published prior to the mid-1970s.
- More coauthor pairs are located in the same organization early in the process, suggesting that within-organization collaboration is being used to limit information flow more early in the diffusion process. The number of same-organization pairs declines steadily over time, again pointing to the declining value of intellectual capital. Figure 6.3 shows the decrease in the percentage of same-institution coauthors.

Specification of Variables and Models. Although these changes over time are suggestive of the relationships we hypothesize, we turn now to multivariate analysis of the collaboration structure in the biosciences. Specifically, as the value of the genetic-sequence discoveries being reported increases, we

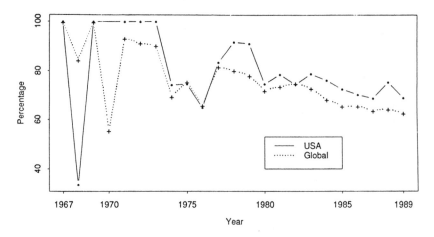

Figure 6.3. Percentage of Coauthors From the Same Institution as the Star, 1967-1989

expect more frequent same-organization collaboration and less frequent collaboration with scientists from different organizations; same-organization collaborations will slow diffusion relative to collaborations outside the same organization. Because our focus here is on the diffusion process, we will limit our analyses primarily to the United States, studying relative diffusion within the 183 different BEA functional economic areas.

The variables designed to operationalize these concepts, including the value of the intellectual capital being produced, the collaboration structure that results, measures of time trends, scientist mobility, and the "birth" of new collaborators, are all described in Table 6.1, along with several control variables. All of the variables are based on characteristics of coauthor pairs, where at least one scientist in each pair must be a star scientist from the United States (except for one analysis, as indicated in the notes to the table), reflecting our sampling frame and U.S. focus for these analyses.

The first seven variables listed in Table 6.1 are indicators of high value in terms of number of discoveries (star), quality of the university program (in biochemistry, molecular biology, and/or microbiology), and high ability to capture rents from discoveries in firms relative to universities and research institutes. Our measures of organizational and geographic location are defined next in the table. We expect more valuable intellectual capital to involve more collaboration within the same organization. The number of times a scientist moves between organizations is expected to widen collaborations to include a larger number of scientists. We define geographic location in terms of the 183 functional economic areas within the United States as defined by the U.S. Bureau of Economic Analysis (here called BEA areas). Our diffusion

TABLE 6.1 Variable Definitions

Value of Intellectual Capital	
$BOTHSTAR_i$	1 if both scientists in coauthor pair i are stars; 0 otherwise
$BOTHTQU_i$	1 if both scientists in coauthor pair i are from top-quality universities; 0 otherwise
$BOTHFIRM_i$	1 if both scientists in coauthor pair i are from firms; 0 otherwise
$BSTARCLB_j$	For each star j, total number of distinct other stars listed as coauthors across all articles
$TQCOLNET_j$	For each star j, total number of distinct coauthors who list affiliation as top-quality universities across all articles
$FIRMLAST_j$	1 if last affiliation of star j was a firm; 0 otherwise
$STAR_{kt}$	Number of stars affiliated with an organization in BEA area k in year t
Location: Organizational and Geographic	
$SAMEORG_i$	1 if both scientists in coauthor pair i list affiliation to the same organization; 0 otherwise
$SAMEOCLB_j$	For each star j, total number of coauthors who list affiliation to the same organization
$DIFFOCLB_j$	For each star j, total number of coauthors who list affiliation to different organizations
$DIFFBEA_{kt}$	Number of coauthor pairs who list affiliations in BEA area k and a different BEA area in year t
$MOBILITY_j$	Number of moves by each star j from one organization to another
Diffusion Measures	
$CLBNET_j$	For each star j, total number of distinct coauthors across all articles
$NCOLLAB_{kt}$	Number of collaborators who are not also stars born in BEA area k in year t
$NCOLLAB1_{kt}$	Lagged 1 year, number of collaborators, stars excluded, born in BEA area k in year t
Control Variables	
$CLBSIZE_i$	Number of authors of the article from which coauthor pair i is drawn
$TOTPUBS_j$	Total number of articles by each star j
$FIRSTYR_j$	Year of entry; calendar year of first article by star j; first year is 1967
$YEAR_i$	Calendar year in which the article with coauthor pair i was published; first year is 1967
$YEARSQ_i$	Calendar year squared; $YEAR_i^2$

measures examine both the size of a star's collaboration network and the "birth" of new collaborators in the same BEA. Control variables include measures of the size of collaborations, years of entry into genetic-sequence publishing, and time trends to capture the declining value of intellectual capital.

For the most part, we select familiar statistical models. But because we are attempting to explain "count" data—that is, data that involve counting the number of new collaborators, first from the perspective of each star (CLBNET) and then by BEA (NCOLLAB)—we rely on a slightly less familiar Poisson regression technique, as suggested by Hausman, Hall, and Griliches (1984). The Poisson process is consistent with count variables: nonnegative

TABLE 6.2 Poisson Regression on the Star's Collaboration Network, Distinct
Coauthors Across All Articles, United States Only, 1967-1990

Constant	21.897***	[6.351]
SAMEOCLB	0.004***	[0.0005]
DIFFOCLB	0.008***	[0.0004]
BSTARCLB	−0.009**	[0.0043]
TQCOLNET	0.005***	[0.0007]
FIRMLAST	0.148***	[0.0476]
MOBILITY	0.071***	[0.0095]
FIRSTYR	−0.010***	[0.0032]
TOTPUBS	0.015***	[0.0022]
Log likelihood = −899.706		

NOTE: Standard errors in square brackets.
*Parameter significant at the 0.05 level.
**Parameter significant at the 0.01 level.
***Parameter significant at the 0.001 level.

integers, often with significant mass at zero. The Poisson process assumes births of new collaborators in a BEA area with a probability l_{it} per unit time. The logarithm of l_{it} is a linear function of the explanatory variables included in the regression. We estimate these regressions using the LIMDEP package (Greene 1992, pp. 539-549).

Collaboration and Trust Production. We begin by examining the predictors of the number of new coauthors in the stars' coauthor network (CLBNET) in Table 6.2. As might be expected from the cosmopolitan or local models of scientific collaboration (Gouldner, 1957-1958), star scientists who possess higher-value intellectual capital generally have larger networks of new coauthors, although the larger the number of collaborators who are also stars (BSTARCLB), the smaller the total number of collaborators (CLBNET). At first glance, the strong, positive effects of both TQCOLNET and FIRMLAST on the network size seem inconsistent with our argument that higher-value intellectual capital is more protected; indeed, even scientists whose last affiliations are with firms (where capturing returns might mean limiting dissemination of the discoveries) have a significant positive effect on network size.

However, these results do not reflect the differential numbers of collaborators drawn from inside the same organization. The number of collaborators from the same or different organizations, SAMEOCLB and DIFFOCLB, both increase the size of collaboration networks significantly, but having more coauthors from different organizations is a much stronger predictor. Also, as expected, the number of times the star scientist moves from one job to the next increases the size of his or her network. All of these effects are measured, controlling for the total number of publications by each U.S. star.

TABLE 6.3 Number of Collaboration Pairs Within the Same Organization and Between Different Organizations: Universities, Research Institutes/Hospitals, and Firms, 1967-1990

	University		Research Institute		Firm	
	Same	Different	Same	Different	Same	Different
University	2,747	771		420		302
Research institute		420	532	141		111
Firm		302		111	346	17
Totals	2,747	1,493	532	672	346	430

NOTE: Location based on affiliation given in the first article published by each pair of scientists. Excludes scientists listing affiliation with more than one institution ($N = 16$).

Table 6.3 shows that over 75% of collaborations within the same type of organization occur within the organizational boundaries, increasing to nearly 95% for firms. Firm scientists very rarely coauthor with scientists at other firms. Most collaboration outside the boundaries of the same organization takes place between university scientists and other scientists located in research institutes and firms. Because universities are the "source," that is, the location of many of the initial discoveries and talent, it is not surprising that both firms and research institutes collaborate frequently with scientists in universities. If we take into account all of these external collaborations, regardless of organization type, the balance shifts somewhat: 43% to 44% of all collaborations involving research institutes and firms take place across organizational boundaries, but 64% of collaborations involving university scientists remain inside the organizational boundaries. Overall, our findings counter assumptions about the open structure of scientific discovery across different universities.

What predicts whether any given coauthor pair is found within the organization's boundary or spans it? In Table 6.4, we find a strong positive effect of higher-value intellectual capital, controlling for collaboration size and time, on the probability that the collaboration pair comes from the same organization. Again, we are examining only pairs in which at least one author is a star and at least one author is from the United States. We find strong support for our hypothesis that intellectual capital of high value—where both coauthors are stars, from top-quality universities, or from firms that can capture value better—is more likely to be within the *information envelope* created by working in the same organization. As expected, the larger the collaboration size, the less likely that any particular pair of coauthors is from the same organization. Time does not have a significant effect, net of the other variables in the equation.

TABLE 6.4 Logit Regression Probability That a Pair of Coauthors Are From the
Same U.S. Organization, 1967-1990

Intercept	1.420**	[.597]
YEAR	−0.001	[.007]
CLBSIZE	−0.249***	[.009]
BOTHFIRM	4.707***	[.246]
BOTHSTARS	0.496***	[.088]
BOTHTQU	2.494***	[.068]

Chi-square for −2 log likelihood (5 d.f.) = 3571.36***
Concordance of predicted probabilities and observations:
Concordant 80.7%, Discordant 16.2%, Tied 3.1%

NOTE: For each coauthor pair, at least one author must be from the United States. Standard errors in square brackets. Results for predicting different organization are opposite signs but have the same magnitude for coefficients.
*Parameter significant at the 0.05 level.
**Parameter significant at the 0.01 level.
***Parameter significant at the 0.001 level.

A minor difficulty in interpreting Table 6.4 arises because the three variables BOTHFIRM, BOTHSTARS, and BOTHTQU all inevitably increase the probability that both coauthors in the pair are from the same institution because all potential authors at a different type of institution are by definition excluded.[15] This effect, however, is relatively small and much smaller than required to explain the large estimated coefficients for these variables in Table 6.4. To take the most extreme case, there are 18 top-quality universities, so if pairs are randomly assigned there is a probability of 1/18 = .0556 that they would be from the same university. Compared to the average probability that the authors are from the same organization (0.639), adding the full .0556 (an overestimate of the increased probability due to this factor) would increase the logit dependent variable from 0.571 to only 0.822. This increase of 0.251 is only a tenth of the size of the coefficient of BOTHTQU. The corresponding estimates of maximum upward bias for the coefficients of BOTHFIRM and BOTHSTARS are 0.0916 and 0.0207, both of which are trivial relative to the size of the estimated coefficients.

Transaction costs provide an alternative—possibly complementary—explanation of the protection of valuable intellectual capital for the high frequency of collaborations inside organizational boundaries. Generally, both protection is lower and other transaction costs are higher for collaborations across organizational boundaries, as compared to within one's own organization. Therefore, all else equal, transactions across organizational boundaries should occur only when sufficient benefits offset the additional costs involved. Looking back at Table 6.3, it appears that the reward/cost ratio of transacting with organizations of the same type seldom makes it worthwhile.

TABLE 6.5 Average Number of Citations to Genetic-Sequence Articles by Location of Collaboration Pair, 1967-1990

	University		Research Institute		Firm	
	Same	Different	Same	Different	Same	Different
University	17.64	29.01		22.00		49.53
Research institute		22.00	18.03	26.45		95.60
Firm		48.53		95.60	69.57	64.18

NOTE: Citation counts are for 1982, 1987, and 1992. Average number of citations is determined by dividing per scientist. Excludes scientists listing affiliation with more than one institution ($N = 16$).

This is especially so for firms, with very rare collaboration with other firms, perhaps in part because of problems concerning property rights that don't emerge when firms collaborate with scientists at universities or research institutes.

But if we examine the average benefits of collaborations in terms of citations that the research receives, occurring within or across organizational boundaries as shown in Table 6.5, the data appear to support the hypothesis that transaction costs (including distrust) increase in interorganizational collaborations: For authors from the same type of organizations, collaborations across organizational boundaries are more highly cited than for those within the same organization, significantly so in universities and research institutes. Interestingly, there is a much greater apparent citation payoff for scientists from universities and research institutes who collaborate with those from firms, which is consistent with the hypothesis that the difference in cultures further reduces trust, but this is also possibly due to selection of the best academic scientists for collaborations by the generally more highly cited firm scientists (some empirical support for selection as a significant factor is provided in Zucker, Darby, & Armstrong, 1994). Our innovation above is that we can use indicators of the value of the information produced to identify collaborations for which reduced trust has a greater impact on the total transaction costs.

Organizational Boundaries and Diffusion. Our final analysis in this chapter is in many respects the most important. The two maps of the geographic location of stars and collaborators in 1980 and 1990 in the United States, displayed as Figure 6.4, provide a clear picture of the rapid diffusion of rDNA techniques. These maps also depict both the dispersion and the local agglomeration of intellectual capital in the biosciences. In Table 6.6, the effects of collaboration with trusted others within the same organization on diffusion of research-reporting genetic-sequence discoveries, measured as the number

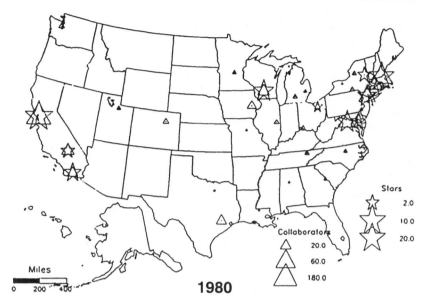

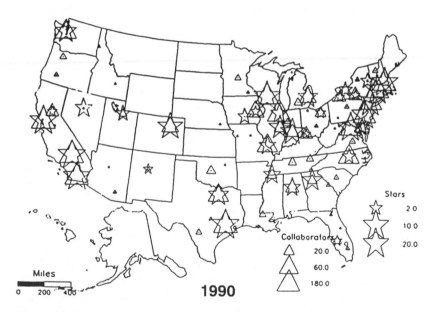

Figure 6.4. Cumulative Geographic Agglomeration and Distribution of Intellectual Capital: Stars and Collaborators in the United States, 1980 and 1990

TABLE 6.6 Poisson Regressions: Determinants of Number of Collaborators Born by BEA Area in the United States and Year, 1967-1989

Dependent variable: $NCOLLAB_{kt}$
Independent Coefficients and Standard Errors

Variables	Model 1	Model 2
CONSTANT	−26.793*	11.429
	(12.500)	(12.840)
SAMEORG	−0.012***	−0.003
	(0.002)	(0.002)
DIFFBEA	0.005	0.039***
	(0.005)	(0.005)
STAR	0.134***	0.121***
	(0.006)	(0.006)
YEAR	0.567	−0.375
	(0.301)	(0.309)
$YEAR^2$	−0.003	0.003
	(0.002)	(0.002)
NCOLLAB1	−0.032***	
	(0.002)	
Log likelihood	−3058.96	−2952.64

NOTE: For each coauthor pair, both authors are from the United States. Each BEA gets ½ birth credit for across BEA collaboration pairs. Standard errors are in parentheses. Results for predicting different organization are opposite signs but have the same magnitude for coefficients.
*Parameter significant at the 0.05 level.
**Parameter significant at the 0.01 level.
***Parameter significant at the 0.001 level.

of new collaborators who coauthor a publication in that year, are estimated within BEAs. As predicted, coauthoring within the same organizational boundaries (SAMEORG) has a *negative* effect, reducing the number of new coauthors "born" in that BEA, but coauthoring across BEA boundaries generally increases the number of new coauthors "born" in that BEA. These results generally hold whether the lagged number of collaborators born in that BEA are entered into the equation, although the positive effect of coauthorship across BEAs (DIFFBEA) is only significant when the lagged dependent variable is included in the equation. The control variable, the number of stars in the BEA, has a positive effect on the "birth" of new collaborators. Effective information boundaries are in fact constructed: Collaboration across geographic boundaries, thus between different organizations, increases diffusion to new collaborators, but in geographic areas, where a higher proportion of coauthor pairs come from the same organization, diffusion to new collaborators is retarded.

Conclusion

Scientists who make breakthrough discoveries can receive above-normal returns to their *intellectual capital,* with returns depending primarily on the degree of "natural excludability," so that at the extreme, privatizing discoveries requires only selecting trusted others as collaborators. Most often these trusted collaborators are scientists working in the same organization where incentives become aligned based on repeat and future exchange that is monitored and enforced by managers serving as third parties to the exchange. We find that high-value intellectual capital paradoxically predicts both a generally larger number of collaborators and more of that network contained within the same organization. Specifically, same-organization collaboration pairs are more likely when both are highly productive "star" scientists, both are located in top-quality bioscience university departments, or both are located in a firm (higher ability to capture returns). Collaboration across organization boundaries, in contrast, is negatively related to the value of intellectual capital and predicted by the number of times the star scientist has moved. As expected, organization boundaries act as information envelopes, such that the more valuable the information produced, the more its dissemination is limited.

At the same time, when collaborations do occur across organizational boundaries, they tend to involve higher-valued output, as measured by citations. Also, as we predicted, diffusion to new collaborators is significantly decreased when collaborations occur within organizational boundaries, effectively slowing the spread of new techniques and related discoveries.

Implications. There are a number of implications of our argument and results, some of which were introduced earlier. First, belonging to the same organization as a potential coauthor appears to be a powerful and effective means of generating trust: Collaboration within organizations is significantly more likely, compared to collaborating across organizational boundaries, especially when the information produced from the collaboration is potentially of high value (both stars, both from top-quality universities or firms). Second, our results suggest that distrust is one of the major costs involved in transacting across organizational boundaries.

Last, and most important, we have evidence that organizational boundaries operate effectively to restrict diffusion. Collaborations across organizational boundaries increase the "birth" of new collaborators in the local geographic area, but collaborations within the same organization significantly retard it. The organizational literature marginalizes organizational boundaries relative to the technical core and the surrounding organizational environment; without making invidious citations, a survey of seven major textbooks on organizations revealed no more than a page or two on organizational boundaries and only a chapter or more on the organizational environment. In sharp contrast, we argue that the organizational boundary, as well as associated repeat or future interactions and monitoring by managers, identifies where trust is being actively produced.

Acknowledgments

We acknowledge very useful comments received from participants in the Stanford Conference on Trust in Organizations, May 1994, and encouraging comments on a preliminary version from participants in the West Coast Conference on Small Group Research, April 1993. Maximo Torero's contributions to graphics development and SAS programming are especially appreciated; Kerry Knight also made substantive contributions to the analysis. We are indebted to a remarkably talented team of research assistants, including Paul J. Alapat, Jeff Armstrong, Cherie Barba, Lynda J. Kim, Edmundo Murrugara, Amalya Oliver, Alan Paul, Alan Wang, and Mavis Wu, and postdoctoral fellows Zhong Deng, Julia Liebeskind, and Hiromi Ono. Any opinions expressed are those of the authors alone.

Notes

1. Indeed, natural excludability has created some problems for making the "enabling disclosure" that is required for a valid U.S. patent application. To obtain the 17-year monopoly granted by a patent, the applicant must make a disclosure that will enable the public to practice the innovation once the patent expires. After some litigation and legislation, patents are now obtainable by biotech inventors who disclose their invention by placing a culture in a recognized public depositary (see Eisenberg, 1987, for a discussion of this history). Disclosure by deposit eliminates the inherent difficulty in disclosing the art used to obtain the invention so that it can be readily replicated.

2. Very little research has examined trust production in organizational settings; most has focused on the effects of trust once it exists (for an excellent review, see Porter & Roberts, 1976). Brewer and Silver (1978) found that in-group members were rated as more trustworthy, honest, and cooperative than their out-group counterparts. Some laboratory research on small groups, simulating organizations has found that members of the same organization are more likely to communicate freely with each other, assuming that reciprocity of communication is more likely (Schneider, 1990; see also Kramer & Brewer, 1984; Sato, 1988). But this increased communication occurs only when individuals believe that the benefits are going exclusively to members of their own group (Dawes, van de Kragt, & Orbell, 1987).

3. In biotechnology, withholding of information has been acknowledged as a common strategy used by both academic and commercial scientists to "retain the exclusive benefits of a discovery for themselves" (Eisenberg 1987, p. 204). As in many other fields of science, recognition and other financial and social awards accrue to the scientist who solves the problem first. As a result, significant deviation from the norms requiring biological materials necessary for replication to be made available to other scientists was acknowledged by a majority of ad hoc committee

members reviewing the publication policy of the *Journal of Biological Chemistry* (Dr. Donald Brown, Department of Embryology, Carnegie Institution of Washington; Dr. I. S. Johnson, Vice President, Lilly Research Laboratories, Eli Lilly; Dr. Daniel Nathans, Department of Microbiology, The Johns Hopkins University School of Medicine; Dr. Jesse C. Rabinowitz, Department of Biochemistry, University of California at Berkeley; as identified in Eisenberg, 1987, pp. 201-202, notes 132, 137, 140).

4. Shapiro (1987) has also outlined some principles of formal structure that increase trust, but her argument is not process focused and doesn't relate directly to the extension of organization theory proposed in our chapter.

5. Explicit agreements, such as joint ventures between organizations, may produce similar trust-enhancing results. We will estimate these equations in later work.

6. It is important to draw a parallel here to economic activity. It is empirically as ubiquitous, but its production is seen as highly variable; when the incentives are not strong, as in the command economies, economic action will be depressed and economic structure will be poorly developed. We need to rethink institutional structure and social action in these terms and consider developing an explicit demand framework. We already know the concept of *resource mobilization,* developed in social movement research, that recognizes the need for resources to work for social change, effectively creating a demand for institutions of a particular sort (McCarthy & Zald, 1977). The concept of *social capital* may also serve as a basis for revising sociological theory if it is redeveloped along the lines suggested here (see Coleman, 1986).

7. By the cost of learning the information, we specifically mean the eventual cost of mastering the information as part of a normal education and/or on-the-job training program of an entering scientist in the field. This cost, not the cost of actually making the discovery, will ultimately determine the returns to the information when equilibrium is reached.

8. In the limit, where the discovery can be easily incorporated into the human capital of any competent scientist, the discoverer(s) cannot earn any personal returns—as opposed to returns to intellectual property, such as patents or trade secrets (see below). In the case of biotechnology, it may be empirically difficult to separate intellectual capital from the conceptually distinct value of cell cultures created and controlled by a scientist who used his or her nonpublic information to create the cell culture.

Besides natural excludability, the value of intellectual capital depends on the novelty and value of the discovery. For example, many discoveries have little or no value—whether monetary or nonmonetary. They are viewed as dead-ends, of interest only within a few collaborations. The techniques and research program crawl along, diffusing slowly, if at all.

9. We used GenBank Release 65.0, which combines data from the DNA Data Bank of Japan (Mishima, Japan), EMBL Data Library (Heidelberg, Germany), and GenBank (Los Alamos, New Mexico). See Bilofsky and Burks (1988) for a description of the GenBank.

10. We excluded unpublished manuscripts and papers published in proceedings and in obscure journals to obtain consistent information on institutional affiliation and location.

11. Gene-splicing machines were initially extremely unreliable. By 1983, the machines had improved in reliability but still were not sufficient for wide adoption (Gebhart, 1983). The high cost remained an additional barrier to adoption until the late 1980s.

12. See U.S. Department of Education, National Center for Education Statistics (1985).

13. The respondents were asked to rate programs using the following scale: 5 for distinguished, 4 strong, 3 good, 2 adequate, 1 marginal, and 0 not sufficient for doctoral education. The reported scores are the averages among respondents.

14. In informal discussion, Ed Penhoet emphasized the role of diffusion in increasing the number of coauthors over time. As an early innovator in the area, both as a founder and the current CEO of Chiron, he has deep insight into the development of the science over the full time period of our study. We will explore this competing hypothesis more adequately in a companion paper that develops a model of the diffusion process underlying rDNA research.

15. We are indebted to Kerry Knight for this point.

References

Bilofsky, H. S., & Burks, C. (1988). The GenBank (R) genetic sequence data bank. *Nucleic Acids Research, 16,* 1861-1864.

Brewer, M. B., & Silver, M. (1978). In-group bias as a function of task characteristics. *European Journal of Social Psychology, 8,* 393-400.

Coase, R. (1937). The nature of the firm. *Economica, 4,* 386-405.

Coase, R. (1988). The nature of the firm: Origin, meaning, influence. *Journal of Law, Economics and Organization, 4,* 3-47.

Cohen, S., Chang, A., Boyer, H., & Helling, R. (1973). Construction of biologically functional bacterial plasmids *in vitro. Proceedings of the National Academy of Sciences, 70,* 3240-3244.

Coleman, J. S. (1986). Social theory, social research, and a theory of action. *American Journal of Sociology, 91,* 1309-1335.

Crane, D. (1969). Social structure in a group of scientists: A test of the invisible college hypothesis. *American Sociological Review, 34,* 335-352.

Crane, D. (1972). *Invisible colleges: Diffusion of knowledge in scientific communities.* Chicago: University of Chicago Press.

Darby, M. R., & Karni, E. (1993). Free competition and the optimal amount of fraud. *Journal of Law and Economics, 16,* 67-88.

Darby, M. R., & Lott, J. R., Jr. (1989). Qualitative information, reputation, and monopolistic competition. *International Review of Law and Economics, 9,* 87-103.

Dawes, R. M., van de Kragt, A., & Orbell, R. (1987). *Not me or thee but we: The importance of group identity in eliciting cooperation in dilemma situations.* Paper presented at the Public Choice Meeting, Tucson, AZ.

Eisenberg, R. S. (1987). Proprietary rights and the norms of science in biotechnology research. *The Yale Law Journal, 97,* 177-231.

Gaston, J. (1973). *Originality and competition in science: A study of the British high energy physics community.* Chicago: University of Chicago Press.

Gebhart, F. (1983). Quality and consistency improved, the automated gene synthesizer market is on the rebound. *GEN, 3*(1), 10.

Geertz, C. (1978). The bazaar economy: Information and search in peasant marketing. *American Economic Review, 68,* 28-32.

Gouldner, A. W. (1957-1958). Cosmopolitans and locals: Toward an analysis of latent social roles. *Administrative Science Quarterly, 2,* 281-306, 444-480.

Granovetter, M. (1985). Economic action and social structure: A theory of embeddedness. *American Journal of Sociology, 91,* 481-510.

Greene, W. H. (1992). *LIMDEP: User's manual and reference guide, version 6.0.* Bellport, NY: Econometric Software.

Hausman, J., Hall, B. H., & Griliches, Z. (1984). Econometric models for count data with an application to the patents—R&D relationship. *Econometrica, 52,* 909-938.

Jones, E. E. (1964). *Ingratiation, a social psychological analysis.* New York: Appleton-Century-Crofts.

Klein, B., Crawford, R., & Alchian, A. (1978). Vertical integration, appropriable rents, and the competitive contracting process. *Journal of Law and Economics, 21,* 297-326.

Kollock, P. (1994). The emergence of exchange structures: An experimental study of uncertainty, commitment, and trust. *American Journal of Sociology, 100,* 313-345.

Kramer, R. M., & Brewer, M. B. (1984). Effects of group identity on resource use in a simulated commons dilemma. *Journal of Personality and Social Psychology, 46,* 1044-1056.

McCarthy, J. D., & Zald, M. N. (1977). Resource mobilization and social movements: A partial theory. *American Journal of Sociology, 82,* 1212-1239.

Merton, R. M. (1938). Motive forces of the new science. In R. M. Merton (Ed.), *Science, technology and society in seventeenth-century England* (pp. 80-111). Bruges, Belgium: Saint Catherine Press.

Merton, R. M. (1957). Priorities in scientific discovery. *American Sociological Review, 22,* 635-659.

Porter, L. W., & Roberts, K. H. (1976). Communication in organizations. In M. D. Dunnett (Ed.), *Handbook of industrial and organizational psychology.* Chicago: Rand McNally.

Sato, K. (1988). Trust and group size in a social dilemma. *Japanese Psychological Research, 30,* 88-93.

Schneider, S. K. (1990). *Communications dilemmas: The effects of social categorization on communication networks.* Unpublished doctoral dissertation, UCLA.

Schneider, S. K., & Brewer, M. B. (1987). *Effects of group composition on contributions to a public good.* Unpublished manuscript, UCLA.

Shapiro, S. P. (1987). The social control of impersonal trust. *American Journal of Sociology, 93,* 623-658.

Taubes, G. (1986). *Nobel dreams: Power, deceit and the ultimate experiment.* New York: Random House.

Tolbert, P., & Zucker, L. G. (1995). Institutional analyses of organizations: Legitimate but not institutionalized In S. Clegg, W. Nord, & C. Harley (Eds.), *Handbook of organizational theory.* Oxford, UK: Basil Blackwell.

U.S. Department of Education, National Center for Education Statistics. (c. 1985). *Higher Education General Information Survey (HEGIS), institutional characteristics, 1983-84* (Machine-readable database, ICPSR 8291). Ann Arbor, MI: Inter-University Consortium for Political and Social Research.

Watson, J. D. (1968). *The double helix: A personal account of the discovery of the structure of DNA.* New York: Norton.

Williamson, O. (1979). Transaction cost economics: The governance of contractual relations. *Journal of Law and Economics, 22,* 3-61.

Williamson, O. (1991). Comparative economic organization: The analysis of discrete structural alternatives. *Administrative Science Quarterly, 36,* 269-296.

Zucker, L. G. (1983). Organizations as institutions. *Research in the Sociology of Organizations, 2,* 1-47.

Zucker, L. G. (1986). Production of trust: Institutional sources of economic structure, 1840 to 1920. *Research in Organizational Behavior, 8,* 53-111.

Zucker, L. G., Darby, M. R., & Armstrong, J. (1994). *Intellectual capital and the firm: The technology of geographically localized knowledge spillovers* (Working Paper No. 4946). Cambridge, MA: National Bureau of Economic Research.

Zucker, L. G., Darby, M. R., & Brewer, M. B. (1994). *Intellectual capital and the birth of U.S. biotechnology enterprises* (Working Paper No. 4653). Cambridge, MA: National Bureau of Economic Research.

Zucker, L. G., & Kreft, I. G. G. (1994). The evolution of socially contingent rational action: Effects of labor strikes on change in union founding in the 1880s. In J. A. C. Baum & J. V. Singh (Eds.), *Evolutionary dynamics of organizations* (pp. 294-313). Oxford, UK: Oxford University Press.

Zuckerman, H. (1967). Nobel laureates in science: Patterns of productivity, collaboration, and authorship. *American Sociological Review, 32,* 391-403.

Zuckerman, H. (1977). *Scientific elite: Nobel laureates in the United States.* New York: Free Press.

Data Sources

Bioscan (Vols. 3-7), 1989-1993.

CITIBASE: Citibank economic database. (1993). (Machine-readable database, 1946-June 1993). New York: Citibank.

GenBank, Release 65.0. (1990, September). (Machine-readable database). Palo Alto, CA: Intelli-Gentics.

Institute for Scientific Information. (various years through 1993). *Science Citation Index* (ISI Compact Disc Editions, machine-readable database). Philadelphia: Institute for Scientific Information.

Jones, L. V., Lindzey, G., & Coggeshall, P. E. (Eds.). (1982). *An assessment of research-doctorate programs in the United States: Biological sciences.* Washington, DC: National Academy Press.

North Carolina Biotechnology Center. (1992, April 16). *North Carolina Biotechnology Center, U.S. companies database* (Machine-readable database). Research Triangle Park: North Carolina Biotechnology Center.

Pratt, S. E. (1982). *Guide to venture capital sources* (6th ed.). Englewood Cliffs, NJ: Prentice Hall.

Pre-Bioscan. (1988). (Biotechnology company database, predecessor source for Bioscan, provided in printout form by a major biotechnology company).

U.S. Department of Commerce, Bureau of the Census. (1982). *County business patterns, 1980: U.S. summary, state, and county data* (Machine-readable database). Washington, DC: Bureau of the Census. [Ann Arbor, MI: Inter-University Consortium for Political and Social Research, 1986 (distributor)]

U.S. Department of Commerce, Economics and Statistics Administration, Bureau of Economic Analysis. (1992a). *National income and product accounts of the United States, Vol. 2, 1959-88.* Washington, DC: Government Printing Office.

U.S. Department of Commerce, Economics and Statistics Administration, Bureau of Economic Analysis. (1992b). *Regional economic information system, version 1.3* (CD-ROM, machine-readable database). Washington, DC: Bureau of Economic Analysis.

U.S. Department of Education, National Center for Education Statistics. (c. 1985). *Higher Education General Information Survey (HEGIS), institutional characteristics, 1983-84* (Machine-readable database, ICPSR 8291). Ann Arbor, MI: Inter-University Consortium for Political and Social Research.

Developing and Maintaining Trust in Work Relationships

ROY J. LEWICKI
BARBARA BENEDICT BUNKER

The past decade has seen dramatic changes in the modern organization. New organizational linkages, strategic alliances, partnerships, and joint ventures are being formed to achieve and maintain competitive advantage in the marketplace. New linkages require organizations to move away from the more traditional hierarchical forms and toward networks and alliances. These new forms are designed to be more responsive to rapid change, enable entrepreneurial activity to flourish within the organization and across its boundaries, and increase the effectiveness of communication and problem solving across departments, locations, functional responsibilities, and organizational boundaries.

In their recent work, *Managing the New Organization,* Limerick and Cunnington (1993) emphasize nine crucial competencies for managing networks, within and across organizational boundaries. Interpersonal dynamics between key actors within a network or alliance are critical elements in this list of competencies, and trust is central to this list:

> The key value in networking, and the one that is most problematic for Western managers, is trust. . . . High levels of trust help reduce transaction costs. . . . Trust

reduces uncertainty about the future and the necessity for continually making provisions for the possibility of opportunistic behavior among participants. . . . Trust lubricates the smooth, harmonious functioning of the organization by eliminating friction and minimizing the need for bureaucratic structures that specify the behavior of participants who do not trust each other. But trust does not come naturally. It has to be carefully structured and managed. (pp. 95-96)

Limerick and Cunnington's work effectively highlights the changes occurring in the contemporary organization and explains the new emphasis on interpersonal skills, particularly trust, in the workplace. The objective of this chapter is to explore how trust is developed, sustained, and repaired in professional work relationships. We will begin the chapter with a definition of trust and a brief review of the various ways that it has been approached and defined in the social science literature. We will then turn our attention to describe a model of trust development that is more complete and complex than previous writings on this subject. Finally, we identify some of the ways that trust is broken in professional relationships and describe the process necessary to repair this trust.

Current Definitions and Research Approaches to Trust

Trust is a concept that has received attention in several different social science literatures—psychology, sociology, political science, economics, anthropology, history, and sociobiology (see Gambetta, 1988; Lewicki & Bunker, 1995; Worchel, 1979, for reviews). As can be expected, each literature has approached the problem with its own disciplinary lens and filters. Remarkably, little effort has been made to integrate these different perspectives or articulate the key role that trust plays in critical social processes (e.g., cooperation, coordination, performance).

Worchel (1979) proposes that these different perspectives can be aggregated into at least three different groups (see also Lewicki & Bunker, 1995, for a more detailed exploration of theory within each category):

1. *The views of personality theorists, who have focused on individual personality differences in the readiness to trust and on the specific developmental and social contextual factors that shape this readiness.* At this level, trust is conceptualized as a belief, expectancy, or feeling that is deeply rooted in the personality and has its origins in the individual's early psychosocial development (see Worchel, 1979).

2. *The views of sociologists and economists, who have focused on trust as an institutional phenomenon.* At this level, trust can be conceptualized as both a phenomenon within and between institutions, and as the trust individuals put in those institutions.

3. *The views of social psychologists, who have focused on the interpersonal transactions between individuals that create or destroy trust at the interpersonal and group levels.* At this level, trust can be defined as the expectation of the other party in a transaction, the risks associated with assuming and acting on such expectations, and the contextual factors that serve to either enhance or inhibit the development and maintenance of that trust.

It is this third approach to trust—the social-psychological perspective, emphasizing the nature of trust in interpersonal transactions—that we wish to emphasize in this chapter. Deutsch (1958) defined *trust* as an expectation of interpersonal events:

> An individual may be said to have trust in the occurrence of an event if he expects its occurrence and the expectations lead to behavior which he perceives to have greater negative motivational consequence if the expectation is not confirmed than positive motivational consequence if it is confirmed. (p. 266)

However, trust is more than simple expectations; as social psychologists note, it is expectations set within particular contextual parameters and constraints. For example, Lewis and Weigert (1985) argue that trust is not mere predictability but confidence in the face of *risk* (a contextual variable that is central to most social-psychological definitions; see also Kahnemann, Knetsch & Thaler, 1986).

Many definitions move beyond expectations to specify the key situational parameters that describe or define situational risk. Deutsch (1960) suggested that a decision to trust is made in situations in which the following situational parameters exist: (a) There is an ambiguous course of action in the future, (b) outcome occurrence depends on the behavior of others, and (c) the strength of the harmful event is greater than the beneficial event. In a subsequent article, Deutsch (1973) refines this decision-making process into a series of hypotheses about the conditions under which trusting choices will be made, noting the positive and negative consequences of the trusting acts. Similarly, Schlenker, Helm, and Tedeschi (1973) defined trust as the "reliance upon information received from another person about uncertain environmental states and their accompanying outcomes in a risky situation" (p. 419). They argued that the situation must contain the following for trust to be demonstrated: (a) a risky situation with regard to whether certain outcomes will be derived in the future; (b) the presence of cues that provide some information as to the probability of various uncertain environmental states occurring, such as the communication of another's intentions; and (c) the resulting behavior of the person demonstrating reliance on this uncertain information (see also Zand, 1972).

In this chapter, we will adopt the definition of trust proposed by Boon and Holmes (1991); their definition is relatively simple, straightforward, and contains most of the elements of other definitions. Boon and Holmes define trust as "a state involving confident positive expectations about another's motives with respect to oneself in situations entailing risk" (p. 194). Boon and Holmes's definition of trust is based on three elements that contribute to the level of trust one has for another: the individual's *chronic disposition* toward trust (see our earlier discussion of personality), *situational parameters* (some are suggested above), and the *history of their relationship*. We will now address this relationship dimension of trust.

Trust in Professional Relationships

Much of the earlier work we have cited thus far assumed that *interpersonal trust* and *relationship* were synonymous and interchangeable. More recent work has attempted to separate the two, although the separation may be indiscernible because many of these studies (e.g., Boon & Holmes, 1991; Holmes, 1991; Rempel, Holmes, & Zanna, 1985) have focused on trust development only in a close, personal relationship (e.g., romantic) context. Clearly, however, not all relationships are romantic ones. Many relationships are best defined as "friendships" or "acquaintances," yet trust is just as essential to sustain these relationships. As we noted earlier, trust is a critical success element to most business, professional, and employment relationships.

The study of personal relationships has been of continuous interest to the field of social psychology (Valley, Neale, & Mannix, 1995). Several recent works have attempted to analyze and understand the fundamental characteristics of relationships (see Duck, 1988, 1993a, 1993b; Duck & Perlman, 1985). Through a comprehensive review of the literature and empirical examination of different types of relationships, Greenhalgh and Chapman (1994, in press) identified 18 empirically different dimensions of relationships. Central to their typology—as it has been to other characterizations of trust (e.g., Davis & Todd, 1985)—is the notion of trust.

Our purpose here is not to explore all of the different dimensions of relationships. Instead, we wish to focus on how trust develops in working relationships, particularly ones that do not entail a romantic component. However, because we have embraced Boon and Holmes's (1991) definition of trust—a definition they developed to explain trust development in intimate, romantic relationships—we will first explain how they propose that trust develops in the context of romantic relationships and then extrapolate this assessment to nonromantic relationships.

Boon and Holmes (1991) suggest that romantic relationships move through three developmental stages or phases: the romantic love stage, the evaluative stage, and the accommodative stage. In the romantic love stage, the parties experience a surge of positive feelings and an idealization of the partner. Boon and Holmes argue that love and trust are fundamentally undifferentiatable at this stage, because the parties' hope that the relationship will prosper over-shadows any fear or caution that it may not. In the evaluative stage, sustained close contact between the parties reveals imperfections in the other, leading them to want to step back and evaluate the relationship more broadly. The "pros and cons" of the relationship are debated, and in the process, Boon and Holmes propose that "real" trust takes root: The parties engage in reciprocal self-disclosure and respond to each other's thoughts and feelings, learning to trust each other and determine whether each other's responsiveness is genuine. Finally, the accommodative stage is marked by a negotiation of conflicting needs, expectations, and perceived incompatibilities. The parties solidify their trust in each other, eventually making a "leap of faith" in which they decide that although they cannot ever know everything about the other, their ability to enjoy compatibilities and resolve differences is likely to sustain the relation-ship for the foreseeable future.

In professional relationships, trust does not begin with the development of intense emotionality. However, the processes of evaluation and information exchange that Boon and Holmes describe are part of relationship development at work. For our purposes, the most important element in Boon and Holmes's description of the evolution of trust is their suggestion that trust dynamics are *different* at each of the three stages. This is a fundamentally different perspec-tive on trust from the view that the essence of trust cannot be captured by a single, "static" definition of its key elements and attributes. Trust is viewed as a dynamic phenomenon that takes on a different character in the early, developing, and "mature" stages of a relationship.

Trust in Professional Relationships

An effort to describe relationship development in a business context was recently proposed by Shapiro, Sheppard, and Cheraskin (1992). These authors suggest that three types of trust operate in the development of a business relationship: deterrence-based trust, knowledge-based trust, and identifica-tion-based trust. *Deterrence-based trust* is based on consistency of behavior— that people will do what they say they are going to do. Behavioral consistency is sustained by the threat of punishment (e.g., loss of relationship) that will occur if consistency is not maintained—that is, people do not do what they say they will do. The second type of trust is *knowledge-based trust*. This type of trust is grounded in behavioral predictability—a judgment of the probability of the other's likely choice of behaviors. Knowledge-based trust occurs when one has enough information about others to understand them and accurately predict their likely behavior. Finally, the third type of trust is called *identification-based trust*. This form of trust is based on a complete empathy with the other party's desires and intentions. At this third level, trust exists because each party effectively understands, agrees with, empathizes with, and takes on the other's values because of the emotional connection between them and thus can act for the other. Identification-based trust thus permits one to act as an "agent" for the other and substitute for the other in interpersonal transactions.

In an earlier paper (Lewicki & Bunker, 1995), we compared this framework to the Boon and Holmes model and significantly expanded on the Shapiro, Sheppard, and Cheraskin framework. We will now review that model and demonstrate its applicability to trust development in professional relationships.

Three Types of Trust

Our earlier paper suggested three specific extensions of the Shapiro, Sheppard, and Cheraskin framework. First, we suggested that the three types of trust are linked in a sequential iteration in which achievement of trust at one level enables the development of trust at the next level. We also proposed that understanding how trust changes and evolves may also help us understand how relationships change and evolve. Finally, our model of transitional stages in trust development creates the necessary groundwork to specify how trust declines and how it may be repaired.

The following three-stage model assumes that two parties are entering into a new relationship. There is no history between them, and thus, although they have no previous "reputations" to overcome, the parties are uncertain about each other, believe they are vulnerable if they disclose too much too quickly, and are uncertain about the future longevity of the relationship.

Calculus-Based Trust

Shapiro, Sheppard, and Cheraskin identified the first kind of trust as deterrence-based trust. These authors argue that this form of trust is based on assuring consistency of behavior; that is, individuals will do what they say because they fear the consequences of not doing what they say. Like any behavior based on a theory of deterrence, trust is sustained to the degree that the deterrent (punishment) is clear, possible, and likely to occur if the trust is violated. Thus, the threat of punishment is likely to be a more significant motivator than the promise of reward.

We have called this form *calculus-based trust* because we believe that deterrence-based trust is grounded not only in the fear of punishment for violating the trust but also in the rewards to be derived from preserving it. In this view, trust is an ongoing, market-oriented, economic calculation whose value is derived by determining the outcomes resulting from creating and sustaining the relationship relative to the costs of maintaining or severing it. Compliance with calculus-based trust is often ensured both by the rewards of being trusting (and trustworthy) and by the "threat" that if trust is violated, one's reputation can be hurt through the person's network of friends and associates. In a business relationship, the professional "reputation" of the other side can serve as a "hostage." If one party begins to violate the other's trust, the violated party can quickly let it be known, throughout the accused's network, that the other is a disreputable individual. "People invest resources for the purpose of building a reputation for honesty" (Dasgupta, 1988, p. 70). Even if you are not an honest person, having a reputation for honesty (or trustworthiness) is a valuable asset that a businessperson would want to maintain. So even if there are opportunities to be dishonest (or untrustworthy), these short-term gains from untrustworthy acts must be balanced (in a calculus-based way) against the longer-run gains of maintaining a good reputation.

Although calculus-based trust may be driven both by the value of benefits or the costs of cheating, we support Shapiro, Sheppard, and Cheraskin's view that at this stage, the deterrence elements will be a more dominant "motivator" than the benefit-seeking elements. The "trust calculus" is made effective, therefore, by the *adequacy and costs of deterrence*. For the threat of deterrence to be effective, the following conditions must exist:

- The potential loss of future interaction with the other must outweigh the profit potential that comes from defecting from the relationship or violating expectations.
- Deterrence requires monitoring the other's behavior for it to work; the parties must continue to monitor each other and be willing to tell each other when a trust violation has been noted.
- The potentially harmed party must be willing to withdraw benefits from, or introduce harm to, the person acting distrustfully. Thus, behavior *control* is central to this form of trust; these control actions are designed to get the other to do what the actor wants them to do.
- The upside and downside calculations of calculus-based trust may be shaped by the actor's orientation toward risk. Trust actions are rational and outcome maximizing, but perceptions of economic rationality are often influenced by orientation to risk (see Bazerman, 1994, for one review). In assessing the benefits of interdependence, costs of cheating, and the associated probabilities, perceptions will be shaped by risk biases that predispose either party toward being exploited (we are naive and "risk seeking," trusting those who do not deserve to be trusted) or toward being suspicious (we are cautious and "risk averse," not trusting those who deserve to be trusted).

Finally, as a developmental process, we believe that the appropriate meta-phor for the growth of calculus-based trust is the children's game *Chutes and Ladders*. Progress is made on the game board by dice throws that permit the player to move ahead in a stepwise fashion; however, if one lands on a "chute," the player is quickly dropped back a number of steps. In calculus-based trust, forward progress is made by ladder climbing in a slow, stepwise fashion; however, hitting a single event of inconsistency may "chute" the individuals back several steps—or, in the worst case, back to square one. At this early stage, trust is partial and quite fragile.

Knowledge-Based Trust

The second form of trust is knowledge-based trust. This form of trust is grounded in the other's predictability—knowing the other sufficiently well so that the other's behavior is anticipatable. Knowledge-based trust relies on information rather than deterrence. It develops over time, largely as a function of the parties having a history of interaction that allows them to develop a generalized expectancy that the other's behavior is predictable and that he or she will act trustworthily (Lindskold, 1978; Rotter, 1971).

According to Shapiro et al. (1992), there are several dimensions to knowledge-based trust. First, and most simply, information contributes to the predictability of the other, which contributes to trust. The better one knows the other, the more accurately he or she can predict what the other will do (Kelley & Stahelski, 1970). Second, predictability enhances trust—even if the other is predictably untrustworthy—because the ways that the other will violate the trust can be predicted. Finally, accurate prediction requires an understanding that develops over repeated interactions in multidimensional relationships (similar to calculus-based trust). In knowledge-based trust, *regular communication* and *courtship* are key processes (Shapiro et al., 1992). Regular communication puts a party in constant contact with the other, exchang-ing information about wants, preferences, and approaches to problems. Without regular communication, one can "lose touch" with the other—not only emo-tionally but in the ability to think alike and predict the reactions of the other. Second, "courtship" is behavior that is specifically directed at relationship development, at learning more about a possible partner. Courtship is con-ducted by "interviewing" the other, watching the other perform in social situations, experiencing the other in a variety of emotional states, and learning how others view this behavior. Courtship permits actors to gain enough information to determine whether the parties can work together well.

In summary, the development of knowledge-based trust is a fundamentally different process of relationship building and testing. The appropriate meta-phor for knowledge-based trust may be from agriculture: Its development is more like "gardening"—tilling the soil year after year to understand it and knowing what will grow in the sandy and moist sections, the shady and sunlit sections. This knowledge comes from experimenting with different plants over the years. In relationships, the parties cultivate their knowledge of each other by gathering data, seeing each other in different contexts, and noticing reactions to different situations. At this level, trust is not necessarily broken by inconsistent behavior. If people believe that they can adequately explain or understand someone else's behavior, they are willing to accept it (even if it has created costs for them), "forgive" that person, and move on in the relationship. Consider the example of two friends who agree to meet at a restaurant at 6 p.m. Person A fails to show up until 6:30 and B is kept waiting. To the degree that their friendship is based simply on calculus-based trust, B will be angry at the high costs she must incur for being "stood up," be upset at A's unreliability, and angry enough to terminate the relationship. If they are operating more on knowledge-based trust, however, B will tolerate A's behavior to the degree that she can muster some adequate explanation for B's behavior—"he must have gotten stuck at work," or "he is caught in heavy downtown traffic," or "he is always running behind and that doesn't bother me because I know he'll get here eventually."

Identification-Based Trust

The third type of trust is based on identification with the other's desires and intentions. At this third level, trust exists because the parties effectively understand and appreciate the other's wants; this mutual understanding is developed to the point that each can effectively act for the other. For example, Kramer (1993; Kramer & Brewer, 1986) argues that a certain form of group-based trust is linked with group membership and develops as individuals identify with the goals espoused by particular groups and organizations. In these situations, salient group identification greatly enhances the frequency of cooperation and provides a far better explanation than self-interest approaches for understanding cooperative behavior.

Identification-based trust thus permits a party to serve as the other's agent and substitute for the other in interpersonal transactions (Deutsch, 1949). The other can be confident that his or her interests will be fully protected and that no surveillance or monitoring of the actor is necessary. A true affirmation of the strength of identification-based trust between parties can be found when one party acts for the other in a manner even more zealous than the other might demonstrate. For example, if Party A is hesitant to defend himself against criticism from an outsider, but Party B is willing to take on the outsider and aggressively protect A, A's trust in B may be affirmed and enhanced by B's willingness to do for A what A could not do for himself. Interestingly, however, if B makes claims about A that exceed even what A might say about himself, A could lose some trust in B because B's exaggeration may show lack of understanding. In identification, B must act *like* A, but not overreact on behalf of A.

A corollary of this "acting for each other" in identification-based trust is that as both knowledge and identification develop, the parties not only know and identify with each other but come to understand what they must do to sustain the other's trust. This process might be described as "second-order" learning. A comes to learn what "really matters" to B and eventually places the same importance on those behaviors as A does. For example, a husband comes to learn how critical the wife believes it is to pick up the children from day care at the appointed hour. The wife has high concern for the children who have been at day care all day and also has high empathy for the teachers in the day care center who want to go home on time. The husband knows that if he is late and fails to pick up the children at the appointed hour, the wife will become very angry and take this lateness as evidence that the husband "can't be trusted" to pick up the children on time (i.e., does not understand how important it is to the wife that the children be picked up on time). Thus, the husband empathizes with the sense of urgency felt by the wife and constantly makes sure that he is not late to pick up the children. If the husband is late, even though the children are never in danger, the wife nevertheless will lose trust in the husband.

Many of the same activities that build and strengthen calculus-based and knowledge-based trust also serve to develop identification-based trust. Four additional types of activities strengthen identification-based trust that supplement those already mentioned (Shapiro et al., 1992): developing a *collective identity* (a joint name, title, logo, etc.); *colocation* in the same building or neighborhood; *creating joint products or goals,* such as a new product line or a new set of objectives; and committing to *commonly shared values,* such that the parties are actually committed to the same objectives and can substitute for each other in external transactions.

In summary, identification-based trust develops as one both knows and predicts the other's needs, choices, and preferences and also shares some of those same needs, choices, and preferences as one's own. Increased identification enables one to "think like" the other, "feel like" the other, and "respond" like the other. People may in fact empathize strongly with the other and incorporate parts of his or her psyche into their own "identity" (needs, preferences, thoughts, and behavior patterns) as a collective identity develops. A suitable metaphor for identification-based trust may be a musical one, such as "harmonizing." The parties learn how to use their voices to sing in a harmony that is integrated and complex. Each knows the others' range and pitch, each knows when to lead and follow, each knows how to play off the others to maximize their strengths, compensate for the others' weaknesses, and create

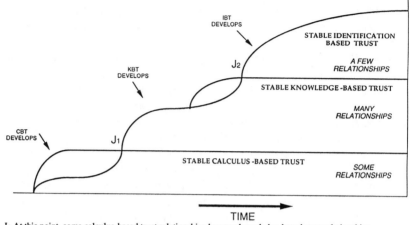

TIME

J₁ At this point, some calculus-based trust relationships become knowledge-based trust relationships

J₂ At this juncture, a few knowledge-based trust relationships where positive affect is present go on to become identification-based trust relationships

Figure 7.1. The Stages of Trust Development

a joint product that is much greater than the sum of its parts. The unverbalized, synchronous chemistry of a cappella choirs, string quartets, highly skilled interactive work groups, or championship basketball teams provide excellent examples of this kind of trust in action.

The Stagewise Evolution of Trust

In professional relationships, trust develops gradually as the parties move from one stage to another. A representation of this development appears in Figure 7.1. The following elements are central to this evolution:

1. Trust evolves and changes. If a relationship goes through its full development into maturation, the movement is from calculus-based, to knowledge-based, to identification-based trust. However, not all relationships develop fully; as a result, trust may not develop past the first or second stage.

2. Relationship building begins with the development of calculus-based trust activities. If these activities develop in a manner that confirms the validity of the trust (the other party is consistent, and deterrence is not frequently required), the parties will also begin developing a knowledge base about the other's needs, preferences, and priorities. This information about the other creates the foundation for a transition to knowledge-based trust and occurs at point J₁ in the figure. However, the parties may *not* move past calculus-based trust, particularly if (a) the relationship does not necessitate more than "business" or "arms-length" transactions, (b) the interdependence between the parties is heavily bounded and

regulated, (c) the parties have already gained enough information about each other to be aware that any further information gathering is unnecessary or likely to be unproductive, or (d) one or more violations of calculus-based trust have occurred.

3. If the parties move into knowledge-based trust, they engage in the activities described above. Some significant percentage of relationships move to this level.[1] The movement from knowledge-based trust to identification-based trust occurs in a similar manner and begins at point J_2 in the figure. As the parties come to learn more about each the other, they may also begin to identify strongly with others' needs, preferences, and priorities and come to see them as their own. Identification leads to a search for more information, which creates a broader foundation for knowledge-based trust and more dimensions on which the parties may identify with each other. However, many productive relationships remain in the knowledge-based trust stage. Relationships at work, for example, are often knowledge-based trust relationships, and identification-based trust may not develop for several reasons: either the parties lack the time or energy to invest beyond the knowledge-based trust level, or the parties may have no desire for a closer relationship.

4. The movement from one stage to another may require a "frame change" in the relationship—that is, a fundamental shift in the dominant perceptual paradigm (Gersick, 1989). In the first case (movement from calculus-based to knowledge-based trust), the frame change is a shift from a perceptual sensitivity to *contrasts* (differences) between self and the other to a perceptual sensitivity to *assimilation* (similarities) between self and the other. A similar frame change (shift) occurs in the evolution from knowledge-based to identification-based trust. In this case, the shift is from simply extending one's *knowledge* about the other to a more personal *identification* with the other.

The Decline of Trust

Trust decline is a general process that reflects the stage of trust development. Sometimes the decline occurs in a single violation that is so severe that it effectively eliminates all trust; other times, the decline is a more gradual erosion of trust. To understand this process, we need a model to describe what happens when trust is violated. This model is proposed in Figure 7.2 and is presented from the perspective of the person who experiences the trust violation. It begins with a relationship in which mutual trust has become established and where the parties have achieved an equilibrium. One of the parties is perceived by the other as acting in such a way that trust is violated. This creates instability and upsets the recipient, who then assesses the situation at both cognitive and emotional levels. Cognitively, the individual thinks about how important the situation is and where the responsibility for it lies. Emotionally, individuals often experience strong feelings of anger, hurt, fear, and frustration; these reactions lead them to reassess how they feel about the other.

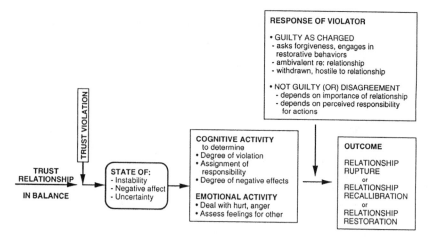

Figure 7.2. The Dynamics of Trust Violation (as seen by the violated person)

Although all of these thoughts and feelings are occurring, the person is probably still interacting with the party who violated the trust and may respond in a number of ways. On the one hand, the violator may accept or deny the other's reactions but also indicate how he or she feels about continuing the relationship. This behavior becomes a factor in the response of the recipient, leading him or her to pursue one of three outcomes: to terminate the relationship, renegotiate the relationship and encourage it to develop on a different basis, or restore the relationship to its former state.

Although one may say, "My trust was violated" to describe many different types of situations, the nature of a violation in each of the stages needs to be examined to help clarify what led to its decline or disruption.

Violations of Calculus-Based Trust

Hirschman (1984) has pointed out that trust is a peculiar resource, one that is increased rather than depleted through use. At the beginning of relationships, trust is very fragile because there is no history to count on. In these relationships, the parties are careful about the degree of risk and build in safeguards to protect themselves. Thus, calculus-based relationships are one way of dealing with the lack of trust characteristic of new relationships. If there is a violation, the relationship can quickly drop down the "chute," back to zero. If one party violates the trust, the other is likely either to renegotiate the contract, to better ensure the desired outcomes, or to seek another relationship. They may be disappointed but not feel deeply aggrieved if trust is broken. The tone might be, "You win some, you lose some."

Violations of Knowledge-Based Trust

Typically, knowledge of the other develops in low-risk situations until some reasonable level of predictability is established (knowledge-based trust). At that point, knowledge of the other and predictability of behavior replaces the contracts, penalties, and legal arrangements more typical of calculus-based trust. Any disconfirmation of expectations is unsettling, not only because the other fails to act as expected, but because this raises questions about one's own perceptual capacity. Trust is perceived as violated only when the person's actions are perceived as freely chosen. When situational factors are perceived to control behavior (and the other can clearly make this attribution), or causal accounts can be made to this end (Bies, 1987, 1989), no violation may be perceived, and trust may be less likely to be disrupted. The considerable literature on causal attribution (Ross, 1977) will help one to predict when to see the behavior as situationally determined, compared to personally determined.

If the violation is freely chosen, the actor must reorganize his or her knowledge base and perceptions of the other in the face of this event. The other may be bewildered—"I don't know you any more"—and experience a diminished willingness to trust. We would expect an active cognitive and emotional reassessment to occur (Figure 7.2) in an effort to both incorporate this information into our understanding of the other person and redefine the relationship in light of this event. If the event can be dismissed as a simple temporary episode, or as situationally caused, then it may be ignored. If not, the individual will revise his or her perception of the other. A certain "tentativeness," characteristic of new relationships, may be experienced for a time. If the new perception solidifies, the relationship will restore itself on this new ground. If, on the other hand, the new information is so disconfirming that the sense of not knowing the other cannot be overcome, the trust in the relationship may be permanently destabilized.

Violations of Identification-Based Trust

Finally, in identification-based trust relationships, violations of trust can be major relationship-transforming events. Violations of trust in identification-based trust are more than unpredictability. They are more than forgetting to bring home the milk, pick up the dry cleaning, or pay the household bills. Because trust at this level is based on identity-sharing and identification, trust violations are actions that go against our common interests or agreements. They tap into values that underlie the relationship and create a sense of moral violation (cf. Kramer, Shah, & Woerner, 1994). They rend the fabric of the relationship and, like "reweaving," they are expensive and time-consuming to repair, such that the fabric may never look quite the same. This kind of trust violation can be asymmetrical. It only requires one person to experience it as a "moral" violation, as a fundamental challenge to the relationship.

Relationships characterized by strong identification-based trust may be able to sustain rather strong challenges to both calculus-based and knowledge-based aspects of the relationship. Thus, events that would destroy the relationship if trust were developed only to these levels may be able to sustain the relationship because identification-based trust is preserved. The capacity of the relationship to sustain calculus-based trust and knowledge-based trust disruptions will be determined, in part, by factors, such as the magnitude of the disconfirmation at these levels, and the dynamics of the cognitive and emotional evaluation that occur after the disconfirming events. We all know people who appear to sustain trust in someone with whom they closely identify—a spouse, a child, or a hero figure—in the face of massive evidence (to others) that the individual's devious or despicable conduct should no longer warrant that trust. In our eyes, the individual cannot be trusted—but we are basing that judgment on calculus-based or knowledge-based trust grounds. To the person with a strong foundation of identification-based trust, the same evidence may not be as compelling. However, we should also recognize that for the truster to accept the invalidating information, he or she must be willing to acknowledge that his or her own decision to trust the other was ill-founded. These dissonant cognitions are identity challenging and may be rejected out of hand as a gesture of self-preservation; to accept them requires a willingness to see oneself as a fool for trusting, which is a self-image most would prefer to reject if alternative cognitions and interpretations can be found.

In summary, trust violations are experienced and reacted to differently at different relationship stages. The more developed the relationship, the more the parties have the capacity to handle violations, especially at "lower" (earlier) stages.

Repairing Trust
That Has Been Broken

We now turn to a discussion of the possibility of repairing a relationship where trust has been violated. We will do this in the context of the model we have proposed. Before spelling out the specific steps, we begin with these assumptions:

Trust has a cognitive and emotional basis. As we noted earlier, trust has a cognitive and emotional component. The cognitive dimensions are most responsible for maintaining the "balance" in calculus-based trust and the knowledge about the other in knowledge-based trust. In contrast, the emotional dimension is most critical in identification-based trust, because feelings of personal attachment toward the other increase. Because the cognitive and emotional bases may be more or less salient in particular stages or phases, some trust repair will require more cognitive work, but other types will require more emotional repair.

Trust violations affect the interpersonal system and hence have an impact on the parties and the fundamental relationship between them. Trust is central to relationships. It is the glue that holds most cooperative relationships together. Hence, a major violation of trust is not simply an isolated interpersonal event; rather, it is a significant event that is likely to have impact on the parties *and* on the relationship. Trust violations in relationships—particularly violations of strong knowledge-based or identification-based trust—can often be viewed as diagnostic signals that the relationship itself is in trouble and that repair work is in order. In fact, we argue that trust is so intimately connected to the fundamental nature of a relationship that trust-shattering events that cannot be repaired will probably be coincident with destroying the essence of the relationship itself. If the relationship does sustain, it is likely to be a "shell" in which only the most formal, emotionally distant, and calculative exchanges can continue to occur.[2] In personal friendships, where there is freedom to initiate or end a relationship, we would predict that the relationship would dissolve. In the workplace, however, termination may not be an option. In that context, we would expect these "shell" relationships to be more prevalent.

Trust repair is a bilateral process. In spite of the fact that a violation of trust is usually committed by one person, a significant amount of work will be required from both the violator and the violated. One party cannot do the work for the other. We now describe the work required of each party.

Committing to the Trust Repair Process

In order for parties to engage in a trust repair process, each must

be willing to invest time and energy into the repair process,
perceive that the short- and/or long-term benefits to be derived from the relationship are highly valued—that is, the payoff is "worth" the investment of additional energy,
perceive that the benefits to be derived are preferred relative to options for having those needs satisfied in an alternative manner.

People may be strongly invested to work on certain relationships because of their fundamental nature and/or because the rewards to be derived from them are centrally important and highly valued. For example, parents and teenagers often fight because teenagers push the limits to define their independence and identity. These relationships can often become quite fragile because both parties do things to violate each other's trust. For example, a boss promises an employee that a confidential conversation will not be divulged but then tells other managers about the conversation. Similarly, a mother cleans a son's room after being told by her son to "stay out of my room." Yet each party recognizes the fundamental and critical importance of a strong parent-child relationship and is willing to work hard to rebuild trust when such events damage it. Few parents (or children) would tolerate similar behavior from those with whom they did not have a long-term relationship. In the workplace, if a trust violation has occurred and both persons expect to be in the same work setting for some years, there may be motivation to improve the relationship. "Hollow shell" relationships, in which at least one party feels antagonism but must display some modicum of cooperation and collegiality, may actually consume more energy than reestablishing a more genuine trust and some consistency between beliefs and feelings.

In addition, the parties evaluate both the anticipated rebuilding work to be done and the expected benefits to be derived from the relationship in comparison to alternative relationships one could establish. Various works on interpersonal dynamics (Thibaut & Kelley, 1959) and negotiation (e.g., Fisher & Ury, 1981; Lewicki, Litterer, Minton, & Saunders, 1994) stress the importance of one's Comparison Level for Alternatives (CLalt), "options," or the Best Alternative to a Negotiated Agreement (BATNA) when one is deciding whether to continue transactions in a relationship, as opposed to pursuing an alternative relationship. The better or more easily accessible the alternative, or the more effort one expects to have to invest to restore and rebuild adequate trust in a relationship, the more that one or both parties may pursue their best alternative. On the other hand, there are constraints against opting out of relationships, even if good options exist. If relationships at work sour, one might be able to get the same job in another city but may have to endure the costs of moving the family, relocating one's life, and so on. Disputing marital partners may consider divorce but may be deterred by the consequences of this action on the children.

Steps Required of Each
Side in the Trust Repair Process

Actions of the Violator. The person who has violated the trust must engage in a series of steps that identify, acknowledge, and assume some "ownership" for the trust-destroying events that occurred. In a study of the impact of apologies on victims of aggression, Ohbuchi, Kameda, and Agarie (1989)

1. Recognize and acknowledge that a violation has occurred.
2. Determine the nature of the violation—that is, what "caused" it—and admit that one has caused the event.
3. Admit that the act was "destructive."
4. Accept responsibility for the effects of one's actions.

Figure 7.3. First Steps in Reciprocal Trust Repair

have shown that an apology effectively mitigates the amount of retaliatory aggression that the victim displays. In addition, the more severe the harm, the more extensive an apology may be needed to alleviate the victim's anger and aggression. More recent work by Ohbuchi (1994) indicates that "accounts" to victims may have a hierarchical structure in which the violator must admit that he or she caused the event in question, acknowledge that the act itself was bad or destructive, and take responsibility for the consequences of the event. Incorporating this research and our own thinking, we propose the following four-step sequence (see Figure 7.3):

Step 1. Recognize and acknowledge that a violation has occurred. Clearly, the violator must first recognize that something has happened to erode or destroy the trust. Often, the violator will recognize it independently, because the violator directly experiences the reaction of the other party or is aware that the act(s) committed are likely to be considered a violation of trust. However, violators may *not* be aware of the violation if they do not know how their actions have been experienced by the other or are blind to the consequences of their actions. If the violator recognizes that events have occurred that damaged interpersonal trust, we argue that it will be easier to repair the trust than if the victim also has to confront the violator with the events and their consequences. If the victim has to do the confrontation, the victim bears a double burden: the consequences of the trust violation and the social awkwardness and embarrassment that may be entailed with confronting the other about his or her actions. In addition, if the victim has to do the work, it may imply that the violator is insensitive and out of touch with his or her actions and the consequences.

Step 2. Determine the nature of the violation—that is, what "caused" the violation—and that one's actions caused it. The violator must be able to identify what caused the violation—that is, what action or collection of actions was responsible for reducing or destroying trust. Frequently, this is not difficult, because the "victim" may already be communicating loudly about the problem and what has happened. Perhaps the violator has not performed in a way that is consistent with expectations; perhaps he or she has done something that the other considers to be a serious violation of their "relationship contract" or has caused some harm or hardship.

If the violators do not know what they have done or are unaware that the victim feels that trust has been violated, they will "go on as though nothing has happened" and the repair process cannot begin. On the other hand, if the violators believe that they truly did not cause the event, or that the behavior in question was only remotely related to the occurrence, then causality may be debatable. For example, if an employee feels that a casual disclosure to the boss by a peer about him has caused the boss to think badly of him, the employee may feel betrayed and angry, but a colleague may view the situation as trivial and not serious.

Step 3. Admit that the event was "destructive" of trust. This follows directly from the earlier stages and, in some ways, is self-evident. If the event was not destructive of trust or the relationship, then it would be difficult to account for the victim's reactions. Yet efforts to rebuild the trust probably necessitate a full discussion of the events themselves and their consequences. Unless the violator fully understands how the victim experienced the events and the ways that aspects of their relationship have been affected by those events, it will be difficult for the parties to decide whether trust can be rebuilt and what types of events must occur.

Step 4. Be willing to accept responsibility for the violation. Finally, key to the process is being willing to accept responsibility for the violation. Even if true causality is still in debate (e.g., the act itself was an accident, unintended, or due to carelessness), and even if the violator was unaware that it happened until so informed by the victim, we argue that "taking responsibility" is a key step in trust repair. Denying that the act happened, claiming that there weren't any consequences, denying any responsibility for it, or claiming that the act was unimportant and should have no impact on the trust level will likely intensify the other's anger and contribute to further trust deterioration rather than to trust repair. If trust has been broken in "the eye of the beholder," it *has* been broken.

Actions of the Victim. We can assume that the "victim" of a trust violation has to engage in the same four steps. In most cases, these assumptions are fairly straightforward. If the victim does not recognize the violation, it is unlikely that there will be any direct threat to the operational level of trust between the parties. Similarly, depending on the specific acts, the victim is most likely to attribute the action to the violator and ascribe motive (i.e., intentionality) to that individual. Finally, if the violator appears to be unsympathetic to the consequences that have occurred to the victim or unwilling to own responsibility for having created the act, then it is unlikely that the victim will want to engage in any actions intended to "rebuild" or "reconstruct" the earlier level of trust.

The Process of Trust Repair: Next Steps

The next critical step in rebuilding trust is for the victim to request, or the violator to offer, some form of forgiveness, atonement, or action designed to undo the violation and rebuild the trust. This is probably the most difficult step in the trust restoration process, although it is difficult to know which side bears the greater burden. The violator must indicate he or she is aware of what has been done and "apologize" or ask for forgiveness. An apology, a symbolic summary of steps 1 through 4, is also an expression of emotional regret that enables the repair process to move forward. The effectiveness of the "account"—that is, (a) how the violator explains what happened and why it happened and (b) how sincere the apology and expressions of regret are—will probably be critical to the victim's willingness to acknowledge and accept the apology (Bies, 1987, 1989; Ohbuchi, 1994; Ohbuchi et al., 1989).

Thus, the violation has caused a temporary shift in the "balance" of the relationship. An exchange theory perspective describes relationships as a negotiated "balance" of rights and obligations, duties and responsibilities. Violations of trust will tend to unbalance the relationship. On both sides, there is the potential for high loss of face and high vulnerability—psychological states that are typically avoided. By apologizing, the violator is offering to engage in actions that will "restore" the balance, and the victim, who has been hurt, is now in the position of dictating whether the relationship can be rebuilt (rebalanced) and the terms and conditions under which that will occur.

After these early first steps, the sequence of actions is so varied that it is impossible to specify one blueprint for trust repair. In general, however, we believe that there are four fundamentally different alternative courses of trust reconstruction:

1. The victim refuses to accept any actions, terms, or conditions for reestablishing the relationship. Several factors may lead to this outcome. The victim may feel so angry or injured that he or she cannot envision any way in which the other could be trusted again. If there have been instances of other trust-destroying actions in recent times, the event in question may be "the straw that broke the camel's back." Thus, either a very severe trust-destroying event or a series of trust-destroying events may be sufficient to render a judgment that the trust is "unrepairable." Alternatively, the victim may believe that the relationship is not "worth" saving—that is, the benefits and gains that were derived from the relationship are not worth recapturing and restoring.

Even though the victim may signal that trust is "unrepairable," the violator may not agree with this assessment. As a result, some violators may, on their own initiative, begin to engage in actions to signal that forgiveness is desired. Verbal apologies may be offered. Symbolic gestures of apology (e.g., letters, cards, flowers) may be proffered. Violators may engage in symbolic acts of "public apology"—that is, letting others know what they have done and how ashamed they are of their actions. Actions may be unilaterally initiated to specifically undo any or all of the negative consequences that accrued to the victim. Acts of outright altruism may be initiated as a way for the violator to "redress" the imbalance created by the trust violation and demonstrate to the victim that a new or restored relationship is desired. For example, Lindskold's (1978) strategy for taking the initiative to build trust, using Osgood's GRIT strategy, could be applied. Under some conditions, these actions may be sufficient to change the victim's perspective and move to one of the other alternatives specified below. Thus, this is a process whose goal is to bring the victim to a readiness to participate in the work of repair.

2. *The victim acknowledges forgiveness and specifies "unreasonable" acts of reparation and/or trust restoration that must be fulfilled by the violator.* In this second alternative, the victim also specifies actions that must be fulfilled for the trust to be repaired, but the violator believes that what is being asked is inappropriate or unreasonable and is unwilling to agree to them. Because the victim is usually in the position of specifying behaviors for the violator, the victim's desire for revenge or retaliation may lead to demands that the violator finds excessive. When this happens, the *violator* is in the position specified in (1) above—that is, refusing to accept the terms for repair. Trust repair is unlikely to be successful, and the relationship will terminate unless the parties can negotiate more viable alternative actions.

3. *The victim acknowledges forgiveness and indicates that no further acts of reparation are necessary.* In this third case, the parties attempt to "pick up where they left off" before the breach occurred. Even though the victim has not required the violator to engage in any specific acts, the relationship will probably continue to experience tension and strain for some time. The violator is likely to continue to feel embarrassed and awkward about what has happened and may expect the victim to attempt revenge or retaliatory action. Thus, even though the violator has been "forgiven," the very act of untrustworthy behavior may create suspiciousness of the other's future motives and intentions (Deutsch, 1958). Similarly, the victim may also be hypervigilant to the violator's future actions to ensure protection from the consequences of future actions that may destroy trust even further. Skipping the process of reparations, a process that allows each party to test the other and restore the balance, may be an additional strain on the trust-rebuilding process.

Interestingly, therefore, acts of true and complete forgiveness without reparations may not be adequate for good trust repair, and we would predict that this alternative would not occur very frequently.

4. The victim acknowledges forgiveness and specifies "reasonable" acts of reparation and/or trust restoration that must be fulfilled by the violator. In the final case, the victim specifies what the violator has to do for trust to be rebuilt. This may be initiated by the violator's request (e.g., "Tell me what I have to do for you to trust me again") or by the victim's edict (e.g., "Here's what you are going to have to do for me to trust you ever again.") These actions may be very specific or quite vague and may extend over a short or long period of time. In general, the actions serve the following functions:

a. the actions are usually designed to demonstrate, to the victim's satisfaction, that the violator is sincere and committed in the desire to rebuild the relationship,

b. the violator demonstrates willingness to incur certain amounts of personal loss or self-sacrifice in the interest of rebuilding the relationship,

c. the actions create an opportunity for the violator to expiate (work out) any guilt or remorse that may be felt as a result of having violated the trust,

d. the victim has an opportunity to judge the sincerity and commitment of the violator in carrying out these actions. In short, both the substance of what is done by the violator and the manner in which it is done are necessary for trust to be reestablished.

Because the specific actions are the result of some "negotiation" between victim and violator, the violator's conduct must be responsive to whatever specific concerns are raised by the victim. These "demands" by the victim may be discussed and negotiated by the violator until both agree to a course of action. Once that course of action is agreed on, both parties must show good faith in enacting it. It is also likely that the parties will undertake occasional monitoring of these actions and will use the opportunities afforded by this monitoring to rebuild calculus-based and knowledge-based trust.

Trust Repair at Different
Levels of Relationship Development

It is our belief that most calculus-based trust can be repaired, using the process that has been described. Repair of this trust assumes that both parties prefer to do so relative to best-alternative relationships for having the same needs met. As the relationship is renegotiated, however, the parties may decide to prepare additional safeguards, such as written contracts, agreements, or legal documents, that delineate the consequences and costs of any subsequent violations. In fact, many calculus-based trust relationships have such agreements negotiated "up front" as a way to ensure that trust violations will not occur, deter the parties from considering such violations, and/or specify exactly how such violations will be handled. Whether they be memoranda of understanding, prenuptial agreements, or extensive legal contracts, the intent is to specify both the exact nature of the parties' expectations and obligations, the consequences for violation of these covenants, and the processes by which such violations will be handled (see Ring & Van de Ven, 1994, for an exploration of the role of such agreements in interorganizational relationships).

In contrast, the repair of knowledge-based trust and identification-based trust is far more problematic. Violations of these two forms of trust present a direct threat to the victim's self-image and self-esteem (the adequacy of his or her knowledge of the other, the predictability of the other's behavior, and/or the identification and emotional commitment made to the other). When someone violates another's trust, it suggests that the victim has been very wrong about the violator—he or she does not know that person as well as previously thought, or the mutual understanding of the expectations and obligations in the relationship is now in question. As a result, a complete restoration of trust to its former state may not be possible. Once trust has been violated this seriously, the victim will always suspect that the violator is capable of doing it again and will never allow him- or herself to be as trusting (and vulnerable) in the relationship as before.

We thus suggest that the capacity to "forgive and forget" is an individual difference variable that is driven by the type and magnitude of trust violation. That is,

- The capacity to "forgive and forget" will vary among individuals, such that the higher the capacity, the more that individual can and will engage in actions that rebuild destroyed trust.
- The bigger the trust violation—that is, the more the violation shakes the very foundation of the relationship or creates very serious negative consequences—the less likely that trust can be effectively rebuilt and restored.
- The more the trust violation creates significant challenges to the "integrity" of the relationship—that is, disturbs the very basis by which one knows and predicts the other's behavior or identifies with the other cognitively and emotionally—the less likely that trust can be effectively rebuilt and restored.

SUMMARY

We began this chapter by noting the many ways that organizations are transforming their mission, function, and structure and the critical role that cooperative and trusting relationships play in these emerging organizational forms. Although the call for developing and sustaining these relationships has been strong, there has been very little research on the process of developing and maintaining these relationships. We need to know far more about how such relationships are created and maintained if we are to help people sustain strong and effective collaboration.

In this chapter, we addressed a core element in these relationships—trust. We suggested that there are different types of trust in business relationships and proposed a model of the ways that these types of trust are related and build on each other. We also described ways that trust can be damaged in relationships and the consequences of these events for trust maintenance. Finally, we proposed a process by which damaged trust can be repaired and the responsibilities of the parties for effectively managing this process.

Future work on trust must be focused on two issues. First, it is necessary to gather data to determine the validity of this model—that is, to determine whether different forms of trust do exist and whether they are related to each other in the developmental manner that we propose. It is also necessary to study trust development and trust repair in more detail to understand the key steps required of each party in the relationship. Second, blueprints for action are needed and can also serve as the basis for further research. How can processes of negotiation and conflict resolution, as well as the therapeutic processes of treating and healing relationships, be brought to bear on trust development and trust repair processes? We believe that the results of this work will offer rich insights into our understanding of how to build, sustain, and repair trust in professional relationships.

Notes

1. We would like to point out that this is not a normative model. We think the stages are very different but not necessarily better than each other. Most people want and have relationships that are in each of the stages because the relationships have different purposes. For example, many business and legal relationships begin and end in calculus-based trust.

2. One can speculate as to what kinds of relationships could be sustained without some form of trust. To the degree that contracts, covenants, and rules can "substitute" for trust, we argue that some transactional relationships could be sustained. See Ring and Van de Ven (1994) for an elaboration of the ways that such contracts and rules function in interorganizational relationships.

References

Bazerman, M. (1994). *Judgment in managerial decision making*. New York: John Wiley.

Bies, R. J. (1987). The predicament of injustice: The management of moral outrage. In B. M. Staw & L. L. Cummings (Eds.), *Research in organizational behavior* (Vol. 9, pp. 289-319). Greenwich, CT: JAI.

Bies, R. J. (1989). Managing conflict before it happens: The role of accounts. In M. A. Rahim (Ed.), *Managing conflict: An interdisciplinary approach* (pp. 83-91). New York: Praeger.

Boon, S. D., & Holmes, J. G. (1991). The dynamics of interpersonal trust: Resolving uncertainty in the face of risk. In R. A. Hinde & J. Groebel (Eds.), *Cooperation and prosocial behavior* (pp. 190-211). Cambridge, UK: Cambridge University Press.

Dasgupta, P. (1988). Trust as a commodity. In D. Gambetta (Ed.), *Trust: Making and breaking cooperative relations.* Oxford, UK: Basil Blackwell.

Davis, K. E., & Todd, M. J. (1985). Assessing friendship: Prototypes, paradigm cases and relationship description. In S. Duck & D. Perlman (Eds.), *Understanding personal relationships.* Beverly Hills, CA: Sage.

Deutsch, M. (1949). A theory of cooperation and competition. *Human Relations, 2,* 129-151.

Deutsch, M. (1958). Trust and suspicion. *Journal of Conflict Resolution, 2,* 265-279.

Deutsch, M. (1960). Trust, trustworthiness and the F-scale. *Journal of Abnormal and Social Psychology, 61,* 138-140.

Deutsch, M. (1973). *The resolution of conflict.* New Haven, CT: Yale University Press.

Duck, S. W. (1988). *Relating to others.* Belmont, CA: Dorsey.

Duck, S. W. (Ed.). (1993a). *Individuals in relationships.* Newbury Park, CA: Sage.

Duck, S. W. (Ed.). (1993b). *Social context and relationships.* Newbury Park, CA: Sage.

Duck, S., & Perlman, D. (Eds.). (1985). *Understanding personal relationships.* Beverly Hills, CA: Sage.

Fisher, R., & Ury, W. (1981). *Getting to yes.* Boston: Houghton Mifflin.

Gambetta, D. (Ed.). (1988). *Trust: Making and breaking cooperative relations.* Oxford, UK: Basil Blackwell.

Gersick, C. (1989). Marking time: Predictable transitions in task groups. *Academy of Management Journal, 32*(2), 274-309.

Greenhalgh, L., & Chapman, D. I. (1994, March). *Joint decision making: The inseparability of relationships and negotiation.* Paper presented at the Stanford Conference on the Social Context of Negotiation, Stanford Graduate School of Business, CA.

Greenhalgh, L., & Chapman, D. I. (in press). The influence of negotiator relationships on the process and outcomes of business transactions. *Academy of Management Journal.*

Hirschman, A. O. (1984). Against parsimony: Three easy ways of complicating some categories of economic discourse. *American Economic Review, 74,* 88-96.

Holmes, J. G. (1991). Trust and the appraisal process in close relationships. *Advances in Personal Relationships, 2,* 57-104.

Kahneman, D., Knetsch, J., & Thaler, R. (1986). Fairness as a constant on profit seeking: Entitlements in the market. *The American Economic Review, 76,* 728-741.

Kelley, H. H., & Stahelski, A. J. (1970). Social interaction basis of cooperators' and competitors' beliefs about others. *Journal of Personality and Social Psychology, 16,* 66-91.

Kramer, R. M. (1993). Cooperation and organizational identification. In K. Murnighan (Ed.), *Social psychology in organizations: Advances in theory and research* (pp. 244-268). Englewood Cliffs, NJ: Prentice Hall.

Kramer, R., & Brewer, M. A. (1986). Social identity and the emergence of cooperation in resource conservation dilemmas. In H. Wilke, C. Rutter, & D. M. Messick (Eds.), *Experimental studies of social dilemmas.* Frankfurt, Germany: Peter Lang.

Kramer, R., Shah, P. P., & Woerner, S. L. (1994). *Why ultimatums fail: Social identity and moralistic aggression in coercive bargaining.* Unpublished manuscript, Stanford University.

Lewicki, R. J., & Bunker, B. B. (1995). Trust in relationships: A model of trust development and decline. In B. B. Bunker & J. Z. Rubin (Eds.), *Conflict, cooperation and justice.* San Francisco: Jossey-Bass.

Lewicki, R. J., Litterer, J., Minton, J., & Saunders, D. (1994). *Negotiation.* Burr Ridge, IL: Irwin.

Lewis, J. D., & Weigert, A. (1985). Trust as a social reality. *Social Forces, 63*(4), 967-985.

Limerick, D., & Cunnington, B. (1993). *Managing the new organization.* San Francisco: Jossey-Bass.

Lindskold, S. (1978). Trust development, the GRIT proposal, and the effects of conciliatory acts on conflict and cooperation. *Psychological Bulletin, 85,* 772-793.

Ohbuchi, K. (1994, September). *The role of apology in accounts to victims of destructive action.* Seminar presented at State University of New York, Buffalo.

Ohbuchi, K., Kameda, M., & Agarie, N. (1989). Apology as aggression control: Its role in mediating appraisal of and response to harm. *Journal of Personality and Social Psychology, 56*(2), 219-227.

Rempel, J. K., Holmes, J. G., & Zanna, M. P. (1985). Trust in close relationships. *Journal of Personality and Social Psychology, 45*(1), 95-112.

Ring, P. S., & Van de Ven, A. (1994). Developmental processes of cooperative interorganizational relationships. *Academy of Management Review, 19,* 90-118.

Ross, L. (1977). The intuitive psychologist and his shortcomings: Distortions in the attribution process. In L. Berkowitz (Ed.), *Advances in experimental social psychology* (Vol. 10, pp. 174-220). New York: Academic Press.

Rotter, J. B. (1971). Generalized expectancies for interpersonal trust. *American Psychologist, 26,* 443-452.

Schlenker, B. R., Helm, B., & Tedeschi, J. T. (1973). The effects of personality and situational variables on behavioral trust. *Journal of Personality and Social Psychology, 25,* 419-427.

Shapiro, D., Sheppard, B. H., & Cheraskin, L. (1992). Business on a handshake. *Negotiation Journal, 8*(4), 365-377.

Thibaut, J., & Kelley, H. H. (1959). *The social psychology of groups.* New York: John Wiley.

Valley, K., Neale, M., & Mannix, B. (1995). Friends, lovers, colleagues, strangers: The effects of relationship on the process and outcome of negotiation. In R. Bies, B. H. Sheppard, & R. J. Lewicki (Eds.), *Research on negotiation in organizations* (Vol. 5, 65-94). Greenwich, CT: JAI.

Worchel, P. (1979). Trust and distrust. In W. G. Austin & S. Worchel (Eds.), *The social psychology of intergroup relations.* Belmont, CA: Wadsworth.

Zand, D. (1972). Trust and managerial problem solving. *Administrative Science Quarterly, 17,* 229-239.

Micro-OB and the Network Organization

BLAIR H. SHEPPARD
MARLA TUCHINSKY

Untermyer: Is not commercial credit based primarily upon money or property?
Morgan: No, sir, the first thing is character.
Untermyer: Before money or property?
Morgan: Before money or anything else. Money cannot buy it. . . . Because a man
    I do not trust could not get money on all the bonds in Christendom.

Ron Chernow, *The House of Morgan* (1990)

The Emerging Role of Relations

If we are to believe the popular press and many recent authors, business is evolving so that the traditional forms of economic exchange are being complemented or replaced by a plethora of new forms. Hierarchy and market are moving aside for the boundaryless firm (Tichy, 1993), the virtual organization (Byrne, 1993), and the network organization (Snow, Miles, & Coleman, 1992).[1] We will leave debate over the merits and nuances of this assertion to those better equipped than us (for a thorough review, see Powell, 1990; Chapter 4, this volume). Instead, in this chapter we would like to entertain the implications for micro-OB to accept the validity of the claim that hierarchy and market are being replaced with more connected, lateral forms of organization. The strongest form of the primary argument contained in this chapter is that Organizational Behavior is missing the intellectual infrastructure to be of much use for understanding the task of surviving in these emerging organizational forms. But we will consider two weaker forms of this argument as well: (a) We have the resident knowledge, but it requires recasting or a shift in emphasis, and (b) our efforts to respond to the implications of alternative organizational forms, although gallant and informative, are inadequate. In some instances, micro-OB is missing the relevant conceptualization; in some cases, the concepts reside in the field but require reframing; in others, we had a valiant but somewhat misdirected start. This view of the field of micro-OB could be considered damning, but we think of it as promising. O'Reilly (1991), in a recent review of research in Organizational Behavior, argued that the field is fallow. The need for a new and reframed set of theories and data to help direct our efforts to live with emerging complex organizations today offers promise for renewing the field. From this review, we hope to illustrate not only the need for a host of new research and ideas but also the primary ways in which research on the microprocesses of network organizations will have to differ from that forming the field's basis to date. First, the context in which the behavior of individuals or pairs of individuals is embedded demands greater consideration than in past research. Second, time in the form of history and the evolution of relationships require far more attention. Third, we will need to borrow from other fields of research, such as political science, communications, clinical psychology, and the emerging field of personal and social relations. We layer under all of these the presumption that often the connection between the parties in a relationship should be the unit of analysis. In sum, this chapter is meant not as a criticism but as an outline of opportunity. As a start, let's begin with the most critical point of view.

Control

Peruse any introductory Organizational Behavior textbook and you will see extensive discussion of topics such as motivation, goal setting, performance appraisal, and leadership. The reader's assumed perspective is that of a manager responsible for directing and controlling subordinates' behavior so that those subordinates achieve the organization's stated ends. Even topics that seem more directly relevant to alternative organizational forms, such as group process and group decision making, are couched in the context of a group, working within a well-established hierarchy and attempting to find the optimal solution for the achievement of an organization's (read shareholders')

ends. Much of Organizational Behavior is about controlling employee behavior, written from the perspective of someone superordinate in a hierarchy.
The levers of control are the capacity to hire and fire; determine job assignments and compensation; allocate other rewards, including granting discretion; set the agenda; and have the voice of legitimate authority. Hackman and
Oldham (1975), Vroom (1964), Maslow (1943), Staw (1977), and even Tyler's
(1990) theories are all cast in the frame of exercising control in the form
of authority. One thing is clear about network organizations, colocated teams,
strategic alliances, and long-term supplier relations: Control is not exercised
in the form of hierarchical authority. You are not your peer's boss, your allies
report through a different authority structure, and suppliers are not your
employees.

Little is said in micro-OB circles about how to exercise control in relationships between relative equals. This void is damning, as we know that without
such control, let's call it trust, alternative organizational forms cannot be
sustained. From both the perspective of economists (see Williamson, 1981)
and institutional theorists (see Powell, 1990), trust is essential if long-term,
nonhierarchical relationships are to be sustained. Economists are quite skeptical about the possibility of developing such trust.

Williamson's (1981) discussion of the early organization of work illustrates this point nicely. Perhaps the crudest mode of organizing work is
putting-out, a form used in the early textile industry. In putting-out,

> [a] merchant-coordinator supplies the raw materials, owns the work-in-process inven-
> tories, and makes contracts with individual entrepreneurs, each of whom performs
> one of the basic operations at his home using his own equipment. Material is
> moved from station to station (home to home) in batches under the direction of
> the merchant-coordinator. (p. 215)

Thus, a merchant-coordinator would "put out" wool or yarn that would be
spun or woven into a more finished product and then transported to another
cottage for further processing. Often more than one step would be done in a
single home. This model is quite different from a pure market, because each
entrepreneur is yoked to a given merchant-coordinator. However, it is not a
hierarchy because the forms of control typical of authority systems do not
exist. There are no budget review processes, accounting periods, or performance appraisals. For early capitalists, this system seemed appealing because
it permitted them to purchase labor in the same manner as raw materials.
Although Williamson refers to many explanations for describing the demise
of putting-out systems, such as slowness, lack of uniformity, uncertainty of
quality, and an inability to change, he emphasizes trust. He quotes Pat Hudson:

Frauds were responsible for "considerable inefficiencies and diseconomies" under the Putting-Out system in the late eighteenth century. They were more severe in the worsted branch than in woolens, mainly, because there were fewer wage workers in woolens "and those there were tended to be closely supervised in small workshops. In the worsted branch, however, woolcombers commonly embezzled their employers' wool and the spinners reeled 'false' or short yarn. Combinations of operatives were often successful in ensuring that these appropriations continued with impunity" (Hudson, 1981, p. 50) The differential ease of embezzlement contributed to the more rapid transition to factory production in the worsted branch (p. 52). (Williamson, 1981, p. 233)

From his analysis of the modes of organizing work it is clear that either trust or the ability to deter cheating is essential if one is to move beyond market transactions to any mode of organization. Although his recent thinking expresses otherwise (see Williamson, 1993), Williamson clearly believed that trust is not sustainable, except in those circumstances in which one party has the forms of control that come with hierarchy. There are two possible explanations for this view: First, that he is correct, and second, that no one has provided an adequate theoretical or empirical infrastructure illustrating alternatives to hierarchical control. His example (cited earlier) involves a situation in which merchants and workers maintained a market or transaction-based exchange process. Yet we now are moving toward relationship-based and trust-based organizations. In fact, it is clear to those studying network organizational forms that trust is essential for such forms to exist, although they do not describe how it arises (see Powell, Chapter 4, this volume; Burt & Knez, Chapter 5, this volume). However, one can draw the beginnings of such an infrastructure from research in the fields of political science, social psychology, economics, and sociology. In an earlier paper, Shapiro, Sheppard, and Cheraskin (1992) summarized the bases of trust that can exist between business partners, derived from the research in these fields. As control mechanisms continue to shift away from hierarchical authority, we need to explore what underlies a possible replacement.

Control in Lateral
Relations: Bases of Trust

The commonsense ideas behind this work are quite straightforward. You can trust those with whom you have a business relationship when three conditions hold: (a) They risk losing too much if they cheat, (b) you can predict your partners well and thus can protect against their cheating, and (c) your partners have adopted your preferences. We refer to these as deterrence-based trust, knowledge-based trust, and identification-based trust, respectively.

Deterrence-Based Trust

Two minimal conditions for most business relationships are that individuals' or firms' actions follow their words and that disclosed information is not shared with the wrong people. When an individual can be trusted to keep his or her word, uncertainty about behavior is reduced and the need to monitor or oversee behavior is minimized. In the case of a subordinate who promises to complete a report by a certain date, periodic updates are unnecessary; and, in the case of an agreement between parties, fewer restrictive penalty clauses and detailed contingencies are needed. The primary advantage of knowing that a partner is reliable (i.e., will keep his or her word) is that one's focus shifts from monitoring to problem solving and exploring additional opportunities. The primary advantage of knowing that a partner will not share information inappropriately is that one can therefore disclose information necessary for successfully conducting affairs.

A primary motivation for keeping one's word and remaining mum is deterrence, or the existence of measures to prevent undesired actions (Deutsch, 1973, termed this notion *calculative trust;* see also Lewicki & Bunker, 1995). In the market, the traditional form of deterrence is the courts; in a hierarchy, it is hierarchical controls. Deterrence in a relationship arises when the potential costs of discontinuing the relationship in whole or in part outweigh the short-term advantage of acting in a distrustful way. This is achieved in a relationship when either many different forms of valuable exchange are being conducted between parties, such that the benefits of cheating in any one exchange pale in comparison to the advantages created through the many other exchanges, or through building future dependency, such that existing investments lose a great deal of value in the future if the other party is not present. This argument is similar but not identical to that of political scientists such as Axelrod (1984), who argues that the long shadow of the future serves to induce cooperative behavior, and of sociologists such as Granovetter (1985), who claims that personal trust arises from continuity and interdependence in relationships (see also Shapiro, 1987).

Knowledge-Based Trust

A second basis of trust is the capacity to predict one's partner. The capacity to predict a partner's behavior means that it is possible to make plans, investments, or other decisions contingent on that partner's behavior. This capacity improves both the speed of decision making, because it is possible to know the other's response and the quality of performance, because the other's likely response can be incorporated into one's actions.

The ability to predict requires understanding. Two approaches described earlier contribute to understanding and predictability: repeated and multi-faceted relationships. The more points of contact parties have, the better the chances they will come to understand and predict each other's behavior. Also useful are regular communication and actively researching one's partner. Firms, functions, and individuals that have the opportunity for ongoing communication improve trust. For example, Bose Corporation has begun stationing a full-time employee in its suppliers' plants. By having someone on site, these suppliers get a feel for Bose's needs and can better meet them. Similarly, Bose develops a deeper understanding of its suppliers' processes and capacities. As one supplier commented, "Any time you get two companies literally sitting with one another and knowing each other's problems and expectations, there are bigger wins than there are almost anywhere else" (Stein, 1993, p. 545).

Identification-Based Trust

The highest order of trust assumes that one party has fully internalized the other's preferences. This type of trust is identification-based trust. In social psychology it has been well demonstrated that people in the same group tend to behave in a more trustworthy manner toward each other than toward others not in the group. Membership in a firm has a similar effect (see Kramer & Brewer, 1984, for a review of this literature). Knowing that someone is from the same company somehow makes him or her more trustworthy. The factors inducing a sense of identity are many. Among the most important are the existence of joint products, goals, and strategy; having a shared name or legal status; proximity; the presence of a long and entangled history; and common values.

The investment required to engender identification-based trust is greater than that required to establish deterrence-based or knowledge-based trust. The rewards, however, are commensurably greater. The benefits go beyond quantity, efficiency, and flexibility that accrue from deterrence and knowledge. When an identity-based relationship exists, it is possible for one's partner to act in his or her stead. Thus, just as knowledge-based and deterrence-based trust allow a person, group, or firm to become more dependent on another person, group, or firm, identity-based trust makes it possible for a person, group, or firm to permit a partner to act independently—knowing its interests will get met. The agency problem is mitigated. Competent employees who know and identify with a firm can be given authority. Team members whose objectives and identity are aligned with the team can be allowed to act on the team's behalf. Suppliers with shared interests with their customers require less oversight. In the absence of such entrusted delegation, serious inefficiencies occur.

TABLE 8.1 Customer-Supplier Partner Relationship

---

1. I know my partner will consider my concerns when making decisions.
2. The quality of our communication is extremely good.
3. We confront issues effectively.
4. We discuss the critical issues of our relationship well.
5. We have frequent face-to-face contact.
6. We speak frequently on the phone.
7. We have a long history.
8. I expect to interact with my partner for a long time in the future.
9. Our contacts entail many different issues.
10. Our goals are the same.
11. We view the world in the same way.
12. We are paid for the same objectives.
13. I frequently think of my partner as a member of the same firm.
14. We have many shared activities.
15. I know well the people important to my partner.
16. My partner knows well the people important to me.
17. I understand well the bases on which my partner is rewarded and compensated.
18. My partner understands well the bases on which I am rewarded and compensated.
19. I understand my partner's primary problems at work.
20. My partner understands my primary problems at work.

Implications for Research in Organizational Behavior

The intention behind reviewing this set of ideas is not to propose an exhaustive or thoroughly correct model of control in lateral relations but instead to illustrate the possibility of trust existing in long-term, nonhierarchical relationships. These ideas have been elaborated on by others (see Lewicki & Bunker, 1995), and many other similar models of trust exist (e.g., see Boon & Holmes, 1991, for a comparable discussion in terms of interpersonal trust). If these ideas hold true, trust is at least somewhat an inherent quality of the relationships parties or firms hold. Moreover, each of these bases of trust can be managed. It is possible to integrate strategies or capital investment decisions between firms. It is possible to let more parts or services to one supplier. It is possible to communicate regularly. It is possible to get to know a firm's other key partners. As preliminary evidence of the effectiveness of these bases of relational trust, we conducted a simple study on 30 pairs of industrial supplier-customer relationships. One member of the pair was asked to indicate on a seven-point scale the degree to which he or she felt the statements in Table 8.1 characterized their relationship. The other partner was asked to indicate on a single-item index how much trust he or she felt existed in the relationship. The survey was counterbalanced so that 15 suppliers and 15 customers responded to each facet of the questionnaires. Two results matter here. First, the items produced a reasonably reliable scale (α = .86). Second, the average score across these questions predicted the partner's reported trust extremely well (r = .68, p < .0001).

The possibility of sustainable trust involving some of the bases just described implies several differences between the micro-OB of network organizations and that of the traditional hierarchy. First, it is much more crucial to incorporate relational history and future into our theories and research than has traditionally been the case. Considerations of the future have been central in many important notions in micro-OB, especially expectancy theory (see Mitchell & Beech, 1976; Staw, 1977; Vroom, 1964) or behavioral decision theory (see Bazerman, 1994, for a straightforward review). However, this has taken the form of expectations or beliefs about likely future events. Such research therefore has been cross-sectional in nature, involving assessing how expectations of future events influence decisions made at a given point in time. Research on trust will need to be more dynamic, evaluating how both expected and unexpected behavior and decisions at one point influence future levels of trust and behavior. Trust is probably most interesting as an evolutionary or devolutionary phenomenon; thus, questions (e.g., How does trust build? What is a credible commitment and how does it play out? Is loss of trust abrupt or slow? Under what conditions and how is trust regained after it is threatened or lost?) are best assessed dynamically. Furthermore, the impact may not always be clearly through expectations; in deterrence-based or calculative trust, decision models probably describe both strategic behavior of someone attempting to engender trust and calculations of the value of cheating, but in identity-based trust, traditional decision models probably miss some of the nuance of trust.

Another way in which research on trust should vary from more traditional OB research is that it should entail consideration of the context in which that relationship is embedded. For example, the discussion of trust earlier is largely predicated on the nature of the connection between the parties themselves. However, this perspective can be extended. The threat of loss of reputation and the resulting loss of business that come from having the word spread about untrustworthy business practice generally are quite effective deterrents. As Dasgupta (1988) argued, people invest a great deal of resources for the purposes of building and maintaining a reputation for honesty. A repairperson in a small town recognizes the importance of this sort of trust. The repairperson cannot afford to act in bad faith.

Others in a relational network can take a direct role in another's relationship. If trust underlies network connections, members work to maintain their and other members' bonds. Those parties can choose to sanction untrustworthy behavior as a mechanism for sustaining the network of relations' viability. Such sanctioning can be quite extended. For example, consider the demands on Frank, whose brother, Guy, is not meeting the important needs of his newborn child. Alan Fiske (1990) explains that an obligation to enforce trust in deeply connected relationships exists at three distinct levels:

> First, the parties immediately and directly participating in the primary relationship have a duty to conform to the model (i.e., meet the needs of a newborn child). Second, people with social links to the primary parties have a duty to react when the primary parties fail to meet their obligations—they must modify their social relationships with the primary parties in suitable ways (e.g., Frank should speak with or sanction Guy for not fulfilling his paternal duties). Third, it is the duty of others with social links to the secondary parties to appropriately modulate their social relationships with the secondary parties if the latter fail to react to the primary parties' breach of duty (Frank's spouse and children should sanction Frank for not speaking with Guy). In other words, people get sanctioned for failing to sanction. (Fiske, 1990, p. 171; items in parentheses our addition)

Such sanctioning behavior occurs because both Guy and Frank have violated a trust with the network of which they are members. Guy violated principles of fair and just behavior, namely adhering to agreed on parenting standards. Frank, as a member of the broader community, must act to enforce those principles necessary for the community to work. To not do so risks undermining the bases of relationships on which the network is built. Similar quadratic forms of trust induction exist when a nurse is berated by her peers for not reporting a doctor's inappropriate use of a medical instrument or when a team member is chided by a peer for not intervening when another member treats colleagues very abusively. Networks only work if the normative basis on which the network rests is sustained through monitoring the behavior of those engaged in the network. A central question in such circumstances concerns what gives someone the right to sanction the behavior of others in one's network. What makes it Frank's business to sanction Guy, or the nurse's business, or the manager's business? An answer to this question may lie in a portion of research in Organizational Behavior, which with some minor adjustments may have a great deal to say about the microbehavior of network organizations, specifically research on organizational justice.

Fairness

The contrast between hierarchical control and lateral trust implied that little can be taken from Organizational Behavior's existing conceptual and empirical infrastructure to help us understand how to manage in alternative organizational forms, but things are not so bleak. Some existing work can be recast to become quite useful. Perhaps the best example of work, which with modest reforming can fit network relationships, is research on justice. Earliest justice research focused on reciprocity or equity as the primary principle on which people make judgments about justice (Adams, 1965; Homans, 1958). The distribution of outcomes was said to be fair when people received back in proportion to what they put in. Those who gave the most should have received the most. Those who gave the least should have received the least. This view of justice is very much predicated on market transactions or exchanges. But many other principles of justice have been identified, most particularly within a hierarchical point of view (Deutsch, 1975; Leventhal, 1980; Lind & Tyler, 1988; Thibaut & Tyler, 1988). In some instances, the perspective is that of a manager or architect of a social system (such as reflected in Deutsch, 1975; Sheppard & Lewicki, 1985). In others, it is the point of view of a judge (see especially Lind & Tyler, 1988; Thibaut & Walker, 1975), who is both a hierarchically advantaged decision maker and a sustainer of exchange contracts (as in contract law). Tyler and Degoey (Chapter 16, this volume) illustrate the pervasiveness of a hierarchical view in this research because they assess the impact of procedural justice on the legitimacy of authorities. But the basic arguments in this research are probably quite useful in discussing sanctioning behavior in network relations. A strong parallel exists between a hierarchical view of justice and the kinds of justice considerations network relations are likely to invoke. To illustrate this point, we consider the dominant notions of distributive justice and then draw their parallel to relationally relevant forms of justice consideration.

The Hierarchical Perspective

For a society or organization[2] to function effectively, three central activities need to occur (see Folger, Sheppard, & Buttram, 1995). The organization or society needs to form and maintain membership, produce efficiently and effectively, and sustain the well-being of its members. Without members, an organization does not exist. Without efficient and effective production, it cannot compete. Without their essential needs met, organizational members will focus on those unmet needs and not the purposes of the organization. It was Deutsch's (1975) view that in distributing a society's or an organization's outcomes, three principles of distributive justice arise from these three essential ingredients of organization: (a) Relative *equality* of distribution ensures a sense of membership, but gross inequality leads to a lack of identification with others in the organization. In essence, through gross inequality, the organization fractionates to become more than one organization. (b) *Equity* engenders the motivation to produce efficiently. Without providing greater reward to those who produce more or better, there is not enough incentive to produce more or better. (c) Distribution of resources according to *need* ensures that the base needs of all societal and organizational members are met.

Subsequent research has well established the validity of equity, equality, and need as the dominant bases of distributive justice (see Greenberg, 1987; Leventhal, 1980; Sheppard, Lewicki, & Minton, 1992). The perspective embedded in Deutsch's functional analysis is that of a society or an organization as a whole. For Deutsch, these three principles of justice are built on the answer to the question, "Under what conditions do societies or organizations function best?" The perspective is thus at the level of the institution as a whole. A leader of a country or a corporate CEO is most likely to adopt such a broad, overall, societal, or corporate view. Those preoccupied at the level of an individual societal member or at the level of a relationship between a few members are less focused on the lofty goals of ensuring that a society remains together, produces effectively, and meets the essential needs of all societal members. These functions are important in the abstract but are not likely to direct the day-to-day activities of most societal members. Thus it is important to consider how the perspectives of social architects and organizations match those of that society's members. Implied in the notion of social goals is a view that individuals evaluating the fairness of a set of outcomes share the goals and/or perspective of the CEO, president, or constitutional author. Is it that people adopt the view of Jefferson, Ghandi, Lenin, Susan B. Anthony, or Jack Welch, or do they have other more personally direct considerations in mind? It is our contention that a complete explanation of the psychology of social justice requires considering how people consider justice when engaged in relations between one another. We do not mean to imply that people are not concerned about social goals or the effective functioning of the society or organization of which they are members—just that other mechanisms are also involved. From the following discussion, it should become clear that surprisingly similar principles evolve when relational forms are considered.

The Interpersonal Perspective

From an exhaustive review of the major thinking on relationships in sociology (such as Blau, 1964; Buber, 1927/1987; Durkheim, 1897/1951; Tönnies, 1887/1988; Weber, 1970), anthropology (such as Polanyi, 1944/1957; Malinowski, 1922/1961; Sahlins, 1965; Udy, 1959), psychology (such as Clark & Mills, 1979; Krech & Crutchfield, 1965; Leary, 1957; Piaget, 1932/1973), and theology (Ricoeur, 1967), Alan Fiske argues for the existence of four elemental forms of human relationships: communal sharing, authority ranking, equality matching, and market pricing. His own definition of these four forms is quite elegant:

> Communal Sharing is a relation of unity, community, undifferentiated collective identity, and kindness, typically enacted among close kin. Authority Ranking is a relationship of asymmetric differences, commonly exhibited in a hierarchical

ordering of statuses and precedence, often accompanied by the exercise of command and complementary displays of deference and respect. Equality matching is a one-to-one correspondence relationship in which people are distinct but equal, as manifested in balanced reciprocity (or tit-for-tat revenge), equal share distributions or identical contributions, in-kind replacement compensation, and turn taking. Market Pricing is based on an (intermodal) metric of value by which people compare different commodities and calculate exchange and cost/benefit ratios. (1991, p. ix)

These four forms surface repeatedly in writing on human relationships and can be found in anthropological research on a diverse set of peoples. His assertion about the pervasiveness and importance of these four forms of human relationships is not a modest one:

My hypothesis is that these models are *fundamental,* in the sense that they are the lowest or most basic-level "grammars" for social relations. Further, the models are *general,* giving order to most forms of social interaction, thought, and affect. They are *elementary,* in the sense that they are the basic constituents for all higher order social forms. It is also my hypothesis that they are *universal,* being the basis for social relations among all people in all cultures and the essential foundation for cross-cultural understanding and intercultural engagement. (1991, p. 25)

Perhaps the simplest illustration of these four elemental relational forms is to consider the developmental experiences of a child. The first experience a baby has is with a mother or father who the child considers an extension of him- or herself. The relationship is built on caring, unity between parent and child, and fulfillment of the child's needs (communal sharing). Often a child's second experience is with authority, in the form of a father or a mother who has switched roles from caregiver to rule setter, who establishes boundaries, sets rules, admonishes bad behavior, and encourages good behavior. Unlike the child's earlier experience, the flow is not to fulfill the child's needs but to develop a sense of right and wrong and mold desirable behavior. Out of love for the parent or in response to the sanctions, the child begins to perceive parental preferences as dominant (authority ranking). The child begins to learn not just that parents fulfill needs but that they are to be obeyed. Still later the child begins to engage peers or siblings, an entity quite distinct from the child her- or himself. The initial exchanges between children generally entail parallel play or joint play. In both instances, the rules of engagement most typically entail sharing or turn taking (equality matching). Finally, children begin to seek things from people who are not family, friends, or neighbors, but are strangers who have desired objects. Stores, restaurants, putt-putt golf places, and videogame halls need some mechanism of exchange that permits the child to make equivalent choices across each. Money is introduced to permit purchasing these goods and allow comparison of unlike things on a single dimension or currency (market pricing). A Big Mac is worth six videogames, because its price is $1.50 and a videogame is worth 25 cents. Such comparisons allow for exchanges across very unlike things.

From this simple illustration it is clear that three of Fiske's relational types produce equity (market pricing), equality (equality matching), and need (community sharing) as principles of fair distribution. Authority ranking has no comparable justice principle described earlier, a point we will return to later. Note the similarity between authority ranking and hierarchy and between market pricing and market as described at the start of this chapter. Fiske argues that hierarchy and market are two fundamental relational forms. Markets are predicated on equity considerations. Note also that Fiske identified two other elemental forms of relationship—communal sharing and equality matching. Both of these exist with regularity in almost all societies but have received very little attention in Organizational Behavior to date. Network organizations entail forms of both. Colocated design teams frequently have resources that participants are expected to use as needed and not to consume unnecessarily. Strategic alliances often entail chit keeping among the participants, such that each partner asks whose opinion dominated most recently. Of course, such relationships are rarely pure. Colocated teams entail elements of hierarchy (often there is a project manager, who is most equal among equals), market (salaries differ for different specialties in the group), equality matching (who least recently did a noxious task), and communal sharing (use of a networked printer). Thus, most interesting relationships are multiplex, involving some components of all four elemental forms.

This elaboration of justice in terms of relational forms illustrates why quadratic trust exists. It is one's right, perhaps obligation, to intervene when a network member has acted inconsistently with the basis on which the network is founded because an injustice has been committed. In our earlier example of two brothers, Frank should sanction Guy because Guy has violated a primary principle of justice among families: Take care of those in need. This principle is part of the basic grammar of families, without which they would not function. Communal sharing has jural qualities in the context of families: Its violation requires restoration. Similarly, violation of dignity such as through abusive treatment is inconsistent with the premise of equality on which many effective teams are founded. In sum, the principles of justice that are derived from a hierarchical, functional view of organizations may be the underpinnings of nonhierarchical organizational forms. How can that be?

First, it is noteworthy that the vast majority of research on justice in organizations has focused on equity. Only recently and somewhat reluctantly has Organizational Behavior begun to look at the need for equality. Equity is a market-oriented principle and thus quite consistent with the field's previous focus on markets and hierarchies. In fact, the focus on equity in organizational decisions implies that hierarchical firms have been quite connected to markets. Second, the absence of a justice principle for hierarchy in its own right implies that the role of hierarchy may be to maintain effective relationships among firm members. That is, one has the right to manage to the degree to which one serves to maintain the relational forms on which the firm is grounded. Managers of groups derive moral authority to the degree to which they preserve equality matching; managers of highly interdependent communities derive authority to the degree to which they maintain communal sharing as a basis of relationships; and managers of individual achievers derive authority to the degree to which they maintain relative equity among employees. Managers derive moral authority as keepers of relational form. This perspective suggests that the limitation of past OB research to the present study of network organizations has involved an overemphasis on equity as a principle of justice. This is not surprising, given that the other form of economic organization historically recognized in organizational research is the market. Hierarchy is not necessarily hostile to colocated teams, strategic alliances, customer-supplier relationships, and boundaryless firms; it just needs reconstrual from a bias toward equity as the primary principle of justice toward need and equality as coequal principles.

This point highlights two of the observations made about how research on network organizations may differ from previous research in Organizational Behavior. Before one can begin to study justice, it will first be necessary to consider the basic relational form in which the issue of justice is embedded. Without knowing the form a relationship takes, it will not be possible to specify which principle of justice is relevant. Second, part of the persuasiveness of Fiske's approach comes from his invocation of rich cross-cultural data. We can learn a great deal about Western business practice by understanding economic exchange in other cultures. Thus, fields such as anthropology may be as important for future OB researchers to be conversant with as psychology or sociology, the two fields from which OB has drawn most in the past. As argued in the beginning of this chapter, in the study of business relationships, context matters and many disciplines have value to add.

Nice Try, but . . .

Research and teaching on negotiation is a growth business (Rubin, 1985). At least part of this growth is a result of the emergence of new organizational forms (Bazerman & Lewicki, 1985; Sheppard, in press). It follows that long-standing relationships between relative equals require bargaining, because formal controls and sanctions do not exist as a means of getting others to do what we wish. In relationships it is necessary to discuss, quibble, exchange, and engage in *quid pro quo* as a way to get someone over whom one does not have power to do what is desired. Partially based on this observation, research on negotiation has been conducted to help fill the void. This research has taken as its model either the bargaining model developed in labor relations (e.g., see Lewicki, Litterer, Minton, & Saunders, 1994), game theory (e.g., see Murnighan, 1991), or decision-theoretic models of negotiation (e.g., see Bazerman & Neale, 1992). Each of these points of view is primarily transactional. They have as their model maximizing return to self in each negotiation. They do not address, as their primary focus, negotiation as a means of establishing and growing long-term relationships nor how the context of a given relationship changes the nature of a negotiation.

Recent research methodologies are also limited. For example, a fairly typical study involves two relative strangers engaging in a simulated negotiation over a few dimensions in which each has been given a set of information outlining the returns to him or her for a set of settlement points on each dimension. The most frequently used simulation is a variant on the two-person, three-issue negotiation developed by Dean Pruitt (1972) for studying integrative bargaining. These are poor proxies for at least three reasons: (a) the negotiation is not in the context of a relationship; (b) the simulation entails a predefined, highly stylized problem; and (c) there is no past and no future. Negotiations among long-term, cross-functional team members, strategic allies, and parties to a long-term customer-supplier relationship have a past and a future, occur in the context of a very elaborate relationship, and entail messy problems. Therefore, the field has attempted to address a very important question—how negotiations occur within the context of an ongoing relationship among relative equals—but given the limiting set of perspectives and methodologies, it really has not. Research has concentrated on transactional exchanges, not relationships. Up to this point, research has inadequately addressed issues unique to relational negotiations. But it is necessary to make this case to illustrate how negotiations in the context of ongoing relationships differ significantly from transactional negotiations. Let us turn to that question now. Much of this thinking is adapted from another chapter specifically written about negotiation in relationships (Sheppard, 1995).

Negotiation in a Partnership

A recently married couple discuss whose parents they will be spending Christmas vacation with. Proctor & Gamble and WalMart discuss who will own the inventory in their new relationship. Price Waterhouse discusses a cost overrun with an extremely important audit client. Members of a new task force determine their new roles only to discover that two wish to serve the same function. Each of these discussions could be modeled quite well as a single-issue, distributive negotiation problem. There are two parties: a single, critical dimension and opposing positions. A great portion of each discussion will entail searching for the other's walkaway point and hiding of one's own. But the discussions are also more complicated than the simple distributive problem.

Using Time to Transform
Distributive Into Integrative Bargains

Most obviously, because a history and a future exist in each of these discussions, ways of identifying integrative potential are not likely to be found in a simple transaction. A one-time distributive problem does not permit introducing other issues into a discussion. However, because a past and a future exist within partnerships, it is possible to transform a single-issue distributive discussion into a multiple-issue integrative discussion. One spouse cares a great deal about where to spend their first married Christmas, but the other harbors strong preferences about where to spend their summer vacation time. Proctor & Gamble wishes WalMart to own any inventory; WalMart wishes to establish a mechanism to ensure a quick response on any future issues arising in the relationship. The customer is very concerned about paying additional costs, but the accountant is concerned about changing client procedures and practices during future audits. Existing procedures result in a slow, unprofitable audit. One member of the task force truly wishes to be the initial point of contact with a critical group, but the other may really wish to be central in the final presentation to that group. In each of these examples, a difficult distributive negotiation problem becomes less difficult as the parties are allowed to logroll over time. Consider a husband and wife, one of whom wishes to vacation in the mountains and the other at the beach. If all else fails, it is possible to go to the mountains one year and the beach the next. To do so, however, there needs to be a next year. In transactional negotiation, a future does not exist, or it exists very tentatively and with no assurances. Thus, a bird in the hand is worth two in the bush. In an ongoing relationship, however, birds in the bush are much less likely to get away.

Distributive Negotiations
Within a Relationship Are Hot

But the future is a double-edged sword. Although integrative potential is raised by the possibility of introducing a second issue into the discussion, there is also potential for the discussion to become very heated and focused on the single issue at hand. Frequently, distributive discussions in ongoing relationships are precedent establishing, where the stakes entail such problems in the future. Thus, a simple one-time distributive negotiation can take on great new import. Who owns the inventory for one Proctor & Gamble product line has clear implications for who owns the inventory for all product lines and all future products. Thus, the discussion is not over just toothpaste for this year, but potentially for the allocation of profits across all brands. Simple allocation questions become questions of precedent and thus more important and more heated. A clear implication of this point is that negotiators within relationships need to be able to handle well emotion-laden or very important issues.

Negotiations Within
Relationships May Never End

Oliver Williamson (1985) best articulated the major reason for not depending on well-specified contracts: People are not infinitely smart. If we could anticipate and plan for all possible contingencies, then a contract could serve our needs. However, people have limited capacity, an especially important complication in today's increasingly complex, ambiguous world. For most interesting negotiations, neither all important contingencies, nor all important aspects of performance, can be identified in advance. This is especially true as changes in products and services occur with increasing rapidity and the focus on customization increases. Moreover, even if we could anticipate all important contingencies, a contract covering them would be too cumbersome. Thus, more open-ended vehicles permit ongoing discussion as a method for responding to changes as they arise. In relationships, exhaustive contracts are unnecessary because parties prefer to rely on a person's word, a handshake, or common honesty and decency.

Of course, there are times when extreme planning is called for in a partnership. When relations falter, behavioral therapists use a typical tactic of getting parties to develop implicit contracts about things on which they can agree. Frequently, incomplete discussions or inaccurate explicit assumptions served as the basis for the relationship failing in the first place. Raising discussion on important little issues and creating agreements on these can set the parties on track to build a more solid base of understanding. Said differently, parties may act as if their relationship is more of a marriage than it is. In such cases, returning to market conditions for a while may be a good idea. A second instance is when coordinating activities is essential and communication is either difficult or very disruptive. A large building project is one example. The client, engineers, architect, contractor, and subcontractors often cannot meet frequently enough to work through a project's details. Moreover, detailed planning permits a level of coordination that ad hoc communication cannot. Thus, planning should take place. Even in such instances, however, it is wise to leave open the possibility of ongoing negotiation. All contingencies cannot be foreseen and it builds stronger relationships.

Integrative Negotiation as an Opportunity for Mutual Development

In discussing integrative negotiation in their important book *Getting to Yes* (1981), Roger Fisher and William Ury admonish the reader to take great care to separate the person from the problem, to be hard on the problem and soft on the person. This is extremely good advice and serves as a cornerstone to effective communication in many difficult discussions. The dilemma of much integrative negotiation in a partnership is that such advice is hard and probably bad to follow. In other words, in negotiations within a relationship the person is often the problem, or the opportunity. In transactional negotiation, discussions are about the exchange of goods, services, or money. Although these issues are central to discussions within ongoing business relationships, they take on a very different cast, relating directly to the reasons why one would develop a close business relationship in the first place. Investment in an ongoing relationship permits the parties in that relationship to accrue real increases in efficiency, quality, and other forms of effectiveness. However, this is only true if investment occurs. Each side of the relationship should be (a) learning about the other, (b) working to improve their value to the other, and (c) developing plans that incorporate the other's interests into those plans. Without doing so, a long-term relationship entails the disadvantage of closing off options, without accruing the benefits of the longer-term commitment. Without mutual development, long-term relationships have no value. This quality of relationship influences the meaning and form of integrative bargaining within them. Integrative bargaining within a partnership is where seeds of mutual development are planted. Therefore, integrative bargaining within a relationship is directly about the people or functions or firms, not about concepts that can be isolated from the parties. Given the notion of mutual development as the cornerstone of effective relationships, how is integrative bargaining different within such a context?

Integrative Bargaining as an Opportunity to Talk

As we just argued, within ongoing, interdependent relationships most discussions present opportunities to discuss improving the relationship or each other in the context of the relationship. We do not mean to imply that pure exchange-based discussions never happen within a relationship. Clearly, they do. For example, a husband and wife in discussing housecleaning discover that one likes cleaning with water, but the other likes dusting, vacuuming, and tidying. The integrative deal entails giving the washrooms and kitchen to one spouse and the rest of the cleaning to the other. In a buyer-seller relationship, the buyer may care about inventory levels, but the seller cares about delivery date. However, we do mean to imply that such pure exchanges are rare and that to consider them distributively is to miss opportunities for improving the value of each partner to the other. They have a static quality to them that minimizes growth. How the partners choose to discuss issues may widen the negotiation's scope and offer chances to enhance their relationship. The couple may wish to talk about means for making cleaning easier: sponging stains that have been allowed to dry is much harder than cleaning as spills occur; tidying throughout the house is harder than tidying in a concentrated area. Separating the discussion of cleaning from the rest of their interchanges loses the opportunity to accrue real efficiencies. If the buyer and seller restrict their discussion only to issues within the confines of existing business practice, they miss opportunities to think about whole new ways of doing ordering, methods for integrating information systems across partners, means for mutually reducing costs, identification of new strategic opportunities, product development possibilities, or identification of competitive threats.

Consider a chief operating officer (COO) of a large electronics firm (call it Firm X) who was very concerned about his company's efforts to improve relations with suppliers as a step in improving overall product quality. Like most of its competition, this firm reduced the number of suppliers of each part to manage better those that remained, increased the number of parts each supplier provided the firm to tie the interests of the supplier better to the firm, put suppliers through a rigorous supplier qualification program, trained suppliers in manufacturing quality processes, and raised dramatically the expected quality of supplied parts. This COO visited his key supplier, where he discovered that his company's program, although having some positive effect, was so poorly implemented that much of the potential benefit was lost. For example, the supplier ran a continuous improvement program in its plants. When a suggested improvement in process or product was made that had implications for Firm X, the supplier was required to submit a large set of drawings at its own expense and wait while its suggested changes underwent a lengthy review process. Often, the supplier did not hear back for 6 months, sometimes not at all. As a result of the cost and difficulty associated with this review process, the supplier did not make many small but important improvements. This was in contrast to one of Firm X's chief competitors, which required no drawings be submitted for most suggestions and provided an answer within a few days on all but the most complicated suggestions. Frequently, this competitor would fly someone at its own expense to the supplier's plant site to clarify any questions. The supplier clearly admitted that this second firm received better and lower-cost materials than did Firm X. In fact, the COO estimated that his parts were 30% more expensive and had far greater quality problems than his competitor. Firm X set up a framework for supplier development but thwarted its effectiveness by not keeping lines of communication open.

In Many Negotiations,
the Person Is the Problem

A corollary of the notion of mutual development and negotiations in marriage is that in such negotiations the person is the problem. Consider the husband and wife discussed earlier. In many instances it behooves the couple to discuss messes throughout the house in a very depersonalized manner. In doing so, no one takes offense and they can discuss the problem of multiple messes to tidy without having a long debate about character or personology. In other words, in marriages it is often important to separate the person from the problem. However, this is impossible or bad advice to follow in two particular instances. First, the problem of distributed mess may simply be part of a larger set of behaviors endemic to the other. The husband may not just leave trails of mess throughout the house but also may not turn his socks right side out before putting them in the laundry; leave paper, money, and other assorted mess in his shirt pocket; bring the dog and children in all muddy and have them traipse throughout the house without concern for the new Oriental rug; and leave coffee cups in every nook and cranny in the house. In sum, he may just be messy. Discussing his messiness, provided it is done with care for his feelings, permits a kind of conversation not permitted by separating the person from the problem. Discussing messiness provides an opportunity to diagnose why he is messy and thus potentially take action on the root cause. Discussing his messiness permits a broad-based discussion on the aspects of messiness that cause his wife real concern and those that are not a problem or are even endearing. Discussing his messiness permits him and his wife to learn something about themselves and about each other. None of these could be easily done if a list of depersonalized local messes was brought up for discussion. Moreover, if the list is too long or different messes are discussed over frequent exchanges, the person has become the problem and in a much less direct passive-aggressive manner.

The example just given is clearly a limited one, not illustrating the full potential of making the person the problem. More important discussions may occur over issues such as self and career, orientation to family, personal values, or the role of one's childhood experiences in his or her present relationship. Consider an extreme example. Parents who were abused as children are much more likely to abuse their own children than are parents who were not abused as children. It appears that a critical determinant of whether abuse will be transferred from generation to generation is the ability of people who were abused as children to confront their views and feelings about relationships with a trusted other (Putallaz, Costanzo, & Klein, 1993). Good marriages are a context in which a person may be able to deal with his or her feelings about relationships and tendencies to abuse. Without recognizing that they are the problem, it is difficult for such abused people to develop truly effective relationships.

Although far less dramatic, equivalent business examples abound. Two people are going to be working together for a long time and one does not trust the other. A key supplier has adopted a long-term strategy inconsistent with a critical customer's needs. A colleague has become too arrogant to work with. A task force chair lacks confidence and is crippling performance. In these instances it may be possible to discuss things in a very indirect, objective manner, but often the other person, business unit, or firm is the problem.

Integrative Negotiations Have Implications for Power and Future Dependence

A related aspect of integrative negotiations is that they entail implications for future power and dependence. In long-term relationships, members are and should be quite concerned about the nature of the dependency between them. Mutual development entails mutual dependence. Long-term commitment entails dependence. Dependence on others means that they wield power over you. Consider the example of the supplier to the electronics company described earlier. One electronics company committed to the supplier over a very long term. In doing so, it shared critical information about its processes, strategy, and upcoming product design. It invested heavily in developing capabilities in that supplier so the supplier could meet better and better the electronics company's material needs. It got to learn well the supplier's processes and incorporated its unique abilities into product development efforts. As a result, the electronics company has higher-quality, less expensive, and better-integrated parts than its competitor, who did none of those things. However, it is also more dependent on the supplier. Because of information and abilities unique to their two-party relationship, the supplier provides better, less-expensive, and more integrated parts. As a result, the electronics company needs that supplier to sustain existing quality, cost, and integration. Williamson (1985) refers to this phenomenon as the development of firm-specific skills—that is, skills that have value only in relation to a particular company. The other electronics company has no such advantages, but it also is not as dependent. In the argot of 1950s teenagers, one firm is going steady, while the other is playing the field.

Dependence can take many forms (Pfeffer & Salancik, 1978; Tichy, 1973). We can depend on others for information, goods, services, money, clout, personal support, or counsel. We can become dependent due to relationship-specific abilities. We can become dependent because we develop a sense of attachment or identity. In each instance, dependence implies power. Where power exists, there is potential for abuse. This argument is simply a variant on Williamson's concern for opportunistic behavior, but in strong form. A solution is to develop mechanisms and relational qualities that permit trust.

Do These Differences Matter?

One can grant that negotiations in relationships have somewhat different qualities yet not believe that our basic approach to researching negotiation needs to change. It is useful to consider this question by realizing how our research questions and our theoretical and methodological approaches might change if we take seriously the differences between negotiating in a relationship and the more traditionally studied transactional negotiations. Table 8.2 outlines a series of research questions suggested by the unique qualities of negotiating in a relationship. This list is not intended to be exhaustive, but it is both long and interesting. Because we do not know much about many of these questions, we cannot address well the questions practitioners of network organizations pose to us. Clearly, we know something about each of them, but far less than we do about cognitive processes in negotiations, behavior in the prisoner's dilemma game, and how people discern integrative potential in a one-time stylized negotiation.

These questions also suggest how our theories and methodologies need adjustment. Taken together, they suggest the following:

- The context in which the negotiation is embedded demands greater attention.
- Dynamic models and methods incorporating time, history, and anticipated future interaction are essential.
- Many relatively untapped fields have insights to provide, including anthropology, communications, political science, interpersonal processes, and clinical and family psychology.
- The relationship should often be the unit of analysis.

Thus, they return us to the beginning of the chapter.

Conclusion

It was our intent in this chapter to provide a glimpse at how micro-OB might change if we were to take seriously the proposition that network organizational forms are of increasing importance. We attempted to provide examples of how new, adapted, and redirected thought are all necessary if we

TABLE 8.2 Research Questions Concerning Negotiations in Relationships

1. What is the impact of anticipated, deep, future interaction on
   - the nature of discourse between negotiators?
   - the substance of negotiation?
   - choice of negotiation partner?
2. How do open-ended, ongoing negotiations differ from discreet, closed negotiations?
3. What is the impact of the existence of a past and related history on
   - the emergence of patterns in negotiation?
   - evolution of negotiations?
   - frames adapted in negotiation?
4. How do parties conduct parallel but related negotiations?
5. What sorts of artificial walls effectively permit appropriate bleeding of discussion across related negotiations?
6. What do people consider appropriate transgressions to become involved in? What is my business, and what is private between parties in my network?
7. When do people sanction network members?
8. How do people restart negotiations?
9. How do negotiations change as external relationships change?
10. How do power asymmetries change the structure of ongoing negotiations?
11. What is the impact of the addition of a new member to an ongoing relationship?
12. What types of social networks exist, and how do they influence negotiation behavior?
13. How does the integration of information systems between firms or functions within a firm influence negotiation?
14. How are negotiations different when the subject is essential qualities of the other person or firm?
15. How do people negotiate the giving up of a critical skill?
16. How do we negotiate so as to ensure growth in another and not smothering?
17. How do distinct cultures merge or accommodate over time?
18. What is sustainable trust?
19. How do different forms of trust color a negotiation?
20. How do people fight productively?
21. Is negotiation the right metaphor for considering discussions among partners?

are to provide the theoretical underpinnings necessary to providing meaningful advice to those attempting to make such organizations work. It is our sincere belief that efforts to address these issues can help to revitalize a "fallow" field.

Notes

1. Purists would disagree with the juxtaposition of the two terms *network* and *organization*, because this is literally not possible. However, for want of a better word, we will engage in such academic license.

2. We will use the term to mean all manner of social organization that has some production requirement for the organization to survive.

References

Adams, J. S. (1965). Inequity in social exchange. In L. Berkowitz (Ed.), *Advances in experimental social psychology* (Vol. 2). New York: Academic Press.

Axelrod, R. (1984). *The evolution of cooperation.* New York: Basic Books.

Bazerman, M. H. (1994). *Judgment in managerial decision making.* New York: John Wiley.

Bazerman, M. H., & Lewicki, R. J. (1985). Contemporary research directions in the study of negotiation in organizations: A selected overview. *Journal of Occupational Behavior, 6,* 1-17.

Bazerman, M. H., & Neale, M. A. (1992). *Negotiating rationally.* New York: Free Press.

Blau, P. M. (1964). Justice in social exchange. *Social Inquiry, 34,* 193-206.

Boon, S. D., & Holmes, J. G. (1991). The dynamics of interpersonal trust: Resolving uncertainty in the face of risk. In R. A. Hinde & J. Groebel (Eds.), *Cooperation & prosocial behavior* (pp. 190-211). Cambridge, UK: Cambridge University Press.

Buber, M. (1987). *I and thou* (R. G. Smith, Trans.). New York: Collier-MacMillian. (Original publication 1927)

Byrne, J. A. (1993, February 8). The virtual corporation. *Business Week,* pp. 98-102.

Chernow, R. (1990). *The house of Morgan.* New York: Atlantic Monthly Press.

Clark, M. S., & Mills, J. (1979). Interpersonal attraction in exchange and communal relationships. *Journal of Personality and Social Psychology, 37,* 12-24.

Dasgupta, P. (1988). Trust as a commodity. In D. Gambetta (Ed.), *Trust: Making and breaking cooperative relations* (pp. 49-72). Oxford, UK: Basil Blackwell.

Deutsch, M. (1973). *The resolution of conflict.* New Haven, CT: Yale University Press.

Deutsch, M. (1975). Equity, equality and need: What determines which value will be used as the basis of distributive justice? *Journal of Social Issues, 31,* 137-149.

Durkheim, E. (1951). *Suicide.* Glencoe, IL: Free Press. (Original publication 1897)

Fisher, R., & Ury, W. (1981). *Getting to yes.* New York: Houghton Mifflin.

Fiske, A. P. (1990). Relativity within Moose culture: Four incommensurable models for social relationships. *Ethos, 18,* 180-204.

Fiske, A. P. (1991). *Structures of social life: The four elementary forms of social relationships.* New York: Free Press.

Folger, R., Sheppard, B. H., & Buttram, R. (1995). Equity, equality and need: Three faces of social justice. In B. B. Bunker & J. Z. Rubin (Eds.), *Conflict, cooperation and justice: Essays inspired by the work of Morton Deutsch.* San Francisco: Jossey-Bass.

Granovetter, M. (1985). Economic action and social structure: The problem of embeddedness. *American Journal of Sociology, 91,* 481-510.

Greenberg, J. (1987). A taxonomy of organizational justice theories. *Academy of Management Review, 12,* 9-22.

Hackman, J. R., & Oldham, G. R. (1975). Development of the job diagnostic survey. *Journal of Applied Psychology, 60,* 159-170.

Homans, G. (1958). Social behavior as exchange. *American Journal of Sociology, 63,* 597-606.

Hudson, P. (1981). Proto-industrialization: The case of the West Riding World Textile Industry in the 18th and early 19th century. *History Workshop, 12,* 34-61.

Kramer, R. M., & Brewer, M. B. (1984). Effects of group identity on resource use in a simulated commons dilemma. *Journal of Personality and Social Psychology, 46,* 1044-1057.

Krech, D., & Crutchfield, R. S. (1965). *Elements of psychology.* New York: Knopf.

Leary, T. F. (1957). *Interpersonal diagnosis of personality: A functional theory and methodology for personality evaluation.* New York: Ronald Cress.

Leventhal, G. S. (1980). What should be done with equity theory? New approaches to the study of fairness in social relationships. In K. J. Gergen, M. S. Greenberg, & R. H. Willis (Eds.), *Social exchange: Advances in theory and research.* New York and London: Plenum.

Lewicki, R. J., & Bunker, B. B. (1995). Trust in relationships: A model of trust development and decline. In B. B. Bunker & J. Z. Rubin (Eds.), *Conflict, cooperation and justice: Essays inspired by the work of Morton Deutsch.* San Francisco: Jossey-Bass.

Lewicki, R. J., Litterer, J. A., Minton, J. W., & Saunders, D. M. (1994). *Negotiation* (2nd ed.). Burr Ridge, IL: Irwin.

Lind, E. A., & Tyler, T. R. (1988). *Social psychology of procedural justice.* New York: Plenum.

Malinowski, B. (1961). *Argonauts of the western Pacific: An account of native enterprise and adventure in the Archipelagoes of Melanesian New Guinea.* New York: Dutton. (Original publication 1922)

Maslow, A. H. (1943, July). A theory of human motivation. *Psychological Review,* pp. 370-396.

Mitchell, T. R., & Beech, L. R. (1976). A review of occupational preference and choice research using expectancy theory and decision theory. *Journal of Occupational Psychology, 99,* 231-248.

Murnighan, J. K. (1991). *The dynamics of bargaining games.* Englewood Cliffs, NJ: Prentice Hall.

O'Reilly, C. A., III. (1991). Organizational behavior: Where we've been, where we're going. *Annual Review of Psychology, 24,* 427-458.

Pfeffer, J., & Salancik, G. R. (1978). *The external control of organizations.* New York: Harper & Row.

Piaget, J. (1973). *Le jugement moral chez l'enfant. Bibliothèque de philosophie contemporaine.* Paris: Presses Universitaries de France. (Original publication 1932)

Polanyi, K. (1957). *The great transformation: The political and economic origins of our time.* New York: Holt, Rinehart & Winston. (Original publication 1944)

Powell, W. W. (1990). Neither market nor hierarchy: Network forms of organization. In B. M. Staw & L. L. Cummings (Eds.), *Research in organizational behavior* (pp. 295-336). Greenwich, CT: JAI.

Pruitt, D. (1972). Methods for resolving differences of interest: A theoretical analysis. *Journal of Social Issues, 28,* 133-154.

Putallaz, M., Costanzo, P. R., & Klein, T. P. (1993). Parental childhood social experiences and their effects on children's relationships. In S. Duck (Ed.), *Understanding relationship processes. Vol. 2: Learning about relationships.* Newbury Park, CA: Sage.

Ricoeur, P. (1967). *The symbolism of evil* (E. Buchanan, Trans.). Boston: Beacon.

Rubin, J. Z. (1985). Editor's introduction. *Negotiation Journal, 1*(1).

Sahlins, M. (1965). On the sociology of primitive exchange. In M. Banton (Ed.), *The relevance of models for social anthropology* (Association of Social Anthropologist, Monograph 1). London: Tavistock.

Shapiro, D., Sheppard, B. H., & Cheraskin, L. (1992, October). Business on a handshake. *The Negotiation Journal,* pp. 365-378.

Shapiro, S. P. (1987). The social control of interpersonal trust. *American Journal of Sociology, 93,* 623-658.

Sheppard, B. H. (1995). Negotiating in long term relationships among relative equals. In B. Bies, R. J. Lewicki, & B. H. Sheppard (Eds.), *Research on negotiation in organizations* (Vol. 5, pp. 3-44).

Sheppard, B. H., & Lewicki, R. J. (1985). Choosing how to intervene: Factors influencing the use of process and outcome control in third party dispute resolution. *Journal of Occupational Behavior, 6,* 49-64.

Sheppard, B. H., Lewicki, R. J., & Minton, J. W. (1992). *Organizational justice.* New York: Free Press.

Snow, C. C., Miles, R. E., & Coleman, H. J., Jr. (1992). Managing 21st century organizations. *Organizational Dynamics, 20*(3), 5-20.

Staw, B. M. (1977). Motivation in organizations: Towards a synthesis and redirection. In B. M. Staw & G. R. Salancik (Eds.), *New directions in organizational behavior.* Chicago: St. Clair Press.

Stein, M. M. (1993). The ultimate customer-supplier relationship at Bose, Honeywell and AT&T. *National Productivity Review, 12*(4), 543-548.

Thibaut, J., & Walker, L. (1975). *Procedural justice: A psychological analysis.* Hillsdale, NJ: Lawrence Erlbaum.

Tichy, N. (1973). An analysis of clique formation and structure in organizations. *Administrative Science Quarterly, 18,* 194-208.

Tichy, N. M. (1993). Revolutionizing your company. *Fortune, 128*(15), 114-118.

Tönnies, F. (1988). *Community and society* (C. P. Loomis, Trans.). New Brunswick and Oxford: Transaction Books. (Original publication 1887)

Tyler, T. R. (1990). *Why people obey the law.* New Haven, CT: Yale University Press.

Udy, S. H. (1959). *Organization of work: A comparative analysis of production among nonindustrial peoples.* New Haven, CT: HumanRelations Area Files Press.

Vroom, V. H. (1964). *Work and motivation.* New York: John Wiley.

Weber, M. (1970). *The Protestant ethic.* London: George Allen and Unwin.

Williamson, O. E. (1981). The economics of organization: The transaction cost approach. *American Journal of Sociology, 87,* 548-577.

Williamson, O. E. (1985). *The economic institution of capitalism.* New York: Free Press.

Williamson, O. E. (1993). Calculativeness, trust, and economic organization. *Journal of Law and Economics, 36,* 453-486.

Swift Trust and Temporary Groups

DEBRA MEYERSON
KARL E. WEICK
RODERICK M. KRAMER

January 1, 1991. The Grand Kempinski Hotel, Dallas, Texas. 9:00 a.m. "Crew Call." About 35 people gather. Some are local. Some flew in overnight from here or there. Some drove in. The 35 encompass almost that many different technical disciplines. Many are meeting each other for the first time. Ten and one-half hours from now they will tape a two hour lecture (given by the author), which will become the centerpiece of an hour-long public television show. They'll tape it again the next day. Then they'll disperse, never again to work together in the same configuration.

Peters, *Liberation Management*
(1992, p. 190)

This is the "Dallas Organization." As Peters and others have noted, temporary groups of this sort are becoming an increasingly common form of organization

AUTHORS' NOTE: We gratefully acknowledge comments and suggestions provided by Joel Brockner, Robert Cialdini, Jim March, Joel Podolny, Gene Webb, and Mayer Zald at various stages in the writing of this chapter. An earlier version of this work was presented at the conference on trust in organizations, held at the Graduate School of Business, Stanford University, May 14-15, 1994.

(Kanter, 1989; Peters, 1992). In many respects, such groups constitute an interesting organizational analog of a "one-night stand." They have a finite life span, form around a shared and relatively clear goal or purpose, and their success depends on a tight and coordinated coupling of activity.

As an organizational form, temporary groups turn upside down traditional notions of organizing. Temporary groups often work on tasks with a high degree of complexity, yet they lack the formal structures that facilitate coordination and control (Thompson, 1967). They depend on an elaborate body of collective knowledge and diverse skills, yet individuals have little time to sort out who knows precisely what. They often entail high-risk and high-stake outcomes, yet they seem to lack the normative structures and institutional safeguards that minimize the likelihood of things going wrong. Moreover, there isn't time to engage in the usual forms of confidence-building activities that contribute to the development and maintenance of trust in more traditional, enduring forms of organization. In these respects, temporary groups challenge our conventional understandings regarding the necessary or sufficient antecedents of effective organization.

These observations come together in a fascinating puzzle. Temporary systems exhibit behavior that presupposes trust, yet traditional sources of trust—familiarity, shared experience, reciprocal disclosure, threats and deterrents, fulfilled promises, and demonstrations of nonexploitation of vulnerability—are not obvious in such systems. In this respect, temporary systems act as if trust were present, but their histories seem to preclude its development.

In the following discussion we argue that one way to resolve this puzzle is to look more closely at the properties of trust and of temporary systems. A closer look suggests that temporary groups and organizations are tied together by trust, but it is a form of trust that has some unusual properties.[1] In other words, we propose that the trust that occurs in temporary systems is not simply conventional trust scaled down to brief encounters among small groups of strangers. There is some of that. But as we will show, the trust that unfolds in temporary systems is more accurately portrayed as a unique form of collective perception and relating that is capable of managing issues of vulnerability, uncertainty, risk, and expectations. These four issues become relevant immediately, as soon as the temporary system begins to form. We argue that all four issues can be managed by variations in trusting behavior, and if they are not managed, participants act more like a permanent crowd than a temporary system. It is the configuration of these variations in behavior that accounts for the unique form that trust assumes in temporary systems, a form that we call *swift trust*.

The argument that swift trust is a useful concept for understanding the functioning of temporary systems will be developed in the following way. First, borrowing from Goodman and Goodman (1976), we describe social constraints and resources found in temporary systems that provide the context for trust and influence its form. Second, we describe three concepts of trust to explain referent situations other than temporary systems. Accompanying each description, we suggest how each concept could be adapted to the conditions of a temporary system and help us understand better how that system is held together and what effect these ties have on outcomes. Third, having discussed systems and trust separately, we interweave them to capture the unique configuration we call swift trust in temporary systems. Finally, we consider the social and cognitive mechanisms that may contribute to the resilience and fragility of swift trust. In doing so, we begin to grasp what makes for more and less successful temporary systems and we begin to gain a better understanding of how trust in general unfolds, builds, and dissipates in organized settings.

Temporary Systems

Goodman and Goodman were among the earliest investigators to think systematically about temporary systems—and among the few to do so. These authors based their ideas predominantly on the systems that formed around theater productions (Goodman, 1981, chap. 4; Goodman & Goodman, 1972), although they also examined auditing teams and research and development projects. They define a temporary system as "a set of diversely skilled people working together on a complex task over a limited period of time" (Goodman & Goodman, 1976, p. 494). Such a system differs from a more stable system in several ways. The tasks as well as the personnel are less well understood in a temporary system, which means they cannot be assigned in ways traditionally relied on to achieve the most effective use of resources. Furthermore, although a temporary system resembles an organic system (Burns & Stalker, 1961), it also differs because it includes "members who have never worked together before and who do not expect to work together again" (p. 495) and members who represent a diversity of functions or skills.

Goodman and Goodman suggest that four concurrent problems provide the context within which any temporary system forms and operates. The first problem, and the one that is most central in our analyses, involves interdependence. "The task is complex with respect to interdependence of detailed task accomplishment, so that it is not easy to define tasks clearly and autonomously. The members must keep interrelating with one another in trying to arrive at viable solutions" (1976, p. 495). This continuous "interrelating" keeps the issue of trust salient throughout the life of a temporary system. The other three components of context include the uniqueness of the task relative to routine procedures available in the organization, the significance of the task in that the organization is willing to create a new structure to deal with it, and the use of clear goals to define the task and impose a time limit for its completion.[2]

Examples of temporary systems described by Goodman and Goodman (1976, p. 495) include presidential commissions, Senate select committees, theater and architectural groups, construction, auditing, negotiating teams, juries, and election campaign organizations.[3] In thinking through the issues of trust and temporary systems, we have also considered film crews (Kawin, 1992), auctions (e.g., Clark & Halford, 1980), cockpit crews in planes (Weiner, Kanki, & Helmreich, 1993), paramedics (e.g., Mellinger, 1994), music composition in films (e.g., Faulkner, 1983), investment banking (Eccles & Crane, 1988), fire-fighting crews (e.g., Klein, 1993), diagnostic teams (e.g., Orr, 1990), nuclear power plant operators (e.g., Gaddy & Wachtel, 1992), and AIDS outreach work (e.g., Suczek & Fagerhaugh, 1991). Although these represent specific settings in which "a set of diversely skilled people work together on a complex task over a limited period of time," part of the impetus for this chapter has arisen from the observation that an increasing number of settings in all organizations involve temporary systems. Temporary systems have become common as a result of more subcontracting, fewer people to handle more diverse assignments, time compression in product development, more use of temporary workers, intensified competition that requires immediate adaptability, loss of valuable experience in response to early retirement programs, and more "network" organizations.

The characteristics of temporary systems, which have potential relevance for the formation of trust, include the following:

1. Participants with diverse skills are assembled by a contractor to enact expertise they already possess.
2. Participants have limited history working together.
3. Participants have limited prospects of working together again in the future.
4. Participants often are part of limited labor pools and overlapping networks.
5. Tasks are often complex and involve interdependent work.
6. Tasks have a deadline.
7. Assigned tasks are nonroutine and not well understood.
8. Assigned tasks are consequential.
9. Continuous interrelating is required to produce an outcome.

To convert the individual expertise of strangers into interdependent work, when the nature of that interrelating and work is not obvious, people must reduce their uncertainty about one another through operations that resemble trust. Interdependent strangers faced with a deadline also face the need to handle issues of vulnerability and risk among themselves. As we will see shortly, people handle these three issues by the ways in which they entrust their fate to others and the way they act when others entrust their fate to them. To trust and be trustworthy, within the limits of a temporary system, means that people have to wade in on trust rather than wait while experience gradually shows who can be trusted and with what: Trust must be conferred presumptively or *ex ante*.

In temporary systems, there is a premium on making do with whatever information is available in advance of close monitoring so that interdependent work is initiated quickly. Swift judgments about trustworthiness can't be avoided, because they enable people to act quickly in the face of uncertainty. People have to make consequential presumptions: no system, no performance. It's as basic as that. Which is not to say it's as simple as that. By no means is this conversion simple. But neither is it slow. To see some of what is involved, we turn next to three quite different accounts of trust, each of which helps us understand better what role trust plays in a temporary system and how that trust develops.

On Framing Swift Trust

In this section we examine three definitions of trust and suggest how swift trust might be represented using the imagery of each definition.

Trust and Vulnerability

The first set of definitions comes from Baier (1986). Her first approximation of a definition of trust is "accepted vulnerability to another's possible but not expected ill will (or lack of good will) toward one" (p. 235). Trust, in this view, is defined by two things: (a) the grounds for expecting that others will not take advantage of one's vulnerability and varieties of vulnerabilities and (b) the grounds for expecting that one will not be harmed by those who are entrusted with the valued items, even though they could derive from such diverse sources as the reality of the interdependence, implicit or explicit threats from the truster or from the network in which the activity occurs, norms in the setting, institutional and cultural categories, role clarity, inability of trustee to conceal harm-doing, and prospect of repeated interactions.

Vulnerability is defined in terms of the goods or things one values and whose care one partially entrusts to someone else, who has some discretion over him or her. Because self-sufficiency is rare in interdependent activities, divisions of labor, and complex tasks, vulnerability is common. Goods entrusted include reputations, conversation, health, safety, investments, political position, and music. Some of these goods are "intrinsically shared" (e.g., chamber music, conversation) and some rely on the behavior of others during certain situations (e.g., safety during fire-fighting missions, health during a serious illness). These situations require us to "allow many other people to get into positions where they can, if they choose, injure what we care about, since those are the same positions that they must be in order to help us take care of what we care about" (Baier, 1986, p. 236).

Given these ideas, the challenge is to see if swift trust can be singled out by the unique goods that are entrusted in these situations and/or the unique grounds that are invoked for expecting others to not take advantage of these vulnerabilities. In the case of the Dallas Organization, reputations are entrusted and the realities of task interdependence forestall intentional harm-doing to those reputations. The Dallas Organization forms around a task that cannot be executed by any one person. The organization is assembled by a "contractor" who may be the link pin (Likert) on which trust is focused (each of the 35 people trusts the contractor's selection criteria for the other 34). Thus, the contractor's reputation as much as the reputation of the performers is at stake—if the 35 or any significant subset foul up, future opportunities for the contractor to assemble an organization will dry up. In the Dallas Organization, individuals know that their specialty is crucial *and* worthless without links to other specialties. They also know of the implicit threat imposed on their own reputations if they don't perform. When all of these pieces are combined, they suggest the existence of vulnerabilities (e.g., reputations and outputs are at stake) and significant grounds for expectations of good will (e.g., threats, the reality of interdependence, and prospects for future interactions).

If membership in a temporary system is a one-shot event with little prospect of future interaction, and if there is low dependence on any one project for continuing work, as well as limited diffusion of information about the project outcomes outside the system, then little is at stake reputationally. Vulnerability is low, as is the need for trust. However, as the size of the pool from which members are selected gets smaller, talent becomes thinner, and information about performance diffuses more effectively, then reputations become vulnerable. In the words of one studio executive, "If someone in, say, makeup doesn't show up or shows up drunk to the set, they will be dead. They won't work for a very long time" (personal communication, 1993). Also, because the prospect of future interaction among the members within this limited labor pool is relatively high, grounds for expectations that members will not act with ill will increases.

Newcomers with fewer opportunities for work and those on the periphery of a network are more vulnerable than veterans who have more opportunities and are central. Well-positioned, high-status, seasoned individuals have more resilient reputations (and are therefore less vulnerable) and can withstand periodic failures or self-centered behaviors. This is a familiar pattern in

Hollywood. And people who work in systems tied together by weak ties (acquaintances and contacts) have less control over the diffusion of their reputations and are more vulnerable than those in networks of *strong* ties (friendship and family). Networks characterized by weak ties should result in wider dissemination of information because networks are less likely to overlap with one another. Here, an implicit threat of significant reputational damage imposed by the nature of the social network increases vulnerability, yet this threat can create the grounds for expecting trustworthy behavior among participants.

In general, we suggest that perceptions of the nature of the network and labor market available for temporary systems can have an impact on the form and incidence of trust in temporary systems through its effects on perceptions of vulnerability. People who are scarce freelance specialists and tied into minimally overlapping networks should perceive their position in temporary systems to be more vulnerable. Their reputation is entrusted to others who can do considerable damage in multiple networks. But in a situation of high interdependence, everyone is comparably vulnerable. Each controls the other's fate and thereby imposes the same threat. Although such a mutual threat may produce wariness, it could also lay the grounds for participants to expect and be receptive to trust and trustworthy behavior. In some temporary systems there is a high need to trust, partly because that is the only viable option. Overtures that address this need, such as short-term promises that are kept (Kouzes & Posner, 1987), should trigger reciprocal behavior.

If we assume that a condition of vulnerability is unsettling and people try to reduce it, then they can do so in one of three ways. First, they can reduce their dependence on others by cultivating alternative partners, projects, and networks. This is a form of "hedge," which we will discuss later. However, that avenue is often blocked, especially for newcomers. Second, because (inter)dependence may be inherent in the nature of the task, the vulnerability can be reduced by cultivating adaptability and the feeling of mastery that "I can handle anything they throw at me" (Faulkner, 1971, p. 136), coupled with "distancing" oneself (Faulkner, 1983, p. 153) from the settings. The feeling of mastery can be a cognitive illusion of sorts, which will also be discussed as a mechanism that can build resilience into the system. Third, one can presume that the other people in the setting are trustworthy. If one acts toward them in a trusting manner, the presumption of trust often acts like a self-fulfilling prophecy and creates the trusting behavior that was presumed to be there (Baier, 1985, chap. 15). The choice among these paths is driven as much by one's own social position, background expectancies generated by the context, and disposition as it is by any characteristics of one's associates. The nature of this choice is one way in which swift trust in temporary systems assumes a distinctive form.

When people in temporary systems entrust important things, such as reputation, to the care of others, they accept the possibility of ill will but usually do not expect it. This suggests that a closer look at the grounds of their expectations may give further clues regarding the shape of trust in temporary systems. We have already seen two possible reasons why people do not expect ill will even though they are vulnerable: implicit threats within the system (e.g., mutual fate control) and the prospect of future interaction. A third reason is role clarity. If people in temporary systems deal with one another more as roles than as individuals—which is likely because the system is built of strangers interacting to meet a deadline—then expectations should be more stable, less capricious, more standardized, and defined more in terms of tasks and specialties than personalities. Moreover, those roles are predicated, in turn, on a stable body of effective principles and practices. As Dawes (1994) noted,

> We trust engineers because we trust engineering and believe that engineers are trained to apply valid principles of engineering; moreover, we have evidence every day that these principles are valid when we observe airplanes flying. We trust doctors because we trust modern medicine, and we have evidence that it works when antibiotics and operations cure people. (p. 24)

What is ironic, if we set the issue of expectations up this way, is that people who enact roles (Fondas & Stewart, 1994) in an innovative, idiosyncratic manner could incur distrust. Because it is harder to draw boundaries around their apparent unpredictability, this could mean that this same unpredictability could extend to how they handle whatever one entrusts to them.

The scenario suggests that an increase in role clarity leads to a decrease in expected ill will, and an increase in trust presumes that roles in temporary systems are clear, that people act toward one another in terms of roles and have a clear understanding of others' roles. Change in any of these three variables should produce a change in trust. Again, we want to underline the general argument. What is often distinctive about temporary systems is that they form among people who represent specialties, and the relating in a temporary system is among roles as much as people. The content of any role description largely excludes expectations of "ill will" and highlights, instead, contributions that can legitimately be expected of the role occupant.

There are, of course, exceptions to this line of argument, and some of the most glaring ones occur in Hollywood. There is role clarity in film production, just as there is in other temporary systems, but with one big difference. The background expectancy among occupations within the industry is often one of expected ill will. Stories of hollow promises and backstabbing characterize the industry, as a conversation (paraphrased) with one Hollywood executive illustrates:

I have lots of friends in the industry, but these are friends because we have something to offer each other. I don't expect anyone to be my friend when things aren't going well or when I stop having something they want. I expect people to backstab me anytime and the only reason they don't is that I could backstab them back. (personal communication, 1993)

If people in Hollywood talk the talk of cooperation but walk the talk of competition and self-interest, then role clarity is a predictable mixture of hyperbole, euphemism, hollow promises, and side bets. Trust of sorts could still develop in this context, but it would require other grounds, such as network-based threats or prospects of future interactions, to mediate the background expectations of ill will. But trust based on mutual expectations of hype is likely to translate into distancing and hesitant interdependence, which means the temporary system is not really much of a system. Dubious credibility is especially likely when high expectations are institutionalized as part of the everyday rhetoric and uttered noncontingently in the context of budgets and deadlines by people who don't know what they are talking about (as one producer said, "Now, since this story is set in France, we should hear lots of French horns," Faulkner, 1983, p. 141). These are the realities of filmmaking.

More generally, expectations of ill will or good will form in temporary systems just as they do in other sites. Because there is insufficient time for these expectations to be built from scratch, they tend to be imported from other settings and imposed quickly in categorical forms. Expectations defined in terms of categories are especially likely because people have little time to size up one another (Fiske & Taylor, 1991). Categories invoked to speed up perception reflect roles, industry recipes, cultural cues, and occupational- and identity-based stereotypes. As Brewer (1981) has noted in her observations of the "minimal group paradigm," social categories, such as those derived from common membership in a social identity group,

can serve as a rule for defining the boundaries of low-risk interpersonal trust that bypasses the need for personal knowledge and the costs of negotiating reciprocity with individual others. As a consequence of shifting from the personal level to the social group level of identity, *the individual can adopt a sort of "depersonalized trust" based on category membership alone.* (p. 356, emphasis added)

These categorization effects appear to be quite robust, emerging even when the basis of social unit formation is arbitrary, transient, and objectively meaningless.

With some exceptions (such as in the film industry and stereotypes of some social identity groups), most social categories invoke expectations of good will rather than ill will from one's associates. Trust (or distrust) in temporary systems can develop swiftly because the expectations that are invoked most quickly tend to be general, task based, plausible, easy to confirm, and stable, all of which implies that the care of valuable things can be entrusted to individuals who seem to fit these institution-driven categories.

We see that the fate of trust in temporary systems is disproportionately influenced by the context in which the system forms. Context defines vulnerability and expectations. And context affords or withholds the resources that encourage or discourage people from managing their vulnerability, quickly, with overtures of trust. Trust, in response to vulnerability, is mediated by conditions of the labor pool from which the system forms, and trust in response to expectations of ill will is mediated by background expectancies consisting of categorical assumptions and interpretive frames (Zucker, 1986, pp. 57-59) derived from the context of the temporary system.

Before moving to other formulations of trust, we want to highlight the quality of interdependence that may be found in temporary systems. Swift trust in temporary systems seems to flow from the nature and magnitude of the interdependence in the setting and the implicit threat that stems from this interdependence. We suspect that a key variable in temporary systems is the degree to which interdependence is in fact high. So far we have assumed that interdependence is high, which means that vulnerability of any one person is high because that person's contribution and reputation are affected by others, as are their contributions and reputations.

In temporary systems, interdependence is crucial. But it should not be extreme. Variations in interdependence affect the extent to which trust is a big deal. It is our hunch that swift trust occurs when the demands of interdependence are in line with the importance of what is being entrusted and the probability that others will care for what is entrusted with good will. There are no certainties anywhere in these calculations, only implicit probabilities. Modest interdependence leaves actors with sufficient control over their contributions, which means the actors are only moderately vulnerable to associates who probably will not take advantage of those vulnerabilities. That's enough to trigger trust. And to do so quickly. If modest dependence is sufficient, then vulnerability and expectations also will be manageable, as will the amount of trust that must be initiated to tie the setting together.

Trust and Uncertainty

A second portrait of trust is found in Gambetta (1988), who argues that

trusting a person means believing that when offered the chance, he or she is not likely to behave in a way that is damaging to us, and trust will *typically* be relevant when at least one party is free to disappoint the other, free enough to avoid a risky relationship, *and* constrained enough to consider that relationship an attractive option. (p. 219)

For Gambetta, trust is an issue of monitoring, as it often is for economists and game theorists:

> Trust (or, symmetrically, distrust) is a particular level of the subjective probability with which an agent assesses that another agent or group of agents will perform a particular action, both *before* he can monitor such action (or independently of his capacity ever to be able to monitor it) *and* in a context in which it affects his own action. (p. 217)

Trust involves an estimation about whether the trustee will do something beneficial or detrimental before the truster can really know for sure. And the estimate itself is focused. It is a

> threshold point, located on a probabilistic distribution of more general expectations [expectations expressing such things as the reputation of others], which can take a number of values suspended between complete distrust (0) and complete trust (1), and which is centered [*sic*] around a mid-point (0.50) of uncertainty. (p. 218)

Trust, in other words, is coincident with uncertainty. And uncertainty is coincident with temporary structures enacted to deal with transient events singled out from ongoing change. The uncertainty tends to focus on the ease with which others can disappoint our expectations.

> If other people's actions were heavily constrained, the role of trust in governing our decisions would be proportionately smaller, for the more limited people's freedom, the more restricted the field of actions in which we are required to guess *ex ante* the probability of their performing them. (Gambetta, 1988, p. 219)

A ruler of a slave society, for example, only has to trust that slaves are not going to commit mass suicide. As coercion and power diminish from this point, there are more ways in which trustees can disappoint. As the number of different ways in which trustees can disappoint increases (i.e., their freedom of action increases), so too should the probability that one or more of these ways could be activated immediately (e.g., an actor may disappoint in numerous ways—by walking off the movie set, through inattention to the director's suggestions, failure to follow the producer's timetable, or failure to say the writer's scripted lines). Disappointments take varying spans of time to develop. If there is a preponderance of swift, immediate disappointments that could unfold in a relationship, then we would expect to find a more rapid development of trust (or distrust). What we would not expect to see is a postponement of choices involving trust. The open field of actions does not allow that luxury.

Gambetta contributes a simple but important insight to our emerging view of swift trust and temporary systems. Uncertainty on matters of trust is highest when there is a 50-50 chance ("a midpoint of uncertainty") that an unmonitored person will take advantage of our trust. This suggests at least two things. First, it suggests that people should be motivated to avoid the uncertainty of a .5 probability of harm, because this requires monitoring that uses up valuable information-processing capability (Brehmer, 1991, p. 196). In a temporary system with deadlines and specific goals, anything that subtracts from task performance, such as distracted attention, should be a glaring threat. Faced with high uncertainty, people should be inclined either toward complete trust (1.0) or complete distrust (.0), both of which provide more certainty and use up less attention in monitoring. Swift trust, then, might occur when uncertainty is high and unacceptable and when some cues in the setting favor an interpretation of the other as trustworthy rather than as untrustworthy. That is, in an effort to avoid uncertainty, the person is likely to be more trusting or more distrusting than the data warrant, simply in the interest of reducing uncertainty and getting on with the task. Such acts reflect the necessary willingness to suspend doubt. In this way, temporary systems may be suggestible systems.

A second implication of Gambetta's analysis is that if people find it hard to resolve uncertainty quickly with a move toward either unwarranted trust or unwarranted distrust, then we would expect to see more idiosyncratic resolutions of trust uncertainty consistent with personality predispositions and a priori implicit theories of trust. There is widespread agreement that when faced with uncertainty and weak situations, people respond dispositionally. In particular, we would expect that a priori tendencies toward high or low trust (Rotter, 1980) would have a strong impact in determining the pattern of trust to be observed in a temporary system, especially when uncertainty is high. Furthermore, implicit theories of trust should exert more influence. Here we take our lead from Good (1988, p. 33), who argued that "trust is based on an individual's theory as to how another person will perform on some future occasion, as a function of that target person's current and previous claims, either implicit or explicit, as to how they will behave." As uncertainty increases, not only should implicit theories, predispositions, and categorical assumptions be more influential, but people should try more urgently to confirm them.

Thus, to understand swift trust in temporary systems is to appreciate the fact that relative strangers are uncertain caretakers of one's goods, especially when opportunities for early and continuous monitoring of their actions are negligible. To reduce this uncertainty, people fall back on predispositions, categorical assumptions, and implicit theories to move them toward the greater certainty of clear trust or clear distrust. Trust that flows from dispositions, assumptions, and theories is swift because to some extent it occurs independent of the object of perception. An individual's associates in a temporary system function essentially as a pretext to access over-learned tendencies and cognitive structures that provide guidelines for trust or mistrust.

Trust and Risk

The final suggestion of how to conceptualize trust, and by extension how to conceptualize swift trust, is Luhmann's (1988) rich distinction between confidence and trust. Luhmann argues that trust and confidence are different ways of asserting expectations that may lapse into disappointment. Trust and confidence are also different ways in which people gain a sense of self-assurance, or in Gambetta's terms, act in the face of uncertainty.

For Luhmann, trust is about risk, and risk is about the choice to expose oneself to a situation where the possible damage may be greater than the advantage that is sought (p. 98). This stipulation is crucial because, without it, whatever risks one faces are within the acceptable limits of rational choice, and trust plays no part in the decision to proceed. Luhmann alerts us to look more closely at risk in temporary systems.

The close relationship between trust and systems we are trying to work out is anticipated by Luhmann's (1988) observation that "a system requires trust as an input condition in order to stimulate supportive activities in situations of uncertainty or risk" (p. 103). Trust, which is a way people assert expectations, presupposes a situation of risk and the possibility of disappointment, which depends in part on our own previous behavior and choices. Luhmann pulls these strands together this way: Trust "requires a previous engagement on your part. It presupposes a situation of risk." You may or may not buy a used car that turns out to be a "lemon." You may or may not hire a baby-sitter for the evening and leave him or her unsupervised in your apartment; he or she may be a "lemon." You can avoid taking the risk, but only if you are willing to waive the associated advantages. You do not depend on trusting relations in the same way you depend on confidence, but trust also can be a matter of routine and normal behavior. The distinction between confidence and trust thus depends on perception and attribution. If you do not consider alternatives (every morning you leave the house without a weapon!), you are in a situation of confidence. If you choose one action in preference to others in spite of the possibility of being disappointed by the actions of others, you define the situation as one of trust. In the case of confidence, you will react to disappointment by external attribution and alienation. In the case of trust, you will have to consider an internal attribution and eventually regret your trusting choice (pp. 97-98). Situations of confidence can turn into situations of trust if it becomes possible to avoid the relationship (p. 98), and trust can change into confidence if people lose their ability to influence the relationship. Trust, therefore, "is an attitude that allows for risk-taking decisions" (p. 103). Without trust, risk is avoided, innovative activities dry up, only routine actions are available for retrospective sensemaking, and uncertainty remains unresolved.

These observations about trust, in general, when adapted for temporary systems, alert us to several issues. To understand trust in temporary systems, one should not overrely on the fact that such systems are short-lived, transient, and fleeting. To do so is to miss the equally important point that in a temporary system, everything is risked, every time. It is rare for risks to be small and for disappointments to be a mere nuisance. Temporary systems form in the context of large risks where the damage incurred could outrun the advantages gained. Trust, rather than rational calculation, is necessary to deal with this imbalance. In film production, for example, the exact nuance needed from an actor may be given only once. If it is missed by the person running the camera, it is missed forever. Sidney Pollack noted that because movies are shot out of sequence, only the director knows where the emotional tone of the picture has to be at the moment any scene is shot. This is what creates the high stakes in the temporary system of film production. Nicholas Kent (1991, p. 170), citing a Pollack remark, shows how small moments can be monumental in filmmaking:

> "In film, as opposed to theater, an actor doesn't have to understand at all how they did what they did or why they have to do what they do. You just have to do it once and the camera has to be rolling." The tragedy [for Pollack] is seeing an actor give him what he wants before he can capture the moment on film.

What all of this has to do with trust is that the potential for damaged reputations and failed investments is substantial in temporary systems devoted to filmmaking. This in turn suggests that something more than rational choice is necessary for success in such a system. That something more is trust—trust in the cinematographer, the actor's willingness to take direction, and the executives staying out of the editing suite while the film is being cut.

The more general point we want to make is that "temporary" does not mean "trivial." Typically, the formation of a temporary system signals the un-availability of any existing structure to handle what has become a significant but nonroutine issue that needs a novel set of specialists who can meet a deadline. Failure to handle the issue means big losses for the people who authorize the system and the people who run it. In Luhmann's terminology, the magnitude of potential damage is greater than the potential gain. So trust is an issue right from the start. The moment the system is envisioned, assessments of potential damage figure into its design: "Unless the system is formed things will get worse, but even if it is formed, there are no guarantees that we'll be better off" (Luhmann, 1988, p. 103). The system is formed in spite of these threats, which is itself an exercise of trust because the output could turn out to be a "lemon." The temporary system itself must comprise trust because it faces a future of potential disappointments and unstable collaboration among near strangers.

Luhmann's ideas about risk also point to a different aspect of temporary systems—namely, their preoccupation with action. Swift trust may be a by-product of a highly active, proactive, enthusiastic, generative style of action. This possibility comes about because risks, choices, actions, and trust have an unusual, self-reinforcing character, as suggested earlier. Luhmann puts it this way:

> Trust is based on a circular relation between risk and action, both being com-
> plementary requirements. Action defines itself in relation to a particular risk as
> external (future) possibility, although risk at the same time is inherent in action
> and exists only if the actor chooses to incur the chance of unfortunate consequen-
> ces and to trust. (1988, p. 100)

To act one's way into an unknown future is to sharpen the element of risk in that projected action, which gives character to the action and substance to the risk. Each creates the necessity for trust, the grounds to validate it, and the potential for invalidation and disappointment. All of this gets triggered basically because forceful action can never guarantee a specific outcome. That's the risk that is made tolerable by trust.

Our point is simply that as action becomes more forceful, the qualities of risk associated with that action become clearer, which then clarifies the action even more and adds to its forcefulness, which further sharpens perceptions of risk, and so on. As these "complementary requirements" build on one another, the person becomes more willing to incur the chance of unfortunate conse-quences and to trust. The more forceful the action, the greater the willingness to trust and the more rapidly does trust develop. Hence, temporary systems that are high in their capability to generate activity and whose cultures value the generation of activity could, by virtue of these tendencies, also heighten perceptions of risk, the willingness to take risks, and the willingness to trust.

Interweaving Trust
and the Temporary

There is no shortage of claims that trust is indispensable to social life. Simmel (1978) is representative:

Without the general trust that people have in each other, society itself would disintegrate, for very few relationships are based entirely upon what is known with certainty about another person, and very few relationships would endure if trust were not as strong as, or stronger than, rational proof or personal observation. (pp. 178-179)

Relative to such abundant and strong claims about the importance of trust, our theories about it remain few and weak. As we said at the beginning of this chapter, our interest here is in the increasingly common collective known as a temporary system in which trust appears to flourish even though its usual antecedents seem to be missing. Having taken a closer look at properties of temporary systems and trust, we feel that trust does appear in temporary systems, but it does so in response to a different set of antecedents than investigators usually examine. Furthermore, because swift trust forms in response to a different set of antecedents, its development is also as different as is its effect on outcomes.

An inquiry into swift trust in temporary systems starts with propositions such as the following ones, which restate themes introduced earlier:

Proposition 1. The smaller the labor pool or network from which personnel in a temporary system are drawn, the more vulnerable the people who are drawn; the stronger the grounds for not expecting harmful behavior, the more rapidly will trust develop among people. The presumption here is that people in a small labor pool have a higher chance of interacting with one another again in the future, which means their reputations as competent or incompetent people whom others can trust or distrust will follow them and shape these future contacts. Reputations are implicitly threatened in any given project to the extent that chances of future interaction increase. In Axelrodian (Axelrod, 1984) terms, the "shadow of the future looms larger" in such groups. However, people in overlapping networks or networks of weak ties may face more reputational vulnerability because a damaged reputation would disseminate across a wider group of people.

Proposition 2. Role-based interaction leads to more rapid development of trust than does person-based interaction. This presumes that role expectations tend to be more stable, less capricious, more standardized, and defined more in terms of tasks and specialties, all of which diminish the anticipation of ill will and help reinforce and sharpen expectations.

Proposition 3. Inconsistent role behavior and "blurring" of roles will lead to a slower build of trust. This presumes that role blurring heightens uncertainty. People who exhibit inconsistent role behavior raise questions about what they will do with whatever is entrusted to them. Attempts to answer these questions slow the development of trust.

Proposition 4. People under time pressure in temporary systems make greater use of category-driven information processing, emphasizing speed and confirmation rather than evidence-driven information processing that is focused on accuracy. The presumption here is that interpersonal perception in temporary systems is subject to the same patterns in a speed-accuracy tradeoff as is perception in other kinds of systems. The time-limited nature of a temporary system tends to be reflected in perceptual tradeoffs that favor speed.

Proposition 5. Category-driven information processing in temporary systems is dominated by institutional categories that are made salient by the context in which the systems form. The presumption here is that categories imported to accelerate interpersonal perception disproportionately reflect local organizational culture, industry recipes, and cultural identity-based stereotypes. These categories affect expectations of good will or ill will and encourage swift trust or swift distrust. In some cases, trust may develop even more swiftly when imported categories also produce behavioral confirmation. When this happens, not only do perceivers look for data that confirm their initial categorization, but their behavior itself increases the likelihood that the target will behave in the manner anticipated. This combination of selective perception and behavioral confirmation produces data relevant to trust more quickly, which means trust itself is enacted sooner.

Proposition 6. Greater reliance on category-driven information processing in temporary systems, with its attendant pressure for confirmation, leads to a faster reduction of the uncertainty associated with trust but to a higher risk that subsequent action will disconfirm the trust and produce damage. The presumption here is that swift trust, especially in response to category-driven perception, overlooks a great deal. Although these oversights leave room for behavioral confirmation and self-fulfilling prophecies, they also allow for actions that disrupt trust (Zucker, 1986, p. 59) and for errors in misplaced trust.

Proposition 7. Swift trust is more likely at moderate levels of interdependence than at either higher or lower levels. The presumption here is that moderate interdependence creates moderate vulnerability, which can be handled with the moderately strong expectations of good will that flow from placement of a trustee in a salient institutional category. People who fit salient categories are to be trusted more so as the degree of trust needed is modest.

At higher levels of interdependence, conformity of action with expectations based on general categories alone is too little data for too high stakes. This combination represents a greater amount of perceived vulnerability than the data can address. Trust will be shaky rather than solid, slow rather than swift, and actions will be tentative rather than firm.

Although this sampler of propositions suggests something of the mind-set necessary to interweave trust and the temporary, it does not direct sufficient attention toward what we regard as a critical ingredient in the emergence and maintenance of swift trust in many temporary groups: the role of the contractor. Below, we focus briefly on the contractor and revisit this role in subsequent sections.

The Role of the Contractor in Temporary Systems

In discussing the teamwork necessary for film production crews to function productively, Kawin (1992) notes the following about the director:

> Of all the people on the set, the director is the one who ought—who needs—to respect the contributions of every member of the production team. The director provides artistic and practical guidance—in a word, *direction*—for the project. The director's guiding vision can inspire the crew, can give them the sense that they are all working together on a good and worthwhile picture, not just putting in their time and building up their résumés. When a studio executive says "Trust me," there may be something in the voice that suggests piranha in the swimming pool. When a director says "It'll work" and it doesn't—when a stunt kills an actor, to take an extreme example—trust can be forfeited permanently. Most people know not to trust executives who say "Trust me," just as it is difficult to believe someone who keeps saying "To tell you the truth. . . ." But on the set, where time is money, nerves may be frayed, and reputations are at stake, the director and the heads of the production categories must be able to be trusted. (pp. 403-404)

Faulkner (1983) comes at the same setting from the other side when he remarks that the conflicts and uncertainties of filmmaking "are locked into a short-term contracting arrangement which places the filmmaker in a position of dependence on outsiders—freelance specialists—with the attendant risk of having to trust the professional judgments and craft instincts of these employees" (p. 121). Each party in filmmaking is dependent on the other, which creates vulnerability, uncertainty, and risk. The trust necessary to act in the face of vulnerability will be there quickly, depending on the perceptual categories that are imported for sizing up one another and the probability for good or ill will associated with the category. The reputation of the contractor and the expectation of good will on his or her part may be all that is necessary to create the general background expectation of good will, independent of information about the other participants.

Swift Trust: Fragile or Resilient?

An analysis that presumes swift trust plays a central role in the life of the temporary group should consider whether such trust is fragile or resilient. To be efficacious, swift trust should be resilient enough to survive those moments and incidents that occur during the life of a temporary group and call into question or threaten to disrupt trust. At the same time, swift trust must not be so resilient as to lead individuals to trust beyond the point where doing so is adaptive or sensible.

Researchers have generally argued that different forms of trust vary considerably in their fragility and resilience. For example, the trust associated with close personal relationships has generally been characterized as a "thick" form of trust that is relatively resilient and durable: Once in place, it is not easily disrupted, and once shattered, it is not easily restored (cf. Janoff-Bulman, 1992; Putnam, 1992). Other forms of trust, in contrast, have been characterized as fragile or "thin" because they are conferred gingerly and withdrawn readily. One might observe this kind of trust in a newly formed exchange relation or collaboration: Expectations are high, but so are reservations. One foot is in the water, but the other is braced firmly on solid ground.

The question of the thickness or thinness of trust that is appropriate in a given social or organizational context raises difficult and also revealing questions about how individuals initially calibrate and update their expectations about others' trustworthiness. With respect to temporary systems, this entails deciding, among other things, when there is a lesson to be learned from a specific experience with another group member and when there isn't. In other words, it includes knowing or deciding when one should suspend or rescind further trust and when one should put aside one's doubts for another day.

Most conceptions of how trust gets developed and updated have emphasized that trust is a history-dependent process (Lindskold, 1978; Rotter, 1980) in which individuals operate like Bayesian statisticians drawing inferences based on relevant but limited samples of experience. Boyle and Bonacich's (1970) characterization is typical: Individuals' "expectations about trustworthy or cooperative behaviors will change in the direction of experience and to a degree proportional to the difference between this experience and the initial expectations applied to them" (p. 130). According to such conceptions, trust builds incrementally and accumulates.

Such perspectives imply that, to the extent it entails expectations about the possible benefits of collaboration, along with attendant fears about vulnerability and exploitation, swift trust should thicken or thin as history unfolds. However, as noted earlier, temporary groups typically lack the requisite history on which such incremental and accumulative confidence-building measures are predicated. There is, quite literally, neither enough time nor opportunity in a temporary group for the sort of experience necessary for thicker forms of trust to emerge. It may be useful to consider, therefore, how history—or, more accurately, substitutes or proxies for history—might contribute to the development of trust in temporary systems.

There is substantial evidence that the "mere" process of group formation alone may provide an initial foundation for the emergence of a protean sort of swift trust. As suggested earlier, even when the basis for group formation appears arbitrary, a presumptive, depersonalized form of trust may emerge (Brewer, 1981).

The existence of such cognitive bases for conferring trust on other group members is augmented, of course, by other psychological mechanisms that reduce perceptions of vulnerability as well as expectations of disappointment in groups. First, and quite obvious, is the simple fact that the formation of a temporary group is neither arbitrary nor meaningless. Individuals enter such groups with a strong and reasonable presumption that the boundary that defines inclusion or exclusion is informative. Inclusion is presumed to imply selectivity on the part of the contractor, and these judgments, in turn, are presumed to be predicated on sensible and more or less conscious criteria.

Here, the credibility of the contractor—in terms of his or her reputation for creating and composing successful temporary groups—serves as a useful substitute for interpersonal history. For example, certain directors such as Woody Allen, John Cassavettes, and Francis Ford Coppola have established strong reputations for assembling remarkable and successful ensemble casts and crews. Based on such reputations, individual actors at the margin are often willing to "sign on" to their films, knowing very little about the concrete details of their projects. They simply trust things to work out.

We suspect further that, on top of whatever reputational capital such directors enjoy, they are skillful at conveying the criteria for inclusion and its legitimacy. In putting together a film crew for the making of *House of Games,* David Mamet chose a cast and crew that consisted only of close friends. Doing so allowed each member of the group to focus on the task at hand and not worry about problems of trust. "That energy (small or large, but inevitable)," he noted, "that is devoted to establishing bona fides in an artistic collaboration between strangers ('How much does this other guy know? Can I trust him, is he going to hurt me?') was in our movie devoted to other things" (cited in Kent, 1991, p. 164). By using such criteria—and using them explicitly—the contractor solves his or her trust dilemma. They also go a long way toward solving the trust dilemma that other group members confront when deciding whether to join a temporary group.

Other psychological mechanisms may help reduce initial perceptions of vulnerability, allowing swift trust to get a toehold. Recent research on positive illusions (Taylor & Brown, 1988), for example, identifies a number of psychological mechanisms that presuppose individuals toward trusting their environments and their experiences. In particular, research on illusions of control and perceived invulnerability suggests that most individuals have in place an array of cognitive strategies that help them maintain confidence that they will be masters rather than victims of their experience. Along similar lines, research on unrealistic optimism (Weinstein, 1980) has shown that individuals often expect their own futures to be significantly better and brighter than others. Even when they view the world as a place in which bad things might happen, they underestimate the likelihood such things will happen to them. Thus, even in a world in which they know trust can be violated, they tend, all else equal, to assume that others will be disappointed and not themselves (cf. Janoff-Bulman, 1992).

Recent research further suggests that these illusions of control, invulnerability, and optimism extend to individuals within group settings. Evidence suggests that individuals enter groups expecting better things to happen to them compared to the average group member. Moreover, they often feel, *ex post,* that they did better and got more from their participation compared to the average other group member (see Paulus, Dzindolet, Poletes, & Camacho, 1993; Polzer, Kramer, & Neale, 1993; Schlenker, Soraci, & McCarthy, 1976). These attributional tendencies should contribute to the resilience of swift trust in a temporary group.

There is also an important sense in which evidence of the reasonableness and appropriateness of swift trust (in terms of positive expectation of benefits and reduced risks from participation) is provided by the actions of the temporary group itself. In a temporary group, people often act *as if* trust were in place. And, because trust behaviors are enacted without hesitation, reciprocally and collectively, they may provide what Cialdini (1993) has termed *social proof* that a particular interpretation of reality is correct. Thus, by observing others acting in a trusting manner, individuals can infer that such a stance is neither foolish nor naive. In this respect, each individual enactment of swift trust in the group, no matter how small, contributes to the collective perception that swift trust is reasonable. In this sense, the individuals in the temporary group, especially early in its life, when expectations are still fragile and forming, resemble the bystanders at the scene of an emergency who look around at the impassive faces of other bystanders and decide not to act because the others act as if there is no emergency (Darley & Latane, 1968). This cognitive process serves as another trigger to self-fulfilling cycles that further increase the resiliency of swift trust.

These psychological orientations and social mechanisms are well-known and do not provide special insight into the dynamics of swift trust in temporary systems, other than to suggest the readiness with which individuals might be predisposed toward conferring trust swiftly, on relatively minimal grounds, and setting off cycles that build trust. There are, however, other bases for swift trust.

First, although the members of a temporary group may lack history with respect to previous contact with each other, there is a sense in which the temporary group itself is not without history. As suggested earlier, there is a collective presumption that each member's inclusion in the group is predicated on a rich and relevant history. Each member assumes that the contractor has either had the requisite experience with others, or, at the very least, that he or she has "asked around" and "checked them out." Thus, trust in the contractor's presumed care in composing the temporary group serves as a proxy for individual knowledge or experience with others' reliability or competence. In this sense, the relevant history of the temporary group resides outside the group: It is tacitly understood by all group members that the necessary experience and learning were gained elsewhere but are nonetheless in place and do not need to be verified or negotiated.

In this regard, the contractor's reputation for putting together the "right kind" of group to get the work of the temporary group done is similar in function to the sorts of institutional mechanisms, such as board certifications and professional degrees, that enhance trust in various professional encounters (Zucker, 1986). For example, we trust board-certified medical specialists because certification signals professional competence, as judged by other competent specialists. Such reputational proxies are quite effective in professional encounters and within industries such as filmmaking in that individuals are often willing to commit to joining a temporary group, knowing very little about what they are getting into and relying only on the judgment of another professional.[4]

Hedges also play an important role in the development and maintenance of swift trust. The aim of a hedge is to reduce the perceived risks and vulnerabilities of trust by reducing interdependence and thus its perceived costs. Hedges guard against or minimize the dangers of misplaced trust, when, in Baier's terms, the goods are of high value. Hedges imply an attitude that is somewhat equivocal: One trusts the other, but not completely. The existence of a hedge allows one to enter into a risky activity because the "worst-case" outcome is anticipated and covered. In this respect, hedges function much like the Best Alternative to a Negotiated Agreement (BATNA) in a negotiation. BATNAs free negotiators to press their case because they reduce the perceived downside should bargaining fail. The "backup" job offer has the same liberating effect in a job interview when it comes to pressing one demand's for a better salary.[5]

As a cognitive process, hedging entails the creation of psychological "fail-safe" mechanisms that provide reassurance, reducing dependence and vulnerability to a moderate level. The posture of hedging is reflected in Weick and Roberts's (1993) observation, based on their research on accidents in flight operations off nuclear carriers, that people who avoid accidents in such situations live by the credo, "Never get into anything without making sure you have a way out" (p. 640). Having a way out allows one to act in a trusting manner because there is a way out. A simple example illustrates this approach: Most people would be very reluctant to trust someone with the sole copy of a manuscript. Creating a backup of the manuscript as a hedge enables one to trust others, even others with whom people have had little or no prior experience. Hedges imply an orientation that resembles the attitude of wisdom described by Meacham (1983) as a stance of simultaneously believing and doubting, understanding and questioning.

This initial trusting behavior can set off a familiar cycle in which trust becomes mutual and reinforcing: Trust allows one to engage in certain behaviors, and these behaviors, in turn, reinforce and strengthen members' trust in each other. There is, of course, a functional irony here in that hedges, which represent acts of partial distrust, allow cycles that enact and reinforce trust within groups to get started.

Although we view hedges as contributing significantly to the resilience of swift trust, we should note that the process of hedging is not without its own risks and disadvantages. First, if others discover that what they initially believed was an act of trust was, in actuality, predicated on a hedge or an act of partial distrust, the self-reinforcing cycle we described earlier may be undermined. In this respect, contractors and others who acquire a reputation for playing it *too* safe by covering all of their bases, including always having a backup, may not inspire much trust at all. Second, having a hedge may sometimes reduce or diminish commitment to the group. When the going gets a little rough, those with attractive alternatives may decide to act on them and go elsewhere. Hedged trust may be abandoned too readily precisely because it *can* be abandoned. This is the intuition behind behavioral self-management strategies that posit that decision makers who want to maximize their commitment to a course of action should "burn their bridges" so that retreat from commitment is not possible (see Schelling, 1984).

Additionally, hedges may contribute to a false sense of invulnerability and security by fostering an exaggerated confidence in one's ability to manage whatever problems are encountered during the life of the temporary group. If perceived risk and vulnerability decrease sufficiently, according to Luhmann, one becomes confident (and sometimes overconfident) and need not rely on trust. As Steven Bach's (1985) account of the making of the film *Heaven's Gate* documents, decision makers who *think* they have control over all of their risks and vulnerabilities may fail to protect themselves or question their confidence when it would be appropriate. Steven Bach and David Field, studio executives, continually underestimated their dependence on director Michael Cimino, thinking they could, at any time, call his bluff. They therefore felt inappropriately secure because they failed to realize the full extent to which they were, in fact, unable to control Cimino. Thus, their *perceived* hedge was not really a hedge at all.

Another potential danger associated with hedging is perhaps less obvious. The process of creating hedges requires anticipatory ruminations about things that might go wrong. Although intended as an adaptive form of preemptive pessimism (cf. Norem & Cantor, 1986), there is evidence that the cognitive strategy of engaging in such "worse-case" thinking can lead to unintended effects, such as unrealistically diminished expectations (e.g., see Kramer, 1994; Kramer, Meyerson, & Davis, 1990).

We have described several cognitive and social processes that contribute to the development of swift trust. The question of the fragility or resilience of swift trust also entails, however, questions about how trust is sustained throughout the life of the temporary group. Groups that have clear expectations and stable role systems would seem less vulnerable to problems of disruption of trust than those lacking such clarity and stability. However, by their very nature, the relatively "thin" expectations and role systems associated with the temporary group almost inevitably must lapse or break down on occasion. In temporary groups, such as filmmaking groups on location, many things happen or fail to happen, and they do so quickly and often. For this reason, we suspect that collective trust may be more resilient within those temporary groups in which members are skilled in the art and *attitude* of improvisation. The attitude of improvisation requires careful attention, listening, and mutual respect. In other words, truly competent role performance of the sort we have associated with behavior in temporary groups often entails doing something different when something different has to be done.

Although our argument here may seem somewhat tautological (i.e., swift trust allows for improvisation, which in turn predicts swift trust), our observation may be more revealing of a double interact than faulty logic. As Putnam (1992) noted, trust not only "lubricates cooperation," but "cooperation itself breeds trust" (p. 171). This "steady accumulation of social capital" plays a central role in the maintenance of collective trust.

Temporary systems engaged in filmmaking illustrate this point nicely. The ability of the director, cinematographer, lighting technicians, and others to improvise inspires confidence that unexpected but unavoidable setbacks, difficulties, and crises are surmountable and survivable. Examples of this dynamic abound in filmmaking lore, and Robert Altman, Francis Ford Coppola, and Steve Spielberg are among those reputed to have especially keen improvisational skills (and, equally important, skill at eliciting improvisations from others when needed!). For example, during the filming of *Raiders of the*

Lost Ark, director Steven Spielberg had planned a marvelous fight scene between the whip-wielding Indiana Jones (played by Harrison Ford) and an Arabian swordsman (recounted in Taylor, 1992). He had carefully scripted this scene to be the best sword fight ever, "the most definitive whip versus sword fight in cinematic history" (p. 107). When the time came to shoot the scene on location in Tunisia, both Spielberg and Ford were suffering from heat exhaustion. In addition, Ford had developed gastroenteritis and was not up to the arduous physical demands of the proposed scene. On the spot, they improvised a scene in which Indiana Jones, confronted by the swordsman, simply pulls out his gun and shoots the swordsman. What was to become one of the most memorable scenes in the film was entirely improvised. The ability and *willingness* of the director to retreat from his original vision and discover a superior one, we suggest, can inspire a powerful kind of collective trust that things will work out, especially when they have to.

Another feature of temporary groups, we argue, may contribute to the maintenance of swift trust—a structural feature that, a priori, one might argue would hinder it. This is the constrained time a temporary group has to do its work. The pace at which activity unfolds in many temporary groups and the required focus of attention on the task at hand may obviate the chance for certain kinds of dysfunctional group dynamics to occur. Because time is short and concentration is crucial, there may be less opportunity in temporary groups for the kinds of corrosive interpersonal and group dynamics that often plague more enduring groups. All of the messy things that go along with "thicker" interpersonal relationships (conflicts, jealousy, misunderstandings, hurt feelings, revenge fantasies, and pursuit of hidden agendas) have less opportunity to surface and play themselves out in the life cycle of temporary social systems. There is simply not enough time for things to go wrong. In contrast, groups that have more time for their tasks also have more time to develop complex relations that could go sour. Thus, the bounded life of the temporary group may make the mind concentrate on the task at hand and thereby keep interpersonal relations out of trouble.

Because swift trust is often centered around and bounded by trust in each individual's competent and faithful enactment of a critical *role,* out-of-role behavior can breed distrust. Individuals' expectations surrounding their own and others' behavior in temporary groups, as we noted earlier, are predicated on what Barber (1983) has characterized as a form of fiduciary trust. The "expectation of technically competent role performance for those involved with us in social relationships and systems," he observes, reflects an "expectation that partners in interaction will carry out their duties" (p. 9). In this sense, the act of conferring swift trust entails rendering judgments more about other individuals' professionalism than their character. Deviations from or violations of group norms and presumptions about competent role behavior call into question the "professionalism" of the transgressor. Not only are they noted and frowned on, but they are likely to be punished.

Again, we suspect the contractor may play an important role here in being not only the architect and facilitator of swift trust but also its centurion. In talking about the highly effective and cohesive film production team he had put together, Alan Ladd, Jr. noted, "When it's your money, and someone isn't performing, you get rid of them, no matter how much you like them; you've got a responsibility to others, including yourself, and you can't afford to let a ship sink because one person can't pull his or her weight" (quoted in Barsh, 1982, p. 19). A contractor must be cooperative and forgiving but also provocable (Axelrod, 1984).

The net result of all of this is that, in an odd sort of way, the very lack of time, along with the collective impatience for lapses in role performance it necessitates, may work in favor of the temporary group's mission. Although such factors may hinder the development of thicker forms of trust, they may sustain swift trust.

As we have tried to suggest in this section, the development and maintenance of trust in temporary groups depend on a variety of subtle psychological processes and social mechanisms. To the extent that such factors operate convergently, swift trust is overly determined. In this regard, swift trust may be subtle, but it also may be rather resilient.

Conclusion

Our analysis suggests a rather rich and complex phenomenology associated with trust in temporary systems. In closing, we should note that what may be most distinctive about swift trust in temporary systems is that it is not so much an interpersonal form as it is a cognitive and action form. Trust work, in the preceding analyses, largely was tied to the level of interdependence. We suggested that swift trust is most likely when interdependence is kept modest through a combination of distancing, adaptability, resilience, interacting with roles rather than personalities, and viewing one's participation as partly voluntary (trust) and partly involuntary (confidence). In short, swift trust is less about relating than *doing*.

The portrait we have drawn of swift trust in temporary systems may be a little too "cool" for some people's taste. There is less emphasis on feeling, commitment, and exchange and more on action, cognition, the nature of the network and labor pool, and avoidance of personal disclosure, contextual cues, modest dependency, and heavy absorption in the task. That's what seems to give swift trust its distinctive quality. Swift trust is not surrender. But neither is it calculated aloofness. Instead, it is artful making do with a modest set of general cues from which inferences are drawn about how people might care for what we entrust to them. Those inferences are driven by generic features of the setting rather than by personalities or interpersonal relations. In this sense, swift trust is a pragmatic strategy for dealing with the uncertainties generated by a complex system concocted to perform a complex, interdependent task using the specialized skills of relative strangers. Given those complexities, unless one trusts quickly, one may never trust at all.

Ultimately, of course, knowing when to confer trust quickly, and when to withhold or withdraw it, may be crucial to the success of the temporary system.

Notes

1. So much so that Robert Cialdini (personal communication, 1994) suggested that the form of trust-like behavior observed in temporary groups might more accurately be characterized as a sort of pseudo-trust or "trustoid" behavior. This is a provocative suggestion. However, for reasons that will become more obvious as our analysis unfolds, we regard trust in temporary groups as a very real form of trust and not merely trust-like.

2. Somewhat unexpected as a characteristic of such systems is the high probability that experience in temporary systems may *not* promote professional growth and learning and may, in fact, slow career progress. Because people are selected to apply their special knowledge to a specific problem, they tend to be selected "for their current capabilities rather than for any learning value the assignment may have for them" (Goodman & Goodman, 1976, p. 496). Repetition of what people already know is especially likely when the temporary system functions with a structure of clarified roles in which specialties interact with specialties. This contrasts with a system in which people interact, at least for some portion of the time, on the basis of blurred roles or changing expectations. High role clarity and stability of expectations are associated with an adequate performance that tends to be low on innovation and individual learning. A move toward more blurred roles, as when members interact in a manner more like Likert's participative system four (Goodman, 1981, pp. 7, 135; Goodman & Goodman, 1976, pp. 499-500), produces more innovation and learning.

3. There are a variety of spontaneous or "ephemeral" organizations and groups, such as improvisational jazz ensembles or pick-up basketball teams, in which swift trust seems to play an important role (Eisenberg, 1990; Lanzara, 1983; Weick, 1990; Weick & Roberts, 1993). However, we wish to focus in this chapter on temporary groups whose products or outputs are more consequential.

4. There is irony and danger here. As March (1994) notes, those who rise to positions of leadership, such as contractors, may do so on a history of accidental successes that, although giving themselves and others a sense of confidence, is predicated at best on shaky evidence and ambiguous performance.

5. There is an important asymmetry here, of course, in that most group members probably prefer that they have good alternatives in place themselves while preferring that others *don't*. They want others to have no choice but be *really* committed, and they prefer to hedge our own bets.

References

Axelrod, R. (1984). *The evolution of cooperation*. New York: Basic Books.

Bach, S. (1985). *Final cut: Dreams and disaster in the making of* Heaven's Gate. Beverly Hills, CA: Sage.

Baier, A. (1985). *Postures of the mind*. Minneapolis: University of Minnesota.

Baier, A. (1986). Trust and antitrust. *Ethics, 96,* 231-260.

Barber, B. (1983). *The logic and limits of trust*. New Brunswick, NJ: Rutgers University Press.

Barsh, J. (1982). *The Ladd company* (Harvard Business School Case 9-482-122). Boston: Harvard Business School Press.

Boyle, R., & Bonacich, P. (1970). The development of trust and mistrust in mixed-motive games. *Sociometry, 33,* 123-139.

Brehmer, B. (1991). Modern information technology: Timescales and distributed decision making. In J. Rasmussen, B. Brehmer, & J. Leplot (Eds.), *Distributed decision making: Cognitive models for cooperative work* (pp. 193-200). Chichester, UK: Wiley.

Brewer, M. B. (1981). Ethnocentrism and its role in interpersonal trust. In M. B. Brewer & B. E. Collins (Eds.), *Scientific inquiry and the social sciences*. San Francisco: Jossey-Bass.

Burns, T., & Stalker, G. M. (1961). *The management of innovation*. London: Tavistock.

Cialdini, R. (1993). *Influence*. New York: Morrow.

Clark, R. E., & Halford, L. (1980). Reducing uncertainty and building trust: The special case of auctions. In S. Fiddle (Ed.), *Uncertainty: Behavioral and social dimensions* (pp. 305-322). New York: Praeger.

Darley, J. M., & Latane, B. (1968). Bystander intervention in emergencies: Diffusion of responsibility. *Journal of Personality and Social Psychology, 8,* 377-383.

Dawes, R. M. (1994). *House of cards: Psychology and psychotherapy built on myth*. New York: Free Press.

Eccles, R. G., & Crane, D. B. (1988). *Doing deals*. Boston: Harvard Business School Press.

Eisenberg, E. M. (1990). Jamming! Transcendence through organizing. *Communication Research, 17,* 139-164.

Faulkner, R. R. (1971). *Hollywood studio musicians*. Chicago: Aldine.

Faulkner, R. R. (1983). *Music on demand*. New Brunswick, NJ: Transaction Books.

Fiske, S. T., & Taylor, S. F. (1991). *Social cognition* (2nd ed.). New York: McGraw-Hill.

Fondas, N., & Stewart, R. (1994). Enactment in managerial jobs: A role analysis. *Journal of Management Studies, 31,* 83-103.

Gaddy, C. D., & Wachtel, J. A. (1992). Team skills training in nuclear power plant operations. In R. W. Swezey & E. Salas (Eds.), *Teams: Their training and performance* (pp. 379-396). Norwood, NJ: Ablex.

Gambetta, D. (1988). Can we trust trust? In D. Gambetta (Ed.), *Trust: Making and breaking cooperative relationships* (pp. 213-237). Oxford, UK: Basil Blackwell.

Good, D. (1988). Individuals, interpersonal relations, and trust. In D. Gambetta (Ed.), *Trust: Making and breaking cooperative relations* (pp. 31-48). Oxford, UK: Basil Blackwell.

Goodman, L. P., & Goodman, R. A. (1972). Theater as a temporary system. *California Management Review, 15*(2), 103-108.

Goodman, R. A. (1981). *Temporary systems*. New York: Praeger.

Goodman, R. A., & Goodman L. P. (1976). Some management issues in temporary systems: A study of professional development and manpower—The theatre case. *Administrative Science Quarterly, 21,* 494-501.

Janoff-Bulman, R. (1992). *Shattered assumptions: Towards a new psychology of trauma*. New York: Free Press.

Kanter, R. M. (1989). *When giants learn to dance*. New York: Simon & Schuster.

Kawin, B. F. (1992). *How movies work.* Berkeley: University of California Press.

Kent, N. (1991). *Naked power: Money and power in the movies today.* New York: St. Martin's Press.

Klein, G. A. (1993). A recognition-primed decision (RPD) model of rapid decision making. In G. A. Klein, J. Orasanu, R. Calderwood, & C. E. Zsambok (Eds.), *Decision making in action: Models and methods* (pp. 138-147). Norwood, NJ: Ablex.

Kouzes, J. M., & Posner, B. Z. (1987). *The leadership challenge.* San Francisco: Jossey-Bass.

Kramer, R. M. (1994). The sinister attribution error: Paranoid cognition and collective distrust in organizations. *Motivation and Emotion, 18,* 199-230.

Kramer, R. M., Meyerson, D., & Davis, G. (1990). How much is enough? Psychological components of "guns versus butter" decisions in a security dilemma. *Journal of Personality and Social Psychology, 58,* 984-993.

Lanzara, G. F. (1983). Ephemeral organizations in extreme environments: Emergence, strategy, extinction. *Journal of Management Studies, 20,* 71-95.

Lindskold, S. (1978). Trust development, the GRIT proposal, and the effects of conciliatory acts on conflict and cooperation. *Psychological Bulletin, 85,* 772-793.

Luhmann, N. (1988). Familiarity, confidence, trust: Problems and alternatives. In D. Gambetta (Ed.), *Trust: Making and breaking cooperative relations* (pp. 94-108). Oxford, UK: Basil Blackwell.

March, J. G. (1994). *A primer on decision making.* New York: Free Press.

Meacham, J. A. (1983). Wisdom and the context of knowledge: Knowing that one doesn't know. *Contributions in Human Development, 8,* 111-134.

Mellinger, W. M. (1994). Negotiated orders: The negotiation of directives in paramedic-nurse interaction. *Symbolic Interaction, 17*(2), 165-185.

Norem, J. K., & Cantor, N. (1986). Defensive pessimism: Harnessing anxiety as motivation. *Journal of Personality and Social Psychology, 51,* 1208-1217.

Orr, J. E. (1990). Sharing knowledge, celebrating identity: Community memory in a service culture. In D. Middleton & D. Edwards (Eds.), *Collective remembering* (pp. 169-189). London: Sage.

Paulus, P. B., Dzindolet, M. T., Poletes, G., & Camacho, L. M. (1993). Perception of performance in group brainstorming: The illusion of group productivity. *Personality and Social Psychology Bulletin, 19,* 78-89.

Peters, T. (1992). *Liberation management.* New York: Knopf.

Polzer, J., Kramer, R. M., & Neale, M. (1993). *Individual and group illusions: Antecedents and consequences.* Unpublished manuscript.

Putnam, R. (1992). *Making democracy work.* Princeton, NJ: Princeton University Press.

Schelling, T. C. (1984). The intimate contest for self-command. In T. C. Schelling (Ed.), *Choice and consequence.* Cambridge, MA: Harvard University Press.

Schlenker, B. R., Soraci, S., & McCarthy, B. (1976). Self-esteem and group performance as determinants of egocentric perceptions in cooperative groups. *Human Relations, 29,* 1163-1176.

Rotter, J. B. (1980). Interpersonal trust, trustworthiness, and gullibility. *American Psychologist, 35,* 1-7.

Simmel, G. (1978). *The philosophy of money.* Boston: Routledge & Kegan Paul.

Suczek, B., & Fagerhaugh, S. (1991). AIDS and outreach work. In D. R. Maines (Ed.), *Social organization and process* (pp. 159-173). New York: Aldine De Gruyter.

Taylor, P. M. (1992). *Steven Spielberg.* New York: Continuum.

Taylor, S. E. (1989). *Positive illusions: Creative self-deception and the healthy mind.* New York: Basic Books.

Taylor, S. E., & Brown, J. D. (1988). Illusion and well-being: A social psychological perspective on mental health. *Psychological Bulletin, 103,* 193-210.

Thompson, J. D. (1967). *Organizations in action.* New York: McGraw-Hill.

Weick, K. E. (1993). Collective mind in organizations: Heedful interrelating on flight decks. *Administrative Science Quarterly, 38,* 357-381.

Weick, K. E., & Roberts, K. H. (1993). Collective mind in organizations: Heedful interrelating on flight decks. *Administrative Science Quarterly, 38,* 357-381.

Weiner, E. L., Kanki, B. G., & Helmreich, R. L. (Eds.). (1993). *Cockpit resource management.* San Diego: Academic Press.

Weinstein, N. D. (1980). Unrealistic optimism about future life events. *Journal of Personality and Social Psychology, 39,* 806-820.

Zucker, L. G. (1986). Production of trust: Institutional sources of economic structure, 1840-1920. In B. M. Staw & L. L. Cummings (Eds.), *Research in organizational behavior* (Vol. 8, pp. 53-111). Greenwich, CT: JAI.

The Road to Hell

The Dynamics of
Distrust in an Era of Quality

SIM B SITKIN
DARRYL STICKEL

Trust has long been recognized as a fundamental feature of interpersonal and intergroup relations in a number of social science disciplines. Sociologists and psychologists have proposed that trust is an element that makes work in organizations possible (Barnard, 1938) through its effect on cooperation (Axelrod, 1984; Deutsch, 1962; Kramer, 1993), interpersonal and group solidarity (Barber, 1983; Blau, 1964; Fox, 1974), and facilitating social infrastructure (Williamson, 1981; Zucker, 1986).

Until a recent resurgence of interest, trust received much less sustained, systematic attention historically among organizational scholars (see Mayer, Davis, & Schoorman, 1995). As a result, the link between trust and organizational features—such as structure, formal role relations, or task characteristics—only has begun to be examined systematically. Recent scholarly attention

AUTHORS' NOTE: The authors gratefully acknowledge support from the National Science Foundation (Grant No. SBR-94-22367) for the research reported in theis chapter. We would like to thank Michal Tamuz for her help in the critical framing of several analyses used in this chapter, Rod Kramer for his suggestions, and several members of the organization studied for helpful comments on an earlier version of this chapter.

in at least two areas, however, has highlighted the central role of trust in organizational affairs. First, scholars who have studied cooperation within and among organizations (e.g., Kramer, 1993; Powell, 1990; Ring & Van de Ven, 1992; Sheppard & Tuchinsky, Chapter 8, this volume) have stressed how trust is an essential feature of effective cooperative relationships.

A second body of research has examined the growing "legalization" of organizational procedures and activities (Edelman, 1990; Sitkin & Bies, 1994). Scholars with this focus have pointed to the use of formal organizational mechanisms as substitutes for interpersonal trust (Shapiro, 1987; Zucker, 1986). This work makes clear the potential importance of formal mechanisms as both facilitators of (Matthews, Kordonski, & Shimoff, 1983; Sitkin, 1995) and impediments to trust (Fox, 1974; Sitkin & Roth, 1993). Furthermore, although past work has explored the constructive role of formal mechanisms in some depth (e.g., the extensive work on formal situational features in fostering cooperative behavior), the work to date has traced only the barest outlines of the mechanisms by which formal procedures, standards, and so on can lead to distrust.

In this chapter, we wish to extend recent work on trust in organizations by exploring how a specific set of situational features can give rise to distrust. Specifically, our goal in this exploratory study is to focus attention on the varied mechanisms through which distrust can arise when employees perceive a mismatch between the tasks they perform and the management control systems they must accommodate.

A grounded theory approach was taken in an organization in which a total quality management (TQM) program stressed highly precise measurement and standardized task routines in a setting characterized by a high degree of task ambiguity. The TQM program was being studied for other purposes, but issues of distrust arose consistently during the course of the data collection effort. Thus, the goal of the analysis reported in this chapter was to identify any links between perceived mismatches and distrust. Although this research represents a serendipitous theory-development effort, it was at least initially guided by Sitkin and Roth's (1993) propositions concerning the role of formal control mechanisms in fostering distrust (e.g., that formal controls instituted to enhance trust by increasing performance reliability can undermine trust and thus deter achievement of the very goals they were put in place to serve). However, as a grounded theory effort, this theoretical starting point was quickly outstripped by the implications of the data.

This chapter will be structured into three parts. First, we will briefly review several key theoretical issues that initially motivated the analysis. Second, we will describe the empirical context of the study and summarize key observations from the data. Finally, we will discuss the implications of our observations for further work in the area.

Theoretical Underpinnings

Model of the Determinants of Trust

A growing body of trust research (e.g., Granovetter, 1985; Meyer, 1983; Shapiro, 1987; Sitkin & Bies, 1994; Yudof, 1981; Zucker, 1986) has suggested that one reason that organizations adopt legalistic mechanisms is to attempt to restore damaged trust within the organization and across its boundaries. According to Sitkin and Roth (1993), legalistic mechanisms (e.g., formal, contract-like arrangements, such as formalization, standardization, or precise outcome measures) are likely to be effective in fostering trust in organizations only when task requirements are understood well enough to identify and codify reliability-related inputs, transformation procedures, or outputs (Fox, 1974; March & Simon, 1958; Perrow, 1967; Williamson, 1975). For example, game theorists have identified circumstances under which formal constraints can be introduced in ways that induce trusting behavior (e.g., Matthews et al., 1983).

The introduction of formal remedies can backfire, however, when trust problems are grounded in perceived value incongruence. According to Sitkin and Roth (1993, p. 370), "Legalistic responses are more or less effective depending upon the specific nature of the expectations that have been violated. They can restore trust expectations effectively when violations are specific to a particular context or task."

Under such conditions, the formalization of relations will introduce (or stress) a sense of distance and differentness that will not only make differences more salient than similarities but will also foster the interpretation of even superficial differences as indicative of deeper-value incongruities.

> Distrust is engendered when an individual or group is perceived as not sharing key cultural values. When a person challenges an organization's fundamental assumptions and values, that person may be perceived as operating under values so different from the group's that the violator's underlying world view becomes suspect (Gabarro, 1978; Lindskold, 1978). . . . The person is now seen as a cultural outsider. (Sitkin & Roth, 1993, p. 371)

In this formulation, the cues used to judge an individual as an "outsider" can be insignificant as long as they are perceived as indicating a lack of acceptance of one or more key cultural principles. Such stereotyping or stigmatization can taint the violator and lead to a generalized sense of distrust that goes far beyond the narrow, superficial, or otherwise insignificant cues that may have initially raised "the values question."

Matching Formal Systems to Task
Characteristics: A Hypothesized Effect on Trust

Sitkin and Roth (1993), Mayer et al. (1995), and others allude only very generally to specific aspects of the formal system that are associated with trust in organizations (and, almost universally, suggest that further work is needed in this area). To be able to look more concretely at how trust problems arise, we narrowed our attention to the degree to which trust-related problems are associated with mismatches between how employee perceptions of their tasks and the use of formal control systems—in this case a TQM system. In doing so, we were following through on the logic articulated by Sitkin and Roth when they posited that managerial responses that did not fit the employee's values or worldview could lead to escalating cycles of distrust. In the case of a formal control system, this suggested to us that if employees perceive a precise and highly formalized management control system as *fundamentally* mismatched to what they perceive to be the nature of their work (e.g., a highly ambiguous task), then Sitkin and Roth's hypothesized effect on trust could be examined, and the mechanisms associated with any observed trust effect could be surfaced.

In focusing on the importance of task congruence, we drew on prior work that has suggested TQM programs as a fertile ground for such research. In proposing a contingency theory of TQM effectiveness, Sitkin, Sutcliffe, and Schroeder (1994) hypothesize that many of the recent failures of TQM may be attributable to programs that were mismatched to the tasks being performed.[1] In a series of studies of TQM programs used in the air traffic safety control system, Tamuz (1987, 1988a, 1988b, 1989) examined how such a mismatch between a TQM program and the work done by air traffic controllers and pilots affected the collection of safety-related information by the FAA and by NASA's Aviation Safety Reporting System. Tamuz's studies exhibit the attributes predicted by Sitkin et al. (1994), with respect to the inappropriate use of precise and deterministic TQM measurement and monitoring systems under nonroutine conditions characterized by high levels of uncertainty. Her research findings suggest that when a quality control program imposes precise performance standards on situations employees perceive as ambiguous and links these performance measures to multiple incentive systems, it can affect the amount (Tamuz, 1987) and the quality (Tamuz, 1988b) of information provided about potential hazards to aviation safety.

With the exception of the works cited earlier, the extant literature on trust does not reflect the potential importance of perceived mismatches between managerial systems and employee task perceptions as a factor in escalating cycles of distrust. As noted earlier, a substantial body of work exists that has explored the positive effects of formalization in supporting trust-like relations—for example, work drawing on game theory, agency theory, or transaction cost economics. However, the role of formal managerial systems as a stimulus for distrust appears in critiques of the inhumane effects of bureaucratization (e.g., Braverman, 1974), which have remained largely detached from the work on trust. Among those who have focused on trust and formalization (e.g., Fox, 1974; Shapiro, 1987; Sitkin & Roth, 1993; Zucker, 1986), the proposition that perceived task management system mismatches could fuel distrust is quite consistent with their theories, but they leave unexplored the mechanisms underlying this potentially basic link to organizational contexts.

Case Study: Applying a Formal
TQM Program to Scientists in a
Corporate Basic Research Laboratory

Background on Research Site Selection

The selection of the site from which these data were drawn was serendipitous. Data were being collected for a broader study for which trust issues were not a focal concern. Nonetheless, in interviews conducted for that study, trust issues kept surfacing in the comments of those being interviewed. This occurred at the same time as the criteria for this analysis were being formulated. It quickly became clear that there was no need to search for a new site because data appropriate for this analysis had already been collected (albeit for another purpose). However, the site selection criteria described below were defined prior to site selection and were used to determine the appropriateness of this site and these data. One benefit of using this data set, however, is that because the issue of trust was not a focal one in the interviews, we can have more confidence that the trust-related issues raised by study participants were not elicited by the interview format or interviewer expectations.

Methodology

Site Selection Criteria. Although Sitkin and Roth (1993) propose a model of the process by which trust and distrust arise in organizational settings, the framework they propose was developed in an extreme context involving a high level of stigmatization (i.e., responses to AIDS in the workplace). Thus, in addition to selecting settings in which employees were likely to recognize task or monitoring system mismatches, another goal in selecting research sites was to focus on contexts that were more readily generalizable (than the focus on responses to AIDS).

The goal was to join Sitkin and Roth's (1993) hypothesis that perceived value incongruence generalizes into distrust with Sitkin et al.'s (1994) predictions concerning the effects of misusing highly structured TQM programs in highly ambiguous work contexts. Specifically, our conjecture was that distrust would be engendered when highly structured and precise control mechanisms were implemented in settings characterized by ambiguous task requirements and reliance on sophisticated professional judgment. It was our hope that examining individual reactions in such a setting would help us to trace the factors that influenced the emergence of distrust—and, more specifically, would allow us to search for evidence of Sitkin and Roth's "value incongruence effect."

Characteristics of the Research Site. The chosen setting (the basic research laboratory of a high-technology company) exhibited all of the key features targeted. As the basic research lab for a major U.S. technology corporation, the scientific work being done was of a highly ambiguous nature, as is usually the case for cutting-edge research. Furthermore, the corporation had a highly developed, widely used, and well-known TQM program. Despite its remarkable success in implementing its Total Quality Program (TQP)[2] in its manufacturing, marketing, and other routine operations, the company had met with only partial success in implementing TQP in its corporate research laboratories—an outcome that suggested that at least some of Sitkin, Sutcliffe, and Schroeder's theoretical musings might be applicable.

Data. The study examined the problems (and successes) encountered in implementing TQP in this corporate research setting by including interviews with research scientists, lab managers, and research executives as well as a review of videotapes and written materials associated with the program (e.g., written training evaluations were on file). A total of 30 scientists, lab managers, and research administrators were interviewed. Most interviews involved a single interviewee, although in a few cases, two or three scientists who had worked closely on a project were interviewed together to discuss the use of TQP in their project. Only one interview lasted less than 30 minutes; most lasted between 45 and 60 minutes, with a few taking several hours in one or more sessions. All interviews were taped and transcribed.

Data Collection Method. The core of the data used in this study was derived from the interview transcripts, with other data sources used for embellishment or cross-checking interpretations. Those being interviewed were asked intentionally open-ended questions about their experience with TQP. Most of the interview time was spent asking for more elaborate or clearer explanations of exactly what happened in an incident being described or how they interpreted an incident. In addition, individuals were asked to discuss why they thought things were handled as they were and to assess the parts of the program they found most and least valuable for them in their own work and for others in the laboratories.

Framing the Observations

The events and interpretations reported by those interviewed manifested patterns consistent with Sitkin and Roth's (1993) distinction between predictability-based and value-based trust or Sheppard and Tuchinsky's (Chapter 8, this volume) distinction between knowledge-based and identification-based trust. Furthermore, the case also was consistent with their notion that when distrust is elicited, predictability problems will tend to be interpreted as providing evidence of fundamental value incongruence and will fuel a cycle of escalating distrust.

Misunderstanding Scientific Research

Lab staff (scientists and administrative staff) repeatedly reported the sense that those involved with TQP did not understand what research involved or what it was that scientists did. There was almost a universal sense that proponents of TQP—and the management of the corporation more generally—viewed basic research as an exotic mystery. They suspected that their corporate "parent" had only the most superficial sense of or appreciation for research—much like an academic's parents, who are proud of their professorial child but secretly hope that nobody asks them anything specific about their son's or daughter's expertise or job.

On the corporate side, there was a similar history of research lab staff (and especially scientists) being perceived as "prima donnas" who were neither aware of nor concerned about operating a business. Whether it was issues of meeting schedules, developing practical (as opposed to esoteric) solutions, or costs, the managers in the corporate office and in the product divisions viewed the research labs as being unconnected to the core business of the corporation. To follow the earlier parental analogy, they viewed the labs as being like a child who takes financial support with no sense of responsibility to explain why the funds are needed and who isn't even involved as an active member of the family.

When TQP was first introduced to the research lab, this background of mutual suspicion was present and both sides became wary of the intentions of the "other" side, leading to particularly salient incidents that were consistent with these views. These attributes fit well with those Brewer (1979), Kramer (1991), Lindskold (1978), and Stephan and Stephan (1985) identify as likely to foster or sustain intergroup conflict and distrust. When coupled with the fundamental problems encountered in applying most TQM programs to basic research settings (Sitkin et al., 1994), the situation was ripe for sparking a cycle of distrust.

Two distinct forms were reported concerning management or TQP proponent misunderstanding of the core work of the lab: misunderstanding of the research task and a lack of appreciation for scientific expertise.

Perceived Misunderstanding of the Research Task. Although some of the precise measurement tools associated with TQP were viewed as routine and reasonable, others were seen as a misfit with the core tasks of research:

> We all knew that TQP was developed for routine situations and that what was special about [our research lab] and its activities was nonroutine.

Scientists in the research labs recognized that TQP, if imposed on them, could force them to change their behavior in ways that did not fit with what they saw as the best way to do research. Furthermore, they did not see any effort on the part of TQP proponents to grasp what the scientists saw as unique about doing basic research. According to one scientist,

> We're supposed to be professional problem solvers, but they don't understand the nature of the task in which we're engaged. The method they proposed for problem solving is inappropriate *within* research. . . . It could have been linked usefully to our interaction with the Product Divisions, but it never was.

As part of the TQP effort, a series of specific research productivity measures and targets were articulated. These were frequently viewed by researchers as unthinkingly "transplanted" solutions. The scientists' response reflects the problems anticipated in Francis's (1992, p. 22) warning to TQM advocates: "Unless [measurements involving uncertainty] . . . are made with scrupulous care . . . critics may discount the results and the whole effort may lose credibility."

As one lab manager put it, "finding measures is easy" as long as you don't care whether they are "real." But, he continued, "you need courage to find real indicators" of research productivity. In another lab, a scientist expanded on this idea:

> Not knowing how to measure quality, we were forced to count instances of PSP and QIP [formal procedures used for problem solving and quality improvement that are common in many TQM programs]—without any sense that they would improve the quality of research.

In fact, this perception of a "form-over-substance" approach was parodied by some scientists, who referred to the program as TQC (Total Quality Through Conformity). Reflecting a common theme in many of the interviews, one lab manager argued that corporate management and TQP proponents never took the time even to attempt to understand what basic research work was about. Instead, he suggested TQP was advocated by those whose work "looked good" when TQP indicators were used. For not recognizing this as a problem, he placed the blame on corporate management rather than on the TQP representatives:

> The predisposition toward quantitative metrics [in measuring research outcomes] is reinforced by . . . those who have good quantitative outcomes. . . .

As this manager emphasized, when continued funding is based on inappropriate measures, this funding can lead to unquestioned adoption (so as to retain corporate support), and such a budgeting system, he argued, "pushed us over the abyss" into "mindlessly focusing on metrics." Perhaps the most telling illustration, however, came from another lab manager, who responded to the specification of numerical patent goals for each laboratory by not telling his researchers what their official goal was. He reported feeling that making such goals so precise and explicit was "dysfunctional." When scientists in his lab heard that other labs had been given specific targets and asked him about it, he dismissed their questions and refused to disclose the targets to them. He explained during an interview that he worried that telling them what specific objectives had been set for them could have "distorted their good judgment" about what they should work on—leading them to pursue "more boring but patentable paths in their research."

Lack of Appreciation of Scientific Expertise. The second type of response reported by lab staff concerned their sense that corporate management in general and TQP trainers in particular did not demonstrate an appropriate appreciation for the degree of knowledge, skill, and judgment that goes along with being a world-class scientist. As a lab administrator put it, "If you look at [our interaction] with TQP, a lot of us were put off by the highly stylized . . . [and] presumptuous approach" taken by them in trying to capture what pioneering researchers actually do.

When operating in any new domain, feelings of uncertainty and insecurity engender what Kramer (1994) describes as "self-consciousness," "paranoia," and "collective distrust." In the case of TQM, Wolff (1992, p. 14) describes a similar phenomenon: "Bring in the 'quality experts' and you can expect reactions ranging from polite skepticism to an angry 'Don't they think I'm technically competent?' " Although Wolff highlights the fear and anger that such a lack of appreciation can engender in many employees, our data suggest a somewhat different response exhibited by the well-known and highly respected research scientists who participated in this study. Their self-confidence and assurance remained unshaken when the TQP trainers treated them "like children," but their respect for TQP proponents was fundamentally undermined.

As world-class scientists, these individuals were quite used to defending their ideas. They viewed themselves as being among the best in the world in their own areas of expertise and were not inclined to let those they perceived to be ill-informed nonscientists tell them how to do their jobs. In public training sessions and in private meetings, researchers challenged the scientific basis for what was asserted as "fact" by proponents of TQP (i.e., trainers and corporate executives) and were "outraged" at what they perceived as a complete lack of recognition on the part of TQP proponents that inadequate scientific support was problematic. Even worse, according to some, was the obvious inattention to even the appearance of respecting the practice of scientific research.

Furthermore, there was the sense that what was being offered was not new to scientists but was already a part of their professional arsenal. In interviews and in the written evaluations of TQP training sessions, participants noted the degree to which links to the scientific method they all believed in could have been made but were not. The following are examples from two scientists:

> People wind up in a place like this because, one way or another, without quite realizing it, they have learned to solve the problems that TQP is all about solving.

> Researchers have been trained for years in problem solving. Most of the specific tools mentioned were variations on what I already use . . . [but this was never acknowledged in the training].

Not above sarcastically using the rhetoric of TQP to skewer its proponents, one researcher suggested, "They forgot we were their 'customers.' " In the end, the scientists almost universally seemed to conclude that anyone who "couldn't distinguish science from religion" could not be expected to recognize world-class researchers. As another scientist characterized the reactions of those in his training group, because the TQP trainers didn't exhibit the proper deference to science, the scientists in the group concluded that those who supported TQP could not possibly share the basic values essential for dialogue with serious researchers.

Perceived Value Incongruence

The imposition of TQP on the research labs represented a situation in which a lack of trust and understanding was a bilateral problem. The Sitkin and Roth

(1993) model would suggest that under such conditions we should see evidence of perceived value incongruity from the researchers toward the corporate staff and management and also from the corporate representatives toward the researchers. With the caveat that the data came almost entirely from the research lab and thus present an inevitably skewed view of the corporate perspective, there seems to be evidence of the predicted, mutually perceived value incongruence. Not only is there evidence of the "other" group in such terms, but there are numerous reports of efforts to enforce in-group conformity by both the corporation and the research community.

Corporate Uniformity and the "You're With Us or You're Against Us" Mentality. A common argument found in the TQM literature is reflected by Francis (1992, p. 35), who advised TQM proponents that resistance to TQM efforts should be dismissed: "Lay aside all the old excuses for not measuring and baselining R&D effectiveness, and do it anyway—*because it is the right thing to do.*"

This viewpoint, reflected in the training materials on TQP, was what lab employees described as the rationale they were given. Illustrating this point of view, a corporate quality officer described a key value of TQP for the company as a whole in one of the archival sources of data, stressing how this was an important factor to consider in implementing TQP in the research laboratory:

> More important than a uniform culture, what we're talking about is a uniform set of values.

In effect, TQP (like many TQM programs) was viewed by many of the scientists as an attempt at proselytizing them. Although the trainers did convey to the scientists the sincerity of their belief that TQP was "the right thing to do," evidently the trainers, like many other members of the company, were persuaded that TQP had led to significant improvements for the company. In fact, many "true believers" had direct experience with the dramatic improvements TQP had fostered in other parts of the firm.

Although TQP may have achieved a born-again quality for many of the company's employees, such revelations were met with a grim skepticism by most researchers in the labs. What was unquestionably "right" to others in the firm apparently did not feel "right" to the researchers. Furthermore, although TQM typically emphasizes that decisions should be made based on careful analysis of problems, the systematic use of data to trace causes, and the use of experiments, it was not at all clear to them that TQP reflected the fundamental values that research scientists saw as their own—or as appropriate for their work. Like Janis and Mann's (1977) description of the process of "spreading the alternatives" or Kramer's (1993) description of the selective confirmation of "worst fears and suspicions," the scientists focused selectively on those aspects of TQP that did not fit with their values and practices while ignoring other equally obvious and important aspects that did fit. As Sitkin and Roth and earlier trust researchers had predicted, once the seeds of distrust were sown they were self-generating.

The clash of values that captured the scientists' attention concerned the notion of enforced uniformity. In particular, the idea that TQP was simply to be accepted without challenge elicited immediate suspicion. Especially damaging was the limited face validity of the claims of TQP proponents when applied to basic research activities.

According to the scientists, the applications of TQP, cited by the firm's TQP trainers and management, were either irrelevant to basic research or served as evidence that it should not work for such endeavors. Scientists reported that throughout this process, even carefully articulated and reasoned opposition to TQP was viewed by TQP proponents as representing an unwillingness to solve problems systematically, follow procedural guidelines, or coordinate with others. As one said, acceptance of "TQP is seen as a membership card in the rest of the organization." In short, although scientists may have objected to the very idea that there is a single best way to approach ambiguous problems or that pathbreaking researchers should have to follow a common approach, they felt that their rational resistance was viewed irrationally as heretical.

None of the lab staff thought that TQP was inapplicable under the right circumstances—even within the labs. But being forced to adopt what they perceived as conformity-based values was clearly unacceptable to them. As one lab manager put it,

> The scope of TQP should be carefully limited to those things for which it is useful. It should not be seen as a way of creating uniformity, but as a way of creating understanding.

Although this vision was articulated by many of those interviewed, one scientist expressed a slightly more extreme version that linked the TQP response to his more general perspective on the corporation. He said that there was resistance to any suggestion that any specific subgroup or subtask within the company had special or different needs. Although the research labs had long been recognized as "special," it was nonetheless "politically incorrect" to discuss differences—whether the special requirements applied to a specific substantive area of research or the distinct focus and needs of different research centers. He noted that whenever he (or others) tried to focus discussion on important differences, he was "shot down because of the focus on retaining a sense of uniformity." In fact, he linked this experience to the previously mentioned "Quality Through Conformity" moniker cited by others.

Reactive Nonconformity in the Research Lab as Another Form of the "You're With Us or You're Against Us" Mentality. Although acceptance and skill in using the formalities of TQP were viewed as a "membership card" within the corporation, acceptance of TQP was viewed with extreme suspicion in the research laboratory. So strong was the rejection of TQP that one researcher reported that when he had recommended the use of a TQP technique to help resolve an impasse encountered in a meeting, he was chastised publicly by others at the meeting and was told disdainfully that "*we* don't use that *here.*" Recalling the resultant sense of cultural insecurity, he quickly learned that to even hint that "TQP applies here" would lead to what he labeled "death in a meeting"—and the threat of one's membership status being questioned. In effect, he (and others) reported the presumption that one who held the "right values" would immediately come into question if seen as accepting—or even being open to—*any part* of TQP. The core values of the scientists related to world-class research and came to be viewed as antithetical to what they viewed as the managerial or engineering values that dominated TQP. Furthermore, they came to exhibit some of the attributes of "groupthink" identified by Janis (1972) or out-group stereotyping (Kramer, 1994). At times this was particularly ironic, for example, when scientists reported that their nonconforming views were squelched as a reaction against the forced conformity that TQP was perceived as representing. Although ironic, such resistance has been predicted in earlier research that found that conformity pressures were especially strenuous in settings containing experts compared with groups without experts.

This incident was reinforced by the experience of one of the authors in collecting data for the study. Specifically, when nearly all interviewees were told that the topic of the interview concerned the TQP program, they were usually visibly put off and suspicious. Their bodies sometimes physically drew back, their tone of voice changed, answers became more terse and were more carefully worded, and even their smiles disappeared. Only after they were told that the project was aimed at "understanding both the value *and the limitations* of TQP" [intentionally stressing the italicized words] did their smiles return, their bodies relax and move closer, and their tone and language become less stilted and controlled. These observed shifts took place even in several instances where the individual being interviewed was a familiar colleague to the interviewer. Furthermore, the shifts were sudden and very striking and they took place in less than a minute of elapsed time in otherwise routine and cordial interviews.

Other Issues Raised in the Interviews

Deskilling and Demystification. As Messick and Mackie (1989) note, a critical factor that fuels intergroup distrust and degradation is the degree to which individual group member identity is tied to the core values and status of the groups to which they belong. Thus, any threats to group identity are likely to engender strong negative responses. In fact, Kramer (1991, 1993) and Sheppard and Tuchinsky (Chapter 8, this volume) highlight support for a sense of identity as critical to establishing trust and, by implication, threats to identity as an important potential stimulus for distrust.

There was some evidence of such identity-related responses in this case. In addition to the distrust that arose from hurt feelings and a sense of not being appreciated, there was some evidence that the use of precise measures and structured procedures was seen as actually threatening to undermine the scientists' claim to professionalism. In part, this seemed to result from a fear that the explication of the details involved in exercising professional judgment could in fact lead to a "demystification" of what it meant to do basic research—a potentially crucial defense for long-range, high-risk science in a resource-constrained and highly competitive corporate climate.

It also reflected a fear that the work itself was less magical than its PR might suggest. For example, one researcher reflected on his personal experience, his observation of others, and in particular his own resistance to the TQP process:

> [We] may have been frightened by the prospect that what was nonroutine could become routine [if it was analyzed] . . . and then anybody could do it. We wouldn't be so special anymore.

This idea was supported by the lab manager, cited earlier, who refused to inform his research staff about their patent goals. He also defended his decision by noting that he was sensitive to the fact that his staff "might have felt cheapened" by the use of such precise indicators to characterize their intellectual efforts. Although there is no evidence that these scientists actually believe that what they and their colleagues do is routine (nor do the authors of this chapter believe it), there is little doubt that in such a climate of distrust such fears may surface from even the most eminent among us.

Discussion

This chapter reports on an exploratory effort to understand the dynamics of distrust—and, in particular, to trace the roots of distrust in organizations to features of the formal organization that are typically offered as "remedies" for trust problems. Consistent with Sitkin and Roth's (1993) critique of formal "remedies," we were able to identify several mechanisms by which highly formalized management control systems can lead to escalating distrust if they are ill-suited to the task at hand—they can undermine a sense of value congruence, convey disrespect and thus create hurt feelings, threaten a sense of professional autonomy and competence, and lead to self-sealing cycles of escalating in-group conformity and out-group resistance.

In the case analyzed here, the proposition that task and skill mismatches would foster distrust was generally supported and did surface several mechanisms that merit further study. Even though the case was quite different from the situation originally examined by Sitkin and Roth (1993), similar patterns of concerns and arguments were spontaneously raised by individuals interviewed.

Sitkin and Roth (1993) posited the role of perceived reliability and perceived value congruence as a factor influencing trust. The patterns observed in this case were consistent with the mechanisms they suggested by which mismatched formalization should fuel distrust. In the next section, we will first suggest how the questions that motivated the research were addressed by the data. Then we will offer an additional theoretical perspective that can help to explain the observed patterns but was not part of the original motivation for the study.

Supportive Evidence
for Previously Cited Research

The case generally supported the importance of perceived value congruence and a sense of knowledge-based predictability. In this situation, where both these features were lacking, already high levels of distrust were exacerbated.

Misunderstanding as a Determinant of Distrust. As we noted earlier, the link between trust and the use of inappropriately precise management systems has received sparse attention in the past. A sense that management (or the technical specialists) misunderstood the task fueled distrust in both cases. In both cases, the issue included the development of precise measures and highly structured procedures that were viewed as fundamentally inappropriate for the highly ambiguous and uncertain tasks involved. This argument is consistent with a recent analysis (Sitkin et al., 1994) of the way in which many TQM programs are applied inappropriately, without a recognition of the structural contingencies involved.

Although Sitkin and Roth (1993) imply that perceived reliability can be grounded, in part, in a presumption of competence, the examples examined here go much further in suggesting that the use of inappropriately precise or rigid measurement schemes can lead employees to conclude that they are not understood or valued as professionals. Although this finding is clearly related to the familiar deskilling arguments, what we observed is largely an emotional or defensive reaction that lies outside the heart of the deskilling perspective. The sense of moral outrage (Bies, 1987) or professional insult (Kramer, 1994) that we observed is a rather distinct link to reactions of distrust and merits further study. One likely theoretical grounding for such work is the literature on perceived justice.

Although an observation that emotional hurt is a stimulus for distrust is hardly surprising once it is articulated, the link between formal system precision, professional pride (or insult), and trust has not been drawn previously. In part, this is because the relevant literatures have been rooted more in issues of power or cognition. Empirically, it seems likely that such emotional reactions could be suppressed and thus difficult to observe—perhaps because the acknowledgment of hurt feelings is not readily accepted as organizationally legitimate, these responses may be couched in more instrumental terms. Future empirical work will need to address the issue of unearthing conditions under which such feelings might arise and have effects on trust independent of the other reactions.

Value Conformity Versus Value Congruence. When distrust splits an organization into warily circling subcommunities, pressures for in-group conformity can escalate and seal off these subgroups from each other (Janis, 1972; Linville & Jones, 1980; see also Fox, 1974). Evidence from the research lab, for example, illustrated how conformity pressures were institutionalized to some extent in both the formal and informal systems, thus solidifying opposing positions and forcing individuals to take sides. The scientist who appealed for the tolerance of nonuniformity may be a key here. For if formal specifications are framed in terms of broad objectives rather than precise measures or highly standardized procedural specifications, it may be more feasible for individual members of the organization to conform to both the spirit and the letter of the rule while adapting that rule to the requirements of their particular task.

Other Issues. Distinct from the sense of hurt that many of those interviewed reported feeling when their competence was unappreciated was the sense that their profession was fundamentally misunderstood. Another effect of formalization, which is quite familiar in the literature on sources of resistance to change, is that it can lead individuals to worry that their special skills are illusory. This effect can also lead to a cycle of escalating distrust if fears of deprofessionalization are fueled through broadstroke challenges to professional autonomy or characterizations of professional competencies as an art or a "black box."

In-Group Perceptions of Out-Groups

The effect of perceived value incongruence on distrust can be usefully informed by extensive psychological studies of social perception and inter-group relations (Messick & Mackie, 1989). We will briefly review some of the findings from this literature and how they inform our interpretation of the case.

Appraisals of Group Characteristics. Although Janis (1972) explained one process by which in-groups will tend to become highly monolithic (see also Messick & Mackie, 1989, for a review of other studies), Linville and Jones (1980) found that group members perceived high levels of heterogeneity within their own group's membership while attributing more extreme characteristics and little diversity to out-group members. These problems were more readily observable when less contact was made between the in-group and out-group members (Linville, Fischer, & Salovey, 1989).

It is interesting to note that in the case examined here there was a historical lack of contact between the research and nonresearch communities. However, in recent years, a concerted effort by the leadership of the research labs to increase such contact has occurred. Based on nonsystematic observation in the period since the data reported here was collected, it appears that the active hostility and distrust exhibited in the interviews have begun to wane (at least for some of the research scientists) as their contact with the rest of the corporation has risen and their perceptions have become more differentiated.

Attributions of Incompetence and Malevolence. Research has also shown that out-groups are stereotyped more readily and negatively than in-groups (Kramer, 1991; Rothbart & Park, 1986). An extreme version of this is the well-known "groupthink" phenomenon (Janis, 1972). These characteristics are exhibited when outsiders are perceived as uniformly unethical or ma-levolent, incompetent, and ill-informed—and the in-group is viewed in the opposite terms. One factor that can fuel groupthink processes is the "halo effect," where modestly negative information about an out-group on one or a few dimensions becomes generalized to all of the group members and to a wide variety of their attributes (Thibaut & Kelley, 1959).

Causal attribution errors can also feed biased perceptions and interpreta-tions of in-group and out-group capabilities, intentions, and actions (Kramer, 1994; Polzer, 1994), which, in turn, can fuel feelings of distrust. Focusing on Sitkin and Roth's (1993) reliability-based trust, out-group members might be judged by the degree to which they are given credit for performance level or performance consistency. But the self-serving attribution bias that has been observed in the social perception of groups mitigates against out-groups getting the sort of credit that leads to enhanced levels of trust. As Polzer (1994) observed, in-group members are seen as being more personally responsible for successes, whereas success for out-group members is attributed to external causes (e.g., circumstances or luck). Negative interactions with out-group members may be more likely to been seen as intentional (Kramer, 1994), but negative interactions with in-group members are more likely to be attributed to external causes.

The Posited Central
Role of Value Congruence

The Sitkin and Roth model (1993) stressed the central role of perceived value incongruence in trust-related problems. Noting that they did not explore several central features of organizations in much depth, we chose to examine their general proposition by focusing on whether mismatches between task and skill requirements and managerial response could be a source of the perceived value incongruity. The idea that task and skill requirements affect trust through value congruence—rather than through the more commonly targeted causal path of perceived reliability—is an interesting one in that tasks and skills are relatively strong candidates for clear standards and measures that typically undergird reliability as a criterion of trust.

As suggested by Sitkin and Roth, escalating cycles of distrust are frequently misunderstood as being rooted in details associated with reliability and competence. The case reported here does illustrate how even when trust-related problems are clearly traceable to seemingly objective correctable errors (e.g., misrepresenting the type of task being performed), the resolution of distrust may lie in attention to perceived value incongruence or repairing hurt pride rather than in the unadorned reversal of a technical error. However, the case data analyzed here do not speak to the relative centrality of value congruence over other potential determinants of distrust. Such determinations will need to be left for future work.

Notes

1. The idea that systems poorly attuned to the task requirements—either by some objective measure or as perceived by employees—are followed by a number of problematic outcomes is a key theme in this work and can be traced to the earlier efforts of Lawrence and Lorsch (1967), Perrow (1967), Thompson (1967), and Woodward (1965).

2. The data reported here have been collected as part of a larger study of organizational TQM efforts. Names, identifiers, and other nonessential details reported here have been changed to preserve confidentiality.

References

Axelrod, R. (1984). *The evolution of cooperation.* New York: Basic Books.
Barber, B. (1983). *The logic and limits of trust.* New Brunswick, NJ: Rutgers University Press.

Barnard, C. I. (1938). *The functions of the executive.* Cambridge, MA: Harvard University Press.

Bies, R. J. (1987). The predicament of injustice: The management of moral outrage. In B. M. Staw & L. L. Cummings (Eds.), *Research in organizational behavior* (Vol. 9, pp. 289-319). Greenwich, CT: JAI.

Blau, P. (1964). *Exchange and power in social life.* New York: John Wiley.

Braverman, H. (1974). *Labor and monopoly capital.* New York: Monthly Review Press.

Brewer, M. B. (1979). In-group bias in the minimal intergroup situation: A cognitive-motivational analysis. *Psychological Bulletin, 86,* 307-324.

Deutsch, M. (1962). Cooperation and trust: Some theoretical notes. In M. Jones (Ed.), *Nebraska symposium on motivation* (pp. 275-320). Lincoln: University of Nebraska Press.

Edelman, L. B. (1990). Legal environments and organizational governance: The expansion of due process in the workplace. *American Journal of Sociology, 95,* 1401-1440.

Fox, A. (1974). *Beyond contract: Work power and trust relations.* London: Faber.

Francis, P. H. (1992). Putting quality into the R&D process. *Research/Technology Management, 35*(4), 16-23.

Gabarro, J. J. (1978). The development of trust, influence and expectations. In A. Athos & J. Gabarro (Eds.), *Interpersonal behavior: Communication and understanding in relationships.* Englewood Cliffs, NJ: Prentice Hall.

Granovetter, M. (1985). Economic action and social structure: The problem of embeddedness. *American Journal of Sociology, 91*(3), 481-510.

Janis, I. L. (1972). *Victims of groupthink.* Boston: Houghton Mifflin.

Janis, I. L., & Mann, I. L. (1977). *Decision making.* New York: Free Press.

Kramer, R. M. (1991). Intergroup relations and organizational dilemmas. In B. M. Staw & L. L. Cummings (Eds.), *Research in organizational behavior* (Vol. 13, pp. 191-228). Greenwich, CT: JAI.

Kramer, R. M. (1993). Cooperation and organizational identification. In K. Murnighan (Ed.), *Social psychology in organizations: Advances in theory and research* (pp. 244-268). Englewood Cliffs, NJ: Prentice Hall.

Kramer, R. M. (1994). The sinister attribution error: Paranoid cognition and collective distrust in organizations. *Motivation and Emotion, 18*(2), 199-230.

Lawrence, P. R., & Lorsch, J. W. (1967). *Organizations and environments.* Cambridge, MA: Harvard University Press.

Lindskold, S. (1978). Trust development, the GRIT proposal, and the effects of conciliatory acts on conflict and cooperation. *Psychological Bulletin, 85*(4), 772-793.

Linville, P. W., Fischer, G. W., & Salovey, P. (1989). Perceived distributions of the characteristics of in-group and out-group members: Empirical evidence and a computer simulation. *Journal of Personality and Social Psychology, 57*(2), 165-188.

Linville, P. W., & Jones, E. E. (1980). Polarized appraisals of out-group members. *Journal of Personality and Social Psychology, 38*(5), 689-703.

March, J. G., & Simon, H. A. (1958). *Organizations.* New York: John Wiley.

Matthews, B. A., Kordonski, W. M., & Shimoff, E. (1983). Temptation and the maintenance of trust: Effects of bilateral punishment capability, *Journal of Conflict Resolution, 27*(2), 255-277.

Mayer, R. C., Davis, J. H., & Schoorman, F. D. (1995). An integrative model of organizational trust. *Academy of Management Review, 20*(3), 709-734.

Messick, D. M., & Mackie, D. M. (1989). Intergroup relations. *Annual Review of Psychology, 40,* 45-81.

Meyer, J. W. (1983). Legalization in education. In J. Meyer & W. R. Scott (Eds.), *Organizational environments: Ritual and rationality.* Beverly Hills, CA: Sage.

Perrow, C. (1967). A framework for the comparative analysis of organizations. *American Sociological Review, 32,* 194-208.

Polzer, J. (1994). *Intergroup negotiations: The effects of negotiating teams.* Manuscript under review.

Powell, W. W. (1990). Neither market nor hierarchy: Network forms of organization. In B. M. Staw & L. L. Cummings (Eds.), *Research in organizational behavior* (Vol. 12, pp. 295-336). Greenwich, CT: JAI.

Ring, P. S., & Van de Ven, A. H. (1992). Structuring cooperative relationships between organizations. *Strategic Management Journal, 13,* 483-498.

Rothbart, M., & Park, B. (1986). On the confirmability and disconfirmability of trait concepts. *Journal of Personality and Social Psychology, 50,* 131-142.

Shapiro, S. P. (1987). The social control of interpersonal trust. *American Journal of Sociology, 93*(3), 623-658.

Sitkin, S. B. (1995). On the positive effects of legalization on trust. In R. J. Bies, R. J. Lewicki, & B. H. Sheppard (Eds.), *Research on negotiation in organizations* (Vol. 5, pp. 185-217). Greenwich, CT: JAI.

Sitkin, S. B., & Bies, R. J. (Eds.). (1994). *The legalistic organization.* Thousand Oaks, CA: Sage.

Sitkin, S. B., & Roth, N. L. (1993). Explaining the limited effectiveness of legalistic remedies for trust/distrust. *Organization Science, 4*(3), 367-392.

Sitkin, S. B., Sutcliffe, K. M., & Schroeder, R. G. (1994). Distinguishing control from learning in Total Quality Management: A contingency perspective. *Academy of Management Review, 19*(3), 537-564.

Stephan, W. G., & Stephan, C. W. (1985). Intergroup anxiety. *Journal of Social Issues, 41,* 157-175.

Tamuz, M. (1987). The impact of computer surveillance on air safety reporting. *Columbia Journal of World Business, 22*(1), 69-77.

Tamuz, M. (1988a). *Monitoring dangers in the air: Studies in ambiguity and information.* Doctoral dissertation, Stanford University.

Tamuz, M. (1988b, August). *Monitoring safety in the skies: A study of ambiguity and information richness.* Paper presented at the Academy of Management Meetings, Anaheim, CA.

Tamuz, M. (1989, August). *Control and the air traffic controllers: A longitudinal study of a safety information system.* Paper presented at the Academy of Management Meetings, Washington, DC.

Tamuz, M., & Sitkin, S. B. (1992). *The invisible muzzle: Organizational and legal constraints on the disclosure of information about health and safety hazards.* Manuscript under review.

Thibaut, J. W., & Kelley, H. H. (1959). *The social psychology of groups.* New York: John Wiley.

Thompson, J. D. (1967). *Organizations in action.* New York: McGraw-Hill.

Williamson, O. E. (1975). *Markets and hierarchies: Analysis and antitrust implications.* New York: Free Press.

Williamson, O. E. (1981). The economics of organization: The transaction cost approach. *American Journal of Sociology, 87,* 548-577.

Woodward, J. (1965). *Industrial organization: Theory and practice.* London: Oxford University Press.

Wolff, M. F. (1992). Quality in R&D: It starts with you. In M. Wolff (Ed.), *Quality in R&D: Selected papers from Research/Technology Management, 1987-1992.* Washington, DC: Industrial Research Institute.

Yudof, M. G. (1981). Law, policy, and the public schools. *Michigan Law Review, 79*(4), 774-791.

Zucker, L. G. (1986). Production of trust: Institutional sources of economic structure, 1840-1920. In B. M. Staw & L. L. Cummings (Eds.), *Research in organizational behavior* (Vol. 8, pp. 53-111). Greenwich, CT: JAI.

Divergent Realities and Convergent Disappointments in the Hierarchic Relation

Trust and the Intuitive Auditor at Work

RODERICK M. KRAMER

I get the willies whenever I see closed doors. Even at work, where I am doing so well now, the sight of a closed door is sometimes enough to make me dread that something horrible is happening behind it, something that is going to affect me adversely.

Joseph Heller, *Something Happened* (1966, p. 1)

AUTHOR'S NOTE: This research owes a special debt to Jim Baron, who organized a stimulating interdisciplinary faculty seminar on trust and norms several years ago, and to Jeffrey Pfeffer, who prompted me to think further about the structural bases of organizational trust. I am also grateful to Susan Ashford, Bill Barnett, Jon Bendor, Bob Bies, Ron Burt, Bob Cialdini, Jane Dutton, Roberto Fernandez, Alice Isen, Bob Kahn, Margaret Levi, Jim March, Joanne Martin, Debra Meyerson, Michael Morris, Joel Podolny, Rick Price, Woody Powell, Bob Sutton, Tom Tyler, Gene Webb, Karl Weick, and Mayer Zald for their constructive comments at various stages of this research. Generous financial support was provided by the Fletcher Jones Foundation, the Miller Fund, and research funds provided by the Graduate School of Business, Stanford University. Earlier versions of this research were presented at the University of Michigan Graduate School of Business, 1993 Academy of Management meetings, the 1992 Asilomar Conference on Organizations, and a conference on trust in organizations held at the Graduate School of Business, Stanford University.

Hierarchical relationships are among the most important and prevalent form of intraorganizational relation. As a form of organizing, the virtues of hierarchy are numerous and long noted by organizational theorists. As with many virtues, however, hierarchy enjoys its share of problems, the catalogue of which varies depending on where in the hierarchical relationship one happens to be situated. From the perspective of individuals who occupy the lower-status position in such relationships (i.e., those on the proverbial "bottom"), fear of exploitation and the nagging suspicion they are being treated unfairly by those above them are real and recurring concerns in many organizations. For individuals in high-status positions (i.e., those "on top"), on the other hand, the suspicion that individuals for whom they are responsible are shirking when performing their duties or engaging in acts that might endanger the organization's welfare creates vexing managerial dilemmas.

Such concerns draw attention to the central role that trust plays in the hierarchical relationship (e.g., see Barber, 1983; Hill, 1992; Kanter, 1977; Miller, 1992; Sitkin & Roth, 1993; Tyler & Lind, 1992). They also remind us of its elusive quality: Despite the obvious need for trust, distrust and suspicion often travel widely over the hierarchical landscape (e.g., Fox, 1974; Kanter, 1977; Kramer, 1994; Sitkin & Roth, 1993; Tyler, 1993).

The importance of trust and the problems that attend it derive at least partially from the reciprocal vulnerabilities and uncertainties that are inherent in hierarchical relationships. In their prototypical form, such relationships are characterized by profound and consequential differences in the power, status, dependence, and control that those on top and bottom enjoy. Although these asymmetries create opportunities for jointly beneficial outcomes, they also give rise to the prospect of disappointment and betrayal.

The present research focuses on two central questions regarding the dynamics of trust in hierarchical relationships. First, what are the antecedents or determinants of trust in such relationships? Second, why does trust sometimes fail? Previous research on these questions has focused primarily on the social and structural determinants of trust and distrust within hierarchical systems (e.g., see Barber, 1983; Fox, 1974; Kanter, 1977). For example, Kanter's (1977) influential work highlighted the impact of certain social categories such as gender on interpersonal relations within hierarchical contexts. Although prior theory and research on hierarchy have generally acknowledged the importance of psychological processes, their role has not been systematically explored. In particular, many questions regarding the perceptual and judgmental bases of trust within such relations remain unanswered. Although there a number of general cognitive theories of trust (Lindskold, 1978; Rotter, 1980), few attempts have been made to understand how structural features of the hierarchical relation influence trust-related cognitions. A primary aim of the present research is to address these important and unresolved questions by exploring how trust-related cognitions are influenced by hierarchical social structures.

Intent and Scope of the Research

To understand how trust works—and why it sometimes fails—the present research imports insights from three streams of theory and research: (a) social information-processing theory (Salancik & Pfeffer, 1978), (b) research on categorization and mental accounting (Kahneman & Tversky, 1984; Kramer, 1989; Kramer, Meyerson, & Davis, 1990; Thaler, 1985, 1992), and (c) research on paranoid cognition (Fenigstein & Vanable, 1992; Kramer, 1994). By blending conceptual insights and empirical findings from these distinct streams of research, the present study indicates how cognitive and structural features of hierarchical relations influence individuals' judgments about trust. Specifically, I show how organizational actors' structural position or location in a hierarchical relationship affects the processing of trust-related information. I further demonstrate that location is correlated with systematic and predictable asymmetries in how individuals construe trust in their relationships.[1]

To advance these claims, it will prove useful to characterize people in organizations as "intuitive auditors." A primary task of the intuitive auditor is to monitor the ongoing stream of interactions and exchanges that constitute, quite literally, the give-and-take of a hierarchical relationship, and which provide, in turn, the raw data from which inferences about trust and distrust are forged. Because of the vulnerabilities and uncertainties they confront, I argue, individuals tend to be vigilant and ruminative auditors, ever attentive to evidence that their trust in the other party is either firmly set on solid ground or built as a house of cards on shifting sand.

Trust and the Intuitive Auditor

Theoretical models of trust development (e.g., Deutsch, 1958; Erikson, 1968; Lindskold, 1978; Pilisuk & Skolnick, 1968; Rotter, 1980) have frequently noted that judgments about others' trustworthiness (or lack of it) are largely history-dependent processes. According to such models, trust thickens or thins as a function of the cumulative history of interaction between interdependent parties.

Evidence of the importance of interpersonal history in judgments about trust comes from several sources. First, there is a substantial body of experimental research that links specific patterns of behavioral interaction with changes in trust. For example, studies by Lindskold (1978) and Pilisuk and

Skolnick (1968) demonstrate that reciprocity in exchange relations enhances trust, but the absence of reciprocity erodes it. Related work on the evolution of cooperation suggests very similar conclusions (Axelrod, 1984; Bendor, Kramer, & Stout, 1991).

In noting the formative role that interactional histories play in the emergence of trust, these models draw attention to the fact that individuals' judgments about others' trustworthiness are anchored, at least in part, on their a priori expectations about others' behavior and the extent to which subsequent experience supports or discredits those expectations. Boyle and Bonacich's (1970) analysis of trust development is representative of such arguments. Individuals' expectations about trustworthy behavior, they posit, tend to change "in the direction of experience and to a degree proportional to the difference between this experience and the initial expectations applied to it" (p. 130).

In support of such assertions, empirical studies show, perhaps not surprisingly, that interactions reinforcing individuals' expectations about others' trustworthiness increase trust, but interactions disconfirming or violating those expectancies tend to undermine trust (Deutsch, 1958, 1973; Messick et al., 1983; Rotter, 1980).

Other research demonstrates that the attributions individuals make about others' behavior also play an important role in judgments regarding their trustworthiness (e.g., Deutsch, 1973; Hilton, Fein, & Miller, 1993; Kramer, 1994; Vorauer & Ross, 1993). In particular, attributions appear to be centrally involved in the process of drawing inferences about others' motives, intentions, and dispositions. These inferences, in turn, are critical for deciding whether someone can be trusted and, if so, how much.

The portrait of the organizational actor that emerges from this research is that of a vigilant and fastidious bookkeeper who maintains a rather strict accounting of the various exchanges and transactions that constitute the history of relationship with another person. From this perspective, individuals' judgments about trust tend to be calculative and cumulative. In their purest form, such models imply a rather straightforward "arithmetic" to trust, with some actions by self and other adding to the accumulation of mutual trust and others subtracting from it. The reservoir of trust in a relationship fills or empties as a function of the parties' aggregate experience.

Although this rather pristine portrait of the intuitive auditor seems plausible enough on *prima facie* grounds, several streams of research cast doubt on its veridicality. First, a number of recent studies demonstrate that individuals' judgments about such things as the gains and losses or benefits and costs associated with transactions are influenced by the "mental accounts" used when evaluating those transactions (Kahneman & Tversky, 1984; Thaler, 1985, 1992). Second, emerging research on paranoid social cognition calls into question the accuracy of individuals' causal attributions and social inferences in certain social and organizational contexts (Fenigstein & Vanable, 1992; Kramer, 1994, 1995a, 1995b, in press-a, in press-b). Third, a substantial body of social-psychological theory and research suggests that individuals' renditions of the interpersonal past are often far from faithful (e.g., see Allison, Messick, & Goethals, 1989; Brown, 1986; Goethals, Messick, & Allison, 1990; Greenwald, 1980; Kramer, 1994; Kramer, Newton, & Pommerenke, 1993; Kunda, 1990; Sanitioso, Kunda, & Fong, 1990; Taylor, 1989).

In the sections that follow, I weave bits and pieces of this evidence together to suggest how the cognitive machinery of the intuitive auditor sometimes undermines the process of making judgments about trust and distrust.

Mental Accounting and
the Arithmetic of Trust

Research on judgment and decision making shows that the perceived value of outcomes individuals obtain (or anticipate obtaining) is often influenced by the mental accounts in terms of which those outcomes are framed and evaluated (see Kahneman & Tversky, 1984; Thaler, 1985, for some clever and delightful examples of this process). This research suggests mental accounts influence judgment and choice in a variety of ways (Kahneman & Tversky, 1984; Kramer et al., 1990; Thaler, 1985, 1992). First, they can influence whether losses versus gains loom large during decision making. Second, they can influence the perceived attractiveness or unattractiveness of a given outcome, especially relative to alternative choices with which it might be compared or contrasted. Third, they can influence how rational or acceptable a given transaction appears.

Initial research on mental accounting phenomena focused primarily on judgments involving relatively simple "one-shot" decisions or transactions involving a single decision maker (e.g., a consumer trying to decide how reasonable it was to drive a certain distance to save some money on a purchase). Subsequent research extended these ideas to interdependent (social) decision contexts and decision problems involving repeated or sequential exchanges (Kramer, 1989; Kramer et al., 1990).

Viewed in aggregate, these studies reveal that mental accounting is a complex cognitive process. In particular, they show how individuals' perceptions of even computationally simple transactions may be dramatically influenced by the prominence and salience of certain information over others and the perceptual contrast among decision alternatives that is created or implied by the mental account used to evaluate them. They imply further that the specific cognitive categories or mental accounts individuals use to track and evaluate transactions play a major role in the coding, editing, and framing of outcomes (e.g., Kahneman & Tversky, 1984; Kramer et al., 1990).

Research on mental accounting has a number of potentially important, although largely unexamined, implications for trust theory. For example, it seems reasonable to posit that, if individuals' judgments about trust depend on how they construe interpersonal histories, then the specific psychological accounts in terms of which those histories are encoded and evaluated may exert a profound influence on such judgments.

To some extent, this argument turns on recognition of the fact that trust is a multidimensional construct. For example, distinctions can be drawn between task-focused, fiduciary, and relational forms of trust. Barber (1983) defines task-focused trust as a function of "technically competent role performance" (p. 9). By contrast, fiduciary trust is predicated on notions of obligation and responsibility and entails expectations that "partners in interaction will carry out their duties" (p. 9). Finally, relational trust centers around issues of interactional justice and interpersonal treatment. They encompass, among other things, individuals' beliefs that they will be fairly treated and trust that they will be afforded appropriate respect and dignity in their relationships (e.g., see Bies & Moag, 1986; Tyler & Bies, 1990; Tyler & Lind, 1992). Viewed from the perspective of mental accounting theory and research, one important implication of the multidimensionality of trust is that the specific categories or mental accounts individuals use to cognitively partition and evaluate their exchanges and transactions with others should influence their judgments about trust.

These abstract distinctions and their theoretical implications raise several key empirical questions regarding (a) the content of the cognitive categories or mental accounts that are used to evaluate transactions within hierarchical relations, (b) how those accounts influence judgments about trust, and (c) their symmetry or asymmetry across various forms of social relation. In moving us toward an answer to these questions, it is useful to have a better understanding of how social information in general—and trust-related information in particular—are processed within hierarchical relations. Salancik and Pfeffer's (1978) social information-processing perspective provides a useful starting point for such an analysis.

Social Information Processing and Trust

Salancik and Pfeffer argue that to understand many forms of organizational behavior, it is essential to consider the social context within which that behavior is embedded. "One can learn most about individual behavior," they propose, "by studying the informational and social environment within which that behavior occurs and to which it adapts" (p. 226). They go on to note that one reason social context matters is that it directs or focuses individuals' attention on certain information, "making that information more salient and providing expectations concerning individual behavior and the logical consequences of such behavior" (p. 227).

Recent research shows that a variety of goals, not always compatible, underlie social information processing within organizations. In some instances, individuals may be motivated primarily to obtain accurate information for making more realistic self-assessments of their performance or abilities (Ashford, 1989). In other situations, they may be concerned primarily about obtaining information that will reduce uncertainty regarding their status or standing in the organization (Tyler, 1993). In yet other contexts, they may be concerned with obtaining evidence that will satisfy needs for self-protection (Wood & Taylor, 1991), self-enhancement (Brown, 1986), or reassurance (Kramer, 1994).

These divergent goals can affect social information processing via several distinct routes, including their impact on (a) the set of expectations with which individuals approach their social interactions, (b) the information they find salient during those interactions, and (c) how they subsequently construe a given interaction and encode it in memory.

From the standpoint of the present research, these arguments are useful but limited insofar as they are largely generic (i.e., they assume those on the top and bottom of a hierarchical relation encounter similar difficulties and opportunities with respect to social information processing). Quite obviously, information-processing conditions are typically far from *ceteris paribus* in such relationships. For example, and as noted earlier, an individual's location in a hierarchical relationship has important implications for the kinds of uncertainties and vulnerabilities they encounter. These distinct forms of uncertainty and vulnerability, in turn, are likely to influence how trust-related information is processed, particularly in terms of their impact on attention, search, and construal processes.

To animate this argument, it might be helpful to scrutinize more closely how the landscape of the hierarchical relationship appears to those on top and bottom.

The Dysphoric View From the Bottom

From the standpoint of individuals in positions of low power or status in a hierarchical relationship, trust is critical for a number of reasons. First, those on the bottom depend on those on top for a variety of critical organizational resources. These include many tangible resources, such as promotions, pay increases, space, coveted assignments, support staff, and other resources needed to get one's work done. Thus, for people on the bottom, trust in those above them matters because of its close link to their expectations about the concrete outcomes they are likely to obtain from the organization over time.

Individuals on the bottom also depend on those on top for many less tangible but no less important psychological resources, such as positive reinforcement, empathy, and social support. As a result, another reason that trust matters is that it is closely coupled with individuals' beliefs about the sort of interpersonal treatment they will receive from those who exert control over them (e.g., see Bies & Moag, 1986; Tyler, 1993; Tyler & Bies, 1990; Tyler & Lind, 1992).

All of the reasons adduced thus far for arguing the importance of trust pertain primarily to the kinds of vulnerabilities those on the bottom routinely confront in their hierarchical relations. Another reason that trust matters, however, is that individuals in such positions usually labor under conditions of considerable uncertainty about their status and standing in the organization. They often encounter considerable uncertainty about not only the quality of the outcomes they are receiving (e.g., how well their rewards compare to what others are getting in the organization) but also the fairness and integrity of the procedures used to generate those outcomes. (Of course, organizational decision makers who exercise control over procedures and outcomes have a variety of reasons for creating and sustaining such uncertainties [e.g., see Pfeffer, 1992; Rosovsky, 1990].)

As a result of these uncertainties, individuals in subordinate roles in hierarchical relations lack precisely those types of information needed to make informed judgments about the trustworthiness (or lack of trustworthiness) of those exercising authority over them. Thus, from the standpoint of those on the bottom, decisions regarding how much trust should be conferred on a particular relationship become simultaneously more consequential and more problematic. This observation simply restates, of course, the point made earlier that those on the bottom of the hierarchical relationship routinely encounter both vulnerability and uncertainty, and these are the conditions that make salient concerns about trust. As Gambetta (1988) observes in this regard, "The condition of ignorance or uncertainty about other people's behavior is central to the notion of trust. It is related to the limits of our capacity ever to achieve a full knowledge of others, their motives, and their responses to endogenous as well as exogenous changes" (p. 218).

Such observations invite the question, "How do individuals adapt or respond to such uncertainties and vulnerabilities?" Stated differently, how do they go about deciding whether someone can be trusted and, if so, how much? Recent research on paranoid cognition provides some informative—albeit provocative—perspectives on these questions.

Paranoid Cognition and
the Not-So-Intuitive Auditor

Paranoid cognitions have been defined as false or exaggerated perceptions of persecution and derogation that "cluster around ideas of being harassed, threatened, harmed, subjugated, accused, mistreated, wronged, tormented, disparaged, vilified, and so on, by malevolent others, either specific individuals or groups" (Colby, 1981, p. 518). Early conceptions of paranoid cognition relied on psychodynamic explanations, on the assumption that such cognitions were manifestations of acute and unresolved intrapsychic conflicts. These views were articulated primarily by clinical psychologists trying to explain extreme forms of paranoid ideation (see Colby, 1981, for a thoughtful survey of the clinical terrain).

More recent social-psychological research has advanced a rather different conception of paranoid cognitions—and one that affords considerably more attention to their social and situational origins (e.g., see Fenigstein & Vanable, 1992; Kramer, 1994, 1995a, 1995b, in press-a, in press-b; Zimbardo, Andersen, & Kabat, 1981). This research takes as a starting point the observation that, in milder form, paranoid cognitions appear to be readily evident even among normal individuals. As Fenigstein and Vanable (1992) observe, ordinary people

in their everyday behavior often manifest characteristics—such as self-centered thought, suspiciousness, assumptions of ill will or hostility, and even notions of conspiratorial intent—that are reminiscent of paranoia. . . . On various occasions, one may think one is being talked about or feel as if everything is going against one, resulting in suspicion and mistrust of others. (pp. 130-133)

Paranoid cognitions thus appear to be common, even if peculiar, modes of social cognition.

The prevalence of these comparatively mild forms of paranoid cognition prompts consideration of a more benign epidemiology than clinical accounts imply or allow. Empirical studies support this intuition and identify a variety of psychological, social, and organizational variables that contribute to the emergence of paranoid cognition. Of particular relevance to the present research is evidence that paranoid cognitions are most likely to occur in situations where individuals feel (a) self-conscious, (b) under intense evaluative scrutiny, (c) insecure about their status or standing in a social system, and/or (d) experience a sense of heightened or diffuse accountability from which they perceive no ready avenue of escape (Fenigstein, 1979, 1984; Fenigstein & Vanable, 1992; Kramer, 1994, 1995a, 1995b, in press-a, in press-b).

In addition to implicating a number of psychological and situational factors in the development of paranoid cognition, this research also indicates several cognitive and behavioral consequences of these cognitions. For example, studies have shown heightened self-consciousness often leads individuals to overestimate the extent to which they are the object of others' thoughts or actions. Fenigstein (1984) characterizes this as the *overperception of self-as-target bias*. As a result of this bias, he argues, individuals tend to construe even relatively innocuous social encounters in unrealistically self-referential terms.

Related research has shown that when individuals feel under intense evaluative scrutiny, they tend to overattribute others' behavior to personalistic causes. In other words, even when plausible nonpersonalistic accounts are available, they tend to discount the credibility of such accounts in favor of those that are viewed as more self-relevant and diagnostic. For example, to young faculty members under review for tenure in an academic department, even casual and seemingly benign encounters can take on a significant and sinister import, because they feel the hot lamp of scrutiny turned toward them. Thus, the failure of a senior colleague to return a casual hello as they pass one another in the hall may prompt intense rumination about the cause or "meaning" of the event ("Did I say something at the last faculty meeting that offended the person?" "Wasn't there a bit of a 'chill' in our conversation at the drinking fountain last week?"). Because of this "sinister attribution error," others' behavior tends to be construed in overly personalistic and unrealistically diagnostic terms (e.g, as having implications for their status or standing in the relationship when in fact there are entirely plausible, competing explanations of a nonpersonalistic nature).

What implications does this picture of the paranoid social perceiver have for understanding the cogitations of our intuitive auditor? First, from a social information-processing perspective, perhaps the most important implication of research on paranoid cognition is that it suggests individuals in lower-status positions in organizations tend to be hypervigilant and ruminative information processors. As a consequence of their enhanced vigilance and rumination, they tend to (over)construe others' behavior as diagnostic of trust-related concerns (Kramer, 1995b).

Second, these arguments imply individuals in lower-status positions should develop, over time, more elaborate and differentiated mental accounting systems for tracking trust-related transactions. According to this *cognitive elaboration hypothesis,* we would expect individuals on the bottom of a hierarchical relation (those in the subordinate role) to be able to recall more trust-related incidents and behaviors compared to their superordinate counterparts.

Third, we might expect from these arguments that, all else equal, violations of trust will tend to "loom larger" than confirmations of trust for those in positions of low power or control in such relationships. Several lines of research motivate this conjecture. First, there is evidence that violations of trust are highly salient to victims, and they also prompt intense ruminative activity, including a greater attributional search for the causes of the violation and attempts at retrospective sensemaking to restore a positive and constructive worldview (Janoff-Bulman, 1992). Second, research on prospect theory (Kahneman & Tversky, 1984) documents that, during judgment, losses often loom larger than gains of the same magnitude. To the extent that violations of trust are coded as interpersonal losses, they should loom larger than "mere" confirmations of trust of comparable magnitude (e.g., breaking a promise should have more impact on judgments about trustworthiness than "merely" keeping it). Finally, there is an impressive body of research that demonstrates cognitive responses to positive and negative events are highly asymmetrical. As Taylor (1991) notes in particular, this research suggests that "negative events produce more causal attribution activity than positive events, controlling for expectedness" (p. 70).

Finally, to the extent that concerns about status or standing in the relationship are highly salient to low-status actors, we might expect that issues of relational trust will tend to loom larger than concerns about task-focused trust. This hypothesis is suggested by research on interactional justice (Bies & Moag, 1986; Tyler & Bies, 1990), relational models of authority (Tyler, 1993; Tyler & Lind, 1992), and the effects of status uncertainty on paranoid cognition (Kramer, 1994).

The View From the Top

Although individuals who sit atop the hierarchical relationship enjoy considerable advantages over those on the bottom in terms of relative power and control, they are far from being free of either vulnerability or uncertainty. The form and intensity their vulnerabilities and uncertainties assume, however, are quite different. To begin with, the dimensions along which they construe trust are likely to be quite different from those employed by their subordinate counterparts. For example, individuals in positions of authority in organizations are likely to be primarily concerned about accomplishing the various tasks for which they are specifically responsible (cf. Barber, 1983; Fox, 1974; Hill, 1992). Because accomplishment of these tasks depends on what their subordinates do or fail to do, concerns about trust are likely to be defined in terms of task-focused and fiduciary trust. For this reason, an important and highly salient dimension for authorities when evaluating the trustworthiness of those below them is whether they are likely to perform their work competently and faithfully fulfill their role obligations and duties. Thus, attention should be focused on the search for evidence regarding the competence, motivation, and values of their employees. Accordingly, one can hypothesize that, all else equal, concerns about task-focused and fiduciary trust should dominate concerns about relational trust. This implies, from a mental accounting standpoint, that others' behavior will be categorized and coded primarily in terms of task-focused and fiduciary trust terms.

In arguing that the attention of those on top will be captured primarily by task- and role-related behaviors, I do not mean to imply individuals at the top will be indifferent to questions regarding relational trust. However, to the extent relational trust concerns are salient to those on top, I argue that they are more likely to be construed in instrumental or consequentialist terms. In other words, those on top will tend to define relational trust as a strategic or managerial issue. For example, managers may decide trust is important because it improves the motivation, morale, and compliance of subordinates—all of which are in the service of enhanced organizational performance and help advance the manager's own agenda. Thus, as managers, they may be willing to expend a fair share of their discretionary attentional resources on "building" relational trust with subordinates. However, this expenditure is justified not on grounds that such trust is intrinsically worthwhile or right but rather on purely calculative grounds: By investing in trust now, they hope to garner enhanced payoffs down the road in terms of lower turnover, absenteeism, shirking, and so on (e.g., managers' accounts of trust in Hill, 1992; Melohn, 1994; Whitney, 1994).

Similar arguments can be marshalled to suggest that those on top will tend to care less than their subordinates about individuating characteristics of the other (i.e., the intentions, motives, and dispositions of those below them) except insofar as these characteristics are perceived to be pertinent to deciding how much surveillance or monitoring of their actions is necessary. In other words, social relations will be defined, all else equal, in relatively more strategic terms (e.g., the extent to which subordinates can be trusted to get things done on their own).

In addition to these substantive differences in the mental accounting between those on top and bottom, there may be quantitative differences as well. Individuals who occupy positions of power in organizations typically find their attention held hostage to a diverse and demanding portfolio of concerns. Thus, they may have little spare attentional capacity to allocate to monitor or ruminate about the activities of a specific subordinate, except insofar as such attention advances specific goals they are trying to accomplish. Accordingly, once they have told a subordinate what to do, managers are likely to turn their thoughts elsewhere. Thus, it might be expected that the mental accounting of those on top will show less cognitive elaboration, both in terms of the number of categories (between category complexity) and the number of diagnostic behaviors within those categories (within category differentiation).

In toto, the arguments advanced thus far imply the views from the top and bottom of a hierarchical relation will diverge in a number of substantive and predictable ways, most notably with respect to the organization and degree of elaboration or differentiation of their mental accounting systems. These mental accounting systems constitute implicit reference frames against which the "same" trust-related exchanges or transactions will be evaluated by those on top and bottom of the hierarchical relationship. And, accordingly, one would expect that individuals' construal of interpersonal histories will reflect these theorized differences. The study described next was designed to put these expectations on trial.

The Arithmetic of Trust
in Academic Relationships

The relationship between doctoral students and the faculty members with whom they work embodies many of the prototypical features of a hierarchical relationship. This includes the full panoply of vulnerabilities, uncertainties, and informational asymmetries described earlier (see Kramer & Martin, 1995; Taylor & Martin, 1987; Zanna & Darley, 1987, for general discussions). For example, graduate students progressing toward a doctoral degree depend on their faculty advisers for a variety of critical resources, including financial support, opportunities for coauthorship on scholarly papers, letters of recommendation, and approval of their dissertation research. They rely on their advisers to serve as advocates in departmental meetings in which they are evaluated and hope they will buffer them from departmental politics that might otherwise adversely affect their graduate careers. Finally, they depend on their faculty members for many less tangible psychological resources, such as attention, intellectual encouragement, and emotional support.

All of these dependencies are embedded in a highly evaluative institutional context. During the long and often arduous journey to the doctoral degree, the typical graduate student dwells under an intense, unremitting, and lugubrious spotlight. In fact, there is hardly any dimension of students' intellectual, personal, or social performance that is not subject to some level of scrutiny by faculty members. Given such intense dependence and scrutiny, it is hardly surprising that concerns about trust often loom quite large to students in their faculty relationships.

Although faculty members enjoy the advantageous position in this relationship in terms of power and status, they nonetheless face their own vexing forms of dependence and vulnerability. Among other things, they often rely heavily on students to collect the raw data on which their research careers depend. Moreover, to the extent they are too busy to micromanage the details of these collaborative endeavors, they trust their students to analyze research data accurately and report results honestly.[2] Second, graduate students often have ready access to a faculty member's computer files, office, and lab space—especially at night or on weekends. Because sensitive and valuable proprietary information (e.g., letters of recommendation, grant proposals, referee reports, and confidential memoranda) are often stored at these sites, trust in the student's integrity and discretion is critical. Finally, and although rarer, faculty may sometimes find themselves the target of attempts by disenchanted graduate students to get even with them via formal departmental complaints, lawsuits, and even acts of stalking and physical violence. For these reasons, faculty members are likely to be mindful of the benefits of trust but also far from oblivious to the costs of misplaced trust.

In terms of fully understanding how faculty and students construe trust in their relationship, it is worth emphasizing that the web of interdependence that binds them often extends for years. For example, the success or failure of their relationship can have long-term reputational consequences for both parties. A graduate student's reputation depends, in no small part, on what faculty members with whom they have worked say about them. In turn, the reputation of faculty members, especially if untenured or relatively unknown in their field, is at least partially in the hands of doctoral students with whom they are associated. What their graduate students say about them to other students, especially new prospective graduate students, may affect their ability to attract good students in the future. And what they say about their professors later, after they have moved on to assistant professorships, can enhance or damage a faculty member's reputation in the field. Thus, for both parties the shadow of the future is likely to loom quite large, especially as investments in the relationship increase.

For all of these reasons, the relationship between graduate students and their faculty advisers provides a rich and interesting context in which to investigate the workings of the intuitive (and not-so-intuitive) auditor.

Overview of Methods

To study trust within such relationships, advanced doctoral candidates and their faculty advisers were recruited for a study ostensibly concerned with collaborative research relationships in academia.[3] An autobiographical narrative methodology similar to that used by Baumeister, Stillwell, and Wotman (1990) was employed to obtain sufficiently detailed interpersonal histories.

Autobiographical narratives are generated by asking individuals to recall and describe significant events from their lives. These accounts are then content analyzed in terms of theoretical dimensions of interest to the researcher. For example, the frequency of events falling into a particular category (such as acts of aggression in a personal relationship) might be determined or the accounts analyzed along some specific dimension (such as the kinds of causal attributions offered to explain these acts). As recent studies have shown, autobiographical narratives provide thick and richly textured data regarding how individuals construe past experiences in their lives and the significant lessons they extract from those experiences (e.g., see Baumeister & Newman, 1994; Baumeister et al., 1990).

To produce the micronarratives used in the present research, graduate students and faculty involved in an advisee-adviser relationship were asked to recall and describe all of the significant incidents and behaviors that they felt affected the level of trust between them.[4] After generating these histories, respondents were asked to estimate the amount of time that they spent thinking about their relationship with this person (private rumination). They were also asked to estimate the amount of time they spent talking to others about the relationship (social rumination). They were also asked to estimate how much time they thought the other person spent thinking about these matters. Finally, they were asked to complete a brief questionnaire assessing various dimensions of their relationship, including trust.

Major Results

Twenty-six narratives were obtained, providing detailed trust histories for 13 dyads. The data analysis strategy followed the approach used by Baumeister et al. (1990).

Recall Data. The narrative data were first analyzed in terms of the frequency of behaviors and incidents that respondents identified as having critically influenced the development of trust in their relationship. Overall, students recalled significantly more behaviors and incidents that they construed as having influenced the level of perceived trust in their relationship ($M = 29.40$) compared to faculty members ($M = 19.14$). More detailed content analyses reveal several additional patterns of interest (in some instances, it was difficult to make a determination as to how an incident or behavior should be coded, in which case the observation was dropped from that particular analysis. As a result, the number of observations on which the following conclusions are based varies slightly across analyses).

First, the data were coded in terms of whether the behaviors or incidents described would be expected, on *prima facie* grounds, to produce an increase or decrease in the level of perceived trust in the relationship. An example of an incident described by a student that was coded as decreasing trust in the faculty member was, "[The professor] said he would write a letter of recommendation for a scholarship I was applying for [and] I later learned he didn't do it." An example of an incident recalled by a faculty member that was coded as leading to decreased trust in the student was, "[The student] lost part of a data set that we had spent several weeks collecting. I couldn't believe he hadn't xeroxed a back-up copy of the questionnaires before he took them home."

TABLE 11.1 Recall of Trust-Related Incidents and Behaviors as a Function of Location in the Relationship

| | Framing of Behavior | | |
| | Acts of Commission[a] | | Acts of Omission[b] |
Valence of Behavior	Increased Trust	Decreased Trust	
Perceiver status			
Faculty member			
Self	5.41	1.29	1.55
Other	3.07	3.44	4.38
Student			
Self	8.74	2.32	2.28
Other	4.16	4.33	7.57

a. Actual wording of instruction: List all of the things you have done (and/or have failed to do) since the beginning of your relationship with O that have affected the level of trust between the two of you.
b. Actual wording of instruction: List all of the things O has done (and/or has failed to do) since the beginning of your relationship that have affected the level of trust between the two of you.

As can be seen from Table 11.1, both students and faculty tended to recall more trust-increasing behaviors that they had done compared to behaviors that the other person had done. Similarly, both students and faculty recalled more things the other person had done that had adversely influenced the level of trust between them compared to things they had done. Both of these patterns are consistent with a self-serving bias in recall of positive versus negative traits (Goethals et al., 1990; Kramer, Newton, et al., 1993; Messick, Bloom, Boldizer, & Samuelson, 1985; Messick & Sentis, 1983).

Behaviors that entailed violations or breaches of trust, and presumably regarded as diagnostic of the other party's lack of trustworthiness, also seemed to be readily available in memory and reveal a similar pattern. By aggregating across acts of commission and omission (Table 11.1), it is evident this pattern is especially pronounced for students, who recall more negative things that faculty had done or not done ($M = 11.90$), compared to faculty ($M = 7.82$). Viewed in aggregate, the lists of indicted behaviors generated by faculty and students are not only on average rather long but also impressive in terms of the variety and severity of transgressions they encompass. For example, they range from relatively egregious transgressions, such as "two-faced" behaviors (accounts of individuals saying one thing to the person's face but another behind his or her back) and controversies over paper authorship or research credit, to far more routine and benign lapses in attention and courtesy.

The critical incidents and behaviors were also coded in terms of whether they pertained to issues of task-focused and fiduciary versus relational forms of trust. An example of an act that was coded as contributing to fiduciary trust in the relationship was, "[The student] coded a very complex data set I had given her. It took her only a week and she didn't make a single error. I was pretty impressed." An example of an act that was coded as a violation of fiduciary trust was, "[The student] left town for the holiday break and took some data that I had wanted to use to write up our Academy submission. I didn't know how to get hold of him. When he came back after Christmas, he said he simply forgot." An example of a faculty behavior recalled by a student that was coded as contributing to relational trust was, "When I didn't do as well as I expected on my field exam, [the faculty member] took me to lunch and spent the whole afternoon talking with me about the ups and downs of graduate school. He was very supportive [and] I knew he was really busy that day, too." An example of a behavior coded as decreasing relational trust was, "[The faculty member] never asked me how things were going during the entire time I was supposed to be working on my dissertation. It was like I no longer existed. I felt abandoned."

Statistical analyses of these data reveal some suggestive patterns. First, students recalled significantly more incidents or behaviors—things their advisers had done—that were coded as relational trust ($M = 10.20$) compared to faculty ($M = 4.24$). With respect to fiduciary trust, however, there were more items for faculty ($M = 6.65$) compared to students ($M = 3.06$).

Based on prior research by others (Spranca, Minsk, & Baron, 1991), it was expected that there might be differences in the availability in memory of acts of commission versus omission. Accordingly, the data were coded in terms of whether the incidents or behaviors described reflected something the focal actor had actually done (an act of commission) versus something he or she had failed to do (an act of omission). An example of an act of omission on the part of a faculty member that was coded as decreasing trust was, "She forgot to write a letter of recommendation for me, even though I asked her twice." Another student reported, "[The faculty member] didn't answer my e-mail for a month after I sent him some ideas for my prospectus [and then] after waiting for weeks, his suggestions were all pretty superficial."

Inspection of the quantitative results (Table 11.1) reveal, in the domain of trust-decreasing incidents, that acts of omission loomed larger than acts of commission for students (Ms of 7.57 vs. 4.33, respectively, difference score = 3.24) than for faculty (Ms of 4.38 vs. 3.44, difference score = 0.94). Thus, failures of action seem especially salient for those in the more dependent position. Stated differently, students "notice" many more things that aren't done compared to faculty.

Ad hoc inspection of these data suggests that many of the crimes implicated in these transgressions center around what Jones (1990) terms *reciprocation scripts*. Reciprocation scripts reflect interactants' mutual understandings regarding social interactions. They often call for complementary or tit-for-tat-like responses from interdependent parties. For example, when people in organizations greet others by smiling at them, they generally expect some sort of matching response, such as an equally friendly acknowledgment in return.

Rumination Estimates. Within hierarchical relationships, reciprocation scripts assume special diagnostic significance because of the disparity in the power and status of the interactants. For example, when an offender has low status, failure to reciprocate can be viewed as a lapse in civility that, via augmenting, might assume special attributional significance to the high-status actor (i.e., a "signal" that something is seriously wrong in their relationship). Conversely, when the offender is a high-status actor, failure to reciprocate may connote a repudiation or rejection of the victim's status or standing in the relationship.

Unfortunately, interpretation of such behaviors is problematic because disruptions of reciprocation scripts tend, from an attributional standpoint, to be ambiguous. As noted earlier, such behaviors almost always can be attributed to either personalistic or nonpersonalistic causes. All else equal, one might expect that disruption of reciprocation scripts will invoke more intense ruminative activity (aimed at reducing attributional ambiguity) among low-status actors because of their greater vulnerability and uncertainty (Kramer, 1994). If this interpretation is correct, differential evidence of such tendencies should emerge in respondents' estimates of how much time they spend thinking about such behaviors, incidents, and/or the relationship in general.

Analyses of the rumination data reveal some evidence in support of these arguments. First, as can be seen from Table 11.2, students estimate they spend more time ruminating about their relationship, both privately and socially, compared to faculty members. When asked during debriefing what some of the things they remember ruminating about were, students frequently mentioned incidents involving relatively minor gestures of concern and breaches of courtesy that, although seemingly small in their own right, took on considerable diagnostic import when viewed by their recipient in *toto*.

Another important dimension of rumination is other-focused rumination (Kramer, 1994), which can be defined as "thinking about what you think the other party might be thinking about." In the present context, these social projections (Laing, Phillipson, & Lee, 1966) provide suggestive evidence of the extent to which each individual thinks the other is preoccupied by their relationship. Accordingly, in addition to soliciting estimates about their own ruminative activity, respondents were asked to estimate how much time they thought the other party spent ruminating about these matters. As can be seen in the bottom half of Table 11.2, students predict faculty spend more time thinking about them compared to faculty members' predictions about student ruminative activity.

Comparing respondents' perceptions of their own rumination with their predictions regarding others' rumination suggests a strong pattern of egocentric projection (Goethals, 1986). Thus, faculty estimates of ruminative activity appear to be anchored on the amount of time they report ruminating

TABLE 11.2 Perceived Levels of Rumination as a Function of Location

| | Perceiver Status | |
	Student	Faculty
Dependent variable		
Estimates of own ruminative activity		
Estimated time you spend thinking about your relationship with O	32.4	10.1
How many times per week do you spend thinking about some unresolved problem or issue in your relationship?	8.4	2.2
Estimated time you spend talking about your relationship with O	18.2	2.1
Estimates of other's ruminative activity		
Time you think the other person (O) spends thinking about your relationship	25.3	15.1
How many times per week do you think O spends thinking about some unresolved problem or issue in your relationship?	6.4	3.1
Time you think the other person spends talking about your relationship	9.5	5.1

NOTE: All time estimates are minutes/week.

about the relationship, causing them, in effect, to "underestimate" the extent to which students seem to be ruminating about the relationship. Similarly, students' estimates of faculty member's ruminative activity appear to be anchored on estimates of their own rumination. In effect, this causes them to overestimate the amount of time they think faculty spend thinking about them.[5] These data thus provide a suggestive, even if somewhat indirect, measure of students' perceptions of the degree to which they are under evaluative scrutiny even when not in the presence of faculty.[6]

Judgmental Data. Respondents' general perceptions of trust in the relationship were assessed in several ways. First, they were asked to rate the overall level of trust in the relationship. As can be seen from Table 11.3, students construed the level of trust as lower than faculty ($p < .05$). Second, they were asked to indicate how trustworthy they thought they were in the relationship. As can be seen in Table 11.3, both faculty and students thought they were more trustworthy than the other party, although all means are above the midpoint of the scale. Additionally, they were asked to estimate the trustworthiness of the other party. Again, both students and faculty members predicted the other party views them as more trustworthy than the other party actually does. Thus, as with the previous data, there is evidence of a general self-enhancement bias.

TABLE 11.3 Perceptions and Social Projections on Trust as a Function of Location in the Relationship

	Perceiver Status	
	Student	Faculty
Dependent variable		
Level of trust in the relationship	4.64	5.37
Perception of own trustworthiness	6.68	6.51
Perception of other's trustworthiness	5.01	5.44
Prediction regarding the other person's trust in you	6.59	6.30

To provide an independent assessment of the level of trust in the relationship, coders, blind to the purpose of the study, were asked to rate the level of overall trust they thought existed in the relationship on the basis of the "tone" of the autobiographical narratives on a 7-point scale (1 = very little trust evident in the relationship; 7 = a great deal of trust evident in the relationship). Coders rated student narratives as conveying significantly lower levels of trust ($M = 4.22$) compared to faculty narratives ($M = 5.19$) describing the same relationship.[7]

Summary and Conclusion

In aggregate, these results support several of the general theoretical expectations advanced earlier. First, student narratives evinced greater categorical thinking compared to faculty narratives, consistent with the cognitive elaboration hypothesis. These results are also consistent with the general argument that vigilance and rumination within interdependence relations are motivated at least in part by differences in the parties' relative power or dependence. In particular, the student data suggest that, even when faculty are out of sight, they are often far from out of mind. For faculty, however, when students are out of sight, they tend to be out of mind as well.[8] Although there are clear limitations to these data, this overall pattern is consistent with other recent studies on paranoid social cognition (including Fenigstein, 1979, 1984; Fenigstein & Abrams, 1993; Fenigstein & Vanable, 1992; Fiske, 1993; Kramer, 1994, 1995a, 1995b, in press-a).

Implications and Conclusions

The contributions of the present research can be framed in several ways. First, the results of this study suggest that individuals fall short as both intuitive auditors and intuitive historians. They thus add further testimony to the compelling indictment of the shortcomings of the social perceiver that have amassed over the past several decades of social cognition research (e.g., see Allison et al., 1989; Brown, 1986; Goethals et al., 1990; Greenwald, 1980; Kramer, 1994; Kunda, 1990; Sanitioso et al., 1990; Taylor, 1989). Much of this previous research has applauded the adaptive role of these cognitive illusions and biases (see notably Taylor, 1989), emphasizing their role in self-protection and self-enhancement. By contrast, the present results add to a smaller but growing chorus that calls into question the utility of such illusions in interdependence settings (Kramer, Newton, et al., 1993; Tyler & Hastie, 1991).

Interpretation of the mental accounting results points toward a similar conclusion. Mental accounting processes can be construed as constructive cognitive processes that produce coherent and useful categorical systems for making sense of and ordering our experiences. They simplify and clarify social reality; they provide cognitive systems for assimilation and accommodation of new experience; and they may lead, over time, to integratively complex schema for evaluating new experiences. However, these same cognitive tendencies can also lead to the miscategorization of experience and prompt decision makers to make errors in aggregative judgments.

Along related lines, one can argue that vigilance and rumination are adaptive cognitive processes in terms of helping organizational actors scan their environments and extract useful generalizations from their experience. *Hypervigilance* and *dysphoric* rumination, however, may impede sensemaking and learning (Kramer, in press-a). One essential dimension to this dynamic, and the one that seems to tip the balance toward either adaptive versus mal-adaptive information processing, is the way in which individuals draw experiential evidence into a coherent and meaningful pattern (i.e., how that evidence is used to build a theory or mental model about others). As Baumeister (1991) noted,

> Meaning is a matter of associations—of connecting things up into broad patterns. If the only broad pattern is happy and optimistic, then isolated contradictory events can be dismissed as minor problems and annoyances. Each problem seems minor and trivial in comparison with the totality of positive aspects. The crucial step occurs, however, when these contradictory events link together to form a larger pattern of negative, dissonant thought. (p. 304)

Asymmetries Between Trust and Distrust

Another implication pertains to the evidence of asymmetry in the salience of acts that increase or decrease trust. Researchers have often talked about distrust as if it were simply the absence of trust (i.e., that trust and distrust are symmetric). The present data call into question this assumption. In particular, they suggest a more complicated possibility, but one that is generally consistent with prospect theory's predictions about gains versus losses and research on the differential impact of negative versus positive events. These asymmetries in social information processing generate divergent realities that lead, over time, to the emergence of reciprocal disappointments. They have some implications for understanding how and why trust within close relationships and collaborative relationships unravel.

On the surface, these data might seem to fly in the face of other data suggesting fairly positive views of others' trustworthiness. As Fein and Hilton (1994) observe in a recent discussion of the literature, "Research concerning social perception is brimming with studies that have demonstrated a remarkably robust tendency of perceivers that, on its surface, seems to reflect a rather naive and overly trusting nature" (p. 167). Reconciliation of these seemingly inconsistent conclusions rests on the social situation that is used as a reference point. The present research focuses on a specific organizational context in which doubts about trust are afforded considerable rein to roam.

The Importance of Social Context

This last point underscores the critical importance of social context in the construal of trust. Organizational researchers across a variety of domains have emphasized the need for a better understanding of how social context affects cognition and behavior in organizations (Barley, 1991; Cappelli & Sherer, 1991; Kramer, 1994; Kramer & Messick, 1995b; Kramer, Pommerenke, & Newton, 1993; Salancik & Pfeffer, 1978). As Watzlawick, Beavin, and Jackson (1967) cogently note in this regard,

> A phenomenon remains unexplainable as long as the range of observation is not wide enough to include the context in which the phenomenon occurs. Failure to realize the intricacies of the relationship between an event and the matrix in which it takes place . . . either confronts the observer with something "mysterious" or induces him to attribute to his object of study certain properties the object may not possess. (p. 21)

The call for greater attention to context seems especially germane for contemporary trust theory. To a large extent, social psychological theory on trust and distrust over the past 40 years has remained surprisingly acontextual (unless one considers the mixed-motive game a rich and generative context for studying trust—which has proven a dubious proposition). Although it has undertaken the important task of explicating the cognitive processes that influence peoples' judgments about trust and distrust, research in this tradition has remained largely "inside the head" of the social perceiver. To the extent that it has overrelied on simple mixed-motive games to study trust-related cognitions and behaviors, it has generated relatively little insight into the social and organizational antecedents of trust. In short, although there is often much that is psychological in these studies, there is often remarkably little that is social.

By contrast, sociological research on trust has provided a much richer rendering of context. Indeed, much of the most stunning conceptual progress in trust research in recent years has been on the macro frontier. Unfortunately however, this research has by and large neglected the cognitive side of the trust equation—or presented only a crude, outmoded, and sometimes almost stereotypic portrait of the social perceiver. By ignoring the content of cognitions, these portraits of the social and organizational landscape on which trust travels often seem rather static and two-dimensional.

In this respect, one goal of the present research was to suggest how micro- and macroperspectives might be wedded more productively. As I have tried to show here, conceptualizing how trust-related cognitions are influenced by the specific organizational context within which such cognitions are inevitably embedded allows us to appreciate the interplay of cognition and social structure.

The Need for More Naive Theory

A survey of extant theory and research on trust evokes one other critique. It quickly becomes evident, from even a casual inspection of the large sociological and psychological literatures on trust, that there is a pressing need for more "naive theories" about trust. Naive theories are the theories that individuals, conceptualized as lay epistemologists, carry around inside their heads. The importance of naive theory about social phenomena has long been recognized by social psychologists (e.g., Heider, 1958; Kelley, 1973; Weiner, Amirkhan, Folkes, & Verette, 1987). It is, after all, the naive theory that provides individuals with the perceived links between *their* cognitions and *their* actions. As such, naive theories presumably play a central role in their attempts to retrospectively make sense of, and learn from, their experiences. As Stephan (1985) cogently observes in this regard, it is the "individual's perception of social reality and the processing of information that influences individual behavior [and] the individual's interpretations of social reality that are crucial rather than the 'real' nature of the situation" (p. 599). Research on autobiographical narratives provides a powerful method for investigating the content and structure of these naive theories.

This observation highlights several methodological implications of the present study. Over the past several decades, an impressive social psychological literature on trust has steadily accumulated, providing important evidence regarding the antecedents and consequences of trust and distrust. However, as already noted, much of this research has examined trust behavior in the context of relatively simple mixed-motive laboratory games. The trust-related cognitions and behaviors observed in these experiments often appear calculative and strategic—and the theories generated to explain such perceptions and behaviors tend to be couched in similar terms. However, the decision structure of such games, along with the situated identities they invoke, make salient precisely such calculative and strategic orientations toward others. In experiments of this sort, few degrees of freedom remain for individuals to express more nuanced or more social modes of trust behavior. Thus, the fit between trust theory and data in these experiments is quite good—but good for reasons that, from the standpoint of external validity, are perhaps not so good.

To some extent, survey research on trust overcomes many of these limitations. However, survey studies suffer from other problems, most notably with respect to the ways in which questions and answers are framed. In survey studies, the universe of responses, and even the range they take, is already sharply constrained by the researcher. Thus, even though the data from such surveys might reveal quite accurately how individuals weight and prioritize among the variables that have been selected by the researcher, they may reveal very little about the naturally occurring set of categories, dimensions, or variables that individuals would spontaneously find salient or invoke.

Autobiographical narratives avoid many of these limitations and shortcomings. As Baumeister et al. (1990) have argued, autobiographical narratives are people's "actual accounts of genuine events from their everyday lives" (p. 995). Accordingly, in terms of ecological validity, they provide data that are more representative of how individuals naturalistically operationalize variables such as trust and trustworthiness. Therefore, researchers advocating the technique have generally emphasized its high external validity. Because individuals generate the data in a comparatively unstructured fashion, they potentially provide a rich and detailed picture of how a phenomenon is subjectively construed.

Unfortunately, the internal validity of the data becomes more problematic for these very same reasons. Threats to internal validity take several forms. First, researchers may interpret the narratives in ways that bias interpretation in line with their a priori expectations. Second, the language used by the researcher to elicit the narratives may unintentionally frame the task in ways that bias the kinds of narratives that are subsequently generated. Finally, the cognitive processes that might bias recall and reconstruction of narrative accounts are hard to pinpoint in any given study. One way to reduce these problems is a conjunctive approach that combines survey and narrative data so that the correspondence between qualitative impression and quantitative results can be better triangulated.

Paranoid Cognition,
the Intuitive Auditor, and Trust
Theory: Value Added or Baggage Added?

In concluding, it seems appropriate to ask whether conceptualizing organizational actors as paranoid cogitators and intuitive auditors adds value to
our understanding of trust. There are several grounds for an affirmative answer
to this question. First, as psychologists (Griffin & Ross, 1991), sociologists
(Berger & Luchmann, 1967), and organizational theorists (Weick, 1969) have
often argued, subjective construal processes lie at the heart of human judgment and social perception. As Griffin and Ross (1991) comment, "Faced with
the booming, buzzing confusion of sensory input," individuals routinely
confront the difficulties that attend constructing "one particular coherent
reality from the set of possible alternatives" (p. 319). Problems of construal
also permeate all of the dilemmas that attend deciding *who* can be trusted and
how much in organizations. Such judgments turn on individuals' abilities to
accurately construe not only others' motives and intentions but also how their
own motives and intentions are construed—and misconstrued—by others. As
I have tried to show here, an integrative framework that construes cognitions
as embedded within social structures provides a useful conceptual platform
from which to survey such difficulties.

The evidence reviewed here leaves us far from sanguine about our ability
to generate accurate construals of social reality. Such research forces us to
acknowledge that our attempts to make sense of reality are frequently sabo-
taged by a variety of subtle processes. Of course, the conceptual insights and
gains that accrue from framing these misperceptions as instances of paranoid
cognition should be balanced against the potential drawbacks of such labels.
For example, the term *paranoid cognition* may strike some as excessively
pejorative and harsh. In particular, characterizing the cognitive processes of
individuals who happen to occupy relatively disadvantaged positions within
social or organizational systems as prone to false or exaggerated distrust and
suspicion might seem to minimize the legitimacy of their concerns or plight.
Such labels risk blaming the victim and come close to committing the
"fundamental attribution error." These aca-demic sins are far from the intent
of the present analysis. Rather, the spirit of the present inquiry is to suggest
some of the deleterious cognitive consequences associated with certain organizational roles and locations within hierarchical social systems.

Along related lines, characterizing people as intuitive auditors who maintain detailed, even if imperfect, mental accounts of their interpersonal relations is useful at helping us understand the cognitive categories in terms of
which social perceivers frame, edit, encode, and recall significant experiences
in their lives. In invoking this metaphor, of course, we risk adding yet another

to an already long and unflattering list that has been used to describe the hapless social perceiver. Thus, over the past two decades, people have been characterized in the social science literature as intuitive rats, intuitive scientists, intuitive economists, intuitive politicians, and intuitive lawyers (e.g., see Bell & Tetlock, 1989; Fincham & Jaspars, 1980; Kelley, 1973; Kramer & Messick, 1995a; Tetlock, 1991). In defense of driving yet another thorn into the bosom of the defenseless social perceiver, I would argue that conceptualizing people as intuitive auditors highlights important ways in which our attempts to construe social reality are sometimes corrupted by seemingly innocent and useful categorical systems. Ironically, through empirical scrutiny of this metaphor, we have identified ways in which the workings of the intuitive auditor turn out, on closer inspection, to be not so intuitive after all.

Notes

1. The present research adopts the dyad as an appropriate unit of analysis for studying trust within hierarchical relations. An alternative and conceptually meaningful level of analysis is the intergroup level (see Kramer, in press-a).

2. Anyone doubting the potential sting of misplaced trust in such matters need only scrutinize recent accounts of graduate students and junior research assistants who have faked data to either advance their own research careers or simply not disappoint their advisers (see Broad & Wade, 1982).

3. The participants in the study were graduate students and faculty members from a number of social-psychology and organizational behavior departments. To control for possible gender effects, only same-gender dyads were studied. Participants were informed the study was part of a larger, ongoing research project exploring graduate educational experiences at U.S. universities. To disguise the trust focus and also obtain general information about the relationship itself, the questionnaire also included a variety of questions pertaining to satisfaction with the relationship, levels of perceived conflict and cooperation, and so on. Coders for the study were all second-year MBA students enrolled in an organizational behavior course who were blind to the purpose of the study.

4. I first conducted a pilot study using a between-respondents design (i.e., independent samples of faculty and students). Although this study produced a similar pattern of findings, a within-dyad study obviously provides a stronger and more compelling test of the theoretical arguments.

5. Of course, it is possible to argue that the causal chain runs the other way (i.e., that students "decide" they had better think about the relationship more because they think the other party is doing so). However, this causal logic seems less plausible on *prima facie* grounds.

6. Although these data are consistent with a motivational argument, they are also consistent with a simpler attentional story. In other words, one could argue that faculty simply have less attentional slack to allocate to relationship issues, especially with respect to noninstrumental concerns. Relatedly, they may allocate whatever discretionary attentional resources they do have to rumination about other relationships of greater perceived relevance to them; in other data I collected about tenured versus untenured faculty, I found that untenured faculty tended to ruminate just as much as graduate students—but the object of their rumination tended to be senior colleagues in their departments!

7. All of these means are between- rather than within-dyad measures because I didn't want coders' estimates to be influenced by explicit comparison of the student-faculty narratives generated.

8. As already noted, in a related study I did investigating paranoid cognition among untenured versus tenured faculty in academic departments, I found that junior faculty displayed similar patterns of paranoid cognition with respect to attributions about their senior colleagues' behaviors. In aggregate, these findings suggest that paranoid cognitions, like other organizational cognitions, are usefully conceptualized as nested cognitions (see Kramer, in press-b, for a discussion).

References

Allison, S. T., Messick, D. M., & Goethals, G. R. (1989). On being better but not smarter than others: The Muhammad Ali effect. *Social Cognition, 7,* 275-296.

Ashford, S. J. (1989). Self-assessments in organizations: A literature review and integrative model. In B. M. Staw & L. L. Cummings (Eds.), *Research in organizational behavior* (Vol. 11, pp. 133-174). Greenwich, CT: JAI.

Axelrod, R. (1984). *The evolution of cooperation.* New York: Basic Books.

Barber, B. (1983). *The logic and limits of trust.* New Brunswick, NJ: Rutgers University Press.

Barley, S. R. (1991). Contextualizing conflict: Notes on the anthropology of disputes and negotiations. In M. H. Bazerman, R. J. Lewicki, & B. H. Sheppard (Eds.), *Research on negotiations in organizations* (Vol. 3, pp. 165-202). Greenwich, CT: JAI.

Baumeister, R. F. (1991). *Meanings of life.* New York: Guilford.

Baumeister, R. F., & Newman, L. S. (1994). How stories make sense of personal experiences: Motives that shape autobiographical narratives. *Personality and Social Psychology Bulletin, 20,* 676-690.

Baumeister, R. F., Stillwell, A., & Wotman, S. R. (1990). Victim and perpetrator accounts of interpersonal conflict: Autobiographical narratives about conflict. *Journal of Personality and Social Psychology, 59,* 994-1005.

Bell, N. E., & Tetlock, P. E. (1989). The intuitive politician and the assignment of blame in organizations. In R. A. Giacalone & P. Rosenfeld (Eds.), *Impression management in the organization* (pp. 181-213). Hillsdale, NJ: Lawrence Erlbaum.

Bendor, J., Kramer, R. M., & Stout, S. (1991). When in doubt: Cooperation in a noisy prisoner's dilemma. *Journal of Conflict Resolution, 35,* 691-719.

Berger, P. L., & Luchmann, T. (1967). *The social construction of reality.* London: Penguin.

Bies, R. J., & Moag, J. (1986). Interactional justice: Communication criteria of fairness. In R. J. Lewicki, B. H. Sheppard, & M. H. Bazerman (Eds.), *Research on negotiations in organizations* (Vol. 1, pp. 43-55). Greenwich, CT: JAI.

Boyle, R., & Bonacich, P. (1970). The development of trust and mistrust in mixed-motives games. *Sociometry, 33,* 123-139.

Broad, W. J., & Wade, N. (1982). *Betrayers of the truth.* New York: Simon & Schuster.

Brown, J. (1986). Evaluation of self and others: Self-enhancement biases in social judgment. *Social Cognition, 4,* 343-353.

Cappelli, P., & Sherer, P. D. (1991). The missing role of context in OB: The need for a meso-level approach. In B. M. Staw & L. L. Cummings (Eds.), *Research in organizational behavior* (Vol. 13, pp. 97-111). Greenwich, CT: JAI.

Colby, K. M. (1981). Modeling a paranoid mind. *The Behavioral and Brain Sciences, 4,* 515-560.

Deutsch, M. (1958). Trust and suspicion. *Journal of Conflict Resolution, 2,* 265-279.

Deutsch, M. (1973). *The resolution of conflict.* New Haven, CT: Yale University Press.

Erikson, E. (1968). *Identity: Youth and crisis.* New York: W. W. Norton.

Fein, S., & Hilton, J. L. (1994). Judging other sin the shadow of suspicion. *Motivation and Emotion, 18,* 167-198.

Fenigstein, A. (1979). Self-consciousness, self-attention, and social interaction. *Journal of Personality and Social Psychology, 37,* 75-86.

Fenigstein, A. (1984). Self-consciousness and the overperception of self as a target. *Journal of Personality and Social Psychology, 47,* 860-870.

Fenigstein, A., & Abrams, D. (1993). Self-attention and the egocentric assumption of shared perspectives. *Journal of Experimental Social Psychology, 29,* 287-303.

Fenigstein, A., & Vanable, P. A. (1992). Paranoia and self-consciousness. *Journal of Personality and Social Psychology, 62,* 129-138.

Fincham, F. D., & Jaspars, J. M. (1980). Attribution of responsibility: From man the scientist to man as lawyer. In L. Berkowitz (Ed.), *Advances in experimental social psychology* (Vol. 13, pp. 82-139). New York: Academic Press.

Fiske, S. T. (1993). Controlling other people: The impact of power on stereotyping. *American Psychologist, 48,* 621-628.

Fox, A. (1974). *Beyond contract: Power and trust relations.* London: Faber.

Gambetta, D. (1988). Can we trust trust? In D. Gambetta (Ed.), *Trust: Making and breaking cooperative relationships* (pp. 213-237). Oxford, UK: Basil Blackwell.

Goethals, G. R. (1986). Fabrication and ignoring social reality: Self-serving estimates of consensus. In J. Olsen, C. P. Herman, & M. Zanna (Eds.), *Relative deprivation in social comparison: The Ontario Symposium* (Vol. 4, pp. 321-339). Hillsdale, NJ: Lawrence Erlbaum.

Goethals, G. R., Messick, D. M., & Allison, S. T. (1990). The uniqueness bias: Studies of constructive social comparison. In J. Suls & T. A. Wills (Eds.), *Social comparison: Contemporary theory and research* (pp. 114-131). Hillsdale, NJ: Lawrence Erlbaum.

Greenwald, A. G. (1980). The totalitarian ego: Fabrication and revision of personal history. *American Psychologist, 35,* 603-618.

Griffin, D. W., & Ross, L. (1991). Subjective construal, social inference, and human misunderstanding. In M. P. Zanna (Ed.), *Advances in experimental social psychology* (Vol. 24, pp. 61-94). New York: Academic Press.

Heider, F. (1958). *The psychology of interpersonal relations.* Hillsdale, NJ: Lawrence Erlbaum.

Hill, L. A. (1992). *Becoming a manager.* Boston: Harvard Business School Press.

Hilton, J. L., Fein, S., & Miller, D. T. (1993). Suspicion and dispositional inference. *Personality and Social Psychology Bulletin, 19,* 501-512.

Janoff-Bulman, R. (1992). *Shattered assumptions: Towards a new psychology of trauma.* New York: Free Press.

Jones, E. E. (1990). *Interpersonal perception.* New York: Freeman.

Kahn, R. & Kramer, R. M. (1990). Untying the knot. In R. Kahn & M. Zald (Eds.), *Organizations and nation states* (pp. 139-180). San Francisco: Jossey-Bass.

Kahneman, D., & Tversky, A. (1984). Choices, values, and frames. *American Psychologist, 39,* 341-350.

Kanter, R. (1977). *Men and women of the corporation.* New York: Basic Books.

Kelley, H. H. (1973). Causal schemata and the attribution process. *American Psychologist, 28,* 107-123.

Kramer, R. M. (1989). Windows of vulnerability or cognitive illusions? Cognitive processes and the nuclear arms race. *Journal of Experimental Social Psychology, 25,* 79-100.

Kramer, R. M. (1994). The sinister attribution error. *Motivation and Emotion, 18,* 199-231.

Kramer, R. M. (1995a). The distorted view from the top: Power, paranoia, and distrust in organizations. In R. Bies, R. Lewicki, & B. Sheppard (Eds.), *Research on negotiations in organizations* (Vol. 5, pp. 120-132). Greenwich, CT: JAI.

Kramer, R. M. (1995b). In dubious battle: Heightened accountability, dysphoric cognition, and self-defeating bargaining behavior. In R. M. Kramer & D. M. Messick (Eds.), *Negotiation as a social process* (pp. 95-120). Thousand Oaks, CA: Sage.

Kramer, R. M. (in press-a). Distrust and suspicion in social groups: A self categorization perspective. In B. Markovsky (Ed.), *Advances in group processes* (Vol. 13).

Kramer, R. M. (in press-b). The ties that blind: Collective distrust and self-defeating behavior in small groups. In M. Turner (Ed.), *Groups at work*. Hillsdale, NJ: Lawrence Erlbaum.

Kramer, R. M., & Martin, J. (1995). Transitions and turning points in faculty-doctoral student relationships. In P. Frost & S. Taylor (Eds.), *Rhythms of academic life*. Thousand Oaks, CA: Sage, forthcoming.

Kramer, R. M., & Messick, D. M. (1995a). Ethical cognition and organizational dilemmas: Decision makers as intuitive lawyers. In D. M. Messick & A. Tenbrunsel (Eds.), *Behavioral research and business ethics*. New York: Russell Sage, forthcoming.

Kramer, R. M., & Messick, D. M. (Eds.). (1995b). *Negotiation as a social process*. Thousand Oaks, CA: Sage.

Kramer, R. M., Meyerson, D., & Davis, G. (1990). How much is enough? Psychological components of "guns versus butter" decisions in a security dilemma. *Journal of Personality and Social Psychology, 58,* 984-993.

Kramer, R. M., Newton, E., & Pommerenke, P. (1993). Self-enhancement biases and negotiator judgment: Effects of self-esteem and mood. *Organizational Behavior and Human Decision Processes, 56,* 110-133.

Kramer, R. M., Pommerenke, P., & Newton, E. (1993). The social context of negotiation: Effects of social identity and interpersonal accountability on negotiator decision making. *Journal of Conflict Resolution, 37,* 633-654.

Kunda, Z. (1990). The case for motivated reasoning. *Psychological Bulletin, 108,* 480-498.

Laing, R. D., Phillipson, H., & Lee, A. R. (1966). *Interpersonal perception*. London: Tavistock.

Lindskold, S. (1978). Trust development, the GRIT proposal, and the effects of conciliatory acts on conflict and cooperation. *Psychological Bulletin, 85,* 772-793.

Melohn, T. (1994). *The new partnership*. New York: Random House.

Messick, D. M., Bloom, S., Boldizer, J. P., & Samuelson, C. D. (1985). Why we are fairer than others? *Journal of Experimental Social Psychology, 21,* 480-500.

Messick, D. M., & Sentis, K. P. (1983). Fairness, preference, and fairness biases. In D. M. Messick & K. S. Cook (Eds.), *Equity theory: Psychological and sociological perspectives* (pp. 63-70). New York: Praeger.

Messick, D. M., Wilke, H., Brewer, M. B., Kramer, R. M., Zemke, P. E., & Lui, L. (1983). Individual adaptations and structural change as solutions to social dilemmas. *Journal of Personality and Social Psychology, 44,* 294-309.

Miller, G. J. (1992). *Managerial dilemmas: The political economy of hierarchies*. New York: Cambridge University Press.

Pfeffer, J. (1992). *Managing with power*. Boston: Harvard Business School Press.

Pilisuk, M., & Skolnick, P. (1968). Inducing trust: A test of the Osgood Proposal. *Journal of Personality and Social Psychology, 8,* 121-133.

Rosovsky, H. (1990). *The university: An owner's manual*. New York: Norton.

Rotter, J. B. (1980). Interpersonal trust, trustworthiness, and gullibility. *American Psychologist, 35,* 1-7.

Salancik, G. R., & Pfeffer, J. (1978). A social information processing approach to job attitudes and task design. *Administrative Science Quarterly, 23,* 224-253.

Sanitioso, R., Kunda, Z., & Fong, G. T. (1990). Motivated recruitment of autobiographical memories. *Journal of Personality and Social Psychology, 59,* 229-241.

Sitkin, S. B., & Roth, N. L. (1993). Explaining the limited effectiveness of legalistic "remedies" for trust/distrust. *Organizational Science, 4,* 367-392.

Spranca, M., Minsk, E., & Baron, J. (1991). Omission and commission in judgment and choice. *Journal of Experimental Social Psychology, 27,* 76-105.

Stephan, W. G. (1985). Intergroup relations. In G. Lindsey & E. Aronson (Eds.), *The handbook of social psychology* (3rd ed., pp. 87-143). New York: Random House.

Taylor, S. E. (1989). *Positive illusions.* New York: Basic Books.

Taylor, S. E. (1991). Asymmetrical effects of positive and negative events: The mobilization-minimization hypothesis. *Psychological Bulletin, 110,* 67-85.

Taylor, S. E., & Martin, J. (1987) The present minded professor: Controlling one's career. In M. P. Zanna & J. M. Darley (Eds.), *The compleat academic* (pp. 210-219). Hillsdale, NJ: Lawrence Erlbaum.

Tetlock, P. E. (1991). An alternative metaphor in the study of judgment and choice: People as politicians. *Theory and Psychology, 1,* 451-475.

Thaler, R. (1985). Mental accounting and consumer choice. *Marketing Science, 4,* 199-214.

Thaler, R. (1992). Savings, fungibility, and mental accounts. In R. H. Thaler (Ed.), *The winner's curse: Paradoxes and anomalies of economic life* (pp. 101-113). New York: Free Press.

Tyler, T. R. (1993). The social psychology of authority. In J. K. Murnighan (Ed.), *Social psychology in organizations: Advances in theory and practice* (pp. 141-160). Englewood Cliffs, NJ: Prentice Hall.

Tyler, T. R., & Bies, R. J. (1990). Beyond formal procedures: The interpersonal context of procedural justice. In J. S. Carroll (Ed.), *Applied social psychology and organizational settings* (pp. 119-132). Hillsdale, NJ: Lawrence Erlbaum.

Tyler, T. R., & Hastie, R. (1991). The social consequences of positive illusions. In M. H. Bazerman, R. J. Lewicki, & B. H. Sheppard (Eds.), *Research in negotiation in organizations* (Vol. 3, pp. 334-347). Greenwich, CT: JAI.

Tyler, T. R., & Lind, E. A. (1992). A relational model of authority in groups. In M. Snyder (Ed.), *Advances in experimental social psychology* (Vol. 25, pp. 115-192). New York: Academic Press.

Vorauer, J. D., & Ross, M. (1993). Making mountains out of molehills: An informational goals analysis of self- and social perception. *Personality and Social Psychology Bulletin, 19,* 620-632.

Watzlawick, P., Beavin, J. H., & Jackson, D. D. (1967). *Pragmatics of human communication: A study of interactional patterns, pathologies, and paradoxes.* New York: Norton.

Weick, K. E. (1969). *The social psychology of organizing.* Reading, MA: Addison-Wesley.

Weiner, B., Amirkhan, J., Folkes, V. S., & Verette, J. A. (1987). An attributional analysis of excuse giving: Studies of a naive theory of emotion. *Journal of Personality and Social Psychology, 52,* 316-324.

Whitney, J. (1994). *The trust factor.* New York: McGraw-Hill.

Wood, J. V., & Taylor, K. L. (1991). Serving self-relevant goals through social comparison. In J. Suls & T. A. Wills (Eds.), *Social comparison: Contemporary theory and research* (pp. 15-34). Hillsdale, NJ: Lawrence Erlbaum.

Zanna, M. P., & Darley, J. M. (1987). On managing the faculty-graduate student research relationship. In M. P. Zanna & J. M. Darley (Eds.), *The compleat academic* (pp. 210-219). New York: Random House.

Zimbardo, P. G., Andersen, S. M., & Kabat, L. G. (1981). Induced hearing deficit generates experimental paranoia. *Science, 212,* 1529-1531.

Beyond Distrust

"Getting Even" and the Need for Revenge

ROBERT J. BIES
THOMAS M. TRIPP

Beloved, do not avenge yourselves, for it is written: "Vengeance is mine; I will repay, says the Lord."

Romans 12:19, *The Bible*

Consider the following examples:

1. A boss takes credit for a subordinate's ideas, and the subordinate responds by "bad-mouthing" the boss behind his back.
2. A market manager for a fast-food franchise company is publicly berated by top management for failing to meet efficiency, sales, and profit targets. The manager, humiliated and embarrassed, vows to work harder and longer hours to "prove" the top management wrong.
3. After his group was "passed over" by top management, a project manager at a computer manufacturing firm motivates his group of demoralized engineers with

the thoughts of proving top management wrong by building a computer faster and better than the higher-profile, top management-supported group of engineers.

4. A university reorganization plan is announced by the Office of the University President, despite explicit assurances to affected faculty and students that such a reorganization would not occur. Angry faculty and students have engaged in protest that has led to university investigations into the legitimacy and the fairness of the administrative process that created the reorganization.

5. A graduate student in the Mathematics Department at a prestigious university murders a member of his dissertation committee because he believes that the committee is intentionally blocking his dissertation completion.

Each of these examples share three common themes. First, the examples are true—they actually happened. Second, all of the people believed a trust, implicit or explicit, had been violated. Third, all of the people were motivated by the thoughts and emotions of revenge—that is, to "get even."

Acts of vengeance, or revenge, are typically conceptualized in extreme and violent terms. The image of U.S. postal workers gunning down former coworkers and bosses has become the social exemplar of revenge gone awry in today's organization (Swisher, 1994). Or, in a sports example, Jimmy Johnson quitting the Dallas Cowboys as part of a feud with the owner, Jerry Jones, is another vivid example of revenge that escalated "out of control." Indeed, for most people, the act of revenge is an emotional and volatile behavior with destructive consequences and thus viewed as an irrational response in a "civilized" organization or society (Jacoby, 1983).

Unfortunately, this dominant view of revenge represents an incomplete and skewed picture of it as a motive and behavior. For example, the second and third introductory examples illustrate that revenge can be a potent motivator for constructive change. Indeed, revenge can actually promote cooperation (Axelrod, 1984), and it can be a powerful constraint against power abuse (Bies & Tripp, in press) and injustice (Bies, 1987; Cahn, 1949; Solomon, 1990) in organizations.

Yet revenge, which can and does occur every day, is relatively unexplored as a social phenomenon in organizations. No study has examined systematically the varieties of revenge that occur and the possible different motivations that might underlie a specific act of revenge. The purpose of this chapter is to provide an initial "mapping" of the emotional geography of revenge. Toward that end, we will first summarize the research findings from our study on revenge in organizations. We will follow this analysis with a discussion of the theoretical and empirical implications of the research findings.

Revenge in Organizations:
Antecedents and Aftermath

In this study, we surveyed MBA students (n = 90) and asked them to recount a specific instance "on the job" in which they wanted to "get even" or seek revenge. As a group, the respondents had significant work experiences (3.2 years on average). The sample included 61 men and 29 women, and 31% of respondents were international students.

As part of the survey, we asked the respondents to think of a *specific* time at work when they decided to get even with someone. They were asked to describe the situation in as much detail as possible, including their thoughts and emotions at that time. In addition, the students were asked to specify what factor(s) caused them to seek revenge, what their specific revenge actions entailed, whether they acted alone, and whether they were successful.

The survey responses were subject to a content analysis. The data suggested that a revenge episode could best be understood in terms of (a) the specific actions that violated a trust, (b) the attributions and cognitions in response to the trust violations, and (c) the responses to the trust violations. A more detailed discussion of each aspect of the revenge process is presented below.

Actions That Violate Trust: Harms
to the "Civic Order" and "Social Identity"

Following Sitkin and Roth (1993), we view trust violations as unmet expectations concerning another's behavior, or when that person does not act consistent with one's values. The data suggest two major categories of harm that resulted from trust violations: a damaged sense of *civic order* and a damaged *identity*. A damaged sense of civic order referred to violations of rules and procedures or unmet social expectations and obligations. A damaged identity refers to attacks on or impugning of one's social identity or reputation. The categories and the specific trust violations are discussed below and summarized in Table 12.1.

A Damaged Sense of "Civic Order"

A damaged sense of the "civic order" occurred when people perceived that there were *rule violations, honor violations,* or *abusive authority.* Each of these actions was judged to violate a fundamental trust between the employee and the organization and its management.

Rule Violations. A *violation of the formal rules* was viewed as a clear trust violation by people. Such a rule violation is perceived, for example, when

TABLE 12.1 Actions That Violate Trust

A damaged sense of "civic order"
Rule violation
Violation of formal rules
Changing the rules "after the fact"
Breach of contract
Honor violation
Shirking of job responsibilities
Broken promises
Lying
Stealing of ideas
Disclosure of confidences and secrets
Abusive authority
Intolerable boss
A damaged "identity"
Public criticism
Accused wrongly or unfairly
Insult to self or collective

someone is promoted to a higher position of authority and status, even though that person does not meet the rules and criteria for promotion. Or, as the person who perceived this violation stated, "The rules mean nothing anymore. With this flagrant violation, I no longer trust anybody making decisions." In other words, there was a perception that the existing rules were not enforced.

Changing the rules "after the fact" was another action that created distrust. For example, when one person applied for an evening MBA program, he made sure that he had met all of the company's rigorous rules and criteria for full-tuition reimbursement if he was accepted to the program. Once accepted, he informed the company of his success; they informed him, in return, of "new" rules they added recently that would result in no tuition reimbursement for the employee. The employee was outraged and furious, and he wanted to tell the organization to "take the job and shove it!" This type of violation is an egregious and capricious abuse of authority (Bies & Tripp, in press).

A *breach of a formal contract* was viewed as the most "objective" violation, because the rules and expectations were in writing, reflecting a reciprocal exchange involving promises between each party. An example violation occurred to a person who negotiated a formal contract with his investment bank employer, detailing promotion and salary increase schedules. Neither salary nor promotion schedules were met, because the bank "just decided not to honor the contract." As the affected banker put it, "You can't even trust the paper the contract is written on."

Honor Violations. Dealing "honorably" with others referred to acting consistent within a prevailing code of ethics or community norms. It emerged as an important criterion or standard to assess the trustworthiness of people in organizations. More specifically, when the standard of honor was violated, distrust of the violator occurred. Five such honor violations were identified in this study.

The *shirking of job responsibilities* was viewed as a failure to meet organizational norms of performance, and, as such, as an honor violation. This violation occurred most frequently between coworkers as part of a team or project when one team member did not fulfill the job responsibilities entrusted to him or her, thus leaving the other team members to "carry the load." Such shirking violated an implicit, if not explicit, trust among team members to work, as one person described, "together" and "sharing the load equally."

Broken promises represented another honor violation that created feelings of distrust. In contrast to a breach of contract, there was no reciprocal exchange involved here. As one example, a person received a promise from a coworker friend to "help out" at a difficult client meeting, yet the coworker "backed out" at the last minute with no explanation. As another example, a boss made explicit promises to support a subordinate's candidacy for a promotion in a management meeting determining such moves but did not do so. In response to that broken promise, the subordinate stated, "My boss's word means nothing, absolutely. I'll never trust him again."

Lying was another honor violation that created feelings of distrust and outrage. One example of lying involved a boss stating that a subordinate would receive a raise when, in fact, no raise was forthcoming. Another example involved a coworker who lied about the status of her contribution to a team project, claiming that it was finished when it was not; as a result, the team failed to complete the project on time and incurred the wrath and anger of top management. In the face of being lied to, people typically reacted by saying that they had been "duped" and "manipulated"—reactions also similar to those who were victims of broken promises—and unable to trust the perpetrator again.

Stealing ideas or credit from others, whether it be by the boss or a coworker, was another honor violation that created feelings of distrust and revenge. One example involved a boss who put his name on a subordinate's report and claimed public credit for it. Another example involved a coworker on a team project who claimed primary responsibility for an innovation that she contributed very little to in terms of work. In each of these examples, and others like them, the victim felt "betrayed" and no longer able to trust the perpetrator.

The *disclosure of private confidences and secrets* was an action that violated a fundamental trust between people. Whether it be disclosing a subordinate's private matter that was supposed to be held in confidence by the boss—or a coworker who received secret information disclosed by another but used it to his or her own advantage—such an action was viewed as a "fundamental betrayal" and "a knife in the back," resulting in what one person described as "not just a splintering, but a shattering of trust."

Abusive Authority. The abuse of authority represents a common source of trust violations. One type of abuse of authority is the *intolerable boss;* another type of abuse of authority is the *corrupt boss.*

The *intolerable boss* is a classic example of abuse in action. Specifically, such bosses are hypercritical, overdemanding, overly harsh, and even, in the words of one person, "cruel" in their dealings with subordinates *across time.* There was, for example, the story of the boss who worked his subordinate 16 to 18 hours a week, 7 days a week. In addition, the boss would send his subordinate e-mail messages at home and would call her by phone at home *at all hours.* This subordinate felt "exploited and abused" and the victim of "management by psychosis."

The *corrupt boss* is another classic example of abuse in action, in which the boss uses power for selfish purposes. Such bosses cited were those who "padded expense reports" or made sure they "flew in first class *at company expense* while the rest of the team flew in coach class on the airplane." These bosses would hire their kids or overlook theft of company resources by their "friends." As one person commented in describing her boss, "He thought he should be treated as lord and king and above the law. He called us his 'subjects,' who were lucky to have a job. Little did he realize that his subjects were plotting a revolt."

A Damaged "Identity"

A damaged identity occurred when people viewed that they were the targets of interpersonal attacks, which had the effect of impugning or undermining their social identity or reputation. Such attacks included *public criticism, wrong or unfair accusations,* and *insults to the self or collective.* Each of these attacks was viewed as violating an implicit trust that one's dignity and respect should be inviolate.

Public criticism was viewed as a direct and focused attack on one's social identity as a competent organizational member. The criticism was not only negative but also unusually personalistic and berating. For example, one boss brought the whole department together and singled out one employee for poor performance in "harsh" and "angry" terms, even making "fun" of the employee's lack of skills and abilities. According to the employee, he felt he had "lost face" and felt "belittled and degraded" and "emotionally scarred" as a result of this attack. Note how the language reflects the expression of feeling an altered social identity.

Being *accused wrongly or unfairly* represented another attack on one's identity as a competent person. A wrongful accusation involved a person being blamed for a mistake or failure, when, in fact, that person was not at fault. For example, one person recounted being accused by a boss of stealing ideas, but the boss was the one who had stolen the ideas. An unfair accusation is similar to a wrongful accusation, in that both accusations are not true. But for many people, an unfair accusation typically reflects a "gross misrepresentation of the facts" rather than "I did not do it," as in the case of a wrongful accusation. An example of an unfair accusation involved a boss who blamed her team for failure, even though the team had done its best and in spite of some "questionable" decisions by the boss. With either accusation, there was a feeling by the victim of being "discredited" and that these accusations "did not do justice" to them.

An *insult to one's self or collective* represented another attack on one's social identity as a member of that group. Insults on a personal level typically involved "name-calling," as in questioning the person's intellectual capacities by referring to the employee as a "moron," or in challenging an male employee's lack of assertiveness by stating that he was a "wimp, probably had no balls." Insults to the collective involved sexist and racist remarks that targeted women and African Americans, for example.

Appraisal of Trust Violations:
Attributions and Information Processing

An analysis of the revenge episodes yielded several insights about the importance of the cognitive appraisal of an event and the manifestation of revenge in response to the event. Specifically, *attributional processes* played a key role in the manifestation of revenge. In addition, people described two different information-processing stages: *initial cognitions,* immediately after the harmful action, and *retrospective cognitions,* much later after the harmful action.

Attributions

Attributions of responsibility were prominent in people's explanations of their revenge. Three different types of responsibility attributions were identified: *act responsibility, role responsibility,* and *system responsibility.*

Act responsibility judgments centered around the perceived causality of the perpetrator's actions in causing the harm. In many cases, people gave the perpetrator the "benefit of the doubt" and searched for a plausible external explanation or attribution (i.e., nonpersonalistic) for the harm (e.g., the perpetrator was under a lot of pressure or "forced" to cause the harm by top management). Whether the victim discovered such an explanation through an investigation or was provided an explanation through a social account by the perpetrator, if the cause was believed to be *nonpersonalistic,* then there was no revenge reported by people. However, the absence of a social account or an apology would result in a personalistic attribution and make the revenge motive more salient.

On the other hand, when a *personalistic* attribution was made by the victim, there was always motivation for revenge in response to the harm. Two types of personalistic attributions were identified, both of which perceived the harm to be intentional. One personalistic attribution focused on the *selfishness* of the perpetrator—that is, when one intended harm for personal benefit, but it really didn't matter who was harmed. For example, as one person lamented, "Oh, she meant to do it. No doubt about that. But the irony is, that she would have done it to anybody in my position. Her greed blinded her."

In contrast, another personalistic attribution focused on the *malevolence* of the perpetrator. In this attribution, the perpetrator's actions were perceived not only as intentional but also malicious and done with the explicit purpose of harming that particular victim. As one person described her boss, "She was cruel and sadistic in her treatment of me. I was aware that she was evil." It was this type of personalistic attribution that was associated with "hotter" cognitions and rumination processes that will be described later in this section.

Apart from act responsibility, *role responsibility* judgments were also associated with revenge. The data clearly showed that people form social and moral expectations of others in certain roles, particularly their bosses and most of the other organizational authority figures. When such expectations are not met, and a person is harmed as a result, the motive for revenge is more salient to people. For example, several people expressed the *expectation* that their bosses would support and speak out for them in top-management meetings; yet when the bosses didn't fulfill such role responsibilities, they were blamed and became a target for revenge. Similarly, top management was judged by many to share some of the blame for "undetected" corruption in the organization when they failed to fulfill their oversight and governance responsibilities.

System responsibility emerged as a third attribution of importance. In this attribution, people held organizations responsible for hiring the perpetrator or failing to constrain the perpetrator. Sometimes, this attribution involved the belief that there was a "cover-up and conspiracy" by those in positions of authority such that the harmful act would avoid detection, or more important, that the perpetrator would escape punishment for harm-doing. This attribution was typically associated with paranoid cognitions that will be discussed later in this section.

Information Processing

Initial Cognitions: "Hot" and "Hypersonic." The initial cognitions after the violation could be characterized as *hot* and *hypersonic.* Indeed, as one person reflected, "I felt like I was in a hurricane of thoughts and emotions."

Hot cognitions were felt almost immediately, according to the people in the study, and they reported that they were "mad, angry, and bitter." A feeling of being engulfed in "white-hot" emotions was also clear and evident in people's rhetoric used to describe the experience. For example, one person described herself as "inflamed and enraged" and "consumed by the thought of revenge." Another person described his emotions as follows: "I needed to satisfy the burning desire of revenge . . . [and] I was only a few rational thoughts away from murder."

The hot cognitions of victims centered not only around anger but also reflected a feeling of being "confused" or "stunned" by the harm. A typical comment by people was found in the words of one person, "I couldn't believe what had just happened. I trusted him. When he attacked me in front of my coworkers, I was paralyzed and speechless." As another example, a person described a betrayed confidence as causing her world to be "shattered," because what she assumed to be "sacred and true—the trust of a friend"—was violated, if not destroyed forever.

Retrospective Cognitions: Rumination. A second stage of information processing, *rumination,* often occurred much later after the violation. Rumination, which involved a retrospective analysis of the violation and its causes, typically occurred when a personalistic attribution was made by the victim. In ruminating, the victim revisited the "scene" in memory and would often find new "evidence" and "facts" overlooked in the initial processing of the violation. This retrospective investigation into one's memory often led people to "discover" more personalistic causes of the violation, thus enhancing blame, and seek to confirm their paranoid cognitions.

Rumination was not merely a cognitive process; it was also an affective process. For, as one person described it, "The frustration continued to gnaw at me. I had become more disturbed at what had happened. I began to hate." In addition, the rumination would go on for weeks and months—even years, as reported by some—in which the event "lived inside of the head" of the victim (cf. Matthews, 1988).

Another interesting aspect of rumination was its *social,* not just psychological, character. Contrary to the conventional view of rumination as a solitary and introspective activity, the people reported that their rumination often occurred in the company of coworkers and/or friends. Rumination occurred publicly, in which the victim received social support and reinforcement of the

TABLE 12.2 Responses to Trust Violations

Revenge "fantasies"

Do nothing
    Self-resignation
    Self-advancement
Private confrontation
Identity restoration
    Demand for public apology and "setting the record straight"
    Work harder
Social withdrawal
    Avoidance
    Withhold help or support
    Work less
    Quit job
"Feuding"
    Unauthorized use of company resources
    "Bad-mouthing"
    Public embarrassment and humiliation
    Whistle-blowing
    Litigation
    Violence
Forgiveness

---

suspicion and outrage. Indeed, it was in such a social context that system responsibility attributions emerged, and conspiracy theories and related paranoid cognitions were constructed about the perpetrator and the organization.

Responses to Trust Violations: From Fantasies to Feuds to Forgiveness

A variety of responses to trust violations were identified. The responses could be meaningfully organized into the following seven categories: *revenge fantasies, doing nothing, private confrontation, identity restoration, social withdrawal, feuding,* and *forgiveness.* These specific revenge responses are presented below by category and summarized in Table 12.2.

Revenge Fantasies

Revenge fantasies were a frequent response to trust violations. In these vivid and often violent dream scenarios, the victim would "get even" with the perpetrator. Such dreams were filled with rich detail, so much so that one could almost "feel" the pain inflicted by the victim in the act of revenge. One person described her dream in the following manner:

The frail old man's eyes bulged and his face contorted wildly as he struggled to free his bound arms and legs. Duct tape covered his mouth. I slowly turned towards him and paused thoughtfully. My body trembled in anticipation as I lifted the 50-pound vat over his writhing body. The golden liquid languorously oozed downward. The rich smell of nectar filled the room. Next came the jar. I place it in front of his face and carefully unscrewed the lid. I had worked for weeks gathering my little helpers. His frail, honey-covered body stiffened and his eyes widened in horror, then glazed over in shock. "You never should have provoked me," I said with a rueful smile as I headed for the door. "Never."

Fantasies, like the one above, were not just an intrapsychic phenomenon; as with rumination, these fantasies were shared with coworkers and friends. Indeed, revenge fantasies were just as much social as they were psychological.

Do Nothing

In a few cases, people chose to do nothing—that is, not engage in revenge. The explanations for inaction, however, varied. One explanation was *self-resignation*, in which the person just "gave up" and did not think any act of revenge would be effective.

A second explanation was *self-advancement*, in which the victim chose not to seek revenge out of self-interest. For example, one person wanted to "get a good recommendation for graduate school," so he chose to do nothing and he got his recommendation. This latter approach is reminiscent of the famous adage: "Don't get mad; don't get even; get ahead" (Matthews, 1988, p. 107).

Private Confrontation

Confronting the perpetrator directly was another manner in which revenge was enacted. In such an encounter, the victim typically wanted to know why the perpetrator caused the harm and then vented anger to that person. In addition, victims would want the perpetrator to know that they *knew* the perpetrator was at fault and that other acts of revenge were possible.

Identity Restoration

If damage had been done to one's identity, attempts to restore that identity were often undertaken. One such attempt involved a *demand for a public apology* and *"setting the record straight."* If one's reputation had been damaged, then these efforts were expected to "repair" the damage and "restore" the identity.

If one's identity had been damaged by public criticism of one's performance or motivation, then some people reported that their revenge was to *work harder.* The goal of such an approach was to, in the words of one person, "prove my boss wrong. His characterization of me was flat out wrong, and I would perform so well that he'd have to eat his words."

Social Withdrawal

Social withdrawal, in a variety of forms, emerged as a frequently used strategy for getting even. One form of social withdrawal was *avoidance* of the perpetrator. By minimizing interactions with the perpetrator, victims reported that that was some measure of revenge, particularly if they were friends with the perpetrator. As one person described it, "We always worked out together, socialized together. But after he 'knifed me in the back,' I said 'Screw you,' and avoided him like the plague. He got the message."

Withholding help or support from the perpetrator was another form of social withdrawal. For example, one person stopped "helping my coworker under deadline," even though such help had been forthcoming in the past. Another example involved a person who stopped "standing up" for his boss when the boss was under attack in meetings. As that person reflected, "He didn't stand up for me in the promotion meeting. So I decided why stand up for him when he needed me."

Related to withholding help and support, some people decided to *work less.* This meant that people would only do those things asked of them and occasionally let work "slide," arrive to work a few minutes late, or leave a few minutes early. In a more extreme form of withdrawal, some people *quit their job* in response to the violation. As one person stated, "I got so fed up, I just told them to 'take this job and shove it'!"

Feuding

In some cases, the revenge would escalate and feuding would occur. One common feuding behavior was the *unauthorized use of company resources.* This act of revenge ranged from using the work phone to make private phone calls to charging lunches and dinners with friends as business expenses. Such behavior was viewed as "fair compensation" for harm endured by the victims.

Feuding escalated publicly when the victim engaged in bad-mouthing the perpetrator. *Bad-mouthing* would typically involve attacks on the perpetrator's social identity or reputation that were communicated to as many people as possible. As one person described, "A few bad words about him . . . here, there, and everywhere. Nobody will want to work with that snake."

Related to bad-mouthing were actions intended to *publicly embarrass and humiliate* the perpetrator. For example, subordinates might pass along negative memos about their boss to top management, or they might challenge the boss in public at departmental meetings involving top management. With actions like these, victims hoped to damage the identity of the perpetrator as "justice" for the harm done them.

A more extreme form of feuding was identified by people who engaged in *whistle-blowing* or going to a corporate ombudsman from an outside agency to lodge a complaint of wrongdoing by management or authority figures. Related to whistle-blowing was the filing of a lawsuit or *litigation* as a means of revenge. One person who was terminated from his job felt that litigation was the "only means available for me to get justice publicly. Just filing the lawsuit made the papers."

Finally, there were a couple instances of *violence* reported by people. One person reported, "First, he lied about me to others and then denied that he did. I was so angry, I just let him have it. I know it was wrong, but I felt I had to hit him . . . hard."

Forgiveness

Forgiving the perpetrator was a response invoked by a few people. Forgiveness was given in response to an apology by the perpetrator but also occurred without any response by the perpetrator. Forgiveness seemed to be perceived as a somewhat "noble" response by victims. As one person reflected, "It was time to move on. Hurting him wasn't going to help, so I said it was time to let go. Forgive him and go on."

Some Preliminary Conclusions

In interpreting these data, some interesting, albeit preliminary, conclusions emerge. First, the data suggest a broader range of revenge responses than is typically conceptualized. Although such stereotypical revenge responses as bad-mouthing and violence were identified in this study, other revenge responses such as fantasies, working harder, and forgiveness imply that there is a broader spectrum of revenge responses at the disposal of people. Indeed, in the cases of fantasies and doing nothing, there was no behavioral act of revenge.

Second, the data suggest that revenge has its own moral imperative. For example, while engaging in revenge, people reported their strong belief that they were "doing the right thing" and that they were "doing justice." Although the act of revenge may have served self-interest, it was justified in moral terms.

Third, and related to the moral imperative, revenge appeared to have a rationality. Not only was revenge rooted in an intuitive "sense of justice" as the foundation of its rationality, but it usually reflected a self-controlled response that was not immediate to the harm. Typically, many options were considered and the choice of revenge was "cool and calculated," according to most people. Indeed, these data supported the wisdom of the English proverb, "Revenge is a dish that should be eaten cold."

In fact, our research suggests that the revenge act is more often than not viewed as less than "an eye for an eye" by the victim. In addition, the delayed revenge response, and its disconnection from the hot, initial cognitions, was an unexpected finding. Contrary to the conventional view of revenge as "irrational," it appeared to be quite rational in both deliberation and delivery.

Fourth, even though victims viewed the revenge to be less than "an eye for an eye," the perpetrator may not have shared that view. Indeed, in the cases involving feuding, there was evidence of "different arithmetics" between victim and perpetrator playing a role in the escalation process. For example, when people perceived that their identities were damaged by a perpetrator's actions, they imposed a harm in return that may have been greater than that imposed on them, and then the perpetrator, who felt the victim's response too extreme, would respond even harder. In other words, the "arithmetics" of measuring harm differed between the parties, thus causing the escalation process and a feud out of control. Such different arithmetics may occur because of an egocentric bias in the experience of pain by victims and/or perhaps because some harms are hard to quantify, as when "the principle of the thing" is at stake.

Fifth, cognitive processes play a prominent and mediating role in revenge. For example, rumination, and how it amplifies blame, emerged as an important cognitive "trigger" related to acts of revenge. The rumination-blame relationship is similar to that found by recent research on organizational paranoia (Kramer, 1995). Also related to organizational paranoia was our finding of a system attribution of responsibility, which essentially perceives a conspiracy as the cause of harm. But we also found that these cognitive processes were enacted in "social settings" with others who would help construct and support the victim's view of the event.

Sixth, some harms and violations appear to be irreversible. For example, one person who was the victim of public ridicule by a boss reported, "I felt so angry and betrayed. There was nothing he could say or do to make me feel better after what he did. Nothing." Moreover, such harms may have a lasting psychological impact. For example, in concluding his story about being publicly ridiculed, the person stated, "I can vividly recall the memory to this day [20 years later]."

Finally, the forgiveness response was a surprise and clearly is a phenomenon in need of further investigation. Why people forgive is an intriguing question, and also whether, when they forgive, they also forget. In addition, forgiveness is interesting because the *victim,* not the perpetrator, restores trust. In other words, there is power in forgiveness.

References

Axelrod, R. (1984). *The evolution of cooperation.* New York: Basic Books.

Bies, R. J. (1987). The predicament of injustice: The management of moral outrage. In B. M. Staw & L. L. Cummings (Eds.), *Research in organizational behavior* (Vol. 9, pp. 289-319). Greenwich, CT: JAI.

Bies, R. J., & Tripp, T. M. (in press). The use and abuse of power: Justice as social control. In R. Cropanzano & M. Kacmar (Eds.), *Organizational politics, justice, and support: Managing social climate at work.* New York: Quorum.

Cahn, E. (1949). *The sense of injustice.* New York: New York University Press.

Jacoby, S. (1983). *Wild justice: The evolution of revenge.* New York: Harper & Row.

Kramer, R. M. (1995). Origins and consequences of organizational paranoia: A social cognitive perspective on distrust. In R. J. Bies, R. J. Lewicki, & B. H. Sheppard (Eds.), *Research on negotiations in organizations* (Vol. 5, pp. 119-153). Greenwich, CT: JAI.

Matthews, C. (1988). *Hardball: How politics is played—told by one who knows the game.* New York: Summit.

Sitkin, S. B., & Roth, N. L. (1993). Explaining the limited effectiveness of legalistic "remedies" for trust/distrust. *Organization Science, 4,* 367-392.

Solomon, R. C. (1990). *A passion for justice: Emotions and the origins of the social contract.* Reading, MA: Addison-Wesley.

Swisher, K. (1994, May 8). Working under the gun. *The Washington Post,* p. H1.

Organizational Responses to Crisis

The Centrality of Trust

ANEIL K. MISHRA

Within this division, there is a real problem with the lower-level people not trusting the people at the top, because the people feel that the management doesn't tell them the truth, doesn't level with them, isn't honest, has a hidden agenda, plays games. I could go on and on. I think it's worse today than I have ever seen it in my 33-year career in this company.

Automotive executive

Introduction

In the latter part of the 20th century, organizational crises have become almost routine. Indeed, crises, most of them caused by humans, are occurring

AUTHOR'S NOTE: This chapter is based on my dissertation work at the University of Michigan's School of Business Administration. I would like to thank my dissertation chairperson, Kim Cameron, and committee members Rick Bagozzi, Dan Denison, Jane Dutton, and Marv Peterson for providing invaluable guidance throughout this research. I would also like to thank Jane Dutton, Marta Geletkanycz, Karen Mishra, Gretchen Spreitzer, Gene Webb, and the editors for their helpful suggestions on earlier versions of this chapter. I wish also to acknowledge generous financial support for this research from the Richard D. Irwin Foundation, the Michigan Business School's Executive Education Program, and the University of Michigan Rackham Graduate School.

on a scale not previously encountered, either through faulty decisions (Janis, 1989), technological complexities (Perrow, 1984), or both (Pauchant & Mitroff, 1992). The purpose of this chapter is to develop a midrange theory that explains why organizations respond differently during crisis and how organizational performance may increase rather than decrease during a crisis.

Definition of Crisis

A crisis is defined to be (a) a major threat to system survival with (b) little time to respond (Hermann, 1963), (c) involving an ill-structured situation (Turner, 1976), and (d) where resources are inadequate to cope with the situation (Starbuck & Hedberg, 1977; Webb, Chapter 14, this volume). Although a crisis calls into question the survival of a system, it can lead to either positive or negative organizational outcomes (Marcus & Goodman, 1991; Pauchant & Mitroff, 1992). Some scholars have even argued that the trauma inherent in crisis is developmental for a system by providing individuals within the system opportunities for learning and change (Pauchant & Mitroff, 1992, pp. 99-100). In the framework developed in this chapter, I contend, however, that whether positive, negative, or developmental outcomes follow crisis depends on the nature of organizational behaviors during crisis. In particular, such outcomes depend on those behaviors that shape how resources are allocated, transformed, and acquired and the key factor(s) that moderate those behaviors during crisis.

Prior Research on
Organizational Responses to Crisis

Researchers have posited a variety of behaviors that will occur within organizations faced with crisis. The threat-rigidity effect hypothesizes that in response to crisis, communication complexity is reduced, power and influence become centralized, and concern for efficiency increases, leading to conservation of resources and greater behavioral rigidity in organizations (Staw, Sandelands, & Dutton, 1981). Pfeffer (1978, p. 54) has also posited that "centralization is a likely outcome of organizational threats and crises, which provides a rationale for legitimately reasserting claims to centralized control." Individuals may also underestimate the extent to which their own behavior contributes negatively to an organizational crisis, thus reducing their flexibility of response (Kiesler & Sproull, 1982, p. 563).

Recent empirical research on crises and crisis-related phenomena supports these hypotheses and arguments. D'Aveni (1989) found that in comparison to surviving firms, bankrupt firms suffer from greater centralization of authority and rigid adherence to existing strategies. Moreover, when faced with an external crisis, managers of failing firms pay more attention to input resources,

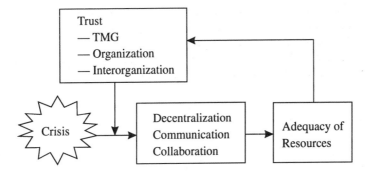

Figure 13.1. Crisis Response Model

such as creditors or suppliers, and internal factors, such as top managers and employees, than do managers of surviving firms (D'Aveni & MacMillan, 1990). Research on organizational decline and downsizing, often involving organizations facing crisis, also provides supporting evidence. Cameron and his colleagues found several negative outcomes of firms that are declining: decreasing levels of slack resources, morale, trust, upward communication, and innovation and increasing levels of conflict, centralization, and scapegoating (Cameron, Kim, & Whetten, 1987; Cameron, Whetten, & Kim, 1987). These same phenomena typically occur in organizations undergoing downsizing (Cameron, Freeman, & Mishra, 1991, 1993).

Prior research, however, has yet to provide an integrative rationale as to why different responses to crisis take place in organizations (e.g., centralization of authority), whether the conservation of resources is adaptive, or why performance suffers in some organizations during crisis but not in others. In addition, some crisis scholars have argued that prior research on crisis response has neglected deeper organizational value systems (such as culture and the values shared by senior managers) or the role of stakeholder relations (Pearson & Mitroff, 1993). This chapter argues that trust represents a key construct that has been neglected in prior research on organizational crises, one that may provide insight into how culture, values, and stakeholder relations influence crisis response and one that constitutes a tentative step toward an integrative crisis response model.

As discussed below, trust is conceptualized as a moderator of three key organizational behaviors that may occur in response to crisis (see Figure 13.1). Two of these behavioral responses, decentralized decision making and undistorted communication, may be viewed as complements to those discussed in previous crisis research: centralization of authority and reduction in communication complexity (D'Aveni & MacMillan, 1990; Staw et al., 1981). The third, collaboration within and across organizations, addresses one aspect of stakeholder relations discussed by several crisis researchers (Janis, 1989; Mitroff, Mason, & Pearson, 1994; Pauchant & Mitroff, 1992). In keeping with the definition of crisis as involving inadequate resources, moreover, each of these behaviors is related to the allocation of resources.

Theoretical Framework

Background

Inductive and deductive approaches were combined in developing the theoretical framework discussed below. A review of the existing literature on trust in sociology, psychology, and organizational studies served to ground the deductive approach. The inductive approach was based on analyzing qualitative data gathered from industry executives during the severe downturn in the automotive industry in the United States and Canada during 1991-1992 in which the survival of many firms was threatened (Flint, 1991; "GM tightens the screws," 1992; Shellum, 1991; White & Stertz, 1991). As such, this crisis is also consistent with those who have incorporated financial adversity (Starbuck & Hedberg, 1977) and significant potential for loss (Billings, Milburn, & Schaalman, 1980) in their depictions of crisis.

During the fall of 1990 and early 1991, I interviewed 33 managers from more than a dozen firms, including one of the "Big Three" (Chrysler, Ford, and GM). Each of the managers occupied top positions in their firms as CEOs, COOs, or heads of major operating units. A semistructured interview protocol was used in which managers were asked to identify the factors that contributed to an organization's performance and chances for survival as the industry became increasingly competitive. During these interviews, trust and distrust were discussed by a number of managers as critical factors affecting their organization's functioning and performance, especially as the industry downturn worsened. To use these discussions systematically in developing a theoretical framework, I searched for all references to trust in the transcripts using computer software (Microlytics, 1989). Findings from these interviews will be used to illustrate the nature of trust and its relationship to several key behaviors during crisis.[1]

The Multidimensional Nature of Trust

Previous research on trust has often been definitionally and conceptually vague (Barber, 1983). Most extant research on trust at the individual, group, and organizational levels of analysis typically suffers from unidimensional conceptualizations and operationalizations and fails to discriminate it from related constructs such as cooperation or familiarity (Barber, 1983; Luhmann, 1988). Indeed, both the research literature and the managers I interviewed typically referred to several different dimensions of trust in their discussions of the concept, often within a short passage, without explicitly stating that they exist together. However, some recent empirical research has begun to treat trust explicitly as a multidimensional construct (Butler, 1991; Swan, Trawick, Rink, & Roberts, 1988).

The review of the trust literature identified four distinct dimensions or components of trust that are discussed below. These four dimensions capture the content domain of the trust literature. Analysis of the 33 manager interview transcripts also yielded these same four dimensions, and representative examples of each trust dimension are provided from the transcripts in discussing each dimension. These four dimensions have been incorporated in the following definition of trust, which is founded on the notions of vulnerability (Barber, 1983; Deutsch, 1973; Luhmann, 1979; Moorman, Zaltman, & Deshpande, 1992) and expectations or beliefs (Barber, 1983; Luhmann, 1979; Moorman et al., 1992):

> *Trust* is one party's willingness to be vulnerable to another party based on the belief that the latter party is (a) competent, (b) open, (c) concerned, and (d) reliable.

Scholars focusing on the concept of trust have defined being vulnerable as taking action where the potential for loss exceeds the potential for gain (Deutsch, 1962, 1973; Luhmann, 1979; Zand, 1972). More recent conceptualizations of trust have also continued to incorporate the notion of vulnerability. Trust by its very nature provides the opportunity for malfeasance on the part of those being trusted (Granovetter, 1985, p. 491; Lewis & Weigert, 1985b, p. 968). Without a situation in which the possible damage may be greater than the advantage one seeks, it would simply be a matter of rational calculation that leads to choosing the course of action because the risks remain within acceptable limits (Luhmann, 1988, p. 98). "Without vulnerability, trust is unnecessary because outcomes are inconsequential for the trustor" (Moorman et al., 1992, p. 82).

This definition of trust as a willingness and a belief subsumes the cognitive, emotional, and behavioral components of trust posited by several scholars (Barber, 1983; Lewis & Weigert, 1985b; Luhmann, 1979) and is consistent with the conceptualization of beliefs as having cognitive, emotional, and behavioral dimensions (Bem, 1970). Trust is distinguished from related behaviors such as cooperation (Deutsch, 1973) or delegation (McGregor, 1967) that follow from one's trust in another (Lewis & Weigert, 1985a, p. 464).

The Competence Dimension of Trust

Within organizations, managers develop relationships with their subordinates and with other managers largely on the basis of trust, where trust is defined in part in terms of competence (Gabarro, 1987, pp. 106-108). Leaders are also characterized by how much their followers trust them to make competent decisions (Kirkpatrick & Locke, 1991). At the organizational and interorganizational levels, the competence dimension of trust is also discussed, especially in the context of exchange relations (Barber, 1983, p. 129; Sako, 1992). As one example, to the extent that a supplier organization's products meets a buying organization's quality standards, the buying organization will no longer inspect those products before accepting delivery, evidencing its greater trust in the supplier organization's competence (Sako, 1992, p. 38).

Competence is one dimension of trust that exists between individuals and organizations, according to the managers I interviewed. When one manager was asked how trust was maintained and developed in his organization, he stated,

> They've got to have some feeling that you're competent to lead them out of this mess. Because, they may like you a lot but if they feel you're a bumbling idiot they say, "%$*&! We can't trust what this guy tells us. He's gonna take us off the end of the cliff." I mean they have to be confident that you're competent. They've got to have some feeling that you know what the hell you're talking about. When you go out there to tell them to do something they've got to have some feeling that it will make a difference.

The Openness Dimension of Trust

Ouchi (1981) discussed trust extensively in describing the nature of the Theory Z organization, often in terms of openness. One key aspect of working relationships between managers and their subordinates is that of trust, where trust is defined in terms of perceptions of openness and honesty, among other dimensions (Gabarro, 1987, pp. 104-108). Openness and honesty are also a dimension of followers' trust in leaders (Kirkpatrick & Locke, 1991; Nanus, 1989). Leaders who are trusted are more effective in acquiring skills, retaining and attracting followers, and promoting change and innovation (Kirkpatrick & Locke, 1991, p. 58). Davis and Lawrence (1977) also conceptualized trust in terms of openness in relating trust to coordination among matrixed departments. In construct validation research, Butler (1991) has found some empirical support for openness as one of several separate conditions of trust.

Managers who I interviewed also discussed trust extensively in terms of openness or honesty. When asked to describe trust between himself and his employees, one manager responded,

If they don't believe what I'm telling them, if they think it's all a bunch of bull, don't expect them to go out there and work a little harder or work a little different. They're not going to be as receptive to change unless they understand and trust that the things that we're talking about are in fact true.

Openness beyond a certain level may, however, serve to impair rather than enhance trust. For example, telling someone the complete truth, with elaborate detail, about his or her character flaws may decrease trust between two parties.[2] Nevertheless, such extreme honesty impairs the overall trust level by lowering trust in terms of the concern or competence dimensions, rather than the openness dimension *per se.*

The Concern Dimension of Trust

At a minimum, this dimension of trust means that one party believes it will not be taken unfair advantage of by another (Bromiley & Cummings, 1993; McGregor, 1967, p. 163). However, greater trust in another party in terms of concern goes beyond believing that the party will not be opportunistic. For example, I can believe that another party will refrain not only from taking unfair advantage of me but will also be concerned about my interests or the interests of the whole (Barber, 1983; Ouchi, 1981). This does not mean that the other party lacks any self-interest. Rather, trust in terms of concern means that such self-interest is balanced by interest in the welfare of others.

Several examples of this dimension exist in the research literature. Middle managers show that they can be trusted by "caring about the company more than anything else" (Kanter, 1977, p. 65). Employees trust top managers in part because they believe that these managers will care about employees' job security (Kanter, 1983, 1989). When management undertakes any organizational change effort, employees evaluate management in terms of whether it can be trusted to be concerned with the employees' own welfare and interests (Kotter & Schlesinger, 1979). Followers' expectations about a leader's degree of concern about the needs of others largely define how much they trust the leader (Nanus, 1989). Moreover, "all leaders require trust as a basis for their legitimacy and as the mortar that binds leader to follower" (Nanus, 1989, p. 101). Trust in terms of concern not only exists in hierarchical relations but also among individuals within the same level in the hierarchy. Pascale (1990, pp. 249-151) has described Honda's culture in terms of employees trusting one another to be concerned with the welfare of the entire organization. This dimension of trust also operates at an institutional level. The assessment of political institutions, which depends on the trust of the electorate, is in part based on their degree of concern for the interests of the whole (March & Olsen, 1989, p. 128).

Managers who were interviewed also referred to trust in terms of concern for another party's welfare or interests.

> I think the trust factor is that you have the best interest of the people at heart, and that they believe in what you're trying to do . . . if they feel that you really care. I have a responsibility for 3,000-plus people and their families. That's an awesome responsibility. My single objective is to make sure that those people have a livelihood, a future, so that they can take care of those families. That's all part of this trust issue.

The Reliability Dimension of Trust

"Inconsistencies between words and action decrease trust" (McGregor, 1967, p. 164). Ouchi (1981, p. 101) has referred to trust in terms of expectations about consistent or reliable behavior. Trust between managers and subordinates is also defined by Gabarro (1987, p. 105) in terms of consistency of behavior and that "judgments about trust in working relationships become specific based on accumulation of interactions, specific incidents, problems, and events" (Gabarro, 1987, p. 104). The trustworthiness of leaders has also been explicitly defined in terms of their reliability. "Nothing is noticed more quickly—and considered more significant—than a discrepancy between what executives preach and what they expect their associates to practice" (Nanus, 1989, p. 102). Kirkpatrick and Locke (1991) also define the trustworthiness of leaders in terms of reliability ("consistency or credibility") and note that during crisis, their reliability is particularly salient for assessments of their trustworthiness. In the marketing literature, Swan et al. (1988) investigated trust that purchasers held in salespeople and validated four distinct dimensions of trust, including reliability, which they labeled dependability.

Reliability, dependability, or consistency between words and action, was another theme in managers' comments when asked what they thought builds trust. When asked to assess the level of trust held in him by his customers, one manager stated,

> I'd say for the most part, our level of trust with our customers is pretty good. Because we, number one, do what we say. If we say we're going to have it on the 17th, we have it on the 17th. If something would prevent that from happening we warn them upfront. We work with them on an early warning system, I hope. There again, customers only trust you because you have a history of delivering what you say.

Another manager from a supplier firm explicitly compared customer firms in terms of their reliability:

In most cases, we've certainly developed more of a trusting relationship with certain companies than we've been able to with this other company. I believe it's because their middle managers are getting consistent messages from the top. These companies are less likely to pull the rug out from under the people we deal with directly. Whereas, this other company's (top managers) will change their minds overnight, and all the things that are put forth by the people that I deal with on a one-on-one basis suddenly aren't valid anymore.

Trust Is a Combination of the Four Dimensions

Several scholars have posited that trust is a set of distinct beliefs or expectations that nevertheless combine in some fashion to represent overall trust. Luhmann (1979, pp. 91-92) articulates how the presence or absence of different expectations marks thresholds between distrust, indifference, and trust. For example, one can be trusted in terms of his or her moral intention but not in terms of his or her ability to report objectively, and therefore the person is not completely trusted (Luhmann, 1979, p. 92). Barber (1983) has explicitly argued that trust is a multidimensional construct, incorporating expectations of both competence and fiduciary responsibility (i.e., concern). These two dimensions of trust operate with respect to many different referents and levels of analysis, including within family groups, between business organizations, and the public's trust in the professions, political leaders, and charitable foundations. Greater trust exists in a particular referent when trust along both dimensions is present, as when a surgeon can be trusted to be both technically competent and concerned for the welfare of the patient (Barber, 1983). Construct validation efforts in both marketing (Swan et al., 1988) and organizational studies (Bromiley & Cummings, 1993) have also provided empirical support for the concept of an overall trust construct composed of multiple dimensions. Moreover, Swan et al. (1988) showed that their separate dimensions of trust explained a sizable fraction of the variance in general trust constructs developed by other researchers.

In this chapter, the separate dimensions of trust are assumed to represent components of an overall trust construct.[3] These dimensions combine multi-plicatively in determining the overall degree of trust that one party has with respect to a given referent. That is, a low level of trust in terms of any of the dimensions offsets high levels of trust in terms of the other dimensions. For example, a manufacturer could trust one of its suppliers to be competent in pro-ducing particular engine components and be reliable in meeting its delivery schedules. But the manufacturer might still suspect that the supplier is not reporting its true cost estimates in order to price-gouge when selling those components to the manufacturer. In other words, the manufacturer may not trust the supplier in terms of openness or concern. The manufacturer in this instance would then be expected to have a low level of trust in that supplier.

Trust is assumed to exist at multiple levels of analysis. It exists within an individual, as in a subordinate's trust for his or her manager (Gabarro, 1987). It also exists within groups or organizations (Ouchi, 1981) and between organizations (Barber, 1983; Sako, 1992).[4] Even at the institutional level trust exists—for example, the public's trust in the political system (Barber, 1983; March & Olsen, 1989) or the professions (Barber, 1983; Zucker, 1986). For a collective of individuals (e.g., a group or an entire organization), trust is operationally defined in terms of the average level of trust among the members of the collective.

Interorganizational Trust
as a Multiconstituency Construct

Trust at the interorganizational level may be important with respect to several different types of organizations. A variety of external stakeholders may affect crisis response in a given organization through their demands for rationality and legitimacy (D'Aveni & MacMillan, 1990; Dutton, 1986; Pauchant & Mitroff, 1992).

In developing the theoretical framework, this chapter will limit its discussion of external stakeholders to customer and supplier organizations. These organizations in particular are critical resources for the focal organization in terms of inputs and as markets for outputs (Pfeffer & Salancik, 1978) and are crucial contingencies for the focal organization (Lawrence & Lorsch, 1967; Thompson, 1967, pp. 26-27). Moreover, effective relationships between customer and supplier firms often depend on trust, even when formal contracts are used extensively (Barber, 1983; Sako, 1992). In evaluating the 1991-1992 automotive industry crisis in the United States and Canada, the business press argued that improving customer-supplier relationships is critical if firms in this industry are to survive (Kirkland, 1991; Shellum, 1991; White, 1991). Not surprisingly, the importance of trust between customer and supplier organizations was often discussed by the interviewed managers.

> We have a relationship with one customer very much like the Japanese do. For a given service, we have a rate that we have agreed on, a target rate, that we charge. They can almost do our quoting for us. The only thing that is really up for discussion is how fast we can do it, not how much we're going to charge for that given rate, but how many parts we'll give per hour. In return they don't send the work that has been designated as our territory out for 1,000 quotes every time it becomes available. We have a very close and trusting relationship with that one customer. They're years ahead of anybody else. I think it's certainly possible to do that; if everybody operated like these guys it would be terrific.

Trust and Organizational Crisis Response

Trust has been discussed as a salient leadership characteristic during crisis (Kirkpatrick & Locke, 1991; Webber, 1987). Theoretical and empirical research, however, have yet to articulate and confirm the processes by which trust affects crisis response in organizations. In this chapter, trust (a) within an organization's top management group (TMG) (Hambrick, 1994), (b) between TMG members and lower-echelon members of a given organization, and (c) between members of that organization and its customers and suppliers are hypothesized to have a positive influence on three key aspects of organizational behavior. Specifically, these behaviors are decentralized decision making (Bowditch & Buono, 1994, p. 297), undistorted communication (Roberts & O'Reilly, 1974), and collaboration (Thomas, 1979) among functional areas or departments within an organization and between organizations (see Figure 13.1).

Decentralized Decision Making

Decentralization is the extent to which decision making is dispersed to individuals at lower levels of an organization's hierarchy (Bowditch & Buono, 1994, p. 297). The extent to which decision making is decentralized is a salient topic in my interviews with the automotive industry managers. The managers I interviewed who headed operating units frequently complained about important decisions being restricted to executives of their corporate parents. Many of the managers also discussed impediments to and the necessity of decentralizing decision making within their own organizations.

Several scholars have conducted research on decision making and crisis and have found support for the proposition that decision making becomes more centralized in organizations in response to crisis (D'Aveni, 1989; Dutton, 1986; Hermann, 1963). Top managers may wish to centralize decision making as a symbolic approach to preserving legitimacy among key internal and external stakeholders (Dutton, 1986, p. 512). Decision making may also become centralized because lower-echelon members wish to disengage themselves to avoid making mistakes that could be punished.

> On the one hand, decision-makers want to enhance their ability to act quickly and decisively in the wake of crisis. On the other hand, lower level members want to disassociate themselves with any responsibility or blame in case resolution attempts fail. (Dutton, 1986, p. 508)

Trust may be a critical factor enhancing decentralized decision making for several reasons. Delegating decision making to others involves both increasing dependence on others and entailing greater risks. Dependence takes the form of ceding one's authority to another who previously did not possess such authority. Action that previously was restricted to the person delegating authority has now been sanctioned to another person or persons. Risk takes the form of ceding authority because these others may behave opportunistically, as agency theorists argue (Arrow, 1985). Even if the assumption of opportunism is removed, risk still remains due to possible incompetence or ignorance on the part of those receiving authority, as critics of agency theory have noted (Donaldson, 1990). As noted earlier, accepting greater dependence or risk is at the core of trusting behavior (Deutsch, 1973; Lewis & Weigert, 1985a), and trust as a belief facilitates trusting behavior. Trust then may be even more important to decentralizing decision making during crisis than in "normal" situations because risk is greater. Risk is greater in a crisis by definition, for the stakes are greater, the goal is organizational survival rather than merely growth or prosperity, and the time constraints are sharper.

In the management literature, researchers have provided initial evidence for the linkage between decentralization of decision making and trust, particularly trust between managers and employees at lower levels of the organizational hierarchy. McGregor (1967, p. 173) argues that managers must be able to trust that their employees are concerned with the organization's interests if they are to delegate decision-making authority to them. Moreover, during crisis, the transformation of an organization based on a mechanistic control system to an organic one depends on the development of trust between the organization's managers and employees (McGregor, 1967, pp. 132-133). Citing case studies of both Japanese and U.S. firms, others more generally state that nonmanagerial personnel will be allowed to make decisions only if they are trusted by those above them in the hierarchy (Davidow & Malone, 1992, p. 176; Ouchi, 1981, p. 81).

The dynamic between decentralization and trust is bottom-up as well as top-down. The effort to move from an autocratic to a democratic style of management depends not only on how much management trusts employees but also on the degree to which employees trust management (Ouchi, 1981, p. 115). More recently, Kirkpatrick and Locke (1991) have found that trustworthy leaders are more likely to develop participation in and commitment to the decision-making process. The managers interviewed also stated that trust facilitated more decentralized decision making. As one manager put it,

> I think to get continuous improvement you have to have the trust and empowerment. I think you have to start trying to get those decision levels down to its lowest possible common denominator—otherwise you get this attitude, "It isn't my job."

Trust among top managers may also be necessary for delegation of decision making to take place (Ancona & Nadler, 1989; Katzenbach & Smith, 1993). Ouchi (1981) notes that an organization's top manager must be able to trust his or her subordinates to be concerned with the best interests of all before decentralizing decision-making authority to them (Ouchi, 1981, p. 105). Members of a TMG must also trust an organization's top manager and one another not to be engaged in self-serving behavior for them to accept decision-making responsibility (Ouchi, 1981, p. 79). Therefore, the hypotheses relating trust to decentralized decision making in organizations are the following:

> Hypothesis 1a: During crisis, the level of trust among TMG members will increase the degree to which decision making is decentralized in an organization.
>
> Hypothesis 1b: During crisis, the level of trust between TMG members and lower-echelon members will increase the degree to which decision making is decentralized in an organization.

Undistorted Communication

Trust is also expected to increase the communication of undistorted, truthful, or candid information. Although the openness dimension of trust, as part of overall trust, is related to undistorted communication, it is conceptually distinct from it. Trust as defined in this chapter includes *beliefs* regarding the openness of another's communication. The extent to which the trusted person engages in undistorted communication then reinforces the trust (in terms of openness) placed in him or her. In contrast, trust in another is reduced when that other engages in outright lying or distortions of the truth.

Undistorted communication, like decentralization, is expected to suffer during crisis unless enhanced by trust. Even though demands for information may increase during crisis (Kiesler & Sproull, 1982), upward communication often suffers (Hermann, 1963). Information may be withheld or distorted due to fear of reprisal among lower-echelon members (Pauchant & Mitroff, 1992, p. 17). To the extent that lying is positively associated with performance pressures stemming from inadequate time or resources (Grover, 1993), it can be expected that the communication of undistorted information will suffer during crisis.

Several scholars have posited that trust facilitates greater use of undistorted communication. At the individual level, Rogers (1961, pp. 50-51) linked trustworthiness and candor of communication. Experiments in group settings have shown that communication is more likely to be distorted, misleading, or deceptive when suspicion rather than trust exists (Deutsch, 1973, p. 165; Zand, 1972, p. 230; see also the review by Golembiewski & McConkie, 1975). Within organizations, scholars have argued that a sufficient level of trust must be present for individuals to speak candidly and honestly to peers, subordinates, and superiors (Beer, 1987; Ouchi, 1981, p. 98; Zand, 1972). Roberts and O'Reilly (1974, p. 208) found that subordinates who had lower levels of trust in their superiors had a greater propensity to withhold information from them and reported a higher degree of distorted upward communication. Thus, trust in TMG members by lower-echelon employees may be important in encouraging them to communicate upward to them, especially in the case of information that is perceived as damaging to TMG members. At the organizational and interorganizational levels, McGregor (1967, p. 163) has argued that "unless mutual trust is a characteristic of the system, the openness of communications will be severely limited." More specifically, trust between customer and supplier organizations is critical to the exchange of open and truthful information, especially proprietary information such as sales, orders, and inventories (Davidow & Malone, 1992, p. 58) or information on future business plans (Sako, 1992, p. 48).

This research is supported by my interviews with managers, in which almost all of them stated the importance of trust as a prerequisite to undistorted communication. The ways in which trust facilitated undistorted communication are illustrated by these managers' comments:

> As far as my boss is concerned, I trust him like I trust a brother. I tell him anything I want. He'll use discretion in how he uses it.

> The way we find [important information] out is, I think, this mutual trust or partnership kind of relationship. One of our people is friends enough with somebody in one of our customer firms that knows that information, who is willing to share it knowing that it is not going to be used in the wrong way and shares it.

The hypotheses articulated below relate trust to undistorted communication about specific information that is especially relevant during crisis. Because a crisis involves scarce resources, information about how resources are currently allocated is critical to individuals' ability to redirect resources to where they are most needed to deal with the crisis. However, sharing such information in a completely honest manner entails risks because costs, inefficiencies, and redundancies may be revealed. For managers and employees to be honest in communicating such information within an organization, they must believe that they will not be adversely harmed (e.g., in the form of reprimands or disciplinary action for not being forthcoming earlier). Moreover, to the extent that norms of reciprocity and equity are operating, individuals will be loathe to disclose potential excess resources unless others are willing to do the same. Sharing information about resource allocation between customer and supplier firms runs the risk that such information will be shared with competitors or will be used by customers to demand price reductions from their suppliers (Sako, 1992; Womack, Jones, & Roos, 1990).

Operating budgets in particular provides decision makers with a key source of information about organizational resource allocation and a key form of managerial control (Bourgeois, 1981; Cyert & March, 1963). Not surprisingly, some scholars of trust have posited that undistorted communication of budgetary information critically depends on trust. For example, Bromiley and Cummings (1993) have argued that a lack of trust between managers causes them to bias their budgetary requests because the budgets are expected to be dishonest in the first place and they are rewarded for performance to budget. Therefore, the hypotheses relating trust to undistorted communication are the following:

Hypothesis 2a: During crisis, the level of trust among TMG members will increase the degree to which they provide to one another honest, undistorted information about operating budgets.

Hypothesis 2b: During crisis, the level of trust between TMG members and lower-echelon members will increase the degree to which lower-echelon members provide to the TMG honest, undistorted information about operating budgets.

Hypothesis 2c: During crisis, the level of trust between members of an organization and its key suppliers will increase the degree to which these parties provide honest, undistorted information to each other about their operating budgets.

Hypothesis 2d: During crisis, the level of trust between members of an organization and its key customers will increase the degree to which these parties provide to each other honest, undistorted information about their operating budgets.

Collaboration

Collaboration is behavior that attempts to satisfy completely the needs of parties that are in conflict with one another (Follett, 1925/1941, p. 35; Thomas, 1979). It is characterized as being highly *cooperative* (attempting to satisfy another party's needs) and highly *assertive* (attempting to satisfy one's own needs) (Thomas, 1979). In particular, collaboration involves the use of problem solving to find alternatives that would satisfy both parties and selecting the most jointly satisfactory alternative (Thomas, 1979).

Collaboration over the allocation of resources is expected to suffer, however, during crisis. Managers responding to crisis often attempt to minimize or ignore the competing resource claims of affected employees, customers, or other stakeholders. If a lack of collaboration results in stakeholders resorting to legal action, even greater claims on the resources may result, as evidenced in Exxon Valdez, Union Carbide/Bhopal, Johns Manville asbestos, and Ford Pinto crises (Pauchant & Mitroff, 1992, pp. 62-63). As the automotive industry downturn deepened in 1990 and 1991 and financial losses grew to record amounts for the Big Three, Ford and GM began demanding unilateral price cuts from their suppliers and Chrysler sharply reduced its collaborative efforts to reduce costs (Fleming, 1991; King, 1991; Shellum, 1991). Not surprisingly, many managers I interviewed during that time period also noted how collaborative approaches suffered:

I'll tell you what bothers me. They [corporate management] put a big scare tactic out there. Right now there are four plants in this company building this car model. Two other plants and my two plants. We look at the forecasted volume in '93 and we need only three. "One of you is going to bite the dust." It's tough to build trust in the three plant managers of those four plants when one of them is fighting for survival—all of us, quite frankly. Do we really share all of our strategies, and all the things we need to know that could help each other in that kind of an environment? That's tough. I sat beside the other two plant mangers, Tom and Bud, for 3 days in New York this week. Fine, fine guys. You know if the three of us ever put our heads together and shared all the success stories each one of us have in our facilities, we could be much better than we are today. But do you do that at the risk of shutting yourself down? That's what is wrong.

Trust, however, has been found to be a critical factor facilitating collaboration. Thomas (1979, p. 217) has argued that "collaboration requires trust in the other party—trust in the other's information and trust that the other will not exploit oneself." Empirical research supports and extends this argument. Trust encourages interdependent individuals and groups to eliminate their fear of exploitation and recognize their existing conflicts (Gibb & Gibb, 1969; Walton & McKersie, 1965), be more cooperative in their behavior (Deutsch, 1962; Ouchi, 1981), and generate suggestions for change focused on the problem itself (Hackman & Oldham, 1980, pp. 234-235). Trust also enhances cross-functional collaboration "by encouraging individuals and groups to rely on one another and to accept each other's judgments when these are based on unique competence and knowledge" (Davis & Lawrence, 1977, p. 107).

Trust is expected to be especially important in the context of crisis and the concomitant scarcity of resources, because trust has also been found to foster collaboration over the allocation of resources within and between firms. Cross-functional collaboration over financial and human resource allocation is often based on trust (Davis & Lawrence, 1977; Lorenz, 1992; Thomas, 1979). Collaboration between firms in the allocation of financial and technical resources also depends critically on trust, whether it is a manufacturer and its suppliers (Davidow & Malone, 1992, pp. 143-145) or even between suppliers selling to the same manufacturer (Sako, 1992, pp. 237-238). Several managers I interviewed also pointed out the benefits of collaboration in the allocation of resources based on trust. As two of them stated,

I trust those people [a division of a major company]. Last year we had significant productivity increases on some of their parts. But we also had some cost increases on some other parts that were out of our control: paint increases, certain types of material increases, some handling issues that came up to prevent damage to parts from going into the plant. We were able to give them cost reductions where improvements are. They in turn gave us our legitimate price increases without any argument. It did come up with a net savings of about $20,000 a year to them. Now $20,000 as we all agree is peanuts. But it's better than having your costs go up. And, we had an open relationship. It was a give-and-take relationship. They ended up with a net reduction in prices. Now, with anybody else, we're not as likely to give them price reductions, and they're not going to be as likely to give us our legitimate price increases. So, it's an adversarial relationship, an animosity on both sides, and these issues never get resolved. It's an absolute 180 degrees the way that company is doing things from one division to another.

One of our fellow plants is our major supplier of metal—our only supplier of metal, basically. They're helping train our guys in synchronous manufacturing, and we're helping train theirs. We're sending out people to each other's plants. I've got a great commitment from this organization. We're talking about saving money. We're looking at tooling fixtures. Why do we have to have duplicate fixtures? I mean it's phenomenal how much redundancy we have in our systems because we don't trust one another. Because we don't have a relationship.

In sum, collaboration over the allocation of resources within organizations and between organizations is expected to be difficult to sustain during crisis in the absence of trust. This is not to say that some forms of competition over resource allocation, even among the plant managers quoted earlier, may also be beneficial during crisis.[5] Indeed, competition that eliminates wasteful practices and results in higher efficiency among all of the competing parties would obviously be useful during a crisis. Indeed, collaboration, as defined by Thomas (1979) and as used in this chapter, incorporates the dimension of competing for one's own interests, which in a crisis means one's survival. It also, however, involves taking into the account the joint interests of both parties and strives to find mutually agreeable outcomes. Thus, the hypotheses regarding trust and collaboration are the following:

Hypothesis 3a: During crisis, the level of trust among TMG members will increase the degree to which a collaborative approach is used to allocate resources within an organization.

Hypothesis 3b: During crisis, the level of trust between TMG members and lower-echelon members will increase the degree to which a collaborative approach is used to allocate resources within an organization.

Hypothesis 3c: During crisis, the level of trust between members of an organization and its key suppliers will increase the degree to which a collaborative approach is used between the organization and these suppliers to reduce costs.

Hypothesis 3d: During crisis, the level of trust between members of an organization and its key customers will increase the degree to which a collaborative approach is used between the organization and these customers to reduce costs.

Trust and Crisis Resolution

Trust is expected to have a positive effect on the degree to which sufficient resources are developed to deal with the crisis in a timely fashion by enhancing decentralization, undistorted communication, and collaboration. Decentralization of decision-making authority increases the flexibility and speed with which resources can be identified and reallocated to where they are most critical to the organization's survival. If, for example, during a crisis, employees are allowed to decide which areas or activities should have resources reduced or eliminated and which areas should receive additional resources, then time that would otherwise be spent seeking management approvals could be devoted to implementing the resource reallocations. This assumes, of course, that the knowledge requisite for making the correct decision resides among these employees (cf. Vroom & Yetton, 1973). Decentralization also frees up resources that would otherwise be devoted to monitoring and control systems, thus enhancing organizational efficiency, because individuals are assumed to not be taking advantage of the system (Bromiley & Cummings, 1993). Thus,

Hypothesis 4: During crisis, decentralized decision making will increase the speed and degree to which adequate resources are developed to resolve the crisis.

Higher-quality communication is also expected to have a positive effect on the degree to which sufficient resources are developed to deal with the crisis in a timely fashion. Effective crisis management depends on open communication channels among hierarchical levels and across divisional units (Pearson & Mitroff, 1993). More specifically, members of an organization will be able to allocate scarce resources more efficiently because they will be able to use honest and complete information about where those resources exist and how they can be employed for the optimal benefit of the entire organization. This same logic applies to allocation of resources between an organization and its suppliers. "Because trust encourages the disclosure of truthful information which might otherwise be withheld or distorted for self-advantage seeking, it may improve allocative efficiency" between an organization and its suppliers (Sako, 1992, p. 47). Moreover, resources can also be allocated more quickly between an organization and its suppliers, because undistorted communication minimizes the time and effort needed for negotiations about resource allocations (Sako, 1992, p. 48).

Hypothesis 5a: During a crisis, undistorted communication within an organization will increase the speed and degree to which adequate resources are developed to resolve the crisis.

Hypothesis 5b: During a crisis, undistorted communication between members of an organization and its key suppliers will increase the speed and degree to which adequate resources are developed to resolve the crisis.

Hypothesis 5c: During a crisis, undistorted communication between members of an organization and its key customers will increase the speed and degree to which adequate resources are developed to resolve the crisis.

Both cross-functional and interorganizational collaboration in the allocation of resources are expected to enhance the speed and degree to which adequate resources are developed during a crisis. Even though collaboration takes longer initially than competitive or unilateral approaches to resolving conflict over resource allocation, commitment to the allocation decisions is greatest using a collaborative approach, thus reducing implementation time (Thomas, 1979; Walton & McKersie, 1965). Evidence for the speed and efficiency of resource allocation based on cross-functional collaboration has been reported by several researchers (Clark & Fujimoto, 1990; Kanter, 1989; Womack et al., 1990). Sako (1992) also found evidence for the efficacy of a collaborative approach to resource allocation between organizations and their suppliers. Consider also the views of one of the managers interviewed:

> In this organization, we have been able to put together a cross-functional team of about 40 people to improve quality and costs. You know, engineering, quality control, finance, materials management people. It's a very good process. We've shown about a 37% improvement in the last year in this organization in reduction of warranty expenses.
> One of the problems that I've had with major customers is the following. I ask them that since they're going to put us close to the edge, by giving them 3% upfront [in price cuts], can I expect them to be more cooperative by processing legitimate price increases in a prompt manner? They said, "No we can't guarantee that." One of the major problems that I have right now is that we'll be donating a lot of money upfront [in price cuts], and in the last 3, 4, or 5 years, we have been totally stonewalled on any price increase whatsoever. Very few [price increase requests], even for legitimate costs, have gone through. Right now I have a price increase that is totally legitimate. I requested it over a year ago. I requested it again last April, and they sent a team out to study it. They shunted it from here to there to some committee somewhere, and I have not heard yet [the outcome]. Now, if I have a cost savings then I'd better hoard it. Because if I give it to them, then they won't reciprocate in good faith in an area where I have a legitimate cost increase. So that's what we have to do.

Thus,

Hypothesis 6a: The degree to which a collaborative approach is used to allocate resources within an organization will increase the speed and degree to which adequate resources are developed to resolve the crisis.

Hypothesis 6b: The degree to which a collaborative approach is used between an organization and its key suppliers to reduce its product costs will increase the speed and degree to which adequate resources are developed to resolve the crisis.

Hypothesis 6c: The degree to which a collaborative approach is used between an organization and its key customers to reduce its product costs will increase the speed and degree to which adequate resources are developed to resolve the crisis.

Extending the
Theoretical Framework

The Dynamics of Trust During Crisis

In addition to influencing several behaviors and the efficacy of resource allocation during crisis, trust itself is also expected to be influenced during a crisis as well. The three behaviors posited to be influenced by trust (decentralized decision making, undistorted communication, and collaboration) are expected to have a subsequent influence on trust, depending on the nature of organizational outcomes. As an example, if decision making has been decentralized to lower-echelon employees during a crisis, and these individuals make good decisions (e.g., the organization develops adequate resources), then they will be trusted by top management to a greater degree in the future. As another example, if an organization collaborates with a key supplier to reduce resource requirements by reducing costs, then the degree of trust between the organization and its supplier will remain the same or even increase. If, however, such collaboration fails to reduce costs, then trust may decline between the two organizations. Trust in the TMG by an organization's employees or other stakeholders may also be influenced as a result of such outcomes. Crises are occasions for managers to demonstrate competence (Kiesler & Sproull, 1982; March, 1981). Accordingly, the TMG that decentralized decision making to lower-echelon employees or championed collaborative efforts with a key supplier, if these actions resulted in positive organizational outcomes, may be perceived as exercising good judgment and therefore trusted to a greater degree in terms of its competence.

Whether trust actually declines when organizational outcomes suffer depends on what attributions are made about them. To extend the example of collaboration between an organization and a key supplier, if participants attribute factors external to the two organizations as influencing these outcomes, then perhaps trust may not suffer. If, instead, participants attribute the failures to internal reasons (e.g., a lack of competence or mutual concern), then trust would be expected to suffer. Indeed, if these internal attributions are strongly negative (e.g., gross negligence on the part of either organization or the selling of confidential cost data or proprietary designs to competitors), then trust may suffer enough to lead to actual distrust between the two organizations.

Negative Consequences of Trust

Trust has been discussed in pathological terms if it is inflexible in the face of changing circumstances (Deutsch, 1973, pp. 170-171; Golembiewski & McConkie, 1975, p. 138). However, it is likely that if trust is violated, then distrust between the parties ensues rather than a continued state of trust, especially if such violations are viewed as deliberate rather than due to circumstances beyond the control of the violating party (Luhmann, 1979). However, in a crisis situation, short-term misallocations of resources based on trust violations could be fatal for an organization. In other words, the vulnerability aspect of trust is even greater in crisis situations than in noncrisis situations. As such, it is likely that reactions to violations of trust are swifter and more pronounced because the stakes are greater. Indeed, Webb (Chapter 14, this volume) has posited that a sense of betrayal rather than disappointment ensues upon trust violations during crisis.

Trust may also have a negative relationship with the efficacy of resource allocation and organizational survival if it leads to feelings of security among organizational members such that they are less motivated to deal with a crisis. Such feelings may be akin to those of invulnerability discussed by Janis (1972). None of the managers interviewed discussed trust as having such negative consequences (or for that matter any negative consequences). Perhaps it is because trust within and between organizations has typically been quite low, at least within a U.S. context (Aktouf, 1992; Davidow & Malone, 1992).

Trust and Distrust:
Opposites or Complements?

To conclude the discussion of extending the theoretical framework, one last issue will be considered—namely, do trust and distrust lie on a contin-uum, as is implied by a number of discussions of trust, or are they functional equivalents for one another? Luhmann (1979) provides arguments for both perspectives. Trust leads to distrust if violations become viewed as gen-eralizable because they occur repeatedly and/or without external attribution (Luhmann, 1979, pp. 73-74). In the context of crisis, repeated or unjustified violations of collaborative agreements to reduce costs between an organiza-tion and a key supplier would turn any existing trust between the two organizations into distrust. In this sense, trust and distrust are opposite ends of a continuum.

Trust and distrust are also complements for one another, because both function to reduce social complexity (Luhmann, 1979, p. 71). In the present context, both trust and distrust help TMG members determine whether employees can be delegated decision-making authority, fellow TMG members can be given confidential budget information, or key suppliers can be offered collaborative agreements. Indeed, greater trust in one particular set of employees, TMG members, or suppliers makes it possible to distrust other employees, groups, or organizations because it becomes easier to make fine-grained distinctions among them in terms of the four dimensions. In the interviews with managers, one sales vice president, who made direct comparisons among various divisions of one customer organization in terms of how much each division was trusted by his firm, stated that his firm was willing to reduce prices for one particularly trusted division but not for the less-trusted divisions. In addition, efforts among the Big Three to collaborate with one another on certain technical issues, such as emissions, product safety testing, and electric car battery development, but to exclude Japanese automotive manufacturers (Miller, 1992a, 1992b; Stertz, 1991) may reflect some common trust in one another at the expense of their Japanese rivals.

The Importance of Trust in Noncrisis Contexts

To conclude, recent discussions by both scholars and the business press suggest that trust is a central factor in organizational behavior and organizational survival for both public and private organizations, even in noncrisis contexts. Several scholars have recently proposed that trust is a central factor enhancing organizations' long-term success and survival, especially because environments have become more uncertain and competitive. Peters (1987, p. 627), for example, argues that "the uncertainty of the environment can be swiftly dealt with only if the firm can fall back upon the certainty of relationships among people and among groups—in other words, upon trust and integrity." If organizations in the next two decades become increasingly flat in their hierarchies and more information based (Drucker, 1989), then trust is expected to become more important in organizational design and development to the extent that it facilitates decentralized decision making and the sharing of information.

The role of trust in other contexts is also important, because trust may be necessary to maintain the vitality of capitalist economies and democratic political systems (March & Olsen, 1989; Waterman, 1987), and it appears to be decreasing, especially with respect to business organizations. "Even to compete, in a mutually non-destructive way, one needs at some level to *trust* one's competitors to comply with certain rules. . . . This applies equally to political and economic undertakings" (Gambetta, 1988, p. 215). Polls show, however, that the public's trust in a variety of institutions over the past 25 years has steadily eroded, with major firms showing the largest decline, ahead of the press, major educational institutions, and even Congress (Benham, 1992). Recent scandals involving Dow Corning, General Electric, and TRW have been explicitly discussed as violations of the public's trust in these firms specifically and in business organizations generally (Gorman, 1992; Miller, 1991; Naj, 1992). In addition, the press has blamed repeated acts of fraud by GE on a lack of trust in top management by lower-echelon employees (Naj, 1992), which has prevented them from identifying the firm's illegalities for fear of reprisal.

Both practitioners and scholars have even proposed that a new paradigm of management and organization must be developed with trust as a core component if organizations, both profit and not-for-profit, are to survive into the 21st century (Sculley, 1987, p. 125). Indeed, Levering (1988), Aktouf (1992), and Davidow and Malone (1992) have asserted that a new paradigm must be developed where distrust is replaced with trust as a key organizing principle if organization theories and management practice are to meet the challenges of the 1990s and beyond.

Notes

1. A detailed description of the interview methodology and results are reported in Mishra (1992).

2. I am indebted to Gene Webb for pointing this out.

3. For an empirical test of the multidimensionality of trust and empirical support for trust comprising the four dimensions in this chapter, see Mishra (1993).

4. Organizations *per se* do not trust one another, individuals do. However, for the sake of brevity, the term *organization* will be used to refer to the collective of individuals within an organization.

5. Thanks to Gene Webb for reminding me of this.

References

Aktouf, O. (1992). Management and theories of organizations in the 1990s: Toward a critical radical humanism? *Academy of Management Review, 17*(3), 407-431.

Ancona, D. G., & Nadler, D. A. (1989, Fall). Top hats and executive tales: Designing the senior team. *Sloan Management Review*, pp. 19-28.

Arrow, K. J. (1985). The economics of agency. In J. W. Pratt & R. J. Zeckhauser (Eds.), *Principals and agents: The structure of business* (pp. 37-51). Boston: Harvard Business School Press.

Barber, B. (1983). *The logic and limits of trust.* New Brunswick, NJ: Rutgers University Press.

Beer, M. (1987). Revitalizing organizations: Change process and emergent model. *Academy of Management Executive, 1,* 51-55.

Bem, D. J. (1970). *Beliefs, attitudes, and human affairs.* Pacific Grove, CA: Brooks/Cole.

Benham, B. (1992, June 12). Why have we lost confidence? *Investor's Business Daily,* p. 1.

Billings, R., Milburn, T., & Schaalman, M. (1980). A model of crisis perception: A theoretical and empirical analysis. *Administrative Science Quarterly, 25,* 300-316.

Bourgeois, L. J., III. (1981). On the measurement of organizational slack. *Academy of Management Review, 6,* 29-39.

Bowditch, J. L., & Buono, A. F. (1994). *A primer on organizational behavior* (3rd ed.). New York: John Wiley.

Bromiley, P., & Cummings, L. L. (1993, August). *Organizations with trust: Theory and measurement.* Working paper, University of Minnesota. Also presented at the 53rd annual meeting of the Academy of Management, Atlanta, GA.

Butler, J. (1991). Toward understanding and measuring conditions of trust: Evolution of a conditions of trust inventory. *Journal of Management, 17*(3), 643-663.

Cameron, K., Freeman, S., & Mishra, A. (1991). Best practices in white-collar downsizing: Managing contradictions. *Academy of Management Executive, 5*(3), 57-73.

Cameron, K., Freeman, S., & Mishra, A. (1993). Organizational downsizing. In G. P. Huber & W. H. Glick (Eds.), *Organizational change and redesign: Ideas and insights for improving performance* (pp. 19-65). New York: Oxford University Press.

Cameron, K., Kim, M., & Whetten, D. (1987). Organizational effects of decline and turbulence. *Administrative Science Quarterly, 32,* 222-240.

Cameron, K., Whetten, D., & Kim, M. (1987). Organizational dysfunctions of decline. *Academy of Management Journal, 30*(1), 126-138.

Clark, K., & Fujimoto, T. (1990). The power of product integrity. *Harvard Business Review, 68*(6), 107-118.

Cyert, R. M., & March, J. G. (1963). *A behavioral theory of the firm.* Englewood Cliffs, NJ: Prentice Hall.

D'Aveni, R. (1989). The aftermath of organization decline: A longitudinal study of the strategic and managerial characteristics of declining firms. *Academy of Management Journal, 32*(3), 577-605.

D'Aveni, R., & MacMillan, I. (1990). Crisis and the content of managerial communications: A study of the focus of attention of top managers in surviving and failing firms. *Administrative Science Quarterly, 35,* 634-657.

Davidow, W. H., & Malone, M. S. (1992). *The virtual corporation.* New York: HarperCollins.

Davis, S., & Lawrence, P. (1977). *Matrix.* Reading, MA: Addison-Wesley.

Deutsch, M. (1962). Cooperation and trust: Some theoretical notes. In M. R. Jones (Ed.), *Nebraska symposium on motivation* (pp. 275-319). Lincoln: University of Nebraska Press.

Deutsch, M. (1973). *The resolution of conflict: Constructive and destructive processes.* New Haven, CT: Yale University Press.

Donaldson, L. (1990). A rational basis for criticisms of organizational economics: A reply to Barney. *Academy of Management Review, 15*(3), 394-401.

Drucker, P. (1989). *The new realities.* New York: Harper & Row.

Dutton, J. (1986). The processing of crisis and non-crisis strategic issues. *Journal of Management Studies, 23*(5), 501-517.

Fleming, A. (1991, April 8). Car makers' demands strain suppliers. *Plastics News,* p. 5.

Flint, J. (1991, October 28). The worst of times. *Forbes,* pp. 59-65.

Follett, M. (1941). Constructive conflict. In H. C. Metcalf & L. Urwick (Eds.), *Dynamic administration: The collected papers of Mary Parker Follett* (pp. 30-49). New York: Harper. (Original publication 1925)

Gabarro, J. (1987). *The dynamics of taking charge.* Boston: Harvard Business School Press.

Gambetta, D. (1988). Can we trust trust? In D. Gambetta (Ed.), *Trust: Making and breaking cooperative relations* (pp. 213-237). Oxford, UK: Basil Blackwell.

Gibb, J., & Gibb, L. (1969). Role freedom in a TORI group. In A. Burton (Ed.), *Encounter theory and practice of encounter groups* (pp. 42-57). San Francisco: Jossey-Bass.

GM tightens the screws. (1992, June 22). *Business Week.*

Golembiewski, R., & McConkie, M. (1975). The centrality of trust in group processes. In C. L. Cooper (Ed.), *Theories of group processes* (pp. 131-185). New York: John Wiley.

Gorman, C. (1992, February 10). Can drug firms be trusted? *Time,* pp. 42-46.

Granovetter, M. (1985, November). Economic action and social structure: The problem of embeddedness. *American Journal Sociology, 91*(3), 481-510.

Grover, S. L. (1993). Lying, deceit, and subterfuge: A model of dishonesty in the workplace. *Organization Science, 4*(3), 478-495.

Hackman, R., & Oldham, G. (1980). *Work redesign.* Reading, MA: Addison-Wesley.

Hambrick, D. C. (1994). Top management groups: A conceptual integration and reconsideration of the "team" label. In B. M. Staw & L. L. Cummings (Eds.), *Research in organizational behavior* (Vol. 16, pp. 171-214). Greenwich, CT: JAI.

Hermann, C. (1963). Some consequences of crisis which limit the viability of organizations. *Administrative Science Quarterly, 8,* 61-82.

Janis, I. L. (1972). *Victims of groupthink: Psychological studies of foreign policy decisions and fiascoes.* New York: Houghton Mifflin.

Janis, I. L. (1989). *Crucial decisions: Leadership in policymaking and crisis management.* New York: Free Press.

Kanter, R. (1977). *Men and women of the corporation.* New York: Basic Books.

Kanter, R. (1983). *The change masters: Innovation and entrepreneurship in the American corporation.* New York: Simon & Schuster.

Kanter, R. (1989). *When giants learn to dance.* New York: Simon & Schuster.

Katzenbach, J. R., & Smith, D. K. (1993). *The wisdom of teams: Creating the high-performance organization.* Boston: Harvard Business School Press.

Kiesler, S., & Sproull, L. (1982). Managerial response to changing environments: Perspectives on problem sensing from social cognition. *Administrative Science Quarterly, 27,* 548-570.

King, A. (1991, May 20). Suppliers: Big 3 price cuts are too deep. *Crain's Detroit Business,* p. 3.

Kirkland, C. (1991, September). Do partnerships work in a recession? *Plastics World,* pp. 44-46.

Kirkpatrick, S., & Locke, E. (1991). Leadership: Do traits matter? *Academy of Management Executive, 5*(2), 48-60.

Kotter, J., & Schlesinger, L. (1979). Choosing strategies for change. *Harvard Business Review, 57,* 106-114.

Lawrence, P., & Lorsch, J. (1967). *Organization and environment.* Boston: Harvard Business School Press.

Levering, R. (1988). *A great place to work.* New York: Avon.

Lewis, J. D., & Weigert, A. (1985a). Social atomism, holism, and trust. *Sociological Quarterly, 26,* 455-471.

Lewis, J. D., & Weigert, A. (1985b). Trust as a social reality. *Social Forces, 63*(4), 967-985.

Lorenz, E. H. (1992). Trust and the flexible firm. *Industrial Relations, 31*(3), 455-472.

Luhmann, N. (1979). *Trust and power.* New York: John Wiley.

Luhmann, N. (1988). Familiarity, confidence, trust: Problems and alternatives. In D. Gambetta (Ed.), *Trust: Making and breaking cooperative relations* (pp. 94-107). Oxford, UK: Basil Blackwell.

March, J. G. (1981). Footnotes to organizational change. *Administrative Science Quarterly, 26,* 563-577.

March, J. G., & Olsen, J. (1989). *Rediscovering institutions: The organizational basis of politics.* New York: Free Press.

Marcus, A. A., & Goodman, R. S. (1991). Victims and shareholders: The dilemmas of presenting corporate policy during a crisis. *Academy of Management Journal, 34*(2), 281-305.

McGregor, D. (1967). *The professional manager.* New York: McGraw-Hill.

Microlytics. (1989). *Gofer: A powerful software utility for searching, finding, and retrieving text.* Pittsford, NY: Author.

Miller, K. (1991, October 15). TRW to give credit reports free of charge. *Wall Street Journal,* p. B1.

Miller, K. (1992a, June 9). Big Three to cooperate on efforts to meet clean-air rules. *Wall Street Journal*, p. B9.

Miller, K. (1992b, July 14). Detroit's Big Three form joint venture destined for disaster. Partnership, to build a better crash dummy, is latest example of cooperation. *Wall Street Journal*, p. A4.

Mishra, A. K. (1992). *Organizational responses to crisis: The role of mutual trust and top management teams*. Unpublished dissertation, The University of Michigan School of Business Administration, Ann Arbor.

Mitroff, I. I., Mason, R. O., & Pearson, C. M. (1994). *Framebreak: The radical redesign of American business*. San Francisco: Jossey-Bass.

Moorman, C., Zaltman, G., & Deshpande, R. (1992). Relationships between providers and users of market research: The dynamics of trust within and between organizations. *Journal of Marketing Research, 29,* 314-328.

Naj, A. (1992, November 18). Auto-parts suppliers call off any recovery parties. *The Wall Street Journal*, p. B2.

Nanus, B. (1989). *The leader's edge: The seven keys to leadership in a turbulent world*. Chicago: Contemporary Books.

Ouchi, W. G. (1981). *Theory Z: How American business can meet the Japanese challenge*. Reading, MA: Addison-Wesley.

Pascale, R. (1990). *Managing on the edge: How the smartest companies use conflict to stay ahead*. New York: Simon & Schuster.

Pauchant, T. C., & Mitroff, I. I. (1992). *Transforming the crisis-prone organization: Preventing individual, organizational, and environmental tragedies*. San Francisco: Jossey-Bass.

Pearson, C. M., & Mitroff, I. I. (1993). From crisis prone to crisis prepared: A framework for crisis management. *Academy of Management Executive, 7*(1), 48-59.

Perrow, C. (1984). *Normal accidents: Living with high-risk technologies*. New York: Basic Books.

Peters, T. (1987). *Thriving on chaos: Handbook for a management revolution*. New York: HarperCollins.

Pfeffer, J. (1978). *Organizational design*. Arlington Heights, IL: Harlan Davidson.

Pfeffer, J., & Salancik, G. (1978). *The external control of organizations*. New York: Harper & Row.

Roberts, K. H., & O'Reilly, C. A., III. (1974). Failures in upward communication in organizations: Three possible culprits. *Academy of Management Journal, 17*(2), 205-215.

Rogers, C. (1961). *On becoming a person*. Boston: Houghton-Mifflin.

Sako, M. (1992). *Prices, quality, and trust: Inter-firm relations in Britain & Japan*. New York: Cambridge University Press.

Sculley, J. (1987). *Odyssey*. New York: Harper & Row.

Shellum, B. (1991, August 8). Caught in a vise. *Detroit Free Press*, pp. F1-F2.

Starbuck, W., & Hedberg, B. (1977). Saving an organization from a stagnating environment. In H. Thorelli (Ed.), *Strategy + Structure = Performance* (pp. 249-258). Bloomington: Indiana University Press.

Staw, B., Sandelands, L., & Dutton, J. (1981). Threat-rigidity effects in organizational behavior: A multilevel analysis. *Administrative Science Quarterly, 26,* 501-524.

Stertz, B. (1991, June 28). In a u-turn from past policy, Big Three of Detroit speed into era of cooperation. *Wall Street Journal*, p. B1.

Swan, J., Trawick, I., Rink, D., & Roberts, J. (1988). Measuring dimensions of purchaser trust of industrial salespeople. *Journal of Personal Selling & Sales Management, 8,* 1-9.

Thomas, K. (1979). Organizational conflict. In Steven Kerr (Ed.), *Organization behavior* (pp. 151-181). New York: John Wiley.

Thompson, J. (1967). *Organizations in action*. New York: McGraw-Hill.

Turner, B. (1976). The organizational and interorganizational development of disasters. *Administrative Science Quarterly, 21,* 378-397.

Vroom, V. H., & Yetton, P. W. (1973). *Leadership and decision making.* Pittsburgh: University of Pittsburgh Press.

Walton, R., & McKersie, R. (1965). *A behavioral theory of labor negotiations: An analysis of a social interaction system.* New York: McGraw-Hill.

Waterman, R. (1987). *The renewal factor.* New York: Bantam Books.

Webber, A. (1987). The statesman as CEO. *Harvard Business Review, 65*(5),76-81.

White, J. (1991, September 8). Japanese auto makers help U.S. suppliers become more efficient. *The Wall Street Journal,* p. A1.

White, J., & Stertz, B. (1991, May 2). Crisis is galvanizing Detroit's Big Three. *Wall Street Journal,* p. B 1.

Womack, J., Jones, D., & Roos, D. (1990). *The machine that changed the world.* New York: Macmillan.

Zand, D. (1972). Trust and managerial problem solving. *Administrative Science Quarterly, 17,* 229-239.

Zucker, L. (1986). Production of trust: Institutional sources of economic structure, 1940-1920. In B. M. Staw & L. L. Cummings (Eds.), *Research in organizational behavior* (Vol. 8, pp. 53-111). Greenwich, CT: JAI.

Trust and Crisis

EUGENE J. WEBB

Prologue: The Secretary and the Bookie

When I think about trust and crises, two neighbors come to mind. Both have operated in crisis settings and both have commented on the centrality of trust in managing routine and crisis situations. The first neighbor is the distinguished Stanford Business School professor George Shultz; the other is less eminent—a rather seedy bookmaker named Al, who makes his living outside the law. An unusual pairing, perhaps, but both have spoken intelligently of the centrality (and fragility) of trust in organizational life—a centrality particularly marked at crisis times.

First, the observations of Shultz. During a long and distinguished public life, he served as the secretary of four different cabinet departments. In aggregate, these roles must have required making thousands of public appearances. Among all of them, Shultz recalls one appearance as generating more public response than any other—a short set of comments contained in his emotionally charged 1987 testimony before the Congressional committee investigating the Iran-Contra affair.

> So . . . I want to send a message out around our country that public service is a
> very rewarding and honorable thing, and nobody has to think they need to lie and

cheat in order to be a public servant or to work in foreign policy. Quite to the contrary: If you are really going to be effective over any period of time, you have to be straightforward and you have to conduct yourself in a basically honest way so people will have confidence and trust in you. . . . Trust's the coin of the realm. Trust is the coin of the realm. (Shultz, 1993)

Al the bookie has written no scholarly books or articles, but he has been thoughtful on the same topic. His precarious occupation generates a continual state of crisis or near-crisis.[1] On each day's table is a new and full plate of risk, uncertainty, and potential wealth. And in that crisis milieu, he asserts, is the centrality of trust. It is not by accident that among the most trustworthy and scrupulously honest occupations is that of an illegal bookie. Those who conduct such illicit business over the telephone are out of business unless they are absolutely trustworthy. The bookie always pays off the winning player, just as there is the clear expectation that the losing player always pays off. The reliability of the transaction and the trustworthiness of the parties are necessary elements for this crisis-prone (or crisis-ridden) financial game to be played. A laconic restatement of this came one day when I asked the bookie about his scrupulous honesty and trustworthiness. He answered, avoiding any invocation of moral aspects of trust, "Hey, how else could you do business?" Indeed, how else?

The Linkage of Trust and Crisis

The magnitude of a crisis and the importance of trust are positively linked. Certainly, trust is a central component in even the most trivial and routine activities of organizational life. But when an unequivocal or threatened crisis surfaces, the saliency of trust (and estimating trustworthiness) is elevated to higher levels. The reasons are clear: Substantial uncertainty is a companion to each crisis, and crisis conditions ratchet up the chance of cognitive and organizational errors. Dependency on others is greater during crises, and with that dependency go premiums on determining trustworthy people and trustworthy coping methods. The importance of the linkage between the two ideas is enhanced because it is during and after crises that the most marked readjustments occur in perceptions of loyalty and betrayal, friendship and treachery. Later in this chapter, I will suggest that crisis is a uniquely flamed crucible for the creation and destruction of trust.

Definitions of
Trust and Crisis

But first a few words on definitions. The concepts of trust and crisis are, unsurprisingly, anchored in perception. Beliefs in the level of trustworthiness or the magnitude of a crisis must, as everything else, be filtered through the common human screens and lenses we all employ (however imperfectly). I leave to readers the more Talmudic distinctions among forms of trust. Here, the rather primitive idea is that trust is a judgment or a confidence estimate that an organization or a person is going to act in a predictable way. Finer-grained views certainly will capture more subtlety, but predictable reliability will have to be adequate here. For a thorough discussion of the dimensionality of trust, see Mishra (Chapter 13, this volume).

Compared to "trust," the definition of "crisis" has been argued less thoroughly; some substantial threat to the organization or the individual is usually at the center of a definition. That's sensible enough, but next question is, "Why is there a threat?" And the answer to that may be more interesting. The view here is that an assessment of resource adequacy defines the presence or absence of a crisis.

Some "triggering event" occurs in the environment, which may signal a potential threat to the organization or to the individual. Is there a crisis? Or is there only a problem? The answer, as usual, is, "It depends." If one believes that available resources are adequate to cope, then there is a problem to be dealt with. If one's resources are seen as not adequate, then there is a crisis. Just as trust is an estimate of predictability, crisis is an estimate of inadequacy.[2] And, of course, estimates can be wrong. One of the more dysfunctional aspects of trust in others and the availability of resources is that the trust estimates can be delusional. One may miscalibrate something as a problem, not a crisis, by underestimating the likelihood of a negative triggering event or the adequacy of available resources to cope. ("Hey, we won't have a really big earthquake for a long while again, and even if we do, we'll get through it.")

Coping With
Resource Inadequacy

If a crisis is defined by resource inadequacy, then the obvious task is to focus resources in the right place. How can one do it? There are at least four classes of managerial moves: reallocation, transformation, collecting, and borrowing. Each of them, in a different way with a different time signature, demands the spending of personal or financial capital.

Reallocate Current Resources. A first step is to move people or material from a less critical area to the crisis area. Such a shift will magnify resources at the critical point. That's good, but, as in any other administrative action, there are potential costs as well as benefits. The reallocation of managers means opportunity costs paid in those normal activities are now being ignored or allowed to slide. A visible realignment of resources can also provide signals to those outside the organization—friends and foes alike. On the positive side, it can show that one is serious and committed to dealing with the issue; visible inattention can have a substantial downside. During the Exxon-Valdez oil spill crisis, the Exxon chairman chose not to go to the site of the spill and his hands-off behavior signaled a cavalier disregard, with attendant heavy costs to the firm.[3]

Transform Resources You Have for Resources You Don't. These transforms entail the shift of resources from one form to another. The best example is the familiar trade of money for information and counsel. That's how consultants make their living.

Consultants can provide the obvious benefits of filling in informational voids, alerting one to dimensions that would otherwise be ignored or undervalued, breaking the usual sets associated with thinking and, nontrivially, giving one an audience to talk to (so one can hear what one is thinking). Loyalty will not be bought with money, but some aids to thinking can be.[4] One can also, in such a competitive game as hostile takeovers, transform money assets in a way to create resource problems for opponents. In a not completely hypothetical case, one could lock up, through retainer agreements, the services of leading proxy mailing firms, preventing access by the opponent and thus producing a resource inadequacy.

Collect Your Debts. If a situation is looming, or if one is already there, then it may be time to spend another class of assets—making a call on old debts or favors owed. Many people hold the view that it is somehow "weak" or inappropriate to ask for repayment. Matthews (1988) suggests the opposite: It is appropriate not only to call but, indeed, that it is a way to build influence.

Borrow on the Future. Just as one can spend what one already has and collect what is currently owed, so too can one borrow on the future. Going into debt to cope better with a crisis can take both formal and informal shapes. One might, for example, borrow money to allow one to buy missing resources. If one doesn't borrow from Peter to pay Paul, he or she might borrow from Citibank to pay McKinsey. Or, one can ask for help with the explicit or implicit understanding that a credit is being established that will be collectible in future time. All of us give and take organizational favors, and a crisis is a time to consider shifting around some of those personal and financial balances of credit.

The Search for Trust:
Selecting Advisers and Implementers

Under the crisis conditions of uncertainty and the need to juggle resources, dependency on others obviously increases. Coping with that dependency usually means going to others for help in both making and executing decisions. At this juncture, trust plays a pivotal role in influencing the choice of who will fill in your missing resources. When you feel shaky about your own ability to cope, it becomes imperative to choose those you can trust.[5]

Adding trustworthy advisers has at least two major advantages. The first, obviously, is that advisers can provide a more textured understanding of facts and consequences than is possible without them.[6] The second is the happy reality, more commonly noted by characteristically suspicious economists, that you don't have to watch trustworthy people as much as you do others.[7] Because crises are commonly marked by a necessary rationing of attention, any energy conservation characteristic becomes a valuable one.

Yet this economy of attention does not come without risks. Although our trustworthy advisers may not have to be monitored closely, our very comfort with them may reduce the change of receiving the variety of thought and action we need. After all, we define people as trustworthy (and increase the chance of their selection as crisis partners) for the same reasons we employ them in so many other social choices: They are people we have had good personal experience with in the past, people who have values and interests similar to our own—in short, people we are comfortable with.[8] Drawing on our comfort estimates and/or reputational views provided by others, we may run the danger of too much comfort.[9] The groupthink risks of in-group cohesion loom larger under crisis or threat conditions; the concern is represented in common phrases: "the embattled enclave," "a circle the wagons mentality," and "the loyal band of true believers." In crisis situations, where uncertainty is high, the temptations are heavy to pick from a narrow band of advisers. It is the old story of the balance between stability and change. When a threatening turbulence surrounds one, the stable component provided by those you know and like is a valued one indeed. If trust is important *during* a crisis—in how it influences the search for advice and the use and transformation of resources, judgments about trust can also be substantially affected *after* a crisis.

Crisis: Amplifying
Trust and Betrayal

Crisis operates as a uniquely heated crucible for the creation of trust and for its destruction. Few other conditions offer so great an opportunity to enhance trust as when one provides an unexpected hand to someone in trouble. Contrarily, failure to provide expected help or resources in a crisis may be viewed not simply as nonperformance but instead as acts of complete betrayal. This amplification effect may be most marked when there is surprise—surprise that expected allies or enemies came forward (or didn't). Surprise of any form occurs when expectations are disconfirmed by experience, and crisis may produce more, rather than fewer, surprises. Our usually effective discounting and interpretation mechanisms may be less on the ready or adequate when infused by the stress and uncertainty of a crisis.

Surprise has enormous perceptual leverage—a happy surprise can ratchet up both joy and trust recalibrations; a disappointing surprise, in turn, can be read as unalloyed treachery. Crisis situations are magnifying loci for the enhancement or dissolution of trust.[10]

The forces behind this amplification effect (if it indeed exists) may rest in nothing more complicated than the primitive observation that a crisis means more chips are on the table. With more chips, the consequence of winning or losing, coping or not coping, goes up. Tied into reliance on others, the greater the dependency on others' help, the greater the appreciation for help extended and the greater the resentment at its nonprovision.[11]

Loyalty and Trust

Given the possible amplification effect and its impact on recalibrations of trust, it may be worthwhile to look on both the bright and dark sides. Trust confirmed, particularly in the super-heated atmosphere of a crisis, is an operational definition of loyalty. Trust disconfirmed, particularly in crises, is the full expression of treachery. First, a look at loyalty and then a look at betrayal.

Loyalty can be generated by a number of forces, prominent among them the influence of reciprocity norms and learned responsibility. The well-known political admonition, "Dance with the one that brung ya," captures the idea. In *Hardball,* Chris Matthews (1988) labels a chapter with that phrase, attributing it to Ronald Reagan:

> He prided himself on sticking with his old crowd through victory as well as defeat. Unabashedly, he appeared at rallies of the most passionate conservative fringe.

Speaking to a convention of ideologues in 1985, Reagan said, "I always see this as an opportunity to dance with the one that brung ya." (Matthews, 1988, p. 77)[12]

An important corollary is noted by George Shultz in the earlier cited quote: "Don't say yes unless you are prepared to work your heart out to get it or think you can deliver it." (Shultz, 1993). Matthews stresses the need to be careful where you put your trust; the downside consequences can be harsh.

When you take a position, in politics or in any other line of work, be very careful. Once you establish a relationship of loyalty, it is hard to back out of it. If you join the wrong side, you will be stuck with the Hobbesian choice of cutting and running or dying in a ditch . . . for a cause that you would never want to be seen alive with. (Matthews, 1988, p. 80)

Two examples will illustrate loyalty at work—how it can transcend narrow parochial interests and display that blend of responsibility and reciprocity we sometimes call honor. One is drawn from the relationship between Nelson Mandela and Fidel Castro, the other from an exchange between Harry Truman and Dean Acheson.

Mandela and Castro

Safire (1992) reported on what many viewed at the time as loyalty gone awry.

Nelson Mandela traveled to Cuba to appear at a rally with Fidel Castro (years after Mandela's release after 27 years in a South African jail). The South African surely knew that the dictator Castro had become a pathetic figure, hoarsely bellowing "Socialism or death!" like mad King Lear on the heath. Public opinion-sensitive colleagues in the African National Congress had surely advised Mr. Mandela that an appearance with this discredited relic of Communist tyranny would offend liberal Mandela-lionizers around the world. Association with a known abuser of human rights might even weaken the ANC's cause.

Yet Mandela went and lifted arms with Castro before the Cuban crowd and world cameras. Why? Because Castro had stood up for him, and his then-ragtag band of followers, at the beginning. Castro had railed and harangued in Mandela's behalf through the decades when the great danger was the world's inattention. To many liberals, that Mandela decision to refuse to abandon one of the last Communist despots was a serious mistake. . . . But I had to admire Nelson Mandela for that display of dogged loyalty, especially since he could do the degenerating dictator little good. (Safire, 1992, p. 99)

Truman and Acheson

Another example illustrates how exceptional loyalties are anchored in profound personal beliefs of responsibility and reciprocity—this time, the actions of a U.S. president, his secretary of state, and a disgraced friend of the secretary. In 1951, President Harry Truman's administration was buffeted by the perjury conviction of Alger Hiss, a prominent Democrat and long-term friend of Secretary of State Dean Acheson.

> Truman and Acheson were not only boss and subordinate. An exceptionally close friendship [existed] between Truman and Acheson. . . . [It] was forged one night in November 1946, when Truman had returned to Washington during one of the lowest moments in his political career, after the midterm sweep by the Republicans of both houses of Congress. There, alone at the train station, to meet him was Acheson.

As part of this mosaic of trust, Acheson knew of Truman's loyalty to his one-time political mentor, Tom Pendergast.

> Shortly after Truman's inauguration as Vice-President, Tom Pendergast died. By that time, Pendergast was a disgraced, bankrupt man recently let out of prison for income-tax evasion, his once considerable fortune squandered on the horses, his physical strength eroded by illnesses. The one thing that had held back Truman's career when he had first arrived in Washington—the one taint on him—was the Pendergast connection. But Truman opted to go to the funeral, a clear sign of his determination to put obligation, as he defined it, over popularity. (Halberstam, 1993, p. 24)

That bond between Truman and Acheson was to be tested by Alger Hiss's perjury conviction. Under substantial political heat, Acheson called a press conference to clarify his stand.

> Feeling that his own beliefs concerning loyalty and obligation were at stake, Acheson thought of what he would say long before [meeting the reporters]. . . . He was the son of an Episcopal bishop, and he believed honor had to be placed above political expediency. There were times when a man had to be counted. . . . He chose his words carefully. "I do not intend to turn my back on Alger Hiss," he told reporter(s). . . . Pressed further, Acheson said to look in their Bible for Matthew 25:36, a passage in which Christ called upon His followers to understand that anyone who turns his back on someone in trouble turns his back on Him: "Naked, and ye clothed me; I was sick and ye visited me; I was in prison and ye came unto me." Later he explained that he was following "Christ's words setting forth compassion as the highest of Christian duties." After the I-shall-not-turn-my-back-on Alger-Hiss statement, he rushed to apologize to the President. Truman

[talked to] him about the Pendergast funeral and [told him] not to worry. (Halberstam, 1993, pp. 17-18, 24)[13]

From another account of the meeting, it is reported that Acheson later wrote to his daughter about Truman's response:

[He] was "wonderful about it . . . [saying] that one who had gone to the funeral of a friendless old man just out of the penitentiary [Pendergast] had no trouble knowing what I meant and proving it. (McCullough, 1992, p. 760)

The political risks for both Truman and Mandela were so great that Acheson and Castro, each a seasoned politician, would have "understood" the "realities" of political life. Had support for them not been forthcoming, it almost certainly would have been shrugged away as understandable and sensible behavior. But it *was* forthcoming, even when it didn't have to be; such acts in both their careers marked Truman and Mandela for what they were: men of honor, men of trust. Mandela and Truman rejected the cautionary advice of their advisers: Don't stick your neck out. Each acted loyally because each honored the principle of paying back what you owe. And each was, and should have been, viewed as leaders demonstrating loyalty and trust.

A Negative Aside:
Trust Can Only Go So Far . . .

But even in these remarkable displays of personal loyalty, of fulfilling a personal trust in times of a crisis, there remains the awkward question: How much loyalty is too much? When does responsibility turn into foolishness or even feed immorality? Again, William Safire is instructive.

In this discussion, I have assumed loyalty to be a value, a good thing in a human being, an obligation in an authority or institution. *But you cannot be a nut about this: Loyalty overdone can cease to be a value and become a corruption of values.* . . . A Mafioso lives and dies by a fearful loyalty to his criminal family; it's a truism that loyalty is a value that can be devalued by fidelity to bad ends. . . . (Safire, 1992, p. 102)

It is difficult to specify how much of anything is enough—much less a culturally prized value such as loyalty. Cialdini (personal communication, 1994) points to a beginning line of thought on bounding the limits of loyalty. He suggests that loyalty is a concept applied to those who are close—typically friends and family. This line of thinking suggests that one cannot be too loyal to one's child or parent; one can be too loyal to an employer. Barney (1990) notes that collective shock can result when norms of trust are violated by family members.

It may be no accident that Safire's example of abuse of loyalty, the Mafia, is a psychological if not a biological "family." With others who are less linked to one, loyalty is not the first consideration, and perhaps it should not be. In these more distant relationships, common interests and obligations (contractual or otherwise) may appropriately dominate. To do otherwise might lead to what common wisdom labels "blind" (and, inferentially, foolish) loyalty. An awkward question is whether one can be inappropriately blind in one's loyalty to those closest.

Betrayal, Surprise, and Crisis

The discussion on loyalty and trust naturally suggests the issue of betrayal and trust. My Stanford colleague Roderick Kramer properly points out that distrust is not necessarily the opposite of trust. Neither is betrayal the opposite of loyalty. Moreover, an extended series of conversations about betrayal and loyalty and a search of the *Psychological Abstracts* suggest a strong asymmetry in the popularity of the two topics. People find it easier to talk about loyalty than betrayal, can spontaneously produce more examples of loyalty than betrayal, and the research literature "favors" loyalty over betrayal. From 1987 to the present, *Psychological Abstracts* shows that the number of abstracts for "loyalty" beat out "betrayal" by a count of 196 to 71. (In a benign comparison, "love" conquered "hate" 1,296 to 104.)

But asymmetric or no, crisis will amplify interpretations of the actions of others—be they coded as reprehensible traitors or heroes. The amplifying quality of the crisis setting applies to betrayal as well as loyalty.

Two features of the setting may be driving this escalated interpretation. The first is the heightened risk, dependency, and emotion of a crisis. As noted earlier, consequences are greater during crises and there is more on the table. The second feature is the characteristic of surprise—surprise because anticipated help is not forthcoming or because we do receive unexpected help from an unforeseen quarter. These surprises can change disappointment into betrayal or gratitude into elation.

Expected responses by others (anticipated help from an ally, no help from an enemy) reinforce earlier views. Predictable help may anneal an already positive relationship, and an expected resistance may yield only a shrug and one more notch to a preexisting negative opinion.

Always is the risk of misattribution. One must be cautious not to confuse betrayal—a violation of a promise or a legitimate expectation of trust—with noncooperation or inconsistent support of one's own view or position. Among the first lessons learned by young politicians is that positions taken against someone else's stand need not represent treachery, stupidity, or personal animosity. Only if a promise is violated is there a fair claim of betrayal. To not be helped does not necessarily imply being rejected. Others might, after all, be unaware that someone requires help. And even when a historical ally defects, one need not, at least in the political world, get too upset. A venerable maxim is, "No permanent friends, no permanent enemies, only permanent interests." Interests change, alliances shift, and reversals can occur without betrayal.[14] Senator Eugene McCarthy watched as his speechwriter Richard Goodwin went to work for Robert Kennedy, McCarthy's adversary for a presidential nomination. Unperturbed, McCarthy approvingly said, "Dick's the kind of man who changes uniforms without giving away the signals" (Matthews, 1988, p. 16).[15]

But to put up a cautionary flag about interpretation is not to suggest that betrayal, treachery, and reprehensible actions do not occur. They do. And massively selfish fair-weather friends properly earn contempt. Yet in the heat of crisis, when so much is at stake, it is easy to overinterpret both loyalty and betrayal. Even under normal conditions, estimating the level of trust is not simple; it is an illusive and brittle commodity that once abused is not easily restored (Rousseau & Parks, 1992). Although folk wisdom abounds, scientific data on the sensible question, "Is it easier to lose trust than to gain it?", remain to be developed.

It may not be accidental that prominent eponyms associated with betrayal are linked to surprising actions during crisis events (war, murder, and tortured conflicts between greed and fidelity). The names of Benedict Arnold and Judas Iscariot have become a shorthand for betrayal of a devastating order. Surprise—here the disconfirmation of positive expectations—marked each. Arnold had been a brilliant Revolutionary general, fighting with distinction against the British; Judas had been one of the first Christian disciples, and some accounts name him as the first treasurer of the Christian church. Their corruption has been interpreted as so massively heinous because each, in earlier and difficult times, had served loyally and well the cause and people he subverted.

So too in Shakespeare, where *Julius Caesar* carries literature's most famous words of betrayal. Surrounded by his assassins, Caesar looks among them and surprisingly sees his beloved friend Brutus; he dies with the words, "Et tu, Brute." Appropriate interpretation of these words is open to literary analysis, but the clear point here is that no betrayal can rival that of the defection of a long-trusted associate.[16]

The follow-on consequences of betrayal may take different forms, one of which is simply the refusal of others to do business. If nobody trusts a traitor, then the traitor cannot hope to enter into very many future transactions—be they economic or social. Bies and Tripp (Chapter 12, this volume) catalog a series of responses to "trust violations," ranging from revenge fantasies to forgiveness. But in the world at large, even at the forgiveness end of the scale, one can find the motto, "Forgive, but don't forget."[17]

And when does a sense of betrayal lead to revenge? Bies and Tripp (Chapter 12, this volume) anchor one (weak) end of a retribution scale with "revenge fantasies." Even in the face of an intellectual awareness that revenge is not sensible, one may fantasize away, courting the temptation of vengeance. Safire wrote of Job's benevolent to response that he "would have hesitated a long moment before interceding [with God] . . . [savoring] the sight of my disloyal ex-supporters . . . thinking about [them] twisting, slowly, slowly in the wind . . . before pleading for mercy on their behalf" (Safire, 1992, p. 97).

Perhaps the other anchor point of response to betrayal is provided in Greek mythology. Medea, enraged by her philandering husband Jason, first sends an enchanted gown to his lover (which burns her to death.) Then Medea kills her two sons by Jason and scornfully displays the dead bodies to him—quite the other end of the scale from fantasies.

Surprise, loyalty, betrayal . . . all intertwined with crisis, all mediated by trust.

SUMMARY

Much of what has been said here may be captured by an old New England proverb: "Trust in God, but keep your powder dry."

Notes

1. The bookie's crisis-prone life can be rocked by both economic and psychological assault. Stanford University recently announced a $5 million gift from a Hong Kong businessman. The money was his windfall profit from a single horse-racing bet (of the multiple quinella form). The economic hit of paying off must have been nontrivial to the bookie, but consider the incremental emotional crisis that might have been produced when the bettor made public that he had intended to make a different bet and gave a "wrong" (but winning) wager over the telephone.

2. Repairing a bleeding four-inch slash in an arm is not a crisis for an emergency room physician with the experience and supplies to cope with this triggering event; it is a simple problem. For the rest of us, it is a crisis. Valid responses both. It is the same wound—with different resources responding to it.

3. In another example of management incompetence during this crisis, the Exxon chairman shrugged off its magnitude by stating publicly, "It only cost a billion dollars." Even today, a billion dollars is real money to some people.

4. A careful writer on the topic properly cautions us about the narrowness of specialists who "can do a few things well, which means that they search the world to see if it needs what they can do. If it doesn't, they do nothing else because they see nothing else" (Weick, 1988, p. 311).

5. One of the consequences of a good social science education may be a diminished faith in one's own performance during a crisis. One is more likely to seek out trusty supporters if one knows how stress and crisis affect thinking and decision making (a reduced set of considered alternatives,

more "primitive" responses, greater likelihood to use historically useful approaches—irrespective of applicability—and the like).

6. In any crisis worth the name, intelligent choice may be so complex that one cannot rely on a single view—even one's own. The canonical text on this is Alexander George's (1980) *Presidential Decision Making in Foreign Policy,* where he reviews a number of methods to counter biases under conditions of conflict and high stress and makes a persuasive argument for "multiple advocacy"—a system in which the executive serves as a judge and evaluates the merits of competing positions. Central to the effective working of this method is that the executive ensures that the different advocates have equivalent resources in the preparation and arguing of their views.

7. The lowered cost of monitoring is central to those analyses of trust grounded in economic transaction costs, a topic discussed by Rousseau and Parks (1992). They have provided an intelligent discussion of the relationship between trust and different forms of contracting, drawing on both economics and organizational literature (e.g., Barney, 1990; Zucker, 1986). Okun, a mainstream economist, had discussed implicit and explicit contracts and the linkage to trust. It will be recalled that he was the coiner of the term *invisible handshake*—a conceptual substitute for the *invisible hand* of the market. He provides a rather disheartening picture of a firm's ability to establish reputations of trust and honesty. "The practice of scrupulous honesty is expensive and not readily demonstrable. . . . Honesty may be the best profit-maximizing policy if the firm's horizon is very long; otherwise, self-interest is likely to create a golden (or leaden) mean between honesty and dishonesty" (Okun, 1981, p. 91).

8. It is conventional wisdom to deride nepotism, which allows the choice of familiar and comfortable partners. But maybe nepotism is getting a bad rap. Perhaps only one's sibling can say to a president, "That's foolish, Jack!" John Kennedy chose his younger brother to be attorney-general of the United States—certainly not because Robert Kennedy held unique administrative skills applicable to running a cabinet department. He was chosen because he could be trusted.

9. For a game-theoretic view of reputation, see Kreps, Milgrom, Roberts, and Wilson (1982) and Fudenberg and Kreps (1987).

10. Robert Cialdini (personal communication, 1994) has pointed out a parallel from the persuasion literature. Reviewing their own and others' work, Eagly, Wood, and Chaiken (1981, p. 59) observe in their review of expectancy and persuasion that "communicators are more persuasive to the extent that they advocate unexpected positions" (see also Eagly, Wood, & Chaiken, 1978.) An allied (if undocumented) phenomenon might be called the "Even Ms. X thinks so" effect. Whenever "even" appears before someone's name in a persuasive message, it usually indicates some surprise element—one working in a direction favorable to the presenter. The common form is a report that an expected opponent has offered support ("Even General LeMay agreed to be conciliatory" or "Even George Ball thought an attack was right").

11. A positive example of this is medical philanthropy's "grateful patient" gift, where the survivor or heirs contribute to a disease-related group or caretaker.

12. Safire (1992) discusses the same maxim but phrases it, "Go home with the one that brung you." This distinction between "dancing with" and "going home with" the one that brung ya (or you) is a delicate intellectual point, perhaps better left to political analysts.

13. "Had he," mused Scotty Reston of the *New York Times* years later, "phrased his thoughts in terms that ordinary men could understand, had he simply said that he would not kick a man when he was down, a great deal less damage might have been done" (Halberstam, 1993, p. 18).

14. Middle Eastern politics is a potent example of this and has produced one of the memorable statements of recent years. Israel's Prime Minister Rabin, after signing an agreement with the Palestine Liberation Organization, noted, "You don't make peace with friends; you make it with very unsavory enemies."

15. The term *fair-weather friends* has a long history. "American patriot and publicist Thomas Paine made objects of his contempt 'the summer soldier and the sunshine patriot,' who shrank from service in the new nation's wintry trial" (Safire, 1992, p. 93).

16. The Shakespearian scholar Ronald Rebholz (personal communication, 1994) notes two dominant interpretations of Caesar's words. The first is one of simple surprise: "You, of all people, Brutus, have betrayed me." The second interpretation is that Caesar's words were intended to induce guilt. Each interpretation is valid and, indeed, each is expressed on the stage. The "surprise" interpretation is an obvious one, but the "guilt" interpretation receives support from action at the end of the play. There, Caesar's words continue their penetrating meaning to the traitor; he sleeps, but sleep cannot protect him from the haunting figure of Caesar in his dreams.

17. A variant of this is, "Don't get mad; don't get even; get ahead." Matthews argues the practicality of such a view and cites Maryland's former governor, Marvin Mandel: "Don't spend your time looking through a rearview mirror." To underscore the importance of looking ahead, Matthews adds, "Always keep your eye on the goal. Accumulate power and the opportunities to render justice will fall onto your plate" (Matthews, 1988, p. 115).

References

Barney, J. (1990). The debate between traditional management theory and organizational economics: Substantive differences or intergroup conflict? *Academy of Management Review, 15,* 382-393.

Eagly, A. H., Wood, W., & Chaiken, S. (1978). Causal inferences about communicators and their effect on opinion change. *Journal of Personality and Social Psychology, 36,* 424-435.

Eagly, A. H., Wood, W., & Chaiken, S. (1981). An attributional analysis of persuasion. In J. H. Harvey, W. Ickes, & R. F. Kidd (Eds.), *New directions in attribution theory* (pp. 37-62). Hillsdale, NJ: Lawrence Erlbaum.

Fudenberg, D., & Kreps, D. M. (1987). Reputation in the simultaneous play of multiple opponents. *Review of Economic Studies, 54,* 541-568.

George, A. (1980). *Presidential decision making in foreign policy.* Boulder, CO: Westview.

Halberstam, D. (1993). *The fifties.* New York: Villard.

Kreps, D., Milgrom, P., Roberts, J., & Wilson, R. (1982). Rational cooperation in the finitely repeated prisoner's dilemma. *Journal of Economic Theory, 27,* 245-252.

Matthews, C. (1988). *Hardball.* New York: Summit.

McCullough, D. (1992). *Truman.* New York: Simon & Schuster.

Okun, A. M. (1981). *Prices and quantities: A macroeconomic analysis.* Washington, DC: Brookings Institution.

Rousseau, D. M., & Parks, J. M. (1992). The contracts of individuals and organizations. In B. M. Staw & L. L. Cummings (Eds.), *Research in organizational behavior* (Vol. 15, pp. 1-43). Greenwich, CT: JAI.

Safire, W. (1992). *The first dissident: The book of Job in today's politics.* New York: Random House.

Shultz, G. (1993). *Turmoil and triumph.* New York: Scribners.

Weick, K. E. (1988). Enacted sensemaking in crisis situations. *Journal of Management Studies, 25,* 305-317.

Zucker, L. (1986). Production of trust: Institutional sources of economic structure, 1840-1920. In B. M. Staw & L. L. Cummings (Eds.), *Research in organizational behavior* (Vol. 8, pp. 53-111). Greenwich, CT: JAI.

The Organizational
Trust Inventory (OTI)

Development and Validation

L. L. CUMMINGS
PHILIP BROMILEY

The purpose of this chapter is to present the conceptual and empirical development, including validation, of a measure of organizational trust. Organizational trust refers to the degree of trust between units of an organization or between organizations.

A number of conceptual and empirical perspectives have been taken on trust, ranging from interpersonal (Helgeson, 1994; Wrightsman, 1991) to intergroup (Zander, 1994) to organizational (Bradach & Eccles, 1989; Gambetta, 1988; Granovetter, 1985; Hosmer, 1995) to societal (Lewis & Weigert, 1985). In addition, trust has been conceptualized as both a behavior and a belief (Shoda, Mischel, & Wright, 1994).

AUTHORS' NOTE: We wish to thank the following for their assistance: Linn Van Dyne, Don VandeWalle, Kathryn Brewer, Hyoung Moon, Seog Kwun, Kimberly Barron, Shoba Das, Charles Flaherty, Tanya Kostova, Mike Latham, and R. P. McDonald.

Conceptual Anchorage:
What Is Trust?

The core of our argument is that trust reduces transactions costs in and between organizations. Optimal expenditures on control, monitoring, and other kinds of transactions costs are a function of opportunism. Opportunism, in turn, depends on and influences the level of trustworthy behavior in an organization. Given that trust reduces transactions costs, we have elsewhere developed hypotheses concerning the impact of trust on internalization, monitoring and evaluation processes and criteria, biases in forecasting, frequency of interdivisional joint projects, effectiveness, and adaptation (Bromiley & Cummings, 1995). We will not repeat our reasoning here. However, the development of the Organizational Trust Inventory (OTI) is based on a formal, explicit definition of trust.

Trust will be defined as an individual's belief or a common belief among a group of individuals that another individual or group (a) makes good-faith efforts to behave in accordance with any commitments both explicit or implicit, (b) is honest in whatever negotiations preceded such commitments, and (c) does not take excessive advantage of another even when the opportunity is available. The rationale for this definition of trust rests on the socially embedded, subjective, and optimistic nature of most interactions within and between organizations that involve trust. Much of organizational interaction rests strongly on these three characteristics and thus makes trust so centrally important. The contrasting position, dominant in many economic formulations of organizational action, depicts individuals acting alone in a strictly self-interested objective fashion and driven by pessimistic assumptions about other individual actors. In particular, Williamson's (1975) transactions costs theory rests on the assumption that organizations must act as if the three forms of trust listed above are completely absent. That is, in transactions cost economics, actors lie in negotiations, cheat on any deals if it is profitable to do so, and exploit opportunities for renegotiation to their utmost. We assert that in many important situations, such a depiction is both inaccurate and inadequate. Consequently, we have chosen to define trust in a manner directly contrary to the assumptions of Williamson. Our definition of trust rests on a view of organizational action based largely on good-faith effort, honesty in exchange, and limited opportunism. Naturally, the measurement of trust as a continuous construct implies that these features will be present in differing amounts in differing organizations and activities.

Trustworthy behavior means that individuals actually behave according to (a), (b), and (c). The first dimension implies the individual being trusted is behaviorally reliable, that is, actually behaves to fulfill commitments. The second dimension implies that the individual's statements and behavior prior to making commitments are consistent with the individual's real desires and facts as the individual knows them. The third dimension implies the individual does not take full, *short-run* advantage of unforeseen opportunities to gain at the expense of the other. It implies that the individual can be counted on to put forward a bargain that is not seen as unreasonable, given the norms of the organization or group.

We define trust in terms of beliefs about negotiating behavior and moderation in exploiting advantages for three reasons. First, this definition conforms to the theoretical structure in which we want to work. Within transaction cost analyses, behavior matters. Second, and nontrivially, our definition avoids the problem of defining the individual's long-term interests. Other definitions of trustworthy behavior often focus on behavior deviating from the individual's self-interest, but these definitions generate the almost insurmountable problem that, given appropriate beliefs about the future, almost everything can be in one's interest. For example, Bradach and Eccles (1989, p. 104) adopt Lewis and Weigert's (1985) definition that "trust is characterized by a cognitive 'leap' beyond the expectations that reason and experience alone would warrant: where opportunism might be rationally expected, trust prevails." Thus, to have trust, the researcher must prove that a behavior clearly cannot be consistent with the subject's reason and experience: Such proof is hard to conceive in most situations. Third, our definition agrees with the common usage of the word *trustworthy*. Part of the reason we may trust a given individual is that we know the individual works within a control and incentive system that makes it very hard for the individual to benefit from cheating us.

Empirical Development

First, we present the rationale for the approach we have taken for the development of the OTI. Second, we describe the exact procedures followed and the results produced in developing and validating the OTI.

Rationale

We base our approach on two decisions. We have proposed a multidimensional definition of trust. The definition includes three dimensions: (a) belief that an individual or group makes good-faith efforts to behave in accordance with any commitments both explicit and implicit, (b) belief that an individual or group is honest in whatever negotiations (more generally, any interactions) preceded such commitments, and (c) belief that an individual or group does not take excessive advantage of another even when the opportunity is available.

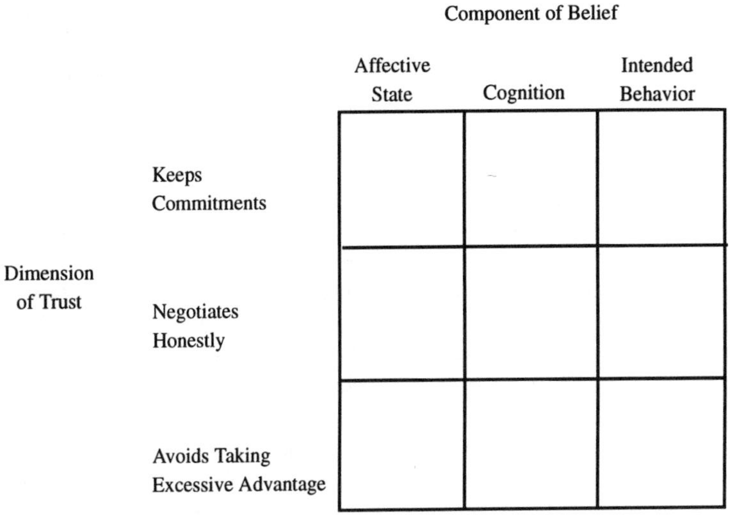

Component of Belief

Figure 15.1. Definitional Matrix of Trust as a Belief

Given the multidimensional definition of trust, we decided to develop survey items to reflect each of these dimensions. As we will demonstrate subsequently, we also tested the items to establish the degree to which they, in fact, array themselves empirically as three distinct but correlated dimensions.

In addition, we have based our theory and measurement of trust as a belief on the assumption that, as a belief, trust should be assessed across three components. These are trust as an *affective state,* as a *cognition,* and as an *intended behavior* (Creeds, Fabrigar, & Petty, 1994). Thus, we decided to construct survey items that reflect each of these three components for each of the three dimensions of the definition of trust.

The Definitional Matrix

These two decisions yielded a three-by-three matrix as the definitional structure of trust (see Figure 15.1).

Thus, we will present survey items fitting into each of the nine cells of the definitional matrix.

Development of the Items
to Measure Interunit Trust

We followed an extensive and very careful process to develop the measure of trust between differing units in organizations. This section describes the process by which the items were developed and their initial validity and reliability assessed. The next section describes the statistical validation of the measure based on survey responses.

Step 1: Development of Items

We began with the three conceptual dimensions of trust identified earlier. Our definition of trust was an individual's belief or a common belief among a group of individuals that another individual or group (a) makes good-faith efforts to behave in accordance with any commitments both explicit and implicit, (b) is honest in whatever negotiations preceded such commitments, and (c) does not take excessive advantage of another even when the opportunity is available.

The questions used for measuring trust dealt with the way people feel (affect), think (cognitive), or intend to behave (intent). We also developed a set of questions on actual behavior to provide some initial checks on the ties between the measure of trust and self-reported behaviors. This will constitute an initial effort to assess the predictive validity of the measure, although, of course, subsequent applications of the instrument in a variety of other nonexperimental and experimental settings will also be needed to fully assess the predictive validity of the instrument.

Under the direction of one of the authors, a group of five doctoral students met over a period of 6 months to develop questions (items) related to each of the three dimensions of trust plus the one area of behavior. As they developed the questions, they worked within the following constraints:

1. The questions could not use the word *trust*.
2. Approximately equal numbers of items should be developed for each dimension.
3. Questions, derived from theoretical and empirical work on defining and measuring attitudes in general, were developed so as to reflect affective, cognitive, and intended behavior components of the attitude labeled *trust*. That is, some questions should be phrased in terms of affect (We feel they . . .), cognitive (We think they . . .) and intended behavior (We will . . .).
4. Items were to be kept as simple as possible—for example, having only one verb to reflect the response mode and avoiding conditional statements.
5. Items needed to be phrased at the group or unit level ("We think that they . . ." rather than "I think that they . . .").

The group developed a list of 273 items. They then reevaluated each question to ensure that all members of the group understood it similarly, that the question matched the dimension it attempted to reflect (i.e., possessed face validity), and that it was simple and not excessively redundant with other questions. Through this process, the original 273 items were reduced to 121 items.

Step 2: Initial Reliability and Validity Assessment

Fifteen items from a previously validated measure (The Organizational Commitment Questionnaire [OCQ]; Mowday, Steers, & Porter, 1979) were added to the list of 121 items to produce a list of 136 items. Each of the 136 items was written on a separate piece of paper and the pieces were randomly ordered. Four cards were put on a table, with the definition of a dimension of trust or organizational commitment on each card. Three doctoral students who had no exposure to the theory or previous work in the area and had no involvement with the group that developed the items were asked to sort the items onto the cards that the item best reflected. The sorters had to place each item into exactly one of the four categories.

The results strongly supported the items developed. Of the 136 items, all three sorters put them into the same category 116 times (85.3%). For another 20 items, two of the three agreed (14.7%). In no case did fewer than two sorters agree on the correct category. We calculated Cohen's kappa (Cohen, 1960), which measures agreement between nominal scales, and all kappas were over .83, which is well above the recommended .7 cutoff. Thus we conclude that the items' reliability reflects the dimensions the items attempted to reflect.

We included the questions from the organizational commitment questionnaire to examine whether the trust items could be distinguished from other items of a related construct. They can be. In no case was a trust item assigned to the commitment category.

In short, the items reliably reflected the constructs they attempted to reflect and discriminated trust from organizational commitment.

To create a survey we could give to a large number of respondents, we needed to reduce the number of questions further. We reviewed all the items to eliminate items that we thought were close in wording. We attempted to retain approximately equal numbers of questions for each dimension and for affect, cognitive, and intended behavior response modes. The final questionnaire had 62 trust questions and 19 behavior questions. The questionnaire included questions where higher levels of trust corresponded to higher-response numbers and where they corresponded to lower-response numbers (i.e., some questions require reverse scoring). This was done in an attempt to minimize response-mode bias.

Step 3: Surveys

We administered the questionnaire to employees and students in under-graduate, day and night MBA, and executive MBA programs at the University of Minnesota. All respondents were asked to fill out the questionnaire only if they had sufficient and appropriate work experience to report their work unit's perceptions of other work units. We obtained a usable sample of 323 responses. A number of questionnaires were not usable because the respondents did not complete them or completed them in a manner clearly indicating they were not reading the questions (e.g., by marking with one line the value 5 for an entire page).

Statistical Methodology to Evaluate the Items. We analyzed the survey responses using latent variable structural equation analysis. Because the questions had been composed to directly represent specific dimensions and response modes, a confirmatory analysis was appropriate rather than an exploratory factor analysis.

The analysis was executed in the following stages: (a) estimation of the items versus the three dimensions of trust; (b) estimation for each dimension of trust of the affect, cognitive, and intent response-mode factors; and (c) estimation of the model that included trust factors and reported behavior.

The model was estimated by maximum likelihood techniques, using the SAS Calis program. Although the sample size falls short of the "10 times the number of parameters" rule of thumb, recent research indicates that this rule is not correct in many cases where accurate estimates can be obtained with smaller samples (Boomsma, 1987). We confirmed this in this sample by estimating the model, with 75% of the data yielding identical results to those reported here, which suggests that the results are not highly sensitive to sample size.

Validity Results. Let us begin by discussing the measurement of the three trust dimensions. Table 15.1 reports the results of this estimation. The model here simply has each item loading on the appropriate dimension. The three trust dimensions are allowed to covary.

The fit of the model was acceptable (Bentler's Comparative Fit Index of .81). All of the questions have highly significant associations with the associated factors; t-statistics are all over 2 and most are in the 15 to 25 range. The level of fit is generally high with all but 11 questions having question-to-factor correlations over .6. The three factors were highly correlated (from .80 to .93). Composite reliability of each dimension's measures was high—.95 to .96.

Although the overall results were extremely strong, some questions were not closely associated with the factors. The questions with lower item-to-factor correlations were generally associated with the behavioral intent response mode.

Although the items strongly load onto the three dimensions of trust, we wished to examine how response modes (affect, cognitive, behavioral intent) influenced the results. For example, do different response modes provide different underlying latent variables? In short, does it matter whether you ask

TABLE 15.1 Initial Estimation Results With All Questions

Question	Estimated Parameter	Standard Error	t-Statistic	Item-to-Factor Correlation	Explanatory Factor
Q24	1.028	0.072	14.22	0.70	Dimension One
Q28	1.051	0.081	12.93	0.65	
Q46	1.082	0.082	13.23	0.66	
Q56	1.427	0.066	21.58	0.92	
Q59	1.009	0.079	12.79	0.64	
Q67	1.262	0.073	17.23	0.80	
Q74	1.292	0.076	17.08	0.79	
Q13	1.188	0.074	16.06	0.76	
Q19	1.159	0.069	16.72	0.78	
Q27	1.359	0.072	18.93	0.85	
Q42	1.39	0.067	20.61	0.89	
Q43	1.406	0.068	20.58	0.89	
Q45	1.317	0.064	20.58	0.89	
Q49	1.306	0.066	19.69	0.87	
Q71	1.24	0.066	18.71	0.84	
Q73	1.462	0.078	18.83	0.85	
Q9	0.511	0.078	6.58	0.36	
Q15	0.494	0.071	6.94	0.38	
Q29	0.582	0.082	7.06	0.38	
Q31	0.142	0.065	2.19	0.12	
Q66	0.378	0.074	5.08	0.28	
Q20	1.293	0.068	18.94	0.85	Dimension Two
Q38	1.416	0.074	19.18	0.86	
Q54	1.341	0.064	20.94	0.90	
Q72	1.22	0.064	19.06	0.85	
Q1	1.112	0.071	15.66	0.75	
Q3	1.094	0.077	14.27	0.70	
Q10	1.026	0.076	13.53	0.67	
Q16	1.093	0.073	14.96	0.72	
Q32	1.273	0.063	20.24	0.88	
Q41	1.258	0.065	19.34	0.86	
Q51	1.19	0.067	17.75	0.81	
Q60	1.112	0.073	15.29	0.73	
Q61	1.225	0.067	18.42	0.83	
Q62	1.346	0.069	19.51	0.86	
Q22	1.1	0.076	14.5	0.71	
Q33	0.728	0.075	9.65	0.51	
Q35	0.953	0.075	12.74	0.64	
Q37	0.221	0.073	3.03	0.17	
Q63	0.683	0.07	9.78	0.51	
Q65	0.563	0.073	7.7	0.41	
Q79	0.56	0.089	6.3	0.34	
Q7	1.271	0.082	15.55	0.74	Dimension Three
Q5	1.324	0.082	16.14	0.76	
Q52	1.474	0.079	18.74	0.84	
Q57	1.282	0.074	17.3	0.80	

(continued)

TABLE 15.1 Continued

Question	Estimated Parameter	Standard Error	t-Statistic	Item-to-Factor Correlation	Explanatory Factor
Q81	1.367	0.080	17.08	0.79	
Q12	1.27	0.087	14.66	0.71	
Q18	1.254	0.077	16.37	0.77	
Q21	1.275	0.076	16.82	0.79	
Q25	1.027	0.088	11.68	0.60	
Q26	1.133	0.074	15.26	0.73	
Q47	1.271	0.085	14.87	0.72	
Q53	1.399	0.074	18.88	0.85	
Q55	1.325	0.073	18.07	0.82	
Q64	1.015	0.076	13.38	0.67	
Q4	0.965	0.085	11.36	0.58	
Q17	1.119	0.079	14.17	0.70	
Q75	1.208	0.071	17.11	0.80	
Q77	1.201	0.079	15.23	0.73	
Q78	1.272	0.073	17.51	0.81	
Q80	1.035	0.078	13.24	0.66	

Covariances Among Factors:
Affect and Cognitive   0.933375
Affect and Intent to Behave   0.803901
Cognitive and Intent to Behave   0.925018

Composite Reliability:
Affect   0.94970
Cognitive   0.95461
Intent to Behave   0.96164
Goodness of Fit Index (GFI)   0.5543
Chi-square = 5332.0252   df = 1826   Prob > chi-squared = 0.0001
Null Model Chi-square: df = 1891   20176.3664
RMSEA Estimate   0.0772 90%C.I.[0.0748, 0.0796]
Bentler's Comparative Fit Index   0.8083
Bentler and Bonnet's (1980) Nonnormed Index   0.8014

in terms of thinking, feeling, or behavioral intent? Such an examination is appropriate to verify the theoretical position articulated earlier; namely, that for each of the three dimensions of our definition of trust, a subdimension (response model) will be confirmed. Three such subdimensions were posited, that is, affective, cognitive, and intended behavior. As noted earlier, these are generally recognized as components of any belief. Given that our conception of trust is as a belief, we wished to establish the existence of each of these components for each dimension of trust.

For Dimension One, the fit improved with a Bentler Comparative Fit Index of .94 (see Table 15.2). The loadings remain high with no item-to-factor loadings below .6. The correlations among the three response-mode factors

TABLE 15.2 Dimension One With Response-Mode Factors

Question	Estimated Parameter	Standard Error	t-Statistic	Item-to-Factor Correlation	Response Mode
Q24	1.026	0.073	14.13	0.69	Affect
Q28	1.065	0.081	13.10	0.65	
Q46	1.099	0.082	13.46	0.67	
Q56	1.424	0.067	21.37	0.91	
Q59	1.024	0.079	13.00	0.65	
Q67	1.273	0.073	17.39	0.80	
Q74	1.305	0.076	17.27	0.80	
Q13	1.200	0.074	16.25	0.77	Cognitive
Q19	1.166	0.069	16.81	0.79	
Q27	1.360	0.072	18.90	0.85	
Q42	1.399	0.067	20.78	0.90	
Q43	1.413	0.068	20.69	0.90	
Q45	1.327	0.064	20.77	0.90	
Q49	1.301	0.067	19.51	0.87	
Q71	1.247	0.066	18.82	0.85	
Q73	1.456	0.078	18.64	0.84	
Q9	1.044	0.073	14.33	0.73	Intent to Behave
Q15	1.034	0.065	15.84	0.79	
Q29	1.209	0.075	16.04	0.80	
Q31	0.709	0.062	11.42	0.61	
Q66	0.842	0.072	11.66	0.63	

Covariances Among Factors:
Affect and Cognitive   0.991526
Affect and Intent to Behave   0.491391
Cognitive and Intent to Behave   0.395585
Composite Reliability, Dimension One:

Affect   0.89637
Cognitive   0.95853
Intent to Behave   0.83856

Goodness of Fit Index (GFI)   0.8585
Chi-square = 535.1133   df = 186   Prob > chi-squared = 0.0001
Bentler's Comparative Fit Index   0.9376
Bentler and Bonnet's (1980) Nonnormed Index   0.9296

indicate that Affect and Cognitive response modes are almost indistinguishable (correlation of .99), but both differ somewhat from Behavioral Intent (correlations of .49 and .40 for Affect and Cognitive correlations with Behavioral Intent). The composite reliability remains high, ranging from .84 to .96.

For Dimension Two, the fit also improved with a Bentler Comparative Fit Index of .92 (see Table 15.3). The loadings remain high, although three item-to-factor loadings are below .6, and one is at .19. The correlations among

TABLE 15.3 Dimension Two With Response-Mode Factors

Question	Estimated Parameter	Standard Error	t-Statistic	Item-to-Factor Correlation	Response Mode
Q20	1.311	0.068	19.28	0.86	Affect
Q38	1.422	0.074	19.21	0.86	
Q54	1.351	0.064	21.09	0.91	
Q72	1.232	0.064	19.27	0.86	
Q1	1.124	0.071	15.82	0.75	Cognitive
Q3	1.094	0.077	14.19	0.70	
Q10	1.021	0.076	13.39	0.67	
Q16	1.076	0.074	14.58	0.71	
Q32	1.293	0.063	20.69	0.90	
Q41	1.256	0.065	19.20	0.86	
Q51	1.217	0.067	18.30	0.83	
Q60	1.130	0.073	15.57	0.75	
Q61	1.221	0.067	18.23	0.83	
Q62	1.330	0.070	19.06	0.85	
Q22	1.237	0.077	16.14	0.79	Intent to Behave
Q33	0.887	0.077	11.57	0.62	
Q35	1.191	0.073	16.29	0.80	
Q37	0.254	0.077	3.30	0.19	
Q63	0.619	0.075	8.27	0.46	
Q65	0.823	0.073	11.28	0.60	
Q79	0.791	0.091	8.68	0.48	

Covariances Among Factors:
Affect and Cognitive   0.992943
Affect and Intent to Behave   0.790352
Cognitive and Intent to Behave   0.786342

Composite Reliability, Dimension Two:
Affect   0.92694
Cognitive   0.94192
Intent to Behave   0.77604

Goodness of Fit Index (GFI)   0.8321
Chi-square = 595.0067   df = 186   Prob > chi-squared = 0.0001
Null Model Chi-square: df = 210   5338.1398
Bentler's Comparative Fit Index   0.9202
Bentler and Bonnet's (1980) Nonnormed Index   0.9100

the three response-mode factors indicate that Affect and Cognitive response modes are almost indistinguishable (correlation of .99) but both differ somewhat from Behavioral Intent (correlations of .79 and .79 for Affect and Cognitive with Behavioral Intent). The composite reliability remains high, ranging from .78 to .94.

TABLE 15.4 Dimension Three With Response-Mode Factors

Question	Estimated Parameter	Standard Error	t-Statistic	Item-to-Factor Correlation	Response Mode
Q7	1.269	0.082	15.41	0.74	Affect
Q5	1.327	0.083	16.08	0.77	
Q52	1.494	0.079	19.02	0.86	
Q57	1.273	0.075	17.01	0.80	
Q81	1.386	0.080	17.31	0.80	
Q12	1.277	0.087	14.69	0.72	Cognitive
Q18	1.265	0.077	16.50	0.78	
Q21	1.249	0.077	16.24	0.77	
Q25	1.046	0.088	11.87	0.61	
Q26	1.147	0.074	15.43	0.74	
Q47	1.289	0.086	15.08	0.73	
Q53	1.425	0.074	19.33	0.86	
Q55	1.344	0.073	18.40	0.84	
Q64	1.040	0.076	13.74	0.68	
Q4	1.012	0.086	11.81	0.61	Intent to Behave
Q17	1.138	0.080	14.23	0.71	
Q75	1.253	0.070	17.78	0.82	
Q77	1.266	0.079	16.13	0.77	
Q78	1.344	0.072	18.76	0.85	
Q80	1.109	0.078	14.24	0.71	

Covariances Among Factors:
Affect and Cognitive   0.990829
Affect and Intent to Behave   0.925019
Cognitive and Intent to Behave   0.921548

Composite Reliability, Dimension Three:
Affect   0.89495
Cognitive   0.91997
Intent to Behave   0.88408

Goodness of Fit Index (GFI)   0.7906
Chi-square = 766.7082   df = 167   Prob > chi-squared = 0.0001
Null Model Chi-square: df = 190   5217.8091
Bentler's Comparative Fit Index   0.8807
Bentler and Bonnet's (1980) Nonnormed Index   0.8643

For Dimension Three, the fit was slightly below that of the previous two, with a Bentler Comparative Fit Index of .92 (see Table 15.4). The loadings remain high, with no item-to-factor loadings below .6. The correlations among the three response-mode factors indicate that Affect and Cognitive response modes are almost indistinguishable (correlation of .99). Oddly enough, for Dimension Three, the Affect and Cognitive to Behavioral Intent

TABLE 15.5 Measurement Model and Behavior Questions

Question	Estimated Parameter	Standard Error	t-Statistic	Item-to-Factor Correlation	Response Mode
Affect, Cognitive, and Intent to Behave Questions					
Q24	1.013	0.073	13.84	0.69	Dimension One— Affect
Q28	1.060	0.082	12.93	0.65	
Q46	1.096	0.082	13.45	0.67	
Q56	1.429	0.068	21.17	0.92	
Q59	1.046	0.080	13.11	0.66	
Q67	1.284	0.073	17.55	0.82	
Q74	1.314	0.076	17.21	0.80	
Q13	1.173	0.075	15.67	0.75	Dimension One— Cognitive
Q19	1.146	0.071	16.25	0.77	
Q27	1.353	0.072	18.69	0.85	
Q42	1.381	0.067	20.50	0.90	
Q43	1.404	0.069	20.28	0.89	
Q45	1.307	0.064	20.34	0.89	
Q49	1.294	0.067	19.29	0.87	
Q71	1.239	0.068	18.32	0.84	
Q73	1.463	0.079	18.63	0.85	
Q9	0.545	0.078	6.97	0.38	Dimension One— Intent
Q15	0.518	0.071	7.31	0.40	
Q29	0.613	0.083	7.35	0.40	
Q31	0.197	0.066	3.00	0.17	
Q66	0.427	0.075	5.66	0.32	
Q20	1.291	0.070	18.52	0.84	Dimension Two— Affect
Q38	1.424	0.075	18.92	0.86	
Q54	1.329	0.065	20.37	0.89	
Q72	1.208	0.065	18.73	0.85	
Q1	1.119	0.072	15.44	0.75	Dimension Two— Cognitive
Q3	1.107	0.078	14.16	0.70	
Q10	1.045	0.077	13.59	0.68	
Q16	1.109	0.074	14.90	0.73	
Q32	1.266	0.064	19.85	0.88	
Q41	1.26	0.066	19.12	0.86	
Q51	1.175	0.068	17.21	0.80	
Q60	1.094	0.073	14.96	0.73	
Q61	1.216	0.068	17.96	0.83	
Q62	1.345	0.069	19.40	0.87	
Q22	1.145	0.076	14.99	0.73	Dimension Two— Intent
Q33	0.757	0.075	10.05	0.53	
Q35	1.006	0.074	13.54	0.68	
Q37	0.237	0.073	3.24	0.18	
Q63	0.718	0.071	10.16	0.54	
Q65	0.606	0.073	8.26	0.45	

Q79	0.603	0.09	6.72	0.37	
Q7	1.288	0.083	15.59	0.75	Dimension Three— Affect
Q5	1.330	0.083	16.02	0.77	
Q52	1.448	0.080	18.08	0.83	
Q57	1.285	0.076	16.97	0.80	
Q81	1.354	0.082	16.52	0.78	
Q12	1.292	0.088	14.71	0.72	Dimension Three— Cognitive
Q18	1.247	0.078	15.97	0.76	
Q21	1.290	0.077	16.74	0.79	
Q25	1.044	0.089	11.78	0.61	
Q26	1.148	0.075	15.36	0.74	
Q47	1.272	0.086	14.71	0.72	
Q53	1.377	0.075	18.35	0.84	
Q55	1.304	0.074	17.51	0.81	
Q64	1.006	0.077	13.03	0.66	
Q4	0.976	0.085	11.52	0.60	Dimension Three— Intent
Q17	1.151	0.078	14.74	0.72	
Q75	1.231	0.072	17.16	0.80	
Q77	1.248	0.079	15.80	0.76	
Q78	1.299	0.074	17.64	0.82	
Q80	1.069	0.078	13.69	0.68	

Behavioral Questions

Q30	0.448	0.075	5.98	0.33	Dimension One
Q36	0.310	0.072	4.29	0.24	
Q48	0.258	0.071	3.61	0.20	
Q50	0.146	0.067	2.18	0.12	
Q68	0.852	0.081	10.57	0.55	
Q70	0.549	0.074	7.40	0.41	
Q8	1.063	0.081	13.19	0.66	Dimension Two
Q34	1.007	0.073	13.70	0.68	
Q40	0.884	0.078	11.33	0.59	
Q44	0.513	0.073	7.01	0.38	
Q58	0.594	0.093	6.37	0.35	
Q69	1.234	0.077	16.00	0.76	
Q76	0.549	0.073	7.49	0.41	
Q2	1.283	0.085	15.15	0.74	Dimension Three
Q6	1.043	0.080	13.08	0.66	
Q11	1.093	0.078	13.99	0.69	
Q14	1.324	0.074	17.87	0.83	
Q23	1.219	0.077	15.77	0.76	
Q39	1.257	0.087	14.44	0.71	

Goodness of Fit Index (GFI)　　　0.3905
Chi-square = 10073.9931　df = 3156　　Prob > chi-squared = 0.0001
Null Model Chi-square: df = 3240　　　27247.2000
Bentler's Comparative Fit Index　0.7118
Bentler and Bonnet's (1980) Nonnormed Index　　0.7042

NOTE: Average item-to-factor correlation for behavioral items .53, with a range from .12 to .83.

TABLE 15.6 Summary of Questions by Dimension and Response Mode

	Affect	Response Modes Cognitive	Intent to Behave
Dimension One	24, 28, 46, 56, 59, 67, 74	13, 19, 27, 42, 43, 45, 49, 71, 73	9, 15, 29
Dimension Two	20, 38, 54, 72	1, 3, 10, 16, 32, 41, 51, 60, 61, 62	22, 33, 35, 65
Dimension Three	5, 7, 52 57,81	12, 18, 21, 25, 26, 47, 53, 55, 64	4, 17, 75, 77, 78, 80

NOTE: The numbers in this table refer to item numbers in the research questionnaire (see Appendix A).

correlations are quite high (.92 and .93). The composite reliability remains high, ranging from .88 to .92.

Finally, we turn to the prediction of behavior. As noted earlier, a set of questions was generated concerning how the group behaves. The model from Table 15.1 was extended by the addition of a set of behavioral questions that will be directly caused by the factors for Dimensions One to Three. The results of estimating this model appear in Table 15.5.

The three trust dimensions are strongly associated with the behavioral questions. With almost no exceptions, parameter estimates on behavior questions are highly significant with only four t-statistics under 6.0 and none under 2.0. Explained variation is also high, with question-to-factor correlations averaging .53 for the behavioral questions (range from .12 to .83).

Although the structural-equation approach presented in Table 15.5 provides the most consistent approach to modeling the measurement of trust along with its influence on behavior, many studies use additive scales instead of structural-equation models. Consequently, we examined the relations between additive scales for trust and for behavior. The items included in each of the three trust dimensions were summed to give a scale for each dimension. Likewise, the behavioral items were summed to create an overall behavioral scale. The correlations between the scales for trust dimensions and the behavior scale were .80, .84, and .86 for Dimensions One, Two, and Three, respectively. Thus, the trust measures represented by an additive scale correlate quite highly with a scale representing trust-related behaviors.

To summarize, the items presented strongly relate to the three trust dimensions. Although Affect and Cognitive response modes provide extremely similar factors, Behavioral Intent questions appear to provide a somewhat less reliable measure, having the lowest composite reliability of the three response modes for all three trust dimensions. Table 15.6 presents the matrix of items by dimension and response mode.

TABLE 15.7 The OTI Short Form

Question	Estimated Parameter	Standard Error	t-Statistic	Item-to-Factor Correlation	Dimension
Q56	1.460	0.067	21.85	0.94	One
Q67	1.270	0.074	17.12	0.81	
Q42	1.368	0.068	20.02	0.89	
Q43	1.419	0.069	20.51	0.90	
Q54	1.381	0.064	21.66	0.93	Two
Q72	1.180	0.066	17.95	0.83	
Q41	1.306	0.065	20.17	0.89	
Q62	1.374	0.069	19.98	0.89	
Q52	1.516	0.079	19.1	0.87	Three
Q81	1.446	0.081	17.92	0.84	
Q47	1.326	0.087	15.29	0.75	
Q53	1.422	0.075	18.98	0.87	

Covariances Among Factors:
Affect and Cognitive   0.924776
Affect and Intent to Behave   0.768428
Cognitive and Intent to Behave   0.902516

Composite Reliability:
Dimension One   0.93508
Dimension Two   0.93578
Dimension Three 0.90088

Goodness of Fit Index (GFI)   0.9457
Chi-square = 110.3177   df = 51   Prob > chi-squared = 0.0001
Null Model Chi-square: df = 66   3880.5259
Bentler's Comparative Fit Index   0.9844
Bentler and Bonnet's (1980) Nonnormed Index   0.9799

The Organizational
Trust Inventory (OTI)—Short Form

Although meeting the necessary measurement standards, the full OTI may be overly long for many uses, so we designed and assessed a short form of the OTI. The procedure for doing so was as follows. First, we discarded the Intended Behavior (IB) items from the long form of the OTI. This was done because the IB items, singularly and on the average, exhibited lower item-to-factor correlations than did the Affective and Cognitive items. Second, we selected the Affective and Cognitive items from the long form that exhibited the highest item-to-factor correlations. Third, within that set of items, we discarded items with redundant wording, maintaining a .70 value as the minimum item-to-factor correlation acceptable. We believe that the resulting

TABLE 15.8 OTI Short Form and Behavior Questions

Question	Estimated Parameter	Standard Error	t-Statistic	Item-to-Factor Correlation	
Trust Items					
Q56	1.436	0.068	21.20	0.92	
Q67	1.299	0.073	17.71	0.82	
Q42	1.367	0.068	19.99	0.89	
Q43	1.409	0.070	20.23	0.90	
Q54	1.346	0.065	20.73	0.91	
Q72	1.182	0.066	18.03	0.83	
Q41	1.285	0.065	19.68	0.88	
Q62	1.361	0.069	19.70	0.88	
Q52	1.473	0.080	18.43	0.85	
Q81	1.389	0.082	17.02	0.80	
Q47	1.305	0.086	15.11	0.74	
Q53	1.388	0.075	18.44	0.85	
Behavioral Items					
Q30	0.418	0.076	5.49	0.31	Dimension One
Q36	0.300	0.073	4.09	0.23	
Q48	0.264	0.072	3.65	0.21	
Q50	0.139	0.068	2.05	0.12	
Q68	0.850	0.082	10.42	0.55	
Q70	0.543	0.075	7.23	0.40	
Q8	1.004	0.082	12.20	0.63	Dimension Two
Q34	0.990	0.074	13.33	0.67	
Q40	0.879	0.079	11.19	0.58	
Q44	0.492	0.074	6.66	0.37	
Q58	0.603	0.094	6.44	0.36	
Q69	1.223	0.078	15.71	0.76	
Q76	0.546	0.074	7.40	0.41	
Q2	1.285	0.085	15.05	0.74	Dimension Three
Q6	1.001	0.081	12.29	0.63	
Q11	1.041	0.080	13.00	0.66	
Q14	1.334	0.074	17.95	0.83	
Q23	1.192	0.079	15.15	0.74	
Q39	1.249	0.088	14.19	0.71	

Goodness of Fit Index (GFI)   0.5723
Chi-square = 1998.4250   df = 431   Prob > chi-squared = 0.0001
Null Model Chi-square: df = 465   7926.4183
Bentler's Comparative Fit Index   0.7899
Bentler and Bonnet's (1980) Nonnormed Index   0.7734

NOTE: Average item-to-factor correlation for behavioral items 0.522, with a range from 0.12 to 0.83.

12-item short form provides a more usable questionnaire without sacrificing substantial measurement assets.

We estimated the measurement model on the 12 questions selected (see Table 15.7). The overall fit of the model was substantially higher than for the longer questionnaire (as would be expected). Bentler's comparative fit index was .98. The three dimensions remained highly correlated. Most important, the composite reliability of the three measures was quite high: Dimension One at .9351, Dimension Two at .9358, and Dimension Three at .9009.

In addition to the reliability statistics, we also examined the fit between items in the short form and the trust behaviors (see Table 15.8). The explanatory power of the short form was almost identical to that of the long form. The average item-to-factor correlation for the behavioral items with the long form was .530, and with the short form it was .522.

As with the long form, we supplemented the structural-equation estimates with an examination of the correlation between additive scales for Dimensions One, Two, and Three and an additive scale including all the behavioral items. The correlations between dimension scales and the behavior scale were .67, .72, and .74 for Dimensions One, Two, and Three, respectively. Thus, the OTI short form also provides trust measures that, when represented by an additive scale, correlate quite highly with a scale representing trust-related behaviors. Note that the short form does have a slightly lower correlation with behavior than the long instrument (where all three scales are correlated over .8 with behavior).

To summarize, the OTI short form has acceptable psychometric properties in terms of reliabilities. Furthermore, it relates almost as strongly as the long form to our measures of behavior.

Conclusions

To summarize, we have developed and demonstrated the reliability of a set of items for measuring trust between units in organizations or between organizations, based on the definitions of trust presented in this chapter. The items have been shown to reflect reliably the three differing dimensions of the construct, validly differ from organizational commitment, and load strongly on the hypothesized factors in a confirmatory factor analysis. Two versions of the OTI resulted. The Organizational Trust Inventory—Long Form (OTI-LF) is presented in Appendix B. The Organizational Trust Inventory—Short Form (OTI-SF) is presented in Appendix C.

Although trust has become an important construct in recent work in organizations, its measurement has been either anecdotal or by unvalidated survey measures. This work provides a properly validated measure of this important construct.

APPENDIX A

Research Items in Instrument to Measure Interorganizational Trust

Items are ordered by factor (Dimension One—Affect, etc.) with the behavioral questions used for validation at the end. The question numbers correspond to the question numbers in the other tables, that is, Qu24 refers to the first question under Dimension One—Affect.

Dimension One—Affect

24. We feel we can depend on _____ to move our joint projects forward.
28. We feel we cannot depend on _____ to fulfill its commitments to us.
46. We worry about the success of joint projects with _____.
56. We feel that _____ will keep its word.
59. We feel uncomfortable about _____'s willingness to stick to the schedule.
67. We feel that _____ tries to get out of its commitments.
74. We worry about _____'s commitment to agreed upon goals.

Dimension One—Cognitive

13. We think _____ keeps commitments.
19. We think _____ behaves according to its commitments.
27. We think that _____ is dependable.
42. We think that _____ meets its negotiated obligations to our _____.
43. In our opinion, _____ is reliable.
45. We think the people in _____ keep their promises.
49. We think _____ keeps the spirit of an agreement.

320

71. We think that commitments made to our _____ will be honored by the people in _____.

73. We think _____ lets us down.

Dimension One—Behavioral Intention

9. We intend to check whether _____ meets its obligations to our _____.
15. We plan to monitor _____'s compliance with our agreement.
29. We don't plan on checking on _____.
31. We intend to check on _____'s progress with our project.
66. We intend to monitor _____'s behavior for timeliness.

Dimension Two—Affect

20. We feel we can depend on _____ to negotiate with us honestly.
38. We feel that _____ is straight with us.
54. We feel that _____ negotiates with us honestly.
72. We feel that _____ negotiates joint expectations fairly.

Dimension Two—Cognitive

1. We think the people in _____ are fair in their negotiations with us.
3. We think that _____ fairly represents its capabilities.
10. We think _____ misrepresents its demands during negotiations.
16. We think _____ misrepresents its capabilities in negotiations.
32. We think that _____ negotiates agreements fairly.
41. We think the people in _____ tell the truth in negotiations.
51. We think _____ negotiates important project details fairly.
60. We think _____ is open in describing its strengths and weaknesses in negotiating joint projects.
61. We think _____ negotiates realistically.
62. We think _____ does not mislead us.

Dimension Two—Behavioral Intention

22. We intend to negotiate cautiously with _____.
33. We intend to question _____'s statements regarding their capabilities.
35. We intend to watch for misleading information from _____ in our negotiations.
37. We intend to misrepresent our capabilities in negotiations with _____.
63. We intend to speak openly in our negotiations with _____.
65. We intend to check on the reasoning given by _____ during negotiations.
79. We plan to document all aspects of our negotiations with _____.

Dimension Three—Affect

5. We feel that _____ takes advantage of our _____.
7. We feel that _____ takes advantage of us.
52. We feel that _____ tries to get the upper hand.
57. We feel confident that _____ won't take advantage of us.
81. We feel that _____ takes advantage of people who are vulnerable.

Dimension Three—Cognitive

12. We think that the people in _____ manipulate others to gain a personal advantage.
18. We think that _____ takes advantage of ambiguous situations.
21. We think _____ tries to take advantage of us.
25. We think that the people in _____ use confidential information to their own advantage.
26. We think that _____ takes advantage of a changed situation.
47. We think that the people in _____ succeed by stepping on other people.
53. We think that _____ takes advantage of our problems.
64. We think that people in _____ interpret ambiguous information in their own favor.
55. We think that _____ takes advantage of our weaknesses.

Dimension Three—Behavioral Intention

4. We intend to monitor changes in situations because _____ will take advantage of such changes.
17. We intend to monitor _____ closely so that they do not take advantage of us.
75. We intend to work openly with _____ because they will not take advantage of us.
77. We intend to share information cautiously with _____ to avoid having them use it to their advantage.
78. We plan to share information openly with _____ because they do not take advantage of us.
80. We intend to check _____'s actions to avoid being taken advantage of.

Dimension One—Behavior

30. We monitor the compliance of _____ in fulfilling our joint agreements.
36. We watch to see whether _____ meets its deadlines.
48. We check to make sure that _____ continues to work on our joint projects.
50. We check _____'s progress with our project.
68. We prod _____ to ensure that they fulfill their commitments to us.
70. We check whether _____ meets its obligations to our _____.

Dimension Two—Behavior

8. In negotiations, we question _____'s statements regarding their capabilities.
34. We watch for misleading information from _____ in our negotiations.
40. We speak openly in negotiations with _____.
44. We check on the reasoning given by _____ during negotiations.
58. We document all aspects of our negotiations with _____.
69. We negotiate cautiously with _____.
76. We misrepresent our capabilities in negotiations with _____.

Dimension Three—Behavior

2. We share information openly with _____ because they do not take advantage of us.
6. We monitor changes in situations so that _____ will not take advantage of such changes.
11. We check _____'s actions to avoid being taken advantage of.
14. We work openly with _____ because they will not take advantage of us.
23. We monitor _____ closely so that they cannot take advantage of us.
39. We share information cautiously with _____ to avoid having them use it to their advantage.

To summarize, to measure trust from an *affective* perspective, one would use questions 24, 28, 56, 59, 67, and 74 for Dimension One; questions 20, 38, 54, and 72 for Dimension Two; and questions 5, 7, 46, 52, 57, and 81 for Dimension Three. To measure trust from a *cognitive* perspective, one would use questions 13, 19, 27, 42, 43, 45, 49, 71, and 73 for Dimension One; questions 1, 3, 10, 16, 32, 41, 51, 60, 61, and 62 for Dimension Two; and questions 12, 18, 21, 25, 26, 47, 53, 64, and 55 for Dimension Three. To measure trust from an *intention to behave* perspective, one would use questions 9, 15, and 29 for Dimension One; questions 17, 22, 33, 35, and 65 for Dimension Two; and questions 4, 75, 77, 78, and 80 for Dimension Three.

APPENDIX B

Organizational Trust Inventory—Long Form (OTI-LF)

Please choose the unit or department about which you can most knowledgeably report the opinions of members of your department or unit.

1. *Your* department or unit is _____. (enter name of department/unit)
2. The *other* department or unit about which you are responding is_____. (enter name of department/unit)

Please circle the number to the right of each statement that most closely describes the opinion of members of your department toward the other department. Interpret the blank spaces as referring to the other department about which you are commenting.

Strongly Disagree	Disagree	Slightly Disagree	Neither Agree nor Disagree	Slightly Agree	Agree	Strongly Agree
1	2	3	4	5	6	7

1. We think the people in _____ are fair in their negotiations with us.   1 2 3 4 5 6 7
2. We think that _____ fairly represents its capabilities.   1 2 3 4 5 6 7
3. We intend to monitor changes in situations because _____ will take advantage of such changes.   1 2 3 4 5 6 7
4. We feel that _____ takes advantage of our department.   1 2 3 4 5 6 7
5. We feel that _____ takes advantage of us.   1 2 3 4 5 6 7
6. We intend to check whether _____ meets its obligations to our department.   1 2 3 4 5 6 7

Strongly Disagree	Disagree	Slightly Disagree	Neither Agree nor Disagree	Slightly Agree	Agree	Strongly Agree
1	2	3	4	5	6	7

7. We think _____ misrepresents its demands during negotiations.　　1 2 3 4 5 6 7

8. We think that the people in _____ manipulate others to gain a personal advantage.　　1 2 3 4 5 6 7

9. We think _____ keeps commitments.　　1 2 3 4 5 6 7

10. We plan to monitor _____'s compliance with our agreement.　　1 2 3 4 5 6 7

11. We think _____ misrepresents its capabilities in negotiations.　　1 2 3 4 5 6 7

12. We intend to monitor _____ closely so that they do not take advantage of us.　　1 2 3 4 5 6 7

13. We think that _____ takes advantage of ambiguous situations.　　1 2 3 4 5 6 7

14. We think _____ behaves according to its commitments.　　1 2 3 4 5 6 7

15. We feel we can depend on _____ to negotiate with us honestly.　　1 2 3 4 5 6 7

16. We think _____ tries to take advantage of us.　　1 2 3 4 5 6 7

17. We intend to negotiate cautiously with _____.　　1 2 3 4 5 6 7

18. We feel we can depend on _____ to move our joint projects forward.　　1 2 3 4 5 6 7

19. We think that the people in _____ use confidential information to their own advantage.　　1 2 3 4 5 6 7

20. We think that _____ takes advantage of a changed situation.　　1 2 3 4 5 6 7

21. We think that _____ is dependable.　　1 2 3 4 5 6 7

22. We feel we cannot depend on _____ to fulfill its commitments to us.　　1 2 3 4 5 6 7

23. We don't plan on checking on _____.　　1 2 3 4 5 6 7

24. We intend to check on _____'s progress with our project.　　1 2 3 4 5 6 7

25. We think that _____ negotiates agreements fairly.　　1 2 3 4 5 6 7

26. We intend to question _____'s statements regarding their capabilities.　　1 2 3 4 5 6 7

27. We intend to watch for misleading information from _____ in our negotiations.　　1 2 3 4 5 6 7

28. We intend to misrepresent our capabilities in negotiations with _____.　　1 2 3 4 5 6 7

Strongly Disagree	Disagree	Slightly Disagree	Neither Agree nor Disagree	Slightly Agree	Agree	Strongly Agree
1	2	3	4	5	6	7

29. We feel that _____ is straight with us.   1 2 3 4 5 6 7

30. We think the people in _____ tell the truth in
    negotiations.   1 2 3 4 5 6 7

31. We think that _____ meets its negotiated obligations
    to our department.   1 2 3 4 5 6 7

32. In our opinion, _____ is reliable.   1 2 3 4 5 6 7

33. We think the people in _____ keep their promises.   1 2 3 4 5 6 7

34. We worry about the success of joint projects
    with _____.   1 2 3 4 5 6 7

35. We think that the people in _____ succeed by stepping
    on other people.   1 2 3 4 5 6 7

36. We think _____ keeps the spirit of an agreement.   1 2 3 4 5 6 7

37. We think _____ negotiates important project
    details fairly.   1 2 3 4 5 6 7

38. We feel that _____ tries to get the upper hand.   1 2 3 4 5 6 7

39. We think that _____ takes advantage of our problems.   1 2 3 4 5 6 7

40. We feel that _____ negotiates with us honestly.   1 2 3 4 5 6 7

41. We think that _____ takes advantage of our weaknesses.   1 2 3 4 5 6 7

42. We feel that _____ will keep its word.   1 2 3 4 5 6 7

43. We feel confident that _____ won't take
    advantage of us.   1 2 3 4 5 6 7

44. We feel uncomfortable about _____'s willingness to
    stick to the schedule.   1 2 3 4 5 6 7

45. We think _____ is open in describing its strengths
    and weaknesses in negotiating joint projects.   1 2 3 4 5 6 7

46. We think _____ negotiates realistically.   1 2 3 4 5 6 7

47. We think _____ does not mislead us.   1 2 3 4 5 6 7

48. We intend to speak openly in our negotiations
    with _____.   1 2 3 4 5 6 7

49. We think that people in _____ interpret ambiguous
    information in their own favor.   1 2 3 4 5 6 7

50. We intend to check on the reasoning given
    by _____ during negotiations.   1 2 3 4 5 6 7

51. We intend to monitor _____'s behavior for timeliness.   1 2 3 4 5 6 7

52. We feel that _____ tries to get out of its commitments.   1 2 3 4 5 6 7

53. We think that commitments made to our department
    will be honored by the people in _____.   1 2 3 4 5 6 7

54. We feel that _____ negotiates joint expectations fairly.   1 2 3 4 5 6 7

Strongly Disagree	Disagree	Slightly Disagree	Neither Agree nor Disagree	Slightly Agree	Agree	Strongly Agree
1	2	3	4	5	6	7

55. We think _____ lets us down.   1 2 3 4 5 6 7

56. We worry about _____'s commitment to agreed
upon goals.   1 2 3 4 5 6 7

57. We intend to work openly with _____ because they
will not take advantage of us.   1 2 3 4 5 6 7

58. We intend to share information cautiously with _____
to avoid having them use it to their advantage.   1 2 3 4 5 6 7

59. We plan to share information openly with _____
because they do not take advantage of us.   1 2 3 4 5 6 7

60. We plan to document all aspects of our negotiations
with _____.   1 2 3 4 5 6 7

61. We intend to check _____'s actions to avoid being
taken advantage of.   1 2 3 4 5 6 7

62. We feel that _____ takes advantage of people who
are vulnerable.   1 2 3 4 5 6 7

APPENDIX C

Organizational Trust Inventory—Short Form (OTI-SF)

Please choose the unit or department about which you can most knowledgeably report the opinions of members of your department or unit.

1. *Your* department or unit is _____. (enter name of department/unit)
2. The *other* department or unit about which you are responding is _____.
   (enter name of department/unit)

Please circle the number to the right of each statement that most closely describes the opinion of members of your department toward the other department. Interpret the blank spaces as referring to the other department about which you are commenting.

Strongly Disagree	Disagree	Slightly Disagree	Neither Agree nor Disagree	Slightly Agree	Agree	Strongly Agree
1	2	3	4	5	6	7

1. We think the people in _____ tell the truth
   in negotiations.   1 2 3 4 5 6 7
2. We think that _____ meets its negotiated obligations
   to our department.   1 2 3 4 5 6 7
3. In our opinion, _____ is reliable.   1 2 3 4 5 6 7
4. We think that the people in _____ succeed by stepping
   on other people.   1 2 3 4 5 6 7
5. We feel that _____ tries to get the upper hand.   1 2 3 4 5 6 7
6. We think that _____ takes advantage of our problems. 1 2 3 4 5 6 7

Strongly Disagree	Disagree	Slightly Disagree	Neither Agree nor Disagree	Slightly Agree	Agree	Strongly Agree
1	2	3	4	5	6	7

7. We feel that _____ negotiates with us honestly.   1 2 3 4 5 6 7

8. We feel that _____ will keep its word.   1 2 3 4 5 6 7

9. We think _____ does not mislead us.   1 2 3 4 5 6 7

10. We feel that _____ tries to get out of its commitments.   1 2 3 4 5 6 7

11. We feel that _____ negotiates joint expectations fairly.   1 2 3 4 5 6 7

12. We feel that _____ takes advantage of people who
    are vulnerable.   1 2 3 4 5 6 7

330   TRUST IN ORGANIZATIONS

References

Bentler, P. M., & Bonnet, D. G. (1980). Significance tests and goodness of fit in the analysis of covariance structures. *Psychological Bulletin, 88,* 588-606.

Boomsma, A. (1987). The robustness of maximum likelihood estimation in structural equation models. In P. Cuttance & R. Ecob (Eds.), *Structural modeling by example* (pp. 160-168). New York: Cambridge University Press.

Bradach, J. L., & Eccles, R. G. (1989). Price, authority and trust: From ideal types to plural forms. *Annual Review of Sociology, 15,* 97-118.

Bromiley, P., & Cummings, L. L. (1995). *Transactions costs in organizations with trust.* In R. Bies, B. Sheppard, & R. Lewicki (Eds.), *Research on negotiations in organizations* (Vol. 5, pp. 219-247). Greenwich, CT: JAI.

Cohen, J. (1960). A coefficient of agreement for nominal scales. *Educational and Psychological Measurement, 20*(1), 37-46.

Creeds, S. L., Fabrigar, L. R., & Petty, R. E. (1994). Measuring the affective and cognitive properties of attitudes: Conceptual and methodological issues. *Personality and Social Psychology Bulletin, 20*(6), 619-634.

Gambetta, D. (Ed.). (1988). *Trust: Making and breaking cooperative relations.* Oxford, UK: Basil Blackwell.

Granovetter, M. (1985). Economic action and social structure: The problem of embeddedness. *American Journal of Sociology, 91*(3), 481-510.

Helgeson, V. S. (1994). Relation of agency and communion to well-being: Evidence and potential explanations. *Psychological Bulletin, 116*(3), 412-428.

Hosmer, L. T. (1995). Trust: The connecting link between organizational theory and philosophical ethics. *Academy of Management Review, 20*(2), 379-403.

Lewis, J. D., & Weigert, A. (1985). Trust a social reality. *Social Forces, 63,* 967-985.

Mowday, R. T., Steers, R. M., & Porter, L. W. (1979). The measurement of organizational commitment. *Journal of Vocational Behavior, 14,* 224-247.

Shoda, Y., Mischel, W., & Wright, J. C. (1994). Intraindividual stability in the organization and patterning of behavior: Incorporating psychological situations into the idiographic analysis of personality. *Journal of Personality and Social Psychology, 67*(4), 674-687.

Williamson, W. E. (1975). *Markets and hierarchies: Analysis and antitrust implications.* New York: Free Press.

Wrightsman, L. S. (1991). Interpersonal trust and attitudes toward human nature. In J. P. Robinson, P. R. Shaver, & L. S. Wrightsman (Eds.), *Measures of personality and social psychological attitudes* (pp. 373-412). New York: Academic Press.

Zander, A. (1994). *Making groups effective* (2nd ed., pp. 185-236). San Francisco: Jossey-Bass.

Trust in Organizational Authorities

The Influence of Motive Attributions
on Willingness to Accept Decisions

TOM R. TYLER
PETER DEGOEY

The focus of this chapter is on the role of trust in authority relations within hierarchical groups. We will discuss a variety of such groups, including nations governed by legal and political authorities, work organizations, and families. In particular, we will examine whether people's judgments about the trustworthiness of group authorities can facilitate the authorities' ability to gain voluntary acceptance for their decisions.

The ability to secure compliance with decisions, more broadly labeled the ability to be authoritative (Tyler, 1990; Tyler & Lind, 1992), is widely recognized as a central characteristic of the effectiveness of organizational authorities. Barnard (1958) argued, for example, that "an essential element of organizations is the willingness of persons to contribute their individual efforts to the cooperative system" (Barnard, 1958, p. 139). Such behavior can be enhanced through the development of a "zone of indifference," within

AUTHORS' NOTE: This chapter was presented at the conference on trust in organizations, Graduate School of Management, Stanford University, May 1994. We would like to thank Robert Cialdini, Rod Kramer, Walter Powell, and other participants in the conference for their comments on our presentation.

which subordinates voluntarily accept an order without consciously questioning its authoritativeness. Herbert Simon (1947) similarly proposed that the willingness to accept an authority's decisions can occur through deference to the organizational role of authorities and can be made "independently of judgments of the correctness or acceptability of the premise [of their decisions]" (Simon, 1947, p. 125).

These organizational theorists recognize that, if authorities must continually explain and justify their decisions, their ability to effectively manage is diminished. Furthermore, these theorists emphasize the importance of the voluntary acceptance of the decisions of authorities and suggest that such acceptance should come about without recourse to reward or coercion. They do not, however, examine the psychology of acceptance. In particular, they do not explore the role that trust in the motives of authorities plays in the willingness to accept decisions.

Recently, sociologists and economists have begun to focus more directly on the role of trust in organizations. Gambetta (1988), Granovetter (1985), and Bradach and Eccles (1989), for instance, argued that trust plays an important role in facilitating economic transactions, especially in transactions embedded in social relations. What these theorists also share in common, however, is that they pay little or no attention to empirically testing their arguments about the importance of trust.

This chapter has two goals. The first is to provide an empirical assessment of the importance of trust in facilitating the voluntary acceptance of an authority's decisions. We will present empirical data showing that people's evaluations of the trustworthiness of organizational authorities shape their willingness to accept the decisions of authorities as well as influencing feelings of obligation to follow organizational rules and laws.

The second goal is to provide information about the psychology of trust in authorities. Here our goal is to contrast a calculative image of the psychological dynamics of trust to a more social conception. The calculative image suggests that people trust others either because these others have acted in favorable ways in the past, or they can be expected to act favorably in the future. This image of trust accords well with the way it has generally been defined in the literature: Trust is seen as a subjective probability calculation of the potential costs and benefits of future interactions (e.g., Gambetta, 1988). As Williamson (1993) has noted, however, trust thus defined adds little to our understanding of human behavior that cannot be explained more parsimoniously by economic theory.

The social conception of trust, on the other hand, suggests that people are influenced by their attributions of the motives of authorities (Tyler, 1990; Tyler & Lind, 1992). According to the social model of trust, an authority's intentions to maintain respectful relations in decision-making processes are central to trust. Attributions of positive intent lead group members to trust the authority and take the obligation to accept his or her decisions onto themselves. The social model further suggests that trust may play an especially important role when people's relationship to an authority is salient. That is, group members are more concerned about trustworthiness when they feel they have a social bond with the authority and when they identify with the group in which the authority operates. We will present empirical data showing that the psychology of trustworthiness is primarily determined by relational and intentional concerns rather than by instrumental concerns for receiving desired outcomes from interactions with authorities.

The Role of Trust
in Dispute Resolution

The research described in this chapter examines the role of trust within the context of disputes within organized groups. In particular, it explores situations in which group authorities are the focus of disputes, either because group members have disputes with authorities or because the authorities mediate among contending parties within the group. Such situations are an ideal arena for exploring the willingness to accept decisions, because the parties involved in the disputes are often faced with difficult conflicts of interest. The parties typically have noncorrespondent interests, hold strongly opposing views, feel hostility and anger, and make exaggerated claims of entitlement. All of these factors lessen their willingness to defer voluntarily to the decisions of authorities.

The work outlined below builds on the classic studies of dispute resolution conducted by Thibaut and Walker (1975) during the 1970s. Their research examined the antecedents of willingness to accept third-party conflict resolution decisions. Thibaut and Walker's work provided the foundations for the field of procedural justice, which focuses on people's perceptions of the manner in which decision-making procedures are enacted. Ironically, Thibaut and Walker did not consider issues of trust. Rather, they focused on people's feelings that they have some degree of control over the authority's decisions and the decision-making process ("voice"). However, subsequent procedural justice research has included the exploration of issues of trust (see Tyler & Lind, 1992).

Tyler (1988, 1990) included assessments of trustworthiness in his analysis of naturally occurring interactions with police officers and judges. He found that trustworthiness was the strongest predictor of evaluations of the fairness of decision-making procedures (see Tyler, 1988). Judgments of trustworthiness explained a striking anomaly in the findings reported by Tyler (1990).

Some people interviewed indicated that police officers and judges were acting in a nonneutral, biased way, yet nonetheless evaluated those authorities to be fair. People seemed willing to forgive surface features of racism and sexism, for example, if they felt that the authorities involved were basically motivated to act in a benevolent manner. It was the trustworthiness of the intentions of the authorities that shaped reactions to the procedures they employed, not surface features of those procedures (e.g., neutrality). These findings suggest that trust may be important in defining people's reactions to authorities.

Other studies have also demonstrated that trust is antecedent to attitudes about the procedural justice of authorities and to beliefs about their legitimacy. Tyler (1994b) demonstrated that trust influences judgments about the fairness of third-party procedures in both legal and managerial settings. Furthermore, Tyler and Degoey (1995b) demonstrated that trust influences views about the legitimacy of authorities in legal, managerial, and familial settings. These social attitudes and views about legitimacy, in turn, have been shown to influence people's willingness to accept voluntarily decisions and to obey group rules.

Trust and Its Consequences

Trust and Voluntary Acceptance of Decisions

Does trust influence the voluntary acceptance of decisions? We will consider three studies that examined this question in the context of conflicts involving authorities. These conflicts occurred in managerial, political, and family settings. Study 1 examined a random sample of workers in Chicago about their recent experiences with their supervisors. In Study 2, citizens of San Francisco were interviewed over the telephone about their views on the San Francisco Public Utilities Commission. The Commission was charged with enacting water conservation policies during the 1991 California water shortage. Study 3 asked undergraduate students at the University of California at Berkeley how recent conflicts with their parents had been resolved. In each study, the dependent variable was the willingness of respondents to voluntarily accept the decisions made by the authority in question. The details of the studies are included in Appendix A.

Two classes of independent variables were included in the regression analyses: (a) calculative/instrumental judgments and (b) relational judgments of the conduct of group authorities. The calculative variables included respondents' assessments that the outcome of the authority's decisions was favorable to them and that they had some degree of control over the decision-making process.[1] Relational judgments included assessments of the trustworthiness of authorities, their willingness to be unbiased in the decision-making

TABLE 16.1   Antecedents of the Willingness to Accept Voluntarily the Decisions of Authorities

	Voluntary Acceptance of Decisions		
	Management	Politics	Family
Instrumental judgments			
Outcome favorability	$.37^{***}$	$.10^{*}$	$.29^{***}$
Control	.07	.07	−.04
Relational judgments			
Trustworthiness	$.30^{***}$	$.47^{***}$	$.33^{***}$
Neutrality	$.21^{**}$	−.13	$.15^{**}$
Status recognition	−.12	.01	.11
R-squared	$45\%^{***}$	$23\%^{***}$	$53\%^{***}$

NOTE: Entries are beta weights and adjusted R-squares. $*p < .05$; $**p < .01$; $***p < .001$.

process, and the degree to which the authorities treated respondents with dignity and respect ("status recognition"). We defined trust in terms of feelings that an authority made a good-faith effort and treated the parties involved in the conflict fairly.

The findings of the three studies are outlined in Table 16.1. They indicate that attributions about trustworthiness are central to the willingness to accept decisions within all three arenas. In the management setting, trustworthiness and outcome favorability were the most important factors shaping voluntary decision acceptance ($\beta = .30$ and $.37$, $p < .001$, respectively), as they were in the family setting ($\beta = .33$ and $.29$, $p < .001$, respectively). In both studies, the differences between the magnitude of the effects of trustworthiness attributions and outcome judgments were not significant. In the political setting, trustworthiness was the major factor shaping willingness to accept decisions ($\beta = .47$, $p < .001$).

Trust and Feelings
of Obligation to Obey Laws

We can also consider the influence of trust on people's feelings of obligation to obey rules. To do so, we review three studies that examined this question. Study 4 explored the antecedents of willingness to obey the law among a sample of citizens in Chicago who were interviewed about their personal experiences with police officers and judges. Study 5 examined feelings of obligation to obey federal laws among citizens of San Francisco who were interviewed about their views on the U.S. Congress. Study 6 explored feelings of obligation to obey federal laws among citizens of San Francisco interviewed about their views on the U.S. Supreme Court. The details of each study are also included in Appendix A.

TABLE 16.2 Antecedents of Feelings of Obligation to Obey the Law

	Obligation to Obey the Law		
	Police	Congress	Supreme Court
Instrumental judgments			
Outcome favorability	.22**	−.04	.14*
Control	.02	−.09	.07
Relational judgments			
Trustworthiness	.28**	.20***	.18*
Neutrality	−.09	.23***	.06
Status recognition	.13	.08	−.07
R-squared	6%**	15%***	10%***

NOTE: Entries are beta weights and adjusted R-squares. *$p < .05$; **$p < .01$; ***$p < .001$.

The results of regression analyses are shown in Table 16.2. They indicate that trust consistently influences feelings of obligation to obey organizational rules and laws. In the Chicago study, trust significantly shaped feelings of obligation to the police and the courts ($\beta = .28$, $p < .01$), as did outcome favorability ($\beta = .22$, $p < .01$; the difference is not significant). Trust also shaped feelings of obligation to obey the laws enacted by the U.S. Congress ($\beta = .20$, $p < .001$). In this case, judgments about the neutrality of Congress also had an influence ($\beta = .23$, $p < .001$). In terms of the U.S. Supreme Court, trustworthiness and outcome favorability both influenced feelings of obligation ($\beta = .18$ and $.14$, $p < .05$).

Summary

Overall, these findings point to a strong, widespread influence of trustworthiness attributions on people's reactions to authorities. This influence is robust across a variety of contexts and groups. In all of the settings studied, inferences about the trustworthiness of the motives of authorities had a powerful effect on whether people voluntarily deferred to third-party decisions and group rules.

The finding that people focus on the motive inference of trustworthiness when reacting to authorities is striking, because the conventional wisdom in cognitive psychology is that people are "cognitively lazy" and do the least amount of processing of their experiences that is possible. Thus, people prefer to develop incomplete but satisfactory answers rather than engage in complex cognitive processing of events. Because trustworthiness attributions are inferences made about the motives of authorities, they require people to consider the implications of surface behaviors for deeper issues of intent—a complex cognitive task. The studies reported here suggest that people tend to engage in this complicated task, even when they could rely on surface features such as neutrality or bias. People seem to value information about benevolent intentions enough to be willing to undergo extra cognitive efforts to obtain them (see Tyler, 1988).

Psychological Models
of Trustworthiness

The findings reported earlier point to the importance of trust in authorities. But which psychological models explain this importance? One model of the psychology of trustworthiness is instrumental and suggests that trustworthiness should be linked to individual beliefs about the likelihood of receiving positive outcomes from interactions with authorities. The other is relational and suggests that trust is related to the nature of the social bond to authorities.

Although Thibaut and Walker (1975) did not speak to trustworthiness directly, their general control model is easily extended to an instrumental model of trustworthiness. The model suggests that people trust authorities who are judged to be motivated to share control. In other words, trustworthiness can be viewed from an instrumental perspective as the belief that one will have a reasonable degree of control over outcomes. Trust in con- trol, in turn, is grounded in expectations that desired outcomes will be received.

This argument has also recently been made by Williamson (1993), who suggested that trust may "have the appearance of being noncalculative" (p. 486) but in fact is a response to environmental contingencies. His analysis considers trust as one aspect of rational "risk analysis"—that is, estimations of the likelihood that others will perform a particular action. "When we say we trust someone or that someone is trustworthy, we implicitly mean that the probability that he [or she] will perform an action that is beneficial or at least not detrimental to us is high enough for us to consider engaging in some form of cooperation with him [or her]" (p. 463). Similarly, Bradach and Eccles (1989) argued that trust is the expectation that an economic exchange partner will not act opportunistically (see also Dasgupta, 1988).

A similar argument has been developed within the literature on social dilemmas. That literature examines situations in which groups or communities are faced with a scarcity of shared, communal resources. Much social dilemma research has focused on developing an understanding of the conditions under which individuals will forgo their short-term self-interests and voluntarily restrain their actions. Widespread evidence suggests that people behave cooperatively when they trust that others will reciprocate cooperative behavior (Brann & Foddy, 1988; Brewer & Kramer, 1986; Komorita, Chan, & Parks, 1993; Komorita, Parks, & Hulbert, 1992; Kramer & Goldman, 1988;

Kramer, Goldman, & Davis, 1989; Kramer, McClintock, & Messick, 1986; Messick et al., 1983). In these studies, trustworthiness is essentially viewed as a probability analysis of the likely consequences of acting cooperatively.

In contrast to the calculative or instrumental models of trust that have been outlined, recent approaches to studying procedural justice effects suggest an alternative perspective. The models propose that trust is linked to the sense of identity people derive from their relationships with authorities. One identity-based model of procedural justice is the relational model of authority (Tyler, 1989; Tyler & Lind, 1992). It suggests that people are concerned about the benevolence of authorities because the way they are treated by these authorities can provide them with important information about themselves, that is, has implications for self-esteem and self-worth. Particularly within groups, which can be an important source of identity for people (Tajfel, 1978; Turner, Hogg, Oakes, Reicher, & Wetherell, 1987), relational aspects of authority conduct may serve an important symbolic role in communicating information about identity. Deference, neutrality, and treatment with dignity by an authority can communicate high status in the group, but rudeness and disrespect can communicate marginal status (Tyler & Lind, 1992).

Recent studies have supported the relational model of authority. Tyler and Degoey (1995a; Tyler, 1994c) showed that relational judgments about group authorities are strongly linked to people's willingness to accept the authorities' decisions. In contrast, judgments about the favorability of outcomes and control over the authority's decision-making process were weakly linked only to decision acceptance. Furthermore, Tyler and Degoey (1995b) showed that relational judgments had a strong effect on people's assessments that they were respected individuals within their group. This latter finding accords well with recent work that has been conducted on the influence of procedural justice on feelings of self-esteem. In experimental contexts, for instance, subjects' self-esteem is influenced by the fairness of the procedures with which they are treated (Koper, Van Knippenberg, Bouhuijs, Vermunt, & Wilke, 1993). Students' self-esteem during their college years has also been found to be related to how fairly they remember being treated by their parents (Joubert, 1991).

Interestingly, research in the social dilemma literature has also yielded results that are consistent with the reasoning just outlined. Studies of trust in social dilemmas have suggested, for instance, that high-trusting subjects will continue to restrict their consumption of a shared, communal resource, even when they are presented with information that others are not restricting their actions (Messick et al., 1983; see Tyler & Dawes, 1993). Furthermore, identification with a group has been linked to a willingness to conserve communal resources (Brewer, 1979; Brewer & Kramer, 1986; Hogg & Abrams, 1988; Messick & Mackie, 1989). Finally, Tyler and Degoey (1995a) have demonstrated that identification itself interacts with relational judgments about group authorities, but not with instrumental judgments, in affecting voluntary decision acceptance.

We will contrast the instrumental and relational models of trust by examining the managerial data set (Study 1; Tyler, 1994c) in three ways. First, we will examine when trust is important. The instrumental model suggests that people will care about trustworthiness when they are dependent on the organization or vulnerable to harm. The relational model suggests that trustworthiness is central when people have a personal connection with authorities or identify with the organization.

Second, we will consider which behaviors of authorities lead to inferences about their trustworthiness. If trust is instrumental in character, then it should be linked to satisfaction with the authority's decisions and to employees' judgments about the degree of control they have over the decision-making process.[2] If trust is relational in character, it should be linked to judgments about the neutrality of authorities and the degree to which these authorities treat their subordinates with dignity and respect.

Finally, we will explore a second aspect of trust—trust in the competence of authorities. In the two types of analyses already outlined, we examined whether voluntary decision acceptance is linked to judgments about the benevolent intentions of authorities. If trust is instrumental in character, however, judgments about the competence of authorities should be more strongly linked to people's willingness to accept an authority's decisions than judgments about the benevolence of authorities. In other words, people should be primarily focused on whether or not their authorities will be able to deal effectively with organizational problems, not on their benevolent intentions. For example, citizens should focus on whether political authorities can solve the water shortage problem, not on whether they are benevolently motivated to distribute water fairly. Similarly, they should be concerned about whether their supervisor can effectively manage their work unit, not whether they are motivated to treat workers fairly.[3]

When Trustworthiness Is Important

Previous research has suggested that people become more concerned about issues of trustworthiness when they have a social relationship with the authorities with whom they are dealing. Tyler and Degoey (1995b) showed that in family settings, trust in authorities is more central than in community settings. Tyler and Degoey suggested that this finding reflects the strength of social bonding to parents in family settings, but in community settings, bonds to community authorities are less clearly established. Similarly, Tyler, Huo, and Lind (1994) used the logic of the relational model to suggest that people's

TABLE 16.3 The Importance of Relationships in the Centrality of Trustworthiness

	Willingness to Accept Decisions			
	Supervisor Is a Friend		Expected Future Relationship	
	No	Yes	No	Yes
Instrumental judgments				
Outcome favorability	.40***	.35***	.40***	.31***
Control	.10	.03	−.01	.16
Relational judgments				
Trustworthiness	.20	.34***	.17	.36**
Neutrality	.08	.35***	.37***	.02
Status recognition	−.04	−.25**	−.07	−.16
R-squared	40%***	46%***	53%***	34%***

NOTE: Entries are beta weights and adjusted R-squares. $*p < .05$; $**p < .01$; $***p < .001$.

orientations toward authorities change once they have established a social bond with those authorities. Although these studies are directed at when people care about procedural justice, they also have implications for when people care about trustworthiness, because trustworthiness is typically highly correlated with procedural justice. The studies suggest that establishing a relationship will heighten concerns over the trustworthiness of authorities.

We will look at a situation in which employees are evaluating their supervisors (Tyler, 1994c). The dependent variable is willingness to accept supervisors' decisions. The instrumental predictor variables are subordinates' judgments about control and the favorability of previous outcomes. Relational predictor variables are judgments about the trustworthiness of the supervisor, neutrality of the decision-making process, and perceived standing with the supervisor. We examine whether trustworthiness has a greater impact on voluntary acceptance of decisions when subordinates feel they have a personal relationship with the supervisor.

The predictions of the relational model are supported by the results shown in Table 16.3. Both the establishment of a current relationship (i.e., thinking of your supervisor as a friend) and the expectation of a future relationship heighten the centrality of trustworthiness. When the supervisor is seen as a friend, trust judgments have an important influence on voluntary decision acceptance ($\beta = .34$, $p < .001$), but they have only a marginal influence if there is not a perceived friendship ($\beta = .20$, n.s.). Similarly, trust significantly shapes decision acceptance when there is an expected future relationship ($\beta = .36$, $p < .001$), but only marginally when there is no expected future relationship ($\beta = .17$, n.s.)

TABLE 16.4 The Influence of Identification on the Centrality of Trustworthiness

| | Willingness to Accept Decisions | | | |
| | Share the Organization's Values | | Get Identity From Work | |
	No	Yes	No	Yes
Instrumental judgments				
Outcome favorability	.31***	.43***	.62***	.30***
Control	.21*	−.15	.16	.04
Relational judgments				
Trustworthiness	.15	.39***	.21	.32***
Neutrality	.19*	.23**	.02	.23***
Status recognition	−.08	−.17	−.21	−.12
R-squared	38%***	47%***	53%***	44%***

NOTE: Entries are beta weights and adjusted R-squares. $*p < .05$; $**p < .01$; $***p < .001$.

The existence of a relationship clearly influences the basis on which people evaluate the decisions of authorities. But this finding can be interpreted in two ways: Trust matters more when a relationship exists because (a) a social bond has been created between the subordinate and his or her supervisor, and (b) the relationship between supervisor and subordinate has shifted to a more resource-dependent one. It is possible to test more directly the relational model by examining the influence of sharing values with one's work organization and using work as a source of self-identity on the importance of trustworthiness.

The results are shown in Table 16.4. As predicted by the relational model, value congruence with the organization heightens the influence of trustworthiness on voluntary decision acceptance ($\beta = .39$, $p < .001$ vs. $\beta = .15$, n.s.). Similarly, getting a sense of identity from work heightens the influence of trust ($\beta = .32$, $p < .001$ vs. $\beta = .21$, n.s.).

Finally, it is possible to test the instrumental model by examining how instrumental aspects of belonging to a work organization influence the importance of trustworthiness. Two aspects are considered: whether subordinates felt they needed to keep their job and whether they felt their job was secure. The analysis, shown in Table 16.5, suggests that these instrumental aspects do not influence the role of trust in the willingness to accept decisions. Trustworthiness attributions had an equally strong influence on subordinates' willingness to accept decisions whether they felt they did or did not need to keep their job or felt their job was or was not secure.

This situational analysis provides two types of support for the relational model of trustworthiness. First, the social bond between respondents and their supervisor and between respondents and their work organization influences the role of trustworthiness in shaping voluntary decision acceptance. When

TABLE 16.5 The Influence of Instrumental Concerns on the Centrality of
Trustworthiness

	Willingness to Accept Decisions			
	Need to Keep the Job		Position Is Secure	
	No	Yes	No	Yes
Instrumental judgments				
Outcome favorability	.33***	.40***	.33***	.39***
Control	.14	.00	.07	.07
Relational judgments				
Trustworthiness	.27***	.28*	.28*	.29**
Neutrality	.27**	.11	.28*	.19**
Status recognition	−.27**	.02	.09	.16*
R-squared	44%***	45%***	38%***	45%***

NOTE: Entries are beta weights and adjusted R-squares. $*p < .05$; $**p < .01$; $***p < .001$.

the bond is stronger, trustworthiness plays a more central role. Second, analyses of the role of instrumental dimensions of organizational membership do not show an influence of these dimensions on the role of trustworthiness in the willingness to accept decisions.

The Link Between the Behaviors of Authorities and Judgments About Trustworthiness

It is also possible to test psychological models of trustworthiness by examining the influence of the actions of authorities on judgments about their trustworthiness.

Instrumental models would predict that authorities are considered trustworthy when they provide favorable outcomes and when people feel they have been given some degree of control over the decision-making process. The relational model suggests that trustworthiness is primarily determined by neutral and unbiased decision making and by the degree to which individuals feel they are treated with respect ("status recognition"). The central idea of the relational model is that people are concerned about the benevolence of the motives of authorities: Neutral and respectful treatment suggests that authorities have good intentions and will not violate a person's sense of dignity and self-worth.

We examined the instrumental and relational antecedents of trustworthiness attributions in three data sets: workers evaluating their supervisors (Study 1), children evaluating their parents (Study 3), and Americans evaluating the Supreme Court (Study 6). The results, shown in Table 16.6, suggest that trustworthiness attributions are predominantly made on the basis of the

TABLE 16.6 Antecedents of Trustworthiness Attributions

	Trustworthiness of Authorities		
	Law	Management	Family
Instrumental antecedents			
Outcome favorability	.14***	.11**	.16***
Control	.22***	.09	.20***
Relational antecedents			
Neutrality	.19***	.31***	.28***
Status recognition	.41***	.49***	.44***
Unique R-squared for instrumental variables	8%	3%	6%
Unique R-squared for relational variables	28%	30%	22%
Total R-squared	71%***	76%***	78%***

NOTE: Entries are beta weights and adjusted R-squares. $*p < .05$; $**p < .01$; $***p < .001$.

relational aspects of authority behaviors. On average, relational characteristics explained 27% of the unique variance in trustworthiness attributions, whereas instrumental variables explained only 6%.

The important role of treatment with respect and dignity is especially noteworthy. In all three settings it is the most important predictor of trustworthiness and more important than either outcome favorability or control. In other words, people find authorities to be trustworthy because those authorities treat them politely, not because they make favorable decisions or share power ("control"). This influence is striking because treatment with respect is directly relational in character. In contrast, neutrality has both relational and instrumental components, because neutral procedures may be viewed as yielding favorable outcomes and indicating social status.

The Characteristics of Trustworthiness

Finally, we examined whether the construct of trustworthiness can be distinguished from issues of competence. In the analyses reported earlier, we defined trustworthiness attributions as judgments that authorities make a good-faith effort and treat all parties involved in the dispute fairly (a relational issue). Judgments about the competence of authorities, however, are more instrumental in nature: Competence indicates there is a reasonable likelihood that authorities will provide the disputing parties with good solutions.

We tested the importance of both conceptions of trust within the managerial data examined by Tyler (1994c). Competence was indexed with judgments that the supervisor tried to reach good solutions and tried to end the

TABLE 16.7 The Influence of Managerial Competence and Integrity on
Willingness to Accept Decisions

	Willingness to Accept Managerial Decisions
Competence of supervisor	$.24^{**}$
Trustworthiness of supervisor	$.38^{***}$
R-squared	$34\%^{***}$

NOTE: Entries are beta weights and adjusted R-squares. $*p < .05$; $**p < .01$; $***p < .001$.

conflict. Trustworthiness attributions were indexed by judgments that the
supervisor showed intentions to maintain positive relations with all the parties
involved in the dispute. The key dependent variable is the willingness to
accept decisions. The results, shown in Table 16.7, indicate that decision
acceptance is related to both trustworthiness judgments and to judgments about
competence. However, trustworthiness judgments have the strongest relationship ($\beta = .38$ vs. $\beta = .24$ for competence).

Again, the findings support a relational model of authority by indicating
that attributions about the social motives of authorities are the crucial component of voluntary acceptance of an authority's decisions, not problem-solving
competence. However, the instrumental model also receives some support.
People are more willing to accept the decisions made by competent authorities.

Summary

Three approaches were used to test between the instrumental and relational
conceptions of trustworthiness. All three support the relational conception of
trustworthiness. Hence, the data presented here suggest that the economic
conception of trust as the calculation of personal gain is inadequate to explain
observed variations in the importance and meaning of trust. Instead, the findings
suggest that people's feelings about trust are more social in nature. Social
relationships to groups and group authorities, and particularly treatment with
respect and dignity, provide the basis for trustworthiness attributions.

Discussion

The idea that trust matters has been widely articulated in the literature on
organizational functioning. The findings outlined provide strong empirical
support for these claims. They do not, however, support the way in which trust
has generally been defined. The economic perspective, which has dominated
sociology, law, political science, and management, places primary emphasis
on calculations of the degree to which authorities may serve the self-interests

of individuals affected by their decisions (Bradach & Eccles, 1989; Dasgupta, 1988; Williamson, 1993). As Oliver Williamson (1993) argued, trust defined in this way may be a misnomer and its use in the research literature of little theoretical value (Williamson, 1993). Others have also recognized that the calculative interpretation of trust may be mistaken (e.g., Dunn, 1988). March and Olson, for instance, argued that "the core idea of trust is that it is *not* based on an expectation of its justification" (March & Olson, 1989, p. 27, emphasis added).

Three types of evidence support the suggestion that trust is a social commodity. First, we presented evidence about when trust matters. The data suggested that trustworthiness attributions are affected by relational issues and become more important when social bonds exist. Conversely, they are not influenced by instrumental issues, such as whether workers are dependent on their job. Second, we presented evidence about how trust is influenced by the actions of authorities. People respond to social information communicated by authorities, not instrumental outcomes. In particular, information about respect and standing with authorities is a prime determinant of trustworthiness attributions. Finally, we presented evidence about the meaning of trust. People respond to benevolent intentions to a greater degree than they do to competence when reacting to authorities. In other words, an empirical evaluation of three distinct aspects of trust suggests that trust is, at least to a considerable extent, a social resource.

The findings suggest that trust—if defined in terms of positive intent rather than calculated risk—is especially important during times of crisis and conflict. During such times, the survival of a group depends on deference to authorities, but resources needed to compel deference and/or monitor compliance may be lacking. Hence, authorities heavily depend on the goodwill of those within the group. That goodwill has been found to be linked to trust. In a variety of dispute situations, the findings suggest that trustworthiness attributions affect people's willingness to accept decisions and obey the law. In previous articles, the trustworthiness of authorities has also been shown to affect indirectly people's willingness to accept conflict resolution decisions through judgments about procedural justice (Tyler, 1994b). In summary, then, being trusted by others appears to be a valuable social resource that gives authorities a "cushion of support" during difficult times.

A word of caution seems in order, however. The relational, identity-based character of trust suggests that it is difficult to build trust in the short-term. Both identification with an organization and feelings of trust in organizational authorities build over time. Hence, organizations without social bonds between authorities and those within the group will have difficulty during periods of scarcity and conflict. Material resources cannot easily compensate for the lack of social identity and relational bonding. In this respect, the social conception of trust is disappointing to organizational authorities looking for a quick fix for their problems. The lure of calculative models is their suggestion that changes in resource allocations and incentives can quickly change behavior in groups. A similar lure is found in social policies about difficult issues such as crime (see Tyler & Degoey, 1995b). Just as increasing penalties for drug use cannot compensate for the effects of poor education, declining family stability, increasing poverty, and other social changes, so organizations cannot quickly compensate for failures to build a favorable organizational culture and create positive bonds with authorities.

The Determinants of
Trustworthiness Attributions

Our exploration of the determinants of trustworthiness attributions was based on propositions made by the relational model of procedural justice (Tyler, 1989; Tyler & Lind, 1992). That model suggests that people care about fair treatment by authorities because they derive a sense of identity from such treatment. Authorities who represent a threat to that sense of self-worth and identity are considered unfair.

Extended to the arena of trustworthiness, a similar argument can be made: Authorities are considered trustworthy if they aid individuals in maintaining a positive self-identity. The findings reported in this chapter provide strong support for our hypothesis: Feelings of trustworthiness are most strongly linked to treatment with dignity and respect by an authority. Instrumental judgments, such as the degree to which an authority delivers favorable decisions or shares some kind of control over those decisions with others, are not as important for trustworthiness attributions. Furthermore, people care most about trustworthiness when they derive a sense of identity from group membership (i.e., identify with their work or their work organization) and when they have developed a social bond with the group authority.

Our findings support the views of sociologists such as Granovetter (1985) and Bradach and Eccles (1989), who have theorized that economic transactions are particularly governed by feelings of trust if those transactions are embedded in social relations. Similarly, industrial psychologists have argued that the personal contact between rater and ratees in a performance appraisal process may be an important variable in understanding the outcomes of that process.

Our findings do not square well, however, with Williamson's (1993) views about the nature of trust in social relations. Williamson wrote, "Trust, if it is obtained at all, is reserved for very special relations between family, friends, and lovers. . . . *Commercial relations do not qualify*" (Williamson, 1993, p. 484, emphasis added). Thus, Williamson distinguishes between two classes of relationships: commercial relationships, in which trust, if it exists, is primarily calculative in nature, and "very special" relationships, in which trust is mostly noncalculative. In contrast, our data suggest that even in commercial relations (i.e., relations between managers and employees), noncalculative trust is an important issue.

Directions for Future Research

The final analysis presented in this chapter examined whether a second aspect of trust—judgments about the competence of authorities—potentially played a role in people's willingness to accept authority decisions. The analysis showed a dominance of judgments about the benevolent intentions of authorities, at least in this particular data set, although judgments about competence also mattered.

This finding is particularly interesting because much previous theorizing has been concerned with the perceived expertise or competence of authorities. Hollander's (1958) work on "idiosyncrasy credit," for example, suggested that group members may become more lenient in their judgments about authorities when those authorities have proven their competence. Similarly, French and Raven (1959) suggested that authorities derive their power, in part, from their perceived expertise. And industrial psychologists have been much preoccupied with examining the ability of managers to be, and be viewed as, farsighted problem solvers who make accurate judgments about work performance.

Future research needs to examine under which conditions judgments about competence or trustworthiness are most salient when people decide whether to cooperate with group authorities. Our findings that benevolent intentions are particularly important when a relationship exists between authorities and their subordinates suggests that, when such a relationship is not perceived to exist, judgments about competence may take on a dominant role. In a work situation, for example, cooperation with one's immediate supervisor may be largely determined by trustworthiness judgments, but cooperation with a more distant departmental head may be driven by competence judgments. In an interesting analysis of leadership, Hogan, Curphy, and Hogan (1994) argued that subordinates judge supervisors in terms of trustworthiness, but bosses judge them in terms of technical competence. This may reflect the greater feeling of relationship between employees and supervisors. Bosses may have a more distant relationship.

Trustworthiness and competence may also play a differential role in intergroup conflict. Our analyses suggested that identification with a group raises the importance of trustworthiness judgments. Hence, when an authority is a member of one's in-group, issues of trustworthiness may be particularly central to a willingness to cooperate. Out-group members may be held to a more competency-based standard. Studies have already indicated that people who identify more strongly with groups and group authorities evaluate them in more strongly relational terms (Huo, Smith, Tyler, & Lind, in press; Smith & Tyler, in press; Tyler & Degoey, 1995a). This suggestion may help explain why people are more willing to forgive fellow group members for mistakes or transgressions than they are willing to forgive out-group members.

Future research is also needed to explore more fully how judgments about trustworthiness change over time. As was noted, our exploration of the antecedents of trust started from the basis of procedural justice theory, particularly from the relational model of procedural justice. The relational model suggests an identity-based perspective of trustworthiness: actions by authorities that indicate individuals are respected, and dignified group members drive judgments about trust. How respect and dignity are communicated and, more important, how changes occur in people's judgments about trustworthiness need to be explored in depth.

Finally, it is also still unclear how people's judgments about authorities link up to their judgments about the institutions that the authorities represent— that is, do feelings of trust in authorities explain anything about how people judge institutional arrangements in a society? A large literature already exists that addresses how institutions can take on a "taken-for-granted" character— that is, acquire legitimacy (Weatherford, 1992). Institutional theorists (e.g., Meyer & Rowan, 1977; see Powell & Dimaggio, 1991) and organizational ecologists (e.g., Hannan & Carroll, 1992) both propose that the viability of institutional arrangements is largely determined by the degree to which they are viewed as legitimate.

The essential question is whether an institutional form can acquire legitimacy based on perceptions about the trustworthiness of its representing authorities. Powell and Dimaggio (1991) suggested that an institution is considered legitimate to the extent that its structure and procedures follow the dictates of prevailing rules and beliefs—"rationalized myths" (Meyer & Rowan, 1977). According to institutionalists, then, conformity with some set of rules or norms leads to legitimation. Possibly, the degree to which an authority behaves in accordance with a given set of beliefs or "rationalized" norms is also an important source of trustworthiness judgments. Or trustworthiness judgments and legitimation may have different antecedents: Respectful interpersonal treatment determines trustworthiness judgments of authorities, but conformity with norms and rules determines the legitimacy of institutions.

A different scenario is plausible as well, however. Because authorities represent institutional arrangements, trust in authorities that is derived from respectful treatment may eventually lead to feelings that the institutions they represent are legitimate. In this scenario, authorities put a "face" on institutions: In the absence of any direct information about how institutional arrangements deal with individuals, people turn to how they are treated by authorities to decide whether they believe the institution to be legitimate. In other words, the way that procedures are implemented may influence their legitimacy (Tyler & Bies, 1990).

Finally, institutionalists may have overlooked another important source of institutional legitimacy: the degree to which the institution respects the dignity of the groups of individuals it represents. People draw their sense of identity, in part, from the groups to which they belong (Tajfel, 1978; Turner et al., 1987). Making this argument raises the level of analysis from the one-on-one relationship between an authority and a subordinate to the collective level of the relationship between groups and institutional arrangements. Future research that finds its joint basis in the microlevels of analysis of psychology and the macrolevels of institutional theory and organizational ecology is needed to unravel these questions.

In summary, our analyses suggest that trust is an important concept to examine in organizational settings. If nothing else, the centrality of its influence on organizational behaviors—accepting decisions, obeying rules—is striking. People seem to be affected strongly by their judgments about the motives of leaders, a finding that is important to anyone who wants to influence the effective functioning of organizations.

The findings outlined also suggest that previous research that defined trust as calculative probability judgments has been at least oversimplified and potentially misguided. However, as Williamson (1993) has also noted, "Tautologies are frequently on the trail of something more important and foreshadow much deeper analysis. Conceivably, the trust tautology will lead to precisely that" (Williamson, 1993, p. 302). The redefinition of trust in terms of benevolent intentions may foreshadow such deeper analysis and open up many avenues of fruitful research.

Notes

1. We also conducted an additional analysis that included expectations of future reciprocity as an instrumental variable. This judgment corresponds more directly to the instrumental variable identified by Williamson. However, expectations of future reciprocity were not found to be important, so they were not included in the analyses presented.

2. As has been noted, instrumental judgments may also include judgments about future reciprocity. However, an analysis of expectations about whether supervisors would help in the future "if needed" (in the managerial setting) or about whether other citizens would reciprocate cooperation (in the local political setting) were not found to be linked to trust, so they were not included in the analyses outlined.

3. The precursors of this distinction can be seen in two prior social-psychological literatures. One is the basis for attitude change (persuasiveness). Two bases have been identified: expertise

and trustworthiness (see Eagly & Chaiken, 1993). Expertise has to do with the competence of one's arguments. People are more persuaded by a speaker if that speaker has some reasonable basis for his or her views—background training, convincing evidence, and so on. Trustworthiness has to do with speaker motives. For example, if people do not believe that a speaker's private attitudes are in line with his or her public positions, they are less persuaded by his or her message.

A second relevant literature is the literature on distributive justice principles—the equity-equality tradeoff. It has been suggested that equity promotes productivity, but equality promotes social harmony. Hence, authorities balance between the motivation of enhancing performance and the motivation of maintaining positive social relations (see Tyler & Belliveau, in press).

APPENDIX A

Study 1: Workers Evaluating Supervisors

A random sample of 409 workers in Chicago were interviewed over the telephone about their recent experiences with their supervisors. For more details about the study, see Tyler (1994b).

Eight questions were asked that indicated trustworthiness judgments:

1. Do you agree or disagree that your supervisor was honest in what he or she said?
2. Did your supervisor do anything that you thought was dishonest or improper? (reverse coded)
3. How hard did your supervisor try to be fair to you?
4. How likely is it that the reasons your supervisor gave for his or her decisions were the real reasons?
5. How hard did your supervisor try to take account of your needs in the situation?
6. Do you agree or disagree that your supervisor . . . tries very hard to be fair?
7. . . . deals with you honestly and ethically?
8. . . . shows a real interest in trying to be fair to you? (Cronbach $\alpha = .93$)

Four questions indicated beliefs about the competence of the supervisor:

1. How good are the decisions your supervisor makes?
2. How good a job is your supervisor doing?
3. How hard did your supervisor try to solve the problem?
4. How hard did your supervisor try to find a settlement that was satisfactory to all of the people involved? (Cronbach $\alpha = .81$)

Study 2: Citizens Evaluating
Local Political Authorities

A random sample of 401 citizens of San Francisco were interviewed over the telephone about their views about the San Francisco Public Utilities Commission, which regulates water use in the city. The respondents were asked to consider how the commission would respond if they went to their meetings to discuss water policy. Trustworthiness was indexed by two questions: "Do you agree of disagree that you would be treated fairly?" and "Do you agree or disagree that the members of the Commission would be honest in the things they said and did?" For further details on this study, see Tyler and Degoey (1995a).

Study 3: Students Evaluating Their Parents

As part of a course requirement, undergraduates ($n = 335$) at the University of California at Berkeley completed questionnaires about recent conflicts with their parents. For more details, see Tyler and Degoey (1995b).

Trustworthiness was indexed by eight items:

1. How hard did your parent(s) try to act in ways that maintained good feelings between you and them?
2. How much consideration was given to your views when decisions were made about how to handle the conflict?
3. How hard did your parent(s) try to do the right thing by you?
4. How hard did your parent(s) try to explain why they made the decisions they made?
5. How likely is it that the reasons your parent(s) gave for their decisions were the real reasons?
6. How hard did your parent(s) try to take account of your needs in the situation?
7. How hard did they try to be fair to you?
8. When you think about your parent(s), to what extent do you trust them? (Cronbach $\alpha = .88$)

Study 4: Citizens Evaluating
Local Legal Authorities

A random sample of 652 adults in Chicago were interviewed about recent experiences with police officers or judges (for more details, see Tyler, 1990). This study directly measured behavior in relationship to the law, so the obligation scale reflects both judgments of obligation to obey the law and actual obedience to the law.

Trust was assessed by asking respondents: "How did the [police, courts] try to be fair to you?" and "How much consideration did they give to your views?" ($\alpha = .79$)

Study 5: Citizens
Evaluating the U.S. Congress

A random sample of 502 white and African American citizens in the San Francisco Bay area were interviewed over the telephone about their views on Congress (for more details, see Tyler, 1994a).

Trustworthiness of Congress was assessed using agreement with three items: "Congress tries to be fair when making decisions," "Congress can usually be trusted to do what is right for most Americans," and "Most of the men and women of Congress try to be fair to the people in their district—not just to special-interest groups" (Cronbach $\alpha = .66$).

Study 6: Citizens Evaluating
the U.S. Supreme Court

A random sample of 502 citizens in the San Francisco Bay area were interviewed over the telephone about their views on the U.S. Supreme Court (for more details, see Tyler & Mitchell, 1994).

Trustworthiness of the Supreme Court was assessed using seven items:

1. Do you agree or disagree that the Supreme Court considers the concerns of average citizens when making decisions?
2. Do you agree or disagree that the Supreme Court tries to be fair when making decisions?
3. Do you agree or disagree that the Supreme Court justices are generally honest— giving the real reasons for their decisions?
4. Suppose that you joined a group that wanted to present its views to the Court. How likely do you think it is that . . . your group would be treated fairly?
5. . . . the justices would consider your group's views before making a decision?
6. . . . the justices would try to be fair in considering your group's issues?
7. . . . the justices would genuinely care about the group's position on its issues? (Cronbach $\alpha = .81$)

References

Barnard, C. I. (1958). *The functions of the executive.* Cambridge, MA: Harvard University Press.

Bradach, J. L., & Eccles, R. G. (1989). Price, authority, and trust: From ideal types to plural forms. *Annual Review of Sociology, 15,* 97-118.

Brann, P., & Foddy, M. (1988). Trust and consumption of a deteriorating common resource. *Journal of Conflict Resolution, 31,* 615-630.

Brewer, M. B. (1979). In-group bias in the minimal intergroup situation: A cognitive-motivational analysis. *Psychological Bulletin, 86,* 307-324.

Brewer, M., & Kramer, R. (1986). Choice behavior in social dilemmas: Effects of social identity, group size, and decision framing. *Journal of Personality and Social Psychology, 50,* 543-549.

Dasgupta, P. (1988). Trust as a commodity. In D. Gambetta (Ed.), *Trust: Making and breaking cooperative relations* (pp. 49-72). Oxford, UK: Basil Blackwell.

Dunn, J. (1988). Trust and political agency. In D. Gambetta (Ed.), *Trust: Making and breaking cooperative relations* (pp. 73-93). Oxford, UK: Basil Blackwell.

Eagly, A. H., & Chaiken, S. (1993). *The psychology of attitudes.* New York: Harcourt Brace.

French, J. R. P., & Raven, B. (1959). The bases of social power. In D. Cartwright (Ed.), *Studies in social power.* Ann Arbor, MI: Institute for Social Research.

Gambetta, D. (1988). Can we trust trust? In D. Gambetta (Ed.), *Trust: Making and breaking cooperative relations* (pp. 213-238). Oxford, UK: Basil Blackwell.

Granovetter, M. (1985). Economic action and social structure: The problem of embeddedness. *American Journal of Sociology, 91,* 481-510.

Hannan, M. T., & Carroll, G. R. (1992). *Dynamics of organizational populations.* New York: Oxford University Press.

Hogan, R., Curphy, G. J., & Hogan, J. (1994). What we know about leadership: Effectiveness and personality. *American Psychologist, 49,* 493-504.

Hogg, M. A., & Abrams, D. (1988). *Social identifications.* New York: Routledge & Kegan Paul.

Hollander, E. P. (1958). Conformity, status, and idiosyncrasy credit. *Psychological Review, 65,* 117-127.

Huo, Y. J., Smith, H. J., Tyler, T. R., & Lind, E. A. (in press). Superordinate identification, subgroup identification, and justice concerns: Is separatism the problem, is assimilation the answer? *Psychological Science.*

Joubert, C. E. (1991). Self-esteem and social desirability in relation to college students' retrospective perceptions of parental fairness and disciplinary practices. *Psychological Reports, 69,* 115-120.

Komorita, S. S., Chan, D. K. S., & Parks, C. D. (1993). The effects of reward structure and reciprocity in social dilemmas. *Journal of Experimental Social Psychology, 29,* 252-267.

Komorita, S. S., Parks, C. D., & Hulbert, L. G. (1992). Reciprocity and the induction of cooperation in social dilemmas. *Journal of Personality and Social Psychology, 62,* 607-617.

Koper, G., Van Knippenberg, D., Bouhuijs, F., Vermunt, R., & Wilke, H. (1993). Procedural fairness and self-esteem. *European Journal of Social Psychology, 23,* 313-325.

Kramer, R. M., & Goldman, L. (1988). *Expectations that bind: Group-based trust, causal attributions, and cooperative behavior in a commons dilemma.* Unpublished manuscript, Stanford University.

Kramer, R. M., Goldman, L., & Davis, G. (1989). *Social identity, expectations of reciprocity, and cooperation in social dilemmas.* Unpublished manuscript, Stanford University.

Kramer, R. M., McClintock, C. G., & Messick, D. M. (1986). Social values and cooperative response to a simulated security dilemma. *Journal of Psychology, 54,* 576-592.

March, J., & Olson, J. (1989). *Rediscovering institutions.* New York: Free Press.

Messick, D. M., & Mackie, D. (1989). Intergroup relations. *Annual Review of Psychology, 40,* 45-81.

Messick, D. M., Wilke, H., Brewer, M. B., Kramer, R. M., Zemke, P. E., & Lui, L. (1983). Individual adaptations and structural change as solutions to social dilemmas. *Journal of Personality and Social Psychology, 44,* 294-309.

Meyer, J. W., & Rowan, B. (1977). Institutionalized organizations: Formal structure as myth and ceremony. *American Journal of Sociology, 83,* 340-63.

Powell, W. W., & Dimaggio, P. J. (1991). *The new institutionalism in organizational analysis.* Chicago: University of Chicago Press.

Simon, H. A. (1947). *Administrative behavior.* New York: Macmillan.

Smith, H. J., & Tyler, T. R. (in press). Justice and power: Can justice motivations and superordinate categorizations encourage the advantaged to support policies which redistribute economic resources and encourage the disadvantaged to willingly obey the law. *European Journal of Social Psychology.*

Tajfel, H. (1978). *Differentiation between social groups: Studies in the social psychology of intergroup relations.* London: Academic Press.

Thibaut, J., & Walker, L. (1975). *Procedural justice: A psychological analysis.* Hillsdale, NJ: Lawrence Erlbaum.

Turner, J. C., Hogg, M., Oakes, P., Reicher, S., & Wetherell, M. (1987). *Rediscovering the social group: A self-categorization theory.* Oxford, UK: Basil Blackwell.

Tyler, T. R. (1988). What is procedural justice? *Law and Society Review, 22,* 301-355.

Tyler, T. R. (1989). The psychology of procedural justice: A test of the group value model. *Journal of Personality and Social Psychology, 57,* 830-838.

Tyler, T. R. (1990). *Why people obey the law.* New Haven, CT: Yale University Press.

Tyler, T. R. (1994a). Governing amid diversity. *Law and Society Review, 28,* 701-722.

Tyler, T. R. (1994b). Psychological models of the justice motive. *Journal of Personality and Social Psychology, 67,* 850-863.

Tyler, T. R. (1994c). *The psychology of legitimacy: Instrumental and relational motives underlying deference to organizational authorities.* Unpublished manuscript, University of California at Berkeley.

Tyler, T. R., & Belliveau, M. (in press). Dealing with tradeoffs among justice principles: The motivational antecedents of definitions of fairness. In J. Rubin & B. Bunker (Eds.), *Conflict, cooperation, and justice: Essays in honor of Morton Deutsch.* San Francisco: Jossey-Bass.

Tyler, T. R., & Bies, R. (1990). Interpersonal aspects of procedural justice. In J. S. Carroll (Ed.), *Applied social psychology in business settings* (pp. 77-98). Hillsdale, NJ: Lawrence Erlbaum.

Tyler, T. R., & Dawes, R. (1993). Fairness in groups: Comparing the self-interest and social identity perspectives. In B. Mellers & J. Baron (Eds.), *Psychological perspectives on justice: Theory and applications* (pp. 87-108). Cambridge, UK: Cambridge University Press.

Tyler, T. R., & Degoey, P. (1995a). Collective restraint in social dilemmas: Procedural justice and social identification effects on support for authorities. *Journal of Personality and Social Psychology, 69*(3).

Tyler, T. R., & Degoey, P. (1995b). Community, family, and the social good: The psychological dynamics of procedural justice and social identification. In G. Melton (Ed.), *Nebraska symposium on motivation* (Vol. 42, pp. 53-92). Lincoln: University of Nebraska Press.

Tyler, T. R., Huo, Y. J., & Lind, E. A. (1994). *Preferring, choosing, and evaluating dispute resolution procedures: The psychological antecedents of feelings and choices.* Unpublished manuscript, University of California at Berkeley.

Tyler, T. R., & Lind, E. A. (1992). A relational model of authority in groups. In M. Zanna (Ed.), *Advances in experimental social psychology* (Vol. 25, pp. 115-191). New York: Academic Press.

Tyler, T. R., & Mitchell, G. (1994). Legitimacy and the empowerment of discretionary legal authority: The United States Supreme Court and abortion rights. *Duke Law Journal, 43,* 703-815.

Weatherford, M. S. (1992). Measuring political legitimacy. *American Political Science Review, 86,* 149-166.

Williamson, O. E. (1993). Calculativeness, trust, and economic organization. *Journal of Law and Economics, 34,* 453-500.

Collective Trust and Collective Action

The Decision to Trust as a Social Decision

RODERICK M. KRAMER
MARILYNN B. BREWER
BENJAMIN A. HANNA

When each individual perceives the same sense of interest in all his fellows, he immediately performs his part of any contract, as being assur'd that they will not be wanting in theirs. All of them, by concert enter into a scheme of actions, calculated for common benefit, and agree to be true to their words; nor is there anything requisite to form this concert or connection, but that every one have a sense of interest in the faithful fulfilling of engagements, and express that sense to other members of the society.

David Hume, *A Treatise on Human Nature* (1740/1969)

Problems of collective action pervade organizational life. Individuals are expected to contribute their time and attention toward the achievement of collective goals (Latane, 1986; Murnighan, Kim, & Metzger, 1994; Olson, 1965), share useful information with other organizational members (Bonacich & Schneider, 1992), and exercise responsible restraint when using valuable

357

but limited organizational resources (Kramer, 1991; Tyler & Degoey, 1995). Organizations cannot recognize and reward every cooperative act, nor can they detect and punish every failure to cooperate. Consequently, successful cooperation depends, at least in part, on the willingness of individuals to engage voluntarily in behaviors that further collective aims (Barnard, 1938/ 1968; Olson, 1965; Organ, 1988).

Although most people recognize that failure to cooperate with others can lead to collectively undesirable outcomes, they also realize that isolated acts of cooperation are not likely to have much impact on the collective outcome. Moreover, unilateral acts can be quite costly, because the person who cooperates bears all of the burdens of cooperation while the benefits are enjoyed by all. In the absence of some basis for thinking that others will reciprocate, therefore, individuals may find it hard to justify the decision to cooperate themselves.

Recognizing this difficulty, researchers have frequently argued that trust plays a prominent role in the emergence of cooperation in such situations (e.g., Dawes, 1980; Edney, 1980; Kramer & Brewer, 1984; Messick & Brewer, 1983; Messick et al., 1983). In particular, they have proposed that individuals' willingness to cooperate is conditioned, at least partially, on a belief or expectancy that other members of a group or organization will do the same (Brann & Foddy, 1988; Kramer, 1991; Messick et al., 1983).

Although its importance is readily apparent, the contours of trust in collective contexts are much less obvious. The decision to trust in collective settings is different from, and in many respects more problematic than, decisions about trust that arise in other social contexts. Because of the size and structural complexity of large organizations, for example, individuals do not have the opportunity to engage in the sort of incremental and repeated exchanges that have been shown to facilitate the development of trust in more intimate settings, such as dyadic relationships (Lindskold, 1978; Pilisuk & Skolnick, 1968; Rotter, 1980). Similarly, many of the informal social mechanisms and interpersonal processes that contribute to the development of trust and cooperation in small, homogeneous groups (e.g., Golembiewski & McConkie, 1975) lose their efficacy in the more complex and socially diverse environments of large organizations (cf. Brewer & Kramer, 1986; Kramer, 1989; Olson, 1965). Finally, the competitive nature of organizational life increases greatly the costs of misplaced trust: Getting the sucker's payoff is

AUTHORS' NOTE: Development of these ideas benefited greatly from an interdisciplinary seminar on trust and norms organized by Jim Baron. Discussions with Jon Bendor, Bob Bies, Ron Burt, Robert Cialdini, Margaret Levi, Jim March, Joanne Martin, Debra Meyerson, Michael Morris, Jeff Pfeffer, Woody Powell, Tom Tyler, Gene Webb, Dave Whetten, Karl Weick, and Mayer Zald were also very helpful. Earlier versions of this chapter were presented at the Asilomar Conference on Organizations the Society of Experimental Social Psychology meetings, and a conference on trust in organizations, held at the Graduate School of Business, Stanford University, May 14-15, 1994. Comments from participants at those gatherings are acknowledged as well.

not only aversive, it can be fatal to one's career. As a consequence, it is often difficult for collective trust to obtain even a toehold, let alone flourish.

On what basis, then, is the decision to trust in collective contexts predicated? Under what circumstances are individuals likely to assume that other members of an organization will act in a trustworthy fashion? When are they willing to engage in trust behavior themselves? These are the central questions we engage in this chapter.

Contemporary organizational theory and research provide a number of useful perspectives on these questions. For example, considerable attention has been afforded to the role that social networks play in the emergence and maintenance of trust (e.g., Burt & Knez, Chapter 5, this volume; Granovetter, 1985; Powell, 1990; Putnam, 1993). Other research has emphasized the efficacy of various institutional mechanisms and governance structures that contribute to the production of trust within organizations (e.g., Powell, Chapter 4, this volume; Sitkin & Roth, 1993; Yamagishi & Sato, 1986; Zucker, 1986).

Although drawing on these contributions, the present chapter adopts a very different point of departure for conceptualizing the origins of collective trust in organizations. Specifically, we examine the role organizational identification plays in trust-related judgment and decision-making processes. We argue that the willingness of individuals to engage in trust behavior in situations requiring collective action is tied to the salience and strength of their identification with an organization and its members. This approach is derived from recent social psychological theory and research on the relationship between group identification and cooperation (Brewer, 1981; Brewer & Kramer, 1986; Brewer & Schneider, 1990; Dawes, van de Kragt, & Orbell, 1988, 1990; Kramer, 1991, 1994; Kramer & Brewer, 1984, 1986; Kramer & Goldman, 1995; Tyler & Dawes, 1993; Tyler & Degoey, 1995). Extrapolating from this work, we propose that psychological and social processes associated with organizational identification increase individuals' propensity to confer trust on others and their willingness to engage in trust behavior themselves.

This chapter will advance this general argument and is organized as follows: First, we explore the anatomy of the decision to trust in collective contexts, describing some of the essential and also distinctive problems surrounding trust in such settings. Next, we introduce a framework for conceptualizing how organizational identification influences trust-related judgment and decision-making processes. Using this framework, we describe several distinct forms of identity-based trust behavior. We conclude by considering some of the implications of an identity-based conception of trust for organizational theory.

		Outcomes to Self	Self-Behavior
		T_s	$\overline{T}_s$
Other Behavior	T_o	$I + B - C$	$I + B$
	$\overline{T}_o$	$I - C$	I

Figure 17.1.

The Decision to
Trust in Collective Contexts

When individuals decide to engage in trust behavior, they create for themselves both opportunity and vulnerability. The opportunity surrounds the perceived gains, both individual and collective, that accrue if and when their acts of trust are reciprocated by others. The vulnerabilities derive from the potential costs associated with misplaced trust. From a judgment and decision-making perspective, such behavior is interesting because it entails a more or less conscious decision by individuals to expose themselves to risk. A central question in trust research, accordingly, is the basis on which such "exposure" is predicated. Brewer (1981) provides a useful analysis of this question at the dyadic level, which we reproduce here and use as a framework for generalizing to the collective case.

Decision Structure of Trust Dilemmas

The basic structure of a trust dilemma, Brewer notes, can be represented using a 2×2 matrix. Each decision maker has to decide whether or not to engage in trust behavior. The trade-offs associated with this decision can be formulated in terms of the perceived consequences (costs and benefits) of trust versus distrust. If I denotes the outcomes that accrue to the individual independent of what the other person involved does, C the costs of engaging in trust, and B the net benefits received from the other's actions, then the logically possible outcomes to self are mapped by the four cells depicted in Figure 17.1.

In its deterministic form, this matrix has the structure of a one-trial prisoner's dilemma game, where, if choices are made independently, pure self-interest always dictates the T choice. No matter which behavior the other chooses, each individual's own outcomes are better in the T column, even though mutual $\overline{T}$ choices result in less than optimal joint outcomes. However, when the possibility of contingent behavior is added, perceived contingent probabilities should be taken into account when individuals make their choice (See Figure 17.2).

		Self-Behavior	
		$\overline{T}_s$	T_s
Other Behavior	$\underline{T_o}$	$p(T_o \backslash \overline{T}_s)$	$p(T_o \backslash T_s)$
	$\overline{T}_o$	$p(\overline{T}_o \backslash \overline{T}_s)$	$p(\overline{T}_o \backslash T_s)$

where

$$p(T_o \backslash T_s) + p(\overline{T}_o \backslash T_s) = 1.00 \text{ and}$$

$$p[(\overline{T}_o \backslash T_s) + p[(T_o \backslash \overline{T}_s)]] = 1.00$$

Figure 17.2.

If the choices of self and other are nonindependent, then there is some degree of reciprocity (either sequential or simultaneous) in the system; reciprocity is defined here as cases in which

$$p(T_o \backslash T_s) > p(T_o \backslash \overline{T}_s),$$

and the degree of reciprocity as:

$$p(T_o \backslash T_s) - p(T_o \backslash \overline{T}_s) = p(\overline{T}_o \backslash \overline{T}_s) - p(\overline{T}_o \backslash \overline{T}_s) = 1.00 - p(T_o \backslash \overline{T}_s) - p(\overline{T}_o \backslash T_s).$$

If reciprocity were perfect, then the probability of symmetric choices ($T_o \backslash T_s$) and ($\overline{T}_o \backslash \overline{T}_s$) would be 1.00, and the probability of asymmetric choices ($T_o \backslash \overline{T}_s$) and ($\overline{T}_o \backslash T_s$) would be 0.00. In this case, the self-interest of both parties dictates a T choice for mutual benefit. However, if reciprocity is imperfect, there is uncertainty in the system—that is $p(T_o \backslash T_s) < 1.00$—and risks are introduced that tend to favor distrust ($\overline{T}$) over trust (T).

This representation of the dyadic trust dilemma draws attention to the two types of decision error an individual can make in such situations: *misplaced trust* (engaging in trust behavior when the other doesn't) and *misplaced distrust* (failing to engage in trust behavior when the other person either did or would have).

Each of these errors entails potential costs, some of which are fairly immediate and some of which are delayed. In the case of misplaced trust, the individual endures the immediate costs associated with his or her willingness to engage in trusting behavior when the other person failed to reciprocate. These include all of the opportunity costs associated with trust. For example, the individual may have squandered scarce attentional resources on a joint venture while the other person devoted his or her time and effort toward pursuit of a personal (nonjoint) aim. The erosion of confidence in others that attends the experience of misplaced trust may have pervasive and long-lasting effects. For example, the psychological residues of misplaced trust may inhibit individuals' willingness to initiate cooperative actions in future encounters where such actions might be reciprocated. Additionally, there are potential social costs associated with misplaced trust, including the possibility of damage to one's reputation. In many organizations, especially those that are highly political or competitive, being labeled by others as naive or gullible may increase the likelihood that opportunists will try to exploit the individual's perceived weakness.

The potential costs associated with misplaced distrust are no less attractive, however. Individuals who routinely distrust others endure the sure losses associated with foregone opportunities and gains. For example, presumptive distrust reduces the likelihood that the incremental benefits of reciprocal exchange will have an opportunity to materialize (cf. Axelrod, 1984; Bendor, Kramer, & Stout, 1991; Lindskold, 1978) because, after all, those who distrust invite distrust in return. Furthermore, individuals who regularly engage in distrust, even if motivated by purely defensive concerns, expose themselves to reputational damage, albeit of a different sort than described earlier: Being labeled by others as distrustful can lead to exclusion from important networks, both formal and informal, within the organization. As a consequence, individuals who adopt distrust as a preemptive, self-protective strategy may end up living in a trustless Pirandellian prison of their own making.

Our intuitions about the trade-offs associated with these decision errors can be expressed more formally as follows. Returning to Brewer's (1981) analysis, the risk of incurring the cost of a trusting choice can be set equal to

$$C[p(\overline{T}_o \backslash T_s)] - (B - C)[p(T_o / T_s)] + B[p(T_o \backslash \overline{T}_s)] = C - B[p(T_o \backslash T_s) - p(T_o \backslash \overline{T}_s)],$$

whereas the risk associated with distrust is

$$(B - C)[p(T_o \backslash T_s)] - C[p(\overline{T}_o \backslash T_s)] - B[p(T_o \backslash \overline{T}_s)] = B[p(T_o \backslash T_s) - p(T_o \backslash \overline{T}_s)] - C.$$

A prototypic example of this kind of trust dilemma at the n-person or collective level is the budget dilemma (Kramer, 1991). In a budget dilemma, individuals from different departments or units in an organization must choose between consumption versus conservation of valuable but limited fiscal resources. From the organization's perspective, it is highly desirable for individuals to conserve such resources to increase organizational efficiency and maintain slack. However, from the individual's perspective, restraint

Outcome Analysis

		Self	
		Show Restraint	*Don't Show*
	Show Restraint	$S + I - R$ $p\,(\,D_o \setminus D_s\,)$	$S + I$ $p\,(\,D_o \setminus \overline{D_s}\,)$
Other			
	Don't Show	S $p\,(\,\overline{D_o} \setminus \overline{D_s}\,)$	$S - R$ $p\,(\,\overline{D_o} \setminus D_s\,)$

Figure 17.3.

makes sense only if others reciprocate. Thus, the dilemma assumes the form shown in Figure 17.3.

Note that restraint in such situations is likely to be forthcoming only if there is sufficient confidence in others, operationalized here as a reasonably high perceived probability of reciprocity. At the very least, there must be an expectation among individuals that their own restraint will not be actively exploited or used to hold future interests hostage.

Much of this analysis, of course, simply reiterates the familiar observation that the decision to trust is largely about decision makers' anticipations of the benefits and risks associated with social acts—anticipations that are shrouded, in turn, in significant uncertainties. In situations where collective trust is high, the benefits of presumptive action may loom large in such anticipations. In situations where suspicion casts its shadow over the expectational landscape, the prospect of both immediate losses and future vulnerabilities may loom large, inhibiting risk taking.

Regardless of their particular form, such anticipations direct our attention to the critical role that individuals' expectations play in the emergence of collective trust. Ultimately, the decision to trust is tied to individuals' expectations, not only about what others will do but also about the expected consequences of their own acts as well. But what form do such expectations take and where do they come from? One answer to this question, although incomplete, is provided by empirical work on the development of trust in interpersonal relationships. A fairly substantial body of empirical data suggests trust development can be conceptualized as a history-dependent process (Lindskold, 1978; Rotter, 1980). According to this evidence, individuals act much like intuitive Bayesians whose judgments about others' trustworthiness are calibrated on the basis of their cumulative experience with them. Boyle and Bonacich (1970) provide a representative view, asserting that expectations about trustworthy behavior will change "in the direction of experience and to a degree proportional to the difference between this experience and the initial expectations applied to them" (p. 130). In addition to these a priori expectations, other research suggests that the causal attributions individuals make about others' actions and inactions play a critical role in the process of deciding whether they can be trusted and, if so, how much. These attributions become, in a sense, the grist from which inferences about others' trust-related intentions, motives, and dispositions are formed (Deutsch, 1973).

The aim of all of this calculative and inferential activity, of course, is an attempt to minimize perceived vulnerability through the reduction of uncertainty. As Gambetta (1988) observes,

> The condition of ignorance or uncertainty about other people's behavior is central to the notion of trust. It is related to the limits of our capacity ever to achieve a full knowledge of others, their motives, and their responses to endogenous as well as exogenous changes. (p. 218)

The Arithmetic of
Trust in Collective Contexts

In dyadic relationships, all of the "arithmetic" of trust—including the calibration of expectations, the aggregation of perceived benefits, and the calculation of risks—is facilitated by the fact that there usually exists a relatively detailed and precise history of interaction with a specific interactional partner. The trustworthiness of this person has been revealed, more or less fully, *ex post* over the course of numerous exchanges and transactions. Thus, even allowing for occasional misperceptions and misunderstandings, the relevant history is comparatively fixed and bounded.

In collective contexts, by contrast, the relevant history is more imperfect and more impoverished. This compounds considerably the inferential difficulties that individuals confront. For example, the task of generalizing about collective attributes is complicated by the fact that individuals typically possess only partial—and selective—historical data. Even under the best of circumstances, individuals in large organizations usually have contact with only a subsample of the population toward which they are attempting to generalize. Moreover, their contact with this population is likely to be quite skewed because of social and structural barriers to interaction (e.g., see Schelling, 1978). As a consequence, the task of drawing reasonable inferences about the *distribution* of trust within an organization is far from easy. For example, how does one go about deciding what the central tendency and variance of a psychological attribute such as trust are in a large, diffuse, and heterogeneous aggregate of social actors?

Relatedly, the process of updating or recalibrating expectations about the trustworthiness of a collective on the basis of incomplete cumulative histories poses daunting computational difficulties for even the most diligent and well-intentioned Bayesian. For example, to what extent should trust in a collective be increased when some, *but not all,* of its members act in a trustworthy fashion? Similarly, to what extent should individuals reduce or rescind trust when evidence becomes available that *a few,* but not all, individuals have violated that trust? When should individuals view evidence of others' lack of trustworthiness as an indication that something is pervasively rotten in a collective, versus merely indicative of a bad apple in the bunch? Stated differently, what is the "tipping point" (Schelling, 1978) at which collective trust does (or should) turn to collective distrust?

In suggesting that the perceptual and attentional burdens associated with trying to track collective trust strain the cognitive capacity of individual decision makers, we seem to be making a rather simplistic argument about the calculus of trust as it arises in collective contexts. One might argue, for example, that individuals will try to remedy such computational hurdles by relying on heuristic modes of information processing. These can include both cognitive heuristics aimed at reducing information overload (Kahneman & Tversky, 1974) and social heuristics (Allison & Messick, 1990) that provide guidelines for expeditious choice and action.

As we argue next, many of these questions can be approached from a perspective that links individuals' perceptions of collective trust to their psychological identification with the group or organization. To animate this argument, some preliminary ground must be covered. First, we need to draw a distinction between the objective representation of a collective trust dilemma and a given organizational decision maker's subjective construal of that dilemma. To do so, it is useful to look at Figure 17.1 again. The representation of the trust dilemma depicted there is crisp insofar as it succinctly captures the different "payoffs" associated with decisions to trust or not trust. However, it obscures the important and obvious fact that people seldom respond to such situations purely as they are given. Instead, they respond in terms of how they subjectively interpret or construe those situations.

This relationship between the objective bases of interdependence, defined in terms of the explicit incentive structure linking social actors, and their subjective representations of that interdependence, has been conceptualized by Kelley (1979), using the notion of *psychological transformations.* According to Kelley, when individuals encounter choice dilemmas of the sort shown in Figure 17.1, they do not act directly in response to the objective or "given" payoff matrix. Instead, this matrix is transformed, via the operation of a variety of psychological processes, into an *effective matrix.* This effective matrix, he argues, is most closely linked to their actual choice behavior.

In social psychological terms, this effective matrix can be viewed as the end result of a complex process of construal (or, more precisely, reconstrual) of a choice dilemma. This transformation process proceeds, it should be emphasized, largely outside individuals' awareness (i.e., it is not assumed they consciously transform a matrix in their minds; rather, the transformed matrix is an expression of their values, motives, goals, and dispositions). In this sense, the transformation process is revealed through behavior and must be inferred rather than observed directly.

Kelley's (1979) formulation of the relationship between the objective and subjective representations of interdependence structures invites the question, "What psychological processes govern this transformation process?" Most of the research to date bearing on this question has focused on individual differences that drive the transformation process (see McClintock & Liebrand, 1988, for a recent review). In several previous papers, however, we argue that social group and organizational identification contribute to transformations (Kramer, 1991, 1994; Kramer & Brewer, 1986; Kramer & Goldman, 1995). Extrapolating from this work, we argue next that identity-based transformations also play an important role in the decision to trust because they affect individuals' beliefs and expectations about the consequences of their own and others' actions.

Linking Organizational
Identification and Collective Trust

To articulate in more concrete terms how identity-based transformations affect people's beliefs about the consequences of trust and distrust, we must first describe the specific form these transformations take. To do so, it is useful to draw a distinction between cognitive, motivational, and affective bases of transformations.[1]

Cognitive Bases of
Identity Transformations

The cognitive transformations associated with organizational identification derive primarily from the effects of categorization on social perception and judgment (see Wilder & Cooper, 1981, for a review). Categorization processes affect not only how individuals perceive other individuals, often referred to as *social categorization effects* (Tajfel, 1969, 1982), but also how they perceive themselves, which have been characterized as *self-categorization effects* (Turner, 1987).

Social categorization processes influence individuals' judgments about the prospects for collective trust in several ways. The first has to do with the effects of social categorization on individuals' perceptions of other people's trustworthiness. Research on in-group bias (Brewer, 1979) has shown that people tend to perceive members of their own social groups in relatively positive terms. In-group members are typically viewed, for example, as being more cooperative, more honest, and more trustworthy than members of other groups. Thus, all else equal, people expect more positive behavior from those with whom they share group membership compared to outsiders.

Second, there is evidence that social categorization enhances perceived similarity among individuals who share membership in a social category (Tajfel, 1969). Because of this enhanced perception of similarity, individuals may presume that other members of a collective perceive a given trust dilemma in similar terms and will act in similar fashion. In other words, common categorization may inflate judgments of consensus about how a dilemma will be construed by other members of the group. These assumptions of similarity and consensus thus provide a basis for presumptive action by reducing the perceived risk that one will be the only person thinking and acting in collective terms (i.e., the only "sucker" in the group).

Organizational identification may be linked to positive expectations about others' trustworthiness in another way. Research on psychological contracts in organizations (Rousseau, 1989) suggests organizational members often possess a variety of more or less tacit understandings regarding the norms, obligations, duties, and rights that govern their relationships with other organizational members. Thus, organizational membership may be taken as *prima facie* evidence that other members of the organization are willing to live by the codes of conduct that bind them together as a group. This may be especially true with respect to those organizations that maintain strong cultures, create significant barriers to entry, and impose substantial socialization costs on their members.

The presumption that a psychological contract is in force helps individual group members solve an important psychological barrier to presumptive action—namely, the fear of exploitation. As Rotter (1980) observed, concerns about fear and gullibility, often more than greed or temptation, underlie the reluctance to trust. Thus, the belief that other group members will not willingly violate the psychological contract may reduce individuals' fears that unilateral initiatives on their part will leave them "exposed" (i.e., at risk of ending up with the sucker's payoff).

In this respect, social categorization creates cognitive benefits that can operate as substitutes for other mechanisms on which trust is more usually predicated. For example, individuals may perceive less of a need to verify or "negotiate" trust before engaging in exchanges or transactions with other organizational members. As Brewer (1981) proposed in this respect,

> Common membership in a salient social category can serve as a rule for defining the boundaries of low-risk interpersonal trust that bypasses the need for personal knowledge and the costs of negotiating reciprocity with individual others. As a consequence of shifting from the personal level to the social group level of identity, the individual can adopt a sort of 'depersonalized trust' based on category membership alone. (p. 356)

There is also evidence that social categorization processes affect individuals' causal attributions about others' dispositions, motives, and intentions. As noted earlier, these attributions often exert a substantial impact on individuals' calculations about the risks of engaging in trusting behavior. Research has shown, for example, that individuals are more likely to attribute in-group members' negative behaviors to external, unstable factors, but the same behavior by an out-group member is more likely to be attributed to stable, internal factors (see Brewer & Kramer, 1985; Hewstone, 1992; Pettigrew, 1979; Weber, 1994, for reviews). Because of these attributional biases, individuals tend to give other in-group members the benefit of the doubt when confronted with information that might otherwise be viewed as diagnostic of a lack of trustworthiness. By discounting such data, trust within the in-group remains intact.

Complementing this evidence that social categorization influences individuals' expectations and attributions about other in-group members' behaviors is evidence that similar processes are at work when individuals view themselves. Turner (1987) characterized these as self-categorization effects. When an individual's identification moves from the personal level to the collective level, he notes that there is a "shift towards the perception of self as an interchangeable exemplar of some social category and away from the perception of self as a unique person" (p. 253). In support of these arguments, research has demonstrated that when individuals are categorized in terms of group or social identities, they are likely to think and act in collective terms. When categorized in terms of more distinctive personal or individualistic identities, however, they are likely to act more in their self-interests (Brewer & Kramer, 1986).

Such findings suggest that self-categorization processes may affect the utility or weight that individuals afford to their own versus others' outcomes (Kramer & Brewer, 1986; Kramer & Goldman, 1995). This line of argument draws attention to the possibility that there are motivational as well as cognitive underpinnings to identity-based transformations.

Motivational Bases of Transformations

Several motivational bases of transformations seem plausible. First, to the extent that common categorization enhances perceptions of similarity with others, it may also reduce perceived social distance between the self and other group members. As a consequence, decision makers may afford more psychological significance to the impact of their actions on others. As Brewer (1979) suggested in this regard, "The reduced differentiation between one's own and other's outcomes associated with in-group formation provides one mechanism for increasing the weight given to collective outcomes in individual decision-making" (p. 322). As a result of common categorization, individuals may draw a less sharp distinction between their own and others' outcomes.

One can imagine additional benefits. In discussing the motivational bases of transformations, Kelley (1979) notes that behavior in interdependence situations is important not only insofar as it materially affects the tangible outcomes that individuals derive from their actions (represented in the given matrix as payoffs) but also in a variety of less tangible but nonetheless important psychological benefits. He proposes, for example, that interdependence dilemmas afford individuals—as social actors—a setting in which to display to others valued interpersonal orientations and behavioral dispositions.

From the standpoint of individuals who identify with an organization and its members, public affirmations and displays of trust serve a number of important social motives. First, they provide a way for individuals to affirm the importance or value that they associate with their membership in their organization (cf. Lind & Tyler, 1988). Second, such behaviors have demonstrative value: Acting as if one trusts other members of one's group communicates respect and liking for them. It thus provides organizational members with an opportunity to communicate the symbolic importance they attach to their shared organizational identity. Finally, it affords them an opportunity to signal to others the importance they assign to the preservation of the collective trust.

From this perspective, the psychological significance of choice in collective trust dilemmas resides not only in the calculus of risks and benefits but also in the social opportunities such situations afford individuals. Thus, a complete theory regarding the decision to trust in collective contexts requires that we take into account not only the direct and obvious benefits of such behavior but also the less visible but not less important self-presentational motives and expressive needs such behavior serves.

Arguments of this sort prompt consideration of other affective correlates of identity-based behavior.

Affective Bases of Transformations

One important implication of our argument regarding the psychological benefits of identification with others is that individuals in organizations may derive substantial hedonic benefits from engaging in collective behavior. For example, to the extent that individuals perceive trust behavior as a mechanism for affirming cherished social identities and positive relationships with others, such affirmations are likely to be perceived as intrinsically pleasurable and self-rewarding. Such linkages, moreover, open the door for powerful secondary reinforcers to come into play. Thus, it is possible individuals may experience additional pleasure when they subsequently learn that presumptive actions predicated on trust in others have been validated. For example, when individuals learn that their own voluntary restraint in a resource crisis has been met by others, they may derive satisfaction from knowing that the risks they willingly assumed *ex ante* have, in a sense, paid off.[2] In this sense, presumptive acts made on the basis of these positive hedonic anticipations may be self-reinforcing and eventually internalized. As Simon (1991) observes in this regard,

> Identification with the "we," which may be a family, a company, a city, a nation, or the local baseball team, allows individuals to experience satisfactions (to gain utility) from successes of the unit thus selected. Thus, organizational identification becomes a motivation for employees to work actively for organizational goals. (p. 36)[3]

And note that such self-control may be pushed back up the temporal chain of action because our ability, as cognitively complex "self-managers," enables us to anticipate and engineer such affective outcomes. As a consequence, these outcomes have a chance to influence our *ex ante* calculations regarding the perceived benefits associated with engaging in them.[4] Elster and Loewenstein (1992) argue that anticipatory cognitions of this sort can exert a potent effect on the self-management of behavior:

> Like memory, anticipated experiences affect current utility through the consumption and contrast effects. Through the consumption effect we are able to, in effect, consume events before they occur through anticipation . . . [our capacity to savor events] acts as multipliers of experience, causing individuals to experience the hedonic impact of events repeatedly before they occur. . . . Anticipated experiences also affect current well-being via the contrast effect, by serving as a reference point against which current consumption is measured. When the future is expected to be superior to the present, the comparison leads to a denigration of the present. (p. 225)

Within the context of the present arguments, consumption and contrast imply socially adaptive cognitive mechanisms that may tip the balance toward presumptive action.

The hedonic consequences associated with identity-based trust and their "strategic" (behavioral) implications are worth highlighting, we feel, because previous work on trust has remained, for the most part, silent about the positive emotional dimensions of trust behavior. Instead, it has focused almost exclusively on negative affective reactions associated with violations of trust. For example, clinical social psychologists (e.g., Janoff-Bulman, 1992) and organizational theorists (e.g., Bies & Tripp, Chapter 12, this volume) have afforded considerable attention to the intense emotional reactions that follow the betrayal of trust. By contrast, the positive emotional consequences that might attend affirmations of trust in social contexts have been largely neglected.

Linking Identity-Based Expectations and Trust

The cognitive, motivational, and affective transformations described thus far can be regarded as important primarily with respect to their influence on individuals' expectations and calculations regarding the consequences (risks and benefits) likely to attend their decisions to trust or not trust. In this section, we elaborate on the logic of this argument, postulating that individuals' willingness to expose themselves to the risks of trust are conditioned on three distinct but related types of expectations. We characterize these as (a) expectations of reciprocity, (b) perceptions of efficacy, and (c) expectations regarding hedonic reinforcement or consequences.

Expectations of Reciprocity

Expectations of reciprocity reflect individuals' a priori beliefs regarding the likelihood that other group members will reciprocate acts of trust. Evidence that generalized expectations of reciprocity play a role in individuals' willingness to trust comes from several sources (see Brann & Foddy, 1988; Lindskold, 1978; Messick et al., 1983). In one demonstration, Messick et al. (1983) found that individuals' willingness to exercise personal restraint when consuming resources from a rapidly depleting common pool was correlated with their belief that others would do so as well.

Although necessary, merely thinking that one's own actions will be reciprocated by others does not necessarily provide sufficient justification for the decision to trust in collective contexts. As Arrow (1974) suggests, "Collective undertakings of any kind . . . become difficult or impossible not only because A may betray B *but because even if A wants to trust B he knows that B is unlikely to trust him*" (p. 26, emphasis added). Gambetta (1988) makes a similar point in arguing that "it is necessary not only to trust others before acting cooperatively, but also to believe that one is trusted *by* others" (p. 216).

In the case of collective contexts, therefore, one must be confident that others also entertain similar expectations—and *enough* others to make a difference. In this respect, trust in collective contexts depends on what Schelling (1960) aptly characterizes as the familiar "spiral of reciprocal expectations" (p. 87). These reciprocal expectations make up the fragile cognitive chain linking perceptions of one's own and others' actions, a chain that may "tip" the collective toward trust.

Perceptions of Efficacy

Perceptions of efficacy reflect individuals' beliefs regarding the agency of their actions (i.e., the extent to which their actions can influence a particular outcome; e.g., see Kaufman & Kerr, 1993; Kerr, 1989, 1992). In the case of collective trust dilemmas, they reflect individuals' judgments regarding the extent to which their own trusting behavior will make a difference in terms of actually influencing the final outcome of the dilemma.

Logically, individuals might conceptualize the links between their own actions and collective outcomes in two distinct but related ways. The first way can be characterized as a form of *causal efficacy*. Causal efficacy has to do with the presumed impact of one's own behavior on a collective dilemma itself (e.g., one's belief that exercising personal restraint during a water shortage will actually help reduce the scarcity rather than be merely an inconsequential drop from the bucket).

The second form of efficacy has to do with the anticipated impact of one's own actions on other group members. With respect to trust, this form of efficacy reflects individuals' beliefs regarding the extent to which they can induce others to engage in trusting behavior by first modeling such behavior themselves. As such, it represents a form of perceived social influence.

Although perceptions of efficacy have received little attention from trust researchers, we think such perceptions may play a critical role in the decision to trust in collective contexts.

Hedonic Expectations

One important consequence of assuming decisions about trust are viewed by group members as, at least partially, social decisions is that individuals may be able to anticipate hedonic benefits from engaging in such acts. Decisions about trust in collective contexts are not only about the calculation of individual risks and profits—they are also about identity and image (cf. March, 1994). Following the work of Tyler and his colleagues (Lind & Tyler, 1988; Tyler, 1993; Tyler & Degoey, 1995), we assume individuals generally care about their standing in social groups. As a consequence, they are likely to care not only about the material benefits they associate with a decision to trust but also its self-presentational implications (see Kramer, Pommerenke, & Newton, 1993). These hedonic anticipations function to discipline and constrain their more self-interested impulses.

As social acts, decisions about trust may also, although not always or necessarily, become linked to group members' perceptions of their obligation to protect cherished group norms and values. For example, individuals may feel the decision to trust is mandated by moral imperatives that dominate or override other more parochial concerns. It is important to note that, in making this argument, we do not intend to suggest (nor do we need to invoke) a principalistic account of social action (cf. Batson, 1994). To explain why individuals engage in such behavior, a purely hedonic argument is more than adequate: The hedonic bases of social acts, and the underlying motivating potential of moral imperatives linked to them, derive from two sources. First, in a positive sense, individuals have the ability to anticipate the pleasurable states associated with prosocial, principalistic behavior when interacting with people within one's social boundaries. Relatedly, our capacity to anticipate the negative hedonic states (guilt and fear) that may attend personal acts that violate the collective trust push us in the same direction.

In terms of the standard payoff matrix, of course, such anticipations are purely exogenous or "extrarational" considerations (cf. Elster, 1989). From the perspective of the transformed matrix, however, they can be construed as anticipations that individuals, as *social* decision makers, routinely incorporate in their calculus.

The Panoply of Motives
Underlying Identity-Based Trust

The social character and importance of identity-based trust emerge most clearly when consideration is given, first, to the distinct ways in which the decision to trust in collective settings can be construed by individuals and, second, to the implications of such differences with respect to their influence on individuals' willingness to engage in trust behavior. In particular, the identity framework advanced in this chapter suggests several distinct motives for engaging in trust behavior, which we will characterize as (a) reciprocity-based trust, (b) elicitative trust, (c) compensatory trust, and (d) noncontingent or moralistic trust.

Reciprocity-Based Trust. The logic of reciprocity-based trust is simply, "I will engage in trust behavior *because* I believe you are likely to do the same." It is explicitly tied to, and thus contingent on, individuals' expectations of reciprocity. In this respect, it is a form of calculative trust not unlike those encountered in a number of recent economic and game-theoretic treatments (see notably, Williamson, 1993).

The strongest evidence for reciprocity-based trust is found in experimental research on interpersonal trust (Lindskold, 1978) and trust in social-dilemma situations (Messick et al., 1983). As noted earlier, these studies demonstrate that individuals' expectations of reciprocity influence their willingness to engage in cooperative behavior themselves (although see Tyler & Degoey, 1995, for a discussion of evidence that expectations of reciprocity alone are not always sufficient).

Elicitative Trust Behavior. Elicitative trust behavior is motivated by the belief or expectation that, by engaging in acts of trust themselves, one may be able to induce others to do the same. Elicitative behavior entails an expectation of reciprocity, but it is an expectation linked to individuals' perceptions of personal efficacy (i.e., their belief that their actions will influence others, especially those who might be reticent to engage in trust because of fear of being the only one to do so). It is thus predicated on individuals' expectation that they can *create* a climate of reciprocal trust through unilateral initiatives. In elicitative trust, the individual acts as a "first mover" or a "missing hero" (Schelling, 1978), an important role if the failure of collective trust is viewed as a problem of volunteer's dilemma (cf. Murnighan et al., 1994) or motivated by fear of ending up with the sucker's payoff.

The notion of elicitative trust behavior is suggested by empirical research on the development of trust (Pilisuk & Skolnick, 1968) and the evolution of cooperation (Axelrod, 1984). Extrapolating from this research, we might expect that elicitative trust behavior is most likely to be observed in situations where expectations of reciprocity are initially low but perceptions of personal agency high.

Compensatory Trust. Perhaps one of the most important implications of our analysis of the effects of organizational identification on individual judgment and decision making is that, through the transformation process, collective trust itself may come to be construed as a public good in its own right. If the collective trust is perceived by organizational members as a valuable shared resource worth protecting, then individuals may be willing to engage in compensatory actions to offset the behavior of other individuals they think might threaten its stability or survival.

Compensatory trust behavior is predicated on the recognition that some, but not all, of the other members of a collective may fail to engage in the needed presumptive behavior. Because most individuals are sophisticated enough to realize that the solution to many collective action problems requires only cooperation from some critical mass or minimal set of decision makers (Schelling, 1978; van de Kragt, Orbell, & Dawes, 1983), compensatory acts (if "replicated" by sufficient others) can offset the harm of anticipated free-riders. Some evidence of such compensatory behavior has been observed in social dilemma experiments (e.g., Brewer, 1985; Brewer & Schneider, 1990).

In making this argument, it is critical to emphasize here, as before, that we are not assuming that individuals who engage in compensatory acts necessarily view such behavior as altruistic. As Lieberman (1964) noted,

> Many views of trust have overlooked what appears to be an essential ingredient in the analysis of trust. . . . [For example,] we trust other nations, but this trust is not based primarily on moral considerations or any notion of the building of positive feelings; [rather,] *it is based on a sophisticated notion of self-interest.* (p. 272, emphasis added)

Thus, it is not necessary to presuppose that decision makers who engage in compensatory acts in collective contexts *ipso facto* perceive themselves as forfeiting their own self-interests on behalf of their group. Instead, we argue, the shift in identity from the personal to the collective level may serve, more simply, to enhance individuals' perception of the tight coupling that exists between their interests and the collective welfare, especially if a sufficiently long-term horizon is adopted. Behavior of this sort reveals, in other words, individuals' willingness to incur personal costs in the near-term to protect a valuable resource that they expect will pay dividends later. In this respect, decisions predicated on compensatory motives resemble calculative trust, but they are more forward-looking (i.e., made with the "shadow of the future" in mind; Axelrod, 1984).

Compensatory behaviors may get even more bite, from a motivational standpoint, vis-à-vis their impact on the cognitive links between self-perception and commitment (cf. Cialdini, 1983). As Boulding (1988) suggests,

> A very important dynamic in the building up of community is what I have called the "sacrifice trap." Once people are coerced, or even better, persuaded, into making sacrifices, *their identity becomes bound up with the community organization for which the sacrifices were made.* Admitting to one's self that one's sacrifices were in vain is a deep threat to identity and is always sharply resisted. (p. 288, emphasis added)

Thus, compensatory acts may lead to self-reinforcing changes in individuals' perceptions not only of themselves but also of their relationship to the collective. In this respect, compensatory behaviors solve not only the individual's immediate decisional dilemma (to engage in collective action this time), they also help resolve a more vexing and recurrent commitment dilemma by breeding attachment to the group.

Moralistic Trust. Moralistic trust constitutes a fourth kind of identity-based trust behavior. Moralistic trust takes the form, "I will act in a trusting and trustworthy fashion irrespective of what others in the group do or don't do." The notion of moralistic trust was originally suggested by Rotter (1980), who argued that trust behavior sometimes reflects an individual's "belief in the moral rightness of trust [rather than] an expectancy of risk in trusting others" (p. 4). In contrast with the first three motives for engaging in trust behavior, which are clearly contingent on various forms of social or causal expectation, we view moralistic trust as noncontingent.[5] It is presumed to be explicitly predicated not on calculations of risks and benefits but rather on general ethical convictions and intrinsic values that individuals associate with group membership.

Within Rotter's framework, we should note, moralistic trust is conceptualized as an individual difference variable. As such, it is presumably linked to individuals' social values and dispositions. By contrast, an identity-based conception of moralistic trust emphasizes its ties to individuals' beliefs about what responsible membership in a social group entails. Moralistic trust is about the identities and images that attend being a "good" group member who cares about maintaining that good standing.

Contributions and Implications

We began this chapter by proposing that the decision to trust in collective contexts differs in a number of ways from decisions about trust that are encountered in other social contexts, such as interpersonal or small-group settings. Taking this intuition as a starting point, we have tried to systematically explicate these differences and their consequences. The contributions of an identity-based conception of trust can be stated more explicitly, however, beginning with some of its theoretical implications.

Resilience (or Fragility)
of Identity-Based Trust

As with other forms of trust, the utility of an identity-based conception can be judged from the standpoint of the resilience or fragility of trust it implies. Social scientists have often noted that forms of trust can be "thick" or "thin," "weak" or "strong," "fragile" or "resilient" (e.g., see Bernard, 1988; Meyerson,

Kramer, & Weick, Chapter 9, this volume; Putnam, 1993). And therein, to a large degree, lies their efficacy. Gambetta (1988) most sharply engages this issue when he asks pointedly, "To what extent can we, and should we, 'trust' trust to make a difference?" (p. 261). If, for example, the cognitive and social processes that produce and sustain identity-based trust are themselves fragile, why not go around such trust? In other words, why not turn to other more robust routes to cooperation?

In approaching this question, we would note first that it is not necessary to assume, as might appear at first glance, that a particularly strong or cohesive bond needs to exist among organizational members for identity-based trust to take hold. It is only necessary to assume that collective identity provides *some* credible basis for individuals to believe that engaging in trusting behavior does not entail unacceptable levels of risk. As Deutsch (1958) observes in this regard, "Mutual trust can occur even under circumstances where the people involved are not overly concerned with each other's welfare, *provided that the characteristics of the situation are such as to lead one to expect one's trust to be fulfilled*" (p. 279, emphasis added).

Thus, our arguments about identity-based trust are not predicated on the assumption that people necessarily care about what happens to others (although we have implied there is some of that present in most social groups). Instead, the cognitive, motivational, and affective processes associated with organizational identification give rise to a number of distinct motives for engaging in acts of trust in collective contexts. To the extent these psychological factors converge to produce trust behavior, identity-based trust can be characterized as an *overdetermined* form of trust. Overdeterminedness alone obviously does not guarantee resilience. The extent to which identity-based trust is fragile or hardy depends also on numerous and often quite subtle organizational actions, cues, and contexts. Identity-based trust can be viewed as a by-product of a variety of organizational factors, including the extent to which socialization practices create strong collective identities; the effectiveness of organizational leaders' symbolic management activities at reinforcing those identities; and the power of the organizational culture to nurture and sustain them. Identity-based trust, like identity itself, is a socially constructed product.

Of course, organizations are often mindful of this fact, as evidenced by their willingness to allocate substantial organizational resources to foster positive identities—identities they hope will forge the necessary perceptual links between individual actions and collective outcomes (cf. Albert & Whetten, 1985; Ashforth & Mael, 1989; Dutton, Dukerich, & Harquail, 1994; Elsbach & Kramer, 1995; Mael & Ashforth, 1992; March, 1994).

Dynamics of Collective
Trust in Organizations

Our arguments about the overdeterminedness of identity-based trust draw attention to the ambiguous nature of trust behaviors, especially as they are enacted in organizational settings. We observe others' acts, but the motive or motives underlying those acts are usually far from clear. Because of this inherent ambiguity, observers can never know for sure what to make of others' trust-like behavior, that is, what it "means" or reveals about them. For example, it is often hard to know whether an observed act of trust is predicated on the other's confidence that he or she won't be exploited (i.e., an example of reciprocal trust), or whether it is intended to move others toward trust (an example of elicitative trust). Thus, it is often difficult to infer whether an instance of trust behavior is indicative of another's confidence, fear, hope, or resignation.

To the extent individuals recognize that inferring motives and intentions from others' behavior is problematic, they are likely to become more attentive and attuned to the nuances of others' actions and inactions. In other words, the ambiguities that surround trust in collective contexts should invite a form of adaptive vigilance (Kramer, 1994). Individuals become willing to pay attention to others' behavior, and how much they are willing to pay (the degree of vigilance) increases as the costs of misplaced trust increase. Thus, we assume individuals do not respond passively to the vulnerabilities and uncertainties they encounter in collective action situations. Rather, they proactively seek information to reduce their perceived vulnerability and uncertainty.

Additionally, to the extent they realize that similar ambiguities attend their own actions (i.e., that their behavior creates interpretive predicaments for others), individuals often proactively undertake initiatives to clarify those actions. In other words, just as people understand the need to *obtain* reassurance, they also recognize the need to *provide* it. Accordingly, we assume that, as with many forms of social behavior, acts of trust are often accompanied by verbal accounts that are aimed at reducing their ambiguity.

Some economists and game theorists argue, of course, that "cheap talk" of this sort is meaningless and should be discounted. Certainly, when the costs of misplaced trust cross some salient threshold, cheap talk should be discounted (e.g., in arms races, actions do speak louder than words). However, in more benign organizational contexts, cheap talk serves a variety of useful social functions, including the reduction of ambiguity and the provision of partial, even if incomplete, reassurance. Thus, although such talk may be cheap, it is often far from worthless.

We further assume that the emergence and maintenance of collective trust are linked to positive and mutually reinforcing cycles of action-reaction among interdependent players (Kahn & Kramer, 1990). In other words, collective trust should be viewed as the end product of a reciprocal-influence process, in which individual actions not only affect collective outcomes, but feedback about collective behavior, in turn, influences individual decisions.

Such dynamics arise, at least in part, from the self-reinforcing properties of cooperative behavior. As Putnam (1993) notes, trust within social communities not only "lubricates cooperation [but] cooperation itself breeds trust" (p. 171). And it is this "steady accumulation of social capital," he suggests, that plays a fundamental role in the development of collective trust and cooperation.[6] Cast in terms of the present analysis, we would argue that the *perception* of common identification—and also the perception that the perception is common—provide the critical cognitive glue that binds interdependent players together and, at the same time, provide a lubricant that enables presumptive actions to diffuse and reverberate throughout the collective.

Miller (1992) offers an excellent example of this kind of socially constructed and self-reinforcing dynamic. In recounting the philosophy of Hewlett Packard founder Bill Hewlett, he noted that the HP way

> consists of the policies and actions that flow from the belief that men and women want to do a good job, a creative job, and that if they are provided with the proper environment they will do so. The reality of cooperation . . . is suggested by the open lab stock policy, which not only allows engineers access to all equipment, but encourages them to take it home for personal use. . . . The open door symbolizes and demonstrates management's trust in the cooperativeness of the employees. . . . The elimination of time clocks and locks on equipment room doors is *a way of building a shared expectation among all the players that cooperation will most likely be reciprocated, [creating] a shared "common knowledge" in the ability of the players to reach cooperative outcomes.* (p. 197, emphasis added)

Because such acts are so manifestly predicated on confidence in others, they tend to breed confidence in turn. As a consequence, collective trust becomes institutionalized over time (at the macrolevel) and internalized (at the microlevel). In this respect, collective trust becomes a potent form of "expectational asset" that group members can rely on to help solve problems of cooperation and coordination (cf. Camerer & Knez, in press). They become, in other words, expectations that bind (Kramer & Goldman, 1995).

The "Dark Sides" of Identity-Based Trust

Although extolling the virtues of identity-based trust, we would be remiss if we failed to consider the possibility that some deleterious consequences might be associated with such trust, both for the individual and the collective. After all, as Brewer and Schneider (1990) aptly note, social identity is a double-edge sword.

Several possibilities regarding the dark sides of identity-based trust suggest themselves. First, we noted earlier that organizational identification can have a variety of positive effects on individuals' a priori expectations about other organizational members. In particular, we suggested that strong identification with a group or organization enhances individuals' trust in other members. If so, it is possible that identification may foster a tendency for individuals, under some conditions, to overestimate reciprocity from others. Similarly, it is possible that the attributional biases described earlier may lead individuals to discount too steeply evidence that other group members are untrustworthy. These judgmental proclivities may push decision makers toward a sort of "leniency" bias (Brewer, 1995) or "benign attribution error" (Kramer, 1994).

Because of these cognitive and attributional biases, individuals sometimes may be slow to learn when their trust in others is misguided, leading them to persevere in cooperating past the point where perseverance is prudent. In this respect, the very properties of identity-based trust that contribute to its resilience might sometimes render individuals more vulnerable to misplaced trust. For example, one might argue that those who "overidentify" with a group relative to the rest of the population are likely to be outlyers with respect to estimating reciprocity from others. As a result, they may underestimate the risks of engaging in trusting behavior and may be slower than others in the collective to recognize when their trust has been breached. Thus, although the perceptual tendencies associated with social identification incline individuals toward presumptive trust, they may also lull them down the slippery slope of misplaced trust.

Consistent with this possibility, one pattern that we observed in the data from our experiments on cooperation in social dilemmas was that decision makers in the "high social identity" conditions cooperated longer than those in the "low social identity" conditions. The interpretation we originally made of this result (Kramer & Brewer, 1986) was that, when the chips were down, those for whom group identification was salient were most willing to forego their own gains to further the collective interests. In other words, we assumed that the behavior we observed in these experiments reflected a compensatory motive of the sort described earlier. However, a less charitable, but equally plausible, interpretation of our data is that these decision makers were simply slower to realize when other group members had abandoned restraint. As a consequence, they were sluggish to adopt appropriate self-protective actions. When social identities are "switched on," recognition and response may be too little and too late.

In addition to these individual-level costs, there may be some deleterious effects of identity-based trust at the collective or organizational level. Throughout this chapter we have implied identity-based trust enhances an organization's ability to solve certain collective action problems, such as free-riding and social loafing. But there is another possibility. In situations where presumptive trust in others is too high, it is possible that individuals may become less likely to engage in collective action precisely because they believe that others will do so. In other words, if individuals trust that others will come forward and take action, then the perceived need for intervention on their part may decrease. The perceived urgency for action is reduced. Thus, one unintended (and ironic) consequence of high levels of presumptive trust in others may be that individuals underestimate the need for personal action.

If so, this dynamic may be most apparent (and have the most disastrous consequences) precisely in those situations where effective presumptive action is most necessary, such as missing hero traps, volunteer dilemmas, and organizational crises (Mishra, Chapter 13, this volume; Schelling, 1978; Webb, Chapter 14, this volume). Such situations create a decision dilemma not unlike those described by Darley and Latane (1968) in their research on the seemingly apathetic bystander: Each individual confronting the emergency decides to take no action, not because of indifference but because a sort of complacency arises from the presumption that someone else has taken the necessary and "collectively obvious" step.

These same arguments have some implications for thinking about problems of collective sensemaking and decision making in organizations (Weick, 1993). If identity-based trust fosters an overconfidence in the collective, as we have suggested, then individuals may sometimes defer too readily to other members. They may, for example, inhibit expressions of doubt or engage in inappropriately severe self-censorship rather than press their claims as vigorously as they might, for example, with comparative strangers. In discussing the results of his famous studies on social influence, Asch pointed out that the behavior of individuals in these experiments demonstrated not only that they were influenced by conformity pressures but also that they had a basic trust in others' perceptions and judgments (see Campbell, 1990, for this discussion). In other words, not only did they trust their own senses, but they also trusted others' as well, leading them to suppress their doubts. Thus, when individuals discovered that their own perceptions were discrepant with those of their fellow group members, they were perplexed and troubled. Rather than simply discount the veridicality of others' perceptions, however, they were motivated to resolve this discrepancy. They thus held back and laid low, trying to make sense of their perceptual predicament rather than drawing attention to it. Collective trust, as much as collective conformity, can lead us to act as if the emperor's new clothes are cut just fine.

Similar lines of argument suggest that identity-based trust might, under some circumstances, impede organizational learning and adaptation. There is an important sense in which the ability of organizations to learn from experience depends not only on individuals' willingness to trust others' views of reality but also their willingness to doubt them. In other words, high-quality decision making requires not only the cooperative pooling of information described by Bonacich and Schneider (1992) but also the collective willingness to challenge claims about the integrity and interpretation of that information (cf. Janis, 1991).

Finally, we should note that many of the benefits we have claimed for identity-based trust operate at the intraorganizational level. In other words, they contribute to the solution of collective-action problems that arise within the social boundaries of a collective. However, these very same dynamics may exacerbate problems of interorganizational distrust and suspicion. In other words, the very things that make trust easy to confer on insiders may render the presumptive trust of outsiders more problematic (see Brewer, 1979). Certain perceptual tendencies, such as perceptual contrast (Cialdini, 1993), may make the boundaries between trust on the inside and outside of social groups even more salient and stark.

The Importance of
Assumptions About Trust

Many contemporary conceptions of trust, especially those encountered in experimental social psychology, game theory, and microeconomics, start with the assumption, either explicitly stated or tacitly assumed, that interdependent decision makers can be conceptualized as asocial game players. As such, their decisions about trust are assumed grounded primarily in strategic and calculative concerns. With these assumptions as starting points, it becomes rather difficult to explain the levels of trust that are routinely observed in both laboratory simulations of collective behavior and real-world organizational settings. Such assumptive frameworks render collective trust surprising, perplexing, and problematic. As we have tried to show here, an identity-based model can more easily explain the origins of collective trust and the presumptive act such trust engenders.

It is easy to discount the theoretical importance of our assumptions about the nature of trust. Questions about whether to conceptualize trust as a social decision versus trust as a calculative decision might seem to be primarily matters of a disciplinary-bent or an academic vogue. However, as organizational theorists have long noted, the assumptive frameworks we adopt greatly influence how the phenomena we study are construed (e.g., Stutman & Putnam, 1994; Tetlock, 1991). The assumptive frameworks from which we start influence not only the problems surrounding trust that we anticipate in our theorizing but also—and in very profound and consequential ways—the kinds of remedies to problems of trust we consider.

In this respect, different models of trust have very different implications regarding how the problems of trust are framed and resolved. Theories about human nature serve as reference points that anchor our expectations about what kinds of behavioral and structural interventions will work and why. Thus, for example, a theory of trust that is predicated on an architecture of rational expectations implies a different elixir than one that views trust as a complex social process that is embedded in complex social contexts.

An informative parallel can be drawn to the history of debate over the comparative efficacy of different approaches to solving social dilemmas (e.g., see Edney, 1980; Hardin, 1968, 1988; Hardin & Baden, 1988; Messick & Brewer, 1983; Olson, 1965; Ostrom, 1990; Schelling, 1978). Much of this debate throughout the 1970s and 1980s swirled around the relative power of individual versus structural solutions—a debate made all the more intense and urgent because it occurred during a decade of acute water shortages, electrical brownouts, and alarming predictions about pending fossil fuel scarcities.

At one end of the continuum in this debate were those who saw little prospect for optimism for solving such dilemmas through individual solutions. For example, starting from a framework that assumed people are relatively self-interested and myopic, Garrett Hardin (1968) was led to the rather bleak conclusion that "the social arrangements that produce responsibility are arrangements that create coercion of some sort" (p. 26). In a subsequent article (Hardin, 1988), he invoked a rather limited—and also limiting—metaphor of the commons as a small, overcrowded lifeboat. Such assumptions, and the metaphors with which they are embellished, invoke Hobbesian images of relentless struggle and competition. They portray social relations as inherently, rather than occasionally, zero-sum.

In so doing, they make it easy to overrepresent the extent to which decision makers are motivated by strategic rather than social concerns. They imply impulses must be constrained and natural tendencies deterred. Given such assumptions, it is hardly surprising that Hardin remained pessimistic about the efficacy of internalized controls and voluntary modes of self-restraint. For him, self-restraint seemed a chimera.

In a similar way, many contemporary models of trust leave us far from sanguine about the extent to which we can "trust" trust to solve problems of collective action. Given the assumptions about human nature with which such theories begin, the glass is already half empty. Such theories imply that we must solve problems of trust by relying on remedies that have more bite to them, such as increased surveillance and tougher deterrents.

A conception of collective trust centered around a more *socialized* view of human action (Granovetter, 1985), by contrast, is inherently more optimistic about the efficacy of internalized forms of self-restraint. Viewed through this lens, collective behaviors might be construed by individuals as rational acts—at least insofar as there are discernible good reasons why they should engage in them. These reasons, we should emphasize once again, do not turn upon any presumption that a mysterious altruistic or prosocial motive undergirds collective action. Rather, they reflect a simpler assumption that decision makers are (sometimes at least) sophisticated enough to recognize that their own welfare and the collective fate are coupled, especially over the long-term. Because of this recognition, individuals may decide it is sensible to act in ways that protect collective trust, just as they decide that many shared resources must be protected. Collective trust, like many social goods, can be thought of as a resource from which individuals can draw benefits only as long as it lasts. In this respect, we argue, individuals sometimes have enough foresight to appreciate that, over the long-term, an organizational world in which collective trust is intact is a better world than one in which it is missing.

On the basis of the arguments and empirical evidence we have assembled here, it might seem as if we think that calculative conceptions of trust are fundamentally flawed. We do not. All decisions about trust, at least to some degree, turn upon calculation—and collective trust is no exception. However, we do regard extant calculative conceptions of trust as incomplete conceptualizations. There is more to trust than meets their eye. A broader construal of calculation, however—and one that makes explicit the social bases of hedonic choice—might move us toward a more integrative and satisfying theory of trust behavior.

Such an integration might be achieved by attempting to build a stronger conceptual bridge between social identity theory and behavioral economics. Several approaches strike us as particularly promising. First, emerging perspectives on intertemporal choice (Elster & Loewenstein, 1992) suggest how and why decision makers might sometimes be able to bring long-term, collective rationalities to bear on their decision making. Second, recent theory and research on self-control and self-management (Ainslie & Haslam, 1992; Schelling, 1984, 1992) suggest a number of interesting mechanisms for decisional self-restraint that, wedded with a social identity conception of the self, might provide a more powerful, more parsimonious, and inherently more social conception of presumptive action.

Notes

1. Although we feel that these processes are distinct enough to warrant independent acknowledgment, we do not assume they are independent of each other.

2. Interestingly, although researchers are often quick to point out the aversiveness of the sucker's payoff (and its motivating potential), they have tended to ignore the possibility that *not* obtaining this outcome might be quite satisfying and motivating as well.

3. Simon goes on to note, "Of course, identification is not an exclusive source of motivation; it exists side by side with material rewards and enforcement mechanisms that are part of the employment contract. But a realistic picture of how an organization operates must include the importance of identification in the motivations of employees" (1991, p. 36).

4. There is an additional motivational "kicker" associated with such acts. By engaging in them, individuals not only have an opportunity to affirm the value they attach to organizational membership, they also have a chance, via downward social comparison, to feel morally superior to those who fail to do so.

5. Having said this, it is important to be clear about the sense in which moralistic trust should be construed as noncontingent. By noncontingent we mean that individuals do not view their actions as conditioned on the expectation they will be reciprocated; nor do they think that they can induce others to follow suit by engaging in trust. Instead, they act in a trustworthy fashion because they believe that's what good group members do. However, there is a sense in which moralistic behavior may be contingent, insofar as the need for such behavior might be most salient in situations where one expects trust to fail. For example, a kind of moral outrage over the failure of others to act in a trustworthy fashion may impel individuals toward acts of moralistic trust.

6. Although Putnam's arguments were aimed at understanding the evolution of cooperation among Italian civic communities, they seem just as relevant to understanding the emergence of trust in large, complex organizations as well. Such organizations resemble, in more ways than we often like to admit, such fiercely competitive tribes and parochial communities.

References

Ainslie, G., & Haslam, N. (1992). Self-control. In G. Loewenstein & J. Elster (Eds.), *Choice over time* (pp. 106-114). New York: Russell Sage.

Albert, S., & Whetten, D. A. (1985). Organizational identity. In B. M. Staw & L. L. Cummings (Eds.), *Research in organizational behavior* (Vol. 7, pp. 263-295). Greenwich, CT: JAI.

Allison, S. T., & Messick, D. M. (1990). Social decision heuristics in the use of shared resources. *Journal of Behavioral Decision Making, 3,* 195-204.

Arrow, K. (1974). *The limits of organization.* New York: Norton.

Ashforth, B. E., & Mael, F. (1989). Social identity theory and the organization. *Academy of Management Review, 14,* 20-39.

Axelrod, R. (1984). *The evolution of cooperation.* New York: Basic Books.

Barber, B. (1983). *The logic and limits of trust.* New Brunswick, NJ: Rutgers University Press.

Barnard, C. I. (1968). *The functions of the executive.* Cambridge, MA: Harvard University Press. (Original publication 1938)

Batson, C. (1994). Why act for the public good? Four answers. *Personality and Social Psychology Bulletin, 20,* 603-610.

Bendor, J., Kramer, R. M., & Stout, S. (1991). When in doubt: Cooperation in a noisy prisoner's dilemma. *Journal of Conflict Resolution, 35,* 691-719.

Bernard, W. (1988). Formal structures and social reality. In D. Gambetta (Ed.), *Trust: Making and breaking cooperative relations* (pp. 263-270). Oxford, UK: Basil Blackwell.

Bonacich, P., & Schneider, S. (1992). Communication networks and collective action. In W. G. Liebrand, D. M. Messick, & H. A. M. Wilke (Eds.), *A social psychological approach to social dilemmas* (pp. 111-121). Oxford, UK: Pergamon.

Boulding, K. E. (1988). Commons and community: The idea of a public. In G. Hardin & J. Baden (Eds.), *Managing the commons* (pp. 1-19). San Francisco: Freeman.

Boyle, R., & Bonacich, P. (1970). The development of trust and mistrust in mixed-motive games. *Sociometry, 33,* 123-139.

Brann, P., & Foddy, M. (1988). Trust and the consumption of a deteriorating resource. *Journal of Conflict Resolution, 31,* 615-630.

Brewer, M. B. (1979). In-group bias in the minimal intergroup situation: A cognitive-motivational analysis. *Psychological Bulletin, 86,* 307-324.

Brewer, M. B. (1981). Ethnocentrism and its role in interpersonal trust. In M. B. Brewer & B. E. Collins (Eds.), *Scientific inquiry in the social sciences* (pp. 214-231). San Francisco: Jossey-Bass.

Brewer, M. B. (1985). Experimental research and social policy: Must it be rigor versus relevance? *Journal of Social Issues, 41,* 159-176.

Brewer, M. B. (1995). In-group favoritism: The subtle side of intergroup discrimination. In D. M. Messick & A. Tenbrunsel (Eds.), *Behavioral research and business ethics* (pp. 101-117). New York: Russell Sage.

Brewer, M. B., & Kramer, R. M. (1985). The psychology of intergroup attitudes and behavior. *Annual Review of Psychology, 36,* 219-243.

Brewer, M. B., & Kramer, R. M. (1986). Choice behavior in social dilemmas: Effects of social identity, group size, and decision framing. *Journal of Personality and Social Psychology, 50,* 543-549.

Brewer, M. B., & Schneider, S. (1990). Social identity and social dilemmas: A double-edged sword. In D. Abrams & M. A. Hogg (Eds.), *Social identity theory: Constructive and critical advances* (pp. 22-41). New York: Springer-Verlag.

Camerer, C. F., & Knez, M. (in press). Creating "expectational assets" in the laboratory: "Weakest link" coordination games. *Strategic Management Journal.*

Campbell, D. T. (1990). Asch's moral epistemology for socially shared knowledge. In I. Rock (Ed.), *The legacy of Solomon Asch* (pp. 135-147). Hillsdale, NJ: Lawrence Erlbaum.

Cialdini, R. (1983). *Influence* (3rd ed.). New York: HarperCollins.

Darley, J. M., & Latane, B. (1968). Bystander intervention in emergencies: Diffusion of responsibility. *Journal of Personality and Social Psychology, 8,* 377-383.

Dawes, R. M. (1980). Social dilemmas. *Annual Review of Psychology, 31,* 169-193.

Dawes, R. M., van de Kragt, A. J. C., & Orbell, J. M. (1988). Not me or thee but we: The importance of group identity in eliciting cooperation in dilemma situations: Experimental manipulations. *Acta Psychologica, 68,* 83-97.

Dawes, R. M., van de Kragt, A. J. C., & Orbell, J. M. (1990). Cooperation for the benefit of us—not me, or my conscience. In J. Mansbridge (Ed.), *Beyond self-interest* (pp. 16-55). Chicago: University of Chicago Press.

Deutsch, M. (1958). Trust and suspicion. *Journal of Conflict Resolution, 2,* 265-279.

Deutsch, M. (1973). *The resolution of conflict.* New Haven, CT: Yale University Press.

Dutton, J., Dukerich, J. M., & Harquail, C. V. (1994). Organizational images and member identification. *Administrative Science Quarterly, 39,* 239-263.

Edney, J. J. (1980). The commons problem: Alternative perspectives. *American Psychologist, 35,* 131-150.

Elsbach, K. E., & Kramer, R. M. (1995). *Cognitive strategies for affirming positive organizational identities under threat: How business school members responded to the Business Week survey.* Unpublished manuscript.

Elster, J. (1989). *The cement of society.* Cambridge, UK: Cambridge University Press.

Elster, J., & Loewenstein, G. (1992). Utility from memory and anticipation. In G. Loewenstein & J. Elster (Eds.), *Choice over time* (pp. 126-134). New York: Russell Sage.

Gambetta, D. (1988). Can we trust trust? In D. Gambetta (Ed.), *Trust: Making and breaking cooperative relations* (pp. 213-237). Oxford, UK: Basil Blackwell.

Golembiewski, R. T., & McConkie, M. (1975). The centrality of interpersonal trust in group processes. In C. L. Cooper (Ed.), *Theories of group processes* (pp. 131-185). London: Wiley.

Granovetter, M. (1985). Economic action and social structure: The problem of embeddedness. *American Journal of Sociology, 91,* 481-510.

Hardin, G. (1968). The tragedy of the commons. *Science, 162,* 1243-1248.

Hardin, G. (1988). Living on a lifeboat. In G. Hardin & J. Baden (Eds.), *Managing the commons.* San Francisco: Freeman.

Hardin, G., & Baden, J. (Eds.). (1988). *Managing the commons.* San Francisco: Freeman.

Hewstone, M. (1992). The "ultimate attribution error"? A review of the literature on intergroup causal attribution. *European Journal of Social Psychology, 20,* 311-335.

Hume, D. (1969). *Treatise of human nature.* Hammondsworth, Middlesex, UK: Penguin. (Original publication 1740)

Janis, I. (1991). *Crucial decisions.* New York: Free Press.

Janoff-Bulman, R. (1992). *Shattered assumptions: Towards a new psychology of trauma.* New York: Free Press.

Kahn, R., & Kramer, R. M. (1990). Untying the knot: Deescalatory processes in international conflict. In R. L. Kahn & M. Zald (Eds.), *Organizations and nation-states: New perspectives on conflict and cooperation* (pp. 139-180). San Francisco: Jossey-Bass.

Kahneman, D., & Tversky, A. (1974). Choices, values, and frames. *American Psychologist, 39,* 341-350.

Kaufman, C. M., & Kerr, N. L. (1993). Small wins: Perceptual focus, efficacy, and cooperation in a stage-conjunctive social dilemma. *Journal of Applied Social Psychology, 23,* 3-20.

Kelley, H. H. (1979). *Personal relationships.* Hillsdale, NJ: Lawrence Erlbaum.

Kerr, N. L. (1989). Illusions of efficacy: The effects of group size on perceived efficacy and group motivation losses: Free rider effects. *Journal of Personality and Social Psychology, 44,* 78-94.

Kerr, N. L. (1992). Efficacy as a casual and moderating variable in social dilemmas. In W. B. G. Liebrand, D. M. Messick, & H. A. M. Wilke (Eds.), *Social dilemmas* (pp. 59-80). New York: Pergamon.

Kramer, R. M. (1989). Windows of vulnerability or cognitive illusions? *Journal of Experimental Social Psychology, 25,* 79-100.

Kramer, R. M. (1991). Intergroup relations and organizational dilemmas: The role of categorization processes. In B. M. Staw & L. L. Cummings (Eds.), *Research in organizational behavior* (Vol. 13, pp. 191-227). Greenwich, CT: JAI.

Kramer, R. M. (1994). The sinister attribution error: Paranoid cognition and collective distrust in organizations. *Motivation and Emotion, 18,* 199-230.

Kramer, R. M., & Brewer, M. B. (1984). Effects of group identity on resource use in a simulated commons dilemma. *Journal of Personality and Social Psychology, 46,* 1044-1057.

Kramer, R. M., & Brewer, M. B. (1986). Social group identity and the emergence of cooperation in resource conservation dilemmas. In H. A. M. Wilke, D. M. Messick, & C. G. Rutte (Eds.), *Experimental social dilemma* (pp. 129-137). Frankfurt, Germany: Verlag Peter Lang.

Kramer, R. M., & Goldman, L. (1995). Helping the group or helping yourself? In D. Schroeder (Ed.), *Social dilemmas* (pp. 49-68). New York: Praeger.

Kramer, R. M., Pommerenke, P., & Newton, E. (1993). The social context of negotiation: Effects of social identity and interpersonal accountability on negotiator decision making. *Journal of Conflict Resolution, 37,* 633-654.

Latane, B. (1986). Responsibility and effort in organizations. In P. S. Goodman (Ed.), *Designing effective work groups* (pp. 241-256). San Francisco: Jossey-Bass.

Lieberman, B. (1964). i-trust: A notion of trust in three-person games and international affairs. *Conflict Resolution, 8,* 271-280.

Lind, E. A., & Tyler, T. R. (1988). *The social psychology of procedural justice.* New York: Plenum.

Lindskold, S. (1978). Trust development, the GRIT proposal, and the effects of conciliatory acts on conflict and cooperation. *Psychological Bulletin, 85,* 772-793.

Mael, F., & Ashforth, B. E. (1992). Alumni and their alma mater: A partial test of the reformulated model of organizational identification. *Journal of Organizational Behavior, 13,* 103-123.

March, J. G. (1994). *A primer on decision making.* New York: Free Press.

McClintock, C. G., & Liebrand, W. B. G. (1988). Role of interdependence structure, individual value orientation, and another's strategy in social decision making: A transformational analysis. *Journal of Personality and Social Psychology, 55,* 396-409.

Messick, D. M., & Brewer, M. B. (1983) Solving social dilemmas: A review. *Review of Personality and Social Psychology, 4,* 11-44.

Messick, D. M., Wilke, H., Brewer, M. B., Kramer, R. M., Zemke, P. E., & Lui, L. (1983). Individual adaptations and structural change as solutions to social dilemmas. *Journal of Personality and Social Psychology, 44,* 294-309.

Miller, G. J. (1992). *Managerial dilemmas: The political economy of hierarchies.* New York: Cambridge University Press.

Murnighan, J. K., Kim, J. W., & Metzger, A. R. (1994). The volunteer dilemma. *Administrative Science Quarterly, 38,* 515-538.

Olson, M. (1965). *The logic of collective action.* New Haven, CT: Yale University Press.

Organ, D. W. (1988). *Organizational citizenship behavior: The good soldier syndrome.* Lexington, MA: D. C. Heath.

Ostrom, E. (1990). *Governing the commons: The evolution of institutions for collective action.* Cambridge, UK: Cambridge University Press.

Pettigrew, T. F. (1979). The ultimate attribution error: Extending Gordan Allport's cognitive analysis of prejudice. *Personality and Social Psychology Bulletin, 5,* 461-477.

Pilisuk, M., & Skolnick, P. (1968). Inducing trust: A test of the Osgood Proposal. *Journal of Personality and Social Psychology, 8,* 121-133.

Powell, W. (1990). Neither markets nor hierarchy: Network forms of social organization. In B. M. Staw & L. L. Cummings (Eds.), *Research in organizational behavior* (Vol. 12, pp. 295-336). Greenwich, CT: JAI.

Putnam, R. (1993). *Making democracy work.* Princeton, NJ: Princeton University Press.

Rousseau, D. M. (1989). Psychological and implied contracts in organizations. *Employee Responsibilities and Rights Journal, 2,* 121-139.

Rotter, J. B. (1980). Interpersonal trust, trustworthiness, and gullibility. *American Psychologist, 35,* 1-7.

Rousseau, D. M. (1989). Psychological and implied contracts in organizations. *Employee Responsibilities and Rights Journal, 2,* 121-139.

Schelling, T. C. (1960). *The strategy of conflict.* Cambridge, MA: Harvard University Press.

Schelling, T. C. (1978). *Micromotives and macrobehavior.* New York: Norton.

Schelling, T. C. (1984). The intimate contest for self-command. In T. C. Schelling (Ed.), *Choice and consequence* (pp. 116-127). Cambridge, MA: Harvard University Press.

Schelling, T. C. (1992). Self-command: A new discipline. In G. Loewenstein & J. Elster (Eds.), *Choice over time* (pp. 186-201). New York: Russell Sage.

Simon, H. A. (1991). Organizations and markets. *Journal of Economic Perspectives, 5,* 34-38.

Sitkin, S. B., & Roth, N. L. (1993). Explaining the limited effectiveness of legalistic "remedies" for trust/distrust. *Organizational Science, 4,* 367-392.

Stutman, R. K., & Putnam, L. (1994). The consequences of language: A metaphorical look at the legalization of organizing. In S. B. Sitkin & R. J. Bies (Eds.), *The legalistic organization* (pp. 351-369). Thousand Oaks, CA: Sage.

Tajfel, H. (1969). Cognitive aspects of prejudice. *Journal of Social Issues, 25,* 79-97.

Tajfel, H. (1982). *Social identity and intergroup relations.* Cambridge, UK: Cambridge University Press.

Tetlock, P. E. (1991). An alternative metaphor in the study of judgment and choice: People as politicians. *Theory and Psychology, 1,* 451-475.

Turner, J. C. (1987). *Rediscovering the social group: A self-categorization theory.* Oxford, UK: Basil Blackwell.

Tyler, T. R. (1993). The social psychology of authority. In J. K. Murnighan (Ed.), *Social psychology in organizations: Advances in theory and practice* (pp. 141-160). Englewood Cliffs, NJ: Prentice Hall.

Tyler, T. R., & Dawes, R. (1993). Fairness in groups: Comparing the self-interest and social identity perspectives. In B. Mellers & J. Baron (Eds.), *Psychological perspectives on justice: Theory and applications* (pp. 80-96). Cambridge, UK: Cambridge University Press.

Tyler, T. R., & Degoey, P. (1995). *Collective restraint in a social dilemma situation: The influence of procedural justice and community identification on the empowerment and legitimation of authority.* Unpublished manuscript, University of California at Berkeley.

van de Kraft, A. J. C., Orbell, J., & Dawes, R. (1983). The minimal contributing set as a solution to public goods problems. *American Political Science Review, 77,* 112-122.

Weber, J. (1994). The nature of ethnocentric attribution bias: In-group protection or enhancement? *Journal of Experimental Social Psychology, 30,* 482-504.

Weick, K. E. (1993). The collapse of sensemaking in organizations: The Mann Gulch Disaster. *Administrative Science Quarterly, 38,* 628-652.

Wilder, D. A., & Cooper, W. E. (1981). Categorization into groups: Consequences for social perception and attribution. In J. H. Harvey, W. Ickes, & R. F. Kidd (Eds.), *New directions in attribution research* (pp. 79-92) Hillsdale, NJ: Lawrence Erlbaum.

Williamson, O. (1993). Calculativeness, trust, and economic organization. *Journal of Law and Economics, 34,* 453-502.

Yamagishi, T., & Sato, K. (1986). Motivational bases of the public goods problem. *Journal of Personality and Social Psychology, 50,* 67-73.

Zucker, L. G. (1986). Production of trust: Institutional sources of economic structure, 1840-1920. In B. M. Staw & L. L. Cummings (Eds.), *Research in organizational behavior* (Vol. 8, pp. 53-111). Greenwich, CT: JAI.

Understanding the Interaction Between Procedural and Distributive Justice

The Role of Trust

JOEL BROCKNER
PHYLLIS SIEGEL

The purpose of this chapter is to discuss how recent developments in the justice literature provide a basis for understanding the role of trust in ongoing social relationships. To facilitate our analysis, a brief historical overview of theory and research on organizational justice is in order. The justice literature has witnessed three major waves over the past 35 years. The first wave centered on distributive justice, in which fairness was defined in terms of the *outcomes* of a resource allocation decision. Outcome-oriented theorists identified a variety of criteria that could be used to define fairness (e.g., see Deutsch's [1985] discussion of the conditions under which equity, equality, and need are appropriate standards of fairness). Empirical research examined how people responded to the outcome of a resource allocation decision as a function of its perceived fairness. For example, studies derived from equity theory measured individuals' work motivation and satisfaction under conditions of underreward, overreward, or equitable reward (Adams, 1965).

AUTHORS' NOTE: The authors thank Rod Kramer, Tom Tyler, and Batia Wiesenfeld for their constructive comments on an earlier version of this chapter.

The second wave was devoted to *procedural* fairness. Thibaut and Walker's (1975) pioneering efforts revealed that individuals were affected not only by the outcomes that they received but also by the fairness of the processes used to plan and implement the decision. Procedural fairness is determined by the structure of the decision process and by the interpersonal behavior of the parties who implement the decision. Structural considerations include process control and decision control (Thibaut & Walker, 1975). The former refers to whether people were allowed to have input or voice into the process, whereas the latter refers to whether people were given any say in the actual rendering of the decision. Leventhal, Karuza, and Fry (1980) identified additional structural aspects of procedural justice, such as whether opportunities existed for the decision to be corrected and whether the procedures were implemented on a consistent basis. The interpersonal component of procedural justice— also known as "interactional justice" (Bies, 1987)—consists of two major factors: (a) whether the reasons for the decision were clearly and adequately explained and (b) whether the implementers treated the parties affected by the decision with dignity and respect.

The second wave of research sought to disentangle the effects of procedural and distributive justice. As a result, research methods were used that differentiated the two constructs. For example, multiple-regression analysis was used in which the dependent variable was examined as a function of distributive and procedural justice (e.g., Lind & Tyler, 1988). In other studies, the two constructs were orthogonally manipulated (e.g., Tyler & Caine, 1981). Results often revealed significant main effects of both procedural and distributive justice. Most recently, research has shown that procedural and distributive justice are differentially related to various categories of dependent variables: The latter is more important than the former in influencing people's satisfaction with the result of the decision, whereas procedural justice is more important than distributive justice in determining their evaluations of the parties or the institution that enacted the decision (e.g., Sweeney & McFarlin, 1993).

The third wave of justice research—currently in progress—evaluates the joint and *interactive* effects of distributive and procedural justice on people's reactions to a decision. The second wave sought to distinguish between the two constructs; hence, the key terms examined were the main effects. The third wave seeks to integrate (the effects of) distributive and procedural justice; hence, the crucial term is the *interaction effect*. The third wave of research is in response to authors such as Cropanzano and Folger (1991), who suggested that

outcomes and procedures work together to create a sense of injustice. A full understanding of fairness cannot be achieved by examining the two constructs

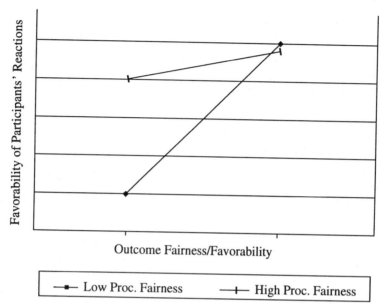

Figure 18.1 Representation of the Modal Interactive Effect of Procedural Fairness and Outcome Fairness/Favorability on Reactions to a Decision

separately. Rather, one needs to consider the interaction between outcomes and procedures. (p. 136)

Brockner and Wiesenfeld (1994) recently reviewed more than 20 field studies in which participants were involved in an ongoing relationship with another person or institution. All of the studies yielded the interactive relationship shown in Figure 18.1. One way to describe the findings is that procedural justice moderated the impact of distributive justice on individuals' reactions to a decision. When procedures were unfair, people responded much more favorably when distributive justice was relatively high. (Such findings are in accordance with classical economic theory in that people were much more likely to benefit materially when distributive justice was relatively high.) When procedures were fair, however, distributive justice had much less of an impact on individuals' reactions. See Table 18.1 for an overview of each study.[1]

Particularly noteworthy is the diversity of the studies in which the interactive pattern was observed. Some studies explored how people reacted to their encounters with legal authorities (Lind & Tyler, 1988). Others examined how employees responded to organizational changes, such as layoffs (Brockner et al., 1994), a pay freeze (Schaubroeck, May, & Brown, in press), relocations (Daly & Geyer, 1995), the introduction of a drug-testing policy (Konovsky &

(text continued on p. 398)

TABLE 18.1 Summary of Studies Yielding Significant Interaction Effects: Field Studies

Study	Site/Event	Participants	Independent Variables	Dependent Variables	Results
Adler, Hensler, & Nelson (1983)	Court-annexed arbitration procedures	Litigants	*Outcome:* Whether subjects won or lost the arbitration *Procedure:* Perceived fairness of arbitration procedure	Satisfaction with experience	Predicted interaction
Bierbauer, Leung, & Lind, reported in Lind (1994a)	Dispute in which a third party intervened	Three samples of undergraduates: one from Germany, one from Hong Kong, and one from the United States	*Outcome:* Perceived favorability of the outcome of the dispute *Procedure:* Fairness with which the third party handled the dispute	Acceptance of the third party	Predicted interaction in all three samples
Brockner, DeWitt, Grover, & Reed (1990)	Layoff at chain of retail stores	597 layoff survivors	*Outcome:* Adequacy of organizational caretaking (e.g., severance pay) if they were to be laid off *Procedure:* Clarity of explanation of reasons for layoff	(1) Organizational commitment (2) Work effort (3) Turnover intention	Predicted interaction on (1) and (3)
Brockner et al. (1994), Study 1	Unemployment line	218 layoff victims applying for unemployment	*Outcome:* Perceived generosity of organization's caretaking (e.g., severance pay) *Procedure:* Advanced notice	Desire for governmental regulation of layoffs	Predicted interaction
Brockner et al. (1994), Study 2	Layoff at a bank	150 layoff survivors	*Outcome:* Layoff severity *Procedure:* Interactional justice	Organizational commitment	Predicted interaction
Brockner et al. (1994), Study 3	Layoff at a manufacturing facility	147 layoff victims who had not yet departed from the organization	*Outcome:* Self-report of how bad the layoff would be for them *Procedure:* Advanced notice	Organizational commitment	Predicted interaction

(continued)

TABLE 18.1 Continued

Study	Site/Event	Participants	Independent Variables	Dependent Variables	Results
Brockner, Wiesenfeld, & Martin (in press)	Layoff at manufacturing facility	193 layoff survivors	*Outcome*: Manipulated through framing: Attention was focused either on those who left (negative frame) or those who remained (positive frame) *Procedure*: Multi-item scale tapping various facets of procedural justice	Organizational trust and support	Predicted interaction
Daly (1994)	7 organizations that had relocated	171 relocated employees	*Outcome*: Reason for the relocation: expansion (positive outcome) or consolidation/decline (negative outcome) *Procedure*: Explanation quality	(1) Distributive justice (2) Procedural justice	Predicted interaction on (1)
Daly & Geyer (in press)	7 organizations that had relocated	171 relocated employees	*Outcome*: Reason for the relocation: expansion (positive outcome) or consolidation/decline (negative outcome) *Procedure*: Procedural fairness in how relocation was handled	Organizational commitment	Predicted interaction
Greenberg (1994)	Smoking ban introduced in a financial services corporation	732 nonunion clerical employees	*Outcome*: Subjects' smoking level prior to the ban (the more they smoked, the more negative the perceived outcome) *Procedure*: (1) Information thoroughness (2) Social sensitivity	(1) Acceptance of ban (organizational commitment, turnover intention, fairness of ban) (2) Fairness of procedure used to	Predicted interactions between each procedural element and outcome on (1)

Study	Setting	Sample	Variables	Dependent variable	Findings
				decide on the ban (3) General attitude toward work smoking bans	
Konovsky & Cropanzano (1994)	Pathology laboratory where drug testing policy was introduced	204 employees	*Outcome*: Perception of severity of consequences for testing positive *Procedure*: (1) Advanced notice (2) Voice (3) Presence of grievance (4) Accuracy (5) Interactional justice (6) For cause testing	Perceived fairness of drug testing (combined procedural and distributive)	Predicted interaction with outcome found for each of the following procedural elements: (1), (2), (5), and (6)
Lind (1994a)	A recent discussion participants had with their supervisors about a problem in the workplace. In all cases, supervisors recommended how to redress the problem.	Two different samples of workers: one from Hong Kong and one from the United States	*Outcome*: Perceived favorability of outcomes associated with following supervisor's recommendation *Procedure*: Procedural fairness of supervisor in discussing participants' problem with them	Willingness to go along voluntarily with the supervisor's recommendation	Predicted interaction in both samples
Lind (1994b)	Court-annexed arbitration program	Litigants	*Outcome*: Perceived favorability of the outcome of the case *Procedure*: Perceived fairness of the arbitration procedure	Acceptance of the decision	Predicted interaction
McFarlin & Sweeney (1992)	Bank	675 employees	*Outcome*: Perception of how fairly they have been rewarded	(1) Organizational commitment	Predicted interaction on (1) and (2)

(*continued*)

TABLE 18.1 Continued

Study	Site/Event	Participants	Independent Variables	Dependent Variables	Results
			in light of contributions *Procedure:* General measure of procedural justice in allocating outcomes (e.g., determination of pay increases)	(2) Evaluation of supervisor (3) Pay level satisfaction	
Mellor (1992)	15 unionized manufacturing organizations	356 blue-collar manufacturing workers	*Outcome:* Layoff severity *Procedure:* Belief in account by the organization implicating the union as cause of layoff	(4) Job satisfaction Union commitment (the opposite of organizational commitment, given the hostile relationship between the organization and the union)	Predicted interaction
Schaubroeck, May, & Brown (in press)	Manufacturing plant in which a pay freeze had been ongoing for 1 year	173 salaried nonunion employees	*Outcome:* Degree of economic hardship caused by freeze *Procedure:* Communication of how and why pay freeze was done	(1) Turnover intention (2) Organizational commitment (3) Trust in management (4) Procedural fairness of pay freeze (5) General job satisfaction	Significant interaction on all five dependent variables
Schroth & Shah (1993), Study 2	Students who had received midterm exam results	69 undergraduates	*Outcome:* Perceived outcome fairness *Procedure:* Perceived fairness of procedures used to judge performance	State self-esteem	"Contrary" interaction

Study	Setting	Sample	Variables	Dependent variables	Results
Trevino (1993)	Variety of organizations in which supervisor had disciplined a subordinate	79 disciplined subordinates	*Outcome*: Perceived harshness of the punishment *Procedure*: (1) Counseling (supportive approach by supervisor) (2) Negative expression (demeanor of the supervisor) (3) Control (process, decision) (4) Explanation adequacy (5) Privacy (6) Arbitrariness (doesn't adhere to rules; is imposed too early)	(1) Performance (2) Organizational citizenship behavior (3) Anticitizenship behavior	5 of 18 possible interactions were significant: (A) Outcome × negative expression on (2) (B) Outcome × explanation on (1) (C) Outcome × explanation on (2) (D) Outcome × privacy on (1) (E) Outcome × arbitrariness on (2) Predicted interaction
Tyler (1987), cited in Lind & Tyler (1988)	Legal institution settings (police, courts)	People who had an encounter with legal institutions	*Outcome*: Favorability of outcome received in the encounter *Procedure*: Perceived fairness of procedure	Affect toward authorities	

397

Cropanzano, 1994), and the onset of a smoking ban (Greenberg, 1994). Distributive justice and procedural justice were operationalized in numerous ways. Moreover, a variety of dependent variables were measured, including organizational commitment (Greenberg, 1994), job performance (Trevino, 1993), citizenship behavior (Trevino, 1993), and turnover intention (Brockner, DeWitt, Grover, & Reed, 1990). Although most of the studies were conducted in the United States, Lind and his colleagues (Bierbrauer, Leung, & Lind, cited in Lind, 1994b; Lind, 1994a) discovered the interactive relationship in two samples of participants from Hong Kong and one from Germany. The fact that the interactive relationship has been observed in many diverse studies attests to the construct validity of the findings.

In this chapter we invoke the construct of trust in an attempt to better understand the interactive relationship between procedural and distributive justice. Our central thesis is that it is not procedural justice per se that is interacting with distributive justice. Rather, it is *the degree of trust engendered by procedural fairness* that interacts with distributive justice to influence reactions to a resource allocation decision.

The remainder of the chapter is divided into three major sections. First, we present the two primary explanations of the interaction effect. Although the explanations differ, the construct of trust is central to both. Second, if trust is the construct that is actually interacting with distributive justice, then it is important to analyze the relationship between procedural justice and trust. For example, how might one account for the hypothesized linkage between procedural justice and trust? Moreover, if trust is the key conceptual variable, then its other determinants (besides procedural justice) should interact with distributive justice (in the way that procedural justice does). Third, we will discuss whether certain determinants of trust are more likely to interact with distributive justice than others. Put differently, whereas the second section of the chapter analyzes a commonality of the antecedents of trust, the third section considers how the determinants of trust may differ.

Explanations of the Interaction Between Distributive and Procedural Justice

The two predominant explanations of procedural justice effects are the self-interest theory (Thibaut & Walker, 1975) and the group value model (Lind & Tyler, 1988). The theories are based on different assumptions of human nature and were originally formulated to account for the main effect of procedural justice—that is, why people generally prefer procedures that are fair rather than unfair. The theories also can account for the interactive relationship between procedural and distributive justice.

The Self-Interest Theory

The self-interest model sees people as motivated to maximize their personal outcomes, particularly outcomes that are concrete, tangible, and material. The outcomes of concern to people are both short- and long-term. According to "informed" self-interest theory (Lind & Tyler, 1988), people may be willing to forego immediate, short-term benefits from an exchange relationship if they believe that the relationship offers the promise of long-term benefits. The role of procedural justice in informed self-interest theory is to shape people's expectations of the outcomes they will receive over the long-term. When procedural fairness is high, people are likely to think that they will receive their share of desired outcomes *over time*. Feeling reassured about their long-term outcomes, they may be less concerned with the distributive fairness of their immediate outcomes.

Unfair procedures, in contrast, provide no such assurances about the outcomes people expect to receive over time. At worst, unfair procedures may lead people to believe that their long-term prospects are negative; at best, the outcomes that they can expect to receive over time are unpredictable. Because low procedural justice prevents people from believing that they will receive their share of material benefits over time, their attitude is likely to be one of, "What have you done for me lately?"

Note that the above reasoning is consistent with the interactive relationship between distributive and procedural justice. Fair procedures make people relatively unconcerned about short-term distributive justice. Given that they assign relatively little significance to their immediate outcomes, their reactions are not likely to vary a great deal in reaction to the distributive justice of the outcomes that they recently received. In contrast, unfair procedures lead people to believe that they cannot trust that they will receive distributive justice over the longer term. Compared to when procedural justice is high, the presence of low procedural fairness may lead people to attach greater significance to, and thus be more affected by, the distributive justice of their current outcomes.

The Group Value Model

Noting the inability of the self-interest model to fully account for the effects of procedural justice, Lind and Tyler (1988) formulated the group value (or relational) model. An underlying assumption of the theory is that people value their group memberships for social and psychological (and not simply economic) reasons. At stake in group memberships are issues of self-identity and self-esteem. A basic tenet of social-identity theory is that people define themselves on the basis of their group memberships (Tajfel & Turner, 1979). Furthermore, the self-esteem of group members partly depends on how they believe that they are evaluated by their groups.

Procedures are one of the major vehicles through which self-relevant information is imparted to group members. Through the two different roles that all group members play—that is, as *agents* and *recipients* of the collective's actions—procedural justice may affect their self-conceptions. As agents of the collective's actions, group members should feel at least somewhat responsible for the behavior of the group. If the collective's decision-making procedures are fair (or unfair), then they may feel, in effect, that *they* acted fairly (or unfairly). The perceived fairness of their own behavior, in turn, may affect their esteem and/or identity. For example, individuals whose group acted procedurally unfairly may wonder, "What does it say about *me* that the group acted this way?"

As recipients of the group's behavior, members may infer from the fairness of the group's procedures the regard in which they are held by the collective: the higher the procedural fairness, the more positively the collective views its members. Through the process of reflected appraisal, in which people evaluate themselves as they believe that they are evaluated by significant others, their self-esteem and/or self-identity may be affected (Mead, 1934).

The self-relevance of procedures sets the stage for the interactive effect of procedural and distributive justice on people's reactions to a decision. When procedural justice is high, individuals' immediate needs for self-esteem and/or identity have been satisfied. Moreover, the presence of procedural fairness suggests that the future relationship with the collective should be self-enhancing. Consequently, whether their current outcomes are distributively fair is relatively unimportant and therefore not so influential. In contrast, low procedural justice thwarts individuals' immediate needs for self-esteem and self-identity and also does not bode well for the future. Why, then, would they be highly affected by the current level of outcome fairness under such circumstances? Recognizing that their self-needs are not being satisfied, they may redefine the nature of their relationship with the collective. They may view their orientation toward the collective as being more "business-like," in which greater importance is assigned to economic outcomes. Said differently, recipients of unfair procedures may introduce psychological distance between themselves and the collective; in the language of psychological contract theory (Rousseau & Parks, 1993), they may view their relationship with the collective as more transactional and/or less relational. Thus, distributive justice—which is highly related to the economic favorability of the outcomes received—will have a more significant impact when procedural fairness is relatively low.

Reconciling Viewpoints: Trust as the Tie That Binds. Self-interest and group value theories are not mutually exclusive. Even the proponents of group value theory (Lind & Tyler, 1988) suggested that the two perspectives are reasonably accurate, if incomplete, descriptions of important aspects of the psychology of procedural justice. . . . We think it is apparent . . . that people react to procedures in ways that clearly reflect self-interest *and* cognitive and attitudinal reactions to group membership. . . . The two sets of psychological processes seem to be functioning at the same time, in parallel, with each set having its effects on the beliefs, attitudes, and behavior that ultimately appear. (p. 240)

One important difference between self-interest and group value theories is the salient "currency of exchange" in the relationship between individuals and collectives. Economic rewards are key to self-interest theory, whereas social and psychological benefits are central to group value theory. In spite of this difference, there are important similarities in how the two viewpoints account for the interactive effect of procedural and distributive justice on reactions to a decision. In both analyses, procedures are considered to be "traits" of the collective: They provide information about how the group or organization is likely to behave over time. Attributions of *trustworthiness* will be made to the collective when it treats its members in procedurally fair ways. That is, people believe that the collective can be counted on to deliver valued rewards over the longer haul. When the collective's procedures are unfair, it will be seen as untrustworthy. Although there are differences in how the two theories account for the interaction—for example, self-interest theory focuses on how people will attach less importance to current economic outcomes when procedural fairness is relatively high, whereas group value theory suggests that people will assign greater significance to current economic outcomes when procedural fairness is relatively low—both highlight the mediating role of trust. In sum, as suggested by both theories, we propose that *it is the degree of trust elicited by the level of procedural fairness* that interacts with distributive justice to affect how people react to a resource allocation decision.

The Relationship Between
Procedural Justice and Trust

The hypothesized causal impact of procedural justice on trust is justifiable on both conceptual and empirical grounds. Trust refers to a belief about a party's future behavior. In deciding whether the party is trustworthy, individuals draw on information about the party that is perceived to be stable—that is, in which the past is believed to be a good predictor of the future. Decision-making procedures are one such source of information. Thus, when current procedures are fair (or unfair), it is reasonable to believe that future procedures also will be fair (or unfair). Trust, in short, is affected by people's estimates of the future level of procedural justice.[2]

Studies in political, legal, and organizational settings have shown that procedural justice positively influences trust. In the political sphere, Lind and Tyler (1988) reported that U.S. citizens' trust in their national government was highly correlated with the perceived fairness of the government's decision-making procedures. In fact, trust judgments were much more sharply affected by procedural justice than by distributive justice (or outcome favorability). Lind and Tyler also found that citizens' trust in legal institutions was strongly related to procedural justice. In the organizational arena, Konovsky and Pugh (1994) discovered a very high correlation between subordinates' judgments of their supervisor's procedural justice and their trust in the supervisor ($r = .77$). Konovsky and Pugh also found that the trustworthiness of the supervisor mediated the relationship between procedural justice and subordinates' organizational citizenship behavior. The mediational findings are consistent with our assertion that it is the trust associated with procedural fairness (rather than procedural fairness per se) that affects important work attitudes and behaviors.

In an experimental study, Sapienza and Korsgaard (1994) manipulated one element of procedural fairness—namely, the timeliness with which individuals received feedback about an important endeavor that they had undertaken (Leventhal et al., 1980). In this role-playing study, participants lent money to an investor. Participants' trust in the investor was strongly affected by the timeliness with which the investor provided feedback about how the investment was faring: As might be expected, investors who gave timely feedback (i.e., investors who were more procedurally fair) were seen as much more trustworthy than those who did not.

Whereas the above findings suggest that procedural fairness influences trust, a recent study by Siegel, Brockner, and Tyler (1995) provides more direct support for the notion that it is the degree of trust produced by procedural fairness that interacts with distributive justice to influence how people respond to a decision. Employees from a wide variety of organizations recalled a recent incident in which they discussed a work-related problem with their immediate manager. The primary dependent variable was employees' voluntary willingness to accept their manager's decision about how to address the problem. Independent variables included (a) the procedural fairness with which their manager handled the situation, (b) trust in the manager, and (c) outcome favorability—that is, the extent to which employees' materially benefited or suffered as a result of the manager's decision. *Separate* multiple regression analyses revealed a significant interaction between (a) procedural fairness and outcome favorability, the nature of which was identical to those found in previous research (i.e., see Figure 18.1), and (b) trust and outcome favorability, such that outcome favorability was less strongly related to voluntary acceptance of the manager's decision when trust in the manager was relatively high. In a subsequent regression analysis, *both* interaction terms were simultaneously entered into the equation. In this case, the interaction between procedural fairness and outcome favorability was no longer significant, but the interaction between trust and outcome favorability retained significance. Such findings suggest that the interaction between procedural and distributive justice actually reflects an interactive relationship between trust and distributive justice.

Processes Through Which
Procedural Justice Affects Trust

Procedural justice depends on the structure of the decision as well as the interpersonal behavior of the implementers of the decision. Both the structural and interpersonal components of procedural justice are likely to influence perceived trust; however, the process may differ for each component. Structural aspects of procedural justice (e.g., decision and/or process control) tend to be stable over time. Thus, it makes perfect sense to form expectations of future behavior on the basis of the structure of the decision. This is not to say that structures cannot be changed. However, due to the inertial nature of institutional forces, the "default option" for structural aspects of procedural justice is to remain as they are.

People also may make trust judgments based on the interpersonal behavior of the parties who implement the decision but for somewhat different reasons. According to the fundamental attribution error, people make (overly) internal attributions about the causes of another's behavior; or, as Heider (1958) suggested long ago, "behavior engulfs the field." Thus, the interactional fairness with which the implementer behaves is likely to be attributed to the implementer's disposition. Like institutional forces that influence the structure of decisions, the implementer's disposition will be viewed as stable over time. Thus, perceivers are apt to believe that they can predict the future (level of interactional fairness) based on the way that they have been treated in the past. In different ways, then, people may view the structural and interpersonal components of procedural justice as indicative of how they are likely to be treated in the future. Procedures that are structurally and interactionally fair will engender trust in the system and in the implementers of decisions, whereas a lack of structural and/or interactional fairness will elicit low levels of trust.

Antecedents of Trust Other
Than Procedural Justice

An important implication of the notion that trust interacts with distributive justice is that determinants of trust other than procedural justice should similarly interact with distributive justice. Antecedents of trust include (but are not limited to) the following: (a) the previous behavior of the people and system that are implementing the current decision, (b) outcome information with longer-term implications, and (c) dispositional tendencies of the perceiver.

Previous Behavior. Allocation decisions often occur in a historical context. In making trust judgments, people rely not only on the present level of procedural justice but also on the past behaviors of the party in question. If the party has a reputation of being trustworthy—perhaps based on a long history of being procedurally fair—then perceivers may be unaffected by the procedural justice level of the current decision. Indeed, the perceived procedural justice of the current event may be seen as similar to (or assimilated by) the existing level of trust, thereby reducing the impact of the current level of procedural justice. If, however, the current level of procedural justice clearly violated perceivers' trust-based expectations, then the ensuing contrast could make the current level of procedural justice particularly influential. For example, Brockner, Tyler, and Cooper-Schneider (1992) found that citizens who were relatively trusting of legal institutions tended to view a recent encounter with the police or courts as more procedurally fair, compared to their less-trusting counterparts (an assimilation effect). The people who did not exhibit such an assimilation effect—that is, those who were trusting at the outset but who felt that they had been treated in a procedurally unfair manner—showed a very sharp decline in subsequent support and trust (a contrast effect). To state the contrast effect differently, the higher they were (in their initial level of trust), the harder they fell (in response to procedurally unfair treatment).

The Anticipation of Favorable Outcomes. Studies showing a significant association between procedural justice and trust often find little or no relationship between distributive justice (or outcome favorability) and trust (e.g., Konovsky & Pugh, 1994; Lind & Tyler, 1988). Perhaps such findings reflect the fact that procedures are more trait-like than outcomes. Outcomes come and go; procedures are more stable. If positive, long-term outcomes were to be seen as more stable or predictable, however, then perceived trust should be high. That is, when trust can be reliably inferred from outcome (rather than procedural) information, degree of trust would be expected to interact with the current level of distributive justice (or outcome favorability) to influence individuals' reactions to the decision.

The results of a recent study by Brockner, Wiesenfeld, and Martin (in press) are consistent with this conjecture. Participants were layoff survivors who indicated their level of support for the organization as a function of procedural justice and perceived outcome favorability. The latter was operationalized through a framing manipulation. In the positive-outcome condition, attention was focused on the people who survived the layoff. The negative-frame condition, in contrast, made salient the people who were laid off. Consistent with the results of many previous studies summarized in Figure 18.1, an interaction between procedural justice and outcome favorability emerged: When procedural justice was low, survivors responded much more favorably in the positive- than in the negative-frame condition. Among those who viewed procedural justice as high, the framing manipulation had no effect.

Survivors also were asked to rate their long-term career opportunities within the organization. Such a judgment may have tapped into feelings of trust. Those who favorably evaluated their career opportunities within the firm in effect were saying that they were counting on the organization to deliver an outcome of importance to them over the long-term. If perceived career opportunities were a proxy for trust, then this factor also should have interacted with the framing variable. In fact, this is precisely what was observed. Those who favorably judged their career opportunities within the firm were unaffected by the framing manipulation. The survivors who were relatively pessimistic about their career opportunities within the firm—much like those who felt that procedural justice was low—responded much more favorably in the positive- than in the negative-frame condition.

Dispositional Tendencies. To this point, the antecedents of trust have been considered to reside within the situation. It is also possible that the tendency to trust is influenced by dispositional factors. Individual difference variables are related to the interaction between procedural and distributive justice in two ways. First, certain individuals simply are more trusting of other people and institutions than are others. Dispositional tendencies to be more or less trusting may operate much like the level of procedural justice in interacting with distributive justice. Like those who receive procedurally fair treatment, individuals who are more dispositionally trusting may be less influenced by the fairness of their current outcomes. High trusters believe that they will receive their share of desired outcomes over time and thus feel that they need not be overly concerned with their most recent outcomes. Individuals who by nature are untrusting—much like those who believe that they have been dealt with in a procedurally unfair way—do not have much faith in their future outcomes; as a result, they should be more influenced by the perceived fairness of their current outcomes.

Second, in addition to having direct effects on trust, individual differences may moderate the relationship between procedural fairness and trust. Consider the trait of delay of gratification (Mischel, 1974), which includes the extent to which people take a longer-term outlook when deciding among preferences. Individuals high in the tendency to delay gratification attach significance to information indicating their likelihood of receiving benefits in the future (Reis, 1986). Level of procedural fairness is one such source of information; the greater the procedural fairness, the more likely people are to believe that they will benefit over the longer haul. If the trait of delay of gratification influences the weight people place on procedural fairness, then the trust levels of people who have a higher tendency to delay gratification should be more affected by the degree of procedural fairness relative to their counterparts with weaker tendencies to delay gratification. Furthermore, if delay of gratification moderates the relationship between procedural fairness and trust, and if trust interacts with distributive justice, then delay of gratification should moderate the interaction between procedural and distributive justice. That is, the typical interaction pattern reported in Figure 18.1 and Table 18.1 should be more pronounced among people with stronger tendencies to delay gratification.

In summary, the analysis of the antecedents of trust (other than procedural justice) illustrates two important points about the interaction between procedural and distributive justice. First, many studies have shown that the level of distributive justice has a greater impact on people's reactions to a decision when procedural fairness is relatively low. The moderating role played by procedural justice may actually be attributable to trust. Second, a noteworthy feature of the studies in Table 18.1 demonstrating the interaction is that procedural justice was operationalized in many different ways. Procedural justice, in turn, may be subsumed by the even larger construct of trust. Procedural justice affects trust, but so may a host of other factors. Therefore, procedural justice may be merely one of a host of determinants of trust that interacts with distributive justice.

Decomposing the Bases of Trust

Trust refers to the beliefs that people maintain about the other party's future behavior. The more that Party A believes that Party B will fulfill the latter's commitments to the relationship, the more trusting Party A will feel toward Party B. The fact that trust refers to expectations about another's *behavior* suggests that its bases can be decomposed into at least two broad categories: motivation (or intent) and ability. Trust should be highest when Party A believes that Party B has both the motivation and the ability to live up to its commitments; trust should be lowest when Party B is seen as lacking both the intent and the ability to behave in a trustworthy fashion.

In the preceding section we implied that trust—however it is determined— should interact with distributive justice to influence people's reactions to a decision. Here, we consider the possibility that the interactive relationship may be affected by whether the perceived level of trust is intent based or ability based. The previous section focused on the commonality of the various antecedents of trust (e.g., procedural justice, the perceiver's disposition, etc.); all were hypothesized to influence trust. The present section calls attention to a difference between procedure-based antecedents of trust that may have implications for the interaction between trust and distributive justice.

Procedures are important because they communicate information about a party's motivation and ability to act in a trustworthy fashion. Procedural justice seems more closely related, however, to the perceived intent than to the perceived ability to be trustworthy. The fairness of procedures says a lot about whether the party's "heart is in the right place." Fair procedures signify that the party "means well," that is, the party appears to want to live up to its commitments. The presence of procedural fairness may indicate less, however, about whether the party has the capabilities to do so.

Procedural attributes other than fairness may be more informative about the party's ability to behave in a trusting manner. Consider the notion of "procedural competence." Competent procedures adhere to the tenets of normative decision making (e.g., Janis, 1989). To enhance decision quality, normative decision theories suggest that it is necessary to (a) define the problem, which includes a clear diagnosis of why the problem is present; (b) generate a variety of possible solutions to the problem; (c) determine the utility of each alternative; (d) implement the alternative with the highest expected utility; and (e) learn from the feedback that results when the alternative is implemented. Competent procedures suggest that the group or organization can be trusted; the collective is likely to be seen as "having its act together." The basis of the trust in this instance, however, is ability. Competence connotes that the collective has the wherewithal to be trustworthy; whether they have the intent to do so may be another matter.

The ability and the intent to be trustworthy are related to one another. Procedures that are fair—which we believe symbolize the party's intent to be trustworthy—also are likely to be "competent," signaling the ability to be trustworthy. For example, in defining the criteria of fair procedures, Leventhal et al. (1980) suggested that decisions should be made on the basis of accurate information. Accuracy seems closely related to (indeed, should even result from) procedural competence. In spite of their overlap, intent and ability as bases of trust are not identical. Suggestive evidence of the distinction between the two is provided in a recent study by Tyler and Degoey (1994). The authors measured employees' willingness to accept managerial decisions voluntarily as a function of their supervisor's (a) competence and (b) integrity. Competence refers to an ability basis of trust, whereas integrity refers to an intent basis. Both factors were significantly related to employees' acceptance of their manager's decisions. However, integrity was a much stronger predictor than was competence.

Tyler and Degoey's (1994) results suggest that to predict the *main* effect of trust on people's acceptance of a decision, it is useful to consider the underlying bases of the trust. In trying to account for the *interaction* between trust and distributive justice—the focal effect of this chapter—researchers also may find it useful to distinguish between the intent versus the ability to be trustworthy. In fact, the two explanations of the interaction between procedural and distributive justice effect—self-interest theory and the group value framework—seem to make different predictions about the usefulness of such a distinction. Self-interest theory assumes that people are outcome maximizers. Thus, *any* factor that enables them to believe that they will receive their share of desired outcomes over the longer haul should lead them to attach less importance to their current outcomes. There is no reason to believe that self-interest theory would assign more or less significance to the intent basis of trust than to the ability basis. In other words, it is not clear that people would be any more or less trusting of the collective that exhibited a high level of ability to be trustworthy (e.g., in which decision-making procedures were "competent") than of the collective that showed high intent to be trustworthy (e.g., in which procedures were fair). As long as the factor affects perceptions of trust, it should interact with distributive justice to influence individuals' reactions to a resource allocation decision.

In contrast, the group value model does appear to differentiate between the bases of trust. Group value theory suggests that people covet the psychological (not simply the economic) rewards of their exchange relationships. Relationships are a vital source of self-esteem and self-identity. In their interchanges with other individuals or collectives, people will be especially interested in information that has relevance to their self-esteem and self-identity. Procedures are one such source of information. The procedures used by individuals and collectives often reflect their motivation and ability to be trustworthy. Although both bases of trust may be relevant to how people perceive and evaluate themselves, we believe that Party A's motivation to be trustworthy is more self-relevant to Party B than is Party A's ability to be trustworthy. The extent to which individuals or groups signal that they *want* to be seen as trustworthy communicates a lot about how they feel toward the recipient of the communication. The symbolic message communicated by parties whose procedures are fair is inherently positive, (i.e., "We think highly enough of you to treat you in a dignified, respectful way."). Moreover, research on self-serving attributional biases shows that people generally make internal attributions for positive outcomes (e.g., Bradley, 1978). In the present context, people may react to procedural fairness in a way that heightens the esteem-increasing impact of the fair treatment.

The symbolic message communicated by parties whose procedures are competent—that is, who show they have the ability to be trustworthy—also is positive. In this case, however, the positive message may be less relevant to the recipients' self-evaluations (than in the case of procedural fairness). It may say more about the communicator than about (a) the recipient or (b) the communicator's relationship with the recipient. In essence, we hypothesize that Party B will see him- or herself as more separate from the actions of Party A when the latter shows the former that it has the ability (rather than the intent) to be trustworthy.

To elaborate on this hypothesis, compare the following two downside situations: one in which Party A shows Party B that Party A lacks the desire to be trustworthy, and one in which Party A shows that it lacks the ability to be trustworthy. Party B is likely to have different beliefs about Party A's control over its own behavior in these two situations. Lack of trustworthiness due to (low) ability should be perceived as less controllable than lack of trustworthiness due to (low) effort (Weiner, 1974). If Party B believes that Party A showed an inability to be trustworthy—for example, if Party A's procedures were incompetent—Party B should be relatively unlikely to take Party A's actions personally; perhaps, Party B may believe, Party A did the best that it could.

If, however, Party A acted in a way that suggested it had little desire to be trustworthy—for example, if its procedures were unfair—then Party B may experience Party A's behavior as more self-relevant. Party B may believe that Party A *could* have chosen to act differently than it did. In thinking about why Party A did not act differently, Party B may believe that it was something about themselves and/or the *relationship between* themselves and Party A that elicited the unfair treatment. Either of these attributions could threaten Party B's sense of themselves.

In summary, group value theory seems to attach more importance to bases of trust that are linked to intent than to ability. Recall that in a study coauthored by one of the architects of group value theory, Tyler and Degoey (1994) found that the main effect of an intention-based factor (i.e., the communicator's integrity) was more important than the main effect of an ability-based factor (i.e., the communicator's competence) in people's voluntary compliance with the communicator. In parallel fashion, it may be that trust factors based on intent are more likely than those based on ability to interact with distributive justice in shaping individuals' reactions to a decision.

Concluding Comments

More than 20 recent studies have shown that procedural and distributive justice interact to influence how people respond to a resource allocation decision. A common theme underlying the two predominant explanations of the interaction effect—self-interest and group value theory—is that level of procedural fairness influences the degree of trust in the exchange relationship. Thus, the findings summarized in Figure 18.1 and Table 18.1 may actually reflect an interaction between trust and distributive justice, as suggested by the results of a recent study (Siegel et al., 1995). Future research may profitably proceed in at least two directions. First, the impact of determinants of trust other than procedural justice needs to be examined. Second, we need to distinguish determinants of trust based on motivation or intent from those based on ability. In so doing, we may be better able to understand whether self-interest or group value theory better accounts for the expected interactive effect of trust and distributive justice in a given instance. Group value theory appears to place far greater emphasis on trust based on motivation than on ability. According to group value theory, therefore, we would expect distributive justice to interact more strongly with motivation-based trust than with ability-based trust.

Self-interest theory suggests that people seek to maximize their economic outcomes. Thus, in trying to predict whether motivation-based trust is more or less likely than ability-based trust to interact with distributive justice, one first needs to ascertain which of these two bases is a more important determinant of individuals' judgments of the economic outcomes that they expect to receive from the exchange relationship over time. If ability-based trust is more important, then it should be more likely than motivation-based trust to interact with distributive justice. A priori, there is no reason to believe that motivation-based trust is more or less likely than ability-based trust to determine individuals' expectations of their longer-term economic outcomes. Thus, from a self-interest perspective, these two bases of trust should be equally likely to interact with distributive justice in shaping how people react to resource allocation decisions.

Notes

1. Many of the studies reviewed in Table 18.1 examined the favorability (rather than the fairness) of the outcome. Outcome favorability is conceptually distinct from outcome (or distributive) fairness. However, outcome favorability and fairness do overlap to a considerable extent. People are much more likely to view favorable (rather than unfavorable) outcomes as fair. Moreover, studies have shown substantial correlations between outcome fairness and favorability (e.g., Tyler & Caine, 1981). Given the evidence of overlap between outcome fairness and favorability—which includes the fact that the results shown in Table 18.1 and Figure 18.1 were similar for both forms of outcome—we will not distinguish between the two for the remainder of the chapter. (Moreover, the terms *distributive justice* and *outcome fairness* will be used interchangeably for the remainder of the chapter.)

2. Brockner and Wiesenfeld (1994) also reported 15 laboratory experiments that yielded the same interactive relationship between procedural and distributive justice as that shown in Figure 18.1. Such findings were excluded from the present analysis, because they might have been driven by a process different from that set forth above. All of the laboratory experiments consisted of one-time encounters for the participants, with no anticipation of future interaction. When future exchange is not anticipated, the role of trust in shaping expectations of how the other party is likely to behave becomes irrelevant. That is, the interaction between procedural and distributive justice probably may be mediated by very different processes when research participants are studied while in the midst of an ongoing relationship (as in the studies reported in Table 18.1), relative to when they are not (e.g., as in a laboratory experiment).

Trust still may be relevant to the interaction between procedural and distributive justice in one-time encounters. A crucial aspect of trust is the perceived benevolence of an actor's intentions. According to Folger (1993), procedural and distributive justice can interact when people use procedural information to make inferences about the benevolence of an actor's intentions, even if they do not form beliefs about the actor's future behavior. Thus, the context of anticipated future interaction—typically absent in laboratory studies—is not necessary for procedural and distributive justice to interact. When the interaction does emerge in the context of an ongoing exchange relationship, however, it is likely to be explained at least in part by how procedural fairness shapes individuals' beliefs of the other party's future behavior.

References

Adams, J. S. (1965). Inequity in social exchange. In L. Berkowitz (Ed.), *Advances in experimental social psychology* (Vol. 2, pp. 267-299). New York: Academic Press.

Adler, J. W., Hensler, D. R., & Nelson, C. E. (1983). *Simple justice: How litigants fare in the Pittsburgh Court Arbitration Program.* Santa Monica, CA: RAND.

Bies, R. J. (1987). The predicament of injustice: The management of moral outrage. In B. M. Staw & L. L. Cummings (Eds.), *Research in organizational behavior* (Vol. 9, pp. 289-319). Greenwich, CT: JAI.

Bradley, G. W. (1978). Self-serving biases in the attribution process: A re-examination of the fact or fiction question. *Journal of Personality and Social Psychology, 36,* 56-71.

Brockner, J., DeWitt, R. L., Grover, S., & Reed, T. (1990). When it is especially important to explain why: Factors affecting the relationship between managers' explanations of a layoff and survivors' reactions to the layoff. *Journal of Experimental Social Psychology, 26,* 389-407.

Brockner, J., Konovsky, M., Cooper-Schneider, R., Folger, R., Martin, C. L., & Bies, R. J. (1994). The interactive effects of procedural justice and outcome negativity on the victims and survivors of job loss. *Academy of Management Journal, 37,* 397-409.

Brockner, J., Tyler, T. R., & Cooper-Schneider, R. (1992). The influence of prior commitment to an institution on reactions to perceived unfairness: The higher they are, the harder they fall. *Administrative Science Quarterly, 37,* 241-261.

Brockner, J., & Wiesenfeld, B. (1994). *The interactive impact of procedural justice and outcome favorability: The effects of what you do depend upon how you do it.* Manuscript under review.

Brockner, J., Wiesenfeld, B., & Martin, C. L. (1995). Decision frame, procedural justice, and survivors' reactions to job layoffs. *Organizational Behavior and Human Decision Processes, 63,* 59-68.

Cropanzano, R., & Folger, R. (1991). Procedural justice and worker motivation. In R. M. Steers & L. W. Porter (Eds.), *Motivation and work behavior* (2nd ed., pp. 131-143). New York: McGraw-Hill.

Daly, J. P. (1994, November). *Explaining changes to employees: The influence of justifications and change outcomes on employees' fairness judgments.* Paper presented to the Southern Management Association, New Orleans, LA.

Daly, J. P., & Geyer, P. D. (1995). Procedural fairness and organizational commitment under conditions of growth and decline. *Social Justice Research, 8,* 137-151.

Deutsch, M. (1985). *Distributive justice: A social psychological analysis.* New Haven, CT: Yale University Press.

Folger, R. (1993). Reactions to mistreatment at work. In J. K. Murnighan (Ed.), *Social psychology in organizations: Advances in theory and research* (pp. 161-183). Englewood Cliffs, NJ: Prentice Hall.

Greenberg, J. (1994). Using socially fair treatment to promote acceptance of a work site smoking ban. *Journal of Applied Psychology, 79,* 288-297.

Heider, F. (1958). *The psychology of interpersonal relations.* New York: John Wiley.

Janis, I. (1989). *Crucial decisions: Leadership in policy-making and crisis management.* New York: Free Press.

Konovsky, M. A., & Cropanzano, R. (1994). *Drug testing practices as determinants of employee fairness perceptions.* Manuscript under review.

Konovsky, M. A., & Pugh, S. D. (1994). Citizenship behavior and social exchange. *Academy of Management Journal, 37,* 656-669.

Leventhal, G. S., Karuza, J., & Fry, W. R. (1980). Beyond fairness: A theory of allocation preferences. In G. Mikula (Ed.), *Justice and social interaction* (pp. 167-218). New York: Springer-Verlag.

Lind, E. A. (1994a, August). *Discussant's comments.* Presented to the Academy of Management Conference, Dallas.

Lind, E. A. (1994b). *Procedural justice and the acceptance of legal authority.* Working paper, American Bar Foundation.

Lind, E. A., & Tyler, T. R. (1988). *The social psychology of procedural justice.* New York: Plenum.

McFarlin, D. B., & Sweeney, P. D. (1992). Distributive and procedural justice as predictors of satisfaction with personal and organizational outcomes. *Academy of Management Journal, 35,* 626-637.

Mead, G. H. (1934). *Mind, self, and society.* Chicago: University of Chicago Press.

Mellor, S. (1992). The influence of layoff severity on postlayoff union commitment among survivors: The moderating effect of the perceived legitimacy of a layoff account. *Personnel Psychology, 45,* 579-600.

Mischel, W. (1974). Processes in delay of gratification. In L. Berkowitz (Ed.), *Advances in experimental social psychology* (Vol. 7, pp. 249-292). New York: Academic Press.

Reis, H. T. (1986). Levels of interest in the study of interpersonal justice. In H. W. Bierhoff, R. L. Cohen, & J. Greenberg (Eds.), *Justice in social relations* (pp. 187-210). New York: Plenum.

Rousseau, D. M., & Parks, J. M. (1993). The contracts of individuals and organizations. In B. M. Staw & L. L. Cummings (Eds.), *Research in organizational behavior* (Vol. 15, pp. 1-43). Greenwich, CT: JAI.

Sapienza, H. J., & Korsgaard, M. A. (1994, June). *Managing investor relations: The impact of procedural justice in establishing and sustaining investor support.* Paper presented at the Babson/Kauffman Foundation Entrepreneurship Conference.

Schaubroeck, J., May, D. R., & Brown, F. W. (in press). Procedural justice explanations and employee reactions to economic hardship: A field experiment. *Journal of Applied Psychology.*

Schroth, H. A., & Shah, P. P. (1993). *Procedures: Do we really want to know them?* Manuscript under review.

Siegel, P., Brockner, J., & Tyler, T. (1995, August). *Revisiting the relationship between procedural and distributive justice: The role of trust.* Paper presented at The Academy of Management Conference, Vancouver.

Sweeney, P. D., & McFarlin, D. B. (1993). Workers' evaluations of the "ends" and the "means": An examination of four models of distributive and procedural justice. *Organizational Behavior and Human Decision Processes, 55,* 23-40.

Tajfel, H., & Turner, J. (1979). An integrative theory of intergroup conflict. In W. G. Austin & S. Worchel (Eds.), *The social psychology of intergroup relations* (pp. 33-47). Pacific Grove, CA: Brooks/Cole.

Thibaut, J., & Walker, L. (1975). *Procedural justice: A psychological analysis.* Hillsdale, NJ: Lawrence Erlbaum.

Trevino, L. (1993). [Unpublished data]. Penn State University.

Tyler, T. R., & Caine, A. (1981). The influence of outcomes and procedures on satisfaction with formal leaders. *Journal of Personality and Social Psychology, 41,* 642-655.

Tyler, T. R., & Degoey, P. (1994, May). *Trust and the legitimacy of group authorities: The influence of motive attributions on procedural justice.* Paper presented at The Stanford Trust Conference, Stanford University, CA.

Weiner, B. (1974). *Achievement motivation and attribution theory.* Morristown, NJ: General Learning Press.

Index

About the Contributors

Robert J. Bies (PhD, Stanford University) is an Associate Professor of Management at the School of Business, Georgetown University, Washington, D.C. His research interests include the delivery of bad news, the "litigation mentality," revenge in organizations, and organizational justice. He has published articles on these topics in the *Academy of Management Journal, Organizational Science, Organizational Behavior and Human Decision Processes, Research in Organizational Behavior,* and *Research on Negotiation in Organizations.* He is also coeditor of *The Legalistic Organization* (1994).

Marilynn B. Brewer is Ohio State Regents Professor of Social Psychology at the Ohio State University. She received her PhD in Psychology from Northwestern University and has written numerous books and articles on the social psychology of person perception, stereotyping, and intergroup relations. In 1993, she was elected President of the American Psychological Society and also has served as President of the Society for Personality and Social Psychology and of the Society for the Psychological Study of Social Issues.

Joel Brockner is Professor of Management at Columbia Business School. After receiving a BA in psychology from SUNY-Stony Brook in 1972, he earned a PhD in Social/Personality Psychology from Tufts University in 1977. Prior to joining Columbia in 1984, he taught in the Psychology Departments at Middlebury College, SUNY-Brockport, and Tufts University, and in the business school at the University of Arizona. His current research interests include self-processes in organizations, the effects of layoffs (and other significant organizational change) on the people who remain, justice theory, and the escalation of commitment to a failing course of action.

Philip Bromiley is a Professor of Strategic Management in the Department of Strategic Management and Organization at the Carlson School of Management, University of Minnesota. His current research interests include risk assessment and risk taking in organizations, with a particular emphasis on commercial lending, techniques to improve strategic thinking, and the measurement of corporate performance. He serves as an associate editor for *Management Science* and is on the editorial board of *Organization Science.*

Barbara Benedict Bunker is Associate Professor of Psychology at the State University of New York at Buffalo. She received her PhD from Teachers College, Columbia University, in 1970. She is the author of numerous books and articles about change processes in organizations, gender and work organizations, theory of practice, and commuting couples. An applied social psychologist, she is a well-known consultant to business, nonprofit, and government organizations. She has held two Fulbright Lectureships in schools of business administration in Japan at Keio University and Kobe University.

Ronald S. Burt is Professor of Sociology and Strategy at the University of Chicago. Recent work includes *Structural Holes: The Social Structure of Competition,* "Contingent Organization as a Network Theory: The Culture-Performance Contingency Function" (with Shaul M. Gabbay, Gerhard Holt, and Peter Moran, *Acta Sociologica*), and "Le capital social, les trous structuraux, et l'entrepreneur" (*Revue Française de Sociologie*).

W. E. Douglas Creed is an Assistant Professor at the Carroll School of Management, Boston College. He received his doctorate in organizational behavior and industrial relations from the Haas School of Business, the University of California at Berkeley, where he worked with Trond Petersen, Karlene Roberts, and Raymond Miles. He also holds an MBA from Berkeley, an MA from Yale Divinity School, and a BA from Yale University.

L. L. Cummings is Professor of Management of the Carlson School of Management, University of Minnesota. His current research focuses on organizational trust, psychological ownership, extra role behaviors, and feedback seeking. He has published widely and serves as coeditor of *Research in Organizational Behavior.* He is a Fellow of the American Psychological Association, the American Psychological Society, The Decision Sciences Institute, and the Academy of Management. He was honored in 1995 by the Academy of Management with its Distinguished Educator Award.

Michael R. Darby is the Warren C. Cordner Professor of Money and Financial Markets and Director of the John M. Olin Center for Policy in the Anderson Graduate School of Management at UCLA. Concurrently he holds appointments as Chairman of The Dumbarton Group, Research Associate with the National Bureau of Economic Research, Adjunct Scholar with the American Enterprise Institute, and Member of the Regulatory Coordination Advisory Committee of the Commodities Futures Trading Commission. Darby received his AB *summa cum laude* from Dartmouth College in 1967. He is the author of seven books and monographs and numerous other professional publications.

Peter Degoey is a doctoral student at the University of California at Berkeley, concurrently completing degrees in Social Psychology and Organizational Behavior. His research focuses on issues of procedural justice, trust in authorities, and collective sensemaking processes within organizations. His first single-author manuscript, which is due to appear in the 1996 volume of the *Research in Organizational Behavior* series, focuses on the social contagion of fairness judgments in social networks. He was a business owner for 10 years before returning to academia.

Benjamin A. Hanna is a doctoral candidate in Organizational Behavior at the Stanford University Graduate School of Business. His interests include the role of social identity and self-categorization on several multilevel phenomena in organizations, including trust behavior, sensemaking during change, and threat perception and reaction. He is currently involved in research on the social-psychological barriers to moving from traditional, hierarchical work arrangements to team-based, high-commitment practices. His dissertation will examine the effects of implementing an employee monitoring system on both managers and employees and how the ideological context of the organization inhibits or facilitates the implementation of the new system.

David Kipnis is at the Department of Psychology at Temple University. His research has examined the use of social power, the relation between social power and technology, and more recently the ways in which technology changes social behavior. His writings include numerous articles and several books (*The Powerholders; Technology and Power*) on these topics.

Marc Knez is Assistant Professor of Behavioral Science and Business Policy at the University of Chicago. Recent work includes "Creating Expectational Assets in the Laboratory: Coordination in Weakest-Link Games" (with Colin Camerer, *Strategic Management Journal*) and "Social Comparison and Outside Options in 3-Player Ultimatum Game Experiments" (with Colin Camerer, under review).

Roderick M. Kramer is an Associate Professor of Organizational Behavior at the Graduate School of Business at Stanford University. Prior to coming to Stanford, he worked for several years as Program Director of the USC Norris Cancer Center's Cancer Information Service and later as Program Director of the UCLA Jonsson Cancer Center's Public and Patient Education Programs. After leaving the Jonsson Center, he earned his PhD in Social Psychology from UCLA. He joined the faculty of the Stanford Business School in 1985. His research focuses primarily on decision making in conflict situations, such as social dilemmas, negotiations, and international disputes. Most recently, his research has focused on the role of cognitive illusions in conflicts and the dynamics of trust and distrust in organizations. His work has appeared in journals such as the *Annual Review of Psychology, Journal of Personality and Social Psychology, Journal of Experimental Social Psychology, Journal of Conflict Resolution,* and *Organizational Behavior and Human Decision Processes.*

Roy J. Lewicki is Professor of Management and Human Resources at the Max M. Fisher College of Business, The Ohio State University. He received his BA in Psychology from Dartmouth College in 1964 and his PhD in Social Psychology from Teachers College, Columbia University, in 1969. He is author and coauthor of numerous books and articles in the fields of negotiation, dispute resolution, organizational justice, and organizational behavior, including *Negotiation* (1994), *Negotiation: Readings, Exercises and Cases* (1993), and *Organizational Justice* (1992).

Debra Meyerson is Adjunct Professor of Organizational Behavior at the University of Michigan's Business School and Lecturer of Organizational Behavior at Stanford University's Graduate School of Business. Her current research interests include the politics and process of change directed at gender and race equity in organizations, alternative conceptions of leadership, cultural responses to ambiguity, and the creation of trust in "temporary" organizations. She received her PhD in Organization Behavior from Stanford University.

Raymond E. Miles is former Dean and Trefethen Professor of Organizational Behavior Emeritus at the Walter A. Haas School of Business at the University of California at Berkeley. He received his PhD in Organizational Behavior from Stanford University. He is the author of five books and numerous articles on managers' theories of management, organization design and change, strategy-structure-process fit, and emerging organizational forms. Dr. Miles is a consultant to organizations in the United States and abroad and is a member of two corporate boards. He is a fellow of the Academy of Management and a frequent participant in its annual programs, including its doctoral consortia.

Aneil K. Mishra is Assistant Professor of Management at the Smeal College of Business at Pennsylvania State University. He received his PhD in Business Administration from the University of Michigan and an AB *cum laude* in economics from Princeton University. His research interests include processes and outcomes of trust within and between organizations, organizational downsizing, and organizational culture. His research has appeared in such journals as the *Academy of Management Executive, Organization Science,* and *Industrial and Labor Relations Review.* Prior to pursuing the PhD, he worked in the automotive industry as a manufacturing engineer and a human resource specialist.

Yusheng Peng received his Master's degree in Sociology from Beijing University in 1986 and his PhD in Sociology from the University of California at Los Angeles in 1993. He is at present a lecturer at the Chinese University of Hong Kong, teaching statistics, methodology, and economic sociology. His research interests include economic institutions, organizational study, and social stratification. Currently he is working on Chinese rural industries. He has published "Wage Determination in Rural and Urban China: A Comparison Between Public and Private Sectors" (1992).

Walter W. Powell is Professor of Sociology at the University of Arizona. He is a coauthor of *Books: The Culture and Commerce of Publishing,* author of *Getting Into Print: The Decision-Making Process in Scholarly Publishing,* and the editor of *The Nonprofit Sector: A Research Handbook.* With Paul DiMaggio, he edited and contributed to *The New Institutionalism in Organizational Analysis. Private Action and the Public Good,* coedited with Elisabeth Clemens, is forthcoming in 1996. He is presently studying the origins and development of the biotechnology industry.

Blair H. Sheppard is a Professor of Management and Associate Dean, Executive Education, at the Fuqua School of Business. He received his BA and MA degrees from the University of Western Ontario and his PhD in Social/Organizational Psychology from the University of Illinois. He taught at the University of Illinois and McGill University prior to coming to Duke. His research interests pertain to the broad topic of managing relations within and between organizations. Specific interests include conflict management, negotiation, organizational justice, and interfirm relations. He has published articles on all of these topics in a range of business and psychology journals and is coeditor of an annual series titled *Research on Negotiation in Organizations.*

Phyllis Siegel is a PhD candidate at Columbia Business School. She graduated with a BA in Psychology and a BS in Management from the University of Pennsylvania in 1991. Her current research interests are threefold: (a) the causes and consequences of justice in organizations, (b) top-management teams, and (c) cross-cultural differences in organizational behavior.

Sim B Sitkin is Associate Professor of Management at the Fuqua School of Business, Duke University. He received his PhD in organizational behavior from the Graduate School of Business, Stanford University, and has previously taught at Carnegie-Mellon University and the University of Texas. His research focuses on the effect of formal and informal organizational control systems on risk taking, accountability, trust, learning, and innovation. His work draws primarily on institutional, impression management, and learning theories to understand the processes by which organizations and their members become more or less capable of change and innovation. He is currently pursuing these interests through two NSF-sponsored projects that examine how formal and informal control systems affect organizational learning—one focusing on the use of TQM programs and the other focusing on the use of rules and documentation in a cross-functional innovation team. He edited with Robert Bies *The Legalistic Organization* (1994).

Darryl Stickel is a PhD student in Management and Organizational Behavior at Duke University's Fuqua School of Business. He completed his BA and MPA degrees at the University of Victoria in Victoria, British Columbia. His research interests include trust, negotiations, labor relations, interpersonal relations, and social justice. He has previously worked for both the federal government of Canada and the provincial government of British Columbia.

Thomas M. Tripp is an Assistant Professor of Management at Washington State University. In 1991, he received his PhD from the Kellogg Graduate School of Management at Northwestern University. In 1985, he received a BS in Psychology from the University of Washington. Dr. Tripp studies conflict resolution, especially how people use fairness to mitigate power differentials during negotiations. He has also written on related issues of power abuse, distrust, revenge, impression management, and defamation within organizations. Nevertheless, he maintains optimism regarding organizational life. His work has appeared in *Organizational Behavior and Human Decision Processes, Journal of Behavioral Decision Making, Social Justice Research, Employee Responsibilities and Rights Journal, Research on Negotiations in Organizations,* and the *Journal of Applied Social Psychology.*

Marla Tuchinsky is a PhD candidate in Management and Organizational Behavior at Duke University's Fuqua School of Business. She earned her BA and MA in Sociology from Stanford University. Her research interests revolve around inter- and intrafirm relationships as well as negotiation and trust issues. She has a forthcoming chapter with Blair Sheppard in *Research in Organizational Behavior,* discussing relational forms as strategic business decisions.

Tom R. Tyler is Professor of Psychology at the University of California at Berkeley. His research explores the social psychology of justice and the dynamics of authority in groups. He is the author of *The Social Psychology of Procedural Justice* (with E. A. Lind) and *Why People Obey the Law.*

Eugene J. Webb was the LANE Professor of Organizational Behavior at the Stanford Graduate School of Business. His early interest in methodological questions helped him to migrate to a concern for public policy. He taught courses in both power politics and philanthropy. He passed away March 14, 1995.

Karl E. Weick, who is the Rensis Likert Collegiate Professor of Organizational Behavior and Psychology at the University of Michigan, is also the former Editor of *Administrative Science Quarterly.* In 1990, Dr. Weick received the highest honor awarded by the Academy of Management, the Irwin Award for Distinguished Lifetime Scholarly Achievement. In the same year, he also received the award for Best Article of the Year in the *Academy of Management Review.* He studies such topics as how people make sense of confusing events, the social psychology of improvisation, high reliability systems, and indeterminacy in social systems.

Lynne G. Zucker is Professor of Sociology and Director of the Organizational Research Program at the Institute for Social Science Research at UCLA. Concurrently she holds appointments as Research Associate with the National Bureau of Economic Research, as Consulting Sociologist with the American Institute of Physics, and in the affiliated faculty of the UCLA School of Education. Zucker is the author of four books and monographs and numerous journal and other articles on organizational theory, analysis, and evaluation, institutional structure, civil service, government spending and services, unionization, science and its commercialization, and permanently failing organizations. She serves or has served as Associate Editor or Editorial Board Member for *Administrative Science Quarterly, American Journal of Sociology, American Sociological Review, Pacific Sociological Review,* and *Symbolic Interaction.*

ADV4511